Journalism

Journalism

The Democratic Craft

G. Stuart Adam
The Poynter Institute
Emeritus, Carleton University

Roy Peter Clark
The Poynter Institute

New York   Oxford
OXFORD UNIVERSITY PRESS
2006

Oxford University Press, Inc., publishes works that further Oxford University's
objective of excellence in research, scholarship, and education.

Oxford   New York
Auckland   Cape Town   Dar es Salaam   Hong Kong   Karachi
Kuala Lumpur   Madrid   Melbourne   Mexico City   Nairobi
New Delhi   Shanghai   Taipei   Toronto

With offices in
Argentina   Austria   Brazil   Chile   Czech Republic   France   Greece
Guatemala   Hungary   Italy   Japan Poland   Portugal   Singapore
South Korea   Switzerland   Thailand   Turkey   Ukraine   Vietnam

Copyright © 2006 by Oxford University Press, Inc.

Published by Oxford University Press, Inc.
198 Madison Avenue, New York, New York 10016
http://www.oup.com

Oxford is a registered trademark of Oxford University Press

Library of Congress Cataloging-in-Publication Data

Journalism : the democratic craft / written and edited by G. Stuart Adam.
    p.   cm.
  Includes bibliographical references and index.
  ISBN-13: 978-0-19-518207-1 (pbk. : alk. paper)
  ISBN-10: 0-19-518207-3 (pbk. : alk. paper)
  1. Journalism.   I. Adam, G. Stuart (Gordon Stuart), 1939–

PN4724.J68 2005
070.4—dc22   2005048821

Printing number: 9 8 7 6 5 4 3 2 1

Printed in the United States of America
on acid-free paper

To Pegie Stark Adam and Karen Clark

CONTENTS

PREFACE

The Why and the How of This Book

This book is a collection of meditations on journalism and closely related subjects that can be read for its own sake by students, teachers, and working journalists. It provides material for the study of what professors of journalism might call "theory," and, in our view, it is an appropriate text for a capstone course in such a subject. But we are hoping that professors who teach reporting and writing courses will also adopt it as a text for their students to read as they undertake increasingly ambitious reporting and writing assignments. Its content and organization are designed to strengthen the practical skills of journalism students by introducing them to a rich version of what we call "the editor's lexicon"—a language providing terms that guide the creation of journalistic texts and direct their correction, repair, and evaluation. It is a language that a master editor might speak and act upon in his or her supervisory role. Regardless of the pedagogical aims of individual instructors, we hope that the lessons contained in the book's essays and articles will promote an understanding that theory in journalism need not be considered a separate and abstract pursuit. In our view, theory should be a clarification of—and an essential aid to—practice.

We first heard the phrase, "the editor's lexicon," in the early 1990s from the late Foster Davis, a former editor at *The Charlotte Observer* and managing editor of *The St. Louis Post-Dispatch*. He said to us at a seminar on reporting and writing at the Poynter Institute, a school for journalists in St. Petersburg, Florida, that as a newly minted editor he discovered the need to learn a special way of talking about journalism. That language and vocabulary, he said, would enable him to communicate successfully with the reporters and writers whose work he was beginning to supervise.

Davis's utterance was fleeting, but on reflection it seemed pregnant with meaning. After thinking about it, we understood that Davis was referring to the words, concepts, and structures of thought that mark the practice of journalism. It is a language that is spoken by editors, to be sure, but it is spoken by writers and reporters as well as they explain what they are doing when they make news judgments, gather evidence, make word choices, compose stories, and interpret events in the here and now. It is a language enriched by the practitioners of photojournalism and design. So Davis was referring to the language and vocabulary of the craft of journalism. He was telling us on that occasion that the editor, more self-consciously perhaps than reporters and writers, must speak it eloquently in order to communicate successfully with fellow journalists who report to him or to her.

The lexicon includes simple terms such as "nut graph" and "lede" or "beat" that classify basic devices of style and organization; it includes grammatical terms such as "the active voice" and "declarative sentences"; or it refers to figures of speech that work such as "metaphors" and those that don't such as "clichés." Such terms and concepts languish in the ether of the places where journalists work, and they mark the conversation that goes—to borrow from the poet W. H. Auden—with the tasks of making, knowing, and judging the things we create.[1] So the lexicon contains phrases that refer to common-places and routine actions, which we assume students will have learned in introductory course work. But it contains also complex notions involving democratic duties and goals, the motivations and moral outlook of authors and editors, the nature of news judgment, the functions and character of journalism and its varieties, its standards and best practices, the conditions of freedom attending its creation, its deficiencies, its achievements and stories—in short, a body of thought contained in a rich literature reflecting the "experience" of writing and producing journalism. To be precise about it, the lexicon, considered as a whole, includes not just the record of such experience; it includes more fundamentally "experience" reconsidered, reflected upon, and thought through. This book constitutes an introduction to that literature. It contains not only the reflections of working journalists on the elements of craft, but also contributions by critics, novelists, and philosophers who have much to say about matters familiar and important to journalists.

We start our voyage in the introduction, with an exploration of the proposition that journalism is the democratic craft par excellence. We argue that it is uniquely born in a system of rights that allows for freedom of expression, and we argue, further, that it operates in a citizens' culture in which practical truth and verifiable fact are essential goods. We take the view that journalists have a social contract with their fellow citizens to bring a real world into view and, as Robert Park once wrote, "to orient man and society in an actual world."[2] We believe that the richer the portrait, the richer the possibilities of democratic life.

We turn then in Part I to a set of reflections on the sources of a writing life in individual personality, in art, and in political life. The essays we have selected are more literary than journalistic, but we are publishing them in the belief that journalists share much with writers of fiction and critics and that apprentice journalists will benefit by looking to their fellow authors for inspiration and ideas about their own craft. A theme running through the readings on authorship and craft is that writers inspire each other.

The introduction and Part I constitute together an inspirational—as well as an analytical—preparation for what follows in Part II. The content of Part II is the book's heart and soul. In it we examine separately and discretely what we view as the fundamental elements of journalism—news judgment in Section A, fact and evidence in Section B, language and narrative in C, and methods of interpretation in D. The selections point to the language of standards and best practices. Section A on news judgment raises not only the question "what is news?" but also the question of what constitutes good and responsible news judgment. Section B explores the status of journalistic knowledge, the conditions under which it is produced, the steps required to produce it, and the rules guarding the boundary between journalism and other literary forms. In Section C we turn to the language of language itself and its moral resonance. In a sense, the readings in Section C are inspired by two observations made by George Orwell. The first is that good prose is "like a window pane"; the second is that "the slovenliness of our language makes it easier to have bad thoughts." In Section D we begin an exploration of the devices that journalists and other writers use to explain why things happen and what they mean.

We conclude in Part III with an epilogue and summation contained in Stuart Adam's essay "Notes Towards a Definition of Journalism." Its purposes are to examine the sources of the book's organization and approach, to reunite its separate and discretely considered elements, and to lay out the foundations for the enterprise of journalism studies considered as a whole.

The master plan, then, involves teaching the language of journalism while, at the same time, teaching journalism as a practice. The essays in the book are intended to provide a special dimension to such teaching by providing a lexicon of terms and judgments that can provide a foundation for a conversation between instructors and students. We have called the language "the editor's lexicon." By doing so, we are not suggesting a permanent hierarchy with the editor on the top and the writer down below. Considered as a whole, this lexical material expresses journalism's methods and values and promotes the stewardship of its best practices. So it is not a possession of the editor alone (although all editors should speak it eloquently); it is the possession of all who seek to practice the craft imaginatively and thoughtfully—or who seek to critique it. It provides a basis for a conversation, as journalism is being produced, about what works and what needs work.

W. H. Auden says poets carry a "Censor" in their heads—an editor who points them toward the ideal and reminds them of technical as well as imaginative components that go into the making of a poem.[3] We have something similar in mind. The Editor/Censor is the critic or judge in the journalist's mind. The task of the Editor/Censor is to inspire rewrites, editing, and refinement across the range of journalism's elements. Through the introduction of these readings (and the voice of the professor) we are promoting the birth of an Editor/Censor in the apprentice journalist such that, in due course, the apprentice will be autonomous and as eloquent as his or her natural talents permit.

At the same time, we are seeking to connect student journalists through these readings to cognate disciplines of the university—particularly literature, philosophy, and politics—where they will have encountered similar material. In this sense, the book is a reminder that a curriculum in journalism works best when it is considered at the crossroads of disciplinary thinking. At such a crossroads, disciplinary thinking doesn't lose its value. It loses rather a tendency to arcane expression and acquires what journalism can give it—namely, a public language for democratic life. So in our view the threads that connect journalism students through these readings back to the disciplines of the university are as important as the readings themselves.

Although we recognize that there are many pathways through a text like this one, we recommend simply that "theory" teachers follow the organization of the book's parts and chapters, asking, over the course of a single semester, that students read and discuss the contents of the essays in their written and oral work. We make suggestions along the way on how these discussions might be organized.

For teachers of professional practices, we suggest something similar, but a little more ambitious. Our recommendation is that each student be assigned a beat, such as city hall, the state legislature, police, education, sports, or theater, and be asked to submit—let's say six—assignments in alternate weeks over the course of a semester. The assignments should be designed to promote understandings central to the outlook of this book. Thus good work should reflect in some sense:

- Journalism's "democratic" purposes;
- An author's sense of responsibility;
- News judgments that matter;
- Reliable facts;
- Elegant language and narrative technique; and
- Thoughtful analysis.

Under such a regime, classroom time would be dedicated to standard forms of feedback on submitted work, but it would also be dedicated—perhaps on alternate weeks—to a close reading of the essays. By the end of the term, students should be able to read their own work and the work of others through the prism of "the editor's lexicon."

Through most of the last century, journalism studies and scholarship have been dominated by two pedagogical movements, best described by the shorthand: the Chi squares versus the green eyeshades, that is, quantitative social science in tension with the teaching of a practical trade or craft. Although we claim no revolutionary intent, this anthology imagines a third way: journalism as a professional practice and a democratic craft. We gained confidence in this approach when the Accrediting Council on Education in Journalism and Mass Communications folded into its accrediting standards the structures of competence—"the editor's lexicon," if you will—that are at the heart of this book. The work of the council—and our work as journalism educators—seeks to answer the question, "What should the product of a sound journalism education be?" In our opinion, the product should be, minimally, a person capable of sound news judgment, a person who understands what constitutes reportorial evidence, who uses language and narrative forms clearly to reveal the world, and who uses powers of criticism and interpretation to help citizens in a democracy understand the world for which they are responsible.

ACKNOWLEDGMENTS

First and foremost, we would like to express our sincere thanks to Dr. Karen Brown Dunlap, President of the Poynter Institute. This project would never have been completed without her blessing, encouragement, and generosity. We also thank Keith Woods, Poynter's academic dean, for his support and encouragement and, equally, Poynter's faculty, who helped us shape and express our ideas. We thank David Shedden, the Librarian of the Poynter Institute, for his able assistance. The Poynter Library, over which Mr. Shedden presides, is a perfect setting in which to study materials related to the practice and study of journalism. Vicki Krueger of the Poynter Institute and Jen Ross, a former Carleton University student of journalism, provided able research assistance along the way and we thank them sincerely. Chris Dornan, the Director of the Carleton University School of Journalism and Communication provided office space and moral support in Ottawa. Paul Attallah, the school's associate director, provided thoughtful commentary, as did Peter Emberley of Carleton's Department of Political Science and Jim Carey of

Columbia University, whose influence is present throughout the volume. Thanks are due as well to Dr. John ApSimon, former Vice President (Research) at Carleton, to Dr. Feridun Hamdullahpur, the current Vice President (Research), and to Richard Van Loon, Carleton's President, who provided funds that got the project started and sustained it in lean years. We also thank Eric Jackman of the Canadian Journalism Foundation for providing seed money for a conference at Carleton University on "The Art of Journalism" when we took our initial steps toward the creation of this text. We would like to thank Trevor Brown, former dean at Indiana University's School of Journalism, who embraced our ideas early in the day and helped to promote them through the Accreditation Council on Education in Journalism and Mass Communication. Finally, we thank the team at Oxford University Press in New York—Sean Mahoney, associate editor, Shiwani Srivastava, assistant editor, and Lisa Grzan, production editor—for their thoughtful and professional guidance. The book is dedicated to our spouses, Pegie Stark Adam and Karen Clark, with much love.

NOTES

1. W. H. Auden, "Making, Knowing and Judging," *The Dyer's Hand and Other Essays* (New York: Random House, 1962).

2. Robert Park's essay, "News as a Form of Knowledge," is reprinted in full in Part II, Section B of this collection. Citations from texts published in the collection are not footnoted.

3. Auden, 33.

INTRODUCTION

Reflections on Journalism and the Architecture of Democracy

Journalism is a large subject, but democracy is many times larger and many times more complex. So it is difficult to lay out in a few short paragraphs why the first matters so much in the consideration of the second. Nevertheless, we would like to say something about the place of journalism in the architecture of democracy and why it should be thought of as a "democratic craft." This claim is so important that it requires two preliminary descriptions of our vantage point, our platform, or, in the vernacular, "where we are coming from."

First, we recognize that locating journalism in the broad setting of democratic culture and practices requires a blending of languages: one language to understand a set of ideals; another to describe experience and practice. In the language of ideals, democracy is a design or foundational template standing more or less on its own. In the language of experience and practice, democracy is an observed pattern of political and social behavior in which there can well be defections from democratic standards. The degree to which a society is democratic depends on the vigor with which it promotes attachment to its fundamental design and renews democratic ways of thinking and acting in each generation. It is possible to imagine a rich legacy of public institutions devoid of any true democratic spirit—swallowed by indifference, indulgence, and diversion. Even a news organization, supposedly devoted to public service, can suffer such a fate.

Second, the analysis that follows depends on the use of terms such as "artifice," "craft," and "design." Such language communicates the idea that the culture and its practices are, whether democratic or not, the products of human design. In this respect, our approach may sound like the lingo of those writers who see the world in terms of the "social construction of reality." Any comparison should end there. Such writers place too much emphasis, we think, on social constraints and the marks of ideology on artifice. We emphasize, instead, the properties of imagination, reason, and truth-seeking that mark the artifacts we are talking about. For example, we believe that accomplished journalists can furnish citizens with reliable maps of the here and now, stripped (or mainly stripped) of ideological content. We believe further that democratic systems are able to respond to knowledge and therefore are open to experience and change. With these qualifications in mind, we can proceed.

When we think of democracy, we speak initially in ideal terms of free individuals connected to one another in systems of familial, communal, and civil association. In its informal aspect, this social order is (or mainly is) regulated by a culture of civility—in the streets, in the places of commerce, on transportation systems, at athletic events and theaters, in queues, or, more intimately, in pub gatherings, book clubs, bowling leagues, and church choirs. But when we think of democratic culture more formally, we think immediately of a set of distinctive institutions and practices of governance that extends from the local to the national level—from city hall to the statehouse to the Capitol—and includes the modern state in all its complexity and richness. In addition to the formal institutions of governance, we think also of nongovernmental and voluntary associations, such as neighborhood crime watches and parent/teacher associations, through which individuals and groups organize their private and public lives.

Central to the concept of democracy are "citizens"—not "subjects," "comrades," or "masses," but "citizens"—who, in the degree to which they share responsibility for society and its welfare, are members of a "public." In democratic theory, "citizens" are morally equal in politics and justice, regardless of wealth and social status. The forms of citizenship and the influence of the public have been well debated by scholars and pollsters. But it is enough to say this: although there is some variation in democratic regimes, republics such as the United States confer sovereignty on their citizens and thereby confer on the public, through the device of elections, the final say on the question of who will govern.

Democratic systems are designed with a view to establishing authority and electing governments that serve at the will of the people. But the will of the people includes the desire to ensure that the power of government, constituted by the democratic principle of majority rule, cannot be used to tyrannize minorities or deprive individuals of fundamental freedoms. Liberal democracies not only authorize the means, methods, and goals of government, but also seek to balance the requirements of collective life with basic and enduring freedoms.

In words expressed initially by the seventeenth- and eighteenth-century philosophers who contributed so much to our understanding of modern politics and government, the balance between freedom and responsibility arises out of a surrender of some portion of individual liberty through a notion called the "social contract." By virtue of this contract, the law—the authority binding all citizens, including those who govern, to rules of conduct—is obeyed and accepted as legitimate. If the system is working, the law draws a boundary around freedom, however much there is. Similarly, a code of civility circumscribes freedom. Together they modify individual freedom in recognition of the requirements of collective life. Thus as John Dewey, a twentieth-century American philosopher and avowed democrat, said, liberty is that "secure release and fulfillment of personal potentialities which take place only in rich and manifold association with others. . . ."[1]

The heart of the social contract is to be found in democratic constitutions. A constitution sanctions the rule of law, the means and ends of government, and democratic rights and freedoms. In the domain of rights and freedoms, democratic constitutions guarantee that the executive and the representatives in the legislatures will be elected by citizens; that elections will be held regularly; that citizenship will be inclusive and universal; that every citizen will have the right to vote; that legal rights will be protected and that citizens will not be deprived of their liberty except through the due processes of law; that the judiciary will be independent; that citizens will be free to organize and associate; and— central to this exposition—that speech, religion, and expression will be free.

Although such principles might not always be obvious in the swirl of activity, advocacy, and competition for power they set in motion, we can say in light of the foregoing that democracies can have an objective existence—as can autocracies and dictatorships. We can also say that each system is artifice, a made thing. By that we mean that each is the product of design, not of the gods or of nature, but of human beings possessed of democratic beliefs and the will to implement them. In the case of liberal democracy, which aims to maximize liberty and justice, the artifice is precious. In this view, democracy is not an edifice that facilitates opportunity, creativity, and pleasure—the dividends of freedom—alone. It also confers a responsibility on all citizens, including journalists, for the well-being of its institutions and practices.

Journalism is one manifestation of the right of free expression, a fundamental democratic freedom. The democratic guarantee in the American Constitution that speech, religion, and expression will be free was not formulated with journalists alone in mind. The right of free expression, sanctioned by the First Amendment, belongs to *all* citizens. Nevertheless, it is from such a guarantee that journalism gains its special ground in the architecture of democracy. In this sense, every act of journalism, regardless of content, is an expression of a freedom guaranteed by the Constitution. In light of this, it is reasonable to ask how—and with what values and ends in mind—journalism is designed.

When journalists reflect on their role, they are likely to see themselves as standing on neutral ground—performing democratic functions, to be sure, but not embedded in the democratic edifice. From this imagined neutral ground, they see themselves watching the swirl of activity that marks modern government, business and commerce, science, society, culture, and civil society, and they describe themselves more as recorders and critics or, more aggressively, as sentinels and watchdogs (even as spies) than as custodians and stewards of democratic life. If they see themselves as custodians and stewards, it is likely to be as stewards of freedom rather than stewards of the project of governance as a whole. There is utility—even some truth—to such a view. It positions the journalist outside the action and places the reporter above the fray—free to record and comment without restriction on all manner of events and subjects. Such a vision makes the journalist not so much a custodian or steward of democracy and its practices as an observer of them.

Our view, exemplified by the essays we have chosen for this collection, is that the ground is not as neutral as it may at first seem. It may feel neutral in a regime of freedom secured by constitutional doctrine and law. It may feel neutral—and even natural—because the constitutional regime, which is a made thing, provides a stable foundation. But its basic character is defined by its place in the democratic design, which itself is artifice. So as a first observation, we would add the corollary that journalism is a practice, a craft, a piece of the artifice we call "democracy." The journalist in this view is a citizen/writer whose autonomy and expression incarnate ideals that promote individual freedom and collective life. Just as the expressive lives of citizens should incarnate such ideals, so, too, should the expressive lives of journalists. Journalism should reflect not only the creative possibilities arising out of individual freedom, but also the values of collective life.

The values that do the job are located in journalism's best practices and protocols: truth is the goal; the evidence of the senses is authoritative; facts should be verified; bias is a weakness; clear writing is a virtue. They are practical values, designed to attune citizens to a common reality that can be known and described. In a world of made things, nothing is value-free. Whatever else journalism might be or do, it should embody the values that make collective life of free citizens possible. John Dewey said as much in 1927 when he wrote that "[c]ommunication can alone create a great community. Our Babel is not one of tongues but of the signs and symbols without which shared experience is impossible."[2]

His observation calls into view the English critic George Orwell's thesis that connects the erosion of political standards to the debasement of language. Orwell says in effect that writers are democracy's stewards. Collective life is dependent on the development of a common and public language. Journalists have a democratic duty to write clearly and in a public language. Furthermore, trust is a core value. It is basic to the idea of journalism and an active public that facts are sacred and should be initially stripped, to the extent it is possible, of their ideological potential. Another way of viewing this is to say that journalists are party to a parallel social contract. The understanding that lies behind such a contract is that as their work goes, so goes democracy. The codes of ethics of various associations of journalists that commit journalists to the virtues of reason, toleration, and—above all—dedicated empiricism are one expression of the terms of the contract that journalists have made with their fellow citizens.

So there are deep moral implications to the view that journalism is artifice. This is not to suggest that we are calling for a debate on the merits of the issues raised by the old phrase "publish and be damned." We approve the democratic courage that the phrase inspires. However, it follows from the view that journalism is an incarnation of democratic ideals that the quality of the journalism always matters. The view we are promoting constitutes not a justification for self-censorship. Rather it constitutes an encouragement to apprentice journalists to do journalism (following Ernest Hemingway's phrasing) well and truly—to bring the here and now to consciousness with care so that citizens can govern themselves and navigate in a free society. We are saying that in order to do journalism well and truly, apprentice journalists must study and master journalism's best practices. Following Northrop Frye, the late Canadian critic, we believe freedom is something earned. Frye wrote in 1962: "Freedom has nothing to do with lack of training. You're not free to move unless you've learned to walk and not free to play the piano unless you practice. Nobody is capable of free speech unless [he or she] learns how to use language, and such knowledge is not a gift; it has to be learned and worked at."[3]

Journalists make and remake journalism's texts with basic values and protocols in mind. Regardless of the manifold subjects it treats, journalism springs from a fundamental democratic freedom. It is a democratic practice bound up with the continuous creation, renewal, and maintenance of democratic institutions, culture, and civil society. With this in mind, the journalist—to the best of his or her ability—is obliged to make good news judgments, to write well and truly, to create faithful documents, and to reflect thoughtfully on the things he or she brings to light. These are the principal goals associated with the essays and articles of this collection. They reveal the manner in which journalism is a democratic craft. Put differently, journalism is not value-neutral or value-free. Conceived as artifice, it is value-laden. The values are those that promote the vitality of democratic life.[4]

NOTES

1. John Dewey, *The Public and Its Problem; An Essay in Political Inquiry* (Chicago: Gateway Books Press, 1946), 150 (originally published by Henry Holt and Co., 1927).

2. Dewey, 142.

3. Northrop Frye, *The Educated Imagination* (Bloomington: University of Indiana Press, 1964), 148–49.

4. For a further exploration of these themes, see G. Stuart Adam, "A Preface to the Ethics of Journalism," *Journal of Mass Media Ethics*, Vol. 19, Nos. 3–4, 2004, 247–257.

AUTHORSHIP AND CRAFT

INTRODUCTION

The essays in Part I direct attention to the motives, inclinations, goals, and duties of authors. Their purpose is to mark the moral and aesthetic seriousness with which good writers, including journalists, construct texts. They include reflections by George Orwell and Joan Didion, who are known for journalism as well as for fiction; V. S. Naipaul, Salman Rushdie, and Robert Stone, who are novelists; and Maya Angelou, who has written novels, poems, and memoirs.

The decision to include novelists and poets in a book directed at journalists turns on a belief that reporters, as much as writers of other literary forms, are authors. Journalists create original texts; they authorize a view of events and reality on the basis of their own work and reflection; they publish (or broadcast) what they write. So in our view, apprentice journalists will benefit from considering how serious authors—novelists as well as journalists—reflect on their work.

In seeing journalists as authors, we must never ignore the crucial distinctions between journalism and fiction, which are explored elsewhere in this anthology. Poets and novelists are free to pursue an expression of truth that may be detached from verifiable fact. The nonfiction author has no such luxury. The journalist's authority depends upon adherence to a social contract with readers that the work has not been fabricated or plagiarized.

We start with George Orwell, whose reputation derives mainly from his political writing. For those familiar with Orwell's work, it may come as a surprise to learn that it was his preoccupation with beauty—"with the perception of beauty in the external world, or . . . in words and their right arrangement"—that led him to become a writer. To be sure, his aesthetic sensibilities were joined in due course to strong political impulses. In 1946, the year in which he published "Why I Write," he said forthrightly that what "I have most wanted to do throughout the past ten years is to make political writing into an art."

The aesthetic and even technical impulses—what Orwell was referring to when he spoke of words and their right arrangement—are described vividly in Didion's essay. She writes, as Orwell did before her, that "[t]he arrangement of the words matters." She offers a technical insight to aspiring writers by saying that "the arrangement you want can be found in the picture in your mind." Didion, who describes herself as a person who spends solitary hours arranging words on pieces of paper, says she is motivated always by a need to know "[w]hat is going on in these pictures in my mind."

For a writer such as Robert Stone, whose essay concludes this section of the book, the plain fact is that the technical, moral, and aesthetic elements are one. At least, they co-exist in, and are essential to, all literature. So, he asks directly, if a "novelist openly accepts that his work must necessarily contain moral and political dimensions, what responsibilities does [the author] take on?" Stone's answer rings loudly: "He assumes, above all, the responsibility to understand"—that is, to penetrate the complex mix of emotions and actions that marks the human world and then to reveal them with his or her best intellectual and aesthetic equipment.

So the goal of a good writer is a version of the truth—a word and a concept that should not be relativized out of an author's (or editor's) vocabulary. V. S. Naipaul says in his essay "On Being a Writer" that he aims in his work for "truth to a particular experience." In a reply to his critics and enemies, Salman Rushdie says that his aim as a novelist is "to see the world anew." Similarly, Maya Angelou says that writers concern themselves with revealing the truth about human beings—"what we are capable of, what makes us lose, laugh, weep, fall down and gnash our teeth and wring our hands and kill each other and love each other."

Despite the fact that writing (along with researching and thinking) is often a solitary task, the views of it expressed by these writers are social. Put a little differently, one can say that although the moral burdens of a serious writer may seem personal, they are actually borne on behalf of readers—one could say, more ambitiously, of the members of the human race—to whom the contours of reality and truth matter. Furthermore, to serve a community of readers adequately, the work of the journalist—however individual it might sometimes feel—is created in a social context, in a newsroom, with the help of responsible editors and in collaboration with other artisans.

The condition of such acts of responsibility and truth-seeking is freedom. Salman Rushdie, for whom freedom is a practical and personal question since the publication of *The Satanic Verses*, writes that "[h]uman beings understand themselves and shape their futures by arguing and challenging and questioning and saying the unsayable; not by bowing the knee, whether to gods or to men." He goes on to say that "[l]anguage and the imagination cannot be imprisoned, or art dies, and with it, a little of what makes us human." For Rushdie, as for all serious writers, the imagination's capacity to shape human understanding is primary even if its products threaten a particular version of the social order and the doctrines supporting it. In a sense, writers don't sow disorder so much as inscribe a counter- or alternative order in which experience is registered and a democracy of mind preserved. We achieve this state of understanding and mind by telling stories. Stone puts it this way: "Storytelling is not a luxury to humanity; it's almost as necessary as bread. We cannot imagine ourselves without it because each self is a story. . . . We tell ourselves our own stories selectively, in order to keep our sense of self intact."

It will become obvious as these essays are examined that authors give attention to and are inspired by the work of other writers. Orwell's interest in language was awakened by John Milton's *Paradise Lost*, which he read when he was young. Joan Didion's essay borrows not only a title, but also an attitude of assertiveness she finds in the title of George Orwell's essay, "Why I Write." V. S. Naipaul takes inspiration and pleasure from the work of such nineteenth-century British journalists as William Cobbett and such novelists as Anthony Trollope; Maya Angelou has been inspired by black poets, preachers, Shakespeare, and Edna St. Vincent Millay; Robert Stone quotes Ernest Hemingway (who was once a journalist himself) to say that an author should write "well and truly"—that is, in clear and elegant prose. It is our hope that these essays will be equally formative to the apprentice journalists who read them.

The readings that follow have been selected to allow students to begin the study of authorship and a philosophy of writing. They are individually rich and call for careful textual reading.

1

WHY I WRITE

George Orwell

From a very early age, perhaps the age of five or six, I knew that when I grew up I should be a writer. Between the ages of about seventeen and twenty-four I tried to abandon this idea, but I did so with the consciousness that I was outraging my true nature and that sooner or later I should have to settle down and write books.

I was the middle child of three, but there was a gap of five years on either side, and I barely saw my father before I was eight. For this and other reasons I was somewhat lonely, and I soon developed disagreeable mannerisms which made me unpopular throughout my schooldays. I had the lonely child's habit of making up stories and holding conversations with imaginary persons, and I think from the very start my literary ambitions were mixed up with the feeling of being isolated and undervalued. I knew that I had a facility with words and a power of facing unpleasant facts, and I felt that this created a sort of private world in which I could get my own back for my failure in everyday life. Nevertheless the volume of serious—*i.e.* seriously intended—writing which I produced all through my childhood and boyhood would not amount to half a dozen pages. I wrote my first poem at the age of four or five, my mother taking it down to dictation. I cannot remember anything about it except that it was about a tiger and the tiger had "chair-like teeth"—a good enough phrase, but I fancy the poem was a plagiarism of Blake's "Tiger, Tiger." At eleven, when the war of 1914–18 broke out, I wrote a patriotic poem which was printed in the local newspaper, as was another, two years later, on the death of Kitchener. From time to time, when I was a bit older, I wrote bad and usually unfinished "nature poems" in the Georgian style. I also, about twice, attempted a short story which was a ghastly failure. That was the total of the would-be serious work that I actually set down on paper during all those years.

However, throughout this time I did in a sense engage in literary activities. To begin with there was the made-to-order stuff which I produced quickly, easily and without much pleasure to myself. Apart from school work, I wrote *vers d'occasion*, semi-comic poems which I could turn out at what now seems to me astonishing speed—at fourteen I wrote a whole rhyming play, in imitation of Aristophanes, in about a week—and helped to edit school magazines, both printed and in manuscript. These magazines were the most pitiful burlesque stuff that you could imagine, and I took far less trouble with them than I now would with the cheapest journalism. But side by side with all this, for fifteen years or more, I was carrying out a literary exercise of a quite different kind: this was the making up of a continuous "story" about myself, a sort of diary existing only in the mind. I believe this is a common habit of children and adolescents. As a very small child I used to imagine that I was, say, Robin Hood, and picture myself as the hero of thrilling adventures, but quite soon my "story" ceased to be narcissistic in a crude way and became more and more a mere description of what I was doing and the things I saw. For minutes at a time this kind of thing would be running through my head: "He pushed the door open and entered the room. A yellow beam of sunlight, filtering through the muslin curtains, slanted on to the table, where a matchbox, half open, lay beside the inkpot. With his right hand in his pocket he moved across to the window. Down in the street a tortoiseshell cat was chasing a dead leaf," etc., etc. This habit continued till I was about twenty-five, right through my non-literary years. Although I had to search, and did search, for the right words, I seemed to be making this descriptive effort almost against my will, under a kind of compulsion from outside. The "story" must, I suppose, have reflected the styles of the various writers I admired at different ages, but so far as I remember it always had the same meticulous descriptive quality.

When I was about sixteen I suddenly discovered the joy of mere words, *i.e.* the sounds and associations of words. The lines from *Paradise Lost*—

So hee with difficulty and labour hard
Moved on: with difficulty and labour hee,

which do not now seem to me so very wonderful, sent shivers down my backbone; and the spelling "hee" for "he" was an added pleasure. As for the need to describe things, I knew all about it already. So it is clear what kind of books I wanted to write, in so far as I could be said to want to write books at that time. I wanted to write enormous naturalistic novels with unhappy endings, full of detailed descriptions and arresting similes, and also full of purple passages in which words were used partly for the sake of their sound. And in fact my first complete novel, *Burmese Days*, which I wrote when I was thirty but projected much earlier, is rather that kind of book.

I give all this background information because I do not think one can assess a writer's motives without knowing something of his early development. His subject matter will be determined by the age he lives in—at least this is true in tumultuous, revolutionary ages like our own—but before he ever begins to write he will have acquired an emotional attitude from which he will never completely escape. It is his job, no doubt, to discipline his temperament and avoid getting stuck at some immature stage, or in some perverse mood: but if he escapes from his early influences altogether, he will have killed his impulse to write. Putting aside the need to earn a living, I think there are four great motives for writing, at any rate for writing prose. They exist in different degrees in every writer, and in any one writer the proportions will vary from time to time, according to the atmosphere in which he is living. They are:

(1) Sheer egoism. Desire to seem clever, to be talked about, to be remembered after death, to get your own back on grownups who snubbed you in childhood, etc., etc. It is humbug to pretend that this is not a motive, and a strong one. Writers share this characteristic with scientists, artists, politicians, lawyers, soldiers, successful businessmen —in short, with the whole top crust of humanity. The great mass of human beings are not acutely selfish. After the age of about thirty they abandon individual ambition—in many cases, indeed, they almost abandon the sense of being individuals at all—and live chiefly for others, or are simply smothered under drudgery. But there is also the minority of gifted, wilful people who are determined to live their own lives to the end, and writers belong in this class. Serious writers, I should say, are on the whole more vain and self-centred than journalists, though less interested in money.

(2) Esthetic enthusiasm. Perception of beauty in the external world, or, on the other hand, in words and their right arrangement. Pleasure in the impact of one sound on another, in the firmness of good prose or the rhythm of a good story. Desire to share an experience which one feels is valuable and ought not to be missed. The esthetic motive is very feeble in a lot of writers, but even a pamphleteer or a writer of textbooks will have pet words and phrases which appeal to him for nonutilitarian reasons; or he may feel strongly about typography, width of margins, etc. Above the level of a railway guide, no book is quite free from esthetic considerations.

(3) Historical impulse. Desire to see things as they are, to find out true facts and store them up for the use of posterity.

(4) Political purpose—using the word "political" in the widest possible sense. Desire to push the world in a certain direction, to alter other people's idea of the kind of society that they should strive after. Once again, no book is genuinely free from political bias. The opinion that art should have nothing to do with politics is itself a political attitude.

It can be seen how these various impulses must war against one another, and how they must fluctuate from person to person and from time to time. By nature—taking your "nature" to be the state you have attained when you are first adult—I am a person in whom the first three motives would outweigh the fourth. In a peaceful age I might have written ornate or merely descriptive books, and might have remained almost unaware of my political loyalties. As it is I have been forced into becoming a sort of pamphleteer. First I spent five years in an unsuitable profession (the Indian Imperial Police, in Burma), and then I underwent poverty and the sense of failure. This increased my natural hatred of authority and made me for the first time fully aware of the existence of the working classes, and the job in Burma had given me some understanding of the nature of imperialism: but these experiences were not enough to give me an accurate political orientation. Then came Hitler, the Spanish civil war, etc. By the end of 1935 I had still failed to reach a firm decision. I remember a little poem that I wrote at that date, expressing my dilemma:

A happy vicar I might have been
Two hundred years ago,
To preach upon eternal doom
And watch my walnuts grow;

But born, alas, in an evil time,
I missed that pleasant haven,
For the hair has grown on my upper lip
And the clergy are all clean-shaven.

And later still the times were good,
We were so easy to please,
We rocked our troubled thoughts to sleep
On the bosoms of the trees.

All ignorant we dared to own
The joys we now dissemble;
The greenfinch on the apple bough
Could make my enemies tremble.

But girls' bellies and apricots,
Roach in a shaded stream,
Horses, ducks in flight at dawn,
All these are a dream.

It is forbidden to dream again;
We maim our joys and hide them;
Horses are made of chromium steel
And little fat men shall ride them.

I am the worm who never turned,
The eunuch without a harem;
Between the priest and the commissar
I walk like Eugene Aram;

And the commissar is telling my fortune
While the radio plays,
But the priest has promised an Austin Seven,
For Duggie always pays.

I dreamed I dwelt in marble halls,
And woke to find it true;
I wasn't born for an age like this;
Was Smith? Was Jones? Were you?

The Spanish war and other events in 1936–7 turned the scale and thereafter I knew where
I stood. Every line of serious work that I have written since 1936 has been written,
directly or indirectly, *against* totalitarianism and *for* democratic socialism, as I understand it. It seems to me nonsense, in a period like our own, to think that one can avoid
writing of such subjects. Everyone writes of them in one guise or another. It is simply a
question of which side one takes and what approach one follows. And the more one is

conscious of one's political bias, the more chance one has of acting politically without sacrificing one's esthetic and intellectual integrity.

What I have most wanted to do throughout the past ten years is to make political writing into an art. My starting point is always a feeling of partisanship, a sense of injustice. When I sit down to write a book, I do not say to myself, "I am going to produce a work of art." I write it because there is some lie that I want to expose, some fact to which I want to draw attention, and my initial concern is to get a hearing. But I could not do the work of writing a book, or even a long magazine article, if it were not also an esthetic experience. Anyone who cares to examine my work will see that even when it is downright propaganda it contains much that a full-time politician would consider irrelevant. I am not able, and I do not want, completely to abandon the worldview that I acquired in childhood. So long as I remain alive and well I shall continue to feel strongly about prose style, to love the surface of the earth, and to take a pleasure in solid objects and scraps of useless information. It is no use trying to suppress that side of myself. The job is to reconcile my ingrained likes and dislikes with the essentially public, non-individual activities that this age forces on all of us.

It is not easy. It raises problems of construction and of language, and it raises in a new way the problem of truthfulness. Let me give just one example of the cruder kind of difficulty that arises. My book about the Spanish civil war, *Homage to Catalonia*, is, of course, a frankly political book, but in the main it is written with a certain detachment and regard for form. I did try very hard in it to tell the whole truth without violating my literary instincts. But among other things it contains a long chapter, full of newspaper quotations and the like, defending the Trotskyists who were accused of plotting with Franco. Clearly such a chapter, which after a year or two would lose its interest for any ordinary reader, must ruin the book. A critic whom I respect read me a lecture about it. "Why did you put in all that stuff?" he said. "You've turned what might have been a good book into journalism." What he said was true, but I could not have done otherwise. I happened to know, what very few people in England had been allowed to know, that innocent men were being falsely accused. If I had not been angry about that I should never have written the book.

In one form or another this problem comes up again. The problem of language is subtler and would take too long to discuss. I will only say that of late years I have tried to write less picturesquely and more exactly. In any case I find that by the time you have perfected any style of writing, you have always outgrown it. *Animal Farm* was the first book in which I tried, with full consciousness of what I was doing, to fuse political purpose and artistic purpose into one whole. I have not written a novel for seven years, but I hope to write another fairly soon. It is bound to be a failure, every book is a failure, but I do know with some clarity what kind of book I want to write.

Looking back through the last page or two, I see that I have made it appear as though my motives in writing were wholly public-spirited. I don't want to leave that as the final impression. All writers are vain, selfish and lazy, and at the very bottom of their motives there lies a mystery. Writing a book is a horrible, exhausting struggle, like a long bout of some painful illness. One would never undertake such a thing if one were not driven on by some demon whom one can neither resist nor understand. For all one knows that demon is simply the same instinct that makes a baby squall for attention. And yet it is also true that one can write nothing readable unless one constantly struggles to efface one's own personality. Good prose is like a window pane. I cannot say with certainty which of my motives are the strongest, but I know which of them deserve to be followed. And looking back through my work, I see that it is invariably where I lacked a *political* purpose that I wrote lifeless books and was betrayed into purple passages, sentences without meaning, decorative adjectives and humbug generally.

[1946]

2

ON BEING A WRITER

V. S. Naipaul

I do not really know how I became a writer. I can give certain dates and certain facts about my career. But the process itself remains mysterious. It is mysterious, for instance, that the ambition should have come first—the wish to be a writer, to have that distinction, that fame—and that this ambition should have come long before I could think of anything to write about.

I remember, in my first term at Oxford in 1950, going for long walks—I remember the roads, the autumn leaves, the cars and trucks going by, whipping the leaves up—and wondering what I was going to write about. I had worked hard for the scholarship to go to Oxford, to be a writer. But now that I was in Oxford, I didn't know what to write about. And really, I suppose, unless I had been driven by great necessity, something even like panic, I might never have written. The idea of laying aside the ambition was very restful and tempting—the way sleep was said to be tempting to Napoleon's soldiers on the retreat from Moscow.

I felt it as artificial, that sitting down to write a book. And that is a feeling that is with me still, all these years later, at the start of a book—I am speaking of an imaginative work. There is no precise theme or story that is with me. Many things are with me; I write the artificial, self-conscious beginnings of many books; until finally some true impulse—the one I have been working toward—possesses me, and I sail away on my year's labor. And that is mysterious still—that out of artifice one should touch and stir up what is deepest in one's soul, one's heart, one's memory.

All literary forms are artificial, and they are constantly changing, to match the new tone and mood of the culture. At one time, for instance, a person of serious literary inclination might have thought of writing for the theater; would have had somehow to do what I cannot do—arrange his material into scenes and acts; would not have written for the printed page, but would have written "parts" to tempt actors and—as someone who has written

---

V. S. Naipaul, "On Being a Writer," *The New York Review of Books*, April 23, 1987. © V. S. Naipaul. Reprinted with permission from Gillan Actken Associates.

plays has told me—would have visualized himself (to facilitate the playwriting process) as sitting in a seat in the stalls.

At another period, in an age without radio or records, an age dominated by print, someone wishing to write would have had to shape a narrative that could have been serialized over many months, or fill three volumes. Before that, the writer might have attempted narratives in verse, or verse drama, rhymed or unrhymed; or verse epics.

All those forms, artificial as they seem to us today, would have appeared as natural and as right to their practitioners as the standard novel does today. Artificial though that novel form is, with its simplifications and distortions, its artificial scenes, and its idea of experience as a crisis that has to be resolved before life resumes its even course. I am describing, very roughly, the feeling of artificiality which was with me at the very beginning, when I was trying to write and wondering what part of my experience could be made to fit the form—wondering, in fact, in the most insidious way, how I could adapt or falsify my experience to make it fit the grand form.

Literary forms are necessary: experience has to be transmitted in some agreed or readily comprehensible way. But certain forms, like fashions in dress, can at times become extreme. And then these forms, far from crystallizing or sharpening experience, can falsify or be felt as a burden. The Trollope who is setting up a situation—the Trollope who is a social observer, with an immense knowledge both of society and the world of work, a knowledge far greater than that of Dickens—is enchanting. But I have trouble with the Trollope who, having set up a situation, settles down to unwinding his narrative—the social or philosophical gist of which I might have received in his opening pages. I feel the same with Thackeray: I can feel how the need for narrative and plot sat on his shoulders like a burden.

Our ideas of literary pleasures and narrative have in fact changed in the last hundred years or so. All the writing of the past century, and the cinema, and television have made us quicker. And the nineteenth-century English writers who now give me the most "novelistic" pleasure—provide windows into human lives, encouraging reflection—are writers who in their own time would not have been thought of as novelists at all.

I am thinking of writers like Richard Jefferies, whose essays about farming people carry so much knowledge and experience that they often contain whole lives. Or William Hazlitt. Or Charles Lamb, concrete and tough and melancholy, not the gentle, wishy-washy essayist of legend. Or William Cobbett, the journalist and pamphleteer, dashing about the countryside, and in his breakneck prose, and through his wild prejudices, giving the clearest pictures of the roads and the fields and the people and the inns and the food. All of these writers would have had their gifts diluted or corrupted by the novel form as it existed in their time. All of them, novelistic as they are in the pleasures they offer, found their own forms.

Every serious writer has to be original; he cannot be content to do or to offer a version of what has been done before. And every serious writer as a result becomes aware of this question of form; because he knows that however much he might have been educated and stimulated by the writers he has read or reads, the forms matched the experience of those writers, and do not strictly suit his own.

The late Philip Larkin—original and very grand, especially in his later work—thought that form and content were indivisible. He worked slowly, he said "You're finding out what to say as well as how to say it, and that takes time." It sounds simple; but it states a difficult thing. Literature is not like music; it isn't for the young; there are no prodigies in writing. The knowledge or experience a writer seeks to transmit is social or sentimental; it takes time, it can take much of a man's life, to process that experience, to understand what he has been through; and it takes great care and tact, then, for the nature of the experience not to be lost, not to be diluted by the wrong forms. The other man's forms served the other man's thoughts.

I have always been concerned about this problem of form, and even of vocabulary, because I fairly soon got to realize that between the literature I knew and read, the literature that seeded my own ambition, between that and my background, there was a division, a dissonance. And it was quickly made clear to me that there was no question simply of mimicking the forms.

In one of his early books James Joyce wrote of the difficulty for him—or his hero— of the English language. "That language in which we are speaking is his before it is mine. How different are the words *home, Christ, ale, master*, on his lips and mine! I cannot speak or write these words without unrest of spirit. . . . My soul frets in the shadow of his language."

James Joyce was an experimenter in pure form—form divorced from content. And the James Joyce point about language is not the one I am making. I never felt that problem with the English language—language as language. The point that worried me was one of vocabulary, of the differing meanings or associations of words. *Garden, house, plantation, gardener, estate*: these words mean one thing in England and mean something quite different to the man from Trinidad, an agricultural colony, a colony settled for the purpose of plantation agriculture. How, then, could I write honestly or fairly if the very words I used, with private meanings for me, were yet for the reader outside shot through with the associations of the older literature? I felt that truly to render what I saw, I had to define myself as writer or narrator; I had to reinterpret things. I have tried to do this in different ways throughout my career. And after two years' work, I have just finished a book in which at last, as I think, I have managed to integrate this business of reinterpreting with my narrative.

My aim was truth, truth to a particular experience, containing a definition of the writing self. Yet I was aware at the end of that book that the creative process remained as mysterious as ever.

The French critic Sainte-Beuve thought that the personal details of a writer's life made clear many things about the writer. This method of Saint-Beuve's was bitterly assailed by Proust in a strange book—a strange and original and beautiful form, part autobiography, part literary criticism, part fiction—called *Against Sainte-Beuve,* where the criticism of the critic and his method, releasing the writer's love of letters, also releases the autobiographical and fictive elements of the work.

"This method," Proust writes (in the translation by Sylvia Townsend Warner)—and he is talking about the method of Sainte-Beuve—"ignores what a very slight degree of self-acquaintance teaches us, that a book is the product of a different *self* from the self we manifest in our habits, in our social life, in our vices." And a little later on, Proust elucidates: "The implication [is] that there is something more superficial and empty in a writer's authorship, something deeper and more contemplative in his private life. . . . In fact, it is the secretion of one's innermost life, written in solitude and for oneself alone, that one gives to the public. What one bestows on private life—in conversation, however refined it may be . . . —is the product of a quite superficial self, not of the innermost self which one can only recover by putting aside the world and the self that frequents the world."

And it is curious—yet not really surprising—that almost the same thought about the writer's writing self should have been expressed by a quite different writer, Somerset Maugham. In his fictional portrait of Thomas Hardy in *Cakes and Ale*, Maugham, by a wonderful stroke (which earned him much abuse), showed the tragic novelist of Wessex to be in his private life extraordinarily ordinary, and for that reason mysterious. "I had an impression"—this is Maugham's summing up—"that the real man, to his death unknown and lonely, was a wraith that went a silent way unseen between the writer of his books and the man who led his life, and smiled with ironical detachment at the two puppets. . . ."

3

WHY I WRITE

Joan Didion

Of course I stole the title for this talk, from George Orwell. One reason I stole it was that I like the sound of the words: Why I Write. There you have three short unambiguous words that share a sound, and the sound they share is this:

I

I

I

In many ways writing is the act of saying *I*, of imposing oneself upon other people, of saying *listen to me, see it my way, change your mind*. It's an aggressive, even a hostile act. You can disguise its aggressiveness all you want with veils of subordinate clauses and qualifiers and tentative subjunctives, with ellipses and evasions—with the whole manner of intimating rather than claiming, of alluding rather than stating—but there's no getting around the fact that setting words on paper is the tactic of a secret bully, an invasion, an imposition of the writer's sensibility on the reader's most private space.

I stole the title not only because the words sounded right but because they seemed to sum up, in a no-nonsense way, all I have to tell you. Like many writers I have only this one "subject," this one "area": the act of writing. I can bring you no reports from any other front. I may have other interests: I am "interested," for example, in marine biology, but I don't flatter myself that you would come out to hear me talk about it. I am not a

---

scholar. I am not in the least an intellectual, which is not to say that when I hear the word "intellectual" I reach for my gun, but only to say that I do not think in abstracts. During the years when I was an undergraduate at Berkeley I tried, with a kind of hopeless late-adolescent energy, to buy some temporary visa into the world of ideas, to forge for myself a mind that could deal with the abstract.

In short I tried to think. I failed. My attention veered inexorably back to the specific, to the tangible, to what was generally considered, by everyone I knew then and for that matter have known since, the peripheral. I would try to contemplate the Hegelian dialectic and would find myself concentrating instead on a flowering pear tree outside my window and the particular way the petals fell on my floor. I would try to read linguistic theory and would find myself wondering instead if the lights were on in the bevatron up the hill. When I say that I was wondering if the lights were on in the bevatron you might immediately suspect, if you deal in ideas at all, that I was registering the bevatron as a political symbol, thinking in shorthand about the military-industrial complex and its role in the university community, but you would be wrong. I was only wondering if the lights were on in the bevatron, and how they looked. A physical fact.

I had trouble graduating from Berkeley, not because of this inability to deal with ideas—I was majoring in English, and I could locate the house-and-garden imagery in *The Portrait of a Lady* as well as the next person, "imagery" being by definition the kind of specific that got my attention—but simply because I had neglected to take a course in Milton. For reasons which now sound baroque I needed a degree by the end of that summer, and the English department finally agreed, if I would come down from Sacramento every Friday and talk about the cosmology of *Paradise Lost*, to certify me proficient in Milton. I did this. Some Fridays I took the Greyhound bus, other Fridays I caught the Southern Pacific's City of San Francisco on the last leg of its transcontinental trip. I can no longer tell you whether Milton put the sun or the earth at the center of his universe in *Paradise Lost*, the central question of at least one century and a topic about which I wrote 10,000 words that summer, but I can still recall the exact rancidity of the butter in the City of San Francisco's dining car, and the way the tinted windows on the Greyhound bus cast the oil refineries around Carquinez Straits into a grayed and obscurely sinister light. In short my attention was always on the periphery, on what I could see and taste and touch, on the butter, and the Greyhound bus. During those years I was traveling on what I knew to be a very shaky passport, forged papers: I knew that I was no legitimate resident in any world of ideas. I knew I couldn't think. All I knew then was what I couldn't do. All I knew then was what I wasn't, and it took me some years to discover what I was.

Which was a writer.

By which I mean not a "good" writer or a "bad" writer but simply a writer, a person whose most absorbed and passionate hours are spent arranging words on pieces of paper. Had my credentials been in order I would never have become a writer. Had I been blessed with even limited access to my own mind there would have been no reason to write. I write entirely to find out what I'm thinking, what I'm looking at, what I see and what it means. What I want and what I fear. Why did the oil refineries around Carquinez Straits seem sinister to me in the summer of 1956? Why have the night lights in the bevatron burned in my mind for twenty years? *What is going on in these pictures in my mind?*

When I talk about pictures in my mind I am talking, quite specifically, about images that shimmer around the edges. There used to be an illustration in every elementary psychology book showing a cat drawn by a patient in varying stages of schizophrenia. This cat had a shimmer around it. You could see the molecular structure breaking down at the very edges of the cat: the cat became the background and the background the cat, everything interacting, exchanging ions. People on hallucinogens describe the same perception of objects. I'm not a schizophrenic, nor do I take hallucinogens, but certain images do shimmer for me. Look hard enough, and you can't miss the shimmer. It's there. You can't think too much about these pictures that shimmer. You just lie low and let them develop. You stay quiet. You don't talk to many people and you keep your nervous system from shorting out and you try to locate the cat in the shimmer, the grammar in the picture.

Just as I meant "shimmer" literally I mean "grammar" literally. Grammar is a piano I play by ear, since I seem to have been out of school the year the rules were mentioned. All I know about grammar is its infinite power. To shift the structure of a sentence alters the meaning of that sentence, as definitely and inflexibly as the position of a camera alters the meaning of the object photographed. Many people know about camera angles now, but not so many know about sentences. The arrangement of the words matters, and the arrangement you want can be found in the picture in your mind. The picture dictates the arrangement. The picture dictates whether this will be a sentence with or without clauses, a sentence that ends hard or a dying-fall sentence, long or short, active or passive. The picture tells you how to arrange the words and the arrangement of the words tells you, or tells me, what's going on in the picture. *Nota bene:*

It tells you.

You don't tell it.

Let me show you what I mean by pictures in the mind. I began *Play It as It Lays* just as I have begun each of my novels, with no notion of "character" or "plot" or even "incident." I had only two pictures in my mind, more about which later, and a technical intention, which was to write a novel so elliptical and fast that it would be over before you noticed it, a novel so fast that it would scarcely exist on the page at all. About the pictures: the first was of white space. Empty space. This was clearly the picture that dictated the narrative intention of the book—a book in which anything that happened would happen off the page, a "white" book to which the reader would have to bring his or her own bad dreams—and yet this picture told me no "story," suggested no situation. The second picture did. This second picture was of something actually witnessed. A young woman with long hair and a short white halter dress walks through the casino at the Riviera in Las Vegas at one in the morning. She crosses the casino alone and picks up a house telephone. I watch her because I have heard her paged, and recognize her name: she is a minor actress I see around Los Angeles from time to time, in places like Jax and once in a gynecologist's office in the Beverly Hills Clinic, but have never met. I know nothing about her. Who is paging her? Why is she here to be paged? How exactly did she come to this? It was precisely this moment in Las Vegas that made *Play It as It Lays* begin to tell itself to me, but the moment appears in the novel only obliquely, in a chapter which begins:

"Maria made a list of things she would never do. She would never: walk through the Sands or Caesar's alone after midnight. She would never: ball at a party, do S-M unless she wanted to, borrow furs from Abe Lipsey, deal. She would never: carry a Yorkshire in Beverly Hills."

That is the beginning of the chapter and that is also the end of the chapter, which may suggest what I meant by "white space."

I recall having a number of pictures in my mind when I began the novel I just finished, *A Book of Common Prayer*. As a matter of fact one of these pictures was of that bevatron I mentioned, although I would be hard put to tell you a story in which nuclear energy figures. Another was a newspaper photograph or a hijacked 707 burning on the desert in the Middle East. Another was the night view from a room in which I once spent a week with paratyphoid, a hotel room on the Colombian coast. My husband and I seemed to be on the Colombian coast representing the United States of America at a film festival (I recall invoking the name "Jack Valenti" a lot, as if its reiteration could make me well), and it was a bad place to have fever, not only because my indisposition offended our hosts but because every night in this hotel the generator failed. The lights went out. The elevator stopped. My husband would go to the event of the evening and make excuses for me and I would stay alone in this hotel room, in the dark. I remember standing at the window trying to call Bogotá (the telephone seemed to work on the same principle as the generator) and watching the night wind come up and wondering what I was doing eleven degrees off the equator with a fever of 103. The view from that window definitely figures in *A Book of Common Prayer*, as does the burning 707, and yet none of these pictures told me the story I needed.

The picture that did, the picture that shimmered and made these other images coalesce, was the Panama airport at 6 A.M. I was in this airport only once, on a plane to Bogotá that stopped for an hour to refuel, but the way it looked that morning remained superimposed on everything I saw until the day I finished *A Book of Common Prayer*. I lived in that airport for several years. I can still feel the hot air when I step off the plane, can see the heat already rising off the tarmac at 6 A.M. I can feel my skirt damp and wrinkled on my legs. I can feel the asphalt stick to my sandals. I remember the big tail of a Pan American plane floating motionless down at the end of the tarmac. I remember the sound of a slot machine in the waiting room. I could tell you that I remember a particular woman in the airport, an American woman, a *norteamericana*, a thin *norteamericana* about forty who wore a big square emerald in lieu of a wedding ring, but there was no such woman there.

I put this woman in the airport later. I made this woman up, just as I later made up a country to put the airport in, and a family to run the country. This woman in the airport is neither catching a plane nor meeting one. She is ordering tea in the airport coffee shop. In fact she is not simply "ordering" tea but insisting that the water be boiled, in front of her, for twenty minutes. Why is this woman in this airport? Why is she going nowhere, where has she been? Where did she get that big emerald? What derangement, or disassociation, makes her believe that her will to see the water boiled can possibly prevail?

"She had been going to one airport or another for four months, one could see it, looking at the visas on her passport. All those airports where Charlotte Douglas's passport had been stamped would have looked alike. Sometimes the sign on the tower would say "Bienvenidos" and sometimes the sign on the tower would say "Bienvenue," some places were wet and hot and others dry and hot, but at each of these airports the pastel concrete walls would rust and stain and the swamp off the runway would be littered with the fuselages of cannibalized Fairchild F-227's and the water would need boiling.

"I knew why Charlotte went to the airport even if Victor did not.

"I knew about airports."

These lines appear about halfway through *A Book of Common Prayer*, but I wrote them during the second week I worked on the book, long before I had any idea where Charlotte Douglas had been or why she went to airports. Until I wrote these lines I had no character called Victor" in mind: the necessity for mentioning a name, and the name "Victor," occurred to me as I wrote the sentence. *I knew why Charlotte went to the airport* sounded incomplete. *I knew why Charlotte went to the airport even if Victor did not* carried a little more narrative drive. Most important of all, until I wrote these lines I did not know who "I" was, who was telling the story. I had intended until that that the "I" be no more than the voice of the author, a nineteenth-century omniscient narrator. But there it was:

"I knew why Charlotte went to the airport even if Victor did not.

"I knew about airports."

This "I" was the voice of no author in my house. This "I" was someone who not only knew why Charlotte went to the airport but also knew someone called "Victor." Who was Victor? Who was this narrator? Why was this narrator telling me this story? Let me tell you one thing about why writers write: had I known the answer to any of these questions I would never have needed to write a novel.

4

IN GOOD FAITH

Salman Rushdie

It has been a year since I last spoke in defence of my novel *The Satanic Verses*. I have remained silent, though silence is against my nature, because I felt that my voice was simply not loud enough to be heard above the clamour of the voices raised against me.

I hoped that others would speak for me, and many have done so eloquently, among them an admittedly small but growing number of Muslim readers, writers and scholars. Others, including bigots and racists, have tried to exploit my case (using my name to taunt Muslim and non-Muslim Asian children and adults, for example) in a manner I have found repulsive, defiling and humiliating.

At the centre of the storm stands a novel, a work of fiction, one that aspires to the condition of literature. It has often seemed to me that people on all sides of the argument have lost sight of this simple fact. *The Satanic Verses* has been described, and treated, as a work of bad history, as an anti-religious pamphlet, as the product of an international capitalist–Jewish conspiracy, as an act of murder ("he has murdered our hearts"), as the

Salman Rushdie, "In Good Faith," *The Independent*, February 4, 1990, 18–20. © 1990 by Salman Rushdie, reprinted with permission of the Wylie Agency, Inc.

product of a person comparable to Hitler and Attila the Hun. It felt impossible, amid such a hubbub, to insist on the fictionality of fiction.

Let me be clear: I am not trying to say that *The Satanic Verses* is "only a novel" and thus need not be taken seriously, even disputed with the utmost passion. I do not believe that novels are trivial matters. The ones I care most about are those which attempt radical reformulations of language, form and ideas, those that attempt to do what the word *novel* seems to insist upon: to see the world anew. I am well aware that this can be a hackle-raising, infuriating attempt.

What I have wished to say, however, is that the point of view from which I have, all my life, attempted this process of literary renewal is the result not of the self-hating, deracinated Uncle-Tomism of which some have accused me, but precisely of my determination to create a literary language and literary forms in which the experience of formerly colonized, still-disadvantaged peoples might find full expression. If *The Satanic Verses* is anything, it is a migrant's-eye view of the world. It is written from the very experience of uprooting, disjuncture and metamorphosis (slow or rapid, painful or pleasurable) that is the migrant condition, and from which, I believe, can be derived a metaphor for all humanity.

Standing at the centre of the novel is a group of characters most of whom are British Muslims, or not particularly religious persons of Muslim background, struggling with just the sort of great problems that have arisen to surround the book, problems of hybridization and ghettoization, of reconciling the old and the new. Those who oppose the novel most vociferously today are of the opinion that intermingling with a different culture will inevitably weaken and ruin their own. I am of the opposite opinion. *The Satanic Verses* celebrates hybridity, impurity, intermingling, the transformation that comes of new and unexpected combinations of human beings, cultures, ideas, politics, movies, songs. It rejoices in mongrelization and fears the absolutism of the Pure. *Mélange*, hotchpotch, a bit of this and a bit of that is *how newness enters the world*. It is the great possibility that mass migration gives the world, and I have tried to embrace it. *The Satanic Verses* is for change-by-fusion, change-by-conjoining. It is a love-song to our mongrel selves.

Throughout human history, the apostles of purity, those who have claimed to possess a total explanation, have wrought havoc among mere mixed-up human beings. Like many millions of people, I am a bastard child of history. Perhaps we all are, black and brown and white, leaking into one another, as a character of mine once said, *like flavours when you cook*.

The argument between purity and impurity, which is also the argument between Robespierre and Danton, the argument between the monk and the roaring boy, between primness and impropriety, between the stultifications of excessive respect and the scandals of impropriety, is an old one; I say, let it continue. Human beings understand themselves and shape their futures by arguing and challenging and questioning and saying the unsayable; not by bowing the knee, whether to gods or to men.

The Satanic Verses is, I profoundly hope, a work of radical dissent and questioning and reimagining. It is not, however, the book it has been made out to be, that book containing "nothing but filth and insults and abuse" that has brought people out on to the streets across the world.

That book simply does not exist.

This is what I want to say to the great mass of ordinary, decent, fair-minded Muslims, of the sort I have known all my life, and who have provided much of the inspiration for my work: to be rejected and reviled by, so to speak, one's own characters is a shocking and painful experience for any writer. I recognize that many Muslims have felt shocked and pained, too. Perhaps a way forward might be found through the mutual recognition of that mutual pain. Let us attempt to believe in each other's good faith.

I am aware that this is asking a good deal. There has been too much name-calling. Muslims have been called savages and barbarians and worse. I, too, have received my share of invective. Yet I still believe—perhaps I must—that understanding remains possible, and can be achieved without the suppression of the principle of free speech.

What it requires is a moment of good will; a moment in which we may all accept that the other parties are acting, have acted, in good faith.

You see, it's my opinion that if we could only dispose of the "insults and abuse" accusation, which prevents those who believe it from accepting that *The Satanic Verses* is a work of any serious intent or merit whatsoever, then we might be able, at the very least, to agree to differ about the book's real themes, about the relative value of the sacred and the profane, about the merits of purity and those of hotch-potch, and about how human beings really become whole: through the love of God or through the love of their fellow men and women.

And to dispose of the argument, we must return for a moment to the actually existing book, not the book described in the various pamphlets that have been circulated to the faithful, not the "unreadable" text of legend, not two chapters dragged out of the whole; not a piece of blubber, but the whole wretched whale.

Let me say this first: I have never seen this controversy as a struggle between Western freedoms and Eastern unfreedom. The freedoms of the West are rightly vaunted, but many minorities—racial, sexual, political—just as rightly feel excluded from full possession of these liberties; while, in my lifelong experience of the East, from Turkey and Iran to India and Pakistan, I have found people to be every bit as passionate for freedom as any Czech, Romanian, German, Hungarian or Pole.

How is freedom gained? It is taken: never given. To be free, you must first assume your right to freedom. In writing *The Satanic Verses*, I wrote from the assumption that I was, and am, a free man.

What is freedom of expression? Without the freedom to offend, it ceases to exist. Without the freedom to challenge, even to satirize all orthodoxies, including religious orthodoxies, it ceases to exist. Language and the imagination cannot be imprisoned, or art will die, and with it, a little of what makes us human. *The Satanic Verses* is, in part, a secular man's reckoning with the religious spirit. It is by no means always hostile to faith. "If we write in such a way as to pre-judge such belief as in some way deluded or false, then are we not guilty of élitism, of imposing our world-view on the masses?" asks one of its Indian characters. Yet the novel does contain doubts, uncertainties, even shocks that may well not be to the liking of the devout. Such methods have, however, long been a legitimate part even of Islamic literature.

What does the novel dissent from? Certainly not from people's right to faith, though I have none. It dissents most clearly from imposed orthodoxies *of all types*, from the view that the world is quite clearly This and not That. It dissents from the end of debate, of dispute, of dissent. Hindu communalist sectarianism, the kind of Sikh terrorism that blows up planes, the fatuousnesses of Christian creationism are dissented from as well as the narrower definitions of Islam. But such dissent is a long way from "insults and abuse". I do not believe that most of the Muslims I know would have any trouble with it.

What they have trouble with are statements like these: "Rushdie calls the Prophet Muhammad a homosexual." "Rushdie says the Prophet Muhammad asked God for permission to fornicate with every woman in the world." "Rushdie says the Prophet's wives are whores." "Rushdie calls the Prophet by a devil's name." "Rushdie calls the Companions of the Prophet *scum and bums*." "Rushdie says that the whole Qur'an was the Devil's work." And so forth.

It has been bewildering to watch the proliferation of such statements, and to watch them acquire the authority of truth by virtue of the power of repetition. It has been bewildering to learn that people, millions upon millions of people, have been willing to judge *The Satanic Verses* and its author, without reading it, without finding out what manner of man this fellow might be, on the basis of such allegations as these. It has been bewildering to learn that people *do not care about art*. Yet the only way I can explain matters, the only way I can try and replace the non-existent novel with the one I actually wrote, is to tell you a story.*

Threats of violence ought not to coerce us into believing the victims of intimidation to be responsible for the violence threatened. I am aware, however, that rhetoric is an insufficient response. Nor is it enough to point out that nothing on the scale of this controversy has, to my knowledge, ever happened in the history of literature. If I had told anyone before publication that such events would occur as a result of my book, I would instantly have proved the truth of the accusations of egomania. . . .

It's true that some passages in *The Satanic Verses* have now acquired a prophetic quality that alarms even me. "Your blasphemy, Salman, can't be forgiven . . . To set your words against the Word of God." Et cetera. But to write a dream based around events that took place in the seventh century of the Christian era, and to create metaphors of the conflict between different sorts of "author" and different types of "text"—to say that literature and religion, like literature and politics, fight for the same territory—is very different from somehow knowing, in advance, that your dream is about to come true, that the metaphor is about to be made flesh, that the conflict your work seeks to explore is about to engulf it, and its publishers and booksellers; and you.

At least (small comfort) I wasn't wrong.

Books choose their authors; the act of creation is not entirely a rational and conscious one. But this, as honestly as I can set it down, is, in respect of the novel's treatment of religion, what "I knew I was doing".

I set out to explore, through the process of fiction, the nature of revelation and the power of faith. The mystical, revelatory experience is quite clearly a genuine one.

---

* Rushdie continues in the following paragraphs with a summary of the story and characters of *The Satanic Verses*. We have removed these paragraphs and pick up the text when he returns to the main argument—the editors.

This statement poses a problem to the non-believer: if we accept that the mystic, the prophet, is sincerely undergoing some sort of transcendent experience, but we cannot believe in a supernatural world, then *what is going on?* To answer this question, among others, I began work on the story of "Mahound". I was aware that the "satanic verses" incident is much disputed by Muslim theologians; that the life of Muhammad has become the object of a kind of veneration that some would consider un-Islamic, since Muhammad himself always insisted that he was merely a messenger, an ordinary man; and that, therefore, great sensitivities were involved. I genuinely believed that my overt use of fabulation would make it clear to any reader that I was not attempting to falsify history, but to allow a fiction to take off from history. The use of dreams, fantasy, etc. was intended to say: the point is not whether this is "really" supposed to be Muhammad, or whether the satanic verses incident "really" happened; the point is to examine what such an incident might reveal about what revelation is, about the extent to which the mystic's conscious personality informs and interacts with the mystical event; the point is to try and understand the human event of revelation. The use of fiction was a way of creating the sort of distance from actuality that I felt would prevent offence from being taken. I was wrong.

Jahilia, to use once again the ancient Arab story-tellers' formula I used often in *The Satanic Verses*, both "is and is not" Mecca. Many of the details of its social life are drawn from historical research; but it is also a dream of an Indian city (its concentric street-plan deliberately recalls New Delhi), and, as Gibreel spends time in England, it becomes a dream of London, too. Likewise, the religion of "Submission" both is and is not Islam. Fiction uses facts as a starting-place and then spirals away to explore its real concerns, which are only tangentially historical. Not to see this, to treat fiction as if it were fact, is to make a serious mistake of categories. The case of *The Satanic Verses* may be one of the biggest category mistakes in literary history.

Here is more of what I knew: I knew that stories of Muhammad's doubts, uncertainties, errors, fondness for women abound in and around Muslim tradition. To me, they seemed to make him more vivid, more human, and therefore more interesting, even more worthy of admiration. The greatest human beings must struggle against themselves as well as the world. I never doubted Muhammad's greatness, nor, I believe, is the "Mahound" of my novel belittled by being portrayed as human.

I knew that Islam is by no means homogeneous, or as absolutist as some of its champions make it out to be. Islam contains the doubts of Iqbal, Ghazali, Khayyám as well as the narrow certainties of Shabbir Akhtar of the Bradford Council of Mosques and Kalim Siddiqui, director of the pro-Iranian Muslim Institute. Islam contains ribaldry as well as solemnity, irreverence as well as absolutism. I knew much about Islam that I admired, and still admire, immensely; I also knew that Islam, like all the world's great religions, had seen terrible things done in its name.

The original incident on which the dream of the villagers who drown in the Arabian Sea is based is also a part of what I "knew". The story awed me, because of what it told me about the huge power of faith. I wrote this part of the novel to see if I could understand, by getting inside their skins, people for whom devotion was as great as this.

He did it on purpose is one of the strangest accusations ever levelled at a writer. Of course I did it on purpose. The question is, and it is what I have tried to answer: what is the "it" that I did?

What I did not do was conspire against Islam; or write—after years and years of anti-racist work and writing—a text of incitement to racial hatred; or anything of the sort. My golem, my false Other, may be capable of such deeds, but I am not.

Would I have written differently if I had known what would happen? Truthfully, I don't know. Would I change any of the text now? I would not. It's too late. As Friedrich Dürrenmatt wrote in *The Physicists*: "What has once been thought cannot be unthought."

The controversy over *The Satanic Verses* needs to be looked at as a political event, not purely a theological one. In India, where the trouble started, the Muslim fundamentalist MP Syed Shahabuddin used my novel as a stick with which to threaten the wobbling Rajiv Gandhi government. The demand for the book's banning was a power-play to demonstrate the strength of the Muslim vote, on which Congress has traditionally relied and which it could ill afford to lose. (In spite of the ban, Congress lost the Muslims and the election anyway. Put not your trust in Shahabuddins.)

In South Africa, the row over the book served the purpose of the regime by driving a wedge between the Muslim and non-Muslim members of the UDF. In Pakistan, it was a way for the fundamentalists to try and regain the political initiative after their trouncing in the general election. In Iran, too, the incident could only be properly understood when seen in the context of the country's internal political struggles. And in Britain, where secular and religious leaders had been vying for power in the community for over a decade, and where, for a long time, largely secular organizations such as the Indian Workers Association (IWA) had been in the ascendant, the "affair" swung the balance of power back towards the mosques. Small wonder, then, that the various councils of mosques are reluctant to bring the protest to an end, even though many Muslims up and down the country find it embarrassing, even shameful, to be associated with such illiberalism and violence.

The responsibility for violence lies with those who perpetrate it. In the past twelve months, bookshop workers have been manhandled, spat upon, verbally abused, book-shop premises have been threatened and, on several occasions, actually fire-bombed. Publishing staff have had to face a campaign of hate mail, menacing phone calls, death threats and bomb scares. Demonstrations have, on occasion, turned violent, too. During the big march in London last summer, peaceful counter-demonstrations on behalf of humanism and secularism were knocked to the ground by marchers, and a counter-demo by the courageous (and largely Muslim) Women Against Fundamentalism group was threatened and abused.

There is no conceivable reason why such behaviour should be privileged because it is done in the name of an affronted religion. If we are to talk about "insults", "abuse", "offence", then the campaign against *The Satanic Verses* has been, very often, as insulting, abusive and offensive as it's possible to be.

As a result, racist attitudes have hardened. I did not invent British racism, nor did *The Satanic Verses*. The Commission for Racial Equality (CRE), which now accuses me of harming race relations, knows that for years it lent out my video-taped anti-racist Channel 4 broadcast to all sorts of black and white groups and seminars. Readers of *The Satanic Verses* will not be able to help noticing its extremely strong anti-racist line. I have never given the least comfort or encouragement to racists; but the leaders of the campaign against me certainly have, by reinforcing the worst racist stereotypes of

Muslims as repressive, anti-liberal, censoring zealots. If Norman Tebbit has taken up the old Powellite refrains and if his laments about the multi-cultural society find favour in the land, then a part of the responsibility at least must be laid at the door of those who burn, and would ban, books.

I am not the first writer to be persecuted by Islamic fundamentalism in the modern period; among the greatest names so victimized are the Iranian writer Ahmad Kasravi, stabbed to death by fanatics, and the Egyptian Nobel laureate Naguib Mahfouz, often threatened but still, happily, with us. I am not the first artist to be accused of blasphemy and apostasy; these are, in fact, probably the most common weapons with which fundamentalism has sought to shackle creativity in the modern age. It is sad, then, that so little attention has been paid to this crucial literary context; and that Western critics like John Berger, who once spoke messianically of the need for new ways of seeing, should now express their willingness to privilege one such way over another, to protect a religion boasting one billion believers from the solitary figure of a single writer brandishing an "unreadable" book.

As for the British Muslim "leaders", they cannot have it both ways. Sometimes they say I am entirely unimportant, and only the book matters; on other days they hold meetings at mosques across the nation and endorse the call for my killing. They say they hold to the laws of this country, but they also say that Islamic law has moral primacy for them. They say they do not wish to break British laws, but only a very few are willing openly to repudiate the threat against me. They should make their position clear; are they democratic citizens of a free society or are they not? Do they reject violence or do they not?

After a year, it is time for a little clarity.

To the Muslim community at large, in Britain and India and Pakistan and everywhere else, I would like to say: do not ask your writers to create *typical* or *representative* fictions. Such books are almost invariably dead books. The liveliness of literature lies in its exceptionality, in being the individual, idiosyncratic vision of one human being, in which, to our delight and great surprise, we may find our own image reflected. A book is a version of the world. If you do not like it, ignore it; or offer your own version in return.

And I would like to say this: life without God seems to believers to be an idiocy, pointless, beneath contempt. It does not seem so to non-believers. To accept that the world, here, is all there is; to go through it, towards and into death, without the consolations of religion seems, well, at least as courageous and rigorous to us as the espousal of faith seems to you. Secularism and its work deserve your respect, not your contempt.

A great wave of freedom has been washing over the world. Those who resist—in China, in Romania—find themselves bathed in blood. I should like to ask Muslims—that great mass of ordinary, decent, fair-minded Muslims to whom I have imagined myself to be speaking for most of this piece—to choose to ride the wave; to renounce blood; not to let Muslim leaders make Muslims seem less tolerant than they are. *The Satanic Verses* is a serious work, written from a non-believer's point of view. Let believers accept that, and let it be.

In the meantime, I am asked, how do I feel? I feel grateful to the British government for defending me. I hope that such a defence would be made available to any citizen so threatened, but that doesn't lessen my gratitude. I needed it, and it was provided. (I'm still no Tory, but that's democracy.)

I feel grateful, too, to my protectors, who have done such a magnificent job, and who have become my friends.

I feel grateful to everyone who has offered me support. The one real gain for me in this bad time has been the discovery of being cared for by so many people. The only antidote to hatred is love.

Above all, I feel gratitude towards, solidarity with and pride in all the publishing people and bookstore workers around the world who have held the line against intimidation, and who will, I am sure, continue to do so as long as it remains necessary.

I feel as if I have been plunged, like Alice, into the world beyond the looking-glass, where nonsense is the only available sense. And I wonder if I'll ever be able to climb back through the mirror.

Do I feel regret? Of course I do: regret that such offence has been taken against my work when it was not intended—when dispute was intended, and dissent, and even, at times, satire, and criticism of intolerance, and the like, but not the thing of which I'm most often accused, not "filth", not "insult", not "abuse". I regret that so many people who might have taken pleasure in finding their reality given pride of place in a novel will now not read it because of what they believe it to be, or will come to it with their minds already made up.

And I feel sad to be so grievously separated from my community, from India, from everyday life, from the world.

Please understand, however: I make no complaint. I am a writer. I do not accept my condition. I will strive to change it; but I inhabit it, I am trying to learn from it.

Our lives teach us who we are.

5

MAYA ANGELOU

Interviewed by George Plimpton

(This interview was conducted in the summer of 1990 on the stage of the YMHA on Manhattan's Upper East Side. A large audience, predominantly women, was on hand, filling indeed every seat, with standees in the back . . . a testament to Maya Angelou's drawing-power. Close to the stage was a small contingent of black women dressed in the white robes of the Black Muslim order. Her presence dominated the proceedings. Many of her remarks drew fervid applause, especially those which reflected her views on racial problems, the need to persevere, and "courage." She is an extraordinary performer and has a powerful stage presence. Many of the answers seemed as much directed to the

George Plimpton (ed.), "Maya Angelou," *Writers at Work, The* Paris Review *Interviews* (New York: Viking, 1992). © 1990 by *The Paris Review*. Reprinted with permission of the Wylie Agency, Inc.

audience as to the interviewer so that when Maya Angelou concluded the evening by reading aloud from her work—again to a rapt audience—it seemed a logical extension of a planned entertainment.)

INTERVIEWER: You once told me that you write lying on a made-up bed with a bottle of sherry, a dictionary, *Roget's Thesaurus*, yellow pads, an ashtray, and a Bible. What's the function of the Bible?

MAYA ANGELOU: The language of all the interpretations, the translations, of the Judaic Bible and the Christian Bible, is musical, just wonderful. I read the Bible to myself; I'll take any translation, any edition, and read it aloud, just to hear the language, hear the rhythm, and remind myself how beautiful English is. Though I do manage to mumble around in about seven or eight languages, English remains the most beautiful of languages. It will do anything.

INTERVIEWER: Do you read it to get inspired to pick up your own pen?

ANGELOU: For melody. For content also. I'm working at trying to be a Christian, and that's serious business. It's like trying to be a good Jew, a good Muslim, a good Buddhist, a good Shintoist, a good Zoroastrian, a good friend, a good lover, a good mother, a good buddy: it's serious business. It's not something where you think, "Oh, I've got it done. I did it all day, hotdiggety." The truth is, all day long you try to do it, try to be it, and then in the evening, if you're honest and have a little courage, you look at yourself and say, "Hmm. I only blew it eighty-six times. Not bad." I'm trying to be a Christian, and the Bible helps me to remind myself what I'm about.

INTERVIEWER: Do you transfer that melody to your own prose? Do you think your prose has that particular ring that one associates with the King James version?

ANGELOU: I want to hear how English sounds; how Edna St. Vincent Millay heard English. I want to hear it, so I read it aloud. It is not so that I can then imitate it. It is to remind me what a glorious language it is. Then, I try to be particular, and even original. It's a little like reading Gerard Manley Hopkins or Paul Laurence Dunbar, or James Weldon Johnson.

INTERVIEWER: And is the bottle of sherry for the end of the day, or to fuel the imagination?

ANGELOU: I might have it at 6:15 A.M. just as soon as I get in, but usually it's about eleven o'clock when I'll have a glass of sherry.

INTERVIEWER: When you are refreshed by the Bible and the sherry, how do you start a day's work?

ANGELOU: I have kept a hotel room in every town I've ever lived in. I rent a hotel room for a few months, leave my home at six and try to be at work by 6:30. To write, I lie across the bed, so that this elbow is absolutely encrusted at the end, just so rough with callouses. I never allow the hotel people to change the bed, because I never sleep there. I stay until 12:30 or 1:30 in the afternoon, and then I go home and try to breathe; I look at the work around five; I have an orderly dinner: proper, quiet, lovely dinner; and then I go back to work the next morning. Sometimes in hotels I'll go into the room, and there'll be a note on the floor which says, "Dear Miss Angelou, let us change the sheets. We think they are moldy." But I only allow them to come in and empty wastebaskets. I insist that all things are taken off the walls. I don't want anything in there. I go into the room, and I feel as if all my beliefs are suspended. Nothing holds me to anything. No milk-maids, no flowers, nothing. I just want to *feel* and then when I start to work I'll remember. I'll read something, maybe the Psalms, maybe, again, something from Mr. Dunbar, James Weldon Johnson. And I'll remember how beautiful, how pliable the language is, how it will lend itself. If you pull it, it says, "Okay." I remember that, and I start to write. Nathaniel Hawthorne says, "Easy reading is damn hard writing." I try to pull the language in to such a sharpness that it jumps off the page. It must look easy, but it takes me forever to get it to look so easy. Of course, there are those critics—New York critics as a rule—who say, "Well, Maya Angelou has a new book out and, of course, it's good but then she's a natural writer." Those are the ones I want to grab by the throat and wrestle to the floor because it takes me forever to get it to sing. I *work* at the language. On an evening like this, looking out at the auditorium, if I had to write this evening from my point of view, I'd see the rust-red used worn velvet seats, and the lightness where people's backs have rubbed against the back of the seat so that it's a light orange; then, the beautiful colors of the people's faces, the white, pink-white, beige-white, light beige and brown and tan—I would have to look at all that, at all those faces and the way they sit on top of their necks. When I would end up writing after four hours or five hours in my room, it might sound like: "It was a rat that sat on a mat. That's that. Not a cat." But I would continue to play with it and pull at it and say, "I love you. Come to me. I love you." It might take me two or three weeks just to describe what I'm seeing now.

INTERVIEWER: How do you know when it's what you want?

ANGELOU: I know when it's the best I can do. It may not be the best there is. Another writer may do it much better. But I know when it's the best I can do. I know that one of the great arts that the writer develops is the art of saying. "No. No, I'm finished. Bye." And leaving it alone. I will not write it into the ground. I will not write the life out of it. I won't do that.

INTERVIEWER: How much revising is involved?

ANGELOU: I write in the morning, and then go home about midday and take a shower, because writing, as you know, is very hard work, so you have to do a double ablution. Then I go out and shop—I'm a serious cook—and pretend to be normal. I play sane: "Good morning! Fine, thank you. And you?" And I go home. I prepare dinner for myself and if I have houseguests, I do the candles and the pretty music and all that. Then, after all the dishes are moved away, I read what I wrote that morning. And more often than not, if I've done nine pages I may be able to save two and a half, or three. That's the cruelest time you know, to really admit that it doesn't work. And to blue pencil it. When I finish maybe fifty pages, and read them—fifty acceptable pages— it's not too bad. I've had the same editor since 1967. Many times he has said to me over the years, or asked me. "Why would you use a semicolon instead of a colon?" And many times over the years I have said to him things like: "I will never speak to you again. Forever. Goodbye. That is it. Thank you very much." And I leave. Then I read the piece and I think of his suggestions. I send him a telegram that says, "OK, so you're right. So what? Don't ever mention this to me again. If you do, I will never speak to you again." About two years ago I was visiting him and his wife in the

Hamptons. I was at the end of a dining room table with a sit-down dinner of about fourteen people. Way at the end I said to someone, "I sent him telegrams over the years." From the other end of the table he said, "And I've kept every one!" Brute! But the editing, one's own editing, before the editor sees it, is the most important.

INTERVIEWER: The five autobiographical books follow each other in chronological order. When you started writing *I Know Why the Caged Bird Sings* did you know that you would move on from that? It almost works line by line into the second volume.

ANGELOU: I know, but I didn't really mean to. I thought I was going to write *Caged Bird* and that would be it and I would go back to playwriting and writing scripts for television. Autobiography is awfully seductive; it's wonderful. Once I got into it I realized I was following a tradition established by Frederick Douglass—the slave narrative—speaking in the first-person singular talking about the first-person plural, always saying "I" meaning "we." And what a responsibility! Trying to work with that form, the autobiographical mode, to change it, to make it bigger, richer, finer, and more inclusive in the twentieth century has been a great challenge for me. I've written five now, and I really hope—the works are required reading in many universities and colleges in the United States—that people *read* my work. The greatest compliment I receive is when people walk up to me on the street or in airports and say, "Miss Angelou, I *wrote* your books last year and I really—I mean I *read* . . ." That is it: that the person has come into the books so seriously, so completely, that he or she, black or white, male or female, feels, "That's my story. I told it. I'm making it up on the spot." That's the great compliment. I didn't expect, originally, that I was going to continue with the form. I thought I was going to write a little book and it would be fine, and I would go on back to poetry, write a little music.

INTERVIEWER: What about the genesis of the first book? Who were the people who helped you shape those sentences that leap off the page?

ANGELOU: Oh well, they started years and years before I ever wrote, when I was very young. I loved the black American minister. I loved the melody of the voice, and the imagery, so rich, and almost impossible. The minister in my church in Arkansas, when I was very young, would use phrases such as "God stepped out, the sun over his right shoulder, the moon nestling in the palm of his hand." I mean, I just loved it, and I loved the black poets, and I loved Shakespeare, and Edgar Allan Poe, and I liked Matthew Arnold a lot, still do. Being mute for a number of years, I read, and memorized, and all those people have had tremendous influence . . . in the first book, and even in the most recent book.

INTERVIEWER: Mute?

ANGELOU: I was raped when I was very young. I told my brother the name of the person who had done it. Within a few days the man was killed. In my child's mind— seven and a half years old—I thought my voice had killed him. So I stopped talking for five years. Of course I've written about this in *Caged Bird*.

INTERVIEWER: When did you decide you were going to be a writer? Was there a moment when you suddenly said, "This is what I wish to do for the rest of my life."

ANGELOU: Well, I had written a television series for PBS, and I was going out to California. I thought I was a poet and playwright. That was what I was going to do the rest of my life. Or become famous as a real estate broker. This sounds like name-dropping, and it really is—but James Baldwin took me over to dinner with Jules and Judy Feiffer one evening. All three of them are great talkers. They went on with their stories and I had to fight for the right to play it good. I had to insert myself to tell some stories too. Well, the next day, Judy Feiffer called Bob Loomis, an editor at Random House, and suggested that if he could get me to write an autobiography, he'd have something. So he phoned me and I said, "No, under no circumstances; I certainly will not do such a thing." So I went out to California to produce this series on African and black American culture. Loomis called me out there about three times. Each time I said no. Then he talked to James Baldwin. Jimmy gave him a ploy which always works with me—though I'm not proud to say that. The next time he called, he said, "Well, Miss Angelou. I won't bother you again. It's just as well that you don't attempt to write this book, because to write autobiography as literature is almost impossible." I said, "What are you talking about? I'll do it." I'm not proud about this button which can be pushed and I will immediately jump.

INTERVIEWER: Do you select a dominant theme for each book?

ANGELOU: I try to remember times in my life, incidents in which there was the dominating theme of cruelty, or kindness, or generosity, or envy, or happiness, glee . . . perhaps four incidents in the period I'm going to write about. Then I select, the one which lends itself best to my device and which I can write as drama without falling into melodrama.

INTERVIEWER: Did you write for a particular audience?

ANGELOU: I thought early on if I could write a book for black girls it would be good, because there were so few books for a black girl to read that said "This is how it is to grow up." Then, I thought "I'd better, you know, enlarge that group, the market group that I'm trying to reach." I decided to write for black boys, and then white girls, and then white boys.

But what I try to keep in mind mostly is my craft. That's what I really try for; I try to allow myself to be impelled by my art—if that doesn't sound too pompous and weird—accept the impulse, and then try my best to have a command of the craft. If I'm feeling depressed, and losing my control, then I think about the reader. But that is very rare—to think about the reader when the work is going on.

INTERVIEWER: So you don't keep a particular reader in mind when you sit down in that hotel room and begin to compose or write. It's yourself.

ANGELOU: It's myself . . . and my reader. I would be a liar, a hypocrite, or a fool—and I'm not any of those—to say that I don't write for the reader. I do. But for the reader who hears, who really will work at it, going behind what I seem to say. So I write for myself and that reader who will pay the dues. There's a phrase in West Africa, in Ghana; it's called "deep talk." For instance, there's a saying: "The trouble for the thief is not how to steal the chief's bugle, but where to blow it." Now, on the face of it, one understands that. But when you really think about it, it takes you deeper. In West Africa they call that "deep talk." I'd like to think I write "deep talk." When you read me, you should be able to say "Gosh, that's pretty. That's lovely. That's nice. Maybe there's something else? Better read it again." Years ago I read a man named Machado de Assis who wrote a book called *Dom Casmro*: *Epitaph of a Small Winner*. Machado de Assis is a South American writer—black mother, Portuguese father—writing in 1865, say. I thought the book was very nice. Then I went back and read the book and said, "Hmm. I didn't realize all that was in that book." Then I read it again, and again, and I came to the conclusion that what Machado de Assis had done for me was almost a trick: he had beckoned me onto the beach to watch a sunset. And I had watched the sunset with pleasure. When I turned around to come back in I found that the tide had come in over my head. That's when I decided to write. I would write so that the reader says, "That's so nice. Oh boy, that's pretty. Let me read that again." I think that's why *Caged Bird* is in its twenty-first printing in hardcover and its twenty-ninth in paper. All my books are still in print, in hardback as well as paper, because people go back and say, "Let me read that. Did she *really* say that?"

INTERVIEWER: The books are episodic, aren't they? Almost as if you had put together a string of short stories. I wondered if, as an autobiographer, you ever fiddled with the truth to make the story better.

ANGELOU: Well, sometimes. I love the phrase "fiddle with." It's so English. Sometimes I make a character from a composite of three or four people, because the essence in any one person is not sufficiently strong to be written about. Essentially though, the work is true though sometimes I fiddle with the facts. Many of the people I've written about are alive today, and I have them to face. I wrote about an ex-husband—he's an African—in *The Heart of a Woman*. Before I did, I called him in Dar-es-Salaam and said, "I'm going to write about some of our years together." He said, "Now before you ask, I want you to know that I shall sign my release, because I know you will not lie. However, I am sure I shall argue with you about your interpretation of the truth."

INTERVIEWER: Did he enjoy his portrait finally, or did you argue about it?

ANGELOU: Well, he didn't argue, but I was kind, too.

INTERVIEWER: I would guess this would make it very easy for you to move from autobiography into novel, where you can do anything you want with your characters.

ANGELOU: Yes, but for me, fiction is not the sweetest form. I really am trying to do something with autobiography now. It has caught me. I'm using the first-person singular, and trying to make that the first-person plural, so that anybody can read the work and say, "Hmm, that's the truth, yes, *uh-huh*," and live in the work. It's a large ambitious dream. But I love the form.

INTERVIEWER: Aren't the extraordinary events of your life very hard for the rest of us to identify with?

ANGELOU: Oh my God, I've lived a very simple life! You can say, "Oh yes, at thirteen this happened to me, and at fourteen . . ." But those are facts. But the facts can obscure the truth, what it really felt like. Every human being has paid the earth to grow up. Most people don't grow up. It's too damn difficult. What happens is most people get older. That's the truth of it. They honor their credit cards, they find parking spaces, they marry, they have the nerve to have children, but they don't grow up. Not really. They get older. But to grow up costs the earth, the *earth*. It means you take responsibility for the time you take up, for the space you occupy. It's serious business. And you find out what it costs us to love and to lose, to dare and to fail. And maybe even more, to succeed.

What it costs, in truth. Not superficial costs—anybody can have that—I mean in truth. That's what I write. What it really is like. I'm just telling a very simple story.

INTERVIEWER: Aren't you tempted to lie? Novelists lie, don't they?

ANGELOU: I don't know about lying for novelists. I look at some of the great novelists, and I think the reason they are great is that they're telling the truth. The fact is they're using made-up names, made-up people, made-up places, and made-up times, but they're telling the truth about the human being—what we are capable of, what makes us lose, laugh, weep, fall down and gnash our teeth and wring our hands and kill each other and love each other.

INTERVIEWER: James Baldwin, along with a lot of writers in this series, said that "when you're writing you're trying to find out something you didn't know." When you write do you search for something that you didn't know about yourself or about us?

ANGELOU: Yes. When I'm writing, I am trying to find out who I am, who we are, what we're capable of, how we feel, how we lose and stand up, and go on from darkness into darkness. I'm trying for that. But I'm also trying for the language. I'm trying to see how it can really sound. I really love language. I love it for what it does for us, how it allows us to explain the pain and the glory, the nuances and the delicacies of our existence. And then it allows us to laugh, allows us to show wit. Real wit is shown in language. We need language.

INTERVIEWER: Baldwin also said that his family urged him not to become a writer. His father felt that there was a white monopoly in publishing. Did you ever have any of those feelings: that you were going up against something that was really immensely difficult for a black writer?

ANGELOU: Yes, but I didn't find it so just in writing. I've found it so in all the things I've attempted. In the shape of American society, the white male is on top, then the white female, and then the black male, and at the bottom is the black woman. So that's been always so. That is nothing new. It doesn't mean that it doesn't shock me, shake me up. . . .

INTERVIEWER: I can understand that in various social stratifications, but why in art?

ANGELOU: Well, unfortunately, racism is pervasive. It doesn't stop at the university gate, or at the ballet stage. I knew great black dancers, male and female, who were told early on that they were not shaped, physically, for ballet. Today, we see very few black ballet dancers. Unfortunately, in the theater and in film, racism and sexism stand at the door. I'm the first black female director in Hollywood; in order to direct, I went to Sweden and took a course in cinematography so I would understand what the camera would do. Though I had written a screenplay, and even composed the score, I wasn't allowed to direct it. They brought in a young Swedish director who hadn't even shaken a black person's hand before. The film was *Georgia, Georgia* with Diane Sands. People either loathed it or complimented me. Both were wrong, because it was not what I wanted, not what I would have done if I had been allowed to direct it. So I thought, well, what I guess I'd better do is be ten times as prepared. That is not new. I wish it was. In every case I know I have to be ten times more prepared than my white counterpart.

INTERVIEWER: Even as a writer where . . .

ANGELOU: Absolutely.

INTERVIEWER: Yet a manuscript is what arrives at the editor's desk, not a person, not a body.

ANGELOU: Yes. I must have such control of my tools, of words, that I can make this sentence leap off the page. I have to have my writing so polished that it doesn't look polished at all. I want a reader, especially an editor, to be a half-hour into my book before he realizes it's reading he's doing.

INTERVIEWER: But isn't that the goal of every person who sits down at a typewriter?

ANGELOU: Absolutely. Yes. It's possible to be overly sensitive, to carry a bit of paranoia along with you. But I don't think that's a bad thing. It keeps you sharp, keeps you on your toes.

INTERVIEWER: Is there a thread one can see through the five autobiographies? It seems to me that one prevailing theme is the love of your child.

ANGELOU: Yes, well, that's true. I think that that's a particular. I suppose, if I'm lucky, the particular is seen in the general. There is, I hope, a thesis in my work: we may encounter many defeats, but we must not be defeated. That sounds goody two-shoes, I know, but I believe that a diamond is the result of extreme pressure and time. Less time is crystal. Less than that is coal. Less than that is fossilized leaves. Less than that it's just plain dirt. In all my work, in the movies I write, the lyrics, the poetry, the prose, the essays, I am saying that we may encounter many defeats—maybe it's imperative that we encounter the defeats—but we are much stronger than we appear to be, and maybe much better than we allow ourselves to be. Human beings are more alike than unalike. There's no real mystique. Every human being every Jew, Christian, back-slider, Muslim, Shintoist, Zen Buddhist, atheist, agnostic, every human being wants a nice place to live, a good place for the children to go to school, healthy children, somebody to love, the courage, the unmitigated gall to accept love in return, someplace to party on Saturday or Sunday night, and someplace to perpetuate that God. There's no mystique. None. And if I'm right in my work, that's what my work says.

INTERVIEWER: Have you been back to Stamps, Arkansas?

ANGELOU: About 1970, Bill Moyers, Willie Morris, and I were at some affair. Judith Moyers as well—I think she was the instigator. We may have had two or three scotches, or seven or eight. Willie Morris was then with *Harper's* magazine. The suggestion came up: "Why don't we all go back South." Willie Morris was from Yazoo, Mississippi. Bill Moyers is from Marshall, Texas, which is just a hop, skip, and a jump—about as far as you can throw a chitterling—from Stamps, my hometown. Sometime in the middle of the night there was this idea: "Why don't Bill Moyers and Maya Angelou go to Yazoo, Mississippi, to visit Willie Morris? Then why don't Willie Morris and Maya Angelou go to Marshall, Texas, to visit Bill Moyers?" I said, "Great." I was agreeing with both. Then they said Willie Morris and Bill Moyers would go to Stamps, Arkansas, to visit Maya Angelou, and I said, "No way, José. I'm not going back to that little town with two white men! I will not do it!" Well, after a while Bill Moyers called me—he was doing a series on "creativity"—and he said, "Maya, come on, let's go to Stamps." I said, "No way." He continued, "I want to talk about creativity." I said, "You know, I don't want to know where it resides." I really don't, and I still don't. One of the problems in the West is that people are too busy putting things under microscopes and so forth. Creativity is greater than the sum of its parts. All I want to know is that creativity is there. I want to know that I can put my hand behind my back like Tom Thumb and pull out a plum. Anyway, Moyers went on and on and so did Judith and before I knew it, I found myself in Stamps, Arkansas. Stamps, Arkansas! With Bill Moyers, in front of my grandmother's door. My God! We drove out of town: me with Bill and Judith. Back of us was the crew, a New York crew, you know, very "Right, dig where I'm comin' from, like, get it on," and so forth. We got about three miles outside of Stamps and I said, "Stop the car. Let the car behind us pull up. Get those people in with you and I'll take their car." I suddenly was taken back to being twelve years old in a southern, tiny town where my grandmother told me, "Sistah, never be on a country road with any white boys." I was two hundred years older than black pepper, but I said, "Stop the car." I did. I got out of the car. And I knew these guys—certainly Bill. Bill Moyers is a friend and brother-friend to me; we care for each other. But dragons, fears, the grotesques of childhood always must be confronted at childhood's door. Any other place is esoteric and has nothing to do with the great fear that is laid upon one as a child. So anyway, we did Bill Moyers's show. And it seems to be a very popular program, and it's the first of the "creativity" programs. . . .

INTERVIEWER: Did going back assuage those childhood fears?

ANGELOU: They are there like griffins hanging off the sides of old and tired European buildings.

INTERVIEWER: It hadn't changed?

ANGELOU: No, worse if anything.

INTERVIEWER: But it was forty years before you went back to the South, to North Carolina. Was that because of a fear of finding griffins everywhere, Stamps being a typical community of the South?

ANGELOU: Well, I've never felt the need to prove anything to an audience. I'm always concerned about who I am to me first, to myself and God. I really am. I didn't go south because I didn't want to pull up whatever clout I had, because that's boring, that's not real, not true; that doesn't tell me anything. If I had known I was afraid, I would have gone earlier. I just thought I'd find the South really unpleasant. I have moved south now. I *live* there.

INTERVIEWER: Perhaps writing the autobiographies, finding out about yourself, would have made it much easier to go back.

ANGELOU: I know many think that writing sort of "clears the air." It doesn't do that at all. If you are going to write autobiography, don't expect that it will clear anything up. It makes it more clear to you, but it doesn't alleviate anything. You simply know it better, you have names for people.

INTERVIEWER: There's a part in *Caged Bird* where you and your brother want to do a scene from *The Merchant of Venice*, and you don't dare do it because your grandmother would find out that Shakespeare was not only deceased but white.

ANGELOU: I don't think she'd have minded if she'd known he was deceased. I tried to pacify her—my mother knew Shakespeare, but my grandmother was raising us. When I told her I wanted to recite—it was actually Portia's speech—Mama said to me, "Now, sistah, what are you goin' to render?" The phrase was so fetching. The phrase was: "Now, little mistress Marguerite will render her rendition." Mama said, "Now, sistah, what are you goin' to render?" I said, "Mama, I'm going to render a piece written by William Shakespeare." My grandmother asked me, "Now, sistah, who is this very William Shakespeare?" I had to tell her that he was white, it was going to come out. Somebody would let it out. So I told Mama, "Mama, he's white, but he's dead." Then I said, "He's been dead for centuries," thinking she'd forgive him because of this little idiosyncracy. She said, "No Ma'am, little mistress you will not. No Ma'am, little mistress you will not." So I rendered James Weldon Johnson, Paul Laurence Dunbar, Countee Cullen, Langston Hughes.

INTERVIEWER: Were books allowed in the house?

ANGELOU: None of those books were in the house; they were in the school. I'd bring them home from school, and my brother gave me Edgar Allan Poe because he knew I loved him. I loved him so much I called him "EAP." But as I said, I had a problem when I was young: from the time I was seven and a half to the time I was twelve and a half I was a mute. I could speak, but I didn't speak for five years, and I was what was called a "volunteer mute." But I read and I memorized just masses—I don't know if one is born with photographic memory, but I think you can develop it. I just have that.

INTERVIEWER: What is the significance of the title, *All God's Children Need Traveling Shoes*?

ANGELOU: I never agreed, even as a young person, with the Thomas Wolfe title *You Can't Go Home Again*. Instinctively I didn't. But the truth is, you can never *leave* home. You take it with you; it's under your fingernails; it's in the hair follicles; it's in the way you smile; it's in the ride of your hips, in the passage of your breasts; it's all there, no matter where you go. You can take on the affectations and the postures of other places, and even learn to speak their ways. But the truth is, home is between your teeth. Everybody's always looking for it: Jews go to Israel; black-Americans and Africans in the Diaspora go to Africa; Europeans, Anglo-Saxons go to England and Ireland; people of Germanic background go to Germany. It's a very queer quest. We can kid ourselves; we can tell ourselves, "Oh yes, honey, I live in Tel Aviv, actually. . . ." The truth is a stubborn fact. So this book is about trying to go home.

INTERVIEWER: If you had to endow a writer with the most necessary pieces of equipment, other than, of course, yellow legal pads, what would these be?

ANGELOU: Ears. Ears. To hear the language. But there's no one piece of equipment that is most necessary. Courage, first.

INTERVIEWER: Did you ever feel that you could not get your work published? Would you have continued to write if Random House had returned your manuscript?

ANGELOU: I didn't think it was going to be very easy, but I knew I was going to do something. The real reason black people exist at all today is because there's a resistance to a larger society that says, "You can't do it. You can't survive. And if you survive, you certainly can't thrive. And if you thrive, you can't thrive with any passion or compassion or humor or style." There's a saying, a song which says, "Don't you let nobody turn you 'round, turn you 'round. Don't you let nobody turn you 'round." Well, I've always believed that. So knowing that, knowing that nobody could turn me 'round, if I didn't publish, well, I would design this theater we're sitting in. Yes. Why not? Some human being did it. I agree with Terence. Terence said, *"Homo sum: humani nihil a me alienum puto."* I am a human being. Nothing human can be alien to me. When you look up Terence in the encyclopedia, you see beside his name, in italics: "Sold to a Roman senator, freed by that Senator." He became the most popular playwright in Rome. Six of his plays and that statement have come down to us from 154 B.C. This man, not born white, not born free, without any chance of ever receiving citizenship, said, "I am a human being. Nothing human can be alien to me." Well, I believe that. I ingested that, internalized that at about thirteen or twelve. I believed if I set my mind to it, maybe I wouldn't be published, but I would write a great piece of music, or do something about becoming a real friend. Yes, I would do something wonderful. It might be with my next-door neighbor, my gentleman friend, with my lover, but it would be wonderful as far as I could do it. So I never have been very concerned about the world telling me how successful I am. I don't need that.

INTERVIEWER: You mentioned courage . . .

ANGELOU: . . . the most important of all the virtues. Without that virtue you can't practice any other virtue with consistency.

INTERVIEWER: What do you think of white writers who have written of the black experience: Faulkner's *The Sound and the Fury*, or William Styron's *Confessions of Nat Turner*?

ANGELOU: Well, sometimes I am disappointed—more often than not. That's unfair, because I'm not suggesting the writer is lying about what he or she sees. It's my disappointment, really, in that he or she doesn't see more deeply, more carefully. I enjoy seeing Peter O'Toole or Michael Caine enact the role of an upper-class person in England. There the working class has had to study the upper-class, has been obliged to do so, to lift themselves out of their positions. Well, black Americans have had to study white Americans. For centuries under slavery, the smile or the grimace on a white man's face, or the flow of a hand on a white woman could inform a black person: "You're about to be sold, or flogged." So we have studied the white American, where the white American has not been obliged to study us. So often it is as if the writer is looking through a glass darkly. And I'm always a little—not a little— saddened by that poor vision.

INTERVIEWER: And you can pick it up in an instant if you . . .

ANGELOU: Yes, yes. There are some who delight and inform. It's so much better, you see, for me, when a writer like Edna St. Vincent Millay speaks so deeply about her concern for herself, and does not offer us any altruisms. Then when I look through her eyes at how she sees a black or an Asian my heart is lightened. But many of the other writers disappoint me.

INTERVIEWER: What is the best part of writing for you?

ANGELOU: Well, I could say the end. But when the language lends itself to me, when it comes and submits, when it surrenders and says "I am yours, darling"—that's the best part.

INTERVIEWER: You don't skip around when you write?

ANGELOU: No, I may skip around in revision, just to see what connections I can find.

INTERVIEWER: Is most of the effort made in putting the words down onto the paper, or is it in revision?

ANGELOU: Some work flows, and you know, you can catch three days. It's like . . . I think the word in sailing is "scudding"—you know, three days of just scudding. Other days it's just awful—plodding and backing up, trying to take out all the ands, ifs, tos, fors, buts, wherefores, therefores, howevers; you know, all those.

INTERVIEWER: And then, finally, you write "The End" and there it is; you have a little bit of sherry.

ANGELOU: A lot of sherry then.

6
THE REASON FOR STORIES
Robert Stone

Last spring the writer and critic William Gass published an essay in this magazine entitled "Goodness knows Nothing of Beauty," an essay which toyed with the proposition that art and moral aspiration were mutually distant. Statements of this view very often seek to replicate in their style the kind of cool, amoral elegance they claim for good art, and Gass's piece is not in this regard exceptional. It is characterized by paradox, alliteration, and a faintly decadent naughtiness suggestive of intense sophistication. In the end, as such pieces often do, it resolves itself solipsistically; that is, it explains itself away in terms of its own moral and aesthetic definitions. But it is interesting to see this old opposition between art and morality appear again, offered by a commentator usually wise and insightful.

"To be a preacher is to bring your sense of sin to the front of the church," Gass writes, "but to be an artist is to give to every mean and ardent, petty and profound, feature of the soul a glorious godlike shape." If this means that you get no points in art for good intentions, no one would argue. But I find here echoes of an old antinomian tendency that

---

Robert Stone, "The Reason for Stories," *Harper's Magazine*, June 1980, 71–76. (This essay is based on a talk Robert Stone gave at the New York Public Library, sponsored by the Book-of-the-Month Club.) Used by permission of Doradio & Olson, Inc. Copyright © 1980 Robert Stone.

goes back at least to Nietzsche. It has been argued by people as different as José Ortega y Gasset and Oscar Wilde; by Joyce speaking in character as Stephen Daedalus; and by Shaw during the period when he was writing *Major Barbara* and, it now appears, attempting to invent fascism.

In this antinomian vision, morality and art are independent and even in opposition. On the right squats morality. It may be imagined as a neo-Gothic structure—immense, ornate, and sterile. Its self-satisfaction, lack of imagination, and philistine sentimentality are advertised in its every plane and line. Architecturally it resembles the Mormon Temple, the one in downtown Salt Lake City, not the Hollywood-biblical one on Santa Monica Boulevard. It contains drear echoing silences.

And over here—art. Art is nothing but beautiful. Art is like a black panther. It has the glamour of the desperado. Art is radical, the appealing cousin of crime. Never a dull moment with art. Morality, in this view, is not only its opposite but its enemy.

This claim of estrangement between morality and art retains its currency for an excellent reason: it's fun. It's agreeable for an artist to imagine himself as a Zarathustrian rope-dancer, balanced against eternity up in the ozone and thin light, while far below the eunuchs of the brown temple of morality whine platitudes at each other in the incense-ridden noonday darkness: "Look before you leap." "A stitch in time saves nine."

But let us pursue this notion. Let us imagine the novel, for example, freed completely from moral considerations. What would that be like? One thing it might be like is one of the anti-novels Robbe-Grillet gave us during the 1950s and '60s. These are novels without any moral context, but they are similarly without characters and plots, beginnings and endings. Surely such an exercise in *doing without something* serves to reinforce the idea of its necessity. Is it possible to postulate the idea of a successful novel about people, or about animals for that matter, in which the living of life, as reflected therein, exists beyond the signal area of moral reference points?

What about the comic novel? Let's eliminate at the outset the obviously sentimental or political comedies that have a message (that is, a moral point) at their core. Let's take the work of two writers—William Burroughs and Evelyn Waugh—who have written very funny books and who are not usually thought of as kindly humanistic sages.

Naked Lunch is the prototypical Burroughs novel, and like all the others it's full of cruelty—not just sadism, but cruelty. The element of sci-fi political satire it contains is sometimes claimed as representing a moral dimension, but I think that's bogus. The moral element in the work of William Burroughs is in its very humor. In the grimmest imaginable places, in the grammar of drug addiction, in the violence and treachery of the addict's world, Burroughs finds laughter. The laughter itself is a primary moral response. Laughter represents a rebellion against chaos, a rejection of evil, and an affirmation of balance and soundness. One can see this principle at work in the way that laughter undercuts super-serious attempts at self-consciously "wicked" sex. I was once given a description of a waterfront S&M joint that presented itself as the meanest saloon on earth. There was a dress code, and patrons were expected to present to any observer nothing less than a grim mask of depravity. There were two house rules, according to my informant. The first was, no rugby shirts. The second was *no laughing*. We must assume that the people who run places like that know what they're doing.

Evelyn Waugh seems to have been lacking in all the qualities we philanthropists find congenial. A bully, a coward, a fascist, a despiser of minorities and the poor, a groveler before the rich and powerful, Waugh was surely one of the worst human beings ever to become a major novelist. But paradoxically, his life and work provide us with a ringing confirmation of the dependence of serious fiction on morality. By borrowing, spuriously or otherwise (it doesn't matter), the certainties of Catholicism, he was able to infuse his best work with the moral center that makes it great. The worldly lives described in the *Men at Arms* trilogy and *Brideshead Revisited* are constantly being measured against a rigorous neo-Jansenist Christianity. In these books the invisible world becomes the real one, and its meanings constitute the truth that undergirds the confusion of desires with which the characters struggle.

Gass's essay starts by having us ask ourselves whether we'd rescue an infant or a Botticelli painting, if we saw both of them being washed out to sea and could salvage only one. The Botticelli's a masterpiece, the baby's only a "potential" human being. After prescribing this antinomian exercise, he commences to deflate his own balloon by running it on the thorns of common sense. He refers to the author's historical struggle against censorship, as though this somehow establislies art's essentially unmoral character, and then admits that each censoring hierarchy reacts to whatever inadequacies of its moral system are challenged by the work in question. He reminds us that good books were written by bad people—bad people (and crafters of fine moral fiction) like Waugh, I assume. Then he ends with a truism to the effect that propaganda cannot justify bad art or bad writing.

There are few statements in the essay which Gass does not obviate or contradict, but there is one that stays, unforsworn and unqualified, in my recollection. He refers to Keats's identification of beauty with truth and vice versa as "a fatuous little motto." Now it seems to me that Gass is being unkind to a perfectly nice axiom; surely we should meditate for a moment on this most appealing sentiment. Isn't it true?

Concerning life, it is a question we cannot finally answer. I think it *tends* to be true. The explanation at the core of any one of nature's mysteries is often edifying. Job cuts through to the substance of it when he questions the beneficence of God. In the end he learns that God's majesty and holiness suffuse the universe. This is what the medieval mystic Julian of Norwich was referring to when she wrote "all shall be well and all shall be well and all manner of things shall be well." In terms of Western tradition it should be true that truth is beauty. Even if you take God out of it, the grimmest principles of existence have their symmetry. All the same, there can be a hundred different explanations for things and every one of them beautiful and none of them true.

But, in art, isn't it *always* true? Aren't truth and beauty very nearly the same? Surely every aesthetic response entails a recognition. What standard do we hold up to art, other than things themselves? And what do we require from art if not a reflection of things, of our lives, in all their variety?

We in the Western world are what the Moslems call "people of the book." The prototypical book in this culture has been the Bible, regardless of whether or not we are believers. After centuries of being Christians and Jews, our context and our perceptions continue to be conditioned by the Bible's narratives. It's hard to overestimate the impact of the Bible on our civilization and on our language. The novel came into existence with the rise of a literate mass readership, and the greatest vehicle of mass literacy in the English-speaking world has been the King James Bible. It has been the great primer. The

Bible is unique among religious books in the relationship it defines between God and man, and in the view it takes of human life. The narratives about people in the books of the Bible are thought to mean something. They are thought to be significant. This implies that the corporeal world in which people live is not an illusion to be overcome, or a shadowland reflecting the void, but an instrument of God's will. For centuries we have been reflecting on peculiar things—like why Esau was disinherited, and how Abraham could have been ready to sacrifice his son—and asking ourselves: What does this mean? What is at the heart of this strange story? What can I learn from it? How does it bear on my situation?

All our philosophies of history descend from the assumptions bequeathed by our Scriptures: they profess to detect the informing principles at the heart of human events. Life matters, lives matter, because earthly human history is the arena in which the universe acts out its consciousness of itself, displaying its nature as creation. Human annals become charged, they become an entity: history. History then is perceived as a rational process, the unfolding of a design, something with a dynamic to be uncovered.

Stories explain the nature of things. Any fictional work of serious intent argues for the significance of its story. A reader holds the characters in judgment, investing sympathy or withholding it, always alert for recognitions, hoping to see his lonely state reflected across time, space, and circumstance. How then can fiction ever be independent of morality? To be so, it would have to be composed of something other than language.

There is no brown temple where morality resides. There is no high wire above it where the artist whirls in freedom. If there is a wire it's the wire we're all on out here, the one we live on, with only each other for company. Our having each other is both the good news and the bad.

We deceive ourselves, we contemporary people, if we imagine that beneath our feet is a great, sound structure, a vast warehouse called civilization, chock-a-block with boring, reliable truths and insights. Around us there is only deep space. Out here, where we all live with each other, it's mostly impromptu. Right-mindedness is cheap—but goodness? William Gass need not worry about its coming between ourselves and our pleasures.

Most journalists who worked in Vietnam during the war were oppressed by the extreme difficulty of translating what they saw into words. It was not necessarily that it was so uniquely horrible; it was only that the brutality and confusion one experienced seemed to lose something when rendered, when written. Somehow, in describing the situation so that it could be set up in columns of type, one always seemed to be cleaning it up.

As I pondered this process, a moment of illumination struck me. We are *forever* cleaning up our act. Not only in describing ourselves but in imagining ourselves, we project a self-image that is considerably idealized. In all our relationships, we present idealized versions of ourselves so as not to frighten others with our primary processes. And just as we individually cultivate an elevated image of ourselves, so we conspire as nations, peoples—as humankind—to create a fictional exemplar of our collective selves, ourselves as we have agreed to imagine ourselves.

But this is not the whole story. Though we are only what we are, we have the amazing ability to extend, to transcend the grimmest circumstances. Moments occur when we amaze each other with acts of hope, acts of courage that can make one proud to be human. The fact is that we absolutely require the elevated image of ourselves which we indulge. If we did not idealize ourselves, if we only accepted the reality of ourselves as we are most of the time, we would never be capable of the extensions of ourselves that are required of us.

Things are in the saddle, Emerson said, and ride mankind. "Whirl is king." Things happen ruthlessly, without mercy; the elemental force of things bears down upon us. From one moment to the next we hardly know what's going on, let alone what it all means. Civilization and its attendant morality are not structures, they're more like notions, and sometimes they can seem very distant notions. They can be blown away in a second. In the worst of times we often look for them in vain. Sometimes the morality to which we publicly subscribe seems so alien to our actual behavior that it seems to emanate from some other sphere. One might call it a fiction, but it's a fiction that we most urgently require. It is much more difficult to act well than we are ready to admit. It can be extremely hard to act sensibly, let alone well.

Storytelling is not a luxury to humanity; it's almost as necessary as bread. We cannot imagine ourselves without it because each self is a story. The perception each of us has of his own brief transient passage through things is also a kind of fiction, not because its matter is necessarily untrue, but because we tend to shape it to suit our own needs. We tell ourselves our own stories selectively, in order to keep our sense of self intact. As dreams are to waking life, so fiction is to reality. The brain can't function without clearing its circuits during sleep, nor can we contemplate and analyze our situation without living some of the time in the world of the imagination, sorting and refining the random promiscuity of events.

If the practice of fiction is inextricably linked with concerns of morality, what is there to say about the writer's responsibility? The writer's responsibility, it seems to me, consists in writing well and truly, to use a Hemingwayesque locution. The writer who betrays his calling is that writer who either for commercial or political reasons vulgarizes his own perception and his rendering of it. Meretricious writing tries to conventionalize what it describes in order to make itself safer and easier to take. It may do this to conform to a political agenda, which is seen as somehow overriding mere literary considerations, or under commercial pressures to appeal to what are seen as the limitations of a mass audience.

The effect of conventionalized, vulgarized writing is pernicious. Fiction is, or should be, an act against loneliness, an appeal to community, a bet on the possibility of spanning the gulf that separates one human being from another. It must understand and illustrate the varieties of the human condition in order to bring more of that condition into the light of conscious insight. It is part of the process which expands human self-knowledge. Meretricious fiction does the opposite of what fiction is supposed to do. The reassurances it offers are superficial and empty. It presents a reality that is limited by its own impoverishment, and as a result, it increases each individual's loneliness and isolation. In the absence of honest storytelling, people are abandoned to the beating of their own hearts.

It must be emphasized that the moral imperative of fiction provides no excuse for smug moralizing, religiosity, or propaganda. On the contrary, it forbids them. Nor does it require that every writer equip his work with some edifying message advertising progress, brotherhood, and light. It does not require a writer to be a good man, only a good wizard.

Above all, what I wish to argue is that the laws of both language and art impose choices that are unavoidably moral. The first law of heaven is that nothing is free. This is the law that requires the artist to constantly make decisions, to choose between symmetry and asymmetry, restraint and excess, balance and imbalance. Because this law is ruthlessly self-enforcing in art, the quality of the artist's work will depend on his making the right decision. The same law operates the scales the blindfolded woman in the courthouse holds. Artistic quality is related to justice. Grammar is related to logic, which is the engine of conscience. Language is always morally weighted. Nothing is free.

Political situations have always attracted me as a subject, and not because I believe that political pathology is necessarily more "important" than private suffering. During times of political upheaval, the relationship between external "reality" and the individual's interior world is destabilized. Revolutions, wars—such upheavals liberate some people from the prison of the self, even as they invite others to play out their personal dramas on a larger stage. People caught up in things that transcend the personal forever bring their own needs and desires to bear. They make pleasant and unpleasant discoveries about each other and themselves. The elements of drama descend on ordinary people and ordinary lives.

I wrote my first book after spending a year in the Deep South, a time that happened to coincide with the first sit-ins and the beginning of the struggle against segregation and also with the reaction to it. The novel centered on the exploitation of electronic media by the extreme Right, a phenomenon which we have not altogether put behind us. A *Hall of Mirrors* was not a strictly "realistic" book, but as young writers will, I put every single thing I thought I knew into it. I gave my characters names with the maximum number of letters because I thought that would make them more substantial. I had taken America as my subject, and all my quarrels with America went into it.

A few years later, working in Vietnam, I found myself witnessing a mistake ten thousand miles long, a mistake on the American scale. I began to write a novel set in Saigon. As it progressed, I realized that the logic of the thing required that everybody make his or her way back home, into the America of the early 1970s. The early to mid-'70s still seem to me, in retrospect, like a creepy, evil time. A lot of bills from the '60s were coming up for presentation. *Dog Soldiers* was my reaction to the period.

I went to Central America in 1978 to go scuba diving while at work on a new novel, and returned to the region several times thereafter. I became acquainted with a few Americans working there. At that time relatively few people in this country knew where Huehuetenango was, and Managua, Nicaragua, was the title of an old Andrews Sisters song. The Somozas had been running Nicaragua for many years and they seemed quite secure in their power—at least to my touristic eyes. Everything was quiet there. One day I even semi-crashed a party at the Presidential Palace.

The palace stood in the middle of what was literally a fallen city. From a distance, downtown Managua looked like a park—it was so green. When you got a closer look you could see that the green was that of vegetation growing over the rubble where the center of the city had collapsed two days before Christmas in 1972. The palace stood unscathed in the middle of the destruction. Around it was a kind of free-fire zone of scrub jungle where no one was permitted. The palace stood just beyond the effective mortar distance from the nearest habitation.

During my trips to Central America, I began to make a point of listening to as many stories as I could. After a while the stories began to form a pattern that conformed to my sense of Mesoamerica's history. This band of republics between the Andes and the Grijalva seemed placed by its gods in a very fateful situation. The region seemed to have attracted the most violent conquistadors and the most fanatical inquisitors. When they arrived, the Spaniards found holy wells of human sacrifice. Here, racial and social oppression had always been most severe. The fertile soil of the place seemed to bring forth things to provoke the appetite rather than things to nourish—baubles and rich toys, plantation crops for your sweet tooth or for your head.

These lands were eventually yoked to labor-intensive, high-profit products, bananas, of course, and coffee, chocolate, tobacco, chicle, emeralds, marijuana, cocaine. I decided to put down the book I was writing and begin a new one. My subject was again America; the United States had been involved here for so long. The new novel became my third, *A Flag for Sunrise*.

Children of Light, a novel about the movies published in 1986, is also political, in my view. The process of creating Hollywood movies is loaded with examples of how America works. People in the film industry who see *Children of Light* as an attack on movie-making apparently fail to see how movie-struck and reverent it really is.

I do not claim to know much more about novels than the writing of them, but I cannot imagine one set in the breathing world which lacks any moral valence. In the course of wringing a few novels from our *fin-de-siècle*, late-imperial scene, I have never been able to escape my sense of humanity trying, with difficulty, to raise itself in order not to fall. I insist on disputing William Gass's claim that goodness knows nothing of beauty. Nor do I believe that, in his excellent fiction and lucid criticism, he practices the ideas he expressed in his essay of that name.

Just as it's impossible to avoid standards of human action in novels about people, it's difficult to avoid politics. But if a novelist openly accepts that his work must necessarily contain moral and political dimensions, what responsibilities does he take on?

He assumes, above all, the responsibility to understand. The novel that admits to a political dimension requires a knowledge, legitimately or illegitimately acquired, intuitive or empirical, of the situation that is its subject. Political commitment is not required, although eventually most authors maneuver themselves into a stand. I think the key is to establish the connection between political forces and individual lives. The questions to address are: How do social and political forces condition individual lives? How do the personal qualities of the players condition their political direction?

The novelist has to cast the net of his sympathies fairly wide. He should be able to imagine his way into the personae of many different people, with different ways of thinking and believing. The aspiring, overtly political novelist might spend a little time every morning meditation on the interior life of General Noriega, a man who actually exists. As far as political satire goes, it should be remembered that the best satire requires a certain subversive sympathy for one's subject.

The writer must remember the first law of heaven: nothing is free. Commitment can be useful because it brings a degree of passion to bear, but it's also dangerous. To be the contented partisan of one side or another, one has to sell something. Because so much of serious politics in this century has to do with violence, this can be a morally enervating exercise. Moral enervation is bad for writers. Above all, the writer must not sentimentalize. He must remember that sentimentality is the great enemy of genuine sentiment.

I believe that it is impossible for any novelist to find a subject other than the transitory nature of moral perception. The most important thing about people is the difficulty they have in identifying and acting upon what's right. The world is full of illusion. We carry nemesis inside us, but we are not excused.

Years ago, a whimsical friend of mine made up a little ditty that for me sums up the backwards-and-forwards tragi-comical nature of humanity's march. It's a highly moral little ditty and it may contain the essence of every work of serious literature ever written. It goes like this:

> *Of offering more than what we can deliver, we have a bad habit it is true.*
> *But we have to offer more than what we can deliver to be able to deliver what we do.*   □

Study Guide

TALKING POINTS

I.   Why do we tell stories? Discuss the question in light of the meditations on writing and authorship contained in the foregoing section.

II. George Orwell admits that one of his strongest motives in becoming a writer was "political." He says that he means that word in "the widest possible sense." He expresses the belief that "no book is genuinely free from political bias" and that "the opinion that art should have nothing to do with politics is itself a political attitude." Review all the essays in this section and the introduction to the book with an eye toward any theme of authorship that relates directly or indirectly toward "the political." In other words, in what sense is the motivation of Rushdie, Angelou, Didion, or Naipaul political? Now reconsider Orwell's declaration that his work has a democratic purpose and compare that purpose with what you know about the mission and craft of journalism. In what sense can we say that journalists have a "political" purpose? As you discuss this, think about some of the standards adopted by some journalists, standards that are often defined by words such as "objective," "nonpartisan," "neutral," and "unbiased." Can the acts of journalists be political and objective at the same time? Can they, as Orwell said he attempted, reconcile "ingrained likes and dislikes with the essentially public, non-individual activities that this age forces upon us"?

III. Another theme of authorship that runs through these essays is a love for the English language. Orwell testifies to a passion for "words and their right arrangement." Naipaul finds power in "literary forms." Didion puts her faith in the "infinite power" of "grammar." Angelou declares that, after courage, writers need "ears . . . to hear the language." Early in the writer's life, this enthusiasm for language is nurtured by an intensity of reading that eventually kindles the desire for self-expression. Discuss the ways in which the "aesthetic" impulse is expressed by these authors. Discuss, for example, Robert Stone's argument—against William Gass—that the moral effect of writing is the equation of "beauty and truth." Journalists, of course, see themselves as practical truth-tellers and as writers who must work hard to make what matters interesting to readers. Think about and discuss how a passion for language can help journalists fulfill their higher democratic purposes.

IV. Salman Rushdie declares that only freedom can create the conditions for the expression of true art. "What is freedom of expression?" he writes. "Without the freedom to offend, it ceases to exist. Without the freedom to challenge, even to satirise all orthodoxies, including religious orthodoxies, it ceases to exist. Language and the imagination cannot be imprisoned, or art dies, and with it, a little of what makes us human." Apply Rushdie's declaration to the practice of journalism. How do journalists exercise the freedom to offend? The freedom to challenge? The freedom to satirize religious orthodoxies?

V.   Robert Stone says that the "writer's responsibility . . . consists in writing well and truly, to use a Hemingwayesque locution. The writer who betrays his calling is that writer who either for commercial or political reasons vulgarizes his own perception and rendering of it. . . . [The author] assumes, above all, the responsibility to understand." Explore the implications of Stone's statement from the point of view of the journalist and his or her responsibilities.

WORKBENCH

I.   The editors proposed in the preface that the task of preparing apprentice journalists involves presenting and becoming fluent in "the editor's lexicon." The following quotation comes from the preface to this book:

"The lexicon includes simple terms such as 'nut graph' and 'lede' or 'beat' that classify basic devices of style and organization; it includes grammatical terms such as 'the active voice' and 'declarative sentences'; or it refers to figures of speech that work such as 'metaphors' and those that don't such as 'cliches.' Such terms and concepts languish in the ether of the places where journalists work, and they mark the conversation that goes—to borrow from the poet W. H. Auden—with the tasks of making, knowing, and judging the things we create. So the lexicon contains phrases that refer to commonplaces and routine actions, which we assume students will have learned in introductory course work. But it contains also complex notions involving democratic duties and goals, the motivations and moral outlook of authors and editors, the nature of news judgment, the functions and character of journalism and its varieties, its standards and best practices, the conditions of freedom attending its creation, its deficiencies, its achievements and stories—in short, a body of thought contained in a rich literature reflecting the 'experience' of writing and producing journalism. To be precise about it, the lexicon, considered as a whole, includes not just the record of such experience; it includes more fundamentally 'experience' reconsidered, reflected upon, and thought through."

Start building a glossary—it need not be exhaustive—from the readings in this section of the words, phrases, sentences, and concepts that might belong in your own "editor's lexicon."

II. At least three of these authors testify that one motivation for writing is to tell the untold stories, especially those stories that emerge from people or groups who are marginalized by mainstream society. Rushdie, for example, describes himself as a "migrant" author, determined "to create a literary language and literary forms in which the experience of formerly colonized, still-disadvantaged peoples might find full expression." Characterizing herself as a "caged bird," Angelou sees herself as a modern practitioner of "the slave narrative," someone who transforms the "I" of autobiography into the collective "we." V. S. Naipul wonders how he, a writer from an "agricultural colony," can honestly claim the language of an "older literature." One slogan of journalists is that their job is to give "voice to the voiceless." Who are the voiceless in your community? Where are the overlooked communities? Where are the untold stories? Write a story, a work of journalism, that captures an experience likely to be ignored in the mainstream media.

Part II

JOURNALISM'S ESSENTIAL ELEMENTS

NEWS

INTRODUCTION

The first act of journalism is "news judgment." It involves a form of vision, a way of knowing the here and now, that leads reporters and editors to notice the events and things that are likely to matter in a democratic society. Without judgments by reporters and editors that some things are more important or more interesting than others and thereby worthy of publication, the journalism we read, listen to, and see would not exist. Without news judgments, the social, cultural, economic, and political forces that surround us would seem a confusing and chaotic swirl.

So news judgments give birth to the processes of fact gathering, composition, and explaining that mark and distinguish journalism from such kindred forms of expression as fiction and history. Norman Cousins once wrote of *The Saturday Review* that he intended the magazine over which he presided to be an essay in the present tense.[1] By this he meant that his duty as editor was to direct attention not to the past but to the present and to do it meaningfully. His intention—and, we would claim, the intention of most journalists—was to stitch together individual portraits of things that matter into a coherent tapestry of the present.

But which events and ideas matter enough to command the attention of journalists? Editors are expected on an hourly, daily, weekly, or monthly basis to select from what Walter Lippmann described in his essay "The Nature of News" as "an ocean" of possibilities. So in the abstract, the exercise of news judgment may seem unduly arbitrary or simply opportunistic. But it is neither. Journalists have designed the craft's methods and operations so that the fields of action within which news is sought are managed and, to a degree, limited.

News can be classified as civic or literary. These categories are broad and flexible, and they do not have fixed boundaries. News, at its most powerful, can be both. But in the broad sense we are proposing, civic news focuses primarily on the events, issues, and institutions that define public life. On the other hand, literary or human-interest news focuses on the lives of individual humans, their triumphs, foibles, and fates. Stitched into these categories is news of natural events such as tornadoes, wildfires, and floods. But they, like so much of journalism, usually comprise a blend of civic and human-interest elements. The dramatic narrative of people rescued from a wildfire may involve public issues such as the budget for fire prevention or rescue.

In the case of Lippmann, for whom the civic was primary, news is "not a mirror of social conditions," but a report upon an event that has "obtruded itself" onto those conditions. Such reports are likely to come from a journalist "stationed" to notice the event. Journalists are routinely assigned to such beats as the legislature, municipal affairs, labor, business, police, school board, or courts. Placing them strategically in such sentry posts facilitates the process of identifying events that are candidates for news. Making news judgments in such circumscribed zones narrows the "ocean" of possibilities not only to events that stick out, but also to the sites in which, as Lippmann noted, "people's affairs touch public authority."

Something similar may be said of human-interest journalism. It focuses on the fates, sorrows, and successes of individuals against a backdrop provided by institutions and broad social forces. Journalism in the civic realm, by contrast, places the operations of those institutions into the foreground and places individuals into the background. But like the standard, bare-bones civic story, in the human-interest story individuals are likely to have been touched by society's formal or informal structure and therefore pushed into the public sphere, where they are candidates for the attention of journalists. Thus, the civic and the literary converge.

Helen MacGill Hughes describes in her essay how the topics of grassroots gossip and local talk were discovered by journalists and incorporated into the mainstream. The effect was to expand journalism's range so that it entertained as well as educated— to substitute, as Hughes notes, "the market for the mission." But such human-interest journalism did more than entertain. In our view, it added a permanent literary aspect to the craft by promoting the publication of narratives in addition to announcements and arguments. It also democratized journalism further by incorporating working people into the audience for the press and disclosing to them portraits of the events marking their world. In our view, human-interest journalism is no less an instrument for revealing the world than is civic journalism.

So news may be civic or it may be literary, or it may be both. Regardless, it is always timely. The very word "journalism" comes from the French word "jour" meaning "the day." "The one quality of the report which is necessary in order to make it 'news' is timeliness," writes Frank Luther Mott. He goes on to report that there is a consensus amongst writers on the subject that the news value of an event is measured by the element of timeliness and three other tests: prominence, proximity, and probable consequences. Accordingly, the news value of a story, considered as a whole, is dependent in part on its "newness," in part on the reputation or notoriety of the players or institutions it involves, and in part on the consequences or effects the event may have for lives of individuals or the well-being of society. Thus a declaration of peace by the president of a powerful country is big news on the day it occurs. The account of a soldier returning home soon after—a human-interest sidebar—is similarly newsworthy as the consequences of the initial declaration follow.

If the application of these categories and criteria to events seems straightforward, Daniel Boorstin in his essay titled "From News Gathering to News Making: A Flood of Pseudo-Events in America" warns us that what is spontaneous and important may lie buried beneath the maneuvering of press agents and spin doctors or beneath the temptations of journalists to promote excitement and conflict. The news may camouflage the reality it seeks to disclose by focusing on staged, dramatic, easy-to-describe, well-packaged, and well-financed pseudo-events—items cast up in a culture in which expectations for novelty, diversion, and knowledge are inflated. Similarly, Max Ways in "What's Wrong with News? It Isn't New Enough" reminds apprentice journalists that important stories of technological and social change can be unrecognized and untold because the traditional frames within which stories are conceived fail to capture what is truly new and important. Good news judgment calls for the consciousness of such traps and obstacles.

In our view, the editor casts his or her eye over an objective world of institutions, processes, individual lives, and nature. It is against such a world of movement and change that an editor asks: "What's new? What matters? What's interesting? What's real? What happened before?" The application of such questions in the here and now may lead to the creation of broadcasts or the publication of newspapers and magazines that promote, conceived broadly and generously, the forms of consciousness that support a democratic way of life. So we are concerned in this section of the book not only with the empirical question of how news judgments are made, but also with the normative question of how they are made well. The readings reflect the discussion of the element of news, which is the journalist's first specialty and exclusive competence. Elusive as the subject might be, we are hoping to promote good and competent news judgment.

NOTE

1. Norman Cousins, *Present Tense, an American Editor's Odyssey* (New York: McGraw-Hill, 1967).

7

THE NATURE OF NEWS

Walter Lippmann

1

All the reporters in the world working all the hours of the day could not witness all the happenings in the world. There are not a great many reporters. And none of them has the power to be in more than one place at a time. Reporters are not clairvoyant, they do not gaze into a crystal ball and see the world at will, they are not assisted by thought-transference. Yet the range of subjects these comparatively few men manage to cover would be a miracle indeed, if it were not a standardized routine.

Newspapers do not try to keep an eye on all mankind.[1] They have watchers stationed at certain places, like Police Headquarters, the Coroner's Office, the County Clerk's Office, City Hall, the White House, the Senate, House of Representatives, and so forth.

Walter Lippmann, "The Nature of News," Chapter 23 of *Public Opinion* (New York: Free Press Paperbacks, 1997), 214–225. Reprinted with the permission of Scribner, an imprint of Simon & Schuster Adult Publishing Group. Copyright © 1922 by Walter Lippmann; copyright renewed © 1950 by Walter Lippmann.

They watch, or rather in the majority of cases they belong to associations which employ men who watch "a comparatively small number of places where it is made known when the life of anyone . . . departs from ordinary paths, or when events worth telling about occur. For example, John Smith, let it be supposed, becomes a broker. For ten years he pursues the even tenor of his way and except for his customers and his friends no one gives him a thought. To the newspapers he is as if he were not. But in the eleventh year he suffers heavy losses and, at last, his resources all gone, summons his lawyer and arranges for the making of an assignment. The lawyer posts off to the County Clerk's office, and a clerk there makes the necessary entries in the official docket. Here in step the newspapers. While the clerk is writing Smith's business obituary a reporter glances over his shoulder and a few minutes later the reporters know Smith's troubles and are as well informed concerning his business status as they would be had they kept a reporter at his door every day for over ten years."[2]

   When Mr. Given says that the newspapers know "Smith's troubles" and "his business status," he does not mean that they know them as Smith knows them, or as Mr. Arnold Bennett would know them if he had made Smith the hero of a three volume novel. The newspapers know only "in a few minutes" the bald facts which are recorded in the County Clerk's Office. That overt act "uncovers" the news about Smith. Whether the news will be followed up or not is another matter. The point is that before a series of events become news they have usually to make themselves noticeable in some more or less overt act. Generally too, in a crudely overt act. Smith's friends may have known for years that he was taking risks, rumors may even have reached the financial editor if Smith's friends were talkative. But apart from the fact that none of this could be published because it would be libel, there is in these rumors nothing definite on which to peg a story. Something definite must occur that has unmistakable form. It may be the act of going into bankruptcy, it may be a fire, a collision, an assault, a riot, an arrest, a denunciation, the introduction of a bill, a speech, a vote, a meeting, the expressed opinion of a well known citizen, an editorial in a newspaper, a sale, a wage-schedule, a price change, the proposal to build a bridge. . . . There must be a manifestation. The course of events must assume a certain definable shape, and until it is in a phase where some aspect is an accomplished fact, news does not separate itself from the ocean of possible truth.

2

Naturally there is room for wide difference of opinion as to when events have a shape that can be reported. A good journalist will find news oftener than a hack. If he sees a building with a dangerous list, he does not have to wait until it falls into the street in order to recognize news. It was a great reporter who guessed the name of the next Indian Viceroy when he heard that Lord So-and-So was inquiring about climates. There are lucky shots but the number of men who can make them is small. Usually it is the stereotyped shape assumed by an event at an obvious place that uncovers the run of the news. The most obvious place is where people's affairs touch public authority. De minimis non curat lex. It is at these places that marriages, births, deaths, contracts, failures, arrivals, departures, lawsuits, disorders, epidemics and calamities are made known.

   In the first instance, therefore, the news is not a mirror of social conditions, but the report of an aspect that has obtruded itself. The news does not tell you how the seed is germinating in the ground, but it may tell you when the first sprout breaks through the surface. It may even tell you what somebody says is happening to the seed under ground. It may tell you that the sprout did not come up at the time it was expected. The more points, then, at which any happening can be fixed, objectified, measured, named, the more points there are at which news can occur.

So, if some day a legislature, having exhausted all other ways of improving mankind, should forbid the scoring of baseball games, it might still be possible to play some sort of game in which the umpire decided according to his own sense of fair play how long the game should last, when each team should go to bat, and who should be regarded as the winner. If that game were reported in the newspapers it would consist of a record of the umpire's decisions, plus the reporter's impression of the hoots and cheers of the crowd, plus at best a vague account of how certain men, who had no specified position on the field moved around for a few hours on an unmarked piece of sod. The more you try to imagine the logic of so absurd a predicament, the more clear it becomes that for the purposes of newsgathering, (let alone the purposes of playing the game) it is impossible to do much without an apparatus and rules for naming, scoring, recording. Because that machinery is far from perfect, the umpire's life is often a distracted one. Many crucial plays he has to judge by eye. The last vestige of dispute could be taken out of the game, as it has been taken out of chess when people obey the rules, if somebody thought it worth his while to photograph every play. It was the moving pictures which finally settled a real doubt in many reporters' minds, owing to the slowness of the human eye, as to just what blow of Dempsey's knocked out Carpentier.

Wherever there is a good machinery of record, the modern news service works with great precision. There is one on the stock exchange, and the news of price movements is flashed over tickers with dependable accuracy. There is a machinery for election returns, and when the counting and tabulating are well done, the result of a national election is usually known on the night of the election. In civilized communities deaths, births, marriages and divorces are recorded, and are known accurately except where there is concealment or neglect. The machinery exists for some, and only some, aspects of industry and government, in varying degrees of precision for securities, money and staples, bank clearances, realty transactions, wage scales. It exists for imports and exports because they pass through a custom house and can be directly recorded. It exists in nothing like the same degree for internal trade, and especially for trade over the counter.

It will be found, I think, that there is a very direct relation between the certainty of news and the system of record. If you call to mind the topics which form the principal indictment by reformers against the press, you find they are subjects in which the newspaper occupies the position of the umpire in the unscored baseball game. All news about states of mind is of this character: so are all descriptions of personalities, of sincerity, aspiration, motive, intention, of mass feeling, of national feeling, of public opinion, the policies of foreign governments. So is much news about what is going to happen. So are questions turning on private profit, private income, wages, working conditions, the efficiency of labor, educational opportunity, unemployment,[3] monotony, health, discrimination, unfairness, restraint of trade, waste, "backward peoples," conservatism, imperialism, radicalism, liberty, honor, righteousness. All involve data that are at best spasmodically recorded. The data may be hidden because of a censorship or a tradition of privacy, they may not exist because nobody thinks record important, because he thinks it red tape, or because nobody has yet invented an objective system of measurement. Then the news on these subjects is bound to be debatable, when it is not wholly neglected. The events which are not scored are reported either as personal and conventional opinions, or they are not news. They do not take shape until somebody protests, or somebody investigates, or somebody publicly, in the etymological meaning of the word, makes an *issue* of them.

This is the underlying reason for the existence of the press agent. The enormous discretion as to what facts and what impressions shall be reported is steadily convincing every organized group of people that whether it wishes to secure publicity or to avoid it, the exercise of discretion cannot be left to the reporter. It is safer to hire a press agent who stands between the group and the newspapers. Having hired him, the temptation to exploit his strategic position is very great. "Shortly before the war," says Mr. Frank Cobb, "the newspapers of New York took a census of the press agents who were regularly employed and regularly accredited and found that there were about twelve hundred of them. How many there are now (1919) I do not pretend to know, but what I do know is that many of the direct channels to news have been closed and the information for the public is first filtered through publicity agents. The great corporations have them, the banks have them, the railroads have them, all the organizations of business and of social and political activity have them, and they are the media through which news comes. Even statesmen have them." [4]

Were reporting the simple recovery of obvious facts, the press agent would be little more than a clerk. But since, in respect to most of the big topics of news, the facts are not simple, and not at all obvious, but subject to choice and opinion, it is natural that everyone should wish to make his own choice of facts for the newspapers to print. The publicity man does that. And in doing it, he certainly saves the reporter much trouble, by presenting him a clear picture of a situation out of which he might otherwise make neither head nor tail. But it follows that the picture which the publicity man makes for the reporter is the one he wishes the public to see. He is censor and propagandist, responsible only to his employers, and to the whole truth responsible only as it accords with the employers' conception of his own interests.

The development of the publicity man is a clear sign that the facts of modern life do not spontaneously take a shape in which they can be known. They must be given a shape by somebody, and since in the daily routine reporters cannot give a shape to facts, and since there is little disinterested organization of intelligence, the need for some formulation is being met by the interested parties.

3

The good press agent understands that the virtues of his cause are not news, unless they are such strange virtues that they jut right out of the routine of life. This is not because the newspapers do not like virtue, but because it is not worth while to say that nothing has happened when nobody expected anything to happen. So if the publicity man wishes free publicity he has, speaking quite accurately, to start something. He arranges a stunt: obstructs the traffic, teases the police, somehow manages to entangle his client or his cause with an event that is already news. The suffragists knew this, did not particularly enjoy the knowledge but acted on it, and kept suffrage in the news long after the arguments pro and con were straw in their mouths, and people were about to settle down to thinking of the suffrage movement as one of the established institutions of American life.[5]

Fortunately the suffragists, as distinct from the feminists, had a perfectly concrete objective, and a very simple one. What the vote symbolizes is not simple, as the ablest advocates and the ablest opponents knew. But the right to vote is a simple and familiar right. Now in labor disputes, which are probably the chief item in the charges against newspapers, the right to strike, like the right to vote, is simple enough. But the causes and objects of a particular strike are like the causes and objects of the woman's movement, extremely subtle.

Let us suppose the conditions leading up to a strike are bad. What is the measure of evil? A certain conception of a proper standard of living, hygiene, economic security, and human dignity. The industry may be far below the theoretical standard of the community, and the workers may be too wretched to protest. Conditions may be above the standard, and the workers may protest violently. The standard is at best a vague measure. However, we shall assume that the conditions are below par, as par is understood by the editor. Occasionally without waiting for the workers to threaten, but prompted say by a social worker, he will send reporters to investigate, and will call attention to bad conditions. Necessarily he cannot do that often. For these investigations cost time, money, special talent, and a lot of space. To make plausible a report that conditions are bad, you need a good many columns of print. In order to tell the truth about the steel worker in the Pittsburgh district, there was needed a staff of investigators, a great deal of time, and several fat volumes of print. It is impossible to suppose that any daily newspaper could normally regard the making of Pittsburgh Surveys, or even Interchurch Steel Reports, as one of its tasks. News which requires so much trouble as that to obtain is beyond the resources of a daily press.[6]

The bad conditions as such are not news, because in all but exceptional cases, journalism is not a first hand report of the raw material. It is a report of that material after it has been stylized. Thus bad conditions might become news if the Board of Health reported an unusually high death rate in an industrial area. Failing an intervention of this sort, the facts do not become news, until the workers organize and make a demand upon their employers. Even then, if an easy settlement is certain the news value is low, whether or not the conditions themselves are remedied in the settlement. But if industrial relations collapse into a strike or lockout the news value increases. If the stoppage involves a service on which the readers of the newspapers immediately depend, or if it involves a breach of order, the news value is still greater.

The underlying trouble appears in the news through certain easily recognizable symptoms, a demand, a strike, disorder. From the point of view of the worker, or of the disinterested seeker of justice, the demand, the strike, and the disorder, are merely incidents in a process that for them is richly complicated. But since all the immediate realities lie outside the direct experience both of the reporter, and of the special public by which most newspapers are supported, they have normally to wait for a signal in the shape of an overt act. When that signal comes, say through a walkout of the men or a summons for the police, it calls into play the stereotypes people have about strikes and disorders. The unseen struggle has none of its own flavor. It is noted abstractly, and that abstraction is then animated by the immediate experience of the reader and reporter.

Obviously this is a very different experience from that which the strikers have. They feel, let us say, the temper of the foreman, the nerve-racking monotony of the machine, the depressingly bad air, the drudgery of their wives, the stunting of their children, the dinginess of their tenements. The slogans of the strike are invested with these feelings. But the reporter and reader see at first only a strike and some catchwords. They invest these with their feelings. Their feelings may be that their jobs are insecure because the strikers are stopping goods they need in their work, that there will be shortage and higher prices, that it is all devilishly inconvenient. These, too, are realities. And when they give color to the abstract news that a strike has been called, it is in the nature of things that the workers are at a disadvantage. It is in the nature, that is to say, of the existing system of industrial relations that news arising from grievances or hopes by workers should almost invariably be uncovered by an overt attack on production.

You have, therefore, the circumstances in all their sprawling complexity, the overt act which signalizes them, the stereotyped bulletin which publishes the signal, and the meaning that the reader himself injects, after he has derived that meaning from the experience which directly affects him. Now the reader's experience of a strike may be very important indeed, but from the point of view of the central trouble which caused the strike, it is eccentric. Yet this eccentric meaning is automatically the most interesting.[7] To enter imaginatively into the central issues is for the reader to step out of himself, and into very different lives.

It follows that in the reporting of strikes, the easiest way is to let the news be uncovered by the overt act, and to describe the event as the story of interference with the reader's life. That is where his attention is first aroused, and his interest most easily enlisted. A great deal, I think myself the crucial part, of what looks to the worker and the reformer as deliberate misrepresentation on the part of newspapers, is the direct outcome of a practical difficulty in uncovering the news, and the emotional difficulty of making distant facts interesting unless, as Emerson says, we can "perceive (them) to be only a new version of our familiar experience" and can "set about translating (them) at once into our parallel facts."[8]

If you study the way many a strike is reported in the press, you will find, very often, that the issues are rarely in the headlines, barely in the leading paragraphs, and sometimes not even mentioned anywhere. A labor dispute in another city has to be very important before the news account contains any definite information as to what is in dispute. The routine of the news works that way, with modifications it works that way in regard to political issues and international news as well. The news is an account of the overt phases that are interesting, and the pressure on the newspaper to adhere to this routine comes from many sides. It comes from the economy of noting only the stereotyped phase of a situation. It comes from the difficulty of finding journalists who can see what they have not learned to see. It comes from the almost unavoidable difficulty of finding sufficient space in which even the best journalist can make plausible an unconventional view. It comes from the economic necessity of interesting the reader quickly, and the economic risk involved in not interesting him at all, or of offending him by unexpected news insufficiently or clumsily described. All these difficulties combined make for uncertainty in the editor when there are dangerous issues at stake, and cause him naturally to prefer the indisputable fact and a treatment more readily adapted to the reader's interest. The indisputable fact and the easy interest, are the strike itself and the reader's inconvenience.

All the subtler and deeper truths are in the present organization of industry very unreliable truths. They involve judgments about standards of living, productivity, human rights that are endlessly debatable in the absence of exact record and quantitative analysis. And as long as these do not exist in industry, the run of news about it will tend, as Emerson said, quoting from Isocrates, "to make of moles mountains, and of mountains moles."[9] Where there is no constitutional procedure in industry, and no expert sifting of evidence and the claims, the fact that is sensational to the reader is the fact that almost every journalist will seek. Given the industrial relations that so largely prevail, even where there is conference or arbitration, but no independent filtering of the facts for decision, the issue for the newspaper public will tend not to be the issue for the industry. And so to try disputes by an appeal through the newspapers puts a burden upon newspapers and readers which they cannot and ought not to carry. As long as real law and order do not exist, the bulk of the news will, unless consciously and courageously corrected, work against those who have no lawful and orderly method of asserting themselves. The bulletins from the scene of action will note the trouble that arose from the assertion, rather than the reasons which led to it. The reasons are intangible.

4

The editor deals with these bulletins. He sits in his office, reads them, rarely does he see any large portion of the events themselves. He must, as we have seen, woo at least a section of his readers every day, because they will leave him without mercy if a rival paper happens to hit their fancy. He works under enormous pressure, for the competition of newspapers is often a matter of minutes. Every bulletin requires a swift but complicated judgment. It must be understood, put in relation to other bulletins also understood, and played up or played down according to its probable interest for the public, as the editor conceives it. Without standardization, without stereotypes, without routine judgments, without a fairly ruthless disregard of subtlety, the editor would soon die of excitement. The final page is of a definite size, must be ready at a precise moment; there can be only a certain number of captions on the items, and in each caption there must be a definite number of letters. Always there is the precarious urgency of the buying public, the law of libel, and the possibility of endless trouble. The thing could not be managed at all without systematization, for in a standardized product there is economy of time and effort, as well as a partial guarantee against failure.

It is here that newspapers influence each other most deeply. Thus when the war broke out, the American newspapers were confronted with a subject about which they had no previous experience. Certain dailies, rich enough to pay cable tolls, took the lead in securing news, and the way that news was presented became a model for the whole press. But where did that model come from? It came from the English press, not because Northcliffe owned American newspapers, but because at first it was easier to buy English correspondence, and because, later, it was easier for American journalists to read English newspapers than it was for them to read any others. London was the cable and news center, and it was there that a certain technic for reporting the war was evolved. Something similar occurred in the reporting of the Russian Revolution. In that instance, access to Russia was closed by military censorsip, both Russian and Allied, and closed still more effectively by the difficulties of the Russian language. But above all it was closed to effective news reporting by the fact that the hardest thing to report is chaos, even though it is an evolving chaos. This put the formulating of Russian news at its source in Helsingfors, Stockholm, Geneva, Paris and London, into the hands of censors and propagandists. They were for a long time subject to no check of any kind. Until they had made themselves ridiculous they created, let us admit, out of some genuine aspects of the huge Russian maelstrom, a set of stereotypes so evocative of hate and fear, that the very best instinct of journalism, its desire to go and see and tell, was for a long time crushed.[10]

5

Every newspaper when it reaches the reader is the result of a whole series of selections as to what items shall be printed, in what position they shall be printed, how much space each shall occupy, what emphasis each shall have. There are no objective standards here. There are conventions. Take two newspapers published in the same city on the same morning. The headline of one reads: "Britain pledges aid to Berlin against French aggression; France openly backs Poles." The headline of the second is "Mrs. Stillman's Other Love." Which you prefer is a matter of taste, but not entirely a matter of the editor's taste. It is a matter of his judgment as to what will absorb the half hour's attention a certain set of readers will give to his newspaper. Now the problem of securing attention is by no means equivalent to displaying the news in the perspective laid down by religious teaching or by some form of ethical culture. It is a problem of provoking feeling in the reader, of inducing him to feel a sense of personal identification with the stories he is reading. News which does not offer this opportunity to introduce oneself into the struggle which it depicts cannot appeal to a wide audience. The audience must participate in the news, much as it participates in the drama, by personal identification. Just as everyone holds his breath when the heroine is in danger, as he helps Babe Ruth swing his bat, so in subtler form the reader enters into the news. In order that he shall enter he must find a familiar foothold in the story, and this is supplied to him by the use of stereotypes. They tell him that if an association of plumbers is called a "combine" it is appropriate to develop his hostility; if it is called a "group of leading business men" the cue is for a favorable reaction.

It is in a combination of these elements that the power to create opinion resides. Editorials reinforce. Sometimes in a situation that on the news pages is too confusing to permit of identification, they give the reader a clue by means of which he engages himself. A clue he must have if, as most of us must, he is to seize the news in a hurry. A suggestion of some sort he demands, which tells him, so to speak, where he, a man conceiving himself to be such and such a person, shall integrate his feelings with the news he reads.

"It has been said" writes Walter Bagehot,[11] "that if you can only get a middleclass Englishman to think whether there are 'snails in Sirius,' he will soon have an opinion on it. It will be difficult to make him think, but if he does think, he cannot rest in a negative, he will come to some decision. And on any ordinary topic, of course, it is so. A grocer has a full creed as to foreign policy, a young lady a complete theory of the sacraments, as to which neither has any doubt whatever."

Yet that same grocer will have many doubts about his groceries, and that young lady, marvelously certain about the sacraments, may have all kinds of doubts as to whether to marry the grocer, and if not whether it is proper to accept his attentions. The ability to rest in the negative implies either a lack of interest in the result, or a vivid sense of competing alternatives. In the case of foreign policy or the sacraments, the interest in the results is intense, while means for checking the opinion are poor. This is the plight of the reader of the general news. If he is to read it at all he must be interested, that is to say, he must enter into the situation and care about the outcome. But if he does that he cannot rest in a negative, and unless independent means of checking the lead given him by his newspaper exists, the very fact that he is interested may make it difficult to arrive at that balance of opinions which may most nearly approximate the truth. The more passionately involved he becomes, the more he will tend to resent not only a different view, but a disturbing bit of news. That is why many a newspaper finds that, having honestly evoked the partisanship of its readers, it can not easily, supposing the editor believes the facts warrant it, change position. If a change is necessary, the transition has to be managed with the utmost skill and delicacy. Usually a newspaper will not attempt so hazardous a performance. It is easier and safer to have the news of that subject taper off and disappear, thus putting out the fire by starving it.

NOTES

1. See the illuminating chapter in Mr. John L. Given's book (*Making a Newspaper*) on "Uncovering the News," Ch. V.

2. Given, p. 57.

3. Think of what guess work went into the Reports of Unemployment in 1921.

4. Address before the Women's City Club of New York, Dec. 11, 1919. Reprinted, *New Republic*, Dec. 31, 1919, p. 44.

5. *Cf.* Inez Haynes Irwin, *The Story of the Woman's Party*. It is not only a good account of a vital part of a great agitation, but a reservoir of material on successful, non-revolutionary, non-conspiring agitation under modern conditions of public attention, public interest, and political habit.

6. Not long ago Babe Ruth was jailed for speeding. Released from jail just before the afternoon game started, he rushed into his waiting automobile, and made up for time lost in jail by breaking the speed laws on his way to the ball grounds. No policeman stopped him, but a reporter timed him, and published his speed the next morning. Babe Ruth is an exceptional man. Newspapers cannot time all motorists. They have to take their news about speeding from the police.

7. *Cf.* Ch. 11, "The Enlisting of Interest."

8. From his essay entitled *Art and Criticism*. The quotation occurs in a passage cited on page 87 of Professor R. W. Brown's, *The Writer's Art*.

9. *Id., supra.*

10. *Cf. A Test of the News*, by Walter Lippmann and Charles Merz, assisted by Faye Lippmann, *New Republic*, August 4, 1920.

11. On the Emotion of Conviction, *Literary Studies*, Vol. III, p. 172.

8

FROM POLITICS TO HUMAN INTEREST

Helen MacGill Hughes

Newspapermen, though noted for their assurance, have never been able to decide whether the modern newspaper is a "news" paper or a daily magazine. The difference is understood to be between something important and something entertaining.

Publishers, the Tories of the Fourth Estate, cherish the traditional belief that the press somehow promotes the health of the body politic and that great newspaper circulation is the *sine qua non* of an informed electorate. But their circulation managers are remarkably silent about the political functions of journalism; they never use the phrase, "the palladium of our liberties," to stimulate sales. But they do buy billboard space to announce a comic strip or the confessions of a movie star. Yet these delights are hardly a public necessity. Like many another sales promoter, the circulation manager is hugely successful in selling a product that people, it seems, do not need—indeed, Whitelaw Reid, the great editor of the *New York Tribune*, once characterized a thriving class of newspapers as being written for men who cannot read—but which they can be made to want. Now, the circulation managers are realists in a business where realists, though seldom vocal, are far from uncommon. And the greatest support for their view of the matter is found in the newspaper's human interest stories.

As an outstanding characteristic of American newspapers, human interest is relatively new. It was discovered by newspapermen a century ago and, sometime later, given a name. Its invasion of the newspaper and final adoption as a policy of news-writing were accompanied by changes in every aspect of the newspaper's organization. In the course of a revolution which is, one suspects, related to the revolution in life itself, the newspaper of the nineteenth century discarded some functions and added others. It emerges, in the twentieth century, as a new form. The natural history of the newspaper, which, as with an organic phenomenon, is "the history of the surviving species,"[1] is the story of the expansion of the traditional function—originally the publishing of practical, important news—to include the sale of interesting personal gossip. In the long process of discovering and exploiting human interest the press, for the first time, became rich and powerful.

THE TRADITIONAL CONCEPTION OF NEWS

Until a hundred years ago, news in Europe and the United States was conceived of in the way it had been ever since news was bought and sold. It was limited to commercial and political intelligence.

Helen MacGill Hughes, "From Politics to Human Interest," Chapter 1 of *News and the Human Interest Story* (Chicago: Chicago University Press, 1940), 1–29. Reprinted with permission of the University of Chicago Press.

Whenever trade and government has taken men away from home, the successful prosecution of their affairs has required them to know what was going on in their head offices. This is the condition that makes news imperative and gives it value and which, in the first place, gave rise to its regular collection.[2] The political welding of extensive territory under the government of the Roman Empire made it necessary to establish official agents in distant parts. To these representatives the news was first sold systematically. It came to them as newsletters. Provincial officials hired slaves to copy the *Acta Diurna*, which was a public record of the proceedings of the Roman Senate, the law courts, and the army. The scribes added to the manuscript any other news of the Capitol that would be of importance to the subscriber, and sent it off to him. Such news was a practical necessity to absent agents of the government, and worth paying for. Business and politics, in so far as it affected trade, were the subject of the famous newsletters sent to agents of the financial house of the Fuggers, of Augsburg, in the seventeenth century. "Lloyd's List" of shipping news was a private circular that was distributed in the eighteenth century among those London importers and speculators who subscribed to it. The newsletter took a form that was dictated by the demands of the person paying for it. Its contents were confined to what was relevant to the pursuit of professional activity; it corresponds to the house organ and the special departments of the modern newspaper in being technical and related to practical affairs. But it was not a public record; it did not circulate indiscriminately. Eventually news was printed and offered for public sale. The new medium, the newspaper, continued to supply the practical, important tidings of business and politics that had been the subject of the newsletter.

Though printed, the news was still the exclusive possession of men of large affairs. The layman had no access to it. In the smaller world of local concerns, in the countryside, the village, and the neighborhood, gossip circulated the news of interesting events among the illiterate—and others. Its scope was smaller, being the geographical range of the peasant and the villager. Word of mouth was its natural and spontaneous medium. It had no superstructure of professional news-gatherer and purchaser, and no cash value.

The early American newspapers were of the historic type. The first newspaper, the *Boston News-Letter*, originated, as its name suggests, in newsletters which were sent by the Boston postmaster to the governors of the Colonies. There was no machinery for the regular collection of even local reports. Editors, as a rule, were either the postmasters, who took advantage of presiding at the source of news and who were in touch with other public servants, or booksellers and job printers who got out a news chronicle incidentally to their other business. The news was principally a belated account of political happenings in Europe. Its sources were travelers and the crews of packet boats, letters, and the English newspapers. Domestic news had to do with the official acts of the governor and the courts, with the arrival and departure of ships, and with a description of their cargoes. The dullness of the record was occasionally relieved by items of more general interest, such as:

> Piscataqua, April 6th. On Tuesday last five of the Skulking Indian Enemy killed two men about Scotland Garrison at York, viz., Daniel Dill and Joseph Jenkins, the last whereof they also stript and scalpt and after the Enemy withdrew they supposing him dead Jenkins arose and marched to the Garrison, and gave an account of the Action and liv'd but about 10 hours afterwards.[3]

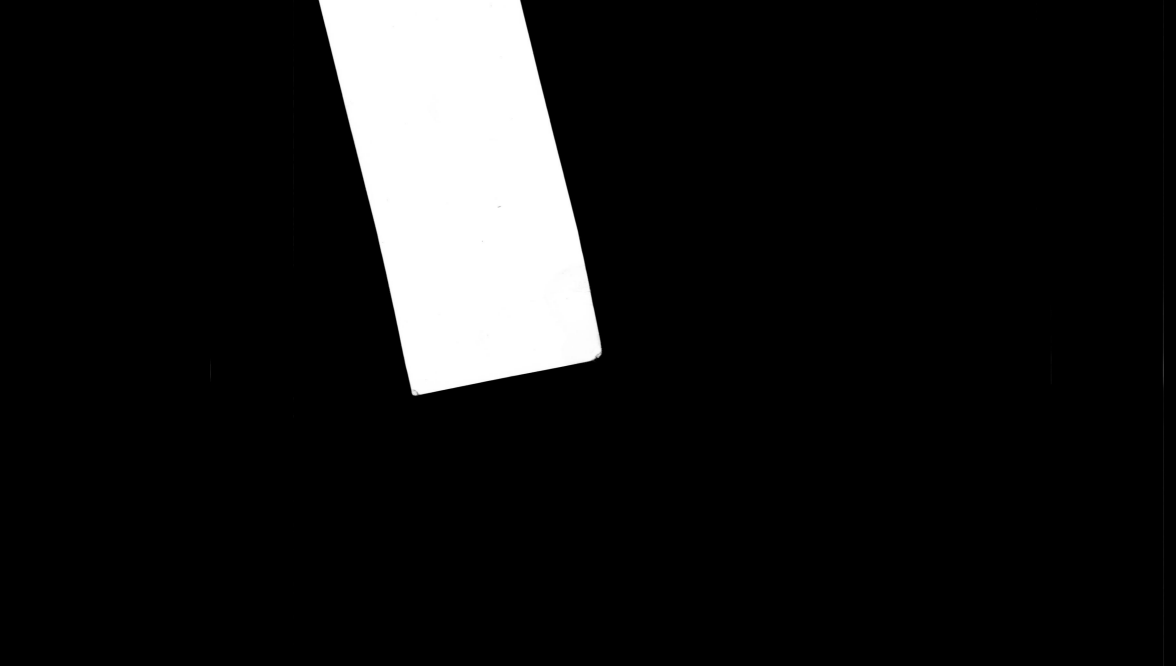

Monkey See, Monkey Read

NEW AND USED BOOKS
BESTSELLERS 20% OFF

425 S. Division St.
Northfield, MN

M-F 10am - 6pm
Sat 10am - 5pm
Sun Noon - 4pm

But this sort of thing was not in keeping with the current conception of news, and so the telling of it was discreetly brief and matter of fact.

THE POLITICAL PARTY PRESS

With the growing enthusiasm for self-government that led to the Revolution, the newspapers became the instruments of public opinion as well as of news. Official printers, who enjoyed the government patronage, printed newspapers endorsed and subsidized by the administration, while Tory sympathizers and the patriots replied to them in their own organs. The few journals that tried to give both sides were short-lived because both sides mistrusted them. After the Revolution the Federalists and the Republicans sought to capture public support by the founding and subsidizing of newspapers, for newspapers had proved themselves more effective than pamphlets in stirring people to action.

The newspaper thus became the agency of a cause. To print the news was the editor's public duty, but, being a "kept" editor, he was not free to tell things indiscriminately; there were tabooed subjects. The qualification for editorship was partisan enthusiasm, for his office was confused with that of the politician; indeed, the reward for fighting a good fight was often a political appointment. The editor held what Will Irwin calls the "professional attitude" to the newspaper: that the press, like the pulpit, should point out to the people where their duty lies, and do so in conformity with its own scheme of values.

The paper that is dominated by its duty to the public interest cannot by the nature of its sacred calling conceive its function as purely commercial. It places its doctrine of the public good above every other consideration—even that of popularity and revenue. Thus Horace Greeley of the *New York Tribune*, a latter-day example, who was said by a fellow-editor to sacrifice everything to principle, once wrote editorially: "We have not sought [advertisements of the theaters] mainly because we consider the Stage, *as it is*, rather an injury than a benefit to the community—vicious, licentious, degrading, demoralizing."[4] The news thus assumes secondary importance in comparison with the editorial; it is subordinated to the propagating of a political or social gospel. Indeed, little or no distinction was made historically between the account of an event and the editor's opinion of it. While the editor's views are now confined to modest dimensions on an inside page, they once pervaded the whole newspaper and, like the communist sheets and the political press of France and Germany,[5] the journal was the mouthpiece of the man or the party behind it. The news was thus turned into a sermon. Now, a sermon is a doctrinaire exposition built on premises on which the faithful agree. In the light of the premises a contemporary event is translated into the familiar moral issue. Although the hearers know it all in advance and are never taken by surprise, the exhorter is under an inner compulsion to speak his piece to the bitter end. The pains taken to give his message the appearance of being new and striking ordinarily spend themselves in a promising opening paragraph.

The organ of opinion, however, has never earned its own living; it has had to be supported by the group whose convictions it expressed. But the party's faithful adherents, knowing these views in advance, often neglected to read what was to them no longer news. They continued, however, to support their paper because they endorsed its policy. They bought it by annual subscription at six dollars or more a year. Circulation was small because of the high price and because the papers were beyond the comprehension of the great mass of the people, for the editor presupposed his reader to be a man of education, interested mainly in affairs of state and in business.

The professional attitude was challenged by the penny press, but it persisted, nevertheless, until after the Civil War in the moral organs edited by the fighting editors—Greeley, Godkin, Manton Marble, and others. There are still editors and readers who, as Lippmann puts it, think of the newspaper "as if it were a church or a school." But the commercial penny press substituted the market for the mission. Its object was to sell, not its influence, but the news, and its customers, therefore, were those who were more interested in the news than in the editor's interpretation of the news.

THE PENNY PRESS AND HUMAN INTEREST

The commercial press began with the penny papers of the 1830's. The *New York Sun*, founded in 1833 by Benjamin Day, a printer, was the first outstanding success.

"The Cheap Press," as Parton, a contemporary, observed, "had, first of all, to create itself, and, secondly, to create its Public."[6] Its public was described as artisans and mechanics, a relatively unlettered class that had never had a newspaper before. Day had no party subsidy and no annual subscribers. His paper had to be self-supporting, with advertisements and cash purchases as the only sources of revenue. The London system of selling papers by newsboy had never been known in America. Irregular purchases had to be made in the newspaper office, but almost all readers got their papers by subscription and delivery. It was Day who introduced street sales. His innovation was greeted with moral indignation, for in taking the news into the market place he was selling "in competition with cakes and apples," as Parton put it,[7] the thing that was called "the tribune of the people and the palladium of our liberties." Therefore he had to offer for sale something his humble clientele would buy. And this was something far removed from the foreign dispatches, politics, and shipping news of the sixpenny contemporary papers.

Giving up the customary public function of the editor, Day made himself a livelihood by selling personal gossip, anecdotes, animal stories, and news of the police courts, told in the main in graphic dialogue form. Reviewing early issues, Frank M. O'Brien discovered the following:

> The removal of William J. Duane as Secretary of the Treasury got two lines on a page where a big shark, caught off Barnstable, got three lines, and the feeding of the anaconda at the American Museum a quarter of a column. Miss Susan Allen, who bought a cigar on Broadway and was arrested when she smoked it while she danced in the street, was featured more prominently than the expected visit to New York of Mr. Henry Clay, after whom millions of cigars were to be named.[8]

These inconsequential items were the first human interest stories in the American press.

New York was too large for oral gossip to circulate everywhere, and the mechanics and artisans bought gossip in the *Sun* and enjoyed it. Day had no philosophy about the popular taste; he discovered it accidentally when he printed the only things he could afford, namely, items detailing the unconsidered trifles of local city life which better-established papers neglected. Economics and politics, which filled the sixpenny papers, were practically ignored in the *Sun*, whose readers had no mind for the abstruse and the remote.

The assassination of the Czar Alexander II of Russia did not sell an extra paper, but the hanging of Foster, the "car-hook" murderer, sent the sales up seventeen thousand. The deaths of Cornelius Vanderbilt and Alexander T. Stewart had no effect on the *Sun's* circulation, the passing of Napoleon III raised it only one thousand for the day, and the death of Pius IX caused only four thousand irregular readers to buy the paper, but the execution of Dolan, a murderer now practically forgotten, sent the sales up ten thousand.[9]

Day's little four-page journal met with instant success. Within four months its sales reached five thousand, which was five hundred more than the *Courier and Enquirer*, the strongest sixpenny paper. When, in two years, it had fifteen thousand readers, the *Sun* claimed it was a "circulation far surpassing that of any other daily paper in the Union, and, with one, perhaps two exceptions in London, in the world."[10]

Day's only assistant was a fellow-printer called George Wisner, whose duties were to attend police-court sessions daily and to write two columns of news of the cases. That may have been because Day suspected his readers would enjoy it, but more probably it was because he had no political connections, no correspondents, and no money, and turned to the police-court reports because they were accessible and cheap. As penny papers were established in other cities, it was usual for the editorial staff to consist of the owner, a collector of news—meaning general city news—and a police reporter.

Out of Day's discovery of the attractiveness of items of purely human interest there grew up, almost at once, a new and lucrative type of journal.

A second penny paper, the *New York Evening Transcript*, appeared in the same year the *Sun* was founded. It was staffed by an editor and a police-court reporter. The *Transcript* was the first paper to recognize the ordinary man's enthusiasm for prize fights, races, and other sporting events, and it created a demand for itself by reporting them. Thus, as though by accident, the newspaper invaded a department of the national life that for decades has yielded it its liveliest, most uproarious—and perhaps its most profitable—columns.

James Gordon Bennett founded the penny *New York Herald* in 1835. Having no financial backing, he proposed, like Day, to print an independent newspaper that would pay for itself. He stated his position in his first issue:

> In debuts of this kind, many talk of principle—political principle—party principle, as a sort of steel trap to catch the public. We mean to be perfectly understood on this point, and therefore openly disclaim all steel traps, all principle, as it is called—all party—all politics. Our only guide shall be good, sound, practical commonsense, applicable to the business and bosoms of men engaged in everyday life. We shall support no party, be the organ of no faction or coterie, and care nothing for any election, or any candidate, from president down to a constable. We shall endeavor to record facts on every public and proper subject stripped of verbiage and coloring with comments when suitable, just, independent, fearless, and good-tempered. If the *Herald* wants the mere expansion which many journals possess, we shall try to make it up in industry, good taste, brevity, variety, point, piquancy, and cheapness. It is equally intended for the great mass of the community—the merchant, mechanic, working people—the private family as well as the public hotel—the journeyman and his employer—the clerk and his principal.[11]

Bennett secured the *Herald* its first great leap in circulation in its first year when a young man about town, named Robinson, murdered Helen Jewett, a prostitute. The six-penny papers reported it in the brief formal way that was conventional in covering crime news. The penny papers, on the other hand, were the only ones to tell people the things that really interested them about the murder. Bennett found out all that an inquisitive person would like to ask, if he dared, and shared it unreservedly with his readers in the columns of the *Herald*. To do so, as he frankly told his readers, he exploited the customary privilege conceded to editors:

> I knocked at the door. A Police Officer opened it, stealthily. I told him who I was. "Mr B., you can enter," said he with great politeness. The crowds rushed from behind seeking also an entrance.
> "No more comes in," said the Police Officer.
> "Why do you let that man in?" asked one of the crowd.
> "He is an editor—he is on public duty."[12]

The fashionable vice resort where Helen Jewett was murdered was a place that his readers could not afford to frequent, but whose aristocratic sinfulness filled them with envy and wonder. When he came to write the story, Bennett abandoned the role of the responsible editor for that of a chattering gossip. He was just the person his readers would have loved to have a long talk with—one who had seen everything and was ready to tell all about it. Describing the scene of the crime, he wrote:

> What a sight burst upon me! There stood an elegant double mahogany bed all covered with burnt pieces of linen, blankets, pillows, black as cinders. I looked around for the object of my curiosity. On the carpet I saw a piece of linen sheet covering something as if carelessly flung over it.
> "Here," said the Police Officer, "here is the poor creature." He half uncovered the ghastly corpse. I could scarcely look at it for a second or two. Slowly I began to discover the lineaments of the corpse as one would the beauties of a statue of marble. It was the most remarkable sight I ever beheld. I never have and never expect to see such another. "My God," I exclaimed, "How like a statue! I can scarcely conceive that form to be a corpse." Not a vein was to be seen. The body looked as white, as full, as polished, as the purest Parian marble. The perfect figure, the exquisite limbs, the fine face, the full arms, the beautiful bust, all, all surpassed in every respect the Venus de Medici, according to the casts generally given of her.

He saw the woman who had discovered the body, asked her everything a curious busy-body could think of, and recounted the conversation in dialogue form to his readers—the first interview. He reconstructed the life of the girl in that "wicked house" and gave a long, full account of champagne parties given in the garden at the back which were attended by some of New York's most notable businessmen.

The popularity of Bennett's *Herald* was as natural as that of a talkative sheriff or coroner. Trifling and gossipy though these reports appeared, they take on importance because, by exploiting the human interest angle in the news, they taught people to read newspapers and made the press popular.[13]

The name "human interest stories" was first used in the office of the *Sun* to designate the chatty little reports of tragic or comic incidents in the lives of the people. Charles Dana, who bought the *Sun* after the Civil War, made human interest, which Day had accidentally discovered, an essential feature of news-writing. Mitchell, his editor-in-chief, in estimating Dana's importance in the history of journalism, wrote:

> From his individual perception of the true philosophy of human interest, more than from any other single source, have come the new general repudiation of the old conventional standards of news importance; the modern newspaper's appreciation of the news value of the sentiment and humor of the daily life around us; the recognition of the principle that a small incident, interesting in itself, and well-told, may be worth a column's space, when a large dull fact is hardly worth a stickful's; the surprising extension of the daily newspaper's province, so as to cover every department of general literature, and to take in the world's fancies and imaginings as well as its actual events.[14]

Bennett was too ingenious to duplicate the field of the existing penny papers, but made a market for himself by extending the news to areas of life not hitherto reported and, by doing so, sought to interest all sorts of people in the news. He was the first to realize the news value of church meetings and of social functions among the wealthy, and the first to cover Wall Street. Occasionally he caused excited comment by illustrating the reports with wood engravings. The paper was pert and bright. "Its power," declares Don Seitz, "grew from its overwhelming lead on the news. . . . His one definite purpose was to tell all that was worth telling about everybody and everything."[15] His free-ranging inquisitiveness led him, as it turned out, to pry into the very things his readers, the "lower half," would have enjoyed exploring. But the newspaper was not supposed to cater to vulgar curiosity. Each innovation provoked a righteous outburst, but Bennett asserted that more people bought and read the *Herald* than bought all the other New York papers together.

The newspaper that furnished these stories addressed itself to the total public and found ready sale among all classes of the people. The reader might be also a subscriber to a party paper who, as Whitelaw Reid complained, often left it with his family at home and bought—though professing to despise it—a more entertaining paper on the way to town. The subscriber supported his paper, but the cash customer felt no moral responsibility for a penny paper's success when he bought it on the street.

The party papers were put to no great cost to obtain their news, but Dana's and Bennett's expenditure for news-gathering was high; sales at a penny did not cover it. Hence, advertising was necessary if the paper was to live. Bennett sent solicitors all over New York to bring in advertisements, for which he insisted on cash payments, since credit had ruined many a newspaper. He not only made the paper the principal vehicle of personals, patent medicine, and classified advertising, but established its financial success at the same time. He was able to say: "At the end of the first three months of its existence, the receipts of the *Herald* pay its expenses, a fact which never happened before in any newspaper enterprise."[16]

The penny papers had now made themselves financially independent of political parties. The publication of political exhortations was supposed to be in the public interest, but Day, Bennett, and Dana, in selling gossip and police-court trivia, did not claim merit on that ground. Though they did not fully foresee it, it transformed the newspaper into a private business run, like any other, for profit. The whole complex of the penny press, its news and its marketing, signalized the commercialization of the newspaper. Contemporary editors called it prostitution. It was the beginning of the independent journal and of a time when, ironically, prostitution would mean the very thing that was the party paper's virtue—propaganda for a cause.

THE INDEPENDENT PRESS: NEWS AND ADVERTISING

In becoming cheap and pervasive the press, as so often happens in a competitive world, grew immensely profitable. But its rich yield was not within the grasp of everyone. Bennett, it is true, had founded the *New York Herald* with no money at all. Ten years later Horace Greeley established the first political penny paper with a capital of a thousand dollars. But ten years after that Henry Raymond, when founding the *New York Times*, required one hundred thousand dollars, and to raise it he organized a company of stockholders. The newspaper was now a capital investment and the change was reflected in its internal economy. By the time the *Tribune* was four months old the traffic in advertising had so increased that Greeley could not direct it and the editorial work, too, and he added a business manager to the staff, dividing the newspaper work into two departments. This had not been necessary until now. It signalized a revolution in journalism. Control was henceforth divided between "upstairs," where the editorial staff wrote the newspaper, and "downstairs," where the counting house or business office solicited advertisers and readers.

What the advertiser bought was circulation, and his money paid the costs of publishing the paper. Sales of the newspaper to readers barely paid for the ink and newsprint paper. But to make advertising space worth paying for, there must be wide circulation. The circulation liar was an inevitable phenomenon in a period when, to survive, it was necessary to boast. Circulation was achieved through the news columns. "The great newspapers," wrote Whitelaw Reid, "are those which look for news, not advertisements. With the news comes circulation, and when circulation demands, the advertisements seek the paper, not the paper the advertisements."[17]

Department stores developed in the eighties from the retail drygoods business, and they found the newspaper was far superior to the circular or signboard as a device for announcing their prices and bargain days. Their advertisements and those of patent-medicine firms, stove factories, and land agents were so extensively printed that the newspapers added pages indefinitely. They tried to undercut each other's rates, and the younger Bennett complained to Whitelaw Reid: "The growth of this advertising troubles me. Whole columns of it I print now at a loss and would gladly throw part of it out, if it were not that some of you fellows would pick it up."[18]

At that time production costs were high. But newsprint paper fell in price when pulp replaced rags as the base.[19] Then Richard Hoe perfected his quadruple press, which, by 1890, was printing, cutting, folding, pasting, and counting seventy-two thousand eight-page papers an hour. Expenses were lowered and newspaper establishments were stable businesses, soon to become Big Business.

When a newspaper is sold on the street corner, there is always the danger that a more interesting paper may usurp its market. Since the readers are not subscribers, they can change their paper every day. In order to live, then, the paper found itself drawn into a race for scoops or beats. Whitelaw Reid wrote his correspondent during the Franco-Prussian War:

For the next two months, if the War should last so long, remember that we look to you to keep us ahead of any other paper in New York on war news, and place no limitation upon your expenditures. . . . The first battle will doubtless be the occasion for the sharpest competition. If we can make a hit on that, it will be of incalculable advantage to us, both for the actual news and as an advertisement. If we can give a complete account of the first battle in advance of everybody else we shall make the *Tribune* the recognized authority on foreign news. But with the *Herald* lies our greatest danger. If they see a chance to get ahead they will willingly spend $50,000 in doing it.[20]

But Reid never advertised, in the modern sense, the beats his paper scored. The *Tribune* capped the news with heads of one-column width and printed long paragraphs of close type. When Pulitzer, in 1883, entered the New York field by buying the *World*, the modern tricks of news treatment had their beginning.

THE YELLOW PRESS

Emboldened by his success with the *St. Louis Post-Dispatch*, Pulitzer bought the *New York World* from Jay Gould. It was, at that time, a decrepid, conservative little sheet overshadowed by powerful competitors. Pulitzer forced it upon general attention by means of unconventional devices, some of which he had developed in St. Louis.

He had learned, for one thing, that a newspaper crusade engrosses people's interest as though it were a horse race; they will buy the paper from day to day to follow its progress. In the *World*, he crusaded against political malpractices. But what brought the paper even more readers were sensational campaigns, such as a drive to expose an astrologer active in white slavery. They were typically to get justice for some obscure but representative individual. To be the people's champion used to mean to trumpet party philippics; now it signified sponsoring the claims of inarticulate victims. People took an interest in this sort of thing and it advertised the paper. It was the first manifestation of that tendency to make the newspaper a personal document, close to the lives of the readers, which shows itself at present in the blatant inquisitiveness of the tabloids.

The staff filled the *World* with breezy news and features. Interviewing had become a common practice of the political press, but such interviews were pontifical in tone and substance, with the stress on some public issue. Pulitzer, recognizing that the ordinary man was curious about the personal characteristics of notable people, wrote to his managing editor:

> Please impress on the men who write our interviews with prominent men the importance of giving a striking vivid pen-sketch of the subject; also a vivid picture of his domestic environment, his wife, his children, his animal pets, etc. . . . Those are the things that will bring him more clearly home to the average reader than would his imposing thoughts, purposes or statements.[21]

Another device to make the paper interesting and easy to read was illustrations. People were attracted to them, even when they could not read.[22] Diagrams increased the lure of crime stories. To simplify complicated issues, pictures were used in the political field; this was the first series of cartoons.

In three years the *World* had two hundred and fifty thousand readers and was the most sensational newspaper in the country. Sightless himself, Pulitzer tried to resist the more spectacular innovations, but he was bent on making the *World* a Democratic power, which meant gaining the attention of the masses for his editorials. In doing so he found his paper turning into something which he never intended and which did violence to his notions of propriety.

Hearst bought the *New York Journal* in 1895. From the very beginning he recognized Pulitzer as his rival among New York publishers, for Pulitzer had the kind of market he coveted—the custom of the common people. He bought Pulitzer's cleverest men for his own paper and waged war against the *World* by using its own weapons. The term, "Yellow Press," was contemptuously coined to describe the freakish journalism developed by each, in competition with the other. To call attention to the wonders and horrors which filled the two dailies, headlines came into use that were larger than ever printed before. Dana had said that news was anything that made people talk—Chamberlain, a Hearst editor, defined news as something sensational:

> I used to go home from the office in the wee, sma' hours on the Hyde Street cable car. At my corner, a starter stood all night on post. Often, he got his morning *Examiner* just as I descended. Sometimes as he looked at the front page by the light of the lantern, he whistled and said, "Gee Whiz!" Then I knew that we had hit it. I've kept my eye on that car starter ever since. The ideal of this paper is to raise that "gee whiz!" emotion every day.[23]

If what actually occurred was not exciting enough to build circulation, news was made to happen. This was called stunt journalism; Bennett had proved its effectiveness in 1872 when he sent Henry Morton Stanley to Africa to find Livingstone. The paper that causes the news is naturally sure of scoring a beat. The *Journal* engaged in a succession of stunts so that every issue might be a surprise when it came on the street. If not by manufacture, then by exaggeration, news could be made that would be big enough to float the headlines.

Always with an eye to the unplumbed East Side, Hearst's men reported fashionable social functions at great length and sometimes with drawings that took up the whole front page. This was news, but to the dazzled *Journal* readers it was more like a tale from the *Arabian Nights*. Shop girls saved the pictures.

In the evening edition Hearst developed the human interest angle to heroic proportions by dramatizing the big stories, as the chief items were now called. His reporters effected this with unabashed curiosity, vigorous writing, and a theatrical flair in the text and the headlines. One such story was headed: "Fight for Fair One; Both Lads in Limbo." There were many human interest stories culled from the police-court news or from anything else that came to the city desk. There were some every day; they were described as "News Novelettes from Real Life: Stories Gathered from the Live Wires of the Day and Written in Dramatic Form." They were said to be written by professional writers like Julian Hawthorne and Edward W. Townsend. Winkler, one of Hearst's several biographers, states that the paper specialized in fictionized news because it had to compensate for the lack of an Associated Press franchise,[24] but, whatever might have been the reason at the time, an editorial at the end of the *Journal*'s first year maintained: "The public is even more fond of entertainment than it is of information."[25] The staff prescribed "sport for the men, love and scandal for the women."

With the feature stuff which they printed in their Sunday issues, Pulitzer and Hearst directly invaded the field of the magazines in the hope of capturing their readers. The feature story is inspired by something that is in the news, but it is an account in which the local and particular aspects are minimized and the subject is expanded to include similar instances so as to be of very general interest. Winifred Black, who became celebrated in the profession as Annie Laurie, the first sob sister, wrote features for the Sunday Magazine, as the feature section was called, on such subjects as "Why Young Girls Kill Themselves." An article of this sort interests all readers and has human interest, though it is not, strictly speaking, a human interest story, for nothing has happened. The oddest feature was the comic strip, which the *World* proved was a dependable circulation-holder. It was the first attempt to interest children in newspapers. Understandable to children, and—at least in the early days—amusing, it was also entertaining to adults and kept them buying the paper.

The layman sometimes speaks of the more lurid and spectacular features invented in this period as human interest or thinks of the latter as constituting the yellowness of the modern daily. But the newspaperman understands the human interest story as a special form of news-writing that has no relation to pornography and is quite as likely to be about law-abiding persons—or manlike behavior in animals—as about notorious characters. The fundamental change in journalism brought about by the Yellow Press was the complete concentration on the production of a commodity, of something that would sell. The missionary conception of his profession that had fortified the political editor had given way to the business attitude, as Will Irwin calls it:

> We are here to supply a commodity—news, and, to a certain extent, views upon that news. We are responsible for furnishing sound news. That is, we will not lie, exaggerate or pad, any more than we would, if we were manufacturing linens, cheapen our product with cotton threads. But we will give the public exactly what it wants, without bothering to elevate the commonwealth. If we find that people prefer murders, then murders they shall have.[26]

Every change in the newspaper, since, has been to perfect it as a commodity—that is, to make it responsive to its market. Sixty years before, "upstairs" had wholly dominated the newspaper, but the balance of power had now shifted in the direction of "downstairs."

THE TABLOIDS

Every new kind of newspaper in the last hundred years was able to claim, for a time, that it had the largest circulation in the country. This happened again in the second decade of the present century when the tabloid appeared—and for the same reasons. For every experiment and technical advance in journalism has been to attain greater public favor or to reach a portion of the public previously indifferent or ignored. The tabloid, being a picture paper, has probably probed to the last level of potential readers.

The *Chicago Tribune*'s publishers founded the first successful New York tabloid, the *Illustrated Daily News*, in 1919. Stating first of all that it would not compete with existing papers but would cover a field all its own, its introductory editorial announced that it would suit the reading habits and the tastes of the modern city dweller:

We shall give you every day the best and newest pictures of the interesting things that are happening in the world. Nothing that is not interesting is news. The story that is told by a picture can be grasped instantly. . . .

The paper is, as you see, of convenient size. You can turn the pages in the subway without having it whisked from your hands by the draft. You can hang to a strap and read it without the skill of a juggler to keep its pages together . . .[27]

The *News* now has over a million and a half readers—the greatest circulation in the United States—and is perhaps the most profitable newspaper property. In its format and in the proportion of pictures to text, the *News* was original, but otherwise it was not radically different from other newspapers. But Hearst set up a tabloid, the *New York Mirror*, and finally, in 1924, Bernarr Macfadden, the oracle of physical culture, founded the *New York Evening Graphic*, now defunct, with the fortune he had made in confession magazines. And now, as all three struggled for the tabloid public, the type took form which has made the word "tabloid" a term of contempt.

The tabloids specialized in confessions. Space and language are the commonest impediments to communication, but the newspaper by now had virtually overcome them by a sensitive news-gathering mechanism and a simple vocabulary. Yet there remains always the fact that people do not easily penetrate each other's minds. Artistic formulation, in poetry or fiction, supplies the entree through the author's intuition. But the newspaperman has no poetic license. Ultimately, then, the most revealing and readable communications a newspaper can print are autobiographical: interviews, diaries, letters, and confessions. The commonest hoax that editors resort to in order to win readers is the ghostwritten "Story of My Experience." Hoaxes are instructive just because they embody empirically reached conclusions about the readers' tastes—that is, about interest.

Macfadden required the news in his paper to be not merely big, in form and substance, but "hot"—which means as near to the threshold of tabooed subjects as public morality allows. It specialized in crime and scandal in the city, making no effort to secure national and foreign news. Indeed, the typical reading matter except for confessions was not news at all, but feature stuff—and this is true of the *News* and of the *Mirror*. The features are written by columnists on sport, on the movies and radio, and their stars, on lovemaking, etiquette, cooking, and on the care of dogs and cats.

By making the columnist popular the tabloids seek to induce people to buy the paper day after day; that is, to stabilize circulation. He writes for that part of the public which Thomas, in discussing the readers of the Yellow Press, described as the "most ignorant, childish and numerous."[28] It is the class without professional interests in whom regular reading can be inculcated only by reference to the pursuits of its leisure time. The tabloid reader is possibly the last reader—the saturation point of circulation.

THE PRESENT STATE OF THE PRESS

Newspapers coexist side by side, but they are not all the same thing. The conception one has of itself varies enormously from that held by another, the reason being that the newspaper is not a unitary thing; it is an omnibus, offering editorials, advertising, news, and human interest stories, and each journal's character depends upon which of the four elements dominates. Thus, some publishers insist on the traditional character of the newspaper as a moral or educational agent, but the one and a half million New Yorkers who read the tabloid *Daily News*, and most of the half million who read the *Times*, want to be interested rather than edified; and when they pay two cents for a newspaper they do not expect their purchase to elevate or educate them. The range of types accounts for the confusion among laymen and within the press itself as to what the newspaper is. At the present time, too, the newspaper appears to be going through an era of transition, the effect of which is to cast doubt on most general statements about it. It is a natural accompaniment of the transformation into a commodity that every aspect of it is re-examined to discover whether it might not be an uneconomic use of space—meaning, by uneconomic, inferior in its power to interest the reader. The experimental spirit dominates it. "The job," says Stanley Walker, "is run by organization, but it must be in some respects unconventional, for news itself is unconventional."[29] The accidents of its history united the four separate functions in the newspaper as we know it, and now the question arises whether under new conditions of competition it still pays to serve all four within the same organization.[30]

In the face of recent threats to the newspaper's market, realistic newspapermen have evinced a willingness to do away with the last monument to their ancient authority. Karl A. Bickel, when president of the United Press said:

> I cannot think of a single newspaper in America that is primarily important today because of its editorial page. I doubt if there is an editorial page in America that is read by five per cent of the paper's readers. On the basis of results the average editorial page is the most expensive in the paper—a loss in white space, composition and editorial labor.[31]

That the newspaper is losing public esteem as a political commentator is suggested in the observation that readers write more often to the sports and financial editors than to the editorial director.[32] Captain Patterson of the *New York Daily News*, who is quicker in sensing the public taste than most publishers, may be the editorial writer's valedictorian; speculating on the mortification of the press on the morning after Roosevelt defeated Landon, he declared as a self-evident truth: "The editorial is dead."

The time has now come when the advertiser yields more than three-quarters of the income of the press.[33] Inevitably, then, though it is in a state of change, the press is unlikely to change in any way that would disturb this agreeable relationship. The newspaper once declared its financial independence of political parties; it has shown no disposition as yet to emancipate itself from business. Radicalism may be endured in the ranks but it is hardly to be expected in the owners and directors of the newspaper industry, which is itself a great capitalistic enterprise. As a matter of fact, advertisers are emancipating themselves from the press. The local advertisers, because they are unwilling to pay for space in several dailies, are bringing about a restriction in the number of newspapers. Their influence, pushed to the logical conclusion, would effect local monopolies, by which a single newspaper commands all the existing circulation.[34] Moreover, the advertisers have discovered that the reader's attention is easiest to hold in the evening, and so the afternoon papers outnumber the morning.[35] But in the evening the newspaper must compete for the reader's time with the radio and the motion picture. It meets the menace of these rivals by constant attempts to restrain the radio in announcing news and by exploiting telephoto news photography.

To keep the favor of the advertiser in competition with the radio, the newspaper has collaborated with him in evolving a new kind of advertisement. It looks like a comic strip, and tells a brief love story in which the advertised commodity plays a fateful part. It is the advertisement with human interest—up to the point where the commercial motive betrays itself. Here, as in every other department, the newspaper seeks to consolidate its position by making itself more readable, more entertaining, and brighter.

The real barrier to greater circulations—if greater are possible—is interest. This is still the fundamental problem of journalism.

The newspaper's machinery for the gathering of news, at least in its mechnical aspects, can hardly be improved upon. What Will Irwin calls news efficiency—"getting the latest event to the furthermost reader in the shortest possible time"—is so perfected now that it may be said that there is practically no physical hindrance to the diffusion of any piece of news from any part of the world to the United States. At times there are obstacles in the form of official censorship or voluntary suppression—such as the press agreed to while Lindbergh tried to communicate with his child's kidnapers—but newspaper competition makes it difficult for them to be intact for long; some paper will tell in order to get a beat. "In America," as the retiring German Ambassador said regretfully in 1917, "everything is told." Illiteracy is negligible as a limit to newspaper reading. On the other hand, the news weeklies, particularly *Time*, being more leisurely in their editing, are able to offer critical readers a more intelligible picture of the world than that of the dailies. To the meaner comprehension the newsreels and the news broadcasts address a less sophisticated version of events. In all these agencies, however, as in the newspaper, the truth is more or less at the mercy of pressure groups. This, at least, is the view of several critics of the press who see in the devious and unacknowledged influence of various industrial and moral interests a worse threat to democracy than in the open and constant bias of the old party organs.

In offering the public human interest stories the newspaper competes with the magazines. The latter, in particular the cheaper monthlies, specialize nowadays in fiction that closely follows contemporary events. The daily newspaper, however, still enjoys the obvious advantages of cheapness and diversity.

To decide categorically whether newspapers in general are "news" papers or literature is difficult and perhaps not vital. While the first term describes a number of successful well-established sheets, the second characterizes a thriving class of daily publications whose popularity is affecting the constitution of all the others. There is no doubt that newspapermen tend to judge much of the news on its human interest—a policy whose effect goes far toward converting the press into a form of popular literature. They customarily print this literature on the front page.

The front page, like a clinical thermometer, has registered every change in the newspaper's constitution; its present form recapitulates the newspaper's natural history. An understanding of it reveals the editor's estimate of the news and human interest stories which he prints there.

NOTES

1. Robert E. Park, "The Natural History of the Newspaper," *American Journal of Sociology*, November, 1923, p. 273.

2. Karl Bücher, *Industrial Evolution*, trans. Morley S. Wickett (New York: Henry Holt & Co., 1901), p. 217.

3. *Boston News-Letter* (an issue of April, 1711).

4. *New York Tribune*, May 11, 1841.

5. For an account of the political press of Republican Germany, which essentially resembled the eighteenth- and nineteenth-century American papers, see the author's "The Lindbergh Case: A Study of Human Interest and Politics," *American Journal of Sociology*, XLII, No. 1 (July, 1936), 32–54.

6. James Parton, *The Life of Horace Greeley, Editor of the "New York Tribune"* (New York: Mason Bros., 1855), p. 145.

7. *Ibid.*, p. 141.

8. *The Story of "The Sun"* (New York: George H. Doran Co., 1918), p. 45. (Used by permission of the author and the publishers.)

9. *Ibid.*, p. 323. This is a retrospective account, mentioning later issues of the *Sun*, when figures were better kept. But the character of the earlier issues was the same (used by permission of the author and the publishers).

10. *Sun*, June 30, 1835 (quoted in Willard Grosvenor Bleyer, *Main Currents in the History of American Journalism* [Boston: Houghton Mifflin, 1927], p. 160).

11. *Herald*, May 6, 1835 (quoted in Don Seitz, *The James Gordon Bennetts, Father and Son* [Indianapolis: Bobbs-Merrill Co., 1928], p. 39).

12. *New York Herald* (an issue of April, 1836).

13. While the population increased 32 per cent in a decade (1830–40), the total sale of newspapers increased 187 per cent (O'Brien, *op. cit.*, p. 136).

14. *Ibid.*, pp. 416–17. (Used by permission of the author and the publishers.)

15. Seitz, *op. cit.*, p. 156.

16. *Herald*, August 7, 1835 (quoted in Bleyer, *op. cit.*, p. 188).

17. Whitelaw Reid, "Journalism as a Career," *American and English Studies* (New York: Charles Scribner's Sons, 1913), II, 220–21.

18. *Ibid.*, p. 237.

19. The price began to fall in 1880. By 1897 large consumers bought paper at less than one-eleventh of the price in the last year of the Civil War; see *ibid.*, p. 292.

20. Royal Cortissoz, *The Life of Whitelaw Reid* (New York: Charles Scribner's Sons, 1921), I, 170–71. (Used by permission of the publishers.)

21. Don Seitz, *Joseph Pulitzer: His Life and Letters* (New York: Simon & Schuster, 1924), p. 422. (Used by permission of the publishers.)

22. "When Joseph Pulitzer went to Europe he was a little undecided about the woodcuts. He left orders to gradually get rid of them, as he thought it tended to lower the dignity of the paper, and he was not satisfied that the cuts helped in its circulation. After Pulitzer was on the

Atlantic, Col. Cockerill [managing editor] began to carry out the expressed wishes of its editor and proprietor. He found, however, that the circulation of the paper went with the cuts, and like the good newspaper general that he is, he instantly changed his tactics. He put in more cuts than ever, and the circulation rose like a thermometer on a hot day, until it reached over 230,000 on the day of Grant's funeral" (*Journalist*, August 22, 1885 [quoted in Bleyer, *op. cit.*, p. 329] [used by permission of the publishers]).

23. Will Irwin, *Propaganda and the News or What Makes You Think So?* (New York: Whittlesey House, McGraw-Hill, 1936), p. 91. (Used by permission of the publishers.)

24. John K. Winkler, *William Randolph Hearst: An American Phenomenon* (New York: Simon & Schuster, 1928), p. 111. (Used by permission of the publishers.)

25. *Journal*, November 8, 1896.

26. "The American Newspaper," *Collier's*, April 1, 1911, p. 18. (Used by permission of the author and *Collier's*.)

27. *Daily News*, July 26, 1919.

28. W. I. Thomas, "The Psychology of Yellow Journalism," *American Magazine*, LXVI (March, 1908), 494.

29. *City Editor* (New York: Frederick Stokes, 1934), p. 3. (Used by permission of the publisher.)

30. "A new type of newspaper" is announced for 1940 in New York. The publisher, Ralph Ingersoll, has been associated with *Time, Fortune*, and the *New Yorker*, publications which have revolutionized—each in its own way—the form and matter of the magazines (*Time*, April 10, 1939, p. 61). Whatever the new journal is, it will be the first innovation in newspapers since the tabloid *Daily News* began its successful career in 1919.

31. "Trends in Training for Newspaper Work," *Proceedings of the Tenth Annual Session of the Ohio State Educational Conference, April, 1931*, p. 307; *Ohio State University Bulletin*, Vol. XXXV, No. 3 (September 15, 1931). (Used by permission of the College of Education, Ohio State University.)

32. Will Feather, "The Pull of the Printed Word," *Atlantic Monthly*, CLVII (May, 1936), 565.

33. Malcolm M. Willey and Stuart A. Rice, *Communication Agencies and Social Life* ("Recent Social Trends Monographs" [New York: McGraw-Hill Co., 1933], p. 175).

34. Where once mere quantity was demanded, the advertiser now makes distinctions on the basis of the readers' purchasing power for specific goods. For some goods class, not mass, circulation is required.

35. Willey and Rice, *op. cit.*, p. 160.

9

WHAT'S THE NEWS?

Frank Luther Mott

Many professors, publicists, and press-men have tried their hands at definitions of the word *news*, and sometimes with amusing results. There was, for example, the ingenious fellow who observed that the word was an anagram, made up of initials of the four major points of the compass—north, east, west, and south—and that it must therefore be defined as happenings in all directions. This naive theory of the origin of the word has actually had a considerable acceptance, and was set forth in an early edition of Haydn's dictionary.

Of course, the word originally meant simply new things, novelties; but recent reports of events were new things, and in the sixteenth century *newes* came into common use for *tidings*. Thus we have it in Lord Berners' translation of *Froissart's Chronicles* in 1523: when the Duke of Lancaster heard some bad reports from France, "he was right pensyue and sore troubled with those news." At that time *newes* meant recent reports of events or situations, and that is still the primary or generic meaning of the word today.

In the interest of sound thinking about the news, it is well to keep in mind this basic meaning. News is always a report. The event itself is not news. When we say the election of a President is "big news," we are speaking figuratively; we are employing what the rhetoricians call synecdoche, that is, reference to the material instead of the thing from which it is made. The American news agencies commonly make up lists each December of what they call the "biggest stories of the year," when what they mean is the most news-worthy events of the year. Such figures of speech are defensible and serviceable, but they should not cause us to forget that news itself is not an event or condition or idea, but the report of such a matter.

The one quality of the report which is necessary in order to make it "news" is timeliness. In other words, news must be new. As we shall see, this truism embodied in the generic definition persists as an essential in the working definitions of news as it is understood by editors and reporters on modern newspapers. For editors eventually took over the news and defined it for themselves and their readers.

We did not need anything more than the simple, generic definition so long as news was anybody's business, and everybody's; but when professional newsmen appeared in the seventeenth century, people began to think of "newes" in terms of what Nicholas Bourne, Nathaniel Butter, and William Archer printed in London, or George Veseler and

Broer Jonson in Amsterdam. The first English newspaper was called *Corante, or Weekely Newes*. For more than a hundred years, it was common usage to refer to a news-sheet as "the newes," so that a man might refer to his "copy of the news," meaning his copy of the current newspaper. Thus the popular concept of what news was came more and more to be formed upon what news was printed.

With this development, the editor assumed a special suzerainty over the news. He decided what was news and what was not. This was not as arbitrary or as absolute an authority as it seemed. The editor was, professionally, in charge of the news, but his control over it was limited sharply by several factors.

Space in the newspaper is always restricted. The first American newspaper, *Publick Occurrences*, contained 5300 words, all told; it could all be printed in half a page of a modern newspaper. But the modern metropolitan newspaper of sixty-four large pages is no more able to publish any considerable proportion of the news reports from all the states in the Union and all the countries of the world than was Ben Harris' tiny sheet. The slogan of the *New York Times*, "All the News That's Fit to Print," is more a sentiment than a fact. The slogan originated in the years when Ochs set his newspaper off sharply from the "yellow journalism" of morbid sensationalism which flowered so nauseously during the competition between the *World* and *Journal* at the turn of the century. The *Times* had two slogans: "It Does Not Soil the Breakfast Cloth" and "All the News That's Fit to Print." The emphasis was on the matter of fitness, not comprehensiveness. The modern news field is so vast that an editor's first task is one of selection. He becomes a specialist in news values. But he is less a dictator than a compromiser of interests.

Second only to space limitations are those imposed by the availability of news reports. News was meager in the early years of the American press, not because important events did not occur, but because the papers had no adequate reports. Mathew Carey in 1785 wrote in his *Pennsylvania Evening Herald* that

> the European news is all, all equally flat, equally insipid. Hard indeed is the lot of the poor Printer! obliged to furnish out his bill of fare, at all events; he must run through piles of papers, glean an article or two amidst heaps of trash, and yet be liable to the charge of stupidity and dulness.

This was in the years when papers received as "exchanges" were an editor's chief reliance. Modern communication has developed only in the last hundred years. But even now, with extraordinarily efficient news-gathering agencies at work, the iron curtains, wars, censorships, and the recalcitrance of sources of information set up many barriers to the free circulation of news.

Moreover, much of the news that is procurable is not usable because it is not of high interest to a given paper's audience. Thus the internal affairs of Chile or a meeting of the Arkansas legislature would reach the columns of the *Baltimore Sun* only in rare instances. They may be important to many thousands of people, but the telegraph editor of the *Sun* has to decide whether they are interesting to his readers.

This imposes the third limitation on news—that of reader interest or disinterest. An editor is, in a considerable degree, the servant of his readers. He is not their slave, and (as we shall try to make clear later) he has responsibilities as a guide and public teacher; but he has to select news, in the main, which he believes his readers want. Unless he can satisfy their desires fairly well, his paper will soon be out of business and he will be out of a job. A good editor is supposed to have a "sixth sense" for news—that is, for knowing what will interest his readers. Some of them have such a sense because they are, by backgrounds and training, a part of the group for which they work, and themselves participate in the ideas, feelings, and interests of their audience. Others of them, through intense study and long experience, have learned to know and understand their readers. Still others have what they think of as an instinct for news; they guess, and if they are lucky they guess right.

These editors with a sixth sense for news have been loath, in some cases, to accept modern methods of measuring readers' interests. Helped on by the advertisers, however, such methods have achieved wide acceptance. George Gallup, working out his doctorate at the State University of Iowa, devised a system whereby interviewers, armed with copies of a given issue of a newspaper, obtained statements from readers of that issue as to exactly what they had read and what they had skipped over; then it was only a clerical task to correlate the information obtained and figure out just what items and what types of news were actually being read. Given a proper sample of readers as respondents, and careful techniques in interviewing, this is a valuable means of supplanting editorial guesswork with facts, though, of course, it does not tell what people might have read if they had been offered something else. Used on many papers (142 in the *Continuing Studies* by 1952) over several years, it has provided useful guidance.

And there are still further limitations on the work of the editors of the news. There are certain controls, pressures, and prejudices, sometimes obvious, sometimes subtle and devious. These will be discussed more fully later, but they must be mentioned here in order to complete our description of the practical background which the newspaperman has when he attempts to define "news." Many of these controls and pressures are not at all sinister. All are a part of the intricately complex pattern in which the editor must work.

When the newsman, then, who is professionally in charge of the gathering, the processing, and the distribution of the news, defines this thing with which he deals, he is thinking of *what he prints*. He is not thinking of all recent reports throughout the habitable globe, or of the *fama* of Virgil's famous passage, or of anything unsuited to his columns; the reports which he recognizes as news are severely limited by the actual conditions of the newspaper.

Thus we have such definitions as that of W. C. Jarnagin, onetime editor of the *Des Moines Capital*: "News is anything that happens in which people are interested." "News is whatever your readers want to know about," wrote a former editor of the *Kansas City Star*. "Anything that enough people want to read is news, provided it does not violate the canons of good taste or the laws of libel," wrote J. J. Schindler, of the *St. Paul Dispatch*, in *Collier's* famous symposium, of March 18, 1911. These are the authentic voices of busy news editors. Or hear Arthur MacEwen, whom W. R. Hearst made editor of the *San Francisco Examiner* when he first took it over: "News is anything that makes a reader say, 'Gee whiz!'" And finally, note the perfect editorial-type definition: "News is whatever a good editor chooses to print."

One expects a definition to be neat and carefully circumscribed. But in view of the extreme diversity of those human beings who edit newspapers, this kind of definition is anything but tidy. Gerald W. Johnson, at the end of his excellent essay, *What Is News*, published by Knopf in 1926, wrote:

the news in which an intelligent [newspaper] man will find most satisfaction is the sort of news which, while it may contribute little to his financial well-being, will test his professional capacity in its presentation; and the severest test of that capacity comes in stripping away the ambiguities and obscurities that have enshrouded some important truth and making it understood by a world in which ignorance, carelessness, and stupidity are far more common than keen delight in the battle of ideas.

That, though, is a definition of the best news. In general practice, news is what is in the newspapers; and newspapers are what newspapermen make them. It is a depressing reflection, rather a terrible reflection. But it is true.

Mr. Johnson was confessedly writing as a newspaperman. Tidy or not, his is the pragmatic definition of news, though we have to keep in mind always that the newspaperman himself is not a dictator, but works under the limitations which have just been reviewed.

What goes on in the editor's head as he tries to evaluate the reports that come in to him, as he makes his choices and processes his material? What criteria does he use in this evaluation? There is general agreement that the "importance" of news (that is, its importance for use in the newspaper) is commonly measured by at least four tests: timeliness, prominence, proximity, and probable consequence.

Timeliness is always one of the editor's chief measuring-sticks. The most recent development or detail of a running story must always take priority. Yesterday's news is no longer "important." This repeats an essential of the simple generic definition of news.

The prominence of the persons involved in a report affords another test. Anything the President of the United States does makes "important" news. The reputation of a movie star may be factitious, but Hollywood personalities and names become so well known that their activities often make "must" stories for the newspapers. Most of us are hero-worshipers at heart, and we want to know how the great ones live. It is true that the newspaper plays a large part in developing a prominence which it must then exploit, as that of a Lindbergh, a Di Maggio, a Capone; but there must have been a dynamic activity which made the personality newsworthy in the first place. Nor can we shrug off the validity of the popular feeling that prominence equals importance; the potency of prominence for good or ill is not to be denied.

Proximity is a third criterion. The news of a paper's home city is of first importance to that paper's audience, and even the largest American newspapers are to a considerable extent local. In spite of modern developments in fast transportation and communication, we have no national newspapers in the United States as they have in some other countries, notably in England. Such a paper is by no means impossible for the future, in view of inventions and technologies presently on the horizon; but thus far the vast scope of our country has prevented such a development. Anyway, readers are primarily interested in their neighbors and their own affairs. Isolationism may be on the wane, but it will be a long time before a massacre in Allahabad will interest the readers of the *Memphis Commercial Appeal* as much as would a bond issue for a new water system in Memphis.

The fourth test which the editor uses to determine what news is important for his paper is probable consequence—the expected or possible effect on his readers of a given event or condition. A congressional debate on a new tax law, the spread of a polio epidemic, a market crash: such events make front-page news, of course. A war overseas in which our nation is engaged, or likely to be engaged, changes the meaning of "proximity": its probable consequences bring it close to all readers.

Editors are, in general, with due allowances for slight divergences in emphasis, pretty surely guided by these four criteria—timeliness, prominence, proximity, and probable consequence. If a story ranks high in these four qualities, it is regarded as important to the reader, and therefore "big news" and a "must" for the newspaper. That the qualities are not actually equal in real importance seems fairly obvious, but that is a question we must postpone for the moment.

Here we must go on to point out that the editor has a second set of tests by which he evaluates the multitudinous happenings of the day. These are tests by types of subject matter which are known to be interesting, and they are founded on well-known feelings and curiosities of the reader. A sex story, for example, will ordinarily draw quick interest. An incident dealing with a large sum of money is likely to attract interest, especially if it is dramatized or associated with persons. Other sure-fire matters in the news are bitter or violent conflict, suspense, disaster, horror, unusualness, appeal to sympathy or pity, romance, "human interest" bits of common life, children, animals. These are interest-provoking factors commonly named in such an enumeration, but we might prolong the list until we have named all the objects of popular curiosity. Indeed, these "elements of reader interest," as MacDougall calls them, might well be arranged in a schedule based on the fundamental human emotions.

Journalism founded on a rule-of-thumb such as the foregoing list suggests is subject to many abuses. Before we criticize news reporting based on such concepts of popular interest, however, let us remind ourselves that (a) it is a proper function of the newsman to serve his public, (b) if he does not do so he will be forced by economic means to give place to someone who will, and (c) by and large, and in the long run, the people are likely to be right and sound in their interests, emotions, and desires. The high-brow berates *demos* too glibly. It is too easy, for example, for the sophisticate to condemn the use of the romance motif as "corny," for the altruist to lambaste the money theme in news as sordid, or for the tender-minded to object to the element of horror in many reports. It is too easy for H. A. Overstreet to allow his aversions to lead him into such a generalization as: "The newspaper has found its vested interest in catastrophe" (*The Mature Mind*, page 108). Of course catastrophes, of which war is the greatest, must be recorded in the newspapers. Reports of mine disasters, destructive fires, and railroad and airplane wrecks point toward investigations and reforms. Popular interest in such things is certainly not wholly morbid, and often useful. Shrillness of faultfinding dies down when we study the basis of such news and try to understand its roots in human needs.

Scolding subsides, perhaps; but there is still plenty of room left for sober and serious thinking about what the newsman is doing with the news in the mid-twentieth century. We have seen how, long ago, naturally and perforce, he took over the definition of news and the news pattern. He has defined it on the run, under the strain of quick decisions, on the edge of a deadline, in the midst of action and noise and multiple pressures. He has made it, day by day, what it is, and has then rationalized the process. Mostly by trial and error, he has approximated the wishes and needs of his public.

The great danger in such a process is that there should be too little sound and philo-sophical thinking about the aims and responsibilities of journalism by the men who are making it. The reporter has too often taken over from his teachers in the newsroom the idea that certain elements of interest, such as we have listed above, form an informal code—the unwritten but accepted rules of the "newspaper game," without much thinking or much wise guidance. He finds a game with such rules exciting and absorbing, and has little opportunity or inclination, in the midst of action and the pressures of competition, to give thought to his obligation of professional service to society.

The lowest and yellowest journalism is that which accepts newspaper work as a game in which a set of obvious "elements of interest" are the counters, and sees no significances in news beyond those immediate emotional appeals. A money-sex story is always a "good" story to the ill-trained and short-sighted reporter who works in such a tradition, especially if there is also an element of unusualness and perhaps some suspense. Indeed a story involving all these factors—a sex-romance built around an heiress to a vast fortune, with a violent contest for her dubious favors through the use of unusual weapons by the suitors, with the outcome of it all in suspense, and with appeals to sympathy, a dash of horror, and something about a pet animal—such a story would seem to such a reporter to deserve an eight-column, front-page banner. Fantastic manipulation of "elements of interest," such as this, have not been lacking in certain sections of the American press. Jazz it up; fake it; make it exciting at whatever cost! Anything to make the reader say, "Gee whiz!" Such myopic and overemphatic use of a small group of themes believed to be exciting to the reader is disgraceful, and makes thoughtful readers question the extent to which aiming at popular interests may be justified.

It comes down to a question of importance in news. There is an obvious importance in the "elements of interest" which the editor is quick to see and to seize upon; their proper use is legitimate and necessary. Though crude overplay of them is silly and outrageous, they always have been and doubtless always will be recognized and used by good newsmen.

But there is another kind of importance in news which is not so immediately obvious. This other kind we shall call, here and in later pages, "significant importance."

It will be helpful in this connection to note Wilbur Schramm's doctrine of immediate and delayed rewards in reading the news, which is itself based on the work of E. L. Thorndike and other psychologists. Schramm says that readers and listeners take their news of crime, accidents and disasters, sports, and human interest for immediate "pleasure reward"; while news of public affairs, economic and social problems, science, and education is generally read for a delayed reward of general preparedness and information.

For example, the reader of sports stories, which are based on interest in conflict, receives an immediate reward in the stimulation of his emotions, though he knows that the Dodgers' victory yesterday has no more than an ephemeral interest for him, though he may forget the very name of Ezzard Charles next year, and though the clowning of the wrestlers on the TV screen means less in his life than the good dinner he has just eaten. But he finds such news easy and diverting, and he forms a taste for it. His attitude is somewhat the same toward most crime stories, news of disasters, Hollywood sex scandals, and so on—the news that centers upon the elements of interest which we have been discussing. These stories bring out his personal partisanship, his shared experience, a quick stimulation of his emotions; he likes them, and therefore the editor of his newspaper and the director of his newscasts know that they are "important."

But there are other kinds of news which are based less on exciting conditions and events. They may involve conflict, as nearly everything in the world does, but not yet open and violent conflict. They deal with matters which may ultimately have vital and tremendous consequences to every reader, but which at the present moment do not seem highly interesting because the situation has not "broken," to use the newsman's term. They have not yet reached the stage of what Walter Lippmann, in his book *Public Opinion*, calls "overt news"; they have not yet come clearly out into the open arena of conflict between recognized leaders, of bitter fight, shock of battle, and frenzied propaganda. And yet these stories may even now be recognizably behind the "overt news," looming up as background, and far more significantly important than most of the thousand little happenings and private scandals and baseball scores that fill so many newspaper columns.

It will be recognized by the patient reader of this chapter (whom we hopefully conceive of as possessing an analytical turn of mind) that this delayed-reward news stands a much better chance of getting into the newspaper or on the air through the first set of editorial tests which we discussed—timeliness, prominence, proximity, and probable consequence—than it does through the criteria of the "elements of interest." Indeed, the test of probable consequence is virtually a measurement of significant importance. Of course, the two categories of immediate-reward news and delayed-reward news are not as sharply defined or mutually exclusive as they may at first seem. But, in general, it must be perceived that the editor works under a double standard: he has to decide what news he will print, on the one hand, because his readers demand it for the easy reading which brings immediate responses, and what he will select, on the other hand, because he thinks it may, in the long run, affect the lives and fortunes of his readers. He has to apportion his news space between the important and the significantly important.

Arthur Hays Sulzberger, publisher of the *New York Times*, speaking on "The Responsibilities of Maturity" at the University of Missouri in 1950, said:

> We have two choices. We can report, and define, and explain, in honest perspective, the great issues which are now before the nation and the world; or we can ignore and minimize these issues and divert our readers to less important, but no doubt more entertaining, matters. My vote goes for the paper that informs.

This is a problem of which thinking newsmen are well aware. They have come to use the terms "hard news" and "soft news." "Hard news" refers to the less exciting and more analytical stories of public affairs, economics, social problems, science, etc.; and "soft news" is that which any editor immediately recognizes as interesting to his readers and therefore "important" for his paper. The two terms represent the double standard of news evaluation with which editors must cope.

The chief fault and failure of American journalism today—and this applies to all media of information—is the disproportionate space and emphasis given to the obviously interesting news of immediate reward ("soft news") at the expense of the significantly important news of situations and events which have not yet reached the stage of being exciting for the casual reader ("hard news"). The divided responsibility for this failure is not easy to place with fairness to all; it is basically that of the reader, but publishers, editors, and news-gatherers cannot escape their share of it.

This is a matter for later chapters, and must await a fuller discussion of the nature of news. Let us now proceed to examine certain great concepts of news which have developed in the journalism of the past, and see how and in what degree they have become fixed in the modern pattern.

10

FROM NEWS GATHERING TO NEWS MAKING: A FLOOD OF PSEUDO-EVENTS

Daniel Boorstin

ADMIRING FRIEND:
"My, that's a beautiful baby you have there!"
MOTHER:
"Oh, that's nothing—you should see his photograph!"

The simplest of our extravagant expectations concerns the amount of novelty in the world. There was a time when the reader of an unexciting newspaper would remark, "How dull is the world today!" Nowadays he says, "What a dull newspaper!" When the first American newspaper, Benjamin Harris' *Publick Occurrences Both Forreign and Domestick*, appeared in Boston on September 25, 1690, it promised to furnish news regularly once a month. But, the editor explained, it might appear oftener "if any Glut of Occurrences happen." The responsibility for making news was entirely God's—or the Devil's. The newsman's task was only to give "an Account of such considerable things as have arrived unto our Notice."

Although the theology behind this way of looking at events soon dissolved, this view of the news lasted longer. "The skilled and faithful journalist," James Parton observed in 1866, "recording with exactness and power the thing that has come to pass, is Providence addressing men." The story is told of a Southern Baptist clergyman before the Civil War who used to say, when a newspaper was brought in the room, "Be kind enough to let me have it a few minutes, till I see how the Supreme Being is governing the world." Charles A. Dana, one of the great American editors of the nineteenth century, once defended his extensive reporting of crime in the New York *Sun* by saying, "I have always felt that whatever the Divine Providence permitted to occur I was not too proud to report."

Of course, this is now a very old-fashioned way of thinking. Our current point of view is better expressed in the definition by Arthur MacEwen, whom William Randolph Hearst made his first editor of the San Francisco *Examiner*: "News is anything that makes a reader say, 'Gee whiz!' " Or, put more soberly, "News is whatever a good editor chooses to print."

We need not be theologians to see that we have shifted responsibility for making the world interesting from God to the newspaperman. We used to believe there were only

Daniel Boorstin, "From News Gathering to News Making: A Flood of Pseudo-Events," Chapter 1 of *"The Image, a Guide to Pseudo-Events in America"* (New York: Atheneum, 1978), 7–44. Reprinted with the permission of Scribner, an imprint of Simon & Schuster Adult Publishing Group. Copyright © 1961 by Daniel Boorstin; copyright renewed © 1989.

so many "events" in the world. If there were not many intriguing or startling occurrences, it was no fault of the reporter. He could not be expected to report what did not exist.

Within the last hundred years, however, and especially in the twentieth century, all this has changed. We expect the papers to be full of news. If there is no news visible to the naked eye, or to the average citizen, we still expect it to be there for the enterprising newsman. The successful reporter is one who can find a story, even if there is no earthquake or assassination or civil war. If he cannot find a story, then he must make one—by the questions he asks of public figures, by the surprising human interest he unfolds from some commonplace event, or by "the news behind the news." If all this fails, then he must give us a "think piece"—an embroidering of well-known facts, or a speculation about startling things to come.

This change in our attitude toward "news" is not merely a basic fact about the history of American newspapers. It is a symptom of a revolutionary change in our attitude toward what happens in the world, how much of it is new, and surprising, and important. Toward how life can be enlivened, toward our power and the power of those who inform and educate and guide us, to provide synthetic happenings to make up for the lack of spontaneous events. Demanding more than the world can give us, we require that something be fabricated to make up for the world's deficiency. This is only one example of our demand for illusions.

Many historical forces help explain how we have come to our present immoderate hopes. But there can be no doubt about what we now expect, nor that it is immoderate. Every American knows the anticipation with which he picks up his morning newspaper at breakfast or opens his evening paper before dinner, or listens to the newscasts every hour on the hour as he drives across country, or watches his favorite commentator on television interpret the events of the day. Many enterprising Americans are now at work to help us satisfy these expectations. Many might be put out of work if we should suddenly moderate our expectations. But it is we who keep them in business and demand that they fill our consciousness with novelties, that they play God for us.

I

The new kind of synthetic novelty which has flooded our experience I will call "pseudo-events." The common prefix "pseudo" comes from the Greek word meaning false, or intended to deceive. Before I recall the historical forces which have made these pseudo-events possible, have increased the supply of them and the demand for them, I will give a commonplace example.

The owners of a hotel, in an illustration offered by Edward L. Bernays in his pioneer *Crystallizing Public Opinion* (1923), consult a public relations counsel. They ask how to increase their hotel's prestige and so improve their business. In less sophisticated times, the answer might have been to hire a new chef, to improve the plumbing, to paint the rooms, or to install a crystal chandelier in the lobby. The public relations counsel's technique is more indirect. He proposes that the management stage a celebration of the hotel's thirtieth anniversary. A committee is formed, including a prominent banker, a leading society matron, a well-known lawyer, an influential preacher, and an "event" is planned (say a banquet) to call attention to the distinguished service the hotel has been rendering the community. The celebration is held, photographs are taken, the occasion is widely reported, and the object is accomplished. Now this occasion is a pseudo-event, and will illustrate all the essential features of pseudo-events.

This celebration, we can see at the outset, is somewhat—but not entirely—misleading. Presumably the public relations counsel would not have been able to form his committee of prominent citizens if the hotel had not actually been rendering service to the community. On the other hand, if the hotel's services had been all that important, instigation by public relations counsel might not have been necessary. Once the celebration has been held, the celebration itself becomes evidence that the hotel really is a distinguished institution. The occasion actually gives the hotel the prestige to which it is pretending.

It is obvious, too, that the value of such a celebration to the owners depends on its being photographed and reported in newspapers, magazines, newsreels, on radio, and over television. It is the report that gives the event its force in the minds of potential customers. The power to make a reportable event is thus the power to make experience. One is reminded of Napoleon's apocryphal reply to his general, who objected that circumstances were unfavorable to a proposed campaign: "Bah, I make circumstances!" The modern public relations counsel—and he is, of course, only one of many twentieth-century creators of pseudo-events—has come close to fulfilling Napoleon's idle boast. "The counsel on public relations," Mr. Bernays explains, "not only knows what news value is, but knowing it, he is in a position to *make news happen*. He is a creator of events."

The intriguing feature of the modern situation, however, comes precisely from the fact that the modern news makers are not God. The news they make happen, the events they create, are somehow not quite real. There remains a tantalizing difference between man-made and God-made events.

A pseudo-event, then, is a happening that possesses the following characteristics:

(1) It is not spontaneous, but comes about because someone has planned, planted, or incited it. Typically, it is not a train wreck or an earthquake, but an interview.

(2) It is planted primarily (not always exclusively) for the immediate purpose of being reported or reproduced. Therefore, its occurrence is arranged for the convenience of the reporting or reproducing media. Its success is measured by how widely it is reported. Time relations in it are commonly fictitious or factitious; the announcement is given out in advance "for future release" and written as if the event had occurred in the past. The question, "Is it real?" is less important than, "Is it newsworthy?"

(3) Its relation to the underlying reality of the situation is ambiguous. Its interest arises largely from this very ambiguity. Concerning a pseudo-event the question, "What does it mean?" has a new dimension. While the news interest in a train wreck is in *what* happened and in the real consequences, the interest in an interview is always, in a sense, in *whether* it really happened and in what might have been the motives. Did the statement really mean what it said? Without some of this ambiguity a pseudo-event cannot be very interesting.

(4) Usually it is intended to be a self-fulfilling prophecy. The hotel's thirtieth-anniversary celebration, by saying that the hotel is a distinguished institution, actually makes it one.

II

In the last half century a larger and larger proportion of our experience, of what we read and see and hear, has come to consist of pseudo-events. We expect more of them and we are given more of them. They flood our consciousness. Their multiplication has gone on in the United States at a faster rate than elsewhere. Even the rate of increase is increasing every day. This is true of the world of education, of consumption, and of personal relations. It is especially true of the world of public affairs which I describe in this chapter.

A full explanation of the origin and rise of pseudo-events would be nothing less than a history of modern America. For our present purposes it is enough to recall a few of the more revolutionary recent developments.

The great modern increase in the supply and the demand for news began in the early nineteenth century. Until then newspapers tended to fill out their columns with lackadaisical secondhand accounts or stale reprints of items first published elsewhere at home and abroad. The laws of plagiarism and of copyright were undeveloped. Most newspapers were little more than excuses for espousing a political position, for listing the arrival and departure of ships, for familiar essays and useful advice, or for commercial or legal announcements.

Less than a century and a half ago did newspapers begin to disseminate up-to-date reports of matters of public interest written by eyewitnesses or professional reporters near the scene. The telegraph was perfected and applied to news reporting in the 1830's and '40's. Two newspapermen, William M. Swain of the Philadelphia *Public Ledger* and Amos Kendall of Frankfort, Kentucky, were founders of the national telegraphic network. Polk's presidential message in 1846 was the first to be transmitted by wire. When the Associated Press was founded in 1848, news began to be a salable commodity. Then appeared the rotary press, which could print on a continuous sheet and on both sides of the paper at the same time. The New York *Tribune*'s high-speed press, installed in the 1870's, could turn out 18,000 papers per hour. The Civil War, and later the Spanish-American War, offered raw materials and incentive for vivid up-to-the-minute, on-the-spot reporting. The competitive daring of giants like James Gordon Bennett, Joseph Pulitzer, and William Randolph Hearst intensified the race for news and widened newspaper circulation.

These events were part of a great, but little-noticed, revolution—what I would call the Graphic Revolution. Man's ability to make, preserve, transmit, and disseminate precise images—images of print, of men and landscapes and events, of the voices of men and mobs—now grew at a fantastic pace. The increased speed of printing was itself revolutionary. Still more revolutionary were the new techniques for making direct images of nature. Photography was destined soon to give printed matter itself a secondary role. By a giant leap Americans crossed the gulf from the daguerreotype to color television in less than a century. Dry-plate photography came in 1873; Bell patented the telephone in 1876; the phonograph was invented in 1877; the roll film appeared in 1884; Eastman's Kodak No. 1 was produced in 1888; Edison's patent on the radio came in 1891; motion pictures came in and voice was first transmitted by radio around 1900; the first national political convention widely broadcast by radio was that of 1928; television became commercially important in 1941, and color television even more recently.

Verisimilitude took on a new meaning. Not only was it now possible to give the actual voice and gestures of Franklin Delano Roosevelt unprecedented reality and intimacy for a whole nation. Vivid image came to overshadow pale reality. Sound motion pictures in color led a whole generation of pioneering American movie-goers to think of Benjamin Disraeli as an earlier imitation of George Arliss, just as television has led a later generation of television watchers to see the Western cowboy as an inferior replica of John Wayne. The Grand Canyon itself became a disappointing reproduction of the Kodachrome original.

The new power to report and portray what had happened was a new temptation leading newsmen to make probable images or to prepare reports in advance of what was expected to happen. As so often, men came to mistake their power for their necessities. Readers and viewers would soon prefer the vividness of the account, the "candidness" of the photograph, to the spontaneity of what was recounted.

Then came round-the-clock media. The news gap soon became so narrow that in order to have additional "news" for each new edition or each new broadcast it was necessary to plan in advance the stages by which any available news would be unveiled. After the weekly and the daily came the "extras" and the numerous regular editions. The Philadelphia *Evening Bulletin* soon had seven editions a day. No rest for the newsman. With more space to fill, he had to fill it ever more quickly. In order to justify the numerous editions, it was increasingly necessary that the news constantly change or at least seem to change. With radio on the air continuously during waking hours, the reporters' problems became still more acute. News every hour on the hour, and sometimes on the half hour. Programs interrupted any time for special bulletins. How to avoid deadly repetition, the appearance that nothing was happening, that news gatherers were asleep, or that competitors were more alert? As the costs of printing and then of broadcasting increased, it became financially necessary to keep the presses always at work and the TV screen always busy. Pressures toward the making of pseudo-events became ever stronger. News gathering turned into news making.

The "interview" was a novel way of making news which had come in with the Graphic Revolution. Later it became elaborated into lengthy radio and television panels and quizzes of public figures, and the three-hour-long, rambling conversation programs. Although the interview technique might seem an obvious one—and in a primitive form was as old as Socrates—the use of the word in its modern journalistic sense is a relatively recent Americanism. The Boston *News-Letter*'s account (March 2, 1719) of the death of Blackbeard the Pirate had apparently been based on a kind of interview with a ship captain. One of the earliest interviews of the modern type—some writers call it the first—was by James Gordon Bennett, the flamboyant editor of the New York *Herald* (April 16, 1836), in connection with the Robinson-Jewett murder case. Ellen Jewett, inmate of a house of prostitution, had been found murdered by an ax. Richard P. Robinson, a young man about town, was accused of the crime. Bennett seized the occasion to pyramid sensational stories and so to build circulation for his *Herald*; before long he was having difficulty turning out enough copies daily to satisfy the demand. He exploited the story in every possible way, one of which was to plan and report an actual interview with Rosina Townsend, the madam who kept the house and whom he visited on her own premises.

Historians of journalism date the first full-fledged modern interview with a well-known public figure from July 13, 1859, when Horace Greeley interviewed Brigham

Young in Salt Lake City, asking him questions on many matters of public interest, and then publishing the answers verbatim in his New York *Tribune* (August 20, 1859). The common use of the word "interview" in this modern American sense first came in about this time. Very early the institution acquired a reputation for being contrived. "The 'interview,'" *The Nation* complained (January 28, 1869), "as at present managed, is generally the joint product of some humbug of a hack politician and another humbug of a reporter." A few years later another magazine editor called the interview "the most perfect contrivance yet devised to make journalism an offence, a thing of ill savor in all decent nostrils." Many objected to the practice as an invasion of privacy. After the American example it was used in England and France, but in both those countries it made much slower headway.

Even before the invention of the interview, the news-making profession in America had attained a new dignity as well as a menacing power. It was in 1828 that Macaulay called the gallery where reporters sat in Parliament a "fourth estate of the realm." But Macaulay could not have imagined the prestige of journalists in the twentieth-century United States. They have long since made themselves the tribunes of the people. Their supposed detachment and lack of partisanship, their closeness to the sources of information, their articulateness, and their constant and direct access to the whole citizenry have made them also the counselors of the people. Foreign observers are now astonished by the almost constitutional—perhaps we should say supra-constitutional—powers of our Washington press corps.

Since the rise of the modern Presidential press conference, about 1933, capital correspondents have had the power regularly to question the President face-to-face, to embarrass him, to needle him, to force him into positions or into public refusal to take a position. A President may find it inconvenient to meet a group of dissident Senators or Congressmen; he seldom dares refuse the press. That refusal itself becomes news. It is only very recently, and as a result of increasing pressures by newsmen, that the phrase "No comment" has become a way of saying something important. The reputation of newsmen—who now of course include those working for radio, TV, and magazines—depends on their ability to ask hard questions, to put politicians on the spot; their very livelihood depends on the willing collaboration of public figures. Even before 1950 Washington had about 1,500 correspondents and about 3,000 government information officials prepared to serve them.

Not only the regular formal press conferences, but a score of other national programs —such as "Meet the Press" and "Face the Nation"—show the power of newsmen. In 1960 David Susskind's late-night conversation show, "Open End," commanded the presence of the Russian Premier for three hours. During the so-called "Great Debates" that year between the candidates in the Presidential campaign, it was newsmen who called the tune.

The live television broadcasting of the President's regular news conferences, which President Kennedy began in 1961, immediately after taking office, has somewhat changed their character. Newsmen are no longer so important as intermediaries who relay the President's statements. But the new occasion acquires a new interest as a dramatic performance. Citizens who from homes or offices have seen the President at his news conference are then even more interested to hear competing interpretations by skilled commentators. News commentators can add a new appeal as dramatic critics to their traditional role as interpreters of current history. Even in the new format it is still the newsmen who put the questions. They are still tribunes of the people.

III

The British Constitution, shaped as it is from materials accumulated since the middle ages, functions, we have often been told, only because the British people are willing to live with a great number of legal fictions. The monarchy is only the most prominent. We Americans have accommodated our eighteenth-century constitution to twentieth-century technology by multiplying pseudo-events and by developing professions which both help make pseudo-events and help us interpret them. The disproportion between what an informed citizen needs to know and what he can know is ever greater. The disproportion grows with the increase of the officials' powers of concealment and contrivance. The news gatherers' need to select, invent, and plan correspondingly increases. Thus inevitably our whole system of public information produces always more "packaged" news, more pseudo-events.

A trivial but prophetic example of the American penchant for pseudo-events has long been found in our *Congressional Record*. The British and French counterparts, surprisingly enough, give a faithful report of what is said on the floor of their deliberative bodies. But ever since the establishment of the *Congressional Record* under its present title in 1873, our only ostensibly complete report of what goes on in Congress has had no more than the faintest resemblance to what is actually said there. Despite occasional feeble protests, our *Record* has remained a gargantuan miscellany in which actual proceedings are buried beneath undelivered speeches, and mountains of the unread and the unreadable. Only a national humorlessness—or sense of humor—can account for our willingness to tolerate this. Perhaps it also explains why, as a frustrated reformer of the *Record* argued on the floor of the Senate in 1884, "the American public have generally come to regard the proceedings of Congress as a sort of variety performance, where nothing is supposed to be real except the pay."

The common "news releases" which every day issue by the ream from Congressmen's offices, from the President's press secretary, from the press relations offices of businesses, charitable organizations, and universities are a kind of *Congressional Record* covering all American life. And they are only a slightly less inaccurate record of spontaneous happenings. To secure "news coverage" for an event (especially if it has little news interest) one must issue, in proper form, a "release." The very expression "news release" (apparently an American invention; it was first recorded in 1907) did not come into common use until recently. There is an appropriate perversity in calling it a "release." It might more accurately be described as a "news holdback," since its purpose is to offer something that is to be held back from publication until a specified future date. The newspaperman's slightly derogatory slang term for the news release is "handout," from the phrase originally used for a bundle of stale food handed out from a house to a beggar. Though this meaning of the word is now in common use in the newsgathering professions, it is so recent that it has not yet made its way into our dictionaries.

The release is news pre-cooked, and supposed to keep till needed. In the well-recognized format (usually mimeographed) it bears a date, say February 1, and also indicates, "For release to PM's February 15." The account is written in the past tense but usually describes an event that has not yet happened when the release is given out. The use and interpretation of handouts have become an essential part of the newsman's job. The National Press Club in its Washington clubrooms has a large rack which is filled daily with the latest releases, so the reporter does not even have to visit the offices which give them out. In 1947 there were about twice as many government press agents engaged in preparing news releases as there were newsmen gathering them in.

The general public has become so accustomed to these procedures that a public official can sometimes "make news" merely by departing from the advance text given out in his release. When President Kennedy spoke in Chicago on the night of April 28, 1961, early editions of the next morning's newspapers (printed the night before for early-morning home delivery) merely reported his speech as it was given to newsmen in the advance text. When the President abandoned the advance text, later editions of the Chicago *Sun-Times* headlined: "Kennedy Speaks Off Cuff . . ." The article beneath emphasized that he had departed from his advance text and gave about equal space to his off-the-cuff speech and to the speech he never gave. Apparently the most newsworthy fact was that the President had not stuck to his prepared text.

We begin to be puzzled about what is really the "original" of an event. The authentic news record of what "happens" or is said comes increasingly to seem to be what is given out in advance. More and more news events become dramatic performances in which "men in the news" simply act out more or less well their prepared script. The story prepared "for future release" acquires an authenticity that competes with that of the actual occurrences on the scheduled date.

In recent years our successful politicians have been those most adept at using the press and other means to create pseudo-events. President Franklin Delano Roosevelt, whom Heywood Broun called "the best newspaperman who has ever been President of the United States," was the first modern master. While newspaper owners opposed him in editorials which few read, F.D.R. himself, with the collaboration of a friendly corps of Washington correspondents, was using front-page headlines to make news read by everybody. He was making "facts"—pseudo-events—while editorial writers were simply expressing opinions. It is a familiar story how he employed the trial balloon, how he exploited the ethic of off-the-record remarks, how he transformed the Presidential press conference from a boring ritual into a major national institution which no later President dared disrespect, and how he developed the fireside chat. Knowing that newspapermen lived on news, he helped them manufacture it. And he knew enough about news-making techniques to help shape their stories to his own purposes.

Take, for example, these comments which President Roosevelt made at a press conference during his visit to a Civilian Conservation Corps camp in Florida on February 18, 1939, when war tensions were mounting:

> I want to get something across, only don't put it that way. In other words, it is a thing that I cannot put as direct stuff, but it is background. And the way—as you know I very often do it—if I were writing the story, the way I'd write it is this—you know the formula: When asked when he was returning [to Washington], the President intimated that it was impossible to give any date; because, while he hoped to be away until the third or fourth of March, information that continues to be received with respect to the international

situation continues to be disturbing, therefore, it may be necessary for the President to return [to the capital] before the third or fourth of March. It is understood that this information relates to the possible renewal of demands by certain countries, these demands being pushed, not through normal diplomatic channels but, rather, through the more recent type of relations; in other words, the use of fear of aggression.

F.D.R. was a man of great warmth, natural spontaneity, and simple eloquence, and his public utterances reached the citizen with a new intimacy. Yet, paradoxically, it was under his administrations that statements by the President attained a new subtlety and a new calculatedness. On his production team, in addition to newspapermen, there were poets, playwrights, and a regular corps of speech writers. Far from detracting from his effectiveness, this collaborative system for producing the impression of personal frankness and spontaneity provided an additional subject of newsworthy interest. Was it Robert Sherwood or Judge Samuel Rosenman who contributed this or that phrase? How much had the President revised the draft given him by his speech writing team? Citizens became nearly as much interested in how a particular speech was put together as in what it said. And when the President spoke, almost everyone knew it was a long-planned group production in which F.D.R. was only the star performer.

Of course President Roosevelt made many great decisions and lived in times which he only helped make stirring. But it is possible to build a political career almost entirely on pseudo-events. Such was that of the late Joseph R. McCarthy, Senator from Wisconsin from 1947 to 1957. His career might have been impossible without the elaborate, perpetually grinding machinery of "information" which I have already described. And he was a natural genius at creating reportable happenings that had an interestingly ambiguous relation to underlying reality. Richard Rovere, a reporter in Washington during McCarthy's heyday, recalls:

> He knew how to get into the news even on those rare occasions when invention failed him and he had no unfacts to give out. For example, he invented the morning press conference called for the purpose of announcing an afternoon press conference. The reporters would come in—they were beginning, in this period, to respond to his summonses like Pavlov's dogs at the clang of a bell—and McCarthy would say that he just wanted to give them the word that he expected to be ready with a shattering announcement later in the day, for use in the papers the following morning. This would gain him a headline in the afternoon papers: "New McCarthy Revelations Awaited in Capital." Afternoon would come, and if McCarthy had something, he would give it out, but often enough he had nothing, and this was a matter of slight concern. He would simply say that he wasn't quite ready, that he was having difficulty in getting some of the "documents" he needed or that a "witness" was proving elusive. Morning headlines: "Delay Seen in McCarthy Case—Mystery Witness Being Sought."

He had a diabolical fascination and an almost hypnotic power over news-hungry reporters. They were somehow reluctantly grateful to him for turning out their product. They stood astonished that he could make so much news from such meager raw material. Many hated him; all helped him. They were victims of what one of them called their "indiscriminate objectivity." In other words, McCarthy and the newsmen both thrived on the same synthetic commodity.

Senator McCarthy's political fortunes were promoted almost as much by newsmen who considered themselves his enemies as by those few who were his friends. Without the active help of all of them he could never have created the pseudo-events which brought him notoriety and power. Newspaper editors, who self-righteously attacked the Senator's "collaborators," themselves proved worse than powerless to cut him down to size. Even while they attacked him on the editorial page inside, they were building him up in front-page headlines. Newspapermen were his most potent allies, for they were his co-manufacturers of pseudo-events. They were caught in their own web. Honest newsmen and the unscrupulous Senator McCarthy were in separate branches of the same business.

In the traditional vocabulary of newspapermen, there is a well-recognized distinction between "hard" and "soft" news. Hard news is supposed to be the solid report of significant matters: politics, economics, international relations, social welfare, science. Soft news reports popular interests, curiosities, and diversions: it includes sensational local reporting, scandalmongering, gossip columns, comic strips, the sexual lives of movie stars, and the latest murder. Journalist-critics attack American newspapers today for not being "serious" enough, for giving a larger and larger proportion of their space to soft rather than to hard news.

But the rising tide of pseudo-events washes away the distinction. Here is one example. On June 21, 1960, President Eisenhower was in Honolulu, en route to the Far East for a trip to meet the heads of government in Korea, the Philippines, and elsewhere. A seven-column headline in the Chicago *Daily News* brought readers the following information: "What Are Ike's Feelings About Trip? Aides Mum" "Doesn't Show Any Worry" "Members of Official Party Resent Queries by Newsmen." And the two-column story led off:

> Honolulu—President Eisenhower's reaction to his Far Eastern trip remains as closely guarded a secret as his golf score. While the President rests at Kaneohe Marine air station on the windward side of the Pali hills, hard by the blue Pacific and an 18-hole golf course, he might be toting up the pluses and minuses of his Asian sojourn. But there is no evidence of it. Members of his official party resent any inquiry into how the White House feels about the whole experience, especially the blowup of the Japanese visit which produced a critical storm.

The story concludes: "But sooner or later the realities will intrude. The likelihood is that it will be sooner than later."

Nowadays a successful reporter must be the midwife—or more often the conceiver—of his news. By the interview technique he incites a public figure to make statements which will sound like news. During the twentieth century this technique has grown into a devious apparatus which, in skillful hands, can shape national policy.

The pressure of time, and the need to produce a uniform news stream to fill the issuing media, induce Washington correspondents and others to use the interview and other techniques for making pseudo-events in novel, ever more ingenious and aggressive ways. One of the main facts of life for the wire service reporter in Washington is that there are many more afternoon than morning papers in the United States. The early afternoon paper on the East Coast goes to press about 10 A.M., before the spontaneous news of the day has had an opportunity to develop. "It means," one conscientious capital correspondent confides, in Douglass Cater's admirable *Fourth Branch of Government* (1959), "the wire service reporter must engage in the basically phony operation of writing the "overnight"—a story composed the previous evening but giving the impression when it appears the next afternoon that it covers that day's events." . . .*

IV

In many subtle ways, the rise of pseudo-events has mixed up our roles as actors and as audience—or, the philosophers would say, as "object" and as "subject." Now we can oscillate between the two roles. "The movies are the only business," Will Rogers once remarked, "where you can go out front and applaud yourself." Nowadays one need not be a professional actor to have this satisfaction. We can appear in the mob scene and then go home and see ourselves on the television screen. No wonder we become confused about what is spontaneous, about what is really going on out there!

New forms of pseudo-events, especially in the world of politics, thus offer a new kind of bewilderment to both politician and newsman. The politician (like F.D.R. in our example, or any holder of a press conference) himself in a sense composes the story; the journalist (like the wire service reporter we have quoted, or any newsman who incites an inflammatory statement) himself generates the event. The citizen can hardly be expected to assess the reality when the participants themselves are so often unsure who is doing the deed and who is making the report of it. Who is the history, and who is the historian?

An admirable example of this new intertwinement of subject and object, of the history and the historian, of the actor and the reporter, is the so-called news "leak." By now the leak has become an important and well-established institution in American politics. It is, in fact, one of the main vehicles for communicating important information from officials to the public.

A clue to the new unreality of the citizen's world is the perverse new meaning now given to the word "leak." To leak, according to the dictionary, is to "let a fluid substance out or in accidentally: as, the ship leaks." But nowadays a news leak is one of the most elaborately planned ways of emitting information. It is, of course, a way in which a government official, with some clearly defined purpose (a leak, even more than a direct announcement, is apt to have some definite devious purpose behind it) makes an announcement, asks a question, or puts a suggestion. It might more accurately be called a "*sub rosa* announcement," an "indirect statement," or "cloaked news."

The news leak is a pseudo-event par excellence. In its origin and growth, the leak illustrates another axiom of the world of pseudo-events: pseudo-events produce more pseudo-events. I will say more on this later.

With the elaboration of news-gathering facilities in Washington—of regular, planned press conferences, of prepared statements for future release, and of countless

---

*In the balance of this section of the essay, Boorstin provides examples of the manner in which interviews generate news, whether or not there are genuine developments in stories. The argument continues in Section IV—the editors.

other practices—the news protocol has hardened. Both government officials and reporters have felt the need for more flexible and more ambiguous modes of communication between them. The Presidential press conference itself actually began as a kind of leak. President Theodore Roosevelt for some time allowed Lincoln Steffens to interview him as he was being shaved. Other Presidents gave favored correspondents an interview from time to time or dropped hints to friendly journalists. Similarly, the present institution of the news leak began in the irregular practice of a government official's helping a particular correspondent by confidentially giving him information not yet generally released. But today the leak is almost as well organized and as rigidly ruled by protocol as a formal press conference. Being fuller of ambiguity, with a welcome atmosphere of confidence and intrigue, it is more appealing to all concerned. The institutionalized leak puts a greater burden of contrivance and pretense on both government officials and reporters.

In Washington these days, and elsewhere on a smaller scale, the custom has grown up among important members of the government of arranging to dine with select representatives of the news corps. Such dinners are usually preceded by drinks, and beforehand there is a certain amount of restrained conviviality. Everyone knows the rules: the occasion is private, and any information given out afterwards must be communicated according to rule and in the technically proper vocabulary. After dinner the undersecretary, the general, or the admiral allows himself to be questioned. He may recount "facts" behind past news, state plans, or declare policy. The reporters have confidence, if not in the ingenuousness of the official, at least in their colleagues' respect of the protocol. Everybody understands the degree of attribution permissible for every statement made: what, if anything, can be directly quoted, what is "background," what is "deep background," what must be ascribed to "a spokesman," to "an informed source," to speculation, to rumor, or to remote possibility.

Such occasions and the reports flowing from them are loaded with ambiguity. The reporter himself often is not clear whether he is being told a simple fact, a newly settled policy, an administrative hope, or whether perhaps untruths are being deliberately diffused to allay public fears that the true facts are really true. The government official himself (who is sometimes no more than spokesman) may not be clear. The reporter's task is to find a way of weaving these threads of unreality into a fabric that the reader will not recognize as entirely unreal. Some people have criticized the institutionalized leak as a form of domestic counter-intelligence inappropriate in a republic. It has become more and more important and is the source today of many of the most influential reports of current politics.

One example will be enough. On March 26, 1955, *The New York Times* carried a three-column headline on the front page: "U.S. Expects Chinese Reds to Attack Isles in April; Weighs All-Out Defense." Three days later a contradictory headline in the same place read: "Eisenhower Sees No War Now Over Chinese Isles." Under each of these headlines appeared a lengthy story. Neither story named any person as a source of the ostensible facts. The then-undisclosed story (months later recorded by Douglass Cater) was this. In the first instance, Admiral Robert B. Carney, Chief of Naval Operations, had an off-the-record "background" dinner for a few reporters. There the Admiral gave reporters what they (and their readers) took to be facts. Since the story was "not for attribution," reporters were not free to mention some very relevant facts—such as that this was the opinion only of Admiral Carney, that this was the same Admiral Carney who had long been saying that war in Asia was inevitable, and that many in Washington (even in the Joint Chiefs of Staff) did not agree with him. Under the ground rules the first story could appear in the papers only by being given an impersonal authority, an atmosphere of official unanimity which it did not merit. The second, and contradictory, statement was in fact made not by the President himself, but by the President's press secretary, James Hagerty, who, having been alarmed by what he saw in the papers, quickly called a second "background" meeting to deny the stories that had sprouted from the first. What, if anything, did it all mean? Was there any real news here at all—except that there was disagreement between Admiral Carney and James Hagerty? Yet this was the fact newsmen were not free to print.

Pseudo-events spawn other pseudo-events in geometric progression. This is partly because every kind of pseudo-event (being planned) tends to become ritualized, with a protocol and a rigidity all its own. As each type of pseudo-event acquires this rigidity, pressures arise to produce other, derivative, forms of pseudo-event which are more fluid, more tantalizing, and more interestingly ambiguous. Thus, as the press conference (itself a pseudo-event) became formalized, there grew up the institutionalized leak. As the leak becomes formalized still other devices will appear. Of course the shrewd politician or the enterprising newsman knows this and knows how to take advantage of it. Seldom for outright deception; more often simply to make more "news," to provide more "information," or to "improve communication."

For example, a background off-the-record press conference, if it is actually a mere trial balloon or a diplomatic device (as it sometimes was for Secretary of State John Foster Dulles), becomes the basis of official "denials" and "disavowals," of speculation and interpretation by columnists and commentators, and of special interviews on and off television with Senators, Representatives, and other public officials. Any statement or non-statement by anyone in the public eye can become the basis of counter-statements or refusals to comment by others. All these compound the ambiguity of the occasion which first brought them into being.

Nowadays the test of a Washington reporter is seldom his skill at precise dramatic reporting, but more often his adeptness at dark intimation. If he wishes to keep his news channels open he must accumulate a vocabulary and develop a style to conceal his sources and obscure the relation of a supposed event or statement to the underlying facts of life, at the same time seeming to offer hard facts. Much of his stock in trade is his own and other people's speculation about the reality of what he reports. He lives in a penumbra between fact and fantasy. He helps create that very obscurity without which the supposed illumination of his reports would be unnecessary. A deft administrator these days must have similar skills. He must master "the technique of denying the truth without actually lying."

These pseudo-events which flood our consciousness must be distinguished from propaganda. The two do have some characteristics in common. But our peculiar problems come from the fact that pseudo-events are in some respects the opposite of the propaganda which rules totalitarian countries. Propaganda—as prescribed, say, by Hitler in *Mein Kampf*—is information intentionally biased. Its effect depends primarily on its emotional appeal. While a pseudo-event is an ambiguous truth, propaganda is an appealing falsehood. Pseudo-events thrive on our honest desire to be informed, to have "all the facts," and even to have more facts than there really are. But propaganda feeds on our willingness to be inflamed. Pseudo-events appeal to our duty to be educated, propaganda appeals to our desire to be aroused. While propaganda substitutes opinion for facts, pseudo-events are synthetic facts which move people indirectly, by providing the "factual" basis on which they are supposed to make up their minds. Propaganda moves them directly by explicitly making judgments for them.

In a totalitarian society, where people are flooded by purposeful lies, the real facts are of course misrepresented, but the representation itself is not ambiguous. The propaganda lie is asserted as if it were true. Its object is to lead people to believe that the truth is simpler, more intelligible, than it really is. "Now the purpose of propaganda," Hitler explained, "is not continually to produce interesting changes for a few blasé little masters, but to convince; that means, to convince the masses. The masses, however, with their inertia, always need a certain time before they are ready even to notice a thing, and they will lend their memories only to the thousandfold repetition of the most simple ideas." But in our society, pseudo-events make simple facts seem more subtle, more ambiguous, and more speculative than they really are. Propaganda oversimplifies experience, pseudo-events overcomplicate it.

At first it may seem strange that the rise of pseudo-events has coincided with the growth of the professional ethic which obliges newsmen to omit editorializing and personal judgments from their news accounts. But now it is in the making of pseudo-events that newsmen find ample scope for their individuality and creative imagination.

In a democratic society like ours—and more especially in a highly literate, wealthy, competitive, and technologically advanced society—the people can be flooded by pseudo-events. For us, freedom of speech and of the press and of broadcasting includes freedom to create pseudo-events. Competing politicians, competing newsmen, and competing news media contest in this creation. They vie with one another in offering attractive, "informative" accounts and images of the world. They are free to speculate on the facts, to bring new facts into being, to demand answers to their own contrived questions. Our "free market place of ideas" is a place where people are confronted by competing pseudo-events and are allowed to judge among them. When we speak of "informing" the people this is what we really mean.

V

Until recently we have been justified in believing Abraham Lincoln's familiar maxim: "You may fool all the people some of the time; you can even fool some of the people all the time; but you can't fool all of the people all the time." This has been the foundation-belief of American democracy. Lincoln's appealing slogan rests on two elementary assumptions. First, that there is a clear and visible distinction between sham and reality, between the lies a demagogue would have us believe and the truths which are there all the time. Second, that the people tend to prefer reality to sham, that if offered a choice between a simple truth and a contrived image, they will prefer the truth.

Neither of these any longer fits the facts. Not because people are less intelligent or more dishonest. Rather because great unforeseen changes—the great forward strides of American civilization—have blurred the edges of reality. The pseudo-events which flood our consciousness are neither true nor false in the old familiar senses. The very same advances which have made them possible have also made the images—however planned, contrived, or distorted—more vivid, more attractive, more impressive, and more persuasive than reality itself.

We cannot say that we are being fooled. It is not entirely inaccurate to say that we are being "informed." This world of ambiguity is created by those who believe they are instructing us, by our best public servants, and with our own collaboration. Our problem is the harder to solve because it is created by people working honestly and industriously at respectable jobs. It is not created by demagogues or crooks, by conspiracy or evil purpose. The efficient mass production of pseudo-events—in all kinds of packages, in black-and-white, in technicolor, in words, and in a thousand other forms—is the work of the whole machinery of our society. It is the daily product of men of good will. The media must be fed! The people must be informed! Most pleas for "more information" are therefore misguided. So long as we define information as a knowledge of pseudo-events, "more information" will simply multiply the symptoms without curing the disease.

The American citizen thus lives in a world where fantasy is more real than reality, where the image has more dignity than its original. We hardly dare face our bewilderment, because our ambiguous experience is so pleasantly iridescent, and the solace of belief in contrived reality is so thoroughly real. We have become eager accessories to the great hoaxes of the age. These are the hoaxes we play on ourselves.

Pseudo-events from their very nature tend to be more interesting and more attractive than spontaneous events. Therefore in American public life today pseudo-events tend to drive all other kinds of events out of our consciousness, or at least to overshadow them. Earnest, well-informed citizens seldom notice that their experience of spontaneous events is buried by pseudo-events. Yet nowadays, the more industriously they work at "informing" themselves the more this tends to be true.

In his now-classic work, *Public Opinion*, Walter Lippmann in 1922 began by distinguishing between "the world outside and the pictures in our heads." He defined a "stereotype" as an oversimplified pattern that helps us find meaning in the world. As examples he gave the crude "stereotypes we carry about in our heads," of large and varied classes of people like "Germans," "South Europeans," "Negroes," "Harvard men," "agitators," etc. The stereotype, Lippmann explained, satisfies our needs and helps us defend our prejudices by seeming to give definiteness and consistency to our turbulent and disorderly daily experience. In one sense, of course, stereotypes—the excessively simple, but easily grasped images of racial, national, or religious groups—are only another example of pseudo-events. But, generally speaking, they are closer to propaganda. For they simplify rather than complicate. Stereotypes narrow and limit experience in an emotionally satisfying way; but pseudo-events embroider and dramatize experience in an interesting way. This itself makes pseudo-events far more seductive; intellectually they are more defensible, more intricate, and more intriguing. To discover how the stereotype is made—to unmask the sources of propaganda—is to make the stereotype less believable. Information about the staging of a pseudo-event simply adds to its fascination.

Lippmann's description of stereotypes was helpful in its day. But he wrote before pseudo-events had come in full flood. Photographic journalism was then still in its infancy. Wide World Photos had just been organized by *The New York Times* in 1919. The first wirephoto to attract wide attention was in 1924, when the American Telephone and Telegraph Company sent to *The New York Times* pictures of the Republican Convention in Cleveland which nominated Calvin Coolidge. Associated Press Picture Service was established in 1928. *Life*, the first wide-circulating weekly picture news magazine, appeared in 1936; within a year it had a circulation of 1,000,000, and within two years, 2,000,000. *Look* followed, in 1937. The newsreel, originated in France by Pathé, had been introduced to the United States only in 1910. When Lippmann wrote his book in 1922, radio was not yet reporting news to the consumer; television was of course unknown.

Recent improvements in vividness and speed, the enlargement and multiplying of news-reporting media, and the public's increasing news hunger now make Lippmann's brilliant analysis of the stereotype the legacy of a simpler age. For stereotypes made experience handy to grasp. But pseudo-events would make experience newly and satisfyingly elusive. In 1911 Will Irwin, writing in *Collier's*, described the new era's growing public demand for news as "a crying primal want of the mind, like hunger of the body." The mania for news was a symptom of expectations enlarged far beyond the capacity of the natural world to satisfy. It required a synthetic product. It stirred an irrational and undiscriminating hunger for fancier, more varied items. Stereotypes there had been and always would be; but they only dulled the palate for information. They were an opiate. Pseudo-events whetted the appetite; they aroused news hunger in the very act of satisfying it.

In the age of pseudo-events it is less the artificial simplification than the artificial complication of experience that confuses us. Whenever in the public mind a pseudo-event competes for attention with a spontaneous event in the same field, the pseudo-event will tend to dominate. What happens on television will overshadow what happens off television. Of course I am concerned here not with our private worlds, but with our world of public affairs.

Here are some characteristics of pseudo-events which make them overshadow spontaneous events:

(1) Pseudo-events are more dramatic. A television debate between candidates can be planned to be more suspenseful (for example, by reserving questions which are then popped suddenly) than a casual encounter or consecutive formal speeches planned by each separately.

(2) Pseudo-events, being planned for dissemination, are easier to disseminate and to make vivid. Participants are selected for their newsworthy and dramatic interest.

(3) Pseudo-events can be repeated at will, and thus their impression can be re-enforced.

(4) Pseudo-events cost money to create; hence somebody has an interest in disseminating, magnifying, advertising, and extolling them as events worth watching or worth believing. They are therefore advertised in advance, and rerun in order to get money's worth.

(5) Pseudo-events, being planned for intelligibility, are more intelligible and hence more reassuring. Even if we cannot discuss intelligently the qualifications of the candidates or the complicated issues, we can at least judge the effectiveness of a television performance. How comforting to have some political matter we can grasp!

(6) Pseudo-events are more sociable, more conversable, and more convenient to witness. Their occurrence is planned for our convenience. The Sunday newspaper appears when we have a lazy morning for it. Television programs appear when we are ready with our glass of beer. In the office the next morning, Jack Paar's (or any other star performer's) regular late-night show at the usual hour will overshadow in conversation a casual event that suddenly came up and had to find its way into the news.

(7) Knowledge of pseudo-events—of what has been reported, or what has been staged, and how—becomes the test of being "informed." News magazines provide us regularly with quiz questions concerning not what has happened but concerning "names in the news"—what has been reported in the news magazines. Pseudo-events begin to provide that "common discourse" which some of my old-fashioned friends have hoped to find in the Great Books.

(8) Finally, pseudo-events spawn other pseudo-events in geometric progression. They dominate our consciousness simply because there are more of them, and ever more.

By this new Gresham's law of American public life, counterfeit happenings tend to drive spontaneous happenings out of circulation. The rise in the power and prestige of the Presidency is due not only to the broadening powers of the office and the need for quick decisions, but also to the rise of centralized news gathering and broadcasting, and the increase of the Washington press corps. The President has an ever more ready, more frequent, and more centralized access to the world of pseudo-events. A similar explanation helps account for the rising prominence in recent years of the Congressional investigating committees. In many cases these committees have virtually no legislative impulse, and sometimes no intelligible legislative assignment. But they do have an almost unprecedented power, possessed now by no one else in the Federal government except the President, to make news. Newsmen support the committees because the committees feed the newsmen: they live together in happy symbiosis. The battle for power among Washington agencies becomes a contest to dominate the citizen's information of the government. This can most easily be done by fabricating pseudo-events.

A perfect example of how pseudo-events can dominate is the recent popularity of the quiz show format. Its original appeal came less from the fact that such shows were tests of intelligence (or of dissimulation) than from the fact that the situations were elaborately contrived—with isolation booths, armed bank guards, and all the rest—and they purported to inform the public.

The application of the quiz show format to the so-called "Great Debates" between Presidential candidates in the election of 1960 is only another example. These four campaign programs, pompously and self-righteously advertised by the broadcasting networks, were remarkably successful in reducing great national issues to trivial dimensions. With appropriate vulgarity, they might have been called the $400,000 Question (Prize: a $100,000-a-year job for four years). They were a clinical example of the pseudo-event, of how it is made, why it appeals, and of its consequences for democracy in America.

In origin the Great Debates were confusedly collaborative between politicians and news makers. Public interest centered around the pseudo-event itself: the lighting, make-up, ground rules, whether notes would be allowed, etc. Far more interest was shown in the performance than in what was said. The pseudo-events spawned in turn by the Great Debates were numberless. People who had seen the shows read about them the more avidly, and listened eagerly for interpretations by news commentators. Representatives of both parties made "statements" on the probable effects of the debates. Numerous interviews and discussion programs were broadcast exploring their meaning. Opinion polls kept us informed on the nuances of our own and other people's reactions. Topics of speculation multiplied. Even the question whether there should be a fifth debate became for a while a lively "issue."

The drama of the situation was mostly specious, or at least had an extremely ambiguous relevance to the main (but forgotten) issue: which participant was better qualified for the Presidency. Of course, a man's ability, while standing under klieg lights, without notes, to answer in two and a half minutes a question kept secret until that moment, had only the most dubious relevance—if any at all—to his real qualifications to make deliberate Presidential decisions on long-standing public questions after being instructed by a corps of advisers. The great Presidents in our history (with the possible exception of F.D.R.) would have done miserably; but our most notorious demagogues would have shone. A number of exciting pseudo-events were created—for example, the Quemoy-Matsu issue. But that, too, was a good example of a pseudo-event: it was created to be reported, it concerned a then-quiescent problem, and it put into the most factitious and trivial terms the great and real issue of our relation to Communist China.

The television medium shapes this new kind of political quiz-show spectacular in many crucial ways. Theodore H. White has proven this with copious detail in his *The Making of the President: 1960* (1961). All the circumstances of this particular competition for votes were far more novel than the old word "debate" and the comparisons with the Lincoln–Douglas Debates suggested. Kennedy's great strength in the critical first debate, according to White, was that he was in fact not "debating" at all, but was seizing the opportunity to address the whole nation; while Nixon stuck close to the issues raised by his opponent, rebutting them one by one. Nixon, moreover, suffered a handicap that was serious only on television: he has a light, naturally transparent skin. On an ordinary camera that takes pictures by optical projection, this skin photographs well. But a television camera projects electronically, by an "image-orthicon tube" which has an x-ray effect. This camera penetrates Nixon's transparent skin and brings out (even just after a shave) the tiniest hair growing in the follicles beneath the surface. For the decisive first program Nixon wore a make-up called "Lazy Shave" which was ineffective under these conditions. He therefore looked haggard and heavy-bearded by contrast to Kennedy, who looked pert and clean-cut.

This greatest opportunity in American history to educate the voters by debating the large issues of the campaign failed. The main reason, as White points out, was the compulsions of the medium. "The nature of both TV and radio is that they abhor silence and 'dead time.' All TV and radio discussion programs are compelled to snap question and answer back and forth as if the contestants were adversaries in an intellectual tennis match. Although every experienced newspaperman and inquirer knows that the most thoughtful and responsive answers to any difficult question come after long pause, and that the longer the pause the more illuminating the thought that follows it, nonetheless the electronic media cannot bear to suffer a pause of more than five seconds; a pause of thirty seconds of dead time on air seems interminable. Thus, snapping their two-and-a-half-minute answers back and forth, both candidates could only react for the cameras and the people, they could not think." Whenever either candidate found himself touching a thought too large for two-minute exploration, he quickly retreated. Finally the television -watching voter was left to judge, not on issues explored by thoughtful men, but on the relative capacity of the two candidates to perform under television stress.

Pseudo-events thus lead to emphasis on pseudo-qualifications. Again the self-fulfilling prophecy. If we test Presidential candidates by their talents on TV quiz performances, we will, of course, choose presidents for precisely these qualifications. In a democracy, reality tends to conform to the pseudo-event. Nature imitates art.

We are frustrated by our very efforts publicly to unmask the pseudo-event. Whenever we describe the lighting, the make-up, the studio setting, the rehearsals, etc., we simply arouse more interest. One newsman's interpretation makes us more eager to hear another's. One commentator's speculation that the debates may have little significance makes us curious to hear whether another commentator disagrees.

Pseudo-events do, of course, increase our illusion of grasp on the world, what some have called the American illusion of omnipotence. Perhaps, we come to think, the world's problems can really be settled by "statements," by "Summit" meetings, by a competition of "prestige," by overshadowing images, and by political quiz shows.

Once we have tasted the charm of pseudo-events, we are tempted to believe they are the only important events. Our progress poisons the sources of our experience. And the poison tastes so sweet that it spoils our appetite for plain fact. Our seeming ability to satisfy our exaggerated expectations makes us forget that they are exaggerated.

11
WHAT'S WRONG WITH NEWS? IT ISN'T NEW ENOUGH

Max Ways

Europe never thrilled to what happened in 1492. Columbus' return from the New World set no fast horses galloping between the great cities. No awed crowds gathered in the streets. The news seeped around so slowly that years later most Europeans probably had only a vague notion of the event. Giant leaps in communication are measured by the contrast with 1969 when a fifth of mankind saw simultaneous TV pictures of explorers walking on the moon and could hear and read lucid explanations of how the feat was accomplished along with shrewd speculation as to what it might mean for the future.

Yet today's network of news may serve the times less effectively than did the fifteenth century's. Then, 99 percent of knowledge was far from new. Basic information,

---

basic economic and social skills, basic beliefs and values descended from parent to child. Against this static and familiar background news could be readily isolated; prodigies of nature, interventions by supernatural or political powers, the novel speculations of savants—these exceptions to the normal course were news. But now this kind of news has been outstripped by reality. The pace, breadth, and depth of twentieth-century change have dissolved the static background. Today's novelty is tomorrow's normality, doomed to be soon discarded. A high proportion of the basic information used by society is new information. The father's skill may be useless in the son's time. Even values and creeds are in flux. Where so much is new, what is news?

Journalism has not fully adjusted itself to the transformed situation. Conditioned by its own past, journalism often acts as if its main task were still to report the exceptional and dramatically different against a background of what everybody knows. News today can concentrate with tremendous impact on a few great stories: a moon landing, a war, a series of civil disorders. But meanwhile, outside the spotlight, other great advances in science and technology, other international tensions, other causes of social unrest are in motion. Yet today's inadequately reported trends will shape tomorrow's reality.

Again and again the twentieth century has been ambushed by crisis. Looking back from the midst of some tumult, like a race riot, or of some quietly desperate frustration, like the present condition of the cities, we are able to see how disaster might have been avoided by more timely and more effective communication. But we have not yet been able to use such hindsight as a spur to foresight.

The most biting and perilous irony of our civilization turns upon knowledge. Expanding knowledge has multiplied power, which has proliferated into the hands of millions of organizations and hundreds of millions of individuals. Now that everyone has some power to effect change, every aspect of life from economics to religion has been set in motion. But at any moment the significance of any specific change will depend in part upon knowledge of other changes that are in train. If communication lags, then the sum of all the changes will seem random and confused. Obviously, the need for better communication does not fall upon journalism alone. The present challenge to education, for instance, is even more severe. But journalism's role, less discussed than education's, is critical in a society that can no longer depend upon tradition to tell it what it is and how it operates.

Certainly news has not declined in quality. Journalists are better trained, more skillful, more serious about their work than they ever were. They have marvelous new media for reaching a larger, better educated audience, which senses its own dependence upon news. With painstaking care and admirable artistry news today brings information about this change or that one. But in actual life these specific changes are colliding and combining with one another, often in ways undreamed of by their originators—and not alertly reported in the news. A relatively simple compound—automobile plus mass prosperity—brings mass ownership of automobiles, a phenomenon that can ruin cities, alter familial relations, and demand new forms and techniques of government. Adequate news analysis of this particular compound is about fifty years overdue and not yet in sight.

When news fails to add up the permutations of change the best-informed men lack confidence that they know what's going on. Many of those who most confidently assert that they know, don't. Radicals and reactionaries both tend to ignore actual change and to derive their passionately held views from a simpler, more static society that isn't here.

The noisiest debates tend to be irrelevant because their informational backgrounds are fragmentary and out of date.

Even the most powerful nation, with the highest production of new knowledge, thus becomes pervaded by a sense of its own ignorance and helplessness because it feels—correctly—that it has no adequate view of its own direction. Lack of confidence in the quality of news could be fatal in our kind of society, as it could not possibly have been in the Europe to which Columbus returned.

A FLY ON THE WALL?

In the last few years there has been a noticeable public disenchantment with news media. It's true that the avidity for news increases and the prosperity of news organs continues on a long upgrade. Nevertheless, many consumers of news voice doubts that the news adds up to an accurate picture of what's going on.

The understandable public anxiety about the adequacy of news cannot by itself be counted upon to generate improvement. The public uneasiness now contributes, for instance, to pressure for greater governmental intervention in television news, an irrelevant therapy that would correct no present defects and create new ones. Nor is public criticism of print journalism more shrewdly aimed. It tends, for instance, to overestimate the distorting effect of the commercial motives of publishers, motives that today do not influence news nearly as much as they formerly did. On the other hand, the public underestimates both the objective difficulty of telling today's news and certain rigidities that are deeply embedded in the craft of journalism itself, as distinguished from the commercial context in which most of it operates.

Among the areas of change that are inadequately discussed is the new situation of journalism. While eagerly reporting and critically appraising the ballerina, the bishop, and the federal budget, journalism has been almost silent about its own performance and its own problems. The pretense that it is an unseen witness, a mere fly on history's wall, becomes less and less plausible as the role of news expands. From the demonstrator on the street to the President of the United States the behavior of the actors in the news is affected by journalism. All the subjects of news tend to conform to journalism's standards of what is reportable.

Many of these standards, mysterious to outsiders, are in fact obsolete in the sense that they were developed to fit a world that exists no more. Why so much of journalism stubbornly clings to outdated patterns and practices is a question that needs analysis. Before turning, however, to this and other imperfections internal to journalism, a closer look at its present environment, at its position in today's world, may be useful.

STRANGERS AND BROTHERS

"Journalism" is used here in a broad sense encompassing newspapers, newsmagazines, radio and television newscasts or "documentaries," press services, trade magazines, corporate house organs, labor-union periodicals—in short, the enormous variety of publications that describe or comment upon the current scene or some segment of it. Along with education and the arts, journalism is one of the three great information systems that account for the bulk of "the knowledge industry," the most rapidly expanding part of every advanced society.

One reason why journalism expands is the amazing diversity of contemporary society. All the nonsense about regimentation to the contrary, there has never been a time when men varied so much in their work, pleasures, beliefs, values, and styles of life. In part, this growing diversity in life is a reflection of the specialization in knowledge and in education. To be "an educated man" no longer denotes participation in a common, circumscribed body of knowledge. Though the total of extant knowledge has multiplied many times, that part of it which "everybody knows" has increased much more slowly. Society cannot afford to imitate the university, where communication between departments is either perfunctory or non-existent. Outside the university, the world becomes smaller in terms of interdependence while it becomes larger in terms of the difficulty of communicating between heterogeneous groups and diverse individuals. Every year we become more like strangers—and more like brothers.

To deal with this difficulty, contemporary journalism has developed along a scale that ranges from publications addressed to as few as a thousand readers up to television and magazine audiences ranging around fifty million. Even in a highly specialized scientific journal some subscribers will have difficulty comprehending an article by a colleague who, in pursuit of the scientific goal of precision, may be developing a different vocabulary to express new concepts. The practitioners of each subspecialty also need to know what's going on in the nearest subspecialty, and beyond that one ad infinitum. As the circles widen, the communication difficulty increases.

FORTUNE, for instance, works in the intermediate range of the scale. Its subject, business, is a valid unit in the sense that its parts are interdependent and have many patterns, practices, problems, and interests in common. A fantastic variety is embraced within this unity. It's a far cry, apparently, from Manhattan's garment trade to the research scientists who developed the laser and the high-technology industries which first used it outside the laboratories. Yet the men on Seventh Avenue needed to be promptly and effectively informed about so fundamental an invention; lasers for cutting fabrics are already in commercial development. To convey such information requires bridging huge gaps between different kinds of information, different habits of mind.

Today every public question—national defense, water pollution, educational policy—involves highly specialized kinds of knowledge. The citizen cannot be adequately informed unless his education and, later, his journalism, give him some access to that essential part of a public question that lies outside his own immediate sphere of interest and competence.

Equally daunting is the journalistic difficulty that arises out of the way contemporary change originates. In a totally planned society (if one were possible) journalism's job would be to focus on the planning authority, reporting its decisions; the sum of these would be the sum of change. But not even the Soviet Union, rigidly authoritarian in theory, works that way. Some shots that the planners call are never made, and new conditions, unforeseen by planners, arise spontaneously.

The dissemination of power implicit in all contemporary society defeats the fondest dreams of centralizers. In the U.S. the decisions of government, important though they are, add up to only a small fraction of the whole impetus of change. Most of the great new government policies of recent decades—social security, welfare, civil-rights programs, increased regulation of business—are secondary changes, efforts to cushion new conditions that had their primary source outside of government. Nor is there in the private sector any one source of change, any establishment of concentrated power, where journalism can find the conscious, deliberate origin of most changes that sweep us onward.

For many years some newsmen and some of their customers have suspected that Washington was overcovered relative to the rest of the American scene. Journalistic tradition partly explains this. In the centuries when political intervention was one of the few sources of what little was new and different, news properly concentrated upon government. Journalism still clings to the legislative act and the presidential decision because they are relatively easy to get into focus. By contrast, such gradual and multicentered changes as the loosening of parental authority or the increase of consumer credit or public acceptance of a new technology of contraception or the rising resentment of black Americans are much more difficult to pinpoint. They are not "events." They didn't happen "yesterday" or "today" or "last week." They do not fit the journalist's cherished notions of a "story."

LOSING THE THREAD

Insofar as journalism solves the problem of where to look for change, it is then confronted with another set of difficulties: the subject will be more complex, intrinsically harder to tell, than news used to be. A scientific advance, for instance, is harder to convey than an explorer's geographical discovery. There was no great communication difficulty in saying that Columbus sailed west for seventy days, that he found a land peopled by naked men. It's all wondrous but it's not opaque. Everybody recognized the terms "sail," "day," "land," "naked." On the other hand, the discovery of deoxyribonucleic acid is, to a non-biologist, more opaque than wondrous. Yet DNA, by unlocking secrets of genetics, may cause more social change than did the age of exploration. And the consequences may follow far more quickly.

In the last ten or fifteen years journalism, thanks to a few very able science reporters, has made tremendous strides in the techniques of communicating to the public the major advances of pure science. A knowledgeable reporter, skilled in translating scientific languages, can sit down with the discoverer and his colleagues and seek ways to penetrate the opacity that surrounds any scientific discovery. Greater difficulty—and less journalistic success—comes when the new discovery begins to move out into use, mingling with technological, economic, psychological, and even moral factors. As a source of information to the reporter the original discoverer may not be of much use at this point. Members of other academic disciplines may not be interested or adroit in bringing their knowledge to bear on the meaning of the change. Journalism may lose the thread because the change has become complex in a way that goes beyond any academic discipline.

Journalism, for instance, has not done well with the economic and social implications of the greatest technological advance of the last twenty years—the computer, symbol of automation. Since its effects spread out to every part of society, everybody needs to know quite a lot about the computer. In the Fifties, when computers and other devices for automating work were coming in, there was an almost hysterical belief that they would sharply increase unemployment. Thousands of economists and social historians were in a position to know better. They not only failed to reach the general public with a more realistic view of automation's impact on employment, they did not even get the message to the rest of the academic community. Even though U.S. employment has increased 36 percent since 1950, millions of people, including many of the best educated, are still walking around with bad cases of computerphobia.

In 1965, Charles E. Silberman, an economist and journalist, undertook in FORTUNE a careful analysis of the actual and probable future effects of computers on the number and kinds of jobs. It would have been possible—though admittedly difficult—to parallel Silberman's explanation at levels of mass-circulation journalism. Newspapers and television have made little effort to explain the economic and social meaning of the computer. Such a subject simply does not fit their working definitions of news. But if in the years ahead there occurs, for some reason unconnected with computers, a sharp and prolonged rise in unemployment, then the press will feel obliged to carry the mouthings of any demagogue who blames computers for the shortage of jobs. A lot of Americans would fall for this because education and journalism, between them, are not getting over to the public enough timely information about the significance of this sort of change.

THE INVISIBLE AMERICANS

In recent decades journalism has missed changes more important and more complex than the effect of the computer. From the end of the post-Civil War Reconstruction period to the mid-Fifties, American journalism was virtually silent on the subject of how black Americans lived. Lynchings were reported and deplored, as were race riots and the more sensational crimes committed by blacks against whites. But crimes by blacks against blacks were regularly ignored as a matter of explicit news policy on most newspapers. This was symptomatic of an implicit journalistic assumption that blacks were not a significant part of the American scene. Journalism bears a considerable share of responsibility for white society's disengagement from the Negro and his problems.

Yet journalists were aware that the position of the blacks in American life was building up tensions. The huge northward migrations during the two world wars created new conditions that seldom got into the news. Much of the material in Gunnar Myrdal's 1944 sociological classic, *An American Dilemma*, came from interviews with American journalists who were interested as individuals in the plight of the Negro, but who collectively and professionally did not consider facts about the condition of Negro life to be news.

In the last few years journalism has been widely denounced for giving undue attention to extreme black militants and to civil disorders arising from racial tension. No doubt there has been some shift over the years in the personal attitudes of newsmen toward racial inequality. But not nearly enough shift to account for a 180° reversal that moved the racial problem from the bottom to the top of the news. One difference is that black militancy found a way to pass the gate of news standards. In the light of the urban riots and fires, newsmen, especially those with TV cameras, suddenly found blacks eminently reportable.

The contrast in news between the past invisibility of blacks as people and the recent hypervisibility of black militants brings us to certain characteristics inherent in the craft of journalism. Why doesn't it try harder to expand its definition of news? Why does so much of journalism remain trapped in "the story," the dramatic, disruptive, exceptional event that properly formed the corpus of news in the generations when the broad background of society was shifting very slowly? Why is journalism still so wrapped up in the deadline, the scoop, the gee-whiz—and so seemingly unable to notice that most of what is new will not fit into a narrative pattern of what happened in the last twenty-four hours?

"The story," and all the bang-bang that went with it, used to be the way "to sell papers" in the days when newsboys crying "Extra" formed the sales force of the press. The business need for this kind of razzle-dazzle has disappeared. The editorial reason for it has diminished to the vanishing point. Yet much of journalism still operates as if its circulation and its usefulness depended on the second hand of the clock rather than the depth of its perception, the accuracy of its report, the relevance of its coverage, and the balance of its judgment.

To understand why news is trapped in its own past, journalism must be looked at in relation to the third great system of social communication mentioned above, the arts. Though most journalists are loath to admit it, what they practice is an art—crude and unbeautiful, but nevertheless an art. Even in the fine arts, where individual originality lies close to the heart of excellence, nearly all artists are influenced by traditions, canons, "schools." Descending the ladder of art toward craftsmanship, originality and novelty become less prominent and tradition becomes stronger. The artifact is acceptable because its design is more or less familiar. This may be especially true of the verbal arts of our day. Language is, after all, a huge network of conventional meanings, a heritage. In slow-moving societies language may have changed as rapidly as the realities it described. In our day, language may be a "conservative" element, lagging behind social change, forcing us to perceive today in terms of the past.

THE ARTISTIC BIAS

The sublanguages of the sciences and other highly specialized activities do change rapidly. But most journalism cannot use these terms because it must transmit information outside the specialized group. In his overriding desire to communicate efficiently, the journalist tends unconsciously to be ruled by precedent in his choice of subject and in the form of presentation. That which is familiar can be communicated more easily than that which is really new. The simple subject is more communicable than the complex. Dramatic conflict, especially when it can be reduced to two sides, is a well established form of communication.

Thus journalism in our time has what might be called a formal bias that causes news to distort reality. Preference for "the story" that journalism *knows* can be communicated leads it to neglect the changes that need to be told but do not fit the standards of familiarity, simplicity, drama. This artistic bias has nothing to do with the ideology or partisanship of the journalist himself. He may take sides concerning the substance of a news story, but such substantive bias will often be overridden by his formal bias. A journalist who sees a story that is attractive—artistically speaking—will tell it even if it runs contrary to his political prejudices, hurts the interests of his friends, and brings sorrow to his mother's heart. This laudable independence exacts, however, a heavy price: if the artistic standards by which the story is selected and shaped are themselves out of phase with reality the consequent distortion may be greater than that produced by a journalist's substantive bias toward one "side" of an issue.

Probably most journalists who handled news produced by the late Senator Joe McCarthy opposed the substance of what he was doing. But McCarthy got enormous attention in the press before he had a large popular following because he played up to the journalistic desire for simplification and dramatization, and had a keen sense of that seven o'clock deadline. On the other hand, most journalists who dealt with John Gardner probably approved of the substance of his influence on public affairs. Yet Gardner, who was Secretary of Health, Education, and Welfare during a critical period, never became a vivid figure in the news. He tended to see life "in the round." Though he recognized the puzzles and problems that engulf government today, he tackled them with an energy derived from a sense of modern society's immense material, intellectual, and moral resources. He did not cast himself as St. George versus the Dragon. He was out of touch with news precisely because he was in touch with contemporary social reality. Gardner's name would have become familiar to every American if, after resigning his post, he had gone along with newsmen who importuned him to launch a series of public attacks on President Johnson.

Ideology and extreme partisanship attract the attention of journalists who are not themselves ideologues or partisans. If news can be simplified into a framework of Cold War or of black extremists against white extremists or of poor against rich, journalists as communicators will be happy although as men and citizens they—along with everybody else—will be depressed at the picture they paint.

BOTH LOCAL AND NATIONAL

In terms of this general view of contemporary journalism's mission, its external difficulties and its internal inhibitions, let us briefly examine some specific media, starting (as a journalistic canon requires) with the most familiar.

Daily newspapers in general do not present an inspiring spectacle of vigorous effort to meet the challenge of change. Most of them go on emphasizing specific events—a crime, an accident, a resolution of the city council—in ways not very different from the journalism of a hundred years ago. Even though crime's incidence has increased to the point where it is a substantial part of the new normality, only a few papers have made a serious effort to explain this change, more important and potentially more interesting than any single crime.

A shift of attention has occurred from local news to national and international news. On most papers this seems to take the heart out of local coverage, while leaving national and international news to the Associated Press and the United Press International, which are the least innovative, most tradition-bound of all journalistic institutions.

Few papers have discovered the category of news that is both local and national. The problems of each city are in some sense unique. Since early in the Johnson Administration, Washington has been aware that decisions made by Congress and carried out by a national Administration will be fruitless unless they are meshed with vigorous and knowledgeable local efforts. Yet each city's problems of transportation, housing, education, poverty, have a wide area of overlap with other cities' problems. The obvious need is for local reporting that will examine what's going on in Pittsburgh and San Francisco in an effort to clarify the problems of Buffalo. Communication, through journalism, between the cities and regions of the U.S. has never been so desperately needed or in worse shape. Efforts to develop a "new federalism" are handicapped by journalism's tradition-bound rigidity that sees national news as one category and local news as an entirely separate category.

The sorry condition of daily newspapers is often blamed on the trend toward local monopoly, a diagnosis that is too easy. In many cities, before mergers occurred, all the papers lacked distinction and leadership. In cities with competing papers journalism is not notably more vigorous than in the monopoly cities. Such notable smaller city papers as the Louisville *Courier-Journal*, the Cleveland *Plain Dealer*, the Minneapolis *Tribune*, and the Charlotte *Observer* are among the very few that really keep trying to improve service to the community.

AWAY FROM THE TRADITIONAL "STORY"

Of yesterday's best-known newspapers the Chicago *Tribune*, the St. Louis *Post-Dispatch*, the New York *Daily News* seem less relevant than they used to be. The most improved large daily (it had lots of room for improvement) is probably the Los Angeles *Times*. In recent years it has developed an ability to cover trends, as well as events, and to relate local subjects to the regional and national scenes. Its intelligent reporting of educational trends, for instance, enabled it to evince clear superiority over the San Francisco press when campus "stories" erupted in the Bay area, at Berkeley and San Francisco State. Because the Los Angeles *Times* was aware of the moving background behind the sensational campus disorders, it reported the events themselves with a far steadier hand than the San Francisco papers.

Two national dailies, the *Christian Science Monitor* and the *Wall Street Journal*, have largely freed themselves from the tyranny of "the story" as traditionally defined. The *Monitor's* interpretive articles are, in fact, more timely than many a front page sprinkled with the words "yesterday" and "today." The *Wall Street Journal*'s two leading front-page articles add up in the course of a year to a better report of what's going on than all the bulletins of the wire services. "Kelly Street Blues," a four-part series on a block in a New York ghetto, put together a mosaic of detail that helps one part of society, the *W.S.J.*'s readers, understand how a very different part lives. Neil Ulman's roundup of protests across the nation against sex education in the schools was an example of the kind of report that conventional newspapers miss. The *W.S.J.*'s foreign news can discuss basically interesting subjects, such as how Soviet citizens can invest their savings or anti-Franco trends in Spain, that are not pegged to any events.

A long way from the *Wall Street Journal* lies the "underground press" that has sprung up in recent years. Its chief significance is to demonstrate that, economically, the proliferation of many publications is now feasible. Unhappily, it cannot be said that the underground press displays much innovative muscle. Its ideology seems moored in nineteenth-century anarchism, and from that viewpoint it can dislike whatever the "straight" press likes. But that hardly helps the job of reducing the lag between journalism and reality. The underground papers are as similar, one to another, as the square papers. An admittedly incomplete survey of underground papers indicates that none of them has invented a new four-letter word.

In a class by itself stands that most aboveground of American newspapers, the New York *Times*. Its influence is by no means confined to its readers. Most journalists, including broadcasters, start their day with it and each journalist assumes that the others have read the *Times* attentively. In the important matter of day-to-day decisions on which stories deserve top play, the *Times* is the greatest single national influence. Its preeminence goes back a long way and it is still steeped in conventional news judgment and traditional journalistic forms. Nevertheless, in recent years the *Times* has produced more and more innovative journalism. Its development of daily biographical sketches of figures in the news abandons the old elitist assumption that everybody knows who these people are. The new managing editor, A. M. Rosenthal, is among those chiefly responsible for an emphasis on "in depth" reporting that breaks away from yesterday's developments. A landmark of this genre was Anthony Lukas' 5,000-word account of a suburban girl who had been found murdered in an East Greenwich Village basement; Lukas' detailed narrative transformed an incomprehensible horror into a memorable insight into the shifting values and life patterns that touch even the most seemingly secure homes. In August, when 300,000 youngsters suddenly converged on Bethel, New York, to hear rock music, the *Times* reports, departing from the conventional emphasis on the disorderly aspects of the scene, made a real effort to understand what had drawn the kids there, what they got out of it, what their values were.

Because of the *Times'* immense influence on journalism that paper's recent willingness to break out of conventional molds is one of the most hopeful signs of long-range improvement of the press. But it may be years before most papers follow such pioneering. They haven't the reporting staffs to do so. Bright, concerned young men and women are loath to go to work for papers that are clearly not alive, not relevant to the great changes and stresses that are sweeping through society.

BROADENING THE SCOPE OF NEWS

Newspapers have been slow to adjust to the liveliness of good TV reportage and the broad-spectrum coverage of newsmagazines.

From its beginning the great distinction of *Time*, the weekly newsmagazine, was not the much-parodied sentence structure of its early years but its broadened concept of news. For example, it looked at religion as a moving part of the total scene. No future historian of the twentieth century's middle decades could possibly omit from an account of the total change the tremendous shifts of religious and ethical belief that color contemporary life. Yet most conventional newspaper journalism still virtually ignores such subjects, except when they surface as dramatic confrontations. The newsmagazines continue to broaden the concept of news. *Newsweek* has added departments on "Life and Leisure" and "The Cities." *Time*'s recent addition of "Behavior" and "Environment" treats other areas that the older journalism assumed to be static. The departmentalization of news itself is more than an orderly convenience for the reader. The departmental structure forces editors to look where they know news ought to be, rather than passively waiting for news to "flow" at them—an attitude that results in today's news being defined as whatever is most like yesterday's news.

All journalism has something to learn from the pioneers of a new journalism of ideas. The quarterly *Daedalus*, under the sensitive editorship of Stephen Graubard, has reached an impressive circulation of 70,000; it provides for a highly educated readership a forum where voices from many disciplines converge in each issue upon a single subject. *The Public Interest*, another quarterly, edited by Daniel Bell and Irving Kristol, is less formidably academic in style, more directly attuned to current problems. One of the most extraordinary publications is the *Kaiser Aluminum News*, whose editor, Don Fabun, delights in translating, primarily for the company's employees, the most difficult contemporary thought into lucid, poetic words and pictures. Fabun never runs a conventional "audience-building story"; and yet the demand for his magazine continues to build because people are fascinated by what he has to say.

Not one of these magazines pursues an ideological shortcut. All are basically periodicals of explanation. They work on the assumption that relevant truths about contemporary society are difficult—but not impossible—to convey.

THE SPECIAL BIAS OF TV

At the other end of the spectrum lies television journalism with its mass audience. Most of its faults have descended from print journalism; it multiplied its inheritance while finding some distortive formal biases of its own. The artistic bias inherent in the TV medium affects the behavior of the actors in the news. The "demonstration" becomes a dominant form of social action rather than the petition, the political debate, the lawsuit. Other media are drawn toward covering, as best they can, the disorderly scenes that television covers so superlatively. There have been months when a consumer of news might wonder whether anything except demonstrations was going on in the U.S. Such overconcentration on one kind of news in a society where thousands of currents are running is a sure way of walking into another ambush, perhaps more grave than that represented by today's disorderly products of yesterday's inattention.

Television is exerting another, more indirect, bias upon news. The generation now of college age is the first that was introduced to news through a medium mainly devoted to dramatized entertainment. The drama is usually highly simplified and one side is morally right, the other wrong. The young viewer expects the news to fall into the same dramatic pattern. It is not surprising if he later becomes a recruit to the new anti-intellectualism apparent in the impatience of campus protesters who regard complex facts as distractions from the "gut commitment," which they hold to be a morally superior approach to public questions. Public expectation of moralistic drama presses all media toward defining news in terms of simple conflict. But what the public needs to know may lie in just the opposite direction. Society's ability to avoid ambush may depend on receiving information before the dramatic conflict develops.

Yet some of the most hopeful signs of tomorrow's journalism are also to be found in television. It has an incomparable ability to convey the integrated *quality* of a personality or of a social situation. Eric Hoffer unobtrusively interviewed by Eric Sevareid was an experience in communication that print journalism could hardly match. C.B.S. also recently did a "documentary" (that blighting word) on Japan as interpreted by former Ambassador Edwin Reischauer, which told more people more about the subject than millions of printed words, including Reischauer's own fine books.

Conventional journalism despairs of communicating such an intrinsically interesting subject as old age in contemporary society. What's the story? What's the event? What's the conflict? What's the issue? Lord Snowdon's beautifully sensitive *Don't Count the Candles* ignores those conventional journalistic questions and brings unforgettable information of what it's like to be old.

Such examples compel the conclusion that television has a great constructive role to play in the journalism of the future upon which society must depend for its sense of cohesion and for the intelligent choice of its own direction.

That poverty in America should have been "discovered" in 1962 by Michael Harrington, an impassioned polemicist, is proof that journalism was not fulfilling its mission. Where were the journalists in the years when Ralph Nader was working on *Unsafe at Any Speed*, an exaggerated indictment of auto manufacturers that is now generally conceded to contain a lot of truth about a matter of universal interest? Nader lately has broadened his attack to other products and services where the buying public is ill-protected and ill-informed. He and Harrington both tend toward governmental remedies for the ills they identify. But the informational problem is more fundamental than the political issue. If society doesn't know about poverty it cannot deal with it governmentally or otherwise; if the consuming public doesn't know enough about what it's buying it cannot protect itself, governmentally or otherwise. The way to defend the market system is to be sure that information, an essential ingredient of any healthy market or any healthy democracy, is adequate.

IT'S UP TO THE NEWSMEN

It ought to be plain, but seemingly it is not, that the quality of journalism depends primarily on journalists—not on government and not on the legal owners of media. Publishers and executives of networks and broadcasting stations now have only a small fraction of the influence on news that owners used to exercise. As commercial bias diminishes, what counts now, for better or worse, is the bias of reporters, cameramen, editors. Their ideological bent is far less important than their artistic bias, the way they select and present what they regard as significant.

Journalism will always need artistry to reach the public's mind and heart. Indeed, what is now required is a higher level of art, a boldness that will get journalism unstuck from forms of communication developed in and for a social context very different from the present. Nobody except journalists can develop such forms. All the public can do is to be wary of existing distortions and appreciative of such efforts as appear to get closer to the current truth.

Study Guide

Talking Points

I.   If, as Walter Lippmann argued, "news is not a mirror of social conditions, but the report of an aspect that has obtruded itself," in what sense is it still a mirror?

II. Is it true to say that the journalist (or the press or the media) occupies the position of the "umpire in an unscored baseball game"?

III. Assess the utility of Frank Luther Mott's criteria for news judgment—timeliness, prominence, proximity, probable consequence, and human interest.

IV. Helen MacGill Hughes says that the "paper that is dominated by its duty to the public interest cannot . . . conceive of its function as purely commercial." She goes on to say that the "commercial penny press substituted the market for the mission." Discuss the subject of news in light of these concepts with a view to assessing the shape of current journalism and the news judgment reflected in it.

V.   Hughes also says a newspaper has a "natural history." What sense do you make of such a concept?

VI. What, if anything, prevents journalists from following the advice of Max Ways and expanding their definition of news?

VII. Do pseudo-events truly flood our consciousness, as Daniel Boorstin argued? Is a news release actually a "news holdback"? What is the difference between pseudo-events and propaganda?

Workbench

I.   For the sake of discussion, imagine that there is a pure kind of news: reporting on events in the public interest. A tornado ravages a town. A mayor is arrested for corruption. A planning board approves construction of a new skyscraper. According to this view, journalists serve as the sentinels of self-government, providing versions of reality upon which citizens can act. As the essays in this section reveal, the matter is a bit more complicated than this. Definitions of news have been influenced by such forces as human interest, marketing to new readers, profit mongering, the development of new technologies, the rise of publicity and public relations, celebrity and sensationalism, the influence of large social movements, and what Boorstin summarized as the "pseudo-event." To determine how these news forces operate in our own time, choose a day to immerse yourself in the news. Divide your class into groups and ask each group to analyze a particular news media platform— for example, a national newspaper, a local newspaper, a local television report, a national news network report, a public radio news broadcast, a twenty-four-hour cable news network, a national news Web site. Discuss how much of the news report is devoted to "reporting on events in the public interest." How much is devoted to other expressions of news? Which of these expressions do you consider "hard"? Which ones would you categorize as "soft"?

II. Add words and concepts to your "editor's lexicon" (see Item I in the Workbench in Section A) based on the readings in this section.

III. Max Ways argues that persistent journalistic routines and patterns of coverage emphasize episodic news over more important, but more gradual developments in societies. Traditional definitions of news, he writes, have been "outstripped by reality." Journalists may place too much emphasis on the workings of government, he suggests, and not enough on other powerful forces of change in society. Stories that require more nuance and explanation get ignored. The steady migration of African Americans from the South to the North and, in some cases, back again; the movement of pornography from the edges of society toward the mainstream; the growing popularity of drug treatments meant to improve lifestyles rather than cure diseases—these are examples of the kinds of stories that are not "events." "They didn't happen 'yesterday' or 'today' or 'last week,'" writes Ways. "They do not fit the journalist's cherished notions of a 'story.'" Interview some professors from disciplines other than journalism who are specialists in fields in which you specialize (or in your beat). Ask them to identify important ongoing movements or changes that may be ignored by journalists suffering from the tyranny of "now." Write a story based on such interviews—be sure it contains a clear and unambiguous nut graph— under the guidance of your professor/editor.

IV. Write two short "hard" news stories under the supervision of your professor/editor on an event in your area of specialization or beat. Pay special attention to the nut graph in which the news and its meaning should be crystallized and expressed precisely.

Facts and Evidence

INTRODUCTION

The essays in this section reflect the natural concern that journalists have with the truth-value of what they publish and the accuracy of the facts that mark their reporting and commentary. The treatments we have selected on this vast and sometimes vexing subject range from the philosophical to the practical. But they are unified by a belief that facts and truth matter to good journalists and are the basis for good journalism.

The discussion of the nature of journalistic "truth" and the reliability of evidence in news has been around for almost as long as there have been journalists and newspapers in our midst. Eighteenth-century English writers and pamphleteers were routinely accused of circulating rumor and gossip, just as journalists in our century are accused of circulating half-truths or bending the truth in favor of their biases.

For our purposes the discussion began in earnest in 1922 when Walter Lippmann published *Public Opinion*. In his chapter, "News, Truth, and a Conclusion," which we have included in this collection, Lippmann challenged the notion that "news and truth are two words for the same thing." He argued instead that the "function of news is to signalize an event" and the function "of truth is to bring to light the hidden facts, to set them in relation with each other, and make a picture of reality on which men can act." Lippmann also said—it may at first seem to contradict his preceding statement—that news itself could be true. He said, for example, there is "reportable truth" in the news that says it is "recorded at the county clerk's office that John Smith has gone into bankruptcy." In other words, news is true if there is a correspondence between the elements of an event, captured typically in a news lead, and the description of that event's main elements.

To be fair, Lippmann was concerned with a broader application of the term "truth." He was comparing reportable evidence in journalism with the standards of evidence that mark science or law. His position was born in an attachment to the empirical sciences and in a deeply held belief that democratic theory calls on citizens—amongst them journalists—to know and to understand their world sufficiently to govern themselves successfully. It was on both scores that his skepticism entered the picture. He remarked, for example, that journalists do not possess a rigorous methodology akin to the one that frees science from "theological control." For the journalist, he said, "[h]is version of truth is only his version." As this relates to democratic life, he said the press "is like the beam of a searchlight that moves restlessly about, bringing one episode and then another out of darkness into vision." But this, he went on, is not enough. Under the circumstances he described, governments and citizens "are compelled to act without a reliable picture of the world. . . ." He wanted to change this by changing our picture of democratic life—including the role of journalists. But regardless of what Lippmann (and others) have said on this subject, journalists continue to speak the language of fact and truth. They assume that facts matter and that practical truth is journalism's most fundamental goal.

They are right. Facts mattered unambiguously, for example, in the week after D-Day in June 1944, When *Life* magazine published photographs of Allied soldiers landing in Normandy as the great battle of World War II began. Facts mattered in a very different but decisive way in 1969 when Seymour Hersh found the soldier who had been charged with leading a massacre of innocent villagers in Vietnam a year before. They mattered in the reporting, reviewed by Christopher Lydon, of a murder case in the late fall of 1989 when a falsehood published in the Boston media disturbed the relations between the races in that city. So in journalism, facts always matter, and truth is always the goal.

This being said, it is obvious that in some circumstances it is easier for journalists to unearth facts and portray them vividly than in others. The eyewitness account is one such circumstance. John Carey writes that good reportage "lays claim directly to the power of the real . . . [It] exiles us from fiction, where disbelief is suspended, into the sharp terrain of truth." In this vein, Roy Peter Clark introduces us to rules that build the firewall between fact and fiction. He argues that although writers of nonfiction can usefully borrow from writers of fiction, the line between the two modes of expression should always be "firm," not "fuzzy"—in the name of the belief that empirical truth matters.

Fact and truth are notions that interest James Ettema and Theodore Glasser, who distinguish thoughtfully between the knowledge claims of beat reporters and those of investigative reporters. They note how investigative reporters engage in a process that allows them to achieve "moral certainty" about the truth of what they publish. The truth they express can come from painstaking research or—what amounts to the same thing—continuous attention to developing and emerging facts. After a long stay in Vietnam, David Halberstam was led by the facts he saw to write the truth. In a later meditation on his experience, he wrote:

> No one becomes a reporter to make friends, but neither is it pleasant in a situation like the war in Vietnam to find yourself completely at odds with the views of the highest officials of your country. The pessimism of the Saigon press corps was of the most reluctant kind: many of us came to love Vietnam, we saw our friends dying all around us, and we would have liked nothing better than to believe the war was going well and that it would eventually be won. But it was impossible for us to believe those things without denying the evidence of our own senses. . . . And so we had no alternative but to report the truth. . . .

So journalists may describe the truth of news and the truth of facts, and they may synthesize true facts into larger truths. The process begins with a disciplined commitment to accuracy. In John Hersey's memorable phrasing, the legend on the license of every journalist should say: "NONE OF THIS WAS MADE UP." He goes on to say that the "ethics of journalism . . . must be based on the simple truth that every journalist knows the difference between the distortion that comes from subtracting observed data and the distortion that comes from invented data." This implies, as Hersey also says, that the facts should be "hard"—a product of corroboration—or, as Bill Kovach and Tom Rosenstiel have said helpfully, of "verification." Journalism, Rosenstiel and Kovach argue, is a discipline of verification. It shares this characteristic with the empirical disciplines with which it sometimes struggles for a reputation.

However, journalists know that there is a tension between the responsibility for facts and truth, on the one hand, and the contexts in which news arises on the other. For example, news is made not only in venues where the elements of an event can be ascertained and verified; it is made also in society's conversation, which is marked as much by guesses and half-truths as it is by hard facts. By "society's conversation," we mean simply the saying, arguing, and claiming—and the record of it in newspapers and broadcasting agencies—by citizens whose reputations or positions make what they say newsworthy. In reporting society's conversation, what is said may be accurately noted and reported—by politicians on the stump, by lawyers or witnesses at a trial, by developers appearing before municipal planning committees, or by representatives of management and labor during negotiations. But the truth of what has been said may not be so easily and quickly verified. It follows that in important cases, the truth of what is said should remain on the media's news agenda until it can be conclusively verified or refuted. In the meantime, much of what is said must be placed on the record even though, in the language of legal evidence, it is hearsay until it is verified. In this respect, every reporter knows about the minefields of rumor and gossip that mark the institutional, political, and social sites where news is made and disagreement rages. Between eyewitness accounts and investigative pieces lies a wide field in which journalists must nevertheless engage in a process of recording, discovering, and disclosing—casting, as Lippmann would say, the beams of their searchlights on the swirl of action and behavior marking our world. Balance and fairness are the ethical standards governing such work, and objectivity—in several meanings of the word—is its formal goal.

By introducing the concept of objectivity, we do not intend to engage the deeper philosophical claims that such a concept suggests. We intend rather to point to a style of journalistic expression in which the journalist distances himself or herself from a subject, points to its principal elements, and leaves the resolution of conflict or disagreement to the parties whose voices figure in a story. In this sense, the word "objectivity" exists in a thesaurus of synonyms such as "neutral," "unbiased," "nonpartisan," and the old-fashioned word "disinterested." That last term does not mean that journalists lack an interest in the commonwealth. It means that a careful exploration of their work will reveal no partisan interest. The "objective" story on abortion, for example, will thus reveal no hint as to the publication's editorial position or where the reporter stands on the issue. Such journalism arises out of an impulse—a respectable one in our view—to portray accurately the voices of those whose views of the facts may differ and, even where there is agreement on facts, differ on the weight they should be given.

The tools that allow reporters to seek facts, to pin them down, and to promote understanding include the cultivation of reliable sources, systematic interviewing, careful observation, and the interrogation of complex documents. They include, amongst the wisest and most thoughtful journalists, arithmetic tools, such as those described by Victor Kohn, that allow good journalists to use such terms as "probability," "variability," and "standard deviation" accurately. They include photographs, which, as Susan Sontag remarks thoughtfully, are the work of the camera—"the ideal arm of consciousness."[1]

So the true representation of reality is the goal, the skepticism of Walter Lippmann and other writers notwithstanding. Lippmann argued that news and truth should be conceptually severed. He argued, in effect, that journalists can reliably signalize events, but cannot reliably synthesize them. We would argue that some can and some cannot. In the meantime, the concepts of news and truth should not be severed. The truth that journalists seek is a practical (not an abstract) truth that arises out of an initial intention to compose pictures of the events that mark the here and now. The intention to compose such pictures produces a practical set of operations such that the pictures that are created are intended to correspond reliably to the elements of the events themselves. To go further and to stake out some philosophical ground, we are sanguine about the truth-claims that arise naturally in the language of journalists not only because truth is essential to journalism's practical operations and democratic responsibilities, but also because we believe that journalists, like other citizens, see with human eyes and speak a common language. A common language makes collective life possible. Although our emotions, our status and capacities, may vary substantially and thus affect how we view the world, our senses and language attune us to a common reality that can be known and described. As helpful as Lippmann's reflections on the subject are, it is our view that he was overly committed intellectually to notions of human singularity and subjectivity. But perhaps we should leave that debate to philosophers.

In the meantime, teasing facts from the swirl of activity that marks institutional and social life is no easy task. But good journalists are committed to doing it well. Their work is motivated by a desire to construct a realistic profile of the here and now, or, as Robert Park would put it, the goal of good journalists is to provide sufficient knowledge—Park has a particular take on that term—to allow human beings to locate themselves in an actual world. To paraphrase and interpret his view, insofar as they succeed, the journalism provided by journalists "tends to preserve the sanity of the individual and the permanence of society."

In the essays that follow, we explore the beliefs and devices that journalists use to pin down facts and tease reality into view—how, in short, truth emerges from hard facts and evidence.

NOTE

1. The arm of consciousness seems to have achieved an even greater reach as the Internet and blogging evolve. See John Schwartz, "Blogs Provide Raw Details from Scene of the Disaster," *New York Times* (nytimes.com), December 28, 2004.

12

NEWS, TRUTH, AND A CONCLUSION

Walter Lippmann

As we begin to make more and more exact studies of the press, much will depend upon the hypothesis we hold. If we assume with Mr. Sinclair, and most of his opponents, that news and truth are two words for the same thing, we shall, I believe, arrive nowhere. We shall prove that on this point the newspaper lied. We shall prove that on that point Mr. Sinclair's account lied. We shall demonstrate that Mr. Sinclair lied when he said that somebody lied, and that somebody lied when he said Mr. Sinclair lied. We shall vent our feelings, but we shall vent them into air.

The hypothesis, which seems to me the most fertile, is that news and truth are not the same thing, and must be clearly distinguished.[1] The function of news is to signalize an event, the function of truth is to bring to light the hidden facts, to set them into relation with each other, and make a picture of reality on which men can act. Only at those points, where social conditions take recognizable and measurable shape, do the body of truth and the body of news coincide. That is a comparatively small part of the whole field of human interest. In this sector, and only in this sector, the tests of the news are sufficiently exact to make the charges of perversion or suppression more than a partisan judgment. There is no defense, no extenuation, no excuse whatever, for stating six times that Lenin is dead, when the only information the paper possesses is a report that he is dead from a source repeatedly shown to be unreliable. The news, in that instance, is not "Lenin Dead" but "Helsingfors Says Lenin is Dead." And a newspaper can be asked to take the responsibility of not making Lenin more dead than the source of the news is reliable; if there is one subject on which editors are most responsible it is in their judgment of the reliability of the source. But when it comes to dealing, for example, with stories of what the Russian people want, no such test exists.

The absence of these exact tests accounts, I think, for the character of the profession, as no other explanation does. There is a very small body of exact knowledge, which it requires no outstanding ability or training to deal with. The rest is in the journalist's own discretion. Once he departs from the region where it is definitely recorded at the County Clerk's office that John Smith has gone into bankruptcy, all fixed standards disappear. The story of why John Smith failed, his human frailties, the analysis of the economic conditions on which he was shipwrecked, all of this can be told in a hundred different ways. There is no discipline in applied psychology, as there is a discipline in medicine, engineering, or even law, which has authority to direct the journalist's mind when he

---

passes from the news to the vague realm of truth. There are no canons to direct his own mind, and no canons that coerce the reader's judgment or the publisher's. His version of the truth is only his version. How can he demonstrate the truth as he sees it? He cannot demonstrate it, any more than Mr. Sinclair Lewis can demonstrate that he has told the whole truth about Main Street. And the more he understands his own weaknesses, the more ready he is to admit that where there is no objective test, his own opinion is in some vital measure constructed out of his own stereotypes, according to his own code, and by the urgency of his own interest. He knows that he is seeing the world through subjective lenses. He cannot deny that he too is, as Shelley remarked, a dome of many-colored glass which stains the white radiance of eternity.

And by this knowledge his assurance is tempered. He may have all kinds of moral courage, and sometimes has, but he lacks that sustaining conviction of a certain technic which finally freed the physical sciences from theological control. It was the gradual development of an irrefragable method that gave the physicist his intellectual freedom as against all the powers of the world. His proofs were so clear, his evidence so sharply superior to tradition, that he broke away finally from all control. But the journalist has no such support in his own conscience or in fact. The control exercised over him by the opinions of his employers and his readers, is not the control of truth by prejudice, but of one opinion by another opinion that it is not demonstrably less true. Between Judge Gary's assertion that the unions will destroy American institutions, and Mr. Gompers' assertion that they are agencies of the rights of man, the choice has, in large measure, to be governed by the will to believe.

The task of deflating these controversies, and reducing them to a point where they can be reported as news, is not a task which the reporter can perform. It is possible and necessary for journalists to bring home to people the uncertain character of the truth on which their opinions are founded, and by criticism and agitation to prod social science into making more usable formulations of social facts, and to prod statesmen into establishing more visible institutions. The press, in other words, can fight for the extension of reportable truth. But as social truth is organized to-day, the press is not constituted to furnish from one edition to the next the amount of knowledge which the democratic theory of public opinion demands. This is not due to the Brass Check, as the quality of news in radical papers shows, but to the fact that the press deals with a society in which the governing forces are so imperfectly recorded. The theory that the press can itself record those forces is false. It can normally record only what has been recorded for it by the working of institutions. Everything else is argument and opinion, and fluctuates with the vicissitudes, the self-consciousness, and the courage of the human mind.

If the press is not so universally wicked, nor so deeply conspiring, as Mr. Sinclair would have us believe, it is very much more frail than the democratic theory has as yet admitted. It is too frail to carry the whole burden of popular sovereignty, to supply spontaneously the truth which democrats hoped was inborn. And when we expect it to supply such a body of truth we employ a misleading standard of judgment. We misunderstand the limited nature of news, the illimitable complexity of society; we overestimate our own endurance, public spirit, and all-round competence. We suppose an appetite for uninteresting truths which is not discovered by any honest analysis of our own tastes.

If the newspapers, then, are to be charged with the duty of translating the whole public life of mankind, so that every adult can arrive at an opinion on every moot topic, they fail, they are bound to fail, in any future one can conceive they will continue to fail. It is not possible to assume that a world, carried on by division of labor and distribution of authority, can be governed by universal opinions in the whole population. Unconsciously the theory sets up the single reader as theoretically omnicompetent, and puts upon the press the burden of accomplishing whatever representative government, industrial organization, and diplomacy have failed to accomplish. Acting upon everybody for thirty minutes in twenty-four hours, the press is asked to create a mystical force called Public Opinion that will take up the slack in public institutions. The press has often mistakenly pretended that it could do just that. It has at great moral cost to itself, encouraged a democracy, still bound to its original premises, to expect newspapers to supply spontaneously for every organ of government, for every social problem, the machinery of information which these do not normally supply themselves. Institutions, having failed to furnish themselves with instruments of knowledge, have become a bundle of "problems," which the population as a whole, reading the press as a whole, is supposed to solve.

The press, in other words, has come to be regarded as an organ of direct democracy, charged on a much wider scale, and from day to day, with the function often attributed to the initiative, referendum, and recall. The Court of Public Opinion, open day and night, is to lay down the law for everything all the time. It is not workable. And when you consider the nature of news, it is not even thinkable. For the news, as we have seen, is precise in proportion to the precision with which the event is recorded. Unless the event is capable of being named, measured, given shape, made specific, it either fails to take on the character of news, or it is subject to the accidents and prejudices of observation.

Therefore, on the whole, the quality of the news about modern society is an index of its social organization. The better the institutions, the more all interests concerned are formally represented, the more issues are disentangled, the more objective criteria are introduced, the more perfectly an affair can be presented as news. At its best the press is a servant and guardian of institutions; at its worst it is a means by which a few exploit social disorganization to their own ends. In the degree to which institutions fail to function, the unscrupulous journalist can fish in troubled waters, and the conscientious one must gamble with uncertainties.

The press is no substitute for institutions. It is like the beam of a searchlight that moves restlessly about, bringing one episode and then another out of darkness into vision. Men cannot do the work of the world by this light alone. They cannot govern society by episodes, incidents, and eruptions. It is only when they work by a steady light of their own, that the press, when it is turned upon them, reveals a situation intelligible enough for a popular decision. The trouble lies deeper than the press, and so does the remedy. It lies in social organization based on a system of analysis and record, and in all the corollaries of that principle; in the abandonment of the theory of the omnicompetent citizen, in the decentralization of decision, in the coördination of decision by comparable record and analysis. If at the centers of management there is a running audit, which makes work intelligible to those who do it, and those who superintend it, issues when they arise are not the mere collisions of the blind. Then, too, the news is uncovered for the press by a system of intelligence that is also a check upon the press.

That is the radical way. For the troubles of the press, like the troubles of representative government, be it territorial or functional, like the troubles of industry, be it capitalist, coöperative, or communist, go back to a common source: to the failure of self-governing people to transcend their casual experience and their prejudice, by inventing, creating, and organizing a machinery of knowledge. It is because they are compelled to act without a reliable picture of the world, that governments, schools, newspapers and churches make such small headway against the more obvious failings of democracy, against violent prejudice, apathy, preference for the curious trivial as against the dull important, and the hunger for sideshows and three legged calves. This is the primary defect of popular government, a defect inherent in its traditions, and all its other defects can, I believe, be traced to this one.

NOTE

1. When I wrote *Liberty and the News*, I did not understand this distinction clearly enough to state it, but *cf.* p. 89 ff.

13
EYEWITNESS TO HISTORY
John Carey

Before editing a book of reportage you need to decide what reportage is, and how you tell the good from the bad. I decided early on that for my purposes reportage must be written by an eye witness, and I have stuck to this most of the time, though occasionally I have let in a piece that is not eye witness itself but based on eye-witness accounts. An example is William of Newburgh's story about two green children who landed on earth out of some other dimension in the middle of the twelfth century. This, like other exceptions to the eye-witness rule, seemed too good to miss, and must surely be based on facts of some sort, however garbled.

One advantage of insisting on eye-witness evidence is that it makes for authenticity. All knowledge of the past which is not just supposition derives ultimately from people who can say "I was there", as the assortment of chance bystanders, travellers, warriors, murderers, victims, and professional reporters I assemble here can. Another advantage is stylistic. Eye-witness accounts have the feel of truth because they are quick, subjective and incomplete, unlike "objective" or reconstituted history, which is laborious but dead.

For the sake of sharp focus I also decided to prefer accounts of happenings that could be dated exactly—day, month, year. Sometimes in the earlier and less time-conscious

---

John Carey, "Introduction," *Eyewitness to History* (Cambridge, Mass.: Harvard University Press, 1987), xxix–xxxviii. © John Carey; reprinted with the kind permission of the author.

eras this requirement had to be waived. Even in later periods I have let in the odd piece which—like W. H. Hudson's memories of a Norfolk-coast holiday—is vague as to date but precise in other ways. However, the general rule about dating holds. The reporter is a private eye working in a public area, and the subject of his report must not be inward or fanciful, but pinned verifiably to the clockface of world time.

That does not mean reportage has to be about "important" happenings. I had to choose, at the start, between a principle of selection that would put a premium on subject matter (is this event of major historical interest?), and one that would be concerned primarily with the qualities of writing and observation displayed. I chose the second, on the grounds that nothing is important—or unimportant—except as it is perceived.

Of course, a lot of the pieces selected are nevertheless about big historical events, because those are the kind people feel incited to record if they are around when they occur. But—to give an instance of the other kind—one of the pieces I should have defended most stubbornly if anyone had suggested leaving it out is Joe Ackerley's diary entry about going rabbiting with a small boy one afternoon. Obviously this is trivial in a sense. But because it tells how one young male began to be acclimatized to killing, it is also momentous—the loss of innocence observed through Ackerley's fastidious lens— and it is germane to all the massacres and atrocities this book logs.

Some definitions of reportage insist it should have been written in the heat of the moment, reflecting the rush and compression and ignorance of what is going to happen next that all reporters have to put up with. There are plenty of these on-the-spot pieces in this collection, and some gain power from the spot they are on—like Samuel Wilkeson's Gettysburg despatch, penned beside the dead body of his son. But to include only instant-response stories seemed too cramping. Rushed reportage can carry the tang of crisis, but it can also be just rushed. So I have drawn as well on autobiographies and travel books, often written long after the event; and when reporters like Richard Harding Davis or Webb Miller have left two accounts of an incident, one in newspaper columns, the other in their memoirs, I have sometimes chosen the later, more worked-at version.

What makes good reportage good? We get some help in answering this from Stendhal's account, in *La Chartreuse de Parme*, of Fabrizio's experiences at Waterloo. Fabrizio is an innocent. He has never been in a battle before. The chaos bewilders him, and since he has no idea what he is supposed to be doing, he simply goes through the same motions as those around him, his mind filled meanwhile with romantic imaginings about Marshal Ney, whom he catches sight of riding by with his escort:

> Suddenly they all moved off at full gallop. A few minutes later Fabrizio saw, twenty paces ahead of him, a piece of tilled land that was being ploughed up in a singular fashion. The bottoms of the furrows were full of water, and the very damp soil that formed the ridges of these furrows was flying about in little black lumps flung three or four feet into the air. Fabrizio noted this curious effect as he was passing; then his mind turned to dreaming of the Marshal and his glory. He heard a sharp cry close by him; it was two hussars falling struck by shot; and when he looked round at them they were already twenty paces behind the escort.
>
> "Ah! so I am under fire at last," he said to himself. "I have seen the firing!" he repeated with a sense of satisfaction. "Now I am a real soldier." At that moment the escort began to go at a tearing pace, and our hero realized that it was shot from the guns that was making the earth fly up all around him.

Stendhal here manages to avoid the usual relations between language and reality. He shows us what Fabrizio actually sees (little black lumps flying in the air), and only afterwards supplies the coded linguistic formula for it ("I am under fire") so that both we and Fabrizio are rather surprised to find that is what was happening. By this means he reminds us how removed from the actual such linguistic formulae are. Fabrizio repeats the formula to himself with satisfaction, because it is language's way of ascribing merit to what he has been through. But it is also language's way of receiving it into the huge collection of known quantities and dead experiences, rubbed smooth and featureless by persistent use, which makes up most everyday discourse.

The power of language to confront us with the vivid, the frightening or the unaccustomed is equalled only by its opposite—the power of language to muffle any such alarms. Either power is available for language-users, but bad reportage opts firmly for the second. Anyone compiling an anthology of this kind will have to trudge through, for example, hundreds of pages of battle accounts filled with sentences like "Our horse inflicted severe punishment on the enemy's right flank" or "Four brigade did tremendous execution with the bayonet"—circumlocutions that, with their bizarre use of singulars for plurals, and their scrupulous exclusion of any mention of killing, are designed to neutralize and conceal experiences the writers felt were too terrible or too unseemly or too prejudicial to the future of good order and military discipline to record directly. Such euphemisms illustrate one major function of language, which is to keep reality at bay.

A distinguishing feature of good reportage is that it combats this inevitable and planned retreat of language from the real. However good it is, good reportage cannot, of course, get beyond language, because it is language itself. It is an axiom of modern critical theory that there are no accessible "realities", only texts that relate to one another intertextually. But even if he believes this, the good reporter must do everything in his power to counteract it, struggling to isolate the singularities that will make his account real for his readers—not just something written, but something seen.

This book is (and is meant to be) full of unusual or indecorous or incidental images that imprint themselves scaldingly on the mind's eye: the ambassador peering down the front of Queen Elizabeth I's dress and noting the wrinkles; Joe Louis's nostrils like a double-barrelled shotgun; Mata Hari drawing on her filmy stockings on the morning of her execution; the Tamil looter at the fall of Kuala Lumpur upending a carton of snowy Slazenger tennis balls; Richard Hillary closing one eye to see his lips like motor tyres; the men at Gallipoli crying because they were dirty; the unsheathed steel at Balaclava like "the turn of a shoal of mackerel"; the assassin Booth catching his boot-heel in the drapery round Lincoln's box; Pliny watching people with cushions on their heads against the ash from the volcano; Mary, Queen of Scots, suddenly aged in death, with her pet dog cowering among her skirts and her head held on by one recalcitrant piece of gristle; the starving Irish with their mouths green from their diet of grass.

It is history these accounts offer, but history deprived of generalizations. The writers are strangers to omniscience. The varnish of interpretation has been removed so we can see people clearly, as they originally were—gazing incredulously at what was, for that moment, the newest thing that had ever happened to them.

To achieve this effect the good reporter's report must be individual. It must restore to his experience the uniqueness it rightly possesses—and which worn-out language tries to rob it of. Nietzsche argued that language was originally developed to shield mankind from the inconceivable welter of pre-linguistic reality in which everything—every tree, stone and breath of wind—was unique. To simplify this mind-jamming variety, language supplied category words—stone, tree, wind—which allowed man to generalize. Though this brought gains, it also entailed losses, because the individuality each creature actually possesses is now hidden beneath the grey blanket of words.

The good reporter must resist this, and resist language's—and reportage's—daily slide into sameness. The results of the slide are portrayed in Michael Frayn's *The Tin Men*. Frayn's novel describes a research institute where a computer is being programmed to produce daily newspapers which will have all the variety and news-sense of the genuine article, but will bear no relation to events that have actually happened. The computer's programmers have organized mass surveys to discover what news stories people like best, how often they want them to recur, and which details they would like included. Should there be an air-crash story every month, or more frequently? Is it preferred, or not, that children's toys should be found lying pathetically among the wreckage? If a murder is reported, should the victim be, preferably, a small girl, an old lady, or an illegitimately pregnant young woman, and should the corpse be naked or clad in underclothes? When the computer has collected and analysed these reader requirements, it will be able to turn out popular daily papers indefinitely without the preliminary bother and expense of actually gathering any news.

Frayn's satire highlights the reporter's difficulty. Massive accumulations of standardized language and hackneyed story-lines lie in wait, ready to leap from his fingers to the typing paper. In a sense this is any writer's problem, but it is worse for the reporter, because he must stay true to the real, yet constantly defamiliarize it. He must see it, and tell it, as if for the first time.

This raises another difficulty. The good reporter must cultivate the innocent eye, but he must not be innocent. What innocence would be like at reporting, we can judge from Tolstoy's description, in *War and Peace*, of Natasha's reaction when, for the first time in her life, she is taken to an opera, and feels ashamed to be present at anything so absurd:

> Smooth boards formed the centre of the stage, at the side stood painted canvases representing trees, and in the background was a cloth stretched over boards. In the middle of the stage sat some girls in red bodices and white petticoats. One extremely fat girl in a white silk dress was sitting apart on a low bench, to the back of which a piece of green cardboard was glued. They were all singing something. When they had finished their chorus the girl in white advanced towards the prompter's box, and a man with stout legs encased in silk tights, a plume in his cap and a dagger at his waist, went up to her and began to sing and wave his arms about.

The good reporter must have something of Natasha's devastating literalism, and must see, like her, what is there, not what is meant to be. But her account would obviously not do as an opera review. She is ignorant, and the reporter cannot be. It is his job to know. He must be Experience simulating Innocence—as Tolstoy was when he put together Natasha's mind.

Why do we need reportage? It is clear we do, for hundreds of thousands of words of it are produced daily to glut the world's appetite. yet this is a comparatively recent development, made possible only by technology and mass literacy. The crucial innovations were the education acts of the late nineteenth century, and the electric telegraph, which was first used by American reporters during the Civil War. When they came to Europe to cover the Franco-Prussian war, they telegraphed battle stories to their papers back home, and British popular papers quickly followed suit.

In September 1870 William Howard Russell, the veteran reporter of the Crimea, travelled in person from the battlefield of Sedan to Printing House Square, writing all night, to get his dramatic story of the slaughter ready for *The Times*. But other London papers, using the telegraph, had printed news of the German victory two days earlier. In the years that followed, the results of this advance were consumed by the new mass readership in ever increasing quantities. Between 1880 and 1900, the number of newspapers doubled.

Arguably the advent of mass communications represents the greatest change in human consciousness that has taken place in recorded history. The development, within a few decades, from a situation where most of the inhabitants of the globe would have no day-to-day knowledge of or curiosity about how most of the others were faring, to a situation where the ordinary person's mental space is filled (and must be refilled daily or hourly, unless a feeling of disorientation is to ensue) with accurate reports about the doings of complete strangers, represents a revolution in mental activity which is incalculable in its effects.

To early-modern man the current situation would have been incomprehensible. Ben Jonson's play *The Staple of News* (acted around 1626) turns on the self-evident absurdity of news-gathering as an activity. History has not supported Jonson's judgement. It is hard for communication-age man to imagine what pre-communication-age man found to think about. But if we ask what took the place of reportage in the ages before it was made available to its millions of consumers, the likeliest answer seems to be religion.

Not, of course, that we should assume pre-communication-age man was deeply religious, in the main. There is plenty of evidence to suggest he was not. But religion was the permanent backdrop to his existence, as reportage is for his modern counterpart. Reportage supplies modern man with a constant and reassuring sense of events going on beyond his immediate horizon (reassuring even, or particularly, when the events themselves are terrible, since they then contrast more comfortingly with the reader's supposed safety). Reportage provides modern man, too, with a release from his trivial routines, and a habitual daily illusion of communication with a reality greater than himself. In all these ways religion suggests itself as the likeliest substitute pre-modern man could have found for reportage, at any rate in the West.

When we view reportage as the natural successor to religion, it helps us to understand why it should be so profoundly taken up with the subject of death. Death, in its various forms of murder, massacre, accident, natural catastrophe, warfare, and so on, is the subject to which reportage naturally gravitates, and one difficulty, in compiling an anthology of this kind, is to stop it becoming just a string of slaughters. Religion has traditionally been mankind's answer to death, allowing him to believe in various kinds of permanency which make his own extinction more tolerable, or even banish his fear of it altogether. The Christian belief in personal immortality is an obvious and extreme example of this. Reportage, taking religion's place, endlessly feeds its reader with accounts of the deaths of other people, and therefore places him continually in the position of a survivor—one who has escaped the violent and terrible ends which, it graphically apprises him, others have come to. In this way reportage, like religion, gives the individual a comforting sense of his own immortality.

If reportage performs these various functions it clearly has a social value comparable to that which religion once had. Its "cultural" value, on the other hand, has generally been considered negligible—with certain favoured exceptions such as Mark Twain's *The Innocents Abroad*, which are allowed to be literature because their authors also wrote respectable literary books. The question of whether reportage is "literature" is not in itself interesting or even meaningful. "Literature", we now realize, is not an objectively ascertainable category to which certain works naturally belong, but rather a term used by institutions and establishments and other culture-controlling groups to dignify those texts to which, for whatever reasons, they wish to attach value. The question worth asking therefore is not whether reportage is literature, but why intellectuals and literary institutions have generally been so keen to deny it that status.

Resentment of the masses, who are regarded as reportage's audience, is plainly a factor in the development of this prejudice. The terms used to express it are often social in their implications. "High" culture is distinguished from the "vulgarity" said to characterize reportage. But the disparagement of reportage also reflects a wish to promote the imaginary above the real. Works of imagination are, it is maintained, inherently superior, and have a spiritual value absent from "journalism". The creative artist is in touch with truths higher than the actual, which give him exclusive entry into the soul of man.

Such convictions seem to represent a residue of magical thinking. The recourse to images of ascent which their adherents manifest, the emphasis on purity, the recoil from earthly contamination, and the tendency towards a belief in inspiration, all belong to the traditional ambience of priesthoods and mystery cults. Those who hold such views about literature are likely, also, to resent critical attempts to relate authors' works to their lives. The biographical approach, it is argued, debases literature by tying it to mere reality: we should release texts from their authors, and contemplate them pure and disembodied, or at any rate only in the company of other equally pure and disembodied texts.

The superstitions that lie behind such dictates are interesting as primitive cultural vestiges, but it would be wrong to grant them serious attention as arguments. The advantages of reportage over imaginative literature, are, on the other hand, clear. Imaginative literature habitually depends for its effect on a "willing suspension of disbelief" in audience or reader, and this necessarily entails an element of game or collusion or self-deception. Reportage, by contrast, lays claim directly to the power of the real, which imaginative literature can approach only through make-believe.

It would be foolish, of course, to belittle imaginative literature on this score. The fact that it is not real—that its griefs, loves and deaths are all a pretence, is one reason why it can sustain us. It is a dream from which we can awake when we wish, and so it gives us, among the obstinate urgencies of real life, a precious illusion of freedom. It allows us to use for pleasure passions and sympathies (anger, fear, pity, etc.), which in normal circumstances would arise only in situations of pain or distress. In this way it frees and extends our emotional life. It seems probable that much—or most—reportage is read as if it were fiction by a majority of its readers. Its panics and disasters do not affect them as real, but as belonging to a shadow world distinct from their own concerns, and without their pressing actuality. Because of this, reportage has been able to take the place of imaginative literature in the lives of most people. They read newspapers rather than books, and newspapers which might just as well be fictional, as Frayn's are.

However enjoyable this is, it represents, of course, a flight from the real, as does imaginative literature, and good reportage is designed to make that flight impossible. It exiles us from fiction into the sharp terrain of truth. All the great realistic novelists of the nineteenth century—Balzac, Dickens, Tolstoy, Zola—drew on the techniques of reportage, and even built eye-witness accounts and newspaper stories into their fictions, so as to give them heightened realism. But the goal they struggled towards always lay beyond their reach. They could produce, at best, only imitation reportage, lacking the absolutely vital ingredient of reportage which is the simple fact that the reader knows all this actually happened.

When we read (to choose the most glaring example) accounts of the Holocaust by survivors and onlookers, some of which I have included in this book, we cannot comfort ourselves (as we can when distressed by accounts of suffering in realistic novels) by reminding ourselves that they are, after all, just stories. The facts presented demand our recognition, and require us to respond, though we do not know how to. We read the details—the Jews by the mass grave waiting to be shot; the father comforting his son and pointing to the sky; the grandmother amusing the baby—and we are possessed by our own inadequacy, by a ridiculous desire to help, by pity which is unappeasable and useless.

Or not quite useless, perhaps. For at this level (so one would like to hope) reportage may change its readers, may educate their sympathies, may extend—in both directions —their ideas about what it is to be a human being, may limit their capacity for the inhuman. These gains have traditionally been claimed for imaginative literature. But since reportage, unlike literature, lifts the screen from reality, its lessons are—and ought to be—more telling; and since it reaches millions untouched by literature, it has an incalculably greater potential. . . .

14

ON THE EPISTEMOLOGY OF INVESTIGATIVE JOURNALISM

James S. Ettema
Theodore L. Glasser

In contrast to "muckraking," a term still used pejoratively to underscore the shady side of journalism, "investigative reporting" enjoys an unmistakably honorable connotation. At least since Bernstein and Woodward (1974) chronicled their now legendary efforts to expose corruption in the Nixon White House, investigative reporting has come to mean journalism of the highest order. Even when it falls short of its ideals, investigative reporting evokes the respect of journalists themselves because it signifies a special enterprise, an extraordinary confluence of time, talent, and resources.

While some data and considerable commentary exist on the status of investigative reporting (Dygert, 1976; Downie, 1976; Behrens, 1977), and while several text books endeavor to explain how reporters "do" investigative reporting (Anderson & Benjaminson, 1976; Williams, 1978; Bolch & Miller, 1978; Wier & Noyes, 1981; Ullmann & Honeyman, 1983), little has been done to examine what is really distinctive about the "best" journalists doing the "best" journalism. In an effort to develop an appreciation for the peculiarities of investigative journalism, this study focuses on how reporters accomplish the fundamental and very practical task of knowing what they know. Our objective is twofold: (i) to review how daily reporters know what they know, and (ii) to contrast that with what we have learned about how investigative reporters accomplish that task. Ultimately, our goal is to contribute to a discussion that began in earnest nearly a half century ago when journalist-turned-sociologist Robert Park (1940) assessed news as a form of knowledge.

What we intend here is an aspect of the sociology of knowledge: a "sociology of epistemology." By sociology of *epistemology* we mean to limit ourselves to a study of how journalists know what they know.[1] And by *sociology* of epistemology we mean to differentiate between a philosophical examination of epistemology, for which we disclaim any pretension, and a phenomological examination of epistemology. Our study thus focuses on what journalists themselves regard as acceptable knowledge claims; it is not an effort to determine whether those knowledge claims are, in fact, valid.

We begin our pursuit of what qualifies as knowledge in the investigative journalism setting with several fundamental definitions and distinctions. Philosophers ordinarily define knowledge as a "justified true belief," where both the truth of the belief as well as its proper justification are regarded as the necessary conditions of knowledge (O'Connor

James S. Ettema and Theodore L. Glasser, "On the Epistemology of Investigative Journalism," *Communication*, Vol. 8, No. 2, 1985, 183–206. Reprinted with the permission of the authors and the publisher, the Institute for Communications Research, the University of Illinois.

and Carr, 1982). To justify a belief required that we identify the grounds for it—that is, the evidence in support of it and the reasons for accepting that evidence. It is important to understand that a true belief may not be justified—it may be, for example, just a lucky guess; and, conversely, a justified belief may not be true. In many practical matters, however, justification is very often the more useful criterion for judging beliefs because verification may be impractical or undesirable even if possible.[2] As Lewis (1946:255– 257) points out, whether a belief can be defended as "rationally credible" is repeatedly a more important issue than whether it has been (or can be) verified. Recognizing this, rhetoricians concerned with the role of argument in practical judgment insist upon standards of justification, not verification, when assessing the quality of an argument (McKerrow, 1977). Phenomologists, of course, also bypass the obdurate question of "genuine" knowledge and focus instead on the whatever passes for "knowledge" in a particular setting, "regardless of the ultimate validity or invalidity (by whatever criteria) of such 'knowledge' " (Berger and Luckman, 1966:3). Their concern is, then, the practical, everyday justification of beliefs.

Our inquiry presupposes no absolute or objective standard of justification; a justified belief is nothing more or less than belief "that has been shown to be legitimate within a context of justification" (Lyune, 1981:148). We expect, therefore, the justification of journalists' knowledge claims to depend upon—and vary according to—the context within which journalists operate. In the remainder of this article we seek to understand what journalists in two different contexts do to create well founded, "rationally credible"— that is to say, justified—stories. We begin with an examination of the context of the daily reporter as that context might reasonably be inferred from the work of Fishman (1980; 1982), Tuchman (1973; 1978), Gans (1979), Sigal (1973) and others. This context serves as a point of comparison for that of the investigative reporter.

THE CONTEXT OF JUSTIFICATION FOR THE DAILY REPORTER: A REVIEW

Although both daily reporters and investigative reporters concern themselves with "hard" news, the characteristics of hard news are very different in the daily reporting and investigative reporting settings. As Tuchman (1973:117) found in her study in the routines of reporting, journalists organize themselves differently and allocate resources differently as they move from one kind of story to another; they "typify"[3] the work they do "along dimensions that reflect practical tasks associated with their work." The hard news produced by the daily reporter tends to be more time-bound than the hard news produced by the investigative reporter, and the daily reporter is not able to utilize as many organizational resources as his or her investigative counterpart. Thus, the hard news of the two reporters are likely to be distinguished by the rigors of inquiry to which each is subjected.

But do the rigors of investigative journalism yield knowledge claims unlike the knowledge claims of daily journalism? Are the methods of investigative reporting a substantial departure from what Phillips (1977) describes as the primitive empiricism of daily reporting? The answer to the question of whether, in fact, daily and investigative reporters employ distinctive epistemologies must begin with an appreciation of what Fishman (1980:27–44) portrays as the principal objective of daily journalism: the beat system.

Fishman (1980:28) defines daily journalism's beat system as "a complex object of reporting consisting of a domain of activities occurring outside the newsroom." As a resource for "routinizing the unexpected," to borrow one of Tuchman's phrases, the beat system is essentially an organizing tool: it establishes a rationale for allocating editorial personnel and, by so doing, it identifies the most appropriate—and by inference, the least appropriate—sources of information (Sigal, 1973; Tuchman, 1973; Fishman, 1980). At least among American daily newspapers, the beat system flourishes as the dominant mode of news coverage. "The beat system of news coverage is so widespread among established newspapers," Fishman argues, "that not using beats is a distinctive feature of being an experimental, alternative, or underground newspaper" (27).

In concept, beats fall into one of two broadly distinguishable categories: *locational*, such as city hall, the police department, and the courts, or *substantive*, such as law, medicine, and education (Gans, 1979:144). In practice, however, virtually all beats are locational, since only locations can offer daily reporters what they need most: "a steady stream of timely information" (Roshco, 1975:64). To be sure, these locations account for the spatial pattern to which Tuchman (1978) applies her "news net" metaphor:

> There is a significant difference between the capacity of a blanket and that of a net to gather fodder for daily newspaper columns and television air time. Each arrangement may capture fresh information daily, thus confirming and reinforcing the old adage "old news is no news." (News grows stale like bread and cakes; it is a depletable consumer item.) But a net has holes. Its haul is dependent upon the amount invested in intersecting fiber and the tensile strength of that fiber. The narrower the intersections between the mesh—the more blanket-like the net—the more can be captured (21).

Daily reporters not only know where information can be found, as the news net metaphor suggests, but they know when to find it. The spatial pattern of the dispersion of reporters, Tuchman (1978:41–42) found, is augmented by the tempo or rhythm of the newsroom: "Just as reporters seek central spatial locations to find potential news events, so, too, reporters are temporally concentrated." Thus the production of news, particularly as news is produced on a daily basis, becomes spatially and temporally synchronized with the very beats to which reporters are assigned.

A well developed system of beats, then, is a remarkably efficient method for deploying personnel and gathering information: if reporters cannot know what will be news each day, they can at least know where and when to find it. As a practical matter, beats are efficient to the degree they can accommodate the exigencies of news by establishing standards for the selection of sources. Put another way, the efficiency of the beat system rests on its capacity to circumscribe *how* reporters will know what they know, an achievement inextricably wedded to *what* journalists will know. Sigal (1973:46) sums it up well: what journalists "know depends to a considerable extent on whom they know, which, in turn, depends on where they are."

For daily reporters, the empirical beliefs or propositions they glean from the beats they cover are ordinarily accepted at face value. As a practical matter, the scheduling characteristics of hard news—at least the hard news with which daily reporters must contend—leave reporters little time for verification. And as a matter of principle, the very idea of verification often implies conduct inimical to the canons of objective reporting

(Tuchman, 1972; Roshco, 1975).[4] Accordingly, daily reporters strive for accuracy, not veracity: they will report propositions "fairly" and "accurately" but they will neither assess nor attest to the veracity of what is reported.

If the veracity of a proposition does not justify its publication, what standards of justification do daily reporters use? Following Fishman (1980), who provides a detailed and insightful examination of the news production process, the justification for a proposition is established by the very bureaucracy through which it appears:

> Information which is bureaucractically organized, produced, and provided is hard fact; it is the stuff that makes up straight reporting. Any other kind of information . . . does not have the character of hard fact; it is stuff that makes up interpretive reports or news analysis (92).

Fishman offers two mutually auxiliary explanations for the acceptance these bureaucratic accounts find among daily reporters. One explanation focuses on what Fishman describes as the "socially sanctioned character of the bureaucrats' competence to know" (94–95); the other focuses on the performative character of bureaucratic documents and preceedings (95–100).

At least within the domain of their bureaucracy, bureaucrats appear to the daily reporter as self-evidently competent knowers. The daily reporter not only views bureaucrats "as having a special vantage point from which they can observe events" (Fishman, 1980:95), but the daily reporter also views bureaucrats as socially and politically "authorized" to know what they know. Moreover, bureaucrats are authorized to know what they know by virtue of their status or position in society, which no doubt enhances their appeal as "efficient" sources of information; "it always remains easier," Gouldner (1976:122–123) reminds us, "to publish accounts consonant with those offered by the managers of social institutions—accounts which thereby reinforce conventional definitions of social reality and the existent system of stratification."

Bureaucratic proceedings (e.g., a city council meeting) and bureaucratic documents (e.g., a deed) are similarly credible, due in large part to their "performative" nature. Following J. L. Austin (1961, 1962, 1971), Fishman defines performatives as utterances that "do something rather than merely say something"; performatives, it follows, "cannot be true or false because they are things in themselves and not statements about things" (1980:96–97). For the daily reporter, therefore, a bureaucratic account of something *becomes* something—just as "a lease *is* the leasing of property" or "an insurance policy *is* the insuring of valuables" (98).[5]

Bureaucratically credible accounts thus find acceptance among daily reporters not only because journalists ordinarily "participate in upholding a normative order of authorized knowers in the society," but because to treat bureaucratic accounts as factual "is also a position of convenience" (Fishman, 1980:96). Daily reporters are therefore predisposed to accept bureaucratic accounts largely because the very organization and structure of newswork define bureaucracies—especially established public bureaucracies —as "the appropriate site at which information should be gathered" (Tuchman, 1978:210); these are the very beats to which daily reporters are assigned.

The beat system is as efficient as it is, therefore, because it offers the daily reporter *pre-justified* accounts of "what is." The beat system not only reduces daily journalism to the coverage of mere appearances,[6] but it enables the reporter to operate within a context of justification that usually requires no independent analysis or evaluation of what passes as knowledge. Ultimately, this abiding faith in the authority of bureaucratically credible accounts allows the daily reporter to apply to the complex and ambiguous realm of public affairs the kind of empiricism Bernstein (1976:112) calls "objectivism": "a substantive orientation that believes that in the final analysis there is a realm of basic, uninterpreted, hard facts that serves as the foundation for all empirical knowledge."[7]

The daily reporter's enduring commitment to the supremacy of bureaucratically credible facts—indeed, the very ethic of objectivity—rests on the belief that news is something journalists are compelled to report, not something journalists are responsible for creating. That is, because news presumably exists "out there"—apparently independent of the reporter—journalists are typically reluctant to accept responsibility for the quality or value of what is reported. The ideology of objective reporting, in short, accounts for what may be fairly termed the amorality of daily journalism (cf. Glasser, 1984).

THE CONTEXT OF JUSTIFICATION FOR THE INVESTIGATIVE REPORTER: A CASE STUDY

The daily reporter's knowledge claims, as we have argued, are usually immediately credible due to the context in which they arise—the news net composed of bureaucratically credible sources. The claims need not, then, be justified by the daily reporter because they are pre-justified. The investigative reporter, however, may not be so epistemologically fortunate. Indeed, as we attempt to show in the case study which follows, the investigative reporter not only shoulders the burden of justification, but also creates a method for doing so.

In this case study we focus on a particular investigative reporting team, a unit within a network-affiliated, major market television station composed of two reporters, a researcher and several clerical workers and student interns. Under the supervision of the station's director of public affairs, who also supervises a documentary production unit, the investigative unit produces four to six stories a year using the mini-documentary format (i.e., five segments each of about five minutes, running on five consecutive nightly newcasts). The topical focus of the investigative stories is wrong-doing of various sorts, what Gans (1979:56–57) calls "moral disorder" news. Indeed, the unit has clearly articulated its investigatory charge in the form of a "manifesto," which each member can recite with only slight variation. Here is one reporter's version:

> The manifesto is, if I can remember it in its original language, "through standard and professional journalistic techniques to investigate and report (with the intention of gaining results) heretofore unknown facts regarding unsolved crime or political corruption which affects the community (and) which others seek to keep secret."

The format and the topical focus of the investigative unit distinguishes it from the documentary unit which produces hour-length programs on social issues, such as the rise of religious cults and the social status of children. The two units do, however, share a track record of outstanding broadcast journalism as recognized by a large number of regional and national citations including several du Pont/Columbia and Peabody awards.

Our method in the study of this investigative unit was the intensive interview. In these interviews we asked each of the members to outline the investigative process and to exemplify the process with one or two recent investigations. Members were asked to pay special attention to when in the course of an investigation they were required to decide whether or not information was true and to how they made that decision. In these interviews one reporter emerged as the most enthusiastic and articulate of the interviewees. This reporter is active in the Investigative Reporters and Editors (IRE) organization and had lobbied the station management for the formation of the investigative unit. Our study focuses on his thinking about this subject and thus attempts to interpret and appreciate the way in which one highly skilled and thoughtful practitioner makes sense of what he does. We do not seek, in other words, to merely describe the work of a random collection of news workers or a single typical worker but instead to learn from the ruminations of a master craftsman.

Justification as Process

While the knowledge claims of the daily reporter are pre-justified by the context in which they arise, the knowledge claims of the investigative reporter and his colleagues are not prejustified in this way. Indeed, their investigations into crime and corruption usually arise outside of the news net and may cite bureaucratically *in*credible sources. We find, however, that this investigative reporter has worked out for himself an elaborate process which justifies to himself and his colleagues the knowledge claims embodied in his stories. This process underscores the active stance of the investigative reporter, who must establish credibility, versus the passive stance of the daily reporter, who merely accepts credibility.

This process of justification is perhaps best conceptualized as a set of intellectual exercises which the reporter, often in concert with his colleagues, goes through at key points in the investigation. These are:

1. Screening the tips.
2. Weighing the evidence.
3. Fitting the pieces.
4. Evaluating the story.

These four points coincide with and reflect several of the steps identified by Bants *et al.* (1980) in the production of daily reportage by a local television station. What follows, however, are not descriptions of investigative production routines but rather of the phenomenology of those routines. They are attempts to describe how a reporter thinks through and characterizes tasks which confront him.

Screening the Tips

For this reporter and his colleagues stories often begin with tips. A story about the fraudulent sales tactics and shoddy work of a basement waterproofing firm, for example, began with a call from an unhappy customer. The firm's refusal to deal with the complaint lead to a brief story by the station's consumer affairs reporter which, in turn, generated a call from a former salesman for the firm who was willing to discuss the sales tactics. The researcher who is responsible for handling the unsolicited tips estimates that he handles about 25 such tips a week. Of these, he opens a file on one or two of them for further inspection by the unit's reporters.

The researcher and then a reporter screen the tips on several criteria and select those to be "pitched" to the entire unit at one of its regular meetings. Here is the reporter's description of the process.

> (You) get a phone call and someone lays out an incredible story for you on the phone. You have absolutely no substantiation for the story, but you may run in the next room and say, "Hey, just got a call and if this thing is right we've got September. Let's pitch it Monday morning at nine in the meantime, this weekend, I'll work to get some more stuff sourced out on this thing to see if it's real."
>
> By Monday you may find out it was not real, or you may find that it is real but impossible to do. You may find out that it's real, perfectly do-able, but will have no effect and doesn't matter to anyone whatsoever.
>
> There are a million things you could find out between your initial idea or the initial discussion and the point you pitch it. But generally you'd give it a week I guess. A week of work before you'd mention it to anyone in a formal way. What usually happens (then) is some table talk in the conference room in a staff meeting. You go around the table and say, "What are your ideas? What have you got?"

In "pitching" the story to his supervisor and colleagues the investigative reporter must be able to show that the tip can meet three criteria. The tip must be (1) "real", and (2) "do-able", as well as (3) promise to result in a story which has an "effect." In practice, meeting the criterion of "real" does not require proof that the story implied by the tip is, in fact, true but merely the display of some additional evidence to that effect. There are indeed "a million things" the report could do, but at this point he need do only enough to show his colleagues that the tip *could be* real. Meeting the criterion of "do-able" requires the display of some plan for collecting enough additional evidence to make a case for the truth of the implied story. The reporter must convince his colleagues that the tip could be *shown* to be real. Finally the criterion of "effect" is akin to the daily journalist's judgment of news value. The story must be not only "real" and "do-able" but promise to make a difference in the community. In this first justificatory exercise, then, the reporter seeks little verification of the tip and the story implied by it. Rather he seeks justification for continuing, for converting the tip into a full-fledged in vestigation.

Weighing the Evidence

The tips which meet these criteria to the satisfaction of the investigative reporter and his colleagues become active investigations. So begins the "legwork" of journalistic legend. Textbook authors have made much of this activity with chapters on the sifting through government records, conducting adversarial interviews and other such investigative tasks. For this investigative reporter, however, such tasks are certainly a good deal of work but not very intellectually problematic:

> There are some things that are just standard in the trade. . . . Paper, documents, signatures, recordings, anything that captures the fact, that certifies the fact. So, always the

first question I ask after some preliminary stuff is there any paper on this? . . . If there's not, I've got a lot more work to do. I would have to skip the paperwork and go directly to interviews.

This collection of evidence does follow a plan; the reporter, after the preliminary "table talk," must produce a "blue sheet" or plan confirming the "do-ability" of the investigation. The reporter, however, does not emphasize planfulness in his accounts of the collection of evidence. Indeed, he likens the collection of evidence to building "a mound."

The collected evidence, if not *dis*organized, is as yet *un*organized. However, each item of evidence collected together into the mound possesses a property which is critical to the completion of the next exercise in justification—an exercise which yields justification for accepting the evidence as *sufficient* even if unorganized. The critical property is that of weight:

> The heaviest evidence would be the act itself captured on videotape. The act itself. ABSCAM. Undeniably these people met with these other people and discussed bribes and money changed hands and went into the pocket. That's a big heavy piece of evidence. There's very little more you have to do to substantiate that the thing happened. You can put facts with it, like what time did it happen, what date did it happen, names of the participants, but the act itself happened. That would be what I would call the number one. Secondarily to that kind of video document would be a paper document that outlined the suspected act which was attested to by the parties involved.

The investigative reporter thus outlines a hierachy of evidence based on the notion of weight, a metaphor which, in turn, reflects the journalist's presumptions about its veracity. Highest in the hierachy are the artifacts produced in the course of the criminal or corrupt act; things which are accepted by the reporter as some aspect of the act itself. The heaviest evidence is a highly iconic representation of the act in the form of videotape. In the case of the waterproofing investigation the sales tactics were recorded by hidden cameras. Of somewhat less weight is "paper." In the waterproofing investigation this included training manuals outlining the tactics.

Lower in the hierarchy are the post-hoc accounts of the act. Accounts by "participatory witnesses," including confessions, are the heavier sort of account. In the waterproofing investigation these included the statements of the former salesmen. Of somewhat less weight are the accounts by the "non participatory witnesses." The statements of experts attesting to the shoddiness of the workmanship of the waterproofer is an example of this sort of evidence.

Below such accounts in the hierarchy is material which could best be described as pre-evidentiary—material which is not itself evidence but may lead to evidence. This includes hunches or "presumptions" as the reporter himself calls them. Of the least weight is the "anonymous phone call—as light as you can get."

Thus the investigative reporter's list of information to be gathered is distinguished from the daily reporter's list less by what is on it than by the hierarchical organization of the list based on "weight." For the daily reporter, weight is an irrelevant concept. When propositions originate in the news net and are embodied in bureaucratically credible "paper" and accounts, they are not more credible or less credible; they are credible—period! The daily reporter is always completely justified in citing such propositions. For the investigative reporter, however, weight is a critical concept because propositions often originate outside of the news net (indeed, they begin with the lowly hunch or phone call) and are embodied in the accounts of alleged criminals and other suspect accounts. The investigative reporter must himself provide justification for citing such propositions. "Heavier" evidence is more credible, more justifiable.

One other property of the evidence is central to the completion of this exercise in justification. This is whether the item of evidence tends to support the charges to be made in the story; whether the evidence is, in the words of the reporter, "inculpatory" or "exculpatory." Like the daily reporter, the investigative reporter feels he must faithfully seek "both sides." Unlike the daily reporter, however, the investigative reporter does not merely repeat both sides. Rather, the investigative reporter proceeds to *weigh* both sides and eventually comes to a judgment:

> It's simply the scales. You take inculpatory evidence and stack it up and you take the exculpatory evidence and stack it up and you have to be very truthful to yourself. You have to be as vigorous in seeking the exculpatory information as you are in seeking the suff that's damning. And once gathered, you watch the way it falls. And you say the preponderance of evidence is that this thing occurs in a damning way (but) sometimes there's perfect balance and your investigation continues. You keep going and going and going . . . It's simply the weight of the evidence.

Using the law as an intellectual resource, the reporter refers to this process of weighing evidence as the "preponderance test," the test used to decide the outcome of civil cases. The reporter uses legal metaphor and imagery often and here the image of the scales of justice is quite real to him. Indeed, he can precisely specify the psycho-physics of evidentiary weight:

> As you go down (the hierarchy of evidence) you need more of each . . . One non-participatory witness, one piece of material evidence, one document weighs as much as the videotape act.

It would be both an oversimplification and an exaggeration to suggest that all of the available evidence is collected and then weighed as would be the goal in a trial. Collecting and weighing evidence is an iterative process which in any particular investigation may be repeated many times. If in this weighing exercise, the scale tips decisively toward the exculpatory evidence or if, after much effort, the scale cannot be made to tip, the investigation is abandoned. If, however, the scale tips decisively toward the inculpatory evidence, the investigation finally becomes a story.

What remains elusive, to us, and apparently even to the reporter himself without recourse to examples from specific investigations, is the weight necessary to make the scale tip decisively. It is clear, however, that the reporter expects to find conflicting evidence. Indeed, he must honestly seek out such evidence. If, however, the preponderence —the weight—of evidence does tend to support the charges of wrong-doing, then the reporter is justified at last in making the investigation into a story.

Fitting the Pieces

The collected evidence must be assembled into a television news story. While the reporter *weighed the evidence* in the course of the investigation now he *fits the pieces* into a story. The reporter invokes the metaphor of the jigsaw picture puzzle and explains some of the ways in which pieces are assembled.

REPORTER: I use chronology. Number the pieces one through a thousand by date and time and put them together starting with piece one. What happens is often you don't have the full sequence. You have one, two, nine and fourteen, eighty-five and that helps you put it together because you or your boss says you really do need pieces seven and eight here in order to even get the full idea . . . So you go out and get seven and eight and put that together. Then you may have 85 through 100 over here which makes another separate picture within the picture itself. It's the mast and you can put that all together and . . . just move the section over the hull that I have already put in place. I think it fits about there. I group chronologically and try to build the piece from the very first piece of information I have going back as far as I can and bring it forward then it gives me a time perspective on how things happen . . .

QUESTIONER: What other rules for fitting can you give us?

REPORTER: What we call the interlocking directorate schematic. Most stories have them. Those are the relationships of the individuals to each other and to the events. The two together, the chronology and the interlocking directorate analogy gives you a pretty good understanding of who knew what when, who did what when, with whom . . . It is simply done by doing a flow chart or a bunch of boxes with lines.

It may be necessary to cycle through the collection of evidence and the weighing exercise again and again before the necessary pieces are present, but eventually the puzzle is complete—or at least complete enough to present a coherent and credible picture. This notion of interlocking pieces of a puzzle is, then, quite necessary to the process of justification because the fit of each piece enhances the credibility of each of the others and, in turn, the whole picture assembled from them (cf. Tuchman, 1978:82–103). Accepting the story as true is increasingly justified as more pieces fit and the story becomes more complete and coherent.

Fitting the pieces into a picture is a point at which the reporter explicitly acknowledges that he must convince his boss of the credibility of what he has discovered. It is also the point at which he expresses the greatest concern for the credibility of the story to the television news audience. He is concerned that the fit of the pieces—the coherence of the story—shine through the completed mini-documentary segments.

He also recognizes, however, that because of broadcast time constraints, only some of the completed puzzle can be shown to the audience:

Mike [the investigative unit's supervisor] takes a look at your completed puzzle and says what is the most definite aspect of this puzzle; what is the most interesting aspect of this puzzle. And now let's take [a frame] and lay it over different portions of your puzzle and see which one is best. We'll just take a frame and move it around until we find a picture that has the most detail and then we will reshape [the picture] maybe. Then we will take your puzzle and we will paint a picture from your puzzle. I like your island but it is not in the [frame]. Let's, in this picture, move the island a little closer. You have well established the island. Let's move it in right behind the boat.

The reporter does, then, recognize that when he and his colleagues produce the story for broadcast, they frame a picture within the larger puzzle which they have assembled. There is even an acknowledgment that the picture can be manipulated—the island can be moved—for best effect. There is, however, no hint that meaning is created, that reality is constructed. The meaning of the story—the pieces of the puzzle and the way each fits with the others—exists quite independently of the reporter and the picture he finally paints. Meaning is there to be discovered and assembled in the most credible way possible within the constraints of the mini-documentary television format.

Evaluating the Story

With the puzzle pieces found and assembled, the picture/story is subject to a final, sometimes dramatic, exercise in justification. The exercise begins by attempting to generate alternative explanations or additional exculpatory evidence which could disconfirm the story:

> You turn yourself into a defense attorney and we do that a lot . . . And it's a lot of fun. We take the facts and turn them around on ourselves. We take our techniques and turn them around on ourselves. We see how it plays. What can they say to disprove them. They'll say, "The guy's out-of-town"
> And I'll say, "Well, have you found out whether he was in town or not?"
> "I haven't."
> "Well, get on your horse and find out whether he was in town."

In this attempt to develop disconfirmatory material the reporter may subject the story to the "moral certainty test."

> I like some of the things that they go through in juries. You know, they struck moral certainty from jury instruction a long time ago because it was just too tough a test. Defense attorneys would say, "You have to be more convinced of this individual's guilt than you are convinced that there is a God." And people couldn't do it . . . We have to be morally certain that what we're saying is true.

A dramatic example of this test occurred in an investigation of a judge who was alledged to have paid children (i.e. underaged male prostitutes) for sex:

> Tuesday afternoon I made a phone call to one of the boys that was going to be on the air Thursday, and I said, "I'm coming out to get you."
> And he said "what for?"
> And I said, "I'll tell you later."
> Now I had lie detected these guys, I had them ID (the judge) out of six very difficult photographs of gray-haired, heavyweight, middle-aged men. I had them describe artifacts in the house (bronze and ducks, titles of books on the bedstead), draw maps of the house, and then compare it with people who have been in the house . . .
> I'm getting ready to go there in two days and accuse the judge of some pretty bad things. These kids are going to accuse him. I brought the kid in. It was 8:00 at night. I drove him to the station, and then I said, "take me to (the judge's) house."
> He said, "Why?"

I said, "I just want you to drive me to (the judge's) house. Do you know where it is?" I said, "you described it, that it's on (a particular street), that it's yellow, that you entered through the back door with a three-car garage. You've given me all that stuff. I want you to take me there."

He says, "OK." Drove right to the house. He's fifteen, the fifteen-year-old.

I said, "thanks," and I took him home.

In the course of the investigation of the judge, this witness' story had been corroborated by other boys. Further, this boy had been examined and cross-examined several times by the reporters to assess the internal consistency of his story. This late night ride to the judge's residence was, however, not merely one more cross-examination. Rather, it is best understood as an exercise in self persuasion—a final attempt to achieve moral certainty made imperative by a tip that the judge was contemplating suicide. This was, then, an attempt to justify the story simultaneously on both epistemological and moral grounds. The term "moral certainty" is, it turns out, very well chosen indeed for it captures the fundamental fusion of epistemological and ethical concerns which the investigative journalist must confront.

Justification and Equivocation

A justified story is, then, one in which the evidence is so "heavy" and the pieces "fit" so well that the reporter has become "morally certain" that he cannot disconfirm it. Despite this painstaking process, however, the reporter does not altogether abandon the rituals of balanced reporting, specifically, he still feels he must "cover the other side"—i.e., repeat the denial of the wrong-doer even though he is morally certain, presumably, that it is untrue:

QUESTIONER: Why did (the judge) have the right to defend himself on the air?

REPORTER: That's the American way. Balance . . . What I'm concerned about is whether I'm true to some real basic ethical considerations. That's just decency . . .

We do not doubt the sincerity of the reporter's decency rationale for the right of response for the accused, but we also find at least one other consideration in his insistence upon that right. While the reporter does not, of course, accept the denial itself as true, he does accept the existence of the denial as one sort of "conflicting fact"—a fact which does not fit well with all of the other puzzle pieces. Significantly, this conflict—this lack of fit—is sufficient to cause the reporter to equivocate about the truth of the story:

I can have a view of the truth but I'm one person. I can say, "my investigation, my finite abilities, my limited number of questions asked, my examination of the facts indicate to me that this is the truth." What I now have just rendered is an opinion . . . When you reach a conclusion in an investigation where you have conflicting fact, what you have arrived at, what you believe to be the truth, is an opinion.

Thus, even after the elaborate exercises reviewed here, the reporter is reluctant to claim that his story faithfully reproduces the truth as it exists "out there." The story is still only his opinion concerning that truth and he is obligated, therefore, to cite the opinion of the accused as well. There is in this feeling of obligation, we suspect, an intuitive sense of the distinction between justification and verification. The reporter has painstakingly developed the grounds, the good reasons, for accepting the story as true. He is, in our terms, willing to claim justification. And yet, in the face of conflicting facts such as the denial of the accused, the reporter wishes to stop short of saying that the story is more than opinion about the truth. The reporter, in other words, is reluctant to claim verification. There is too much at stake to claim certainty and abandon the strategies of objectivity.

THE PRODUCTION OF JUSTIFICATION: CONCLUSION

Whereas the objectivism of daily journalism rests on bureaucratically credible facts that are immediately and uncritically accepted as legitimate knowledge claims, the episte-mology of investigative journalism underscores what Schudson (1978:192) describes as the investigative reporter's "mature subjectivity," a subjectivity "aged by encounters with, and regard for, the facts of the world." Specifically, the knowledge claims of the investigative reporter studied here are firmly grounded in the process of screening tips, assembling and weighing evidence, fitting facts and attempting to disconfirm the result-ing story. In the end, these exercises yield a degree of "moral certainty" about the con-vergence of facts into a truthful report. Taken together these activities constitute what may be called the "production of justification," an achievement generally antithetical to the ideals of daily reporting.

The epistemology of the investigative journalist thus distinguishes itself from that of the daily journalist in three important ways. First, the investigative reporter accom-modates a variety of types of fact, including facts dismissed by the daily reporter as bureaucratically *in*credible. Second, the investigative reporter assesses the relative quality of facts, an essentially rational—even if imprecise—process from which facts emerge as more credible or less credible. And third, the investigative reporter seeks to justify the larger truth of the story, a truth often greater than the sum of the story's facts.

The investigative reporter is thus less burdened by—though not unmindful of—the routines of objective reporting. The reporter, however, has acquired a different, perhaps far heavier, burden: responsibility for the quality of the facts reported as well as a defense of the broader value judgments that effectively define the story's theme. Still, as Gans (1979:183) reminds us, this does not render investigative journalism—at least from the practitioner's perspective—biased or partial: the quintessential investigation—the expose—"typically judges the exposed against their own expressed values, and these can be determined empirically by the reporter; as a result, even his or her value judgment is considered objective."

Investigative reporting is, in short, unabashedly moralistic. It is also highly personalized—even idiosyncratic. The process of justification reviewed here is the creative achievement of a single individual acting in concert with a few colleagues. We fully expect to find other reporters with different backgrounds, interests and assignments to have created different solutions to the epistemological problems of their craft. What we offer here, then, is by no means a model of how, in general, investigative reporters *do* know what they know, but rather an illustration of how investigative reporters *can* come to know what they know. It illustrates what one textbook (Williams, 1978:xi) describes as the investigative reporter's "conscious aversion" to the accepted methods of daily reporting and the standard definitions of news. And, more positively, it illustrates how investigative reporters can—indeed must—move beyond objectivism to develop criteria for assessing the quality and value of what is reported, which in the end translates into a heightened sense of responsibility for the consequences of their conduct.

NOTES

This research was supported in part by The Graduate School of the University of Minnesota and the Gannett Foundation. An earlier version of this paper was presented to the Qualitative Studies Division of the Association for Education in Journalism and Mass Communication, Gainsville, Florida, August 1984.

1. Our task, then, is far less ambitious than the recent studies by Gans (1979), Tuchman (1978), Gitlin (1980), Fishman (1980), Roshco (1975), and others whose work takes a broad sweep across, as Gitlin (1980:15) puts it, "the nature, sources, and consequences of news."

2. From the "Correspondence theory" perspective, which is most sympathetic to journalistic objectivity, an empirical belief is either true or false, depending on whether its denotation or extension is actual or existent and ultimately testable by experience (Lewis, 1946:35–70). For example, to say "the stove is hot" expresses a belief independent of the proposition itself; it *denotes* a "hot stove." To verify the proposition—to determine, that is, whether it is true or false—requires that we experience the "hot stove." But to *justify* our belief by determining what, if any, *credible evidence* exists in support of the proposition "the stove is hot," we note, for instance, a kettle of boiling water and take that as evidence of a hot stove, *credible* evidence because experience has taught us that kettles of water boil on when stoves are hot. We have thus justified—not verified—an empirical belief.

3. By "typify" Tuchman means to underscore the importance of the distinction between "typification" and "category": "Category" denotes a "classification of objects according to one or more relevant characteristics ruled salient by the classifiers" but "typification" implies a phenomenological orientation, a classification in which relevant characteristics are central to the solution of practical tasks or problems at hand and are constituted and grounded in everyday activity" (1973:116–117).

4. Verification is especially problematic for journalists because it involves their own experiences. For no matter how reliable the journalist may be as an observer, when the journalist may be as an observer, when the journalist's observations or experiences conflict with the "official" pronouncements of a presumably authoritative source, the tenets of objective reporting require the journalist to disseminate only the source's version. Molotch and Lester (1975), in a case study of what is probably one of the most extreme examples of the ethic of objectivity interferring with verification, report that journalists could see and smell a beach polluted by a massive oil spill and yet proclaimed the beach clean because President Nixon arrived at the beach and announced that it had fully recovered from the oil spill.

5. The term "performative" is derived from "perform;" and "indicates that the issuing of the utterance is the performing of an action" (Austin, 1962:6). Performatives are especially prevalent in law—when, for example, a court declares a contract void or rules that a statute is unconstitutional. For an interesting examination of the importance of performatives in legal discourse, see Fletcher (1981).

6. As Gans (1967:323) found when he studied the nature of the news media's coverage of local government, reporters were inclined "to cover the performing rather than the actual government." Often ignorant of the intricacies of government, reporters' stories tended to be limited to the government's "decisions and the performances that accompany them."

7. It is the realm of daily public affairs reporting that the routines of objectivity are most widely and consistently practiced. The literature on daily public affairs reporting which we have reviewed here thus contributes to the definition of an ideal type of daily reporting—a conceptualization we have sought to distill in our description of the daily reportorial setting.

15

TUESDAY WAS A GOOD D-DAY FOR *LIFE*

John G. Morris

Something woke me early on the morning of Tuesday, June 6, 1944. I drew the blackout curtain and saw that it was just another dull, gray day, colder than an English spring had any right to be. The streets were empty, and I was alone in the flat I shared with Frank Scherschel on Upper Wimpole Street in London's West End. He had departed—vanished, actually, without saying a word—several days earlier for his battle station, a camouflaged airfield from which he would fly reconnaissance over the English Channel to photograph the largest armada ever assembled. My job was to stay behind, to edit those and other photos for *Life* as picture editor of the London bureau.

I dressed as usual in olive drab, turned on the radio, made tea and read the papers, which of course had nothing to report. Then, at 8:32 London time, the bulletin came over the BBC: "Under command of General Eisenhower, Allied naval forces, supported by strong Allied air forces, began landing Allied armies this morning on the northern coast of France." "This is it," I whispered to myself, uttering the very words that Joe Liebling of *The New Yorker* later called "the great cliché of the Second World War." I hurried to the *Time/Life* office in Soho, even though there wouldn't be much for me to do—for many hours, as it turned out.

I had been waiting eight months for this day. There had been a false alarm on Saturday, when a young telegrapher in the Associated Press London bureau, practicing to get up her speed, had put out an erroneous bulletin: URGENT PRESS ASSOCIATED NYK FLASH EISENHOWER'S HQ ANNOUNCED ALLIED LANDINGS IN FRANCE. It had been corrected within a minute—"Bust that flash"—but it had sent a wave of panic through both Allied and German headquarters. Now it was for real. Tuesday was a good D-Day for

---

John G. Morris, "Tuesday Was a Good D-Day for *Life*," *Get the Picture, a Personal History of Photojournalism* (New York: Random House, 1998), 3–9. © by John Godfrey Morris; reprinted by permission of Lescher & Lescher Ltd. All rights reserved.

Life. Our job was to furnish action pictures for the next issue, dated June 19, which would close on Saturday in New York, and appear the following week. Wirephotos, of poor quality and limited selection, would not do: besides, they would be available to newspapers through the pool. Our only hope to meet the deadline was to send original prints and negatives, as many as possible, in a pouch that would leave Grosvenor Square by motorcycle courier at precisely 9:00 A.M. London time on Thursday. The courier would take it to a twin-engine plane standing by at an airdrome near London. At Prestwick, Scotland, the base for transatlantic flights, the pouch would be transferred to a larger plane. After one or two fuel stops, it would arrive in Washington. D. C., and our pictures would be hand-carried to New York on Saturday.

I had rehearsed my part in every detail, from the moment the raw film arrived in London to the transfer of prints and negatives to the courier who would take them to the States—with a stop at the censor's office in between. Clearing the censors at the Ministry of Information was by now a familiar routine. Their office was on the ground floor of the University of London's tall central building, which backed onto Bedford Square. Available twenty-four hours a day, the censors were cooperative, as censors go, permitting us to sit alongside them as they worked. Our photographers knew to avoid the faces of Allied dead, shoulder patches that revealed unit designations, and "secret" weapons (although by now most were known to the enemy)—so the work was for the most part pro forma. But it was tedious in the extreme, since every single print had to be stamped, after which the censor bundled all the acceptable material into an envelope and sealed it, using a special tape imprinted with the words PASSED FOR PUBLICATION. Without the tape, it could not leave the country.

Getting the packet by car to the courier at Grosvenor Square, about a mile from the ministry, looked simple on the map, but the most direct way, down Oxford Street, was often jammed with double-decker buses, so I devised a parallel route on a series of side streets: Hollen to Noel to Great Marlborough to Hanover to Brook (I can remember every turn five decades later). This put me onto the wrong side of Grosvenor Square, but the final fifty yards could be covered on foot—while running at top speed. I left the little two-door Austin sedan Time Inc. had given me to its own fate. It was not uncommon for joyriders to take it out for a spin when I worked late, but that was no problem. A call to Scotland Yard was all that was necessary. The car would invariably be found as soon as the thief ran out of what little petrol was in the tank.

For the Normandy invasion, there were twelve photographers accredited for the wire services and six for *Life*. Only four press photographers were supposed to land with the first wave of American infantry on D-Day itself, and we managed to get two of the spots, for Bob Landry and Robert Capa. Both were veterans—Capa would be on the fifth front of his third major war. Although often unlucky at cards and horses, Capa nevertheless used a gambling metaphor to describe his situation on D-Day in his 1947 memoir-novel. *Slightly Out of Focus*: "The war correspondent has his stake—his life— in his own hands, and he can put it on this horse or that horse, or he can put it back in his pocket at the very last minute. . . . I am a gambler. I decided to go in with Company E in the first wave."

Bob Landry also felt obliged to accept this dubious privilege. The other *Life* assignments sorted themselves out. Frank Scherschel stuck with his buddies in the Air Force.

David Scherman chose the Navy. George Rodger accompanied the British forces, under General Bernard Montgomery. Ralph Morse's assignment was General George Patton's Third Army, but since it would not hit the beachhead until later, he boarded a landing ship whose job it was to pick up casualties—of which there would be plenty.

Who would get the first picture? Bad weather prevented good general views from either air (Scherschel) or sea (Scherman). Rodger, landing with the British on an undefended beach, "walked ashore in a blaze of anti-climax," as he put it in typically modest understatement. All day Tuesday we waited, and no pictures. It was rumored that one Signal Corps photographer had been killed in the first hours, but it turned out that he had "only" lost a leg. Late on Tuesday night Bert Brandt of Acme Newspictures, having scarcely gotten his feet wet, returned to London with a *first picture!*, but not a terribly exciting one, of a momentarily unopposed landing on the French coast, shot from the bow of his landing craft. Landry's film—and his shoes—somehow got lost. A disaster. I had been told that AP would have the fourth first-wave spot, but not one of their six photographers landed that day. So it was entirely up to Capa to capture the action, and *where was he?* Hour after hour went by. We were now waiting in the gloom of Wednesday, June 7, keeping busy by packaging the "background pictures," all of relatively little interest, that now flooded in from official sources. The darkroom staff—all five of them—had been standing by idly since Tuesday morning, their anxiety about the pressure they would be under growing steadily by the hour. This nervousness would soon result in an epic blunder.

At about 6:30 Wednesday evening, the call came in from a Channel port: Capa's film was on the way. "You should get it in an hour or two," a voice crackled over the line before fading into static. I shared this information with pool editor E. K. Butler of AP, a feisty little martinet whose nickname was "Colonel." He snapped back, "All I want is *pictures*, not promises!" Around nine, a panting messenger arrived with Capa's little package: four rolls of 35-millimeter film plus half a dozen rolls of 120 film ($2^1/_4$ by $2^1/_4$ inches) that he had taken in England and on the Channel crossing. A scrawled note said that the action was all in the 35-millimeter, that things had been very rough, that he had come back to England unintentionally with wounded being evacuated, and that he was on his way back to Normandy.

Braddy, our lab chief, gave the film to young Dennis Banks to develop. Photographer Hans Wild looked at it wet and called up to me to say that the 35-millimeter, though grainy, looked "fabulous!" I replied, "We need *contacts*—rush rush, *rush!*" Again I phoned Butler through the AP switchboard, but he could only bellow. "When do I get *pictures*?" Brandt's wirephoto of troops landing apparently unopposed had scarcely satisfied the West's desperate need to believe in the actuality of invasion.

A few minutes later Dennis came bounding up the stairs and into my office, sobbing. "They're ruined! Ruined! Capa's films are all *ruined!*" Incredulous, I rushed down to the darkroom with him, where he explained that he had hung the films, as usual, in the wooden locker that served as a drying cabinet, heated by a coil on the floor. Because of my order to rush, he had closed the doors. Without ventilation the emulsion had melted.

I held up the four rolls, one at a time.

Three were hopeless; nothing to see. But on the fourth roll there were eleven frames with distinct images. They were probably representative of the entire 35-millimeter take, but their grainy imperfection—perhaps enhanced by the lab accident—contributed to making them among the most dramatic battlefield photos ever taken. The sequence began as Capa waded through the surf with the infantry, past antitank obstacles that soon became tombstones as men fell left and right. This was it, all right. D-Day would forever be known by these pictures.

One more ordeal lay ahead. We now had only a few hours to get our picture packet through the censors, and in addition to Capa's we had hundreds of other photos, the best from Dave Scherman of matters just before the landing. The British and Canadians had covered invasion preparations for days, as had the U.S. Army Signal Corps and the Navy and Air Force photographers. Nobody really cared now about such pictures, but we dutifully sent them on.

At 3:30 on Thursday morning, pictures in hand—including Capa's precious eleven—I drove my Austin through deserted streets to the Ministry of Information, where I had to wait my turn. Ours was the largest picture shipment of the week, and I almost wished I could throw all but the Capa shots overboard in the interest of time. Finally, about 8:30, the censor finished putting his stamp on all the pictures. I stuffed the big envelope, and then it happened. The censor's specially imprinted tape stuck fast to its roll. It simply would not peel off. We tried another roll. Same result. This went on for minutes that seemed hours, and I had to deliver the packet to the courier, a mile away, by nine o'clock—our only chance to make the deadline after eight months!

I left the ministry at about 8:45 and drove like a maniac through the scattered morning traffic, down the little side streets, reaching the edge of Grosvenor Square at 8:59. I ran the last fifty yards and found the courier, in the basement of the Service of Supply headquarters, about to padlock his sack. "Hold it!" I shouted, and he did.

Just after *Life*'s Saturday-night close, the editors cabled, TODAY WAS ONE OF THE GREAT PICTURE DAYS IN LIFE'S OFFICE, WHEN BOB CAPA'S BEACHLANDING AND OTHER SHOTS ARRIVED. I could only think of the pictures *lost*. How was I going to face Capa?

I am a journalist but not a reporter and not a photographer. I am a picture editor. I have worked with photographers, some of them famous, others unknown, for more than fifty years. I have sent them out on assignment, sometimes with a few casual suggestions, other times with detailed instructions, but always the challenge is the same: *Get the picture*. I've accompanied photographers on countless stories; I've carried their equipment and held their lights, pointed them in the right direction if they needed pointing. I've seconded their alibis when things went badly and celebrated with them when things went well. I have bought and sold their pictures for what must total millions of dollars. I have hired scores of photographers, and, sadly, I've had to fire a few. I've testified for them in court, nursed them through injury and illness, saved them from eviction, fed them, buried them. I have accompanied unwed photographers to the marriage license bureau as their witness. Now I am married to one.

Photographers are the most adventurous of journalists. They have to be. Unlike a reporter, who can piece together a story from a certain distance, a photographer must get to the scene of the action, whatever danger or discomfort that implies. A long lens may bring his subject closer, but nothing must stand between him and reality. He must absolutely be in the right place at the right time. No rewrite desk will save him. He must show it as it is. His editor chooses among those pictures to tell it as it was—or was it? Right or wrong, the picture is the last word.

Thus the serious photojournalist becomes a professional voyeur. Often he hates himself for it. In 1936, Bob Capa made a picture of a Spanish Republican soldier, caught in the moment of death. It is one of the most controversial images of the twentieth century. Capa came to hate it, for reasons I will examine later. Don McCullin, the great English photographer who has covered conflict on four continents, says simply, "I try to eradicate the past." He is speaking of how he must deal with what he has seen, because, in fact, he has done his best to preserve the past. And Eddie Adams, whose Pulitzer Prize–winning 1968 photograph of the execution of a Vietcong prisoner by Saigon's chief of police is a kind of ghastly updating of Capa's image, says only, in his trademark staccato, "I don't wanna talk about it."

The picture editor is the voyeurs' voyeur, the person who sees what the photographers themselves have seen but in the bloodless realm of contact sheets, proof prints, yellow boxes of slides, and now pixels on the screen. Picture editors find the representative picture, *the* image, that will be seen by others, perhaps around the world. They are the unwitting (or witting, as the case may be) tastemakers, the unappointed guardians of morality, the talent brokers, the accomplices to celebrity. Most important—or disturbing—they are the fixers of "reality" and of "history." . . .

16

GETTING THE STORY IN VIETNAM

David Halberstam

In most underdeveloped countries the relationship between the American embassy and the American reporter is fairly simple and generally straightforward. A reporter arriving in, say, a country in Africa will go to see officials of the American mission almost immediately. From them he can count on hearing the local American position, but he can also count on getting a relatively detached, if limited, view of the local government, its relations with the U.S., with the Eastern bloc, and with its neighbors. For example, when I was in the Congo for the New York *Times* in 1961 and 1962, the line went something like this: Prime Minister Adoula is better than most people think and considering the kind of country this is, really better than you might expect. As for Tshombe,

---

David Halberstam, "Getting the Story in Vietnam," *Commentary*, Vol. 39, No. 1, January 1965, 30–34. Reprinted by permission of *Commentary*. All rights reserved.

don't be fooled by his anti-Communist stand. He is an anti-Communist, but he is also following a policy which he hopes will turn the rest of the Congo over to the Communists, so that his Katanga secession will look even better to the West.

This was a sensible viewpoint; it was supported, among other things, by the fact that Tshombe's deputies were always voting with the radical left in the assembly in an attempt to topple the moderate government. But it was far from the whole story. The rest of the story was that the Americans wanted to minimize Tshombe's considerable charm and ability and to make him seem just another tribal leader in Katanga, when he actually had far broader support. Thus, when I wrote a long article on him for the Sunday *Times* magazine, the State Department sent a cable to the USIS man in Leopoldville complaining that I had been too sympathetic, and suggesting that I be talked into doing an equally sympathetic piece on Adoula.

But if the State Department often makes the mistake of thinking that New York *Times* reporters are *its* reporters, the relation between American ambassadors and American reporters in most underdeveloped countries is generally one of mutual respect; if anything, reporters—and New York *Times* reporters in particular—may be treated too well. The reporter constantly has to remind himself that an ambassador in a small country where there is no immediate crisis may regard him as the best way to break through State Department channels and get his problems to the White House for breakfast.

In Vietnam, however, relationships such as these simply did not exist. Some were later to claim that the difficulties which arose between the press and the American mission were the result of poor handling or inept news management. But in fact the conflict went much deeper. The job of the reporters in Vietnam was to report the news, whether or not the news was good for America. To the ambassadors and generals, on the other hand, it was crucial that the news be good, and they regarded any other interpretation as defeatist and irresponsible. For beginning in late 1961, when President Kennedy sent General Maxwell D. Taylor to Vietnam on a special mission to see what could be done to keep the country from falling to the Communists, the American commitment there underwent a radical change. From the position of a relatively cool backstage adviser—a position not too different from the one it holds in many other underdeveloped countries—the U.S. became actively involved. Over 16,000 American troops were sent in where there had only been about 600 advisers before, and American aid was boosted to one-and-a-half million dollars a day. Thus the Kennedy administration committed itself fully to Vietnam, placing the nation's prestige in Southeast Asia squarely into the hands of the Ngo family, and putting its own political future in jeopardy.

In effect, the Taylor mission argued that the war could be won, and could be won under the existing government—provided the Vietnamese military were retrained in new methods of counter-guerrilla warfare. Taylor's report recommended that helicopters and amphibious personnel carriers be given to the Vietnamese army to increase its mobility. The report also outlined programs designed to break through Diem's overly centralized and personalized government so that American aid might filter down to the peasants. Finally, Taylor suggested a series of political reforms: broadening the base of the government by taking in non-Ngo anti-Communist elements; making the national assembly more than a rubber stamp; easing some of the tight restrictions on the local press. Above all, Taylor said, the government had to interest itself in the welfare of the peasant, and to this end, Diem, who was not himself corrupt or unjust, must be persuaded to stop tolerating the corruption and injustice of local officials.

The U.S. administration and some of its representatives in the field believed that the Diem government's domestic policies could be changed by all-out American support and that the government could thereby also be led into instituting reforms it had been unwilling to make on its own. Ambassador Frederick Nolting, Jr. emphasized, however, that because of Diem's peculiar psychological makeup, only support which was full and enthusiastic could influence him. It was in line with this position that Vice-President Lyndon Johnson, when visiting Vietnam in the summer of 1961 as Kennedy's personal representative, praised Diem as an Asian Winston Churchill. When, on the plane out of Saigon, a reporter tried to talk to the Vice-President about Diem's faults, Johnson snapped, "Don't tell me about Diem. He's all we've got out there."

It is not surprising, then, that by 1962 the Americans were giving in to the Ngo family on virtually everything. Having failed to get reforms, American officials said that these reforms were being instituted; having failed to improve the demoralized state of the Vietnamese army, the Americans spoke of a new enthusiasm in the army; having failed to change the tactics of the military, they talked about bold new tactics which were allegedly driving the Communists back. For the essence of American policy was: *There is no place else to go.* Backing out of South Vietnam entirely would virtually turn Southeast Asia over to the Communists and could have disastrous repercussions in the next Presidential election. To extend the U.S. commitment would involve the country in another Korean war, and it was by no means certain that the American people were prepared to support such a war. Finding a new leader might be possible, but Diem and Nhu had allowed no national hero to emerge. Consequently, there seemed no alternative to the Taylor-Kennedy policy of helping the country to help itself—sending in advisers, helicopters, pilots, fighter bombers, and pilot-trainers—while stopping short of committing American combat troops to a war against Asians on Asian soil without atomic weapons.

Because a sensitive administration back home wanted to hear that this policy was succeeding, and because of the belief that if the Americans expressed enough enthusiasm Diem would come to trust them and be more receptive to their suggestions for reform, optimism about the situation in Vietnam became an essential element of American policy itself. Not only were members of the mission regularly optimistic in their reports and in their comments to the press, but visiting VIPs were deliberately used to make things look even better. Thus, a general or some other high official from Washington would arrive in Vietnam, spend one day in Saigon being briefed and meeting the Ngo family, and another day or two in the field touring selected strategic hamlets and units. Then at the airport on his way home he would hold a press conference in which he would declare that the war was being won, that the people were rallying to the government, and that he had been impressed by the determination of that great leader, President Diem.

But with the increase in American equipment and American participation, more American reporters also arrived, and they saw little reason to be optimistic. They were told of a new popular enthusiasm for the government; they heard the American officials talk of reforms; they would pick up their American papers and read stories from

Washington about new experts on guerrilla war, about special Washington staffs on counter-insurgency, about books on the subject being rushed into print to inform the American public. Then they would go into the field and see the same tired old government tactics, the same hack political commanders in charge, the same waste of human resources.

I myself arrived in Saigon in September of 1962—a time of singularly bad feeling. François Sully, the *Newsweek* correspondent and for seventeen years a resident of Indo-China, had just been ordered out by the government—or rather by Madame Nhu. Though at first the American authorities had referred to the expulsion as a misunderstanding which would soon be cleared up, it was obvious that there was no misunderstanding at all. As far as anyone could tell, Sully was being expelled because he had offended Madame Nhu in a *Newsweek* article: a quotation from her about the guerrillas—"The enemy has more drive"—had been used under a photo of her paramilitary girl's organization, a cadre which she called "my little darlings," and which drew better pay than the government soldiers in the field. Cables from *Newsweek*'s highest executives pointing out that Sully had nothing to do with writing captions, were of no avail.

The expulsion of a colleague is a serious business for reporters, and in this case the arbitrariness and malice of the decision made it worse. Since Sully's departure was followed shortly by that of Jim Robinson of NBC, and since we all soon began to receive personal warnings of various kinds from agents of the government, we knew that the threat of expulsion hung over all of us. This meant that each man had to censor himself to a certain extent and to decide whether a particular story was important enough to be worth the risk of expulsion. I, for example, tried to avoid stories that would upset the Ngo family without shedding light on the serious issues of the country. On the other hand, in the early spring of 1963, when the military situation was deteriorating in the Delta, and then in June when it became clear that the government lacked the capacity to handle the Buddhist crisis, I decided that it was necessary to take the risk of expulsion and to write very frankly about the events involved.

What was perhaps even more disturbing than Sully's expulsion itself was the reaction of the highest American officials to it; obviously they were not in the least unhappy to see him go. He was, as one of the highest political officers at the time told me, "just a *pied noir*"—a low life. He had caused trouble for the American mission by writing solely about negative aspects of the country, and adopting a doomsday attitude toward the war. From the very beginning, then, I could see that the relation between the American mission and the American press in Vietnam was quite different from that which existed anywhere else in the world. Although the embassy occasionally chided the Ngo government for its attacks on the press, such high officials as Ambassador Nolting, General Paul Donald Harkins, and the CIA chief John H. Richardson were basically more sympathetic to the government viewpoint. They felt we were inaccurate and biased; they thought the war was being won, and they longed for control over us. "The American commitment," said an official mission white paper prepared in January 1963 for General Earle Wheeler, Chief of Staff of the Army, and rewritten once by Nolting because it was not strong enough, "has been badly hampered by irresponsible, astigmatic and sensationalized reporting."

The sources of this conflict between the press and the American mission can be seen very clearly in a comparison of the personalities of Ambassador Nolting and my predecessor as *Times* correspondent in Vietnam, Homer Bigart. Nolting is a gracious and considerate Virginian, a former philosophy professor who went into diplomacy in World War II and has been a career diplomat ever since. He had never been in the Far East before being assigned to Saigon, and because of the pressure from Washington, he badly wanted to take what the Vietnamese government was telling him at face value. If he was shown a piece of paper saying that local officials were going to do something, he was satisfied that it would be done. Though he had held an important job in NATO, he had never been much involved with reporters before, and he had almost no understanding of the press. "You're always looking for the hole in the doughnut, Mr. Halberstam," he once said to me. An extremely hard worker, he was caught in an almost impossible situation: a wartime alliance in which he was bending over backward to alleviate his ally's suspicions, at a time when his every gesture simply convinced the very same ally to take America's continued support for granted. The net effect was of a mythical partnership, for the last thing in the world the Ngo family wanted was a partnership with anyone, particularly the U.S. Still, his position would have been more sympathetic if he had not fed the fire himself. He was reporting that the war was being won, and he was pressuring his subordinates to tell him only good news; to reassure Washington, he had to believe that American policy was more successful than it actually was.

Nolting's job was difficult, but it was made even more difficult by the almost psychotic preoccupation of Diem and his family with the Western press—the one element operating in Saigon other than the Vietcong they could not control. Diem resented any criticism of his family; and since his family was in fact his government, he became angry at a wide assortment of stories. Diem and the Nhus believed that the American press was Communist-infiltrated; paradoxically the Nhus also believed that some of the reporters were CIA agents, and part of a vast underground American conspiracy against them. Hence, for example, when the first Buddhist monk burned himself to death, Diem was convinced that the act had been staged and paid for by an American television team—despite the fact that there had not been a single television man on the scene.

Every time we wrote something Diem disliked he would accuse American officials of having deliberately leaked it to us. (Actually, the source was often one of his own supposedly loyal palace intimates.) Nolting did his best to keep us from finding out anything which reflected badly on the government, but the city was filled with dissident Americans and especially Vietnamese who talked freely; it is a national characteristic of the Vietnamese that they cannot keep a secret. But unlike Diem, who could control the Vietnamese press, Nolting could not get the American reporters "on the team."

The prototype of a non-team player is Homer Bigart. A highly experienced correspondent, winner of two Pulitzer prizes for foreign reporting, Bigart has great prestige among his colleagues. He is no scholar; if he reads books it is a well kept secret, and his facility in foreign languages can be gauged by the legend about him which has it that if a Frenchman were to offer him a cigarette, he would answer: "*Je ne* smoke *pas.*" He is not one of the new breed of reporters—Yale or Harvard and a Nieman fellowship—but wherever he goes in the world he sheds light, writing simply, incisively, and informatively.

In Saigon, Bigart was fifty-five years old, and his stomach frequently bothered him. But in what was essentially a young man's assignment—a relentless, ruthless grind under tropical conditions—basic professional pride drove him on and he outworked every young reporter in town. The embassy officials who accused Sully of being a *pied noir*, and the rest of us of being too young, were obviously dazzled by Bigart's reputation and intimidated by his capacity to find out things they were trying to hide. Eventually they even tried to discredit his reporting by sly allusions to his age and health. When he left Vietnam there was a great sigh of relief from American officials on the scene.

As the situation in Vietnam continued to deteriorate militarily and politically, the antagonism of the chiefs of the American mission toward American reporters grew. In the spring of 1963, the Buddhist protest began, and for four months the reporters—and Washington—watched with a sense of hopelessness Diem's inability to deal with the swelling religious-political protest. The mission's proud boasts that Diem could handle his population and that the embassy could influence the Ngo family were stripped naked during the four-month crisis. On August 21, the entire policy seemed to collapse: after months of promising U. S. officials that he would be conciliatory toward the Buddhists, Nhu—without informing the Americans—raided Vietnam's pagodas in a veritable blood bath. The embassy not only was caught cold and ignorant when it happened, but then was unable to tell who had led the raid and inaccurately blamed it on the military. Reporters, who had predicted that something of this nature was likely to happen, described the raid and identified the raider correctly. In a sense, this meant the end of the old policy, but it ironically unleashed a new wave of criticism against the reporters.

My own first experience of this new wave came in early September, when a friend sent me a column from the New York *Journal-American* in which I was accused of being soft on Communism and of preparing the way through my dispatches in the *Times* for a Vietnamese Fidel Castro. I showed the clipping to a friend in the embassy. "Well, I think you have to expect this sort of thing," he said. "There may be more." He was right; there was more. A few days later, Joseph Alsop, after a brief visit to Vietnam, attacked a group of "young crusaders" in the Saigon press corps who, he said, were generally accurate in their reporting but were responsible for the near-psychotic state of mind among the inhabitants of GiaLong Palace. Being criticized by Alsop is no small honor in this profession; those of us whom he called the "young crusaders" knew that our stock was rising. At the same time, having covered the complex evolution of the Buddhist crisis for four long months, and having spotted the Buddhists as an emerging political force long before the American embassy, we were amazed to see ourselves charged by another visiting reporter with not having understood the political implications of the crisis. And having covered the disintegration of the Delta for more than a year-and-a-half and gone on more than thirty missions in this area, some of us were equally amazed to see ourselves charged by Mr. Alsop with not having visited what he quaintly referred to as "the front."

Alsop was not our only critic. The Kennedy administration—embarrassed by what was beginning to look like a major foreign policy failure, and angered by its ineptitude in allowing the pagoda crackdown to take place, in not having diagnosed it correctly when it did take place, and in not having any answer when it finally did analyze the situation correctly—took to attacking our reporting as inaccurate, the work of a handful of emotional and inexperienced young men. In addition, the President's press secretary, Pierre Salinger, and other White House staff members more interested in their chief's political standing at home than in the status of the war in Vietnam, would knowingly inform White House reporters that we in Vietnam never went on operations.

At the Pentagon, in the higher reaches where the realities of the war rarely penetrated, the criticism was particularly vehement. Defense Department reporters were told by Major General Victor Krulak, the Pentagon's specialist on counter-insurgency, that he simply could not understand what was happening in Vietnam. Experienced correspondents such as the free-lancer Richard Tregaskis and Marguerite Higgins (then of the *Herald Tribune*, now of *Newsday*) were finding that the war was being won, while a bunch of inexperienced young reporters kept writing defeatist stories about the political side. When Maggie Higgins was in Saigon, General Krulak told a representative of *Time* magazine, young Halberstam met her at a bar and showed her a photo of some dead bodies; he asked her if she had ever seen dead bodies, and when she said yes, he burst into tears. Krulak took great delight in passing this story around—whether it was his or Miss Higgins's invention I will never know. In any case, the long knives were really out. "It's a damn good thing you never belonged to any left-wing groups or anything like that," a friend of mine high up in the State Department told me after I left Saigon, "because they were really looking for stuff like that."

On October 22, Arthur Ochs Sulzberger, the new publisher of the *Times*, went by the White House to pay a courtesy call on the President of the United States. It was a time when, except for Vietnam, the administration was riding high and feeling very cocky: Kennedy was sure his 1964 opponent would be Goldwater and was confidently expecting a big victory. Almost the first question the President asked Mr. Sulzberger was what he thought of his young man in Saigon. Mr. Sulzberger answered that he thought I was doing fine. The President suggested that perhaps I was too close to the story, too involved (this is the most insidiously damaging thing that can be said about a reporter). No, Mr. Sulzberger answered, he did not think I was too involved. The President asked if perhaps Mr. Sulzberger had been thinking of transferring me to another assignment. No, said Mr. Sulzberger, the *Times* was quite satisfied with the present distribution of assignments. (At that particular point I was supposed to take a two-week breather, but the *Times* immediately cancelled my vacation.)

But the most curious attack of all on the Saigon press corps came from *Time* magazine. A dispute had long been simmering between *Time*'s editors in New York and its reporters in the field in Vietnam, a far sharper division than the usual one between field and office. The *Time* reporters in the field felt strongly that the magazine was giving too optimistic a view of the war. Periodically, Charles Mohr, *Time*'s chief correspondent in Southeast Asia (who had once been described by Henry Luce himself as "A reporter—and how!") would return to New York for conferences where he would argue for tougher coverage on Vietnam. But his editors, who had lunched with Secretary McNamara and other Pentagon officials and had seen the most secret of charts and the most secret of arrows, would explain patiently to him that he understood only a portion of "the big picture."

In April 1963, Richard M. Clurman, one of the foremost defenders of working reporters among *Time*'s executives, visited Saigon, met with some of the working reporters, talked with their sources, and interviewed Diem, Nhu, and Nolting. After that, matters improved somewhat, and during most of the Buddhist crisis Mohr was relatively pleased with what he was getting into the magazine. But then things took a turn for the worse again. In August 1963, a brilliant cover story he sent in on Madame Nhu was edited to underemphasize her destructive effect on the society, and several weeks later, a long and detailed piece he did on the Saigon press corps analyzing the root of the controversy and praising the work of the reporters was killed.

Finally, in early September, with Washington still searching for answers, Mohr was asked to do a roundup on the entire state of the war in Vietnam. He and his colleague, Mert Perry, put vast amounts of energy into the legwork, and the story he filed was the toughest written to that date by a resident correspondent. It began with this lead: "The war in Vietnam is being lost." Not everyone in Vietnam, Mohr noted, "would be willing to go so far at this point. But those men who know Vietnam best and have given the best of their energies and a portion of their souls to this program are suddenly becoming passionate on this subject." Washington, he continued, had asked all Saigon officials for detailed reports on what was happening, and it had given these officials a chance "to bare their souls. Much of what they write may be diluted by the time it reaches Washington. However, these men realize that they are in the middle of a first class major foreign policy crisis and that history will be a harsh judge. 'I am laying it on the line,' said one. 'Now is the time for the truth. There are no qualifications in what I write.' Another said: 'I am going on the record in black and white. The war will be lost in a year, but I gave myself some leeway and said three years.' Another said that his program in the countryside is 'dead.' One source said American military reporting in the country 'has been wrong and false—lies really. We are now paying the price.' "

This was strong stuff, and it left no doubt that American policy had failed. But it was not what the editors of *Time* magazine wanted to hear. Mohr's story was killed in New York, and an optimistic piece was printed instead bearing no relation to the copy he had filed, and assuring the world that "government troops are fighting better than ever." Since this was not what most sources—the New York *Times*, the AP, the UPI, *Newsweek*, CBS, NBC—were reporting at the time, an explanation was needed. Accordingly, Otto Fuerbringer, the managing editor of *Time*, summoned a writer into his office and (as Stanley Karnow, Mohr's predecessor as *Time* bureau chief in Southeast Asia put it in *Nieman Reports*) with "nothing but his own preconceptions to guide him, dictated the gist of an article for his magazine's Press Section." Karnow called the piece that finally appeared "a devastating compendium of bitter innuendoes and clever generalities, all blatantly impeaching American correspondents in Vietnam for distorting the news." The war, it hinted, was going better than one would gather from the small incestuous clique of reporters who sat around the Caravelle Bar in Saigon interviewing each other and never venturing forth to the countryside. It was a staggering piece, for it not only indicted all of us, but two of *Time*'s own men as well. The upshot was that they both resigned, Mohr eventually going to the *Times*, where he soon became the White House correspondent, and Perry to the Chicago *Daily News*.

No one becomes a reporter to make friends, but neither is it pleasant in a situation like the war in Vietnam to find yourself completely at odds with the views of the highest officials of your country. The pessimism of the Saigon press corps was of the most reluctant kind: many of us came to love Vietnam, we saw our friends dying all around us, and we would have liked nothing better than to believe that the war was going well and that it would eventually be won. But it was impossible for us to believe those things without denying the evidence of our own senses. The enemy was growing stronger day by day, and if nothing else we would have been prevented from sending tranquilizing stories to our papers by a vision of the day when the Vietcong walked into Saigon and *Time* righteously demanded to know where those naïve reporters were now who had been telling the world that all was going well with the war in Vietnam. And so we had no alternative but to report the truth in the hope that we might finally break through the optimism that prevailed so obstinately in high places in America.

17

THE LEGEND ON THE LICENSE

John Hersey

The imminent death of the novel is announced from time to time, but the very repetitiousness of the bulletins testifies to stubborn vital signs. I bring other news from the hospital. Journalism is on a sickbed and is in a very bad way.

The trouble did not begin but came out into the open with the appallingly harmful phrase Truman Capote used in 1965 to categorize *In Cold Blood*. It was, he said, a "nonfiction novel." The blurring of fiction and journalism sanctioned by that phrase is now widely practiced and widely condoned. This has not been particularly good for fiction; it may be mortal to journalism.

In fiction that *is* fiction, no holds need be barred. Novelists may introduce or disguise real people and real events as they choose. Tolstoy disguised all but the generals. Dreiser's *An American Tragedy* was suggested by an actual crime, but he did not feel the need to call his creation "a true-life novel." Malraux, who had an enormous influence on some of the novelists of my generation (e.g., Ralph Ellison), often depicted originals— among others, Chiang Kai-shek in all the splendid irony of his left-wing youth. E. L. Doctorow has had harmless fun with Morgan, Ford, and others. And so on.

The only caution in all this is the one so acutely perceived by Flannery O'Connor (in *Mystery and Manners*): "It's always wrong of course to say that you can't do this or you can't do that in fiction. You can do anything you can get away with, but nobody has ever gotten away with much." In other words, there are tests. A test, for one thing, of quality; of art. Or, to put it more brutally for authors, a test of gifts. But the point is that always, in fiction, there is the saving notice on the license: THIS WAS MADE UP.

As to journalism, we may as well grant right away that there is no such thing as absolute objectivity. It is impossible to present in words "*the* truth" or "the whole story."

John Hersey, "The Legend on the License," *The Yale Review*, Vol. 72, No. 2, February 1986, 289–314. Reprinted by permission of Blackwell Publishing.

The minute a writer offers nine hundred ninety-nine out of one thousand facts, the worm of bias has begun to wriggle. The vision of each witness is particular. Tolstoy pointed out that immediately after a battle there are as many remembered versions of it as there have been participants.

Still and all, I will assert that there is one sacred rule of journalism. The writer must not invent. The legend on the license must read: NONE OF THIS WAS MADE UP. The ethics of journalism, if we can be allowed such a boon, must be based on the simple truth that every journalist knows the difference between the distortion that comes from subtracting observed data and the distortion that comes from adding invented data.

The threat to journalism's life by the denial of this difference can be realized if we look at it from the reader's point of view. The reader assumes the subtraction as a given of journalism and instinctively hunts for the bias; the moment the reader suspects additions, the earth begins to skid underfoot, for the idea that there is no way of knowing what is real and what is not real is terrifying. Even more terrifying is the notion that lies are truths. Or at least these things used to be terrifying; the dulling of the terror that has come about through repeated exposure tells us how far this whole thing has gone.

Let me now drive my own stakes in the ground. I have always believed that the *devices* of fiction could serve journalism well and might even help it to aspire now and then to the level of art. But I have tried to honor the distinction between the two forms. To claim that a work is both fiction and journalism, or to assert, as Doctorow recently did, that "there is no longer any such thing as fiction or nonfiction; there is only narrative"— these are, in my view, serious crimes against the public. In a backward look in *The New Journalism* Tom Wolfe, citing a piece of mine from 1944, remarked, "Here we start getting into the ancestry of the New Journalism." The word "ancestry" makes me feel a bit like the Peking Man, and in laying claim to authority in this field I prefer to think of myself as nothing more remote than a grandfather.

Now. After reading three recent publications—Tom Wolfe's *The Right Stuff*, an entertaining book, Wolfe's best so far; Norman Mailer's *The Executioner's Song*, a powerful work that unquestionably enhances Mailer's claim to the kind of literary top billing he has always so tiresomely whined after; and Truman Capote's "Handcarved Coffins," a gobbet of commercial trash by this once brilliant writer in his new collection, *Music for Chameleons*—I am one worried grandpa. These three hybrids clinch it. The time has come to redraw the line between journalism and fiction.

1

"Handcarved Coffins," which Capote calls both "nonfiction" and "a short novel," belongs here, in the company of the Wolfe and Mailer books, only because of Capote's place in the line of parentage of the hybrid form; it can be dealt with briefly. The story must represent to its author a nostalgic yearning for the remembered powers of *In Cold Blood*, the fine, shapely, hard-fibered novel (as novel) that appears to have been the model Norman Mailer wanted to knock off its pedestal, but couldn't quite, with *The Executioner's Song*. Vivid as *In Cold Blood* was as a novel, it had serious flaws on the nonfiction side, arising from the fact that its actions and dialogue had been reconstructed long after the described events, yet were presented in the book with all assurance as being exactly what had happened; the dialogue, rebuilt from a great distance, stood within the authenticating marks of direct quotation. Besides suffering from troubles like these, which are intrinsic to a genre that claims to be both fiction and not, "Handcarved Coffins" groans under others far more grievous.

For one thing, the tale does something that journalism simply must not do: It strains credulity well beyond the breaking point. There is a much-too-muchness about it, which convinces one that the fictionist has decidedly had the upper hand over the journalist. The story is told in interview form, through a series of dialogues between Capote and a number of characters, the most prominent being a detective from a certain State Bureau of Investigation, who is trying to solve a succession of ghastly murders that have been announced beforehand to the victims, in all cases but one, by the arrival in their hands of beautiful miniature coffins, carved from "light balsam wood" and containing candid photographs of the doomed persons. The murderer has dispatched two of his victims, an elderly pair, by insinuating into their parked car, to await their return to it, nine rattlesnakes that have been "injected with amphetamine." Perhaps we can swallow that one. But try this: A recipient of one of the little coffins, driving along a lonely road in "an eccentric vehicle of his own invention" with no top and no windshield, is cleanly decapitated by "a strong steel wire sharpened thin as a razor" and stretched across the road between a tree and a telephone pole at exactly the right height to catch him just under the chin; the wire "slice[s] off his head as easily as a girl picking petals off a daisy." And so on, murder after murder, until we have been taken far beyond the last shore of belief. (We will come back in due course to this crucial matter of belief.)

An even worse fault of this creaky tale is that it is told as if in a game of blindman's buff. It is the reader who is blindfolded. He has no idea where he is. The story takes place in an invisible place: a nameless town in an unspecified state. The characters are *there*, but they are unseeable as real people. Their names have been changed. Capote says he "had to omit a few identifying things" (*The New York Times*, January 7, 1979)—which implies his having substituted other made-up ones. (The principal suspect "had long simian-like arms; the hands dangled at his knees, and the fingers were long, capable, oddly aristocratic.") Altogether, the ace among rules of reliable reporting—that the facts should be "hard"—is here repeatedly and fatally broken.

2

Tom Wolfe's *The Right Stuff* is a vivid book, a tainted book. It gives an account of the Mercury phase of the United States space program, and its thesis is that test pilots of rocket aircraft, genuinely, and the seven Mercury astronauts, more ambiguously, shared an ineffable quality compounded of spiffy courage, arrogant recklessness, dry-palmed sass, and super-jock male potency (on earth they indiscriminately balled "juicy little girls," and in the sky they whipped around in Pynchonesque flying phalluses), to all of which Wolfe gives the catchy tag "the right stuff." Wolfe's style-machine has never run more smoothly than in this book. The writing is at times wonderfully funny. Some of the passages on flying are classy. A quick and easy read.

Then why tainted? Because Wolfe is the paradigm of the would-be journalist who cannot resist the itch to improve on the material he digs up. The tricks of fiction he uses dissolve now and then into its very essence: fabrication. The notice on the license reads: THIS WAS NOT MADE UP (EXCEPT FOR THE PARTS THAT WERE MADE UP).

The source of the taint is the pair of pieces Wolfe wrote in 1965 for the *Herald-Tribune* Sunday magazine about *The New Yorker*. We must recall them at some length, because in them one finds in gross form the fundamental defect that has persisted ever since in Wolfe's writing, and that is to be found in the work of many of the "new journalists," and also indeed in that of many "nonfiction novelists"—namely, the notion that mere facts don't matter.

In the introduction to *The New Journalism* Wolfe tried to laugh off his *New Yorker* pieces. He called them "some lighthearted fun. . . . A very droll *sportif* performance, you understand." They were nothing of the kind. They made up a vicious, slashing lampoon. Begging the question whether *The New Yorker* may at some point have deserved a serious critique, there seems to be no way to explain the stunningly irresponsible street cruelty of Wolfe's exercise except by guessing that he could not bear to face it that "his" New Journalism would have to be measured sooner or later against the meticulously accurate and vivid reporting of such *New Yorker* writers as A. J. Liebling and Daniel Lang, and against the vivid devices used by the wonderful Joseph Mitchell or, let's say, by Lillian Ross and Truman Capote; who in turn were writing in an honorable tradition, not New at all, reaching back to George Orwell, Henry Mayhew, James Boswell. . . .

Wolfe called his first piece "Tiny Mummies! The True Story of the Ruler of 43rd Street's Land of the Walking Dead." This "true" story was a collage of shameless inventions. Not satisfied with making up lots of little decorative details, such as imaginary colors and types of paper used at *The New Yorker* for memos and manuscripts, Wolfe reached farther into the territory of fiction to devise blunt weapons with which to assault William Shawn, the magazine's editor. He dreamed up a Shawn memorandum which was supposed to have warned the staff against talking to him; he gave a description of the magazine's editorial process which, according to an analysis of Wolfe's pieces by Renata Adler and Gerald Jones, was erroneous "in every particular, large and small"; and he gave a picture of Shawn's role that "was not a little untrue, not half true, but totally, stupefyingly false."

Shawn's "retiring" nature, Wolfe asserted, could be accounted for by "what the records show, actually, in the Cook County (Chicago) Criminal Court"—that Leopold's and Loeb's original intended victim in their famous murder had been "a small and therefore manageable teen-age boy from the Harvard School," whose first name was William ("the court records do not give the last name"), and that the two had decided not to kill William Shawn "only because they had a personal grudge against him and somebody might remember that." Shawn's trauma is totally a Wolfe fantasy. The court records *do* give the last name of the intended victim, and the first as well. It was not a teen-aged William Shawn. It was a nine-and-a-half-year-old boy named John O. Levinson, who testified at the trial.

The coda of the second piece, the climax of the whole charade, is a perfect example of a Wolfe fantasy flying out of control. Wolfe has been building a (false) picture of Shawn slavishly attached to the formulas of the founder of the magazine, Harold Ross. In this scene we see Shawn sitting alone at home, on the very evening when down at the St. Regis the staff is celebrating the magazine's fortieth anniversary. According to Wolfe,

Shawn is listening to "that wonderful light zinc plumbing sound" of Bix Beiderbecke's recording of "I Can't Get Started": "(those other trumpet players, like Harry James, they never played the real 'I Can't Get Started')." At the end of the recording "Bix hits that incredible high one he died on, popping a vessel in his temporal fossa, bleeding into his squash, drowning on the bandstand. . . . *That* was the music of Harold Ross's lifetime. . . . Here, on that phonograph, those days are *preserved.* . . ."

Adler and Jonas:

> The facts are, of course, that "*That*" was not "the music of Harold Ross's lifetime." Or anybody else's. The facts are that "Bix" did not die playing, nor did his death have anything to do with his "temporal fossa." He died in bed, of pneumonia. Nor did Beiderbecke make a recording of "the real 'I Can't Get Started.' " In fact, he never played it—with or without "that incredible high one." It would have been difficult for him to play it. "I Can't Get Started with You" was written in 1935, four years after Beiderbecke's death.

When Wolfe wrote his advertisements for himself in *The New Journalism*, nine years later, he still couldn't suppress his snickers at the reaction to his *New Yorker* caper, and to the subsequent new wave of nonfiction, on the part of "countless journalists and literary intellectuals," who, he said, were screaming, "*The bastards are making it up!* (I'm telling you, Ump, that's a spitball he's throwing. . . .)." But his laughter had an edge of nerves; altogether too many folks in the stands had seen and called attention to his applying a little greasy stuff to the pellet.

In the seven years since then, two things have happened: Wolfe has grown quite a bit more careful (and hard-working), and the public has become increasingly inured, or maybe the word is numb, to the blurring of fiction and journalism. *The Right Stuff* has been accepted as fairly accurate by people in the know. I talked with a number of journalists who had covered the space program, and while one complained of "outright lies" in the book, all the others seemed to think that Wolfe had "made an effort to be as accurate as he could be," that he had "done his homework," that he had made mistakes, but those had been errors of judgment and value that any conventional journalist might have made. Most of them thought he had been too kind to Scott Carpenter and too hard on John Glenn. The official National Aeronautics and Space Administration view was also favorable. Christopher Kraft, in charge of the Johnson Space Center in Houston, declined to talk about the book, but his public relations chief, John MacLeish, said after consultation with others that despite a number of technical errors there was "a high degree of accuracy" in the book. The two astronauts I talked with, John Glenn and Deke Slayton, said, respectively, that Wolfe was "accurate on the details of my flight" and "mostly pretty accurate."

Taint, then? Well, alas, yes. Some questions remain. Enough to add up. Enough so that, in the end, one cannot help wondering whether even these interested parties, in their numbed acceptance of the premise that there is no difference between fiction and nonfiction, between real life and a skillfully drawn image of a dream of it, haven't been to some extent taken in. I give you the example of the way in which Senator Glenn, in speaking to me, paid tribute to the hypnotic ambiguity of Wolfe's prose. Glenn is pictured in the book as an insufferable prig, a prude, a killjoy, yet he said to me, "I came out pretty good in the book, so I can't complain." NASA seemed to think it had come out pretty well, too. Did it?

Wolfe's fiction-aping journalism, he wrote in 1973, "enjoys an advantage [over fiction] so obvious, so built in, one almost forgets what a power it has: the simple fact that the reader knows *all this actually happened.* . . . The writer is one step closer to the absolute involvement of the reader that Henry James and James Joyce dreamed of and never achieved. . . ." Whew. That *is* a big advantage. But let's focus for a moment on much smaller things, such as that little word "all."

In defining the New Journalism, Wolfe wrote that a journalist need use just four devices of fiction to bring this amazing power to the page: scene-by-scene construction, dialogue, point of view, and what he called "status details." But the resources of fiction are by no means so barren as all that. One essential requisite and delight of fiction, for example, is the absolute particularity it can give to every individual, every character. Wolfe has apparently ruled this out; he is a generalizer. Let him find a vivid or funny trait in more than one member of a class, then without exception the whole class has it. Thirty-six military pilots show up at the Pentagon to apply for the space program; without exception they wear "Robert Hall clothes that cost about a fourth as much as their watches." "They had many names, these rockets, Atlas, Navajo, Little Joe, Jupiter, but they all blew up." All test pilots talked something he calls Army Creole. All seven astronauts went in for Flying and Drinking, Drinking and Driving, Driving and Balling. All Russian space vehicles were launched "by the Soviet's mighty and mysterious Integral"—though, as Wolfe knows, Integral was not a person or a state organ but a space ship in Evgeny Zamyatin's novel, *We.* "Every wife . . ." "Every young fighter jock . . ." "Everyone . . ." "Invariably . . ." "All these people . . ." "All . . ." (*"All this actually happened . . ."*)

Another big advantage over other writers that Wolfe apparently feels he has is that since he is using fictional modes, he is, even though dealing with nonfictional matter, freed from the boring job of checking verifiable details. If something turns out to have been dead wrong—well, that was just the free play of fancy. Some of the many details Wolfe should have checked but obviously did not are: The kind of car John Glenn drove. Whether Slayton, pictured as an active partisan at the meeting Wolfe calls the Konokai Seance, was even present. What operant conditioning means. The Latin name for the chimpanzee. What jodhpurs are. What cilia means. When the compass was invented. . . .

But there are disadvantages in the method, too, at least for the reader. One is the frequent juxtaposition of passages that are wholly made up with others that are only partly made up or, beyond the use of one of the four devices, not made up at all. Side by side, for example, are a long parody of an airline pilot's voice reassuring the passengers on the last leg of a flight from Phoenix to New York when the landing gear won't lock, and an account of how the test pilot Chuck Yaeger gets drunk, breaks two ribs falling off a horse on a moonlight gallop, doesn't tell the base doctor, and two days later goes up in an X-1 and buffets through the sound barrier, hurting so badly his right arm is useless. (Right stuff.) Both passages are funny, wildly hyperbolic interchangeable in voice and tone. It is not hard to tell which of these is mostly made up (or is it wholly made up?). But what becomes not so easy, after many such oscillations, is to perceive exactly where the line between reporting and invention in any "real-life" episode actually lies.

This difficulty is immensely reinforced by the way Wolfe uses his third fictional device: point of view. At will, he enters the consciousness of his characters. We have the stream (or in Wolfe's case one has to say river) of consciousness of wives of astronauts, waiting out re-entry. We find ourselves in each astronaut's mind as he barrels across the sky. For an awful moment we become Lyndon Johnson. We may be dismayed to find ourselves suddenly trapped in a chimpanzee's head. Finally (James and Joyce certainly never gave us *this* pleasure) we are right there in God's mind, out of patience with John Glenn and barking at him, "Try the automatic, you ninny." Beyond the dicey issue of freely inventive re-creation of thoughts and dialogue, long after their transaction, a further trouble is that Wolfe never makes the slightest attempt, which any novelist would make as a matter of course, to vary the voice to fit each character. What we hear throughout, ringing in every mind, is the excited shout of Tom Wolfe. Each astronaut in turn *becomes* Tom Wolfe. Without even a little jiggle of lexical sex-change each astronaut's wife becomes Tom Wolfe. Right Stuffers who are alleged to speak nothing but Army Creole are garlanded with elegant tidbits like *esprit, joie de combat, mas allá!* The chimp talks pure Wolfe. God help us, God becomes Tom Wolfe and with His sweet ear chooses the Wolfeish "ninny."

"Class has always been Tom Wolfe's subject," John Gregory Dunne has written (*The New York Review of Books*, November 8, 1979). Dunne sees Wolfe as exposing the unmentionable in a purportedly egalitarian society: the existence of class. Wolfe is always on the side of the outsider, the underdog. Low Rent is good. He declares himself a literary lumpenprole, one of "the Low Rent rabble at the door," of "the Kentucky Colonels of Journalism and Literature." Placing such great emphasis on status seems to have affected Wolfe's decibel range. Whispering, as any outsider knows, is genteel. Understatement is upper class. A consequence of such understandings is the central disaster of this gifted writer's voice: He never abandons a resolute tone of screaming. The test of every sentence is: Will its sound waves shatter a wine glass at twenty feet? It is not surprising that he writes so beautifully about the rupture of the sound barrier.

While he has largely cooled his typographical excesses in this book (there are only three exclamation points, and no italicized words at all, on the first page), the aural and psychological overamplification is still very much there. The voice of every character, even that of a quiet woman like Glenn's wife, is Jovian. One can say that the charm in Wolfe is his enthusiasm. On nearly every page, though, this attractive quality sends him floating off the ground. When he is establishing the driving part of Flying and Drinking, Drinking and Driving, Driving and Balling, in which "all" the astronauts indulged, his excitement over their recklessness at the wheel leads him to write, doubtless in a *sportif* spirit: "More fighter pilots died in automobiles than airplanes." No time period. According to Navy statistics which Wolfe himself cites, there was a 23 percent probability that a Navy career pilot would die in an aircraft accident. Did one in four die on the road? In 1952, sixty-two American Air Force pilots died in crashes in thirty-six weeks of flying at Edwards Air Force Base, 1.7 per week. Did two a week die in cars? The point is not that this little example of possibly humorous overkill announces in itself the death of journalism. The point is that this one happened to be readily catchable. How many others are not? Are they on every page? How can we know? How can we ever know?

And so we come through many cumulative small doubts back to the issue of "accuracy." Let us grant that among Wolfe's works, this book is relatively "accurate" (perhaps because relatively much of it is based on written records, notably the NASA official history, *This New Ocean: A History of Project Mercury*). But "relatively 'accurate' " may not be good enough, when we look for the whole meaning of the work.

By now we are thoroughly skeptical, and, remembering John Glenn's having read the abuse he took at Wolfe's hand as praise, we begin to see abysses of ambiguity, of ambivalence, in the book. Wolfe loves what he loathes. The individual words mock and slash and ridicule; the sentences into which they are combined somehow ogle and stroke and admire. As Eric Korn put it (*Times Lilerary Supplement*, November 30, 1979), "If there's one thing more unlovable than the man of letters showing his contempt for physical valor, it's the man of letters fawning on physical valor. Wolfe contrives to do both at once." Glenn and NASA are both right and awfully wrong to think they come out "pretty good."

Looking back, we see that this double-think has been there, off and on, all through Wolfe's work. His class struggle seems to be in his own heart. The New Journalism was a product of the sixties, and like much of what hit the kids in that decade, Wolfe's struggle seems to have been a generational one. To adopt his voice: Young and new are good, old and old are bad; but O I love you Mummy and Daddy, you bitch and bastard. This lumpenprole affects beautifully tailored white suits and his prose often gives off a donnish perfume—*prima facie*, *Beruf*, pick your language. If Tom Wolfe is at all interested in class, it is in a new elite of those few "outsiders" who, at any given moment, are "in." The quasi-fictional method allows Wolfe to be both out and in.

Precisely this ambiguity makes for really zippy entertainment—the dazzle of the magic show. Great fun. But. It leaves us with serious doubts about a mode of journalism that straddles in its ambiguities the natural and obligatory substance of such a book: the horrendous issues of the space program, its cost, philosophy, technological priorities, and impact on national jingoism and machismo in a cold-war atmosphere which, as we saw in the winter of 1979–1980, could so easily be brought to dangerous warmth.

I believe that the double-think flaw is intrinsic to Wolfe's method. One who gets the habit of having it both ways in form slips into the habit of having it both ways in attitude and substance. The legend on the license really does matter.

As to deeper and subtler forms of social harm that this journalism also may cause, more later.

3

The case of Norman Mailer is much more complicated, because Mailer is so richly talented and so grossly perverse.

Readers know by now that the first half of *The Executioner's Song* is based on the horrifying story of two wanton murders in Utah by a bright, sick, witty, cowboyish paroled recidivist named Gary Gilmore, who, having been condemned to death for the crimes, staunchly insisted on being executed. The second half tells how the strong smell of money given off by this death-row drama drifted east with the weather systems and attracted New York's media vultures, the swiftest among them being one Lawrence Schiller, who had already picked the bones clean from other carrion: Jack Ruby, Marina Oswald, Susan Atkins, for examples. (Schiller had also—though Mailer finds it convenient to omit this from 1,056 pages which seem to leave absolutely nothing else out—arranged for Mailer to make bucks cleaning the dear flesh from the skeleton of poor Marilyn Monroe; and was, of course, to arrange the same for Mailer with Gilmore's remains.) . . .*

In fiction, the writer's voice matters; in reporting, the writer's authority matters. We read fiction to fortify our psyches, and in the pleasure that that fortification may give us, temperament holds sway. We read journalism—or most of us still do, anyway—to try to learn about the external world in which our psyches have to struggle along, and the quality we most need in our informant is some measure of trustworthiness. *The Executioner's Song* may satisfy us as fiction—it does me—precisely because the author's voice is so pungent, so active, so eloquent, so very alive. But there is deep trouble when we come to the journalistic pretensions of this novel, precisely because the temperament of the reporter is so intrusive, so vaunting, and, considering the specific story being told, so hard to trust.

When we read a novel of Mailer's, the wild shenanigans of his private life are none of our business, really; the art is there to speak for itself, and so is the strong voice of the weaver behind the arras. With good fiction, those are enough. But when we are told that a tale with the massive social implications of *The Executioner's Song* is "a model of complete, precise, and accurate reporting," we are entitled to know a bit more about the mind and temperament that have shaped our instruction. The facts about Mailer's life—and he himself has been the trumpeting source of most of our knowledge of them—raise some questions about the trustworthiness of the authority behind the book.

Like Hemingway before him, Norman Mailer has made himself at home in a fantasy of pugilism, and has challenged all champs and all pretenders in all weights to fifteen rounds in the ring of letters; he has scattered his macho boasts and seed among a flock of wives, mistresses, and bare acquaintances; near dawn after a night of carousal and quarrels he made a pretty fair attempt on the life of one of these ladies with a cheap knife; he has romanticized marijuana, "the smoke of the assassins," and rewrote one novel "bombed and sapped and charged and stoned with lush, with pot, with benny, saggy, Miltown, coffee, and two packs a day"; in a rage while directing a pseudo-movie he tried to bite an earlobe off an actor with the right name for the scene, Rip Torn; considering a mayoral run in New York he advocated jousting in Central Park as a therapy for muggers.

Can we trust a reporter with such a bizarre history of brutality, insecurity, mischief, and voguishness when he gives us, thinly, just three implied reasons (do they seem to be *justifications*?) for Gary Gilmore's crimes: (1) the desperation of a young lover afraid of losing his beloved; (2) the damage done him by psychiatrists in, for instance, having transiently administered to him, long before the murders, a drug called Prolixin; and (3) a vague possibility, only glancingly hinted at, of a strain of infantilism in the killer?

---

*In the next paragraphs Hersey provides detail on Lawrence Schiller's research, which Mailer mined, as he makes the case that Mailer's commitment to art leads him to take liberties with the facts of the story and the voices of the principal characters. For example, he provides examples of dialogue from Mailer's text and then asks if it represents projection or reporting. We pick up the argument where Hersey has turned to the distinction between journalism and fiction and the sources of trust in a journalist's word—the editors.

Or can we trust this reporter when he devotes so much energy and space to rendering the sex and violence in the story—making of it not *Romeo and Juliet* but a mongrel, out of *Tristan and Isolde* by *Bonnie and Clyde*—and skimps the intricate, fascinating, and socially consequential questions of law and philosophy that hovered over the first execution in the country in many years?

Or when, in his eagerness to give us a dope-smoky, drive-in, stick-shift, gang-bang Western romance, he does not do anything like justice to the vision of the kindly people of the town of Provo, firmly (and perhaps, in the context of this drama, disastrously) fixed and drenched in Mormon ideas of the correctional effects of love and decency; or to their views of proper sexual conventions, and of the regions beyond death?

Am I saying that we can accept what Mailer says as a novelist and cannot accept what he says as a journalist? Baffled by the impossibility of knowing when he is which, I am. When we read a novel, we are asked to suspend disbelief, and as soon as we close the book we can be expected in normal circumstances to bring the suspension to an end along with the story, for in fiction, as Auden wrote is the case in poetry (in *The Dyer's Hand*), "all facts and beliefs cease to be true or false and become interesting possibilities." But when we read an ambitious journalistic work, we are asked to believe, and to carry belief away with the book. This is a crucial difference.

Why does Mailer claim so much? He has repeatedly said over the years that he would rather be known as a novelist than as a journalist. In a *Paris Review* interview some years ago, which he liked well enough to include in *Cannibals and Christians*, he said:

> If what you write is a reflection of your own consciousness, then even journalism can become interesting. One wouldn't want to spend one's life at it and I wouldn't want ever to be caught justifying journalism as a major activity (it's obviously less interesting to write than a novel), but it's better, I think, to see journalism as a venture of one's ability to keep in shape than to see it as an essential betrayal of the chalice of your literary art. Temples are for women.

Disregard that last line. That was just Norman being a bad boy. But since the publication of *The Executioner's Song*, he has insisted over and over, that, yes, the book is both fiction and journalism. Asked how that could be, he said on one occasion (*The New York Times*, October 26, 1979): "A writer has certain inalienable rights, and one is the right to create confusion."

At the risk of taking Mailer seriously at a moment when we can see his tongue poking his cheek out, I would flatly assert that for a reporter that right is distinctly and preeminently alienable. If there is any one "right" a journalist never had to begin with, it is purely that one. This perversity of Mailer's brings us straight home: The widespread acceptance of *The Executioner's Song* as a "true-life story" is an ominous sign of journalism's ill-health these days.

4

Good writers care about what words mean. Francis Steegmuller said not long ago (*The New York Times*, March 26, 1980) that when Auden died his Oxford English Dictionary was "all but clawed to pieces." The better the writer, it seems, the more frequent the appeals to the lexicographer. Yet some very good writers have lately seemed to want to ignore what the dictionaries say about matters essential to their craft: That "fiction" means something; which something is excluded from "non-fiction." Both the OED and Webster's point to original, central, and rather copious meanings of "fiction": fashioning, imitating, or inventing. Both dictionaries, in elaborating the active, current definition of the word, lay stress on a fundamental antithesis. OED: "invention as opposed to fact." Webster:"that which is invented, feigned, or imagined . . .—opposed to *fact or reality*" (emphasis Webster's).

Our grasp on *reality*, our relationship with the real world, is what is at stake here. We have to grope our way through that world from day to day. To make sense of our lives, we need to know what is going on around us. This need plunges us at once into complicated philosophical issues, having to do with trees falling in distant forests. Can we always rely on what others tell us about what is "really" going on? A suspicion that we cannot has led to the great fallacy, as I see it, of the New Journalism, and indirectly to the blurring in recent years of fiction and nonfiction.

That fallacy can be crudely stated as follows: Since perfect objectivity in reporting what the eyes have seen and the ears have heard is impossible, there is no choice but to go all the way over to absolute subjectivity. The trouble with this is that it soon makes the reporter the center of interest rather than the real world he is supposed to be picturing or interpreting. A filter of temperament discolors the visible universe. The report becomes a performance. What is, or may be, going on in "reality" recedes into a backdrop for the actor-writer; it dissolves out of focus and becomes, in the end, fuzzy, vague, unrecognizable, and false.

The serious writer of fiction hopes to achieve a poetic truth, a human truth, which transcends any apparent or illusory "reality." And in good novels, the temperament of the author, as expressed through the complex mix of elements that writers call "voice," subtly becomes part of the impression of human truth that the reader gets. The fictionist may at times use real people or real events, sometimes deliberately remaking and transforming them, in order to flesh out imitation or make invention seem like reality. This sleight of hand works beautifully if the novelist is gifted, artful, and inventive; it is a disaster (and an open invitation to libel suits) when the writing is bad, when the invention is weak or nonexistent—in short, when fiction is not fiction.

Two kinds of grave social harm, beyond those already suggested, come from works like Capote's and Wolfe's and Mailer's.

The first is that their great success, whether in kudos or cash or both, attracts imitators. The blurring of the crafts becomes respectable, fashionable, profitable, enviable. The infection spreads. If the great Mailer can do it, so can any tyro, and the only certainty is that the tyro will fuzz things up worse than Mailer does. Headlines tell us that Capote has sold "Handcarved Coffins" to the movies for "nearly $500,000." The blurring has long since made its way into investigative journalism, which, of all forms of reporting, bears the heaviest weight of social responsibility. In *The Brethren*, the Woodward and Armstrong book on the Supreme Court which recently spent some time at the top of the bestseller list, the processes of filtration we have seen in the Mailer novel are similarly at work. Clerks vouch for Justices' subjective states, moods, thoughts, and exact words—mostly recaptured in distant retrospect. Chief Justice Burger refused all contact with the authors, yet: "Burger vowed to himself that he would grasp the reins of power immediately. . . ."

The second harm, related to the first, is far more serious. It is that these blurrings lead to, or at the very least help soften the way for, or confirm the reasonableness of, public lying. The message of Jules Feiffer's *Little Murders* is that tiny symbolic killings, done with the tongue, lead to big actual ones, done with guns. Habitual acceptance of little fibs leads to the swallowing whole of world-shaking lies. In the Dodge Aspen commercial, we are told we are watching two people in a following car through a hidden camera; what we watch (and overhear, as a hidden camera in a leading van could not possibly over-hear) is a carefully rehearsed advertising routine. We write that off; it's just a formula; we're used to all that stuff. But have we also gotten used to writing off big lies? Did we write off—I am afraid the vast majority of Americans *did* write off—being told in official announcements that bombs were being dropped on North Vietnam, when in fact they were being dropped on Cambodia?

It would be preposterous, of course, to hold Mailer's and Wolfe's recent inventions responsible, retroactively, for lies told a decade ago. But the point is that the two phenomena—the blurring of fiction and journalism, as Mailer and Wolfe and many others have practiced it (for quite a bit more than a decade), and public lying, as Kissinger and Nixon and many others have practiced it (and some still do)—the two have had something like a symbiotic relationship with each other. Each has nourished and needed the other. Each in its way has contributed to the befogging of the public vision, to subtle failures of discrimination, and to the collapse of important sorts of trust.

But how could the blurring possibly be corrected at this late date? Hasn't the process gone too far? Isn't all this much too complicated? Aren't the shadings too subtle?

Not at all. It is very simple. To redraw the line we need merely think clearly about the legends on the licenses. All we need do is insist upon two rules.

The writer of fiction must invent. The journalist must not invent.

18
HOW I BROKE THE MYLAI 4 STORY

Seymour Hersh

It was a young man—not in the military—who called me on the afternoon of October 22, 1969, to report that the Army was "court-martialing some lieutenant in secrecy at Fort Benning. He's supposed to have killed seventy-five Vietnamese civilians."

I still don't completely know why I believed my caller; catastrophe via telephone tip is a cheap commodity in Washington, D.C. Two factors, I guess, were important. First,

Seymour Hersh, "How I Broke the Mylai 4 Story," *Saturday Review*, July 11, 1970, 46–49. Reprinted with the kind permission of the author.

I hated the war in Vietnam and knew that the full story of its nature was not known to most Americans. Second, I had had the experience of publishing a book on chemical and biological warfare in 1968 telling, among other things, of huge Army nerve gas depots and the outdoor testing of lethal bacteria and viruses by Strangelovean military scientists. Although the book eventually helped the White House change its mind about biological warfare, its impact was slow in coming: Americans simply did not believe such things went on in America.

I instinctively knew I was not the first reporter to hear about the charge against the lieutenant, whoever he was, but I also knew I was probably one of the few who would believe it. So I simply stopped all other work (I was then researching a book on the Pentagon for Random House) and began chasing down the Mylai 4 massacre story.

I began at the beginning: Who was being court-martialed? For obvious reasons, I did not telephone the Pentagon press office with my query. So I called friends in and out of the military (some were retired) all over Washington. I made at least twenty-five calls a day for two or three days until I got a lead. An old friend on Capitol Hill, a hawk, knew about the case. He gave me a few sketchy details, but urged me not to do anything about the story. "It'll hurt the Army, Sy." I had gone to the hawks in Congress for information on the assumption, usually sound, that they would have been informed in advance by the Army, which could ill afford to have its boosters read about mass murder charges in the newspapers.

My hawk friend also told me that there was as yet no court-martial under way. I then took a chance and telephoned the public information office at Fort Benning, Georgia, and asked for the names of any men being held for court-martial. Someone told me that a Lt. William L. Calley of Miami, Florida was being held on murder charges "for offenses allegedly committed against civilians while serving in Vietnam in March 1968." I was told that an Associated Press dispatch about the charges could be found on page 38 of *The New York Times* for September 8. The officer on the other end of the telephone was courteous and helpful; he, perhaps, knew even less about the case than I did.

I was sure that Lieutenant Calley was the one accused of the mass murder. I went back to my friend in Congress and began the standard newspaperman's bluffing operation: pretending to know more than I did. I then learned that Lieutenant Calley was indeed the officer charged with the murder of more than seventy-five civilians; my source thought the correct number was over ninety. He also told me that the lieutenant not only had ordered his men to open fire, but also had fired at civilians himself. I was told that this group of men were obviously psychotic and urged once again not to write anything (at no time, however, did anyone threaten me in connection with my investigation).

I then talked to some officers at the Pentagon, all of whom knew something about the case. Most refused to say anything, but one colonel, who also told me not to write about Mylai 4, indignantly slammed the edge of his hand against his knee and said, "Don't tell me kids this high are Vietcong." The implication was plain: Calley and his men had gone berserk. It was an aberration.

By now, less than two weeks after getting the tip. I suspected that there had been a massacre of civilians in Vietnam that went far beyond Calley; and I knew that many members of Congress and many Pentagon officers knew a great deal about it. Only the public hadn't been told. But as a reporter, I was still far away from being able to write about the massacre. Who was Calley? When did it happen? What happened? What were the charges?

I had to find Calley's lawyer and then the lieutenant. There was no more information available—at least to me—in Washington. After some frustrating attempts; I telephoned my original source and asked if he could help. A day later, he came back with the name "Latimer." That was all he knew; Calley's lawyer was named Latimer. There was only one lawyer named Latimer in the Washington directory; no, he wasn't representing a Lieutenant Calley in a court-martial case, but perhaps I meant George Latimer of Salt Lake City, a former judge on the Court of Military Appeals. I did. I called Salt Lake City to interview Latimer, but suddenly made another instinctive decision—I wouldn't talk over the telephone to any potential source about the case. Not because of any fear of wiretapping or such, but simply to ensure that I gave myself every chance to get as much information as possible. Latimer agreed, somewhat reluctantly, to see me—he couldn't be sure how much I knew.

In early November, I flew out (aided by a $2,000 travel grant from the Philip Stern Fund for Investigative Journalism), and Latimer and I talked. It was a major step forward. I learned Calley was officially charged with six specifications of murder, where the offenses allegedly took place, something about Calley and his family, and quite a bit about what Latimer thought of the Army charges. I agreed not to publish anything about the case until I contacted Latimer, who made the request before discussing the case with me. There was no reason for me not to make such a pact: Latimer, as long as he did not initiate a newspaper story, had nothing to lose by publication of the charges against his client. The lawyer was convinced the Army was railroading the young lieutenant. He was going to make another attempt in Washington to have the charges dropped, but acknowledged in advance that it would be fruitless. Would I wait at least until then? Sure.

After seeing Latimer, I called *Life* magazine and told a personal friend there about the story. The friend, one of *Life*'s many editors, took it up immediately with his superiors. A day later, came the word: "Out of the question." *Life* had already heard something about the case, my friend said, and had decided not to pursue. He was disappointed. (Later, I learned that Ronald Ridenhour, the GI whose letter prompted the Army inquiry in March 1969, had contacted the magazine.) I next tried *Look* magazine, even drafting—at an editor's request—a memo outlining the salient facts of the story. They, too, passed it by.

For lack of anywhere else to turn, I kept on researching. All I now needed to begin writing was to find Calley and confirm—once again—the essential details of the case. I knew, from my conversation with Latimer in Salt Lake City, that Calley had been shipped back from Vietnam (where he was serving his third tour) to the United States in midsummer 1969, and was stationed at Benning, one of the Army's largest training centers, near Columbus, Georgia. I decided to go blindly looking for him.

On November 11, I took an early morning flight from Washington's Dulles Airport directly to Columbus, where I rented a car and drove onto the base (like the vast majority of Army installations around the country, Fort Benning is an "open base," available to visitors). Where to begin my hunt? Not the public relations office, certainly. Calley wasn't listed in the base telephone directory, the information operator couldn't find his name under "new" listings, and there was no William Calley listed on any register in the bachelor officers' quarters. I was convinced the Army was hiding him somewhere on the base, nonetheless, and I began with the prisoners' stockade under the jurisdiction of the Army Provost Marshal. The basic assumption was that only a few high-ranking officers would know the significance of my questions about Calley; thus, I asked directly for him when I went to the main Provost Marshal's office on the base. The officers were helpful and checked their records, but no William Calley. There were a dozen or so military police (MP) detachments scattered throughout the huge fort; perhaps Calley was locked up covertly in one of them. So I began visiting those units, parking my car in front, grabbing my brief case; and calmly strolling in, saying to the sergeant invariably on duty, "Hi. I'm looking for Bill Calley." No one asked who I was or why I was looking; I assumed they assumed I was a lawyer (since, after all, not too many civilians with brief cases walk into MP offices).

After about four stops, it was clear that no prisoners were being kept in those small MP units, so I gave that up. By now I had been on the base more than three hours, driven more than a hundred miles, and checked most of the obvious places—with no sign of Calley.

He was not listed in any military directories (I even checked the directory at Infantry Hall, the large office building that serves as a focal point for training at Benning). Calley was not a prisoner, at least not in any of the regular detention centers. Yet, his lawyer had made clear he was at Fort Benning, and even indicated that the two were in regular telephone communication.

To reassure myself that Calley did, indeed, exist, I made a reckless move. I walked into the Judge Advocate General's office (JAG serves as the Army's lawyer and would be prosecuting the Calley case) and asked a "lifer," the elderly sergeant at the desk, if he knew where Calley could be reached. The sergeant quickly wanted to know who I was. When I said reporter, he grabbed a telephone and started to place a call to a colonel. I walked out, saying, "It's okay. It's okay." He probably did not complete the call; since I was no longer actually in his office, I was no longer his problem. In the Army, the buck does not stop with sergeants.

By now it was after lunch and I had no clue, except I was pretty sure that Calley was around. At least the sergeant in the JAG office knew who he was. Latimer had also given me the name of Calley's military lawyer at Fort Benning, Major Kenneth A. Raby, but a morning's visit with him did nothing for me, and got the major visibly agitated. The buck doesn't stop with majors, either.

I had a depressing sandwich at an Army cafeteria and thought briefly of giving up. But then I had a better thought. I had noticed that the Fort Benning telephone directory was dated September 1969, at least one month *after* Calley was sent back to the base. His name had been struck from that directory, but perhaps it would still be shown under the "new" or "additional" listings category for the earlier telephone directory. Army telephone books are usually published four times a year, a reflection, unfortunately, more of the constant flux of personnel than of efficiency.

After some explanation, the information operator checked an old book, and found a "new" listing for a William L. Calley, Jr., who was attached to a company in The Student Brigade (TSB), the main training unit for recruits at Fort Benning. I dashed over there, and luckily found the unit's company commander, Captain Charles Lewellen, in his office. (Getting there wasn't so simple, largely because the combination of Army abbreviations and Southern dialect made it impossible to easily understand directions. It took nearly one precious hour to travel the scant two or three miles to Lewellen's office.)

Lewellen had a broad smile for me when I announced I was a journalist. It faded when I said I was looking for Bill Calley. He, too, quickly grabbed for the telephone and asked for some colonel. He explained that he wasn't authorized to speak about Calley. Was the lieutenant still in his company? "I can't tell you anything," the captain said. I knew I was finally getting close. Calley was around. I quickly walked out, not wanting to meet up with any colonels—yet. Lewellen hung up and followed me outside the barracks (a standard three-story concrete and steel Army structure of the type that replaced the World War II prefabs). He grabbed my arm and said, almost conspiratorially: "Look, give me a break. I'm just a captain trying to mind my own business. If you've got any questions about Calley, take them someplace else." (Six months later, I learned that Lewellen had been in the same brigade as Calley at the time of Mylai 4, and had made an extensive tape recording of all the radio messages during the assault by Calley's unit, Charlie Company. The tape, made not in expectation of the slaughter, but because of Lewellen's interest in recording the sounds of combat, was later described by one officer who heard it as an "instant replay" of the massacre. But Lewellen delayed turning over his tape to Fort Benning's JAG office and, in fact, had done so only two months before I dropped in on him—almost eighteen months after the assault.)

The captain's advice only made me bolder. The closer I got to Calley, the more chances I would take. I waited for Lewellen to walk back into the barracks and then followed, only dodging past his office and up the stairs that led to the empty sleeping quarters above. The trainees were out in the field. I walked through corridor after corridor of empty beds. I was sure the Army was keeping Calley penned up somewhere in the barracks. On the third floor, I saw a young GI sleeping in a bunk. I walked over and kicked the bed. "Wake up, Calley." A blond youth rolled over, yawned, and said, "What the hell, man?" The name tag on his fatigues said something like Petri. He, it turned out, was from Ottumwa, Iowa, a National Guardsman serving his compulsory six months of active duty at Fort Benning. The Army had lost his files, so he was spending his days in bed. "Been in the God-damned Army for three-and-a-half months, and all I do is sleep," the GI said. We began talking. He'd heard a little bit about Calley: "You mean that guy that killed all those people?" But Calley hadn't been around, and my new-found friend had no idea where he could be found. But he did have a friend who worked in the message center of the battalion sorting most of the mail. The friend, Jerry, had just been busted from sergeant to private the day before; he might be in the mood to help. By now it was nearly 4 p.m., and the working day was almost over. Would the GI lead me to his friend? Nope. He didn't want to get involved. But I knew how to handle that. I said, as rapidly as possible: "Look. It's 3:35. Synchronize our watches, and I'll meet you behind the barracks in exactly seven minutes—at 3:42. I'll be driving a blue Ford and will pick you up as soon as you get out the door. No one will see." Without giving him a chance to protest, I dashed off to my car. I knew that any kid who had been sleeping for three-and-a-half months wouldn't pass up any kind of action. He showed up at 3:42 on the dot and led me to the battalion message center.

The busted private was working in a small, run-down former barracks converted into a mail room. I left my car, motor running, in the parking lot directly in front of it, grabbed my brief case, straightened my tie, and walked in. "I want to see Jerry outside in my car in two minutes flat," I said crisply and angrily to the first sergeant sitting nearby. The sergeant giggled happily (one could hear him thinking: "What has that dumb son of a bitch done now?") and went off. I walked back to my car, and two minutes later Jerry appeared, looking apprehensive. I motioned him inside, and told him whom and what I wanted. Gee, he was sorry, but he didn't know anything much about Calley. In fact, there was a big batch of undelivered mail waiting for the lieutenant now. Calley had been around, the ex-sergeant said, but no one knew where he was now. The only way Jerry could find out anything would be to steal Calley's personnel file. There was a long pause.

"Well?" I said.

"I'll try, Mister."

In less than five minutes he returned with a short information sheet the battalion commander kept on each officer. The sheet included a local address in Columbus for Calley. By now it was after working hours—nearly 5 p.m.—and again I raced off. The address turned out to be a small house Calley and a number of other young officers had rented in a residential area near Fort Benning. As I drove up, some officers were climbing out of a car in the driveway. I parked behind them and again simply explained who I was and what I wanted. After some hesitation, the officers—angry at what they considered the mistreatment of Calley—told me what they knew.

As they described it, Calley had not deliberately killed any civilians that day, but large numbers had been slain during a bitter battle with the Vietcong who were defending Mylai 4 (known to the officers only as "Pinkville"). Calley had been ordered by the Army out of the house in mid-September, they said, and told to live on base in the senior bachelor officers' quarters located near some tennis courts. I sped again to Fort Benning and again checked the roster at the officers' quarters. No Calley. So I drove over to the senior bachelor officers' quarters—by now it was 7 p.m.—and was generally discouraged by what I saw. There were five two-story buildings, each with about fifty rooms. Calley's former roommates had never visited him there and had no idea—so they said— in which room he was billeted. So I did the inevitable. Beginning with the first building, I walked through the maze, knocking on each door and saying brightly with each knock, "Hey, Bill, are you in?" I did this for the next hour or two, finding only a few officers inside and no sign of Calley. Again, I was at the end of my wits, but I wasn't about to quit. If need be, I thought, I'd stay at Benning and knock on these doors for weeks.

Rather than go to a motel, I decided to continue the search at the nearby large parking area for officers' cars. I spent about an hour there, stopping each auto as it drove in saying, "Hey, I'm looking for Bill Calley. You seen him?" No luck. By now it was nearly 10 p.m. I decided to go back to my car and get off the base. Two men were tinkering with the motor of an auto in a far corner of the parking lot; I had not seen them earlier. One last try: "Hey, you guys seen Bill Calley?" "Yeah. He's up in 221," one of them answered, without lifting his head. Long pause. "Um, which building?" Now he turned and gave me a sharp look. Again I explained I was a journalist and told why I wanted to talk to Calley ("To give him a chance to tell his side, if he wants"). The officer invited me into his room for a drink of Scotch. He was a twenty-year veteran of the Army, a guy who had joined up at the age of seventeen and was now beginning to have some doubts about Vietnam. Not that he was a peacenik or troublemaker; he just wasn't sure where the Army—and he—were headed. He wanted to complain to a reporter from Washington.

We drank for an hour, and I did most of the talking, telling him about my visit to attorney Latimer and my search for the lieutenant. The officer, of course, eventually began telling me what he knew. He and Calley were friends and drank together. Calley was probably going to be at a party later that night in town; would I want to come? I sure would. More drinks, and finally we walked but together. Once outside, I was anxious to go and get some sleep, but the officer suddenly yelled to a slight figure walking toward us, "Hey, Rusty, come over here." "Look, I gotta go," I said, wanting no more drinks at that moment. "Wait. That's Calley."

In my book, I've described my impressions of the lieutenant in the following way:

> Calley was apprehensive. All he wanted in life was to stay in the Army and be a good soldier. He reminded me of an earnest freshman one might find at an agricultural college, anxious about making a fraternity. We went to a party at a friend's apartment and had some drinks. I wanted to leave. Calley wanted me to stay. He knew what was coming, and he knew I was the last reporter with whom he would talk, and drink, for many months. He told me, that evening, a little bit about the operation; he also told me how many people he had been accused of killing.

We sat in his room for an hour or so drinking beer. As he talked, I took notes, even jotting down the number of his telephone. He took a shower, and I remember staring at his nude body as he toweled and thinking, "This is the man who shot and killed 109 people." Hell, he was nice. We went out together and drove to the Post Exchange, where Calley bought some bourbon and wine; then we drove to a food store and picked up a steak. Our next stop was his girl's apartment nearby; she cooked us a great dinner. It could have been a night with any old friend.

Calley clinched the Mylai story for me, although I would write about the massacre at first as having taken place in a location called "Pinkville" (actually just an Army map coloring that showed a high population density in the area of Mylai). He had confirmed the essential numbers of the story and provided some essential quotes. I wrote the 1,500-word story—first of five I was to write about Mylai 4—on the airplane going back to Washington the next morning. It began: "Lt. William L. Calley, Jr., twenty-six, is a mild-mannered, boyish-looking Vietnam combat veteran with the nickname of 'Rusty.' The Army says he deliberately murdered at least 109 Vietnamese civilians during a search-and-destroy mission in March 1968, in a Vietcong stronghold known as 'Pinkville.' "

If *Life* or *Look* wouldn't have the story, a small syndicate known as Dispatch News Service would. Run by David Obst, a twenty-four-year-old neighbor of mine in Washington, Dispatch had been placing stories in West Coast newspapers from a small group of correspondents in Vietnam and elsewhere in Asia. Obst, who had moved East to drum up more business a few months earlier, convinced me not so much that he could do anything with the Mylai 4 story, but that he would try. At least the editors would get a chance to read my story, I thought, and perhaps assign someone to check it out. My newspaper experience paid off in this regard, because I knew the only person the reporters would be able to contact would be Latimer, Calley's attorney. The Pentagon would not comment, and Calley was unreachable (unless someone wanted to fly down to Fort Benning and try to find him). So I took the unusual step after reaching Washington of calling Latimer and reading my entire story to him. This normally is a frowned-upon practice in journalism and rightly so, but I knew two things would impress Latimer: the fact that the story was written objectively (all my years with the Associated Press had given me that ability); and the fact that none of the quotes I had from Calley involved specifics about what he had or had not done that day. To this day, I have not written all that Calley told me; he is entitled to make his own defense at a time of his choosing.

Latimer made one helpful addition to my story and, most importantly, stood behind it when the inevitable flood of newspaper calls came the next day. Dispatch had sent the story by wire (collect, no less) to about fifty major newspapers; thirty-six of them purchased it for $100 and ran it on their front page on November 13, 1969, and sent the publishing world scrambling.

The story was out. I would later spend almost five months on the road, interviewing more than fifty of the GIs who were with Calley on that day in March 1968, writing more newspaper stories and my book. Throughout it all, whenever things got hectic and disappointing, I would simply remember that day at Fort Benning when I tracked down William Calley. I'll remember it the rest of my life.

19

JOURNALISM OF VERIFICATION

Bill Kovach
Tom Rosenstiel

As he sat down to write, the Greek correspondent wanted to convince his audience it could trust him. He was not writing an official version of the war, he wanted people to know, nor a hasty one. He was striving for something more independent, more reliable, more lasting. He had been mindful in his reporting of the way memory, perspective, and politics blur recollection. He had double-checked his facts.

To convey all this, he decided to explain the methods of his reporting right at the beginning. This is the dedication to the methodology of truth Thucydides drafted in the fifth century B.C. in the introduction to his account of the Peloponnesian War:

> With regard to my factual reporting of events . . . I have made it a principle not to write down the first story that came my way, and not even to be guided by my own general impressions; either I was present myself at the events which I have described or else heard of them from eye witnesses whose reports I have checked with as much thoroughness as possible. Not that even so the truth was easy to discover: different eye witnesses gave different accounts of the same events, speaking out of partiality for one side or the other, or else from imperfect memories.[1]

Bill Kovach and Tom Rosenstiel, "Journalism of Verification," Chapter 4 of *The Elements of Journalism; What Newspeople Should Know and the Public Should Expect* (New York: Three Rivers Press, 2001), 70–93. Copyright © 2001 by Bill Kovach and Tom Rosenstiel. Used by permission of Crown Publishers, a division of Random House, Inc.

Why does this passage seem so contemporary more than 2,000 years after it was written? Because it speaks to the heart of the task of nonfiction: How do you sift through the rumor, the gossip, the failed memory, the manipulative agendas, and try to capture something as accurately as possible, subject to revision in light of new information and perspective? How do you overcome your own limits of perception, your own experience, and come to an account that more people will recognize as reliable? Strip away all the debate about journalism, all the differences between media or between one age or another. Day to day, these are the real questions faced by those who try to gather news, understand it, and convey it to others.

While not standardized in any code, every journalist operates by relying on some often highly personal method of testing and providing information—his own individual discipline of verification. Practices such as seeking multiple witnesses to an event, disclosing as much as possible about sources, and asking many sides for comment are, in effect, the discipline of verification. These methods may be intensely personal and idiosyncratic. Writer Rick Meyer at the *Los Angeles Times* splices his facts and interviews into note-card-like snippets and organizes them on his office floor. Or they may be institutionalized, like the fact-checking department of *The New Yorker*. But by whatever name, in whatever medium, these habits and methods underlie the third principle:

The essence of journalism is a discipline of verification.

In the end, the discipline of verification is what separates journalism from entertainment, propaganda, fiction, or art. Entertainment—and its cousin "infotainment"—focuses on what is most diverting. Propaganda will select facts or invent them to serve the real purpose—persuasion and manipulation. Fiction invents scenarios to get at a more personal impression of what it calls truth.

Journalism alone is focused first on getting what happened down right.

This is why journalists become so upset with Hollywood moviemakers when they stray into real-life accounts. *60 Minutes* correspondent Mike Wallace was livid in 1999 when the movie *The Insider* put invented words in his mouth and altered time frames to suggest he was worried about his "legacy" when he caved in to the tobacco industry on a story. "Have you ever heard me invoke the word *legacy*? That is utter bullshit . . . and I'm offended."[2] The film's director, Michael Mann, countered that though things were changed to make the story more dramatic, the film was "basically accurate" to some larger definition of truthfulness, since Wallace had indeed caved. If words were invented or if Wallace's motives were different, it didn't matter. In this sense utility becomes a higher value and literal truth is subordinated to necessary fictions.

The two men are talking different languages. Mann is saying Wallace is, in effect, hiding behind the facts to obscure the significance of what he did. Wallace is suggesting the significance can never be detached from an accurate account of the details. In this case both arguments may be defensible. But the journalistic process of verification must take both of these into account.

Journalists often fail to connect their deeply held feelings about craft to the larger philosophical questions about journalism's role. They know how to check a story. They can't always articulate the role that checking a story plays in society. But it resides in the central function of journalism. As Walter Lippmann put it in 1920, "There can be no liberty for a community which lacks the information by which to detect lies."[3]

THE LOST MEANING OF OBJECTIVITY

Perhaps because the discipline of verification is so personal and so haphazardly communicated, it is also part of one of the great confusions of journalism—the concept of objectivity. The original meaning of this idea is now thoroughly misunderstood, and by and large lost.

When the concept originally evolved, it was not meant to imply that journalists were free of bias. Quite the contrary. The term began to appear as part of journalism early in the last century, particularly in the 1920s, out of a growing recognition that journalists were full of bias, often unconsciously. Objectivity called for journalists to develop a consistent method of testing information—a transparent approach to evidence—precisely so that personal and cultural biases would not undermine the accuracy of their work.

In the latter part of the nineteenth century, journalists talked about something called realism rather than objectivity.[4] This was the idea that if reporters simply dug out the facts and ordered them together, the truth would reveal itself rather naturally. Realism emerged at a time when journalism was separating from political parties and becoming more accurate. It coincided with the invention of what journalists call the inverted pyramid, in which a journalist lines the facts up from most important to least important, thinking it helps audiences understand things naturally.

At the beginning of the twentieth century, however, some journalists began to worry about the naïveté of realism. In part, reporters and editors were becoming more aware of the rise of propaganda and the role of press agents. At a time when Freud was developing his theories of the unconscious and painters like Picasso were experimenting with Cubism, journalists were also developing a greater recognition of human subjectivity. In 1919, Walter Lippmann and Charles Merz, an associate editor for the *New York World*, wrote an influential and scathing account of how cultural blinders had distorted the *New York Times* coverage of the Russian Revolution.[5] "In the large, the news about Russia is a case of seeing not what was, but what men wished to see," they wrote. Lippmann and others began to look for ways for the individual journalist "to remain clear and free of his irrational, his unexamined, his unacknowledged prejudgments in observing, understanding and presenting the news."[6]

Journalism, Lippmann declared, was being practiced by "untrained accidental witnesses." Good intentions, or what some might call "honest efforts" by journalists, were not enough. Faith in the rugged individualism of the tough reporter, what Lippmann called the "cynicism of the trade," was also not enough. Nor were some of the new innovations of the times, like bylines, or columnists.[7]

The solution, Lippmann argued, was for journalists to acquire more of "the scientific spirit. . . . There is but one kind of unity possible in a world as diverse as ours. It is unity of method, rather than aim; the unity of disciplined experiment." Lippmann meant by this that journalism should aspire to "a common intellectual method and a common area of valid fact." To begin, Lippmann thought, the fledgling field of journalism education should be transformed from "trade schools designed to fit men for higher salaries in the existing structure." Instead, the field should make its cornerstone the study of evidence and verification.[8]

Although this was an era of faith in science, Lippmann had few illusions. "It does not matter that the news is not susceptible of mathematical statement. In fact, just because news is complex and slippery, good reporting requires the exercise of the highest scientific virtues."[9]

In the original concept, in other words, the method is objective, not the journalist. The key was in the discipline of the craft, not the aim.

The point has some important implications. One is that the impartial voice employed by many news organizations, that familiar, supposedly neutral style of newswriting, is not a fundamental principle of journalism. Rather, it is an often helpful device news organizations use to highlight that they are trying to produce something obtained by objective methods. The second implication is that this neutral voice, without a discipline of verification, creates a veneer covering something hollow. Journalists who select sources to express what is really their own point of view, and then use the neutral voice to make it seem objective, are engaged in a form of deception. This damages the credibility of the whole profession by making it seem unprincipled, dishonest, and biased. This is an important caution in an age when the standards of the press are so in doubt.

Lippmann was not alone in calling for a greater sense of professionalization, though his arguments are the most sophisticated. Joseph Pulitzer, the great innovator of yellow journalism a generation earlier, had just created the Graduate School of Journalism at Columbia University for many of the same, though less clearly articulated, reasons. The Newspaper Guild was founded in large part to help professionalize journalism.

Over the years, however, this original and more sophisticated understanding of objectivity was utterly confused and its meaning lost. Writers such as Leo Rosten, who authored an influential sociological study of journalists, used the term to suggest that the journalist was objective. Not surprisingly, he found that idea wanting. So did various legal opinions, which declared objectivity impossible. Many journalists never really understood what Lippmann meant.[10] Over time, journalists began to reject the term *objectivity* as an illusion.

In the meantime, reporters have gone on to refine the concept Lippmann had in mind, but usually only privately, and in the name of technique or reporting routines rather than journalism's larger purpose. The notion of an objective method of reporting exists in pieces, handed down by word of mouth from reporter to reporter. Developmental psychologist William Damon at Stanford, for instance, has identified various "strategies" journalists have developed to verify their reporting. Damon asked his interviewees where they learned these concepts. Overwhelmingly the answer was: by trial and error and on my own or from a friend. Rarely did journalists report learning them in journalism school or from their editors.[11] Many useful books have been written. The group calling itself Investigative Reporters and Editors, for instance, has tried to develop a methodology for how to use public records, read documents, and produce Freedom of Information Act requests.

By and large, however, these informal strategies have not been pulled together into the widely understood discipline that Lippmann and others imagined. These is nothing approaching standard rules of evidence, as in the law, or an agreed-upon method of observation, as in the conduct of scientific experiments.

Nor have the older conventions of verification been expanded to match the new forms of journalism. Although journalism may have developed various techniques and conventions for determining facts, it has done less to develop a *system* for testing the reliability of journalistic interpretation.

JOURNALISM OF ASSERTION VERSUS JOURNALISM OF VERIFICATION

Now, moreover, the modern press culture generally is weakening the methodology of verification journalists have developed. Technology is part of it. "The Internet and Nexis [plus services developed over the last decade or so for sharing and disseminating video] afford journalists easy access to stories and quotes without doing their own investigating," journalist Geneva Overholser told us at one Committee of Concerned Journalists forum. Facts have become a commodity, easily acquired, repackaged, and repurposed. In the age of the 24-hour news cycle, journalists now spend more time looking for something to add to the existing news, usually interpretation, rather than trying to independently discover and verify new facts. "Once a story is hatched, it's as if all the herd behavior is true. The story is determined by one medium—one newspaper or TV account. . . . Partly because news organizations are being consolidated and partly because of electronic reporting, we all feed at the same trough," said Overholser.[12]

The case of presidential candidate A1 Gore is only one example of how technology can weaken the process of double-checking. As Gore campaigned in the 2,000 election, the press began to focus on his seeming propensity to exaggerate past accomplishments. One account referred to Gore's "Pinocchio problem," another called him a "liar," and a third "delusional."[13] A key bit of evidence was his supposed claim that he had discovered the Love Canal toxic waste site in upstate New York. The problem is, Gore had never made any such claim. He had told a group of New Hampshire high school students that he first learned about hazardous waste dangers when a constituent told him about a polluted town in Tennessee called Toone and Gore wanted to hold hearings. "I looked around the country for other sites like that," he told the students. "I found a little place in upstate New York called Love Canal. Had the first hearing on the issue, and Toone, Tennessee—that was the one that you didn't hear of. But that was the one that started it all."[14]

The next day, however, the *Washington Post* misquoted Gore completely as saying "I was the one that started it all." In a press release, the Republican Party changed the quote to "I was the one who started it all." The *New York Times* printed the same misquote as the *Post*. Soon the press was off and running, relying on the faulty accounts fixed in the Nexis database of the two papers. It didn't catch anyone's attention that the Associated Press had the quote correct. The matter was not cleared up until the high school students themselves complained.

As journalists spend more time trying to synthesize the ever-growing stream of data pouring in through the new portals of information, the risk is they can become more passive, more receivers than gatherers. To combat this, a better understanding of the original meaning of objectivity could help put the news on firmer footing. We are not the only ones to recognize this. "Journalism and science come from the same intellectual roots," said Phil Meyer, University of North Carolina journalism professor, "from the seventeenth- and eighteenth-century enlightenment. The same thinking that led to the First Amendment"—the idea that out of a diversity of views we are more likely to know the truth—also "led to the scientific method. . . . I think this connection between journalism and science ought to be restored to the extent that we can. . . . I think we ought to emphasize objectivity of method. That's what scientific method is—our humanity, our subjective impulses . . . directed toward deciding what to investigate by objective means."[15]

Seen in this light, fairness and balance take on a new meaning. Rather than high principles, they are really techniques—devices—to help guide journalists in the development and verification of their accounts. They should never be pursued for their own sake or invoked as journalism's goal. Their value is in helping to get us closer to more thorough verification and a reliable version of events.

Balance, for instance, can lead to distortion. If an overwhelming percentage of scientists, as an example, believe that global warming is a scientific fact, or that some medical treatment is clearly the safest, it is a disservice to citizens and truthfulness to create the impression that the scientific debate is equally split. Unfortunately, all too often journalistic balance is misconstrued to have this kind of almost mathematical meaning, as if a good story is one that has an equal number of quotes from two sides. As journalists know, often there are more than two sides to a story. And sometimes balancing them equally is not a true reflection of reality.

Fairness, in turn, can also be misunderstood if it is seen to be a goal unto itself. Fairness should mean the journalist is being fair to the facts, and to a citizen's understanding of them. It should not mean, "Am I being fair to my sources, so that none of them will be unhappy?" Nor should it mean that journalist asking, "Does my story seem fair?" These are subjective judgments that may steer the journalist away from the need to do more to verify her work.

Clarifying such common misunderstandings and improving the discipline of verification may be the most important step journalists can take in improving the quality of news and public discussion. In the end, this discipline is what separates journalism from other fields and creates an economic reason for it to continue. A more conscious discipline of verification is the best antidote to the old journalism of verification being overrun by a new journalism of assertion, and it would provide citizens with a basis for relying on journalistic accounts.

What would this journalism of objective method rather than aim look like? What should citizens expect from the press as a reasonable discipline of reporting?

As we listened to and studied the thoughts of journalists, citizens, and others who have thought about the news, we began to see a core set of concepts that form the foundation of the discipline of verification. They are the intellectual principles of a science of reporting:

1. Never add anything that was not there.
2. Never deceive the audience.
3. Be transparent as possible about your methods and motives.
4. Rely on your own original reporting.
5. Exercise humility.

Let's examine them one at a time.

An important parallel to the new journalism of assertion is the rise of fiction posing as nonfiction. It has had different names in different areas. On television, producers have called it docudrama. It is making stuff up. In some cases it is just lying. Oddly, there are some in journalism who believe that narrative nonfiction, the use of literary style to tell nonfiction, needs to blend into the area of invention. A long list of some of the best narrative stylists in nonfiction also doesn't see the problem. But the problem is growing. Ironically, it is also unnecessary. Narrative nonfiction doesn't need to invent to succeed. Mark Kramer at Boston University offers a strong set of rules which any deadline journalist or literary stylist could live with; for example, he speaks to interior monologues: "No attribution of thoughts to sources unless the sources have said they'd had those very thoughts." Steve Lopez, a writer at Time Inc., says the rules and devices may differ depending on the style of story, but the principle does not: If it isn't verified, don't use it. Perhaps John McPhee, a *New Yorker* writer noted for the strength of his narrative style, summarized the key imperatives best: "The nonfiction writer is communicating with the reader about real people in real places. So if those people talk, you say what those people said. You don't say what the writer decides they said. . . . You don't make up dialogue. You don't make a composite character. . . . And you don't get inside their [characters'] heads and think for them. You can't interview the dead. Where writers abridge that, they hitchhike on the credibility of writers who don't."[16]

In 1980, John Hersey, the Pulitzer Prize—winning author of *Hiroshima*, the story of the effects of the first use of the atomic bomb in World War II, attempted to articulate a principle to help make journalism compelling without crossing the line between fact and fiction. In "The Legend on the License," Hersey advocated a strict standard: Never invent. Journalism's implicit credo is "nothing here is made up."[17]

Today, we think Hersey's standard of "never invent" needs to be refined. In his book *Midnight in the Garden of Good and Evil*, John Berendt used composite characters and condensed several events into one for dramatic effect. Ronald Reagan biographer Edmund Morris believed he could make the former president's life more vivid if he, the biographer, were a character in it. But reconstructing dialogue, using composite characters, compressing events, and moving people in time are inventions.

Along with Roy Peter Clark, the senior scholar at the Poynter Institute in St. Petersburg, Florida, we developed an updated set of ideas for journalists trying to navigate the shoals lying between fact and fiction.

Do Not Add

Do not add simply means do not add things that did not happen. This goes further than "never invent" or make things up, for it also encompasses rearranging events in time or place or conflating characters or events. If a siren rang out during the taping of a TV story, and for dramatic effect it is moved from one scene to another, it has been added to that second place. What was once a fact becomes a fiction.

Do Not Deceive

Do not deceive means never mislead the audience. Fooling people is a form of lying and mocks the idea that journalism is committed to truthfulness. This principle is closely related to *do not add*. If you move the sound of the siren and do not tell the audience, you are deceiving them. If acknowledging what you've done would make it unpalatable to the audience, then it is self-evidently improper. This is a useful check. How would the audience feel if they knew you moved that sound to another point in the story to make it more dramatic? Most likely they would feel the move was cheesy.

Do not deceive means that if one is going to engage in any narrative or storytelling techniques that vary from the most literal form of eye-witness reporting, the audience should know. On the question of quoting people, a survey of journalists that we conducted found broad agreement. Except for word changes to correct grammar, the overwhelming majority of journalists believe some signal should be sent to audiences—such as ellipses or brackets—if words inside quotation marks are changed or phrases deleted for clarity.[18]

If a journalist reconstructs quotes or events he did not witness, *do not deceive* suggests the audience should know these specific quotes were reconstructed and how these secondhand quotes were verified. A vague author's note at the beginning or end of a book or story that tells audiences merely "some interviews involved reconstruction" doesn't come close to adequate. Which interviews? Reconstructed how? These kinds of vague disclosures are not disclosures at all. They really amount to evasions.

We believe these two notions, *do not add* and *do not deceive*, serve as basic guideposts for journalists navigating the line between fact and fiction. But how as citizens are we to identify which journalism to trust? Here some other concepts help.

Transparency

If journalists are truth seekers, it must follow that they be honest and truthful with their audiences, too—that they be truth presenters. If nothing else, this responsibility requires that journalists be as open and honest with audiences as they can about what they know and what they don't. How can you claim to be seeking to convey the truth if you're not truthful with the audience in the first place?

The only way in practice to level with people about what you know is to reveal as much as possible about sources and methods. How do you know what you know? Who are your sources? How direct is their knowledge? What biases might they have? Are there conflicting accounts? What don't we know? Call it the Rule of Transparency. We consider it the most important single element in creating a better discipline of verification.

Most of the limitations journalists face in trying to move from accuracy to truth are addressed, if not overcome, by being honest about the nature of our knowledge, why we trust it, and what efforts we make to learn more.

Transparency has a second important virtue: it signals the journalist's respect for the audience. It allows the audience to judge the validity of the information, the process by which it was secured, and the motives and biases of the journalist providing it. This makes transparency the best protection against errors and deception by sources. If the best information a journalist has comes from a potentially biased source, naming the source will reveal to the audience the possible bias of the information—and may inhibit the source from deceiving as well.

Transparency also helps establish that the journalist has a public interest motive, the key to credibility. The willingness of the journalist to be transparent about what he or she has done is at the heart of establishing that the journalist is concerned with truth.

The lie, or the mistake, is in pretending omniscience or claiming greater knowledge than we have.

How does the Rule of Transparency work? It starts at the top, where it may mean public meetings, speeches, or editors' columns, especially during controversy. At the *Washington Post*, editor Leonard Downie wrote a column explaining the separation between news and editorial pages the day the paper made its presidential endorsement. It flows down to individual stories, where it may demand specificity. If a piece reports "experts say," to how many did the reporter actually talk?

Key is this: The Rule of Transparency involves the journalist asking for each event, "What does my audience need to know to evaluate this information for itself? And is there anything in our treatment of it that requires explanation?"

It is the same principle as governs scientific method: explain how you learned something and why you believe it—so the audience can do the same. In science, the reliability of an experiment, or its objectivity, is defined by whether someone else could replicate the experiment. In journalism, only by explaining how we know what we know can we approximate this idea of people being able, if they were of a mind to, to replicate the reporting. This is what is meant by objectivity of method in science, or in journalism.

Even as he began to develop doubts about whether journalists could really sort out the truth, Walter Lippmann recognized this. "There is no defense, no extenuation, no excuse whatsoever, for stating six times that Lenin is dead when the only information the paper possesses is a report that he is dead from a source repeatedly shown to be unreliable. The news, in that instance, is not that 'Lenin is Dead' but 'Helsingfors Says Lenin is Dead.' And a newspaper can be asked to take responsibility of not making Lenin more dead than the source of the news is reliable. If there is one subject on which editors are most responsible it is in their judgment of the reliability of the source."[19]

Unfortunately, the idea of transparency is all too frequently violated. Too much journalism fails to say anything about methods, motives, and sources. Network television newscasts, as a matter of course, will say simply "sources said," a way of saving valuable time on the air. It is also a mistake. It is a standing rule in most offices on Capitol Hill, similarly, that staffers will be quoted anonymously at all times. As citizens become more skeptical of both journalists and the political establishment, this is also a disservice to the public and brings journalism under greater suspicion.

Misleading Sources: A Corollary to Transparency

The Rule of Transparency also suggests something about the way journalists deal with their sources. Obviously journalists should not lie to or mislead their sources in the process of trying to tell the truth to their audiences.

Unfortunately, journalists, without having thought the principle through, all too often have failed to see this. Bluffing sources, failing to level with sources about the real point of the story, even simply lying to sources about the point of stories are all techniques some journalists have applied—in the name of truth seeking. While at first glance candor may seem a handcuff on reporters, in most cases it won't be. Many reporters have come to find that it can win them enormous influence. "I've found it is always better to level with sources, tell them what I'm doing and where I'm going," then *Boston Globe* political correspondent Jill Zuckman told us. *Washington Post* reporter Jay Matthews makes a habit of showing sources drafts of stories. He believes it increases the accuracy and nuance of his pieces.[20]

At the same time, journalists should expect similar veracity from their sources. A growing number of journalists believe that if a source who has been granted anonymity is found to have misled the reporter, the source's identity should be revealed. Part of the bargain of anonymity is truthfulness.

There is a special category of journalists misleading sources. It is called masquerading. This occurs when journalists pose as someone else to get a story by misleading sources. The "undercover" reporting technique is nothing new. Muckrakers like Nellie Bly, who among other remarkable achievements posed as an inmate in an insane asylum to expose mistreatment of the mentally ill, used masquerade at the beginning of the twentieth century. Television today frequently uses masquerade and tiny hidden cameras to expose wrongdoing.

What does avoiding deception and being transparent with audiences and sources suggest about masquerade? We believe these ideas do not preclude journalists' use of masquerade. Rather, they suggest that journalists should use a test similar to the concepts justifying civil disobedience in deciding whether to engage in the technique. Citizens should also apply this test in evaluating what they think of it. There are three steps to this test:

1. The information must be sufficiently vital to the public interest to justify deception.
2. Journalists should not engage in masquerade unless there is no other way to get the story.
3. Journalists should reveal to their audience whenever they mislead sources to get information, and explain their reasons for doing so, including why the story justifies the deception and why this was the only way to get the facts.

With this approach, citizens can decide for themselves whether journalistic dishonesty was justified or not. And journalists, in turn, have been clear with the citizens to whom they owe their first loyalty.

We have dealt at length with this notion of a more transparent journalism because it will help over the long run to develop a more discerning public. This is a public that can readily see the difference between journalism of principle and careless or self-interested imitation. In this way, journalists can enlist the new power of the marketplace to become a force for quality journalism.

This transparency means embedding in the news reports a sense of how the story came to be and why it was presented as it was. During the reporting on the Clinton-Lewinsky scandal, the *New York Times* did just this in explaining to readers why a story about the allegations of a woman named Juanita Broaddrick was held for a time and then played on page 16. Broaddrick was alleging that President Clinton had forced himself sexually on her roughly twenty-one years earlier in Arkansas, though she had not made the allegations at the time, or even earlier in the Lewinsky scandal. Nor was she pressing the case legally.

Reporters Felicity Barringer and David Firestone interviewed their own managing editor, Bill Keller, and included his explanation in the story: The merits of Broaddrick's allegations are ultimately "probably unknowable . . . legally it doesn't seem to go any-where. . . . Congress isn't going to impeach him again . . . and 'frankly we've all got a bit of scandal fatigue,' " Keller reasoned in the story. Some citizens might disagree, but at least they now had some explanation for the news they were receiving, not some false sense that news is an objective reality rather than the product of human judgment.[21]

Two elements are important here. First, the reporters felt it was important to let readers know how news decisions were made and just what standards are applied to those decisions. Second, the atmosphere inside the newsroom of the *New York Times* was such that the reporters felt comfortable questioning the managing editor's decision, pen in hand, with the intention of quoting his comments in the story.

Originality

Beyond demanding more transparency from journalism, citizens and journalists can also look for something else in judging the value of a news report. Michael Oreskes, the Washington bureau chief of the *New York Times*, has offered this deceptively simple but powerful idea in the discipline for pursuing truth: Do your own work.

Throughout the sex and legal scandal involving President Bill Clinton and White House intern Monica Lewinsky, news organizations found themselves in the uncomfort-able position of what to do with often explosive exposés from other news organizations that they could not verify themselves. Usually, to make matters more complicated, these were based on anonymous sources, meaning the news organization had to take even greater responsibility for the veracity of the story than if they were quoting someone. Based on such sourcing, three different news organizations reported that a third-party witness had seen the president and Lewinsky in an intimate encounter—stories that were later found to be inaccurate. Should a news organization report these exposés because they know others might, and that the story will be, in the popular phrase, "out there"?

Oreskes concludes the answer is an adamant no. "The people who got it right were those who did their own work, who were careful about it, who followed the basic standards of sourcing and got their information from multiple sources. The people who worried about what was 'out there,' to use that horrible phrase that justifies so many journalistic sins, the people who worried about getting beaten, rather than just trying to do it as well as they could as quickly as they could, they messed up."[22]

Originality is deeply grounded in journalism. Some ancient axioms of the press say much the same thing: "When in doubt leave it out." The tradition of "matching" stories is rooted in the same idea. Rather than publishing another news outlet's scoop, journalists have tended to require one of their reporters to call a source to confirm it first. In part, this was a way of avoiding having to credit the other news organization. Yet it had another more important effect. Stories that couldn't be independently confirmed would not be repeated.

Humility

A fifth and final concept is that journalists should be humble about their own skills. In other words, not only should they be skeptical of what they see and hear from others, but just as important, they should be skeptical about their ability to know what it really means. Jack Fuller again has suggested that journalists need to show "modesty in their judgments" about what they know and how they know it.[23] A key way to avoid misrepresenting events is a disciplined honesty about the limits of one's knowledge and the power of one's perception.

An incident unearthed in our forum on diversity helps illustrate the point. The event, described by then *New York Times* religion writer Laurie Goodstein, was a Pentecostal prayer revival on the steps of the U.S. Capitol. The gathering featured faith healings, calls for school prayer, condemnations of abortion and homosexuality—a fairly typical evangelical revival meeting. A reporter for a newspaper covering the event related all this, Goodstein explained, but added this sentence: "At times, the mood turned hostile toward the lawmakers in the stately white building behind the stage." Then the reporter quoted a Christian radio broadcaster speaking from the stage: "Let's pray that God will slay everyone in the Capitol."[24]

The reporter assumed the broadcaster meant *slay* as in "kill."

But, Goldstein explained, "any Pentecostal knows that asking God to slay someone means to slay in spirit, slay in the sense of holy spirit, praying that they are overcome with love for God, for Jesus."

The problem was the reporter didn't know, didn't have any Pentecostals in the newsroom to ask, and was perhaps too anxious for a "holy shit" story to double-check with someone afterward whether the broadcaster was really advocating the murder of the entire Congress.

"It made for a very embarrassing correction," said Goodstein. It also makes a strong case for the need for humility.

Together, these five ideas amount to a core philosophy that frames the discipline of verification. They also establish a closer relationship between the journalist and the citizen, which is mutually beneficial. By employing the powerful tools of transparent, narrative storytelling, the journalist engages citizens with important information they might otherwise pass by and does so without sacrificing factual integrity. At the same time, by being more open about his or her work, the journalist is encouraged to be more thoughtful in acquiring, organizing, and presenting the news.

TECHNIQUES OF VERIFICATION

Obviously, these concepts are not specific enough to constitute "a scientific method" of reporting. That is for individual journalists to refine—as long as they are clear about it. But we would like to offer some concrete methods from journalists around the country. While not encyclopedic, any journalist could fashion a superb method of gathering and presenting news from adapting the following few techniques.

Skeptical Editing

Sandra Rowe, the editor of the *Oregonian* in Portland, Oregon, employs a system at her paper that she and executive editor Peter Bhatia call "prosecutorial editing." The term may be an unfortunate one. Reid MacCluggage, editor and publisher of *The Day* in New London, Connecticut, has suggested a better one, "skeptical editing."[25] Regardless, the concept is important for journalists and citizens to understand.

The approach involves adjudicating a story, in effect, line by line, statement by statement, editing the assertions in the stories as well as the facts. How do we know this? Why should the reader believe this? What is the assumption behind this sentence? If the story says that a certain event may raise questions in people's minds, who suggested that? The reporter? A source? A citizen?

Amanda Bennett, an *Oregonian* managing editor, says the notion—which she learned at the *Wall Street Journal*—is designed for "rooting out not so much errors of fact but unconscious errors of assertion and narrative—to root out the things that people put in because 'they just know it's true.' "[26]

If a story says most Americans now have a personal computer, the editor would ask for verification. If a story said "according to sources," the editor would ask, "Who are the sources? Is there more than one?" If there was only one, the story would have to say so.

If a story said that presidential candidate Al Gore's flip-flop on returning six-year-old shipwreck survivor Elián González to Cuba raises questions about his ideological consistency, the editor would ask, "What questions?" and "In whose mind?" If the answer is merely the reporter and his friends, the story would either have to say so, or that line would come out.

Whenever possible, said editor Rowe, this kind of editing involves the editor and the reporter sitting side by side, and the reporter producing original material. "The more of it we did, the more we were sending true fear" through the newsroom, said Rowe.[27] Bennett began teaching it in the newsroom in front of groups of reporters and editors. "People didn't know it was okay to ask these questions," Bennett said. The purpose, in large part, is to "make that role of asking questions okay, and to make it conscious." Rather than including more in stories, more was taken out, unless it could be absolutely verified.[28]

The technique, Bennett and Rowe believe, made editors and reporters better and more thorough. The objective of the *Oregonian*'s skeptical editing is to create an atmosphere in which people can question a story without questioning the integrity of the reporter. It becomes part of an atmosphere of open dialogue in a newsroom, which goes bottom-up as well as top-down.

Accuracy Checklist

David Yarnold, the executive editor of the *San Jose Mercury News*, has developed something he has called an accuracy checklist.

As they move through stories, editors have to answer the following questions among others:

- Is the lead of the story sufficiently supported?
- Has someone double-checked, called, or visited all the phone numbers, addresses, or Web addresses in the story? What about names and titles?
- Is the background material required to understand the story complete?
- Are all the stakeholders in the story identified and have representatives from that side been contacted and given a chance to talk?

- Does the story pick sides or make subtle value judgments? Will some people like this story more than they should?
- Is anything missing?
- Are all the quotes accurate and properly attributed, and do they capture what the person really meant?

The checklist, which Yarnold printed and some editors posted on their computers, began as an experiment. Yarnold gave one team of thirty reporters and editors a checklist to use in producing stories. The group was able to follow the checklist about 80 percent of the time and required 20 percent fewer corrections than another team that worked without the checklist.

Corrections are a fairly subjective measurement, and some editors consider Yarnold's checklist too mechanistic. Still, who would quarrel with the questions being asked? This is a simple, forceful step toward an objectivity of method.

Assume Nothing

David Protess, a professor at Northwestern University's Medill School of Journalism, has used the cases of death row inmates to teach journalism students the importance of verifying presumed facts.

Among the lessons: Don't rely on officials or news accounts. Get as close as you can to primary sources. Be systematic. Corroborate.

Each year Protess receives thousands of letters from people on death row who claim wrongful conviction. Each year he chooses a handful that he assigns his students to examine. In 1999, the appeal of Anthony Porter was one of the cases Protess used to introduce his aspiring journalists to the value of skepticism.

"Maybe the best way to understand my method is what I do for the students when they come into my class," Protess explained in an interview when we sought him out. "I draw a set of concentric circles on the blackboard. In the outermost circle are secondary source documents, things like press accounts. . . . The next circle in is primary source documents, trial documents like testimony and statements. The third circle in is real people, witnesses. We interview them to see if everything matches what's in the documents. We ask them questions that may have come up looking at the documents. And at the inner circle are what I call the targets—the police, the lawyers, other suspects, and the prisoner.

"You'd be surprised how much is in the early documents. There is a lot there, especially early suspects the police passed by."

At the inner circle of the Porter case, Protess and his students found Alstory Simon, a suspect the police quickly overlooked. Using Protess's systematic approach to cross-checking the documents and sources, Protess and his students found a nephew who had overheard Simon confess to the murder on the night of the killings. Simon was ultimately convicted of the crime for which Porter was about to die. On March 19, 1999, Anthony Porter became the fifth prisoner wrongfully convicted of murder in Illinois freed by the work of Protess and his students.

Protess's work is an extraordinary demonstration of the power of methodical journalistic verification.

Tom French's Colored Pencil

If Protess's method is exhaustive, Tom French's is wonderfully simple. French specializes in writing long, deep narrative nonfiction for the *St. Petersburg Times* in Florida. He won the 1998 Pulitzer Prize for Feature Writing. He also writes on deadline.

French has a test to verify any facts in his stories. Before he hands a piece in, he takes a printed copy and goes over the story line by line with a colored pencil, putting a check mark by each fact and assertion in the story to tell himself that he has double-checked that it is true.

Anonymous Sources

As citizens, we all rely on other sources of information for most of what we know. The journalists monitoring the world on our behalf also most often depend on others for the details of their reporting. One of the earliest techniques adopted by journalists to assure us of their reliability was the practice of providing the source of their information. Mr. Jones said so and so, in a such and such a speech at the Elks Lodge, in the annual report, etc. Such dependence on others for information has always required a skeptical turn of mind for journalists. They early on adopt the reminder: "If your mother says she loves you, check it out." If the source of the information is fully described, the audience can decide for itself whether the information is credible. In recent years as dependence on anonymous sources for important public information has grown—as in the case of the Clinton-Lewinsky story—journalists learned the importance of developing rules to assure themselves and their audience they were maintaining independence from the anonymous sources of their news.

Joe Lelyveld, executive editor of the *New York Times*, required that reporters and editors at the *Times* ask themselves two questions before using an anonymous source:

1. How much direct knowledge does the anonymous source have of the event?
2. What, if any, motive might the source have for misleading us, gilding the lily, or hiding important facts that might alter our impression of the information?

Only after they are satisfied by the answers to these questions will they use the source. And then, to the maximum degree possible, they have to share with the audience information to suggest how the source was in a position to know ("a source who has seen the document," for example) and what special interest that source may have ("a source inside the Independent Prosecutor's office," for example). This effort at more transparency was a crucial factor in the degree to which the audience could judge for themselves how much credence to give the report, but more important it signaled the standards of the organization serving up their news.

Deborah Howell, the Washington editor of the Newhouse newspapers, has two other rules for anonymous sources that reinforce Lelyveld's.

1. Never use an anonymous source to offer an opinion of another person.
2. Never use an anonymous source as the first quote in a story.

These serve as two practical instructions for how to write stories, even after you have decided to use what an anonymous source is offering.

TRUTH'S MULTIPLE ROOTS

In the end, everyone in the journalistic process has a role to play in the journey toward truth. Publishers and owners must be willing to consistently air the work of public interest journalism without fear or favor.

Editors must serve as the protector against debasement of the currency of free expression—words—resisting effort by governments, corporations, litigants, lawyers, or any other newsmaker to mislead or manipulate by labeling lies as truth, war as peace.

Reporters must be dogged in their pursuit, and disciplined in trying to overcome their own perspective. Longtime Chicago TV newscaster Carol Marin explained it this way at one committee forum: "When you sit down this Thanksgiving with your family and you have one of the classic family arguments—whether it's about politics or race or religion or sex—you remember that what you are seeing of that family dispute is seen from the position of your chair and your side of the table. And it will warp your view, because in those instances you are arguing your position. . . . A journalist is someone who steps away from the table and tries to see it all."[29]

And, if journalism is conversation, in the end that conversation includes discourse among citizens as well as with those who provide the news. The citizens, too, have a role. They must, of course, be attentive. They also must be assertive. If they have a question or a problem, they should ask it of the news organization. How do you know this? Why did you write this? What are your journalistic principles? These are fair questions to ask, and citizens deserve answers.

Thus journalists must be committed to truth as a first principle and must be loyal to citizens above all so they are free to pursue it. And in order to engage citizens in that search, journalists must apply transparent and systematic methods of verification. The next step is to clarify their relationship to those they report on.

NOTES

1. Thucydides, *History of the Peloponnesian War*, bks. 1 and 2, trans. C. F. Smith (Cambridge: Harvard University Press, 1991), 35–39.

2. Claudia Puig, "Getting Inside the Truth, Filmmakers Accused of Fiddling with Facts Cite Dramatic Accuracy," *USA Today*, 3 November 1999.

3. Walter Lippmann, *Liberty and the News* (New Brunswick, N.J., and London: Transaction Publishers, 1995), 58.

4. Michael Schudson, *Discovering the News* (New York: Basic Books, 1978), 6. Schudson's book has a particularly useful analysis of the move away from naive empiricism of the nineteenth century to the initially more sophisticated idea of objectivity.

5. Walter Lippmann and Charles Merz, "A Test of the News," *New Republic*, 4 August 1920.

6. Walter Lippmann, "The Press and Public Opinion," *Political Science Quarterly*, 46 (June 1931), 170. The fact that Lippmann wrote this last passage in 1931, twelve years after his study of the Russian Revolution, is a sign of how the problem continued to dog him.

7. Lippmann, *Liberty and the News*, 74.

8. Ibid., 60.

9. Ibid., 74.

10. Schudson, *Discovering the News*, 155–56.

11. William Damon, to Committee of Concerned Journalists steering committee, 12 February 1999.

12. Geneva Overholser, at CCJ Minneapolis forum, 22 October 1998.

13. Robert Parry, "He's No Pinocchio," *Washington Monthly*, April 2000; available from www. washingtonmonthly.com.

14. Ibid.

15. Phil Meyer, at CCJ St. Petersburg, Florida, forum, 26 February 1998.

16. Norman Sims, ed., *The Literary Journalists* (New York: Ballantine Books, 1984), 15.

17. Tom Goldstein, ed., *Killing the Messenger* (New York: Columbia University Press, 1989), 247.

18. CCJ and the Pew Research Center for the People and the Press, "Striking the Balance: Audience Interests, Business Pressures and Journalists' Values" (March 1999); Amy Mitchell and Tom Rosenstiel, "Don't Touch That Quote," *Columbia Journalism Review*, January 2000, 34–36.

19. Walter Lippmann, *Public Opinion* (New York: The Free Press, 1965), 226.

20. Jay Matthews, interview by Dante Chinni, 12 September 2000.

21. Felicity Barringer and David Firestone, "On Torturous Route, Sexual Assault Accusation Against Clinton Resurfaces," *New York Times*, 24 February 1999.

22. Michael Oreskes, speech delivered at CCJ Washington, D.C., forum, 20 October 1998.

23. Jack Fuller, *News Values: Ideas from an Information Age* (Chicago and London: University of Chicago Press, 1996), 350.

24. Laurie Goodstein, speech delivered at CCJ Detroit forum, 2 February 1998.

25. MacCluggage in an address to regional editors argued, "Edit more skeptically. If skeptics aren't built into the process right from the start, stories will slide onto page one without the proper scrutiny." Associated Press, "APME President Urges Editors to Challenge Stories for Accuracy," 15 October 1998.

26. Amanda Bennett, interview by author Rosenstiel, 13 April 2000.

27. Sandra Rowe, interview by author Rosenstiel, 13 April 2000.

28. Bennett, interview by author Rosenstiel, 13 April 2000.

29. Carol Marin, speech delivered at CCJ Chicago forum, 6 November 1997.

20

THE BOSTON HOAX: SHE FOUGHT IT, HE BOUGHT IT

Christopher Lydon

The Stuart case—the "media" story—can be told in the misadventures of two Boston reporters who came to personify the frustration and embarrassment surrounding the hoax.

While it lasted the hoax served as a perfect parable for the reign of guns and drugs in American cities. Random, racial mayhem, it seemed, had visited perhaps the best among us—a suburban couple leaving a Lamaze birthing class at one of Boston's great hospitals. Two and a half months later, after his brother squealed, the real villain apparently jumped off a bridge into Boston Harbor. Carol Stuart's death turned out to be the most calculated of family murders—a story the cops didn't investigate and the reporters didn't report.

Michelle Caruso of the *Boston Herald* reacted intuitively at the news last October that Chuck Stuart, burly exfootball player, had survived a shooting, and his pregnant wife had died of a bullet in the head. It didn't make sense, she guessed immediately, no matter Stuart's description of the raspy-voiced, jump-suited black gunman.

Caruso dug for two and half months on the case and never got a serious hint of the true story into print.

And then there is the best-read columnist in town, Mike Barnicle of the *Boston Globe*. Often in error, never in doubt, he whistled the police tune in the case even after the truth was out—through frame-up and whitewash—till the cops and Mike Barnicle stumbled off a cliff.

In short, one reporter got it on instinct, then hit a wall. The other followed his friendly anonymous sources into an abyss.

First, Caruso's story. "From the first day two things were gnawing at me: I could not accept that any criminal was crazed enough—if he'd shot one—to leave a second person alive in that car. I couldn't fathom it. The other thing, from Day One: This was not a customary crime. We have purse snatchings. And armed robberies on the street. An automobile abduction is almost unheard of. It is so much easier to stand out in the parking lot of a fancy restaurant and snap a purse. There's very little work in it, and not much chance of getting caught. So I found the crime unusual, a bit too much."

Michelle Caruso, 34, has been covering the cops around Boston and piloting her own investigations for three years. Gilda Radner might have played her in a movie version of the Stuart case, with Roseanne Roseannadanna's bushy curls. Deborah Winger could suggest her nerwous energy.

Christopher Lydon, "The Boston Hoax: She Fought It, He Bought It," *Washington Journalism Review*, March 1990, 56–60. Reprinted with the kind permission of the author.

Caruso studied German intellectual history at the University of Massachusetts; she taught English for a year in Lesotho and covered the hill towns of western Massachusetts for $10 a story to learn the craft of reporting. Now almost the only thing she does outside of work is read "true crime books—never fiction. Let's face it, crime is my whole life," she says.

When the Stuart shooting hit Boston and the TV networks Monday, October 23 [1989]. Michelle Caruso was finishing up a *Herald* series on organized crime. "The Stuart case was like a fly in my head, buzzing, 'something's wrong, something's wrong, something's wrong.'" A week after it happened, Caruso went to state police head-quarters and copied the tape of Charles Stuart's 13-minute emergency call to 911.

After listening to the tape, "things started jumping out at me," she remembers, "as though they were billboards in red letters that said: I'M GUILTY. Within the first 30 sec-onds of the tape the dispatcher, Gary McLaughlin, said, 'Sir, your wife has been shot as well?' And Chuck Stuart pauses for what I thought was a very long wait. He said, 'Yes,' and then there is a five-second pause—I timed it—and he says, 'Yes, in the head.'"

"I said to myself, 'Buddy, there's something wrong here.' The normal crime victim would have been screaming, 'Yes! My wife!' Blood! Panic! Agony! Hysteria! The normal thing is that you always find the dispatcher in the calming role, and here we have the opposite. The dispatcher had to badger him with questions, because Chuck was so goddamn calm.

"So Chuck pauses when he says, 'Yes. . . . in the head.' There is no followup from Gary McLaughlin, but Chuck blurts out in a nervous kind of way: 'and I ducked down.' And I thought: 'No one asked you, Chuck.' He was offering an explanation for being less seriously injured. Beware of the person who offers you an alibi even before you ask, 'Where were you?' Not a good sign.

"So I go through the tape. There is a section where they ask him for street signs. He said, 'I'm driving with my lights out.' They said: 'Can you turn them on?' He said, 'It's too painful, I can't reach forward.' And then I remembered the Toyota light switch is right under the wheel. I could just feel it: This guy is making excuses.

"Gary said, 'Call the next passerby,' and Chuck got a little testy. He said, 'There aren't that many people.' I rewound the tape and listened again. He says, 'There aren't that many people.' And I said, 'Hey, Chuck, *one* person is all you need, and a hairy, green monster would do! You just need *one* to help you save your wife.'"

Caruso mapped all the routes Chuck Stuart might have driven between the site of the shooting—where police had found his spare set of car keys—and the spot where he was found. And then she drove the distance over and over, listening to the 911 tape on a cassette player in her car. "On the tape he says, 'I'm on Tremont Street, and I know where I am. Should I drive to the hospital?' Gary asks him, 'Are you well enough?' And Chuck says, 'I'm going to try to drive.' He drove all right, but he drove right down into the project, and pulled up near the corner of Horadan Way and parked the car. Straight as a die, six inches from the curb, and says, 'I'm going to black out.' This guy announces it!

"That was the clincher. He'd left an area where help was sure to come and turned down a street where his chances of being found were so much less. He was, in effect, signing his wife's death warrant. She's critically wounded, and the baby, too."

"And there's another point. He never mentioned the baby. Never once on the tape does he say 'help.' Never does he use the word 'hurry.' He barely mentioned his wife, except when Gary pressed him, and he never called out to his wife. 'Help' is the one word people in trouble can't stop saying, and he never said it."

Michelle Caruso is well-respected in the Suffolk County DA's office, not least because two years ago her legwork had cracked what proved to be a double homicide case—the poisoning of two Roxbury tots—after the police had concluded it was natural causes. "That was when I realized you can't have a lot of confidence that crimes get investigated," she says.

She knew the chief of homicide prosecutions, Francis O'Meara, well enough to call him with ideas and suspicions. Wasn't it odd, she had asked O'Meara, that no witness had come forward who'd seen a black man jump into the Stuarts' car? When Caruso and *Herald* reporter Kim Tan re-enacted the hijacking exactly a week after it happened, the site was teeming with cars, buses and pedestrians. Caruso says she had also pressed O'Meara to search the Stuarts' home for property records and phone bills, among other things. An investigator wouldn't have needed a warrant—only Chuck Stuart's consent, which an innocent victim could hardly have denied.

On November 9 Caruso had another long phone talk with O'Meara. "Franny told me the ballistics showed the wounds were consistent with shots from the backseat of the car. Franny was very strong telling me it was a third party, in the rear of the car. I said: 'What if he hired somebody?' Franny said: 'You gotta understand: Seven vital organs have been damaged. This was no surface nick.' I said: 'But Franny, if it was a shot in the leg or foot, no one would have believed him. He had to do *some* damage!' At the end of the conversation I was getting pushy. 'Well, are you going to do anything about it?' I asked. He said, 'I might he inclined to agree with you if we didn't have another lead in another direction.' I said: 'You got a suspect?' He said: 'I'm not talking suspects. I'm talking about a lead in another direction.' "

"I had already done some research on Willie Bennett. I mean, the profile was perfect and therefore had to be wrong. Laughing. I said to Franny: 'You don't mean Willie Bennett, do you?' First he was dead silent, then he said: 'I'm not going to comment on any names you throw at me.' I said: 'Jesus, that's it.' He could have said: 'That name doesn't ring a bell.' and he didn't."

"About Willie Bennett, we knew a number of things. In the Mission Hill housing project, put it this way: If the police are shaking down a person in the project, the street finds out about it. From the street is where we found out they were interested in Bennett. So I looked him up in our morgue. In the 70s he'd shot a legless cabdriver in an armed robbery. He'd shot at two Boston cops and wounded one of them. In 1982 they caught up with Bennett, shot in the hand; he was sentenced to Walpole. By now he's been out of Walpole about a year. And he should be much too smart to do this for a hundred bucks."

Caruso had been shaken, however, by her last talk with Franny O'Meara. "These people are out 24 hours a day, with the full force of the Boston police and the Suffolk County DA's office. And if, after three weeks, this is where they've come to, maybe *I'm* wrong. Chucky's coming out crystal clear. I figured: Maybe they've got Bennett's fingerprints off the car."

Michelle Caruso went with Fran O'Meara and the Boston cops who stormed and searched Willie Bennett's Mission Hill apartment at 2:30 on the morning of November 11. The Sunday *Herald* headline blared "Police Nab #1 Suspect in Stuart-Killing Case."

Both papers unhesitatingly named Bennett as a suspect, though he had not been charged. The only cautionary notes in either of the Boston papers came from Caruso's interviews with a police informant. "The woman claims she told police she had seen Bennett with a gun one night about a week prior to the Stuart shootings, but she denied seeing him on the night of the shootings." Caruso reported. "The woman said police are pressuring her to implicate Bennett. 'They said I seen Willie Bennett running the night of the killing. I know one thing. I didn't see him no night of no murder. I only told police the truth. They think I know more. They are trying to put words in my mouth.' "

As Caruso remembers things now, "The bottom line was: We came one inch away from writing a story about all the doubts I had. I needed an expert in law enforcement, or a forensic guy, to say, 'This case is not what it seems.' A reporter still needs a source. This may be the biggest thing the public doesn't understand. A reporter can't write his own opinions."

Caruso's last long shot was a friendly expert: Dr. Michael Baden, formerly the chief medical examiner in New York City, now the director of forensic sciences for the New York State Police and author of *Unnatural Deaths: Confessions of a Medical Examiner*. "He's very bold, and I thought, maybe if he looks and sees something, he won't be afraid to go against the grain. Would be say, 'I don't believe Chuck Stuart passed out,' or, 'His voice doesn't sound right'? I figured, maybe that's how I can get my story in print if the cops won't give me a hook."

"I Fed Ex'd the clips to him, and a map and the tape, and the very next day Baden called me. He was quite intrigued. He was very curious about the way I had described the gunshot wound. It was not a typical wound when the shooter is in the backseat. He said: 'Some of it does seem strange. The guy sounds calm, but so little is known about stress reactions, and the effect of shock.' I said, 'But it doesn't *sound* like he's in shock.' He said, 'You haven't given me enough. I can't help you.' "

Where was Deep Throat when she needed him? "I mean, if O'Meara had said, 'You're right on the money, we're looking at the guy,' I would have written it, but I was getting the opposite. There wasn't a shred of evidence that they were looking at Chuck Stuart. They might have said, 'Yeah, we're searching Mission Hill, but we're also looking at the husband,' and they never said it."

"They say we failed. Fuck *we* failed. We didn't solve the Stuart murder, but that's not our job. The critics say, 'How come you got buffaloed?' But the cops had the car. They had the ballistics. They had Chuck Stuart, for cryin' out loud. I'd have given anything to spend five minutes with the guy. And they turn around and blame us."

"Now, as I see it, there probably was nobody in the Boston Police Department who believed anything other than what Chuck Stuart said. In any other case, a detective will call and say, 'I've heard you're asking questions about that case. Let me tell you: It stinks.' I never found anybody to say that in the Stuart case."

Caruso thought she'd convinced *Herald* Editor Ken Chandler that Charles Stuart was probably a murderer. But the *Herald*, in fact, never stopped headlining "Camelot Couple" over their pictures of Chuck and Carol. Yet Caruso's digging was never reined in.

"I had my instincts, which had never failed me before, but I couldn't get anybody to take this one on—even off the record. As it turns out, we would have been right about Chuck Stuart. But what if we'd been wrong?"

Mike Barnicle, whose column appears each Tuesday, Thursday and Sunday in the *Globe*, made only one glancing reference to the Stuart case before Chuck Stuart went off the bridge in January. "Some Shots in the Dark" was the headline on his October 29 column, which detailed the routine of ghetto violence on the Friday night before. Like a lot of Barnicle columns it appeared to have been reported from the passenger seat of a police cruiser. Knowing but numb, the tone of voice says: It's a jungle out there. "There were numerous other shootings but no bodies," Barnicle concluded. "Drugs were sold all around the city. A man was robbed at gunpoint on Fenwood Road, close to where Carol Stuart was killed Monday night. A glut of politicians met to discuss measures aimed at fighting crime. The talk shows and many campaign statements featured the electric chair quite prominently. And at one o'clock Saturday morning, a gang of kids, all of them maybe 14 or 15, celebrated by shooting off their guns on Topliff Street in Dorchester. That finishes my report for today."

Mike Barnicle is fascinated by his city, though the message to his readers, as above, is often: Forget it. He is a sentimentalist about wars, World Series games and Boston neighborhoods of the 1940s—when, in fact, Mike Barnicle was growing up in the mill town of Fitchburg 40 miles west. His favorite Red Sox sluggers (like Ted Williams) and politicians (like Tip O'Neill) are in retirement now. And it is common knowledge—and an old target of teasing—that this journalistic stalker of the naked city actually dwells out in the sylvan splendor of suburban Lincoln, hard by George Bush's sister and the top slice of Boston's corporate class.

The morning after Charles Stuart's apparent suicide, Barnicle shared a Page One byline with two other *Globe* reporters on the story. His own column inside the paper gave us the voice of a friend, somebody had told Barnicle. The source was surely a detective or prosecutor who had just heard Matthew Stuart's confession of his brother's perfidy. The cop had just woken up, in effect, and immediately started generating blue smoke.

"Charles Stuart was the coldest, most calculating son-of-a-bitch you've ever seen," the cop told Barnicle. Part of the proof, he said, was that Stuart had hedged his identification of the black suspect in the police lineup, Willie Bennett.

What Stuart had said, according to Barnicle's cop, was, "That looks the most like him of any of them here." This was a convenient revision of what the cops had said, and the *Globe* had reported, late in December, when Bennett was the prime suspect. "It was absolutely crystal clear. That's the guy," the paper's lineup source had said. (The *Herald*'s source had said: "It was as positive an identification as I've ever seen. He didn't hesitate.") Barnicle made no note of the inconsistency. He was angry instead about the "wail of a black community demanding apologies for the fact that a black man was arrested."

Two days later Barnicle's Sunday column had some fresh Stuart family scenes in it, including con man Chuck's last meeting, two nights before his death, with the bereaved father of his wife. "Dad," Stuart was quoted, without attribution, "how about if I come for supper tonight?"

But the passion in Barnicle's piece was in the extended defense of the Boston police who had nailed the wrong suspect, Willie Bennett.

"When this incredibly bizarre story finally comes to an end," Barnicle had written, "it will be shown that detectives from the homicide unit merely covered themselves with glory. Despite having a suspect, Bennett, who had, in a moment of ignorant street swagger, actually claimed carrying out a crime he did not commit—shooting Carol Stuart—and despite testimony from several black resIdents of the project one day after the crime occurred that they had seen Bennett with a gun and jewelry on the evening Carol Stuart was shot, the police balked at charging him with murder."

The point was to banish the thought that Willie Bennett might have been "framed" —a word Barnicle never used—and then to pretty up the process that got police their warrants to arrest Bennett and search his family's apartment. The effect of his columns, in short, was to dismiss the frame-up and lend a hand in the whitewash. Barnicle extended the frame-up in this sense: While police and press had all cast suspicion on Willie Bennett earlier, Barnicle piled on *after* the world knew for sure that Bennett was exonerated. Barnicle's part in the short-lived cover-up was to suggest that the police affidavits against Bennett had been gathered in good faith—when they weren't.

Barnicle's first step was to heap the humiliation of Bennett's childhood on the career criminal he became. Barnicle wrote that the Boston school system had rated Bennett's IQ at 62, and had stamped "mental defective" on his record a quarter century ago. Barnicle listed the Ds and Es on Bennett's final report card and expalined: "The E does not stand for excellent. The man's pathetic, violent history is so much a part of the unyielding issues of race, crime and drugs tearing daily at America that it is amazing how any black minister or black politician could ever stand up and howl in public that his arrest was a product of police bigotry."

Barnicle warmed to the same theme in his next column, Tuesday, January 9. "Maybe all the loudmouths so quick to bang the cops and promote themselves" should have talked to Willie Bennett's real victims of a decade or so earlier," he wrote.

All this was *after* "prime suspect" Willie Bennett had been formally exonerated of the Stuart crime, when the further belaboring of Bennett seemed graceless, irrelevant, even diversionary. Hadn't he overdone it?

"Absotuely not," Barnicle told me in the aftermath. "Willie Bennett has hurt more people than Chuck Stuart ever did."

After working Willie Bennett over again, Barnicle tried another ploy: praising the police work that had found the wrong man. "They had sworn testimony," Barnicle explained in his Thursday column, January 11, "that Willie Bennett himself had admitted to being the shooter." On January 12 Barnicle embellished the story: Willie Bennett's nephew, Barnicle wrote, had told detectives within 24 hours of the Stuart shooting that his uncle had boasted of doing it. "He told the dude not to look in the rear-view window," the nephew had stated, according to Barnicle. Three days after the shooting, Stuart, in his hospital bed, had told cops: "He told me not to look in the rear-view mirror." A close match, it seemed. Significant evidence, Barnicle still urged us to believe.

But the gathering of that "sworn testimony," including the rear-view details, promptly turned out to have been perhaps the saddest and most discrediting part of the whole bad business.

The examination of Willie Bennett's "confession" revealed a big lie that the police had evidently planted among teenagers on Mission Hill. It seems a cop had a girlfriend, and the girlfriend had a son; the son had a friend, and the friend had heard Joey "Toot" Bennett say—laughing and joking —that his Uncle Willie shot the Stuarts. It had taken some fierce intimidation to build affidavits from that wispy joke, but the police got what they wanted.

One reluctant 17-year-old "witness," who asked for a lie detector test to substantiate the truth, said he had been threatened with 20 years in maximum security if he didn't swear he'd heard Willie Bennett's confession. He'd also get a beating then and there. The homicide detective told the kid, "The only lie detector I have is you with Officer Dunn" in a dark 6-by-6-foot room. So the boy said what he was instructed to say, including tell-tale clothing details and "rear-view" phrases. The next day, he said, he came back to the homicide unit to recant, was threatened again and turned away.

It took 10 days after Chuck Stuart's death for the fecklessness and bullying of Boston's police to come clear, and by then Mike Barnicle had stopped writing about the Stuart case.

It has been a strange season in Boston. Michelle Caruso, on Murdoch's racy tabloid Boston *Herald*, had sat on the Greatest Story Never Told. On the good, gray, famously liberal Boston *Globe*, Mike Barnicle had laid down a line that—especially to black sensibilities—added insult to the injury of the Stuart case. Without questions, it seemed, without attribution, without editing, and, to date, without correction.

21
THE SCIENTIFIC WAY

Victor Cohn

To reporters, the world is full of true believers, peddling their "truths." The sincerely misguided and the outright fakers are often highly convincing, also newsy. How can we tell the facts, or the probable facts, from the chaff?

We can borrow from science. We can try to judge all possible claims of fact by the same methods and rules of evidence that scientists use to derive some reasonable guidance in scores of unsettled issues.

As a start, we can ask these questions:

- *How do you know?*
- *Have the claims been subjected to any studies or experiments?*
- *Were the studies acceptable ones, by general agreement?* For example: Were they without any substantial bias?
- *Have results been fairly consistent from study to study?*

Victor Cohn, "The Scientific Way," Chapter 3 of *News and Numbers, a Guide to Reporting Statistical Claims and Controversies in Health and Other Fields* (Ames: Iowa State University Press, 1989), 12–34. Reprinted with permission of Blackwell Publishing (once Iowa State University Press).

- *Have the findings resulted in a consensus among others in the same field? Do at least the majority of informed persons agree? Or should we withhold judgment until there is more evidence?*
- Always: *Are the conclusions backed by believable statistical evidence?*
- *And what is the degree of certainty or uncertainty?* How sure can you be?

Obviously, much of statistics involves attitude or policy rather than numbers. And much, at least much of the statistics that reporters can most readily apply, is good sense.

There are many definitions of statistics as a tool. A few useful ones: The science and art of gathering, analyzing, and interpreting data; a means of deciding whether an effect is real; a way of extracting information from a mass of raw data; a set of mathematical processes derived from probability theory.

Statistics can be manipulated by charlatans, self-deluders, and inexpert statisticians. Deciding on the truth of a matter can be difficult for the best statisticians, and sometimes no decision is possible. Uncertainty will ever rule in some situations and lurk in almost all.

There are rare situations in which no statistics are needed. "Edison had it easy," says Dr. Robert Hooke, a statistician and author. "It doesn't take statistics to see that a light has come on."[1] It did not take statistics to tell 19th-century physicians that Morton's ether anesthesia permitted painless surgery or to tell 20th-century physicians that the first antibiotics cured infections that until then had been highly fatal.

Overwhelmingly, however, the use of statistics, based on probability, is called the soundest method of decision making, and the use of large numbers of cases, statistically analyzed, is called the only means for determining the unknown cause of many events. Birth control pills were tested on several hundred women, yet the pills had to be used for several years by millions before it became unequivocally clear that some women would develop heart attacks or strokes. The pills had to be used for some years more before it became clear that the greatest risk was to women who smoked and women over 35.

The best statisticians, let alone practitioners on the firing line (for example, physicians), often have trouble deciding when a study is adequate or meaningful. Most of us cannot become statisticians, but we can at least learn that there are studies and studies, and the unadorned claim "We made a study" or "We did an experiment" may not mean much. We can learn to ask more pointed questions if we understand some basic concepts and other facts about scientific studies.

These are some bedrock statistical concepts:

- Probability
- "Power" and numbers
- Bias and confounders
- Variability

PROBABILITY

Scientists cope with uncertainty by measuring probabilities. Since all experimental results and all events can be influenced by chance and almost nothing is 100 percent certain in science and medicine and life, probabilities sensibly describe what has happened and should happen in the future under similar conditions. Aristotle said, "The probable is what usually happens," but he might have added that the improbable happens more often than most of us realize.

The accepted numerical expression of probability in evaluating scientific and medical studies is the P (or *probability*) value. The P value is one of the most important figures a reporter should look for. It is determined by a statistical formula that takes into account the numbers of subjects or events being compared in order to answer the question, could a difference or result this great or greater have occurred *by chance alone?* By more precise definition, the P value expresses the probability that an observed relationship or effect or result could have *seemed* to occur by chance *if there had actually been no real effect.* A low P value means a low probability that this happened, that a medical treatment, for example, might have been declared beneficial when in truth it was not.

Here is why the P value is used to evaluate results. A scientific investigator first forms a hypothesis. Then he or she commonly sets out to try to *disprove* it by what is called the *null hypothesis:* that there is no effect, that nothing will happen. To back the original hypothesis, the results must *reject* the null hypothesis. The P value, then, is expressed either as an exact number or as <.05, say, or >.05, meaning "less than" or "greater than" a 5 percent probability that nothing has happened, that the observed result could have happened just by chance—or, to use a more elegant statistician's phrase, by *random variation.*

• By convention, *a P value of .05 or less*, meaning there are only 5 or fewer chances in 100 that the result could have happened by chance, is most often regarded as *low.* This value is usually called *statistically significant* (though sometimes other values are used). The unadorned term "statistically significant" usually implies that P is .05 or less.

• A *higher P value*, one *greater than .05*, is usually seen as not statistically significant. The higher the value, the more likely the result is due to chance.

In common language, a low chance of chance alone calling the shots replaces the "it's certain" or "close to certain" of ordinary logic. A strong chance that chance could have ruled replaces "it can't be" or "almost certainly can't be."

Why the number .05 or less? Partly for standardization. People have agreed that this is a good cutoff point for most purposes. And partly out of old friend common sense. Frederick Mosteller tells us that if you toss a coin repeatedly in a college class and after each toss ask the class if there is anything suspicious going on, "hands suddenly go up all over the room" after the fifth head or tail in a row. There happens to be only 1 chance in 16—.0625, not far from .05, or 5 chances in 100— that five heads or tails in a row will show up in five tosses, "so there is some empirical evidence that the rarity of events in the neighborhood of .05 begins to set people's teeth on edge."[2]

Another common way of reporting probability is to calculate a *confidence level*, as well as a *confidence interval* (or *confidence limits* or *range*). This is what happens when a political pollster reports that candidate X would now get 50 percent of the vote and thereby lead candidate Y by 3 percentage points, "with a 3-percentage-point margin of error plus or minus and a 95 percent confidence level." In other words, Mr. or Ms. Pollster is 95 percent confident that X's share of the vote would be someplace between 53 and 47 percent. Similarly, candidate Y's share might be 3 percentage points greater (or less) than the figure predicted. In a close election, that margin of error could obviously turn a predicted defeat into victory. And that sometimes happens.

An important point in looking at the results of political polls (and any other statements of confidence): In the reports we read, the plus or minus 3 (or whatever) percentage points is often omitted, and the pollster merely mentions a "3-point margin of error." This means there is actually a 6-point range within which the truth *probably* lurks.

The more people who are questioned in a political poll or the larger the number of subjects in a medical study, the greater the chance of a high confidence level and a narrow, and therefore more reassuring, confidence interval.

No matter how reassuring they sound, P values and confidence statements cannot be taken as gospel, for .05 is not a guarantee, just a number. There are several important reasons for this.

• All that P values measure is the *probability* that the results might have been produced by some sneaky random process. In 20 results where only chance is at work, 1, on the average, will have a reassuring-sounding but misleading P value of <.05. One, in short, may be a false positive.

Dr. Marvin Zelen points out that there may be 6,000 to 10,000 clinical (medical) trials of cancer treatment under way today, and if the conventional value of .05 is adopted as the upper permissible limit for false positives, then every 100 studies with no actual benefit may, on average, produce 5 false-positive results. Hence, we may expect 50 false positive results, on average, for every 1,000 trials with no beneficial effects! Zelen in fact has said, "We may now have reached an impasse in cancer chemotherapy in which there are large numbers of false-positive therapies in the clinic,"[3] leading physicians down many false paths.

Amazingly, most false positives probably remain undetected. Scientists do not profit much professionally by reporting negative results. Journal editors are not keen on publishing them. Nor are scientists keen on doing costly and time-consuming studies that merely confirm someone else's work, so "confirmatory studies are rare," Zelen reports.

• Statistical significance alone does not mean there is a cause and effect. *Correlation* or *association* is not causation. Remember the rooster who thought his crowing made the sun rise? Unless an association is so powerful and so constantly repeated that the case is overwhelming, association is only a clue, meaning more study or confirmation is needed.

To statisticians, incidentally, there is this important difference between correlation and association: *Association* means there is at least a possible relation between two variables. A *correlation* is a measure of the association.

• If the number of subjects is too small, an unimpressive P value may simply mean that there were too few subjects to detect something that might have shown an effect in more subjects. Highly "significant" P values can sometimes adorn negligible differences in large samples.

• An impressive P value might also be explained by some other variable or variables—other conditions or associations— not taken into account.

• Statistical significance does not mean biological, clinical—that is, medical—or practical significance, though inexperienced reporters sometimes see or hear the word "significant" and jump to that conclusion, even reporting that the scientists called their study "significant." Example: A tiny difference between two large groups in mean hemoglobin concentration, or red blood count (say, 0.1 g/100 mL, or a tenth of a gram per 100 milliliters), may be statistically significant yet medically meaningless.[4]

• Eager scientists can consciously or unconsciously manipulate the P value by failing to adjust for other factors, by choosing to compare different end points in a study (say, condition on leaving the hospital rather than length of survival), or by choosing the way the P value is calculated or reported.

There are several mathematical paths to a P value, such as the chi-square (χ^2), t, F, r, and paired t tests. All may be legitimate. But be warned. Dr. David Salsburg of Pfizer, Inc., has written in the *American Statistician* of the unscrupulous practitioner who "engages in a ritual known as 'hunting for P values' " and finds ways to modify the original data to "produce a rich collection of small P values" even if those that result from simply comparing two treatments "never reach the magical .05."[5]

"If you look hard enough through your data," contributes an investigator at a major medical center, "if you do enough subset analyses, if you go through 20 subsets, you can find one"—say, "the effect of chemotherapy on premenopausal women with two to five lymph nodes"—"with a P value less than .05. And people do this."

"Statistical tests provide a basis for probability statements," writes Dr. John Bailar, "only when the hypothesis is fully developed before the data are examined. . . . If even the briefest glance at a study's results moves the investigator to consider a hypothesis not formulated before the study was started, that glance destroys the probability value of the evidence at hand." (At the same time, Bailar adds, "review of data for unexpected clues . . . can be an immensely fruitful source of ideas" for new hypotheses "that can be tested in the correct way." And occasionally "findings may be so striking that independent confirmation . . . is superfluous.")[6]

A rather sophisticated—and possibly touchy—line of questioning that some reporters might want to try if they're skeptical: *How did you arrive at your* P *value? Did you use the test planned in advance in your protocol or study design, or did you apply several tests, then report the best-sounding one?*

And you may think of other questions.

The laws of probability also teach us to *expect* some unusual, even impossible-sounding events.

We've all taken a trip to New York or London or someplace and bumped into someone from home. The chance of that? I don't know, but if you and I tossed for a drink every day after work, the chance that I would ever win 10 times in a row is 1 in 1,024. Yet I would probably do so sometime in a four- or five-year period. What I like to call the Law of Unusual Events—statisticians call it the Law of Small Probabilities—tells us that a few people with apparently fatal illnesses will inexplicably recover, there will be some amazing clusters of cases of cancer or birth defects that will have no common cause, and I may once in a great while bump into a friend far from home.

In a large enough population such coincidences are not unusual. They are the rule. They produce striking anecdotes and often striking news stories. In the medical world they produce unreliable, though often cited, testimonial or anecdotal evidence. "The world is large." Vogt notes, "and one can find a large number of people to whom the most bizarre events have occurred. They all have personal explanations. The vast majority are wrong."[7]

"We [reporters] are overly susceptible to anecdotal evidence," Philip Meyer writes. "Anecdotes make good reading, and we are right to use them. . . . But we often forget to remind our readers—and ourselves—of the folly of generalizing from a few interesting cases. . . . The statistic is hard to remember. The success stories are not."[8]

A statistic to ask about is the *denominator*—the number of people or, a statistician would say, the *population* or domain—in whom such an event might happen. Zelen cites this example: The chance of any youngster between ages five and nine developing leukemia is 3 in 100,000 per year. In a school with 100 children of this age group, we would expect only 3 cases in 100 years. But in this nation with thousands of schools, we would occasionally—such is chance—find schools with 3 or more cases in a single year. "Then one is faced with the problem of interpretation," Zelen says. "Is this one of those rare events that is surely going to be observed? Or is it due to some causal factor?"

A reporter in this instance might ask a statistician at the National Cancer Institute or a medical center, What is the chance of such an event in such a population? How many similar unusual events are probably never reported?

"POWER" AND NUMBERS

This gets us to another statistical concept: *power*. Statistically, "power" means the probability of finding something if it's there. Example: Given that there is a true effect, say a difference between two medical treatments or an increase in cancer caused by a toxin in a group of workers, how likely are we to find it?

Sample size confers power. Statisticians say, "Funny things can happen in small samples without meaning very much" . . . "There is no probability until the sample size is there" . . . "Large numbers confer power" . . . "Large numbers at least make us sit up and take notice."*

All this concern about sample size can also be expressed as the *law of large numbers*, which says that as the number of cases increases, the probable truth of a conclusion or forecast increases. The *validity* (truth or accuracy) and *reliability* (reproducibility) of the statistics begin to converge on the truth.

---

*There is another unrelated use of the word "power." Scientists commonly speak of increasing or "raising" some quantity *by a power of* 2 or 3 or 100 or whatever. "Power" here means the product you get when you multiply a number by itself one or more times. Thus, in $2 \times 2 = 4$, 4 is the second power of 2, or to put it another way, there are two 2's in your equation. This is commonly written 2^2 and known as 2 to the second power or just 2 to the second. In $2 \times 2 \times 2 = 8$, 2 has been raised to the third power. When you think about 2^{100}, you see the need for the shorthand.

We already learned this when we talked about probability. But by thinking of power as statisticians do—as a function of both sample size and the accuracy of measurement, since that too affects the probability of finding something—we can see that if the number of treated patients is small in a medical study, a shift from success to failure in only a few patients could dramatically decrease the success rate.

If six patients have been treated with a 50 percent success rate, the shift to the failure column of just one would cut the success rate to 33 percent. And the total number is so small in any case that the result has little reliability. The result might be valid or accurate, but it would not be generalizable—it would not have reliability until confirmed by careful studies in larger samples. The larger the sample, and assuming there have been no fatal biases or other flaws, the more confidence a statistician would have in the result.

One canny science reporter, Lewis Cope, says,

> I have my own "rule of two." If someone makes some numerical claim, I look at the numbers, then see how much I might change the finding by adding or subtracting two from any of the figures. For example, someone says there are five cases of cancer in a community. Would it seem meaningful if there were three?
>
> Or if there were eight cases this year but four the year before—a 100 percent increase—I ask myself, "If I add two cases to last year's total and subtract two from this year's, is there a chance things haven't changed, except by chance?" This approach will never supplant refined analysis. But by playing around with the numbers this way— I sometimes try three instead of two—a reporter can often spot a potential problem or error.

A statistician says, "This can help with small numbers but not large ones." Mosteller contributes "a little trick I use a lot on counts of any size." He explains, "Let's say some political unit has 10,000 crimes or deaths or accidents this year. Has something new happened? The minimum standard deviation . . . for a number like that is 100—that is, the square root of the original number. That means the number may vary by a minimum of 200 every year without even considering growth, the business cycle, or any other effect. This will supplement your reporter's approach."

Looking for error in reported results, statisticians try to spot both false positives and false negatives. The *false positive* (or *Type I* or *alpha error* in statistical language you may see) is to find a result or effect where there is none. The *false negative* (or *Type II* or *beta error*) is to miss an effect where there is one. The latter is particularly common when there are small numbers. "There are some very well conducted studies with small numbers, even five patients, in which the results are so clear-cut that you don't have to worry about power," says Dr. Relman. "You still have to worry about applicability to a larger population, but you don't have to doubt that there was an effect. When results are negative, however, you have to ask, How large would the effect have to be to be discovered?"

Many scientific and medical studies are underpowered—that is, they include too few cases. "Whenever you see a negative result," another scientist says, "you should ask, What is the power? What was the chance of finding the result if there was one?" One study found that an astonishing 70 percent of 71 well-regarded clinical trials that reported no effect had too few patients to show a 25 percent difference in outcome. Half of the trials could not have detected a 50 percent difference.[9]

A statistician scanned an article on colon cancer in a leading journal. "If you read the article carefully," he said, "you will see that if one treatment was better than the other—if it would increase median survival by 50 percent, from five to seven and a half years, say—they had only a 60 percent chance of finding it out. That's little better than tossing a coin!"

The weak power of that study would be expressed numerically as .6, or 60 percent. Scan an article's fine print or footnotes, and you will sometimes find such a *power statement*. Most authors still don't report one, but the practice is growing, especially when results are negative.

How large is a large enough sample? One statistician calculated that a trial has to have 50 patients before there is even a 30 percent chance of finding a 50 percent difference in results.

Sometimes large populations indeed are needed.[10] If some kind of cancer usually strikes 3 people per 2,000, and you suspect that the rate is quadrupled in people exposed to substance X, you would have to study 4,000 people for the observed excess rate to have a 95 percent chance of reaching statistical significance. The likelihood that a 30-to-39-year-old woman will suffer a myocardial infarction, or heart attack, while taking an oral contraceptive is about 1 in 18,000 per year. To be 95 percent sure of observing at least one such event in a one-year trial, you would have to observe nearly 54,000 women.[11]

Even the lack of an effect—statistically sometimes called a zero numerator—can be a trap. Say, someone reports, "We have treated 14 leukemic boys for five years with no resulting testicular dysfunction"—that is, zero abnormalities in 14. The question remains, how many cases would they have had to treat to have any real chance of seeing an effect? The probability of an effect may be small yet highly important to know about.

All this means you must often ask, *What's your denominator? What's the size of your population?** A disease rate of 10 percent in 20 individuals may not mean much. A 10 percent rate in 200 persons would be more impressive. A rate is only a figure. Always try to get both the numerator and the denominator.

The most important rule of all about any numbers: Ask for them. When anyone makes an assertion that should include numbers and fails to give them, when anyone says that most people, or even X percent, do such and such, you should ask, *What are your numbers?* After all, some researchers reportedly announced a new treatment for a disease of chickens by saying, "33.3 percent were cured, 33.3 percent died, and the other one got away."

---

*And know that to a statistician a population does not necessarily mean a group of people. Statistically, a *population* is any group or collection of pertinent units—units with one or more pertinent characteristics in common—people, events, objects, records, test scores, or physiological values (like blood pressure readings). Statisticians also use the term *universe* for a whole group of people or units under study.

BIAS AND CONFOUNDERS

One scientist once said that lefties are overrepresented among baseball's heavy hitters. He saw this as "a possible result of their hemispheric lateralization, the relative roles of the two sides of the brain." A critic who had seen more ball games said some simpler covariables could explain the difference. When they swing, left-handed hitters are already on the move toward first base. And most pitchers are right-handers who throw most often to right-handed hitters.[12]

Scientist A was apparently guilty of *bias*, meaning the introduction of spurious associations and error by failing to consider other influential factors. The other factors may be called *covariables, covariates, intervening* or *contributing variables, confounding variables*, or *confounders*. A simpler term may be "other explanations."

Statisticians call bias "the most serious and pervasive problem in the interpretation of data from clinical trials" . . . "the central issue of epidemiological research" . . . "the most common cause of unreliable data." Able and conscientious scientists try to eliminate biases or account for them in some way. But not everybody who makes a scientific, medical, or environmental claim is that skilled. Or that honest. Or that all-powerful. Some biases are unavoidable by the very difficulty of much research, and the most insidious biases of all, says one statistician, are "those we don't know exist."

Some biases may be uncovered by assiduous investigation. A father noticed that every time one of his 11 kids dropped a piece of bread on the floor, it landed with the buttered side up. "This utterly defies the laws of chance," he exclaimed. Close examination disclosed the cause: The kids were buttering their bread on both sides.

I told this story to one statistician, who said, "I was once called about a person who had won first, second, and third prizes in a church lottery. I was asked to assess the probability that this could have happened. I found out that the winner had bought nearly all the tickets."

He had of course asked the obvious question for both scientist and reporters: *Could the relationship described be explained by other factors?*

Not everyone will tell you, of course, for bias is a pervasive human failing. As one candid scientist is said to have admitted, "I wouldn't have seen it if I hadn't believed it." Enthusiastic investigators often tell us their findings are exciting. But they may be so exciting that the investigators paint the results in over-rosy hues.

Other powerful human drives—the race for academic promotion and prestige, financial connections—can also create conscious or unconscious conflicts of interest or attitudes that feed bias. Dr. Thomas Chalmers of Mount Sinai Medical Center in New York tells of a drug trial, financed by a pharmaceutical firm, in which both the head of the study committee and the main statisticians and analysts were the firm's employees, though not so identified in any credits. He tells of a study of oral drugs for diabetes in which the fact that the first author had previously published 14 articles on the subject, and in 7 had acknowledged support by the drug manufacturers, was "not known to the reader."

In contrast, Chalmers describes a study also financed by a drug firm but with a contract specifying a study protocol designed by independent investigators and monitored by an outside board less likely to be influenced by a desire for a favorable outcome. "It is never possible to eliminate" potential conflicts of interest in biomedical research, he concludes, but they should be disclosed so others can evaluate them.[13]

Even a genius may be biased. Horace Freeland Judson of Johns Hopkins University tells how Isaac Newton experimented with prisms and lenses and developed a theory of color, light, and the solar spectrum. He did not report seeing some dark lines—absorption lines, which mark varying wavelengths—that his instruments must have shown. A modern scientist argues that Newton's theory, not his instruments, had no place for that evidence: "To the observing scientist, hypothesis is both friend and enemy."[14]

For years technicians making blood counts were guided by textbooks that told them two or more "properly" studied samples from the same blood should not vary beyond narrow "allowable" limits. Reported counts always stayed inside those limits. A Mayo Clinic statistician rechecked and found that at least two thirds of the time the discrepancies exceeded the supposed limits. The technicians had been seeing what they had been told to expect and discounting any differences as mistakes. This also saved them from the additional labor of doing still more counting.

Both the *biased observer* and the *biased subject* are common in medicine. A researcher who wants to see a treatment result may see one. A patient may report one out of eagerness to please the researcher. There is also the powerful *placebo effect*. Summarizing many studies, one scientist found that half the patients with headaches or seasickness—and a third of those suffering from coughs, mood changes, anxiety, the common cold, and even the disabling chest pains of angina pectoris—reported relief from a "nothing pill."[15] A placebo is not truly a nothing pill; the mere expectation of relief seems to trigger important effects within the body. But in a careful study the placebo should not do as well as a test medication; otherwise the test medication is no better than a placebo.

Sampling bias is the bugaboo of both political polls and medical studies. Say you want to know what proportion of the populace has heart disease, so you stand on a corner and ask people as they pass. Your sample is biased, if only because it leaves out those too disabled to get around. Your problem, a statistician would say, is *selection*. A political pollster who fails to build a valid probability sample, easy when questioning only a thousand or so people from coast to coast, has equally poor selection.[16]

A doctor in a clinic or hospital with an unrepresentative patient population—healthier or sicker or richer or poorer than average—may report results that do not represent the population as a whole. Veterans Administration hospitals, for example, treat relatively few women; their conclusions may apply only to the disproportionate number of lower-income men who typically seek out the VA hospitals' free care. A celebrated Mayo or Cleveland or Ochsner clinic sees both a disproportionate number of difficult cases and a disproportionate number of patients affluent and well enough to travel. The famed Kinsey reports were valuable revelations of sexual behavior but flawed because the samples consisted disproportionately of upper middle-class men and women and of those willing to talk.

An investigator may also introduce bias by *constraining*, or distorting, a sample—by failing to reveal *nonresponse* or by otherwise "throwing away data." A surgeon cites his success rate in those discharged from the hospital after an operation but omits those who died during or just after the procedure. Many people drop out of studies—sometimes they just quit—or they are dropped for various reasons: They could not be evaluated, they came down with some "irrelevant" disorders, they moved away, they died. In fact, many of those not counted may have had unfavorable outcomes had they stayed in the study.

Mosteller tells of a nationwide study of a possibly dangerous anesthetic. The investigators relied on autopsy results at 38 hospitals. Unfortunately, only about 60 percent of the relevant dead had been autopsied, and "anything could have been explained by the missing 40 percent, so that part of the study wound up with a handful of nothing."

The presence of significant nonresponse can often be detected, when reading medical papers, by counting the number of patients treated versus the number of untreated or differently treated *controls*—patients with whom the treated patients are compared. If the number of controls is strikingly greater in a randomized clinical trial (though not necessarily in an epidemiological or environmental study), there were probably many dropouts. A well-conducted study should describe and account for them. A study that does not may report a favorable treatment result by ignoring the fate of the dropouts—a confounding variable.

Age, gender, occupation, nationality, race, income, socioeconomic status, health status, and powerful behaviors like smoking are all possible confounding—and frequently ignored—variables. In the 1970s, foes of adding fluoride to city water pointed to crude cancer mortality rates in two groups of 10 U.S. cities. One group had added fluoride to water, the other had not, and from 1950 to 1970 the cancer mortality rate rose faster in the fluoridated cities. The National Cancer Institute pointed out that the two groups were not equal: The difference in cancer deaths was almost entirely explained by differences in age, race, and sex. The age-, race-, and sex-adjusted difference actually showed a small, unexplained lower mortality rate in the fluoridated cities.[17]

If you look carefully at the fate of women taking birth control pills, you find that advancing age and smoking are the two great confounders. You must take both into account to find the greatest clusters of ill effects. Smoking has been an important confounder in studies of industrial contaminants like asbestos, in which, again, the smokers suffer a disproportionate number of ill effects.[18]

A 1947 survey of Chicago lawyers showed that those who had mere high school diplomas before entering legal training earned 6.3 percent more, on the average, than college graduates. The confounder here—the real explanation—was age. In 1947 there were still many older lawyers without college degrees, and they were simply older, on the average, and hence more established.[19]

Occupational studies often confront another seeming paradox: The workers exposed to some possible adverse effect turn out to be healthier than a control group of persons without such exposure. The confounder: the well-known *healthy-worker effect*. Workers tend to be healthier and live longer than the population in general.

Some studies of workers in steel mills showed no overall increase in cancer, despite possible exposures to various carcinogens. It took a look at black workers alone to find excess cancer. They commonly worked at the coke ovens, where carcinogens were emitted. This was a case where the population had to be *stratified*, or broken up in some meaningful way, to find the facts. Such findings in blacks often may be falsely ascribed to race or genetics, when the real or at least the most important contributing or ruling variables—to a statistician, the *independent variables*—are occupation and the social and economic plights that put blacks in vulnerable settings. The excess cancer is the *dependent variable*, the result.

"In a two-variable relationship," Dr. Gary Friedman explains, "one is usually considered the independent variable, which affects the other or dependent variable."[20] Take the fact that more people get colds in winter. Here weather is commonly seen as the underlying or independent variable, which affects incidence of the common cold, the dependent variable. Actually, of course, some people, like children in school who are constantly exposed to new viruses, are more vulnerable to colds than others. In the case of these children, then, as in the case of the black workers at the coke ovens, there is often more than one independent variable. Also, some people think that an important underlying reason for the prevalence of colds in winter may be that children are congregated in school, giving colds to each other, thence to their families, thence to their families' coworkers, thence to the coworkers' families, and so on. But cold weather—and home heating?—may still figure, perhaps by drying nasal passages and making them more vulnerable to viruses.

The search for *true variables* is obviously one of the main pursuits of the epidemiologist, or disease detective—or of any physician who wants to know what has affected a patient, or of any student of society who seeks true causes. Like colds, many medical conditions, such as heart disease, cancer, and probably mental illness, have multiple contributing factors. Where many known, measurable factors are involved, statisticians can use mathematical techniques—the terms you will see include *multiple regression, multivariate analysis*, and *discriminant analysis* and *factor, cluster, path, and two-stage least-squares analyses*—to relate all the variables and try to find which are the truly important predictors. Yet some situations, like the striking decline in U. S. heart disease mortality in recent years, defy such analyses. These years have seen several major changes in American life that may play a role: less smoking among men, consumption of a leaner diet, more recreational exercise (though more sedentary work). Medical care is far better, including the treatment of hypertension, which disposes people to heart disease. Many of these variables cannot be well measured, and the effect of some is debatable, so—a common situation in science—the truth remains uncertain.

VARIABILITY

Doctors always say, "Most things are better in the morning," and they're mostly right. Most chronic or recurring conditions wax and wane. We tend to wake up at night when the condition is at its worst. Then, no matter what is done by way of treatment the next day, the odds are that we'll feel better.

This is *regression toward the mean*: the tendency of all values in every field of science—physical, biological, social, and economic—to move toward the average. Tall fathers tend to have shorter sons, and short fathers, taller sons. The students who get the highest grades on an exam tend to get somewhat lower ones the next time. The regression effect is common to all repeated measurements.

Regression is part of an even more basic phenomenon: *variation*, or *variability*. Virtually everything that is measured varies from measurement to measurement. When repeated, every experiment has at least slightly different results. Take a patient's blood pressure, pulse rate, or blood count several times in a row, and the readings will be somewhat different. Take them at different times of day or on different days, and the readings may vary greatly.

The important reasons? In part, fluctuating physiology, but also measurement errors, the limits of measurement accuracy, and observer variation. Examining the same patient, no two doctors will report exactly the same results, and the results may be grossly different. If six doctors examine a patient with a faint heart murmer, only one or two may have the skill or keen hearing to detect it. Experimental results so typically differ from one time to the next that scientific and medical fakers—a Boston cancer researcher, for example—have been detected by the unusual regularity of their reported results, with numbers agreeing too well and the same results appearing time after time, with not enough variation from patient to patient.

Biological variation is the most important cause of variation in physiology and medicine. Different patients, and the same patients, react differently to the same treatment. Disease rates differ in different parts of the country and among different populations, and—alas, nothing is simple—there is natural variation within the same population.

Every population, after all, is a collection of individuals, each with many characteristics. Each characteristic, or *variable*, such as height, has a *distribution* of values from person to person, and—if we would know something about the whole population—we must have some handy summaries of the distribution. We can't get much out of a list of 10,000 measurements, so we need single values that summarize many measurements.

Enter here the familiar *average* or, more exactly, the *mean, median,* and *mode*. These and a few other measures can give us some idea of the look of the whole and its many measurable properties, or *parameters.*

When most of us speak of an average, we mean simply the *mean* or *arithmetic average*, the sum of all the values divided by the number of values. The mean is no mean tool; it is a good way to get a typical number, but it has limitations, especially when there are some extreme values. There is said to be a memorial in a Siberian town to a ficitious Count Smerdlovski, the world's champion at Russian roulette. On the average he won, but his actual record was 73 and 1.[21]

If you look at the average salary in a hospital, you will not know that half the personnel may be working for the minimum wage, while a few hundred persons make $100,000 or more a year. You may learn more here from the *median*, the figure that divides a population into two equal halves. The median can be of value when a group has a few members with extreme values, like the 400-pounder at an obesity clinic whose other patients weigh from 180 to 200 pounds. If he leaves, the patients' mean weight might drop by 10 pounds, but the median might drop just 1 pound.[22]

The most frequently occurring number or value in a distribution is called the *mode*. When the median and the mode are about the same, or even more when mean, median, and mode are roughly equal, you can feel comfortable about knowing the typical value.

You still need to know something about the exceptions, in short, the *dispersion* (or spread or scatter) of the entire distribution. One measure of spread is the *range*. It tells you the lowest and highest values. It might inform you, for example, that the salaries in that hospital range from $10,000 to $250,000.

You can also divide your values into 100 *percentiles*, so you can say someone or something falls into the 10th or 71st percentile, or into *quartiles* (fourths) or *quintiles* (fifths). One useful measure is the *interquartile range*, the interval between the 75th and 25th percentiles—this is the distribution in the middle, which avoids the extreme values at each end. Or you can divide a distribution into *subgroups*—those with incomes from $10,000 to $20,000, for example, or ages 20 to 29, 30 to 39, and so on.

All these values can easily be plotted. With many of the things that scientists, economists, or others measure—IQs, for example, and other test scores—we typically tend to see a familiar, bell-shaped *normal distribution*, high in the middle, low at each end, or *tail*. This is the classic *Gaussian curve*, named after the 19th-century German mathematician Karl Friedrich Gauss. But you may also find that the plot has two or more peaks or clusters, a *bimodal* or *multimodal distribution*.

A widely used number, the *standard deviation*, can reveal a great deal. No matter how it sounds, it is not the average distance from the mean but a more complex figure.* Unlike the range, this handy figure takes full account of every value to tell how spread out things are—how dispersed the measurements. In what one statistician calls a truly remarkable generalization, in most sets of measurement "and without regard to what is being measured" only 1 measurement in 3 will deviate from the average by more than 1 standard deviation, only 1 in 20 by more than 2 standard deviations, and only 1 in 100 by more than 2.57 standard deviations.

"Once you know the standard deviation in a normal, bellshaped distribution," according to Thomas Louis, "you can draw the whole picture of the data. You can visualize the shape of the curve without even drawing the picture, since the larger the variation of the numbers, the larger the standard deviation and the more spread out the curve—and vice versa."

Example: If the average score of all students who take the SAT college entrance test is relatively low and the spread—the standard deviation—relatively large, this creates a very long-tailed, low-humped curve of test scores, ranging, say, from around 300 to 1500. But if the average score of a group of brighter students entering an elite college is high, the standard deviation of the scores will be less and the curve will be high-humped and short-tailed, going from maybe 900 to 1500.

---

*There is more than one way to calculate it, and there are several variations, depending on the statistician's purpose. A common one is to add the squares of the differences between each number and the mean, then divide that number by the total number of squares, often referred to as the *variance* (minus I if you're looking at a sample of a population rather than the whole population). Then calculate the square root of the result. As in

$$s = \sqrt{\frac{\Sigma(X - \bar{X})^2}{n - 1}}$$

Sometimes statisticians calculate the *standard deviation of the mean*—this because the mean, being an average, is less variable than single measurements. Some call this the *standard error* or *standard error of the mean*. As in

$$s_{\bar{x}} = \frac{x}{\sqrt{n}}$$

All the above are measures of dispersion.

"If just told you the means of two such distributions, you might say they were the same," another scientist says. "But if I reported the means and the standard deviations, you'd know they were different, with a lot more variations in one."

From a human standpoint, variation tells us that it takes more than averages to describe individuals. Biologist Stephen Jay Gould learned in 1982 that he had a serious form of cancer. The literature told him the median survival was only eight months after discovery. Three years later he wrote in *Discover*, "All evolutionary biologists know that means and medians are the abstractions," while variation is "the reality," meaning "half the people will live longer" than eight months.

Since he was young, since his disease had been diagnosed early, and since he would receive the best possible treatment, he decided he had a good chance of being at the far end of the curve. He calculated that the curve must be skewed well to the right, as the left half of the distribution had to be "scrunched up between zero and eight months, but the upper right half [could] extend out for years." He concluded, "I saw no reason why I shouldn't be in that small tail. . . . I would have time to think, to plan and to fight." Also, since he was being placed on an experimental new treatment, he might if fortune smiled "be in the first cohort of a new distribution with . . . a right tail extending to death by natural causes at advanced old age."[23]

Statistics cannot tell us whether fortune will smile, only that such reasoning is sound.

NOTES

1. Robert Hooke, *How to Tell the Liars From the Statisticians* (New York: Marcel Dekker, 1983).

2. Frederick Mosteller talk at the Council for the Advancement of Science Writing (CASW) seminar "New Horizons of Science."

3. Zelen, "Innovations in the Design of Clinical Trials in Breast Cancer," in *Breast Cancer Research and Treatment*, no. 3 (1983), Proceedings of Fifth Annual San Antonio Breast Cancer Symposium.

4. Gary D. Friedman, *Primer of Epidemiology*, 3d ed. (New York: McGraw-Hill, 1987).

5. David S. Salsburg, "The Religion of Statistics as Practiced in Medical Journals," *American Statistician* 39, no. 3 (August 1985): 220–22.

6. John Bailar, "Science, Statistics and Deception," *Annals of Internal Medicine* 104, no. 2 (February 1986): 259–60.

7. Thomas M. Vogt, *Making Health Decisions: An Epidemiologic Perspective on Staying Well* (Chicago: Nelson-Hall, 1983).

8. Philip Meyer, *Precision Journalism: A Reporter's Introduction to Social Science Methods.* 2d ed. (Bloomington: Indiana University Press, 1979).

9. J. A. Freiman, cited by Mosteller in *Coping,* ed. Warren.

10. Alvin R. Feinstein, "Epidemiology: Challenges and Controversies," in *1983 Encyclopedia Britannica Medical and Health Annual* (Chicago: Encyclopedia Britannica, 1983).

11. David L. Sackett in *Clinical Trials: Issues and Approaches,* ed. Stanley H. Shapiro and Thomas A. Louis (New York: Marcel Decker, 1983).

12. David Hemenway, quoted in a Harvard School of Public Health staff newsletter, November 1983.

13. Thomas Chalmers in *Clinical Trials: Issues and Approaches*, ed. Stanley H. Shapiro and Thomas A. Louis (New York: Marcel Decker, 1983).

14. Horace Freeland Judson, *The Search for Solutions* (New York: Holt, Rinehart and Winston, 1980).

15. Henry K. Beecher, *Measurement of Subjective Responses: Quantitative Effects of Drugs* (New York: Oxford University Press, 1959).

16. Vogt, *Making Health Decisions.*

17. Hooke, *How to Tell the Liars.*

18. Department of Health, Education and Welfare, *The Health Consequences of Smoking: A Report of the Surgeon-General*, 1980.

19. Hooke, *How to Tell the Liars.*

20. Friedman, *Primer.*

21. James Trifel, "Odds are Against Your Beating the Law of Averages," *Smithsonian*, September 1984, 66–75.

22. Friedman, *Primer.*

23. Stephen Jay Gould, "The Median Isn't the Message," *Discount*, June 1985, 40–42.

22

IN PLATO'S CAVE

Susan Sontag

Humankind lingers unregenerately in Plato's cave, still reveling, its age-old habit, in mere images of the truth. But being educated by photographs is not like being educated by older, more artisanal images. For one thing, there are a great many more images around, claiming our attention. The inventory started in 1839 and since then just about everything has been photographed, or so it seems. This very insatiability of the photographing eye changes the terms of confinement in the cave, our world. In teaching us a new visual code, photographs alter and enlarge our notions of what is worth looking at and what we have a right to observe. They are a grammar and, even more importantly, an ethics of seeing. Finally, the most grandiose result of the photographic enterprise is to give us the sense that we can hold the whole world in our heads—as an anthology of images.

To collect photographs is to collect the world. Movies and television programs light up walls, flicker, and go out; but with still photographs the image is also an object, lightweight, cheap to produce, easy to carry about, accumulate, store. In Godard's *Les*

Carabiniers (1963), two sluggish lumpen-peasants are lured into joining the King's Army by the promise that they will be able to loot, rape, kill, or do whatever else they please to the enemy, and get rich. But the suitcase of booty that Michel-Ange and Ulysse triumphantly bring home, years later, to their wives turns out to contain only picture postcards, hundreds of them, of Monuments, Department Stores, Mammals, Wonders of Nature, Methods of Transport, Works of Art, and other classified treasures from around the globe. Godard's gag vividly parodies the equivocal magic of the photographic image. Photographs are perhaps the most mysterious of all the objects that make up, and thicken, the environment we recognize as modern. Photographs really are experience captured, and the camera is the ideal arm of consciousness in its acquisitive mood.

To photograph is to appropriate the thing photographed. It means putting oneself into a certain relation to the world that feels like knowledge—and, therefore, like power. A now notorious first fall into alienation, habituating people to abstract the world into printed words, is supposed to have engendered that surplus of Faustian energy and psychic damage needed to build modern, inorganic societies. But print seems a less treacherous form of leaching out the world, of turning it into a mental object, than photographic images, which now provide most of the knowledge people have about the look of the past and the reach of the present. What is written about a person or an event is frankly an interpretation, as are handmade visual statements, like paintings and drawings. Photographed images do not seem to be statements about the world so much as pieces of it, miniatures of reality that anyone can make or acquire.

Photographs, which fiddle with the scale of the world, themselves get reduced, blown up, cropped, retouched, doctored, tricked out. They age, plagued by the usual ills of paper objects; they disappear; they become valuable, and get bought and sold; they are reproduced. Photographs, which package the world, seem to invite packaging. They are stuck in albums, framed and set on tables, tacked on walls, projected as slides. Newspapers and magazines feature them; cops alphabetize them; museums exhibit them; publishers compile them.

For many decades the book has been the most influential way of arranging (and usually miniaturizing) photographs, thereby guaranteeing them longevity, if not immortality—photographs are fragile objects, easily torn or mislaid—and a wider public. The photograph in a book is, obviously, the image of an image. But since it is, to begin with, a printed, smooth object, a photograph loses much less of its essential quality when reproduced in a book than a painting does. Still, the book is not a wholly satisfactory scheme for putting groups of photographs into general circulation. The sequence in which the photographs are to be looked at is proposed by the order of pages, but nothing holds readers to the recommended order or indicates the amount of time to be spent on each photograph. Chris Marker's film, *Si j'avais quatre dromadaires* (1966), a brilliantly orchestrated meditation on photographs of all sorts and themes, suggests a subtler and more rigorous way of packaging (and enlarging) still photographs. Both the order and the exact time for looking at each photograph are imposed; and there is a gain in visual legibility and emotional impact. But photographs transcribed in a film cease to be collectable objects, as they still are when served up in books.

Photographs furnish evidence. Something we hear about, but doubt, seems proven when we're shown a photograph of it. In one version of its utility, the camera record incriminates. Starting with their use by the Paris police in the murderous roundup of Communards in June 1871, photographs became a useful tool of modern states in the surveillance and control of their increasingly mobile populations. In another version of its utility, the camera record justifies. A photograph passes for incontrovertible proof that a given thing happened. The picture may distort; but there is always a presumption that something exists, or did exist, which is like what's in the picture. Whatever the limitations (through amateurism) or pretensions (through artistry) of the individual photographer, a photograph—any photograph—seems to have a more innocent, and therefore more accurate, relation to visible reality than do other mimetic objects. Virtuosi of the noble image like Alfred Stieglitz and Paul Strand, composing mighty, unforgettable photographs decade after decade, still want, first of all, to show something "out there," just like the Polaroid owner for whom photographs are a handy, fast form of note-taking, or the shutterbug with a Brownie who takes snapshots as souvenirs of daily life.

While a painting or a prose description can never be other than a narrowly selective interpretation, a photograph can be treated as a narrowly selective transparency. But despite the presumption of veracity that gives all photographs authority, interest, se-ductiveness, the work that photographers do is no generic exception to the usually shady commerce between art and truth. Even when photographers are most concerned with mirroring reality, they are still haunted by tacit imperatives of taste and conscience. The immensely gifted members of the Farm Security Administration photographic project of the late 1930s (among them Walker Evans, Dorothea Lange, Ben Shahn, Russell Lee) would take dozens of frontal pictures of one of their sharecropper subjects until satisfied that they had gotten just the right look on film—the precise expression on the subject's face that supported their own notions about poverty, light, dignity, texture, exploitation, and geometry. In deciding how a picture should look, in preferring one exposure to another, photographers are always imposing standards on their subjects. Although there is a sense in which the camera does indeed capture reality, not just interpret it, photographs are as much an interpretation of the world as paintings and drawings are. Those occasions when the taking of photographs is relatively undiscriminating, promiscuous, or self-effacing do not lessen the didacticism of the whole enterprise. This very passivity—and ubiquity—of the photographic record is photography's "message," its aggression.

Images which idealize (like most fashion and animal photography) are no less aggressive than work which makes a virtue of plainness (like class pictures, still lifes of the bleaker sort, and mug shots). There is an aggression implicit in every use of the camera. This is as evident in the 1840s and 1850s, photography's glorious first two decades, as in all the succeeding decades, during which technology made possible an ever increasing spread of that mentality which looks at the world as a set of potential photographs. Even for such early masters as David Octavius Hill and Julia Margaret Cameron who used the camera as a means of getting painterly images, the point of taking photographs was a vast departure from the aims of painters. From its start, photography implied the capture of the largest possible number of subjects. Painting never had so imperial a scope. The subsequent industrialization of camera technology only carried out a promise inherent in photography from its very beginning: to democratize all experiences by translating them into images.

That age when taking photographs required a cumbersome and expensive contraption —the toy of the clever, the wealthy, and the obsessed—seems remote indeed from the era of sleek pocked cameras that invite anyone to take pictures. The first cameras, made in France and England in the early 1840s, had only inventors and buffs to operate them. Since there were then no professional photographers, there could not be amateurs either, and taking photographs had no clear social use; it was a gratuitous, that is, an artistic activity, though with few pretensions to being an art. It was only with its industrialization that photography came into its own as art. As industrialization provided social uses for the operations of the photographer, so the reaction against these uses reinforced the self-consciousness of photography-as-art.

Recently, photography has become almost as widely practiced an amusement as sex and dancing—which means that, like every mass art form, photography is not practiced by most people as an art. It is mainly a social rite, a defense against anxiety, and a tool of power.

Memorializing the achievements of individuals considered as members of families (as well as of other groups) is the earliest popular use of photography. For at least a century, the wedding photograph has been as much a part of the ceremony as the prescribed verbal formulas. Cameras go with family life. According to a sociological study done in France, most households have a camera, but a household with children is twice as likely to have at least one camera as a household in which there are no children. Not to take pictures of one's children, particularly when they are small, is a sign of parental indifference, just as not turning up for one's graduation picture is a gesture of adolescent rebellion.

Through photographs, each family constructs a portraitchronicle of itself—a portable kit of images that bears witness to its connectedness. It hardly matters what activities are photographed so long as photographs get taken and are cherished. Photography becomes a rite of family life just when, in the industrializing countries of Europe and America, the very institution of the family starts undergoing radical surgery. As that claustrophobic unit, the nuclear family, was being carved out of a much larger family aggregate, photography came along to memorialize, to restate symbolically, the imperiled continuity and vanishing extendedness of family life. Those ghostly traces, photographs, supply the token presence of the dispersed relatives. A family's photograph album is generally about the extended family—and, often, is all that remains of it.

As photographs give people an imaginary possession of a past that is unreal, they also help people to take possession of space in which they are insecure. Thus, photography develops in tandem with one of the most characteristic of modern activities: tourism. For the first time in history, large numbers of people regularly travel out of their habitual environments for short periods of time. It seems positively unnatural to travel for pleasure without taking a camera along. Photographs will offer indisputable evidence that the trip was made, that the program was carried out, that fun was had. Photographs document sequences of consumption carried on outside the view of family, friends, neighbors. But dependence on the camera, as the device that makes real what one is experiencing, doesn't fade when people travel more. Taking photographs fills the same need for the cosmopolitans accumulating photograph-trophies of their boat trip up the Albert Nile or their fourteen days in China as it does for lower-middle-class vacationers taking snapshots of the Eiffel Tower or Niagara Falls.

A way of certifying experience, taking photographs is also a way of refusing it—by limiting experience to a search for the photogenic, by converting experience into an image, a souvenir. Travel becomes a strategy for accumulating photographs. The very activity of taking pictures is soothing, and assuages general feelings of disorientation that are likely to be exacerbated by travel. Most tourists feel compelled to put the camera between themselves and whatever is remarkable that they encounter. Unsure of other responses, they take a picture. This gives shape to experience: stop, take a photograph, and move on. The method especially appeals to people handicapped by a ruthless work ethic—Germans, Japanese, and Americans. Using a camera appeases the anxiety which the work-driven feel about not working when they are on vacation and supposed to be having fun. They have something to do that is like a friendly imitation of work: they can take pictures.

People robbed of their past seem to make the most fervent picture takers, at home and abroad. Everyone who lives in an industrialized society is obliged gradually to give up the past, but in certain countries, such as the United States and Japan, the break with the past has been particularly traumatic. In the early 1970s, the fable of the brash American tourist of the 1950s and 1960s, rich with dollars and Babbittry, was replaced by the mystery of the group-minded Japanese tourist, newly released from his island prison by the miracle of overvalued yen, who is generally armed with two cameras, one on each hip.

Photography has become one of the principal devices for experiencing something, for giving an appearance of participation. One full-page ad shows a small group of people standing pressed together, peering out of the photograph, all but one looking stunned, excited, upset. The one who wears a different expression holds a camera to his eye; he seems self-possessed, is almost smiling. While the others are passive, clearly alarmed spectators, having a camera has transformed one person into something active, a voyeur: only he has mastered the situation. What do these people see? We don't know. And it doesn't matter. It is an Event: something worth seeing—and therefore worth photographing. The ad copy, white letters across the dark lower third of the photograph like news coming over a teletype machine, consists of just six words: ". . . Prague . . . Woodstock . . . Vietnam . . . Sapporo . . . Londonderry . . . LEICA." Crushed hopes, youth antics, colonial wars, and winter sports are alike—are equalized by the camera. Taking photographs has set up a chronic voyeuristic relation to the world which levels the meaning of all events.

A photograph is not just the result of an encounter between an event and a photographer; picture-taking is an event in itself, and one with ever more peremptory rights—to interfere with, to invade, or to ignore whatever is going on. Our very sense of situation is now articulated by the camera's interventions. The omnipresence of cameras persuasively suggests that time consists of interesting events, events worth photographing. This, in turn, makes it easy to feel that any event, once underway, and whatever its moral character, should be allowed to complete itself—so that something else can be brought into the world, the photograph. After the event has ended, the picture will still exist, conferring on the event a kind of immortality (and importance) it would never otherwise have enjoyed. While real people are out there killing themselves or other real people, the photographer stays behind his or her camera, creating a tiny element of another world: the image-world that bids to outlast us all.

Photographing is essentially an act of non-intervention. Part of the horror of such memorable coups of contemporary photojournalism as the pictures of a Vietnamese bonze reaching for the gasoline can, of a Bengali guerrilla in the act of bayoneting a trussed-up collaborator, comes from the awareness of how plausible it has become, in situations where the photographer has the choice between a photograph and a life, to choose the photograph. The person who intervenes cannot record; the person who is recording cannot intervene. Dziga Vertov's great film, *Man with a Movie Camera* (1929), gives the ideal image of the photographer as someone in perpetual movement, someone moving through a panorama of disparate events with such agility and speed that any intervention is out of the question. Hitchcock's *Rear Window* (1954) gives the complementary image: the photographer played by James Stewart has an intensified relation to one event, through his camera, precisely because he has a broken leg and is confined to a wheelchair; being temporarily immobilized prevents him from acting on what he sees, and makes it even more important to take pictures. Even if incompatible with intervention in a physical sense, using a camera is still a form of participation. Although the camera is an observation station, the act of photographing is more than passive observing. Like sexual voyeurism, it is a way of at least tacitly, often explicitly, encouraging whatever is going on to keep on happening. To take a picture is to have an interest in things as they are, in the status quo remaining unchanged (at least for as long as it takes to get a "good" picture), to be in complicity with whatever makes a subject interesting, worth photographing—including, when that is the interest, another person's pain or misfortune. . . .*

Photographs can abet desire in the most direct, utilitarian way—as when someone collects photographs of anonymous examples of the desirable as an aid to masturbation. The matter is more complex when photographs are used to stimulate the moral impulse. Desire has no history—at least, it is experienced in each instance as all foreground, immediacy. It is aroused by archetypes and is, in that sense, abstract. But moral feelings are embedded in history, whose personae are concrete, whose situations are always specific. Thus, almost opposite rules hold true for the use of the photograph to awaken desire and to awaken conscience. The images that mobilize conscience are always linked to a given historical situation. The more general they are, the less likely they are to be effective.

A photograph that brings news of some unsuspected zone of misery cannot make a dent in public opinion unless there is an appropriate context of feeling and attitude. The photographs Mathew Brady and his colleagues took of the horrors of the battlefields did not make people any less keen to go on with the Civil War. The photographs of ill-clad, skeletal prisoners held at Andersonville inflamed Northern public opinion—against the South. (The effect of the Andersonville photographs must have been partly due to the very novelty, at that time, of seeing photographs.) The political understanding that many

---

*In the section that follows, Sontag begins with a remark by photographer Diane Arbus that photography is a "naughty thing to do." Amongst other things, Sontag explores the implication of Arbus's thought by referring to films that reveal sexual impulses in the filmmaker or his or her characters. She goes on to say that the camera is sometimes sold as a kind of gun—"a predatory weapon." These threads lead to a meditation on photography and moral and political impulses—the editors.

Americans came to in the 1960s would allow them, looking at the photographs Dorothea Lange took of Nisei on the West Coast being transported to internment camps in 1942, to recognize their subject for what it was—a crime committed by the government against a large group of American citizens. Few people who saw those photographs in the 1940s could have had so unequivocal a reaction; the grounds for such a judgment were covered over by the pro-war consensus. Photographs cannot create a moral position, but they can reinforce one—and can help build a nascent one.

Photographs may be more memorable than moving images, because they are a neat slice of time, not a flow. Television is a stream of underselected images, each of which cancels its predecessor. Each still photograph is a privileged moment, turned into a slim object that one can keep and look at again. Photographs like the one that made the front page of most newspapers in the world in 1972—a naked South Vietnamese child just sprayed by American napalm, running down a highway toward the camera, her arms open, screaming with pain—probably did more to increase the public revulsion against the war than a hundred hours of televised barbarities.

One would like to imagine that the American public would not have been so unanimous in its acquiescence to the Korean War if it had been confronted with photographic evidence of the devastation of Korea, an ecocide and genocide in some respects even more thorough than those inflicted on Vietnam a decade later. But the supposition is trivial. The public did not see such photographs because there was, ideologically, no space for them. No one brought back photographs of daily life in Pyongyang, to show that the enemy had a human face, as Felix Greene and Marc Riboud brought back photographs of Hanoi. Americans did have access to photographs of the suffering of the Vietnamese (many of which came from military sources and were taken with quite a different use in mind) because journalists felt backed in their efforts to obtain those photographs, the event having been defined by a significant number of people as a savage colonialist war. The Korean War was understood differently—as part of the just struggle of the Free World against the Soviet Union and China—and, given that characterization, photographs of the cruelty of unlimited American firepower would have been irrelevant.

Though an event has come to mean, precisely, something worth photographing, it is still ideology (in the broadest sense) that determines what constitutes an event. There can be no evidence, photographic or otherwise, of an event until the event itself has been named and characterized. And it is never photographic evidence which can construct—more properly, identify—events; the contribution of photography always follows the naming of the event. What determines the possibility of being affected morally by photographs is the existence of a relevant political consciousness. Without a politics, photographs of the slaughter-bench of history will most likely be experienced as, simply, unreal or as a demoralizing emotional blow.

The quality of feeling, including moral outrage, that people can muster in response to photographs of the oppressed, the exploited, the starving, and the massacred also depends on the degree of their familiarity with these images. Don McCullin's photographs of emaciated Biafrans in the early 1970s had less impact for some people than Werner Bischof's photographs of Indian famine victims in the early 1950s because those images had become banal, and the photographs of Tuareg families dying of starvation in the sub-Sahara that appeared in magazines everywhere in 1973 must have seemed to many like an unbearable replay of a now familiar atrocity exhibition.

Photographs shock insofar as they show something novel. Unfortunately, the ante keeps getting raised—partly through the very proliferation of such images of horror. One's first encounter with the photographic inventory of ultimate horror is a kind of revelation, the prototypically modern revelation: a negative epiphany. For me, it was photographs of Bergen-Belsen and Dachau which I came across by chance in a bookstore in Santa Monica in July 1945. Nothing I have seen—in photographs or in real life—ever cut me as sharply, deeply, instantaneously. Indeed, it seems plausible to me to divide my life into two parts, before I saw those photographs (I was twelve) and after, though it was several years before I understood fully what they were about. What good was served by seeing them? They were only photographs—of an event I had scarcely heard of and could do nothing to affect, of suffering I could hardly imagine and could do nothing to relieve. When I looked at those photographs, something broke. Some limit had been reached, and not only that of horror; I felt irrevocably grieved, wounded, but a part of my feelings started to tighten; something went dead; something is still crying.

To suffer is one thing; another thing is living with the photographed images of suffering, which does not necessarily strengthen conscience and the ability to be compassionate. It can also corrupt them. Once one has seen such images, one has started down the road of seeing more—and more. Images transfix. Images anesthetize. An event known through photographs certainly becomes more real than it would have been if one had never seen the photographs—think of the Vietnam War. (For a counter-example, think of the Gulag Archipelago, of which we have no photographs.) But after repeated exposure to images it also becomes less real.

The same law holds for evil as for pornography. The shock of photographed atrocities wears off with repeated viewings, just as the surprise and bemusement felt the first time one sees a pornographic movie wear off after one sees a few more. The sense of taboo which makes us indignant and sorrowful is not much sturdier than the sense of taboo that regulates the definition of what is obscene. And both have been sorely tried in recent years. The vast photographic catalogue of misery and injustice throughout the world has given everyone a certain familiarity with atrocity, making the horrible seem more ordinary—making it appear familiar, remote ("it's only a photograph"), inevitable. At the time of the first photographs of the Nazi camps, there was nothing banal about these images. After thirty years, a saturation point may have been reached. In these last decades, "concerned" photography has done at least as much to deaden conscience as to arouse it.

The ethical content of photographs is fragile. With the possible exception of photographs of those horrors, like the Nazi camps, that have gained the status of ethical reference points, most photographs do not keep their emotional charge. A photograph of 1900 that was affecting then because of its subject would, today, be more likely to move us because it is a photograph taken in 1900. The particular qualities and intentions of photographs tend to be swallowed up in the generalized pathos of time past. Aesthetic distance seems built into the very experience of looking at photographs, if not right away, then certainly with the passage of time. Time eventually positions most photographs, even the most amateurish, at the level of art.

The industrialization of photography permitted its rapid absorption into rational—that is, bureaucratic—ways of running society. No longer toy images, photographs became part of the general furniture of the environment—touchstones and confirmations of that reductive approach to reality which is considered realistic. Photographs were enrolled in the service of important institutions of control, notably the family and the police, as symbolic objects and as pieces of information. Thus, in the bureaucratic cataloguing of the world, many important documents are not valid unless they have, affixed to them, a photograph-token of the citizen's face.

The "realistic" view of the world compatible with bureaucracy redefines knowledge —as techniques and information. Photographs are valued because they give information. They tell one what there is; they make an inventory. To spies, meteorologists, coroners, archaeologists, and other information professionals, their value is inestimable. But in the situations in which most people use photographs, their value as information is of the same order as fiction. The information that photographs can give starts to seem very important at that moment in cultural history when everyone is thought to have a right to something called news. Photographs were seen as a way of giving information to people who do not take easily to reading. The *Daily News* still calls itself "New York's Picture Newspaper," its bid for populist identity. At the opposite end of the scale, *Le Monde*, a newspaper designed for skilled, well-informed readers, runs no photographs at all. The presumption is that, for such readers, a photograph could only illustrate the analysis contained in an article.

A new sense of the notion of information has been constructed around the photographic image. The photograph is a thin slice of space as well as time. In a world ruled by photographic images, all borders ("framing") seem arbitrary. Anything can be separated, can be made discontinuous, from anything else: all that is necessary is to frame the subject differently. (Conversely, anything can be made adjacent to anything else.) Photography reinforces a nominalist view of social reality as consisting of small units of an apparently infinite number—as the number of photographs that could be taken of anything is unlimited. Through photographs, the world becomes a series of unrelated, freestanding particles; and history, past and present, a set of anecdotes and *faits divers*. The camera makes reality atomic, manageable, and opaque. It is a view of the world which denies interconnectedness, continuity, but which confers on each moment the character of a mystery. Any photograph has multiple meanings; indeed, to see something in the form of a photograph is to encounter a potential object of fascination. The ultimate wisdom of the photographic image is to say: "There is the surface. Now think—or rather feel, intuit—what is beyond it, what the reality must be like if it looks this way." Photographs, which cannot themselves explain anything, are inexhaustible invitations to deduction, speculation, and fantasy.

Photography implies that we know about the world if we accept it as the camera records it. But this is the opposite of understanding, which starts from *not* accepting the world as it looks. All possibility of understanding is rooted in the ability to say no. Strictly speaking, one never understands anything from a photograph. Of course, photographs fill in blanks in our mental pictures of the present and the past: for example, Jacob Riis's images of New York squalor in the 1880s are sharply instructive to those unaware that urban poverty in late-nineteenth-century America was really that Dickensian. Nevertheless, the camera's rendering of reality must always hide more than it discloses. As Brecht points out, a photograph of the Krupp works reveals virtually nothing about that organization. In contrast to the amorous relation, which is based on how something looks, understanding is based on how it functions. And functioning takes place in time, and must be explained in time. Only that which narrates can make us understand.

The limit of photographic knowledge of the world is that, while it can goad conscience, it can, finally, never be ethical or political knowledge. The knowledge gained through still photographs will always be some kind of sentimentalism, whether cynical or humanist. It will be a knowledge at bargain prices—a semblance of knowledge, a semblance of wisdom; as the act of taking pictures is a semblance of appropriation, a semblance of rape. The very muteness of what is, hypothetically, comprehensible in photographs is what constitutes their attraction and provocativeness. The omnipresence of photographs has an incalculable effect on our ethical sensibility. By furnishing this already crowded world with a duplicate one of images, photography makes us feel that the world is more available than it really is.

Needing to have reality confirmed and experience enhanced by photographs is an aesthetic consumerism to which everyone is now addicted. Industrial societies turn their citizens into image-junkies; it is the most irresistible form of mental pollution. Poignant longings for beauty, for an end to probing below the surface, for a redemption and celebration of the body of the world—all these elements of erotic feeling are affirmed in the pleasure we take in photographs. But other, less liberating feelings are expressed as well. It would not be wrong to speak of people having a *compulsion* to photograph: to turn experience itself into a way of seeing. Ultimately, having an experience becomes identical with taking a photograph of it, and participating in a public event comes more and more to be equivalent to looking at it in photographed form. That most logical of nineteenth-century aesthetes, Mallarmé, said that everything in the world exists in order to end in a book. Today everything exists to end in a photograph.

23
THE LINE BETWEEN FACT AND FICTION
Roy Peter Clark

Journalists should report the truth. Who would deny it? But such a statement does not get us far enough, for it fails to distinguish nonfiction from other forms of expression. Novelists can reveal great truths about the human condition, and so can poets, film makers and painters. Artists, after all, build things that *imitate* the world. So do nonfiction writers.

To make things more complicated, writers of fiction use fact to make their work believable. They do research to create authentic settings into which we enter. They return us to historical periods and places that can be accurately chronicled and described: the

Roy Peter Clark, "The Line between Fact and Fiction," *Creative Nonfiction*, Vol. 16, 4–15, 2001. Reprinted with the permission of the publisher.

battlefield at Gettysburg, the Museum of Natural History in New York City, a jazz club in Detroit. They use detail to make us see, to suspend our disbelief, to persuade us it was "really like that."

For centuries writers of nonfiction have borrowed the tools of novelists to reveal truths that could be exposed and rendered in no better way. They place characters in scenes and settings, have them speak to each other in dialogue, reveal limited points of view, and move through time over conflicts and toward resolutions.

In spite of occasional journalism scandals that hit the national landscape like plane crashes, our standards are higher than ever. Historical examples of nonfiction contain lots of made-up stuff. It appears as if, 50 years ago, many columnists, sports writers and crime reporters—to name the obvious categories—were licensed to invent. The term *piping*—making up quotes or inventing sources—came from the idea that the reporter was high from covering the police busts of opium dens.

Testimony on our shady past comes from Stanley Walker, the legendary city editor of the New York Herald Tribune. In 1934 he wrote about the "monumental fakes" that were part of the history of journalism and offered:

> It is true that, among the better papers, there is a "general professional condemnation" of fakers. And yet it is strange that so many of the younger men, just coming into the business, appear to feel that a little faking here and there is a mark of distinction. One young man, who had written a good story, replete with direct quotation and description, was asked by the city desk how he could have obtained such detail, as most of the action had been completed before he had been assigned to the story.
>
> "Well," said the young man, "I thought that since the main facts were correct it wouldn't do any harm to invent the conversation as I thought it must have taken place." The young man was soon disabused.

In more recent times and into the present, influential writers have worked in hybrid forms with names such as "creative nonfiction" or "the nonfiction novel." Tom Rosenstiel catalogues the confusion:

> The line between fact and fiction in America, between what is real and made up, is blurring. The move in journalism toward infotainment invites just such confusion, as news becomes entertainment and entertainment becomes news. Deals in which editor Tina Brown joins the forces of a news company, Hearst, with a movie studio, Miramax, to create a magazine that would blend reporting and script writing are only the latest headlines signaling the blending of cultures. Prime time news magazines, featuring soap opera stories or heroic rescue videos, are developing a growing resemblance to reality entertainment shows such as "Cops," or Fox programs about daring rescues or wild animal attack videos. Book authors such as John Berendt condense events and use "composite" characters in supposedly nonfiction work, offering only a brief allusion in an author's note to help clarify what might be real and what might not. Newspaper columnists are found out, and later removed, from the Boston Globe for confusing journalism and literature. A writer at the New Republic gains fame for material that is too good to be true. A federal court in the case of Janet Malcolm rules that journalists can make up quotes if they somehow are true to the spirit of what someone might have said. Writer Richard Reeves sees a deepening threat beyond journalism to society more generally, a threat he calls evocatively the "Oliver Stoning" of American culture.

The controversies continue. Edmund Morris creates fictional characters in his authorized biography of Ronald Reagan; CBS News uses digital technology to alter the sign of a competitor in Times Square during the coverage of the millennium celebration; a purported memoir of a wife of Wyatt Earp, published by a university press, turns out to contain fiction. Its author, Glenn G. Boyer, defends his book as a work of "creative nonfiction."

To make things more complicated, scholars have demonstrated the essential fictive nature of all memory. The way we remember things is not necessarily the way they were. This makes memoir, by definition, a problematic form in which reality and imagination blur into what its proponents describe as a "fourth genre." The problems of memory also infect journalism when reporters—in describing the memories of sources and witnesses —wind up lending authority to a kind of fiction.

The post-modernist might think all this irrelevant, arguing that there are no facts, only points of view, only "takes" on reality, influenced by our personal histories, our cultures, our race and gender, our social class. The best journalists can do in such a world is to offer multiple frames through which events and issues can be seen. Report the truth? they ask. Whose truth?

Caught in the web of such complexity, one is tempted to find some simple escape routes before the spider bites. If there were only a set of basic principles to help journalists navigate the waters between fact and fiction, especially those areas between the rocks. Such principles exist. They can be drawn from the collective experience of many journalists, from our conversations, debates and forums, from the work of writers such as John Hersey and Anna Quindlen, from stylebooks and codes of ethics, standards and practices.

Hersey made an unambiguous case for drawing a bold line between fiction and nonfiction, that the legend on the journalist's license should read "None of this was made up." The author of "Hiroshima," Hersey used a composite character in at least one early work, but by 1980 he expressed polite indignation that his work had become a model for the so-called New Journalists. His essay in the Yale Review questioned the writing strategies of Truman Capote, Norman Mailer and Tom Wolfe.

Hersey draws an important distinction, a crucial one for our purposes. He admits that subjectivity and selectivity are necessary and inevitable in journalism. If you gather 10 facts but wind up using nine, subjectivity sets in. This process of subtraction can lead to distortion. Context can drop out, or history, or nuance, or qualification or alternative perspectives.

While subtraction may distort the reality the journalist is trying to represent, the result is still nonfiction, is still journalism. The addition of invented material, however, changes the nature of the beast. When we add a scene that did not occur or a quote that was never uttered, we cross the line into fiction. And we deceive the reader.

This distinction leads us to two cornerstone principles: Do not add. Do not deceive. Let's elaborate on each:

Do not add. This means that writers of nonfiction should not add to a report things that did not happen. To make news clear and comprehensible, it is often necessary to subtract or condense. Done without care or responsibility, even such subtraction can distort. We cross a more definite line into fiction, however, when we invent or add facts or images or sounds that were not there.

Do not deceive. This means that journalists should never mislead the public in reproducing events. The implied contract of all nonfiction is binding: The way it is represented here is, to the best of our knowledge, the way it happened. Anything that intentionally or unintentionally fools the audience violates that contract and the core purpose of journalism—to get at the truth. Thus, any exception to the implied contract—even a work of humor or satire—should be transparent or disclosed.

To make these cornerstone principles definitive, we have stated them in the simplest language. In so doing, we may cause confusion by failing to exemplify these rules persuasively or by not offering reasonable exceptions. For example, by saying "Do not deceive," we are talking about the promise the journalist makes to the audience. A different argument concerns whether journalists can use deception as an investigative strategy. There is honest disagreement about that, but even if you go undercover to dig for news, you have a duty not to fool the public about what you discovered.

Because these two principles are stated negatively, we decided not to nag journalists with an endless list of "Thou shalt nots." So we've expressed four supporting strategies in a positive manner.

Be unobtrusive. This guideline invites writers to work hard to gain access to people and events, to spend time, to hang around, to become such a part of the scenery that they can observe conditions in an unaltered state. This helps avoid the "Heisenberg effect," a principle drawn from science, in which observing an event changes it. Even watchdogs can be alert without being obtrusive.

We realize that some circumstances require journalists to call attention to themselves and their processes. So we have nothing against Sam Donaldson for yelling questions at a president who turns a deaf ear to reporters. Go ahead and confront the greedy, the corrupt, the secret mongers; but the more reporters obtrude and intrude, especially when they are also obnoxious, the more they risk changing the behavior of those they are investigating.

Stories should not only be true, they should *ring* true. Reporters know by experience that truth can be stranger than fiction, that a man can walk into a convenience store in St. Petersburg, Fla., and shoot the clerk in the head and that the bullet can bounce off his head, ricochet off a ceiling beam, and puncture a box of cookies.

If we ruled the world of journalism—as if it could be ruled—we would ban the use of anonymous sources, except in cases where the source is especially vulnerable and the news is of great import. Some whistleblowers who expose great wrongdoing fall into this category. A person who has migrated illegally into America may want to share his or her experience without fear of deportation. But the journalist must make every effort to make this character real. An AIDS patient may want and deserve anonymity, but making public the name of his doctor and his clinic can help dispel any cloud of fiction.

Fired Boston Globe columnist Mike Barnicle writes:

> I used my memory to tell true tales of the city, things that happened to real people who shared their own lives with me. They represented the music and flavor of the time. They were stories that sat on the shelf of my institutional memory and spoke to a larger point. The use of parables was not a technique I invented. It was established ages ago by other newspaper columnists, many more gifted than I, some long since dead.

A parable is defined as a "simple story with a moral lesson." The problem is that we know them from religious literature or ancient beast fables. They were fictional forms, filled with hyperbole. Mike Barnicle was passing them off as truth, without doing the reporting that would give them the ring of truth.

In the Middle Ages, perhaps, it could be argued that the literal truth of a story was not important. More important were the higher levels of meaning: how stories reflected salvation history, moral truth or the New Jerusalem. Some contemporary nonfiction authors defend invention in the name of reaching for some higher truth. We deem such claims unjustifiable.

The next guideline is to make sure things *check out*. Stated with more muscle: Never put something in print or on the air that hasn't checked out. The new media climate makes this exceedingly difficult. News cycles that once changed by the day, or maybe by the hour, now change by the minute or second. Cable news programs run 24 hours, greedy for content. And more and more stories have been broken on the Internet, in the middle of the night, when newspaper reporters and editors are tucked dreamily in their beds. The imperative to go live and to look live is stronger and stronger, creating the appearance that news is "up to the minute" or "up to the second."

Time frenzy, however, is the enemy of clear judgment. Taking time allows for checking, for coverage that is proportional, for consultation and for sound decision-making that, in the long run, will avoid embarrassing mistakes and clumsy retractions.

In a culture of media bravado, there is plenty of room for a little strategic *humility*. This virtue teaches us that Truth—with a capital T—is unattainable, that even though you can never *get* it, that with hard work you can get *at* it—you can gain on it. Humility leads to respect for points of view that differ from our own, attention to which enriches our reporting. It requires us to recognize the unhealthy influences of careerism and profiteering, forces that may tempt us to tweak a quote or bend a rule or snatch a phrase or even invent a source.

So let's restate these, using slightly different language. First the cornerstone principles: The journalist should not add to a story things that didn't happen. And the journalist should not fool the public.

Then the supporting strategies: The journalist should try to get at stories without altering them. The reporting should dispel any sense of phoniness in the story. Journalists should check things out or leave them out. And, most important, a little humility about your ability to truly know something will make you work harder at getting it right.

These principles have meaning only in the light of a large idea, crucial to democratic life: that there is a world out there that is knowable. That the stories we create correspond to what exists in the world. That if we describe a velvet painting of John Wayne hanging in a barber shop, it was not really one of Elvis in a barbecue joint. That the words between quotation marks correspond to what was spoken. That the shoes in the photo were the ones worn by the man when the photo was taken and not added later. That what we are watching on television is real and not a staged re-enactment.

A tradition of verisimilitude and reliable sourcing can be traced to the first American newspapers. Three centuries before the recent scandals, a Boston newspaper called Publick Occurrences made this claim on September 25, 1690: ". . . nothing shall be entered, but what we have reason to believe is true, repairing to the best fountains for our Information."

We assert, then, that the principles of "Do not add" and "Do not deceive" should apply to all nonfiction all the time, not just to written stories in newspapers. Adding color to a black-and-white photo—unless the technique is obvious or labeled—is a deception. Digitally removing an element in a photo, or adding one or shifting one or reproducing one—no matter how visually arresting—is a deception, completely different in kind from traditional photo cropping, although that, too, can be done irresponsibly.

In an effort to get at some difficult truths, reporters and writers have at times resorted to unconventional and controversial practices. These include such techniques as composite characters, conflation of time, and interior monologues. It may be helpful to test these techniques against our standards.

The use of composite characters, where the purpose is to deceive the reader into believing that several characters are one, is a technique of fiction that has no place in journalism or other works that purport to be nonfiction.

An absolute prohibition against composites seems necessary, given a history of abuse of this method in works that passed themselves off as real. Although considered one of the great nonfiction writers of his time, Joseph Mitchell would, late in life, label some of his past work as fiction because it depended on composites. Even John Hersey, who became known for drawing thick lines between fiction and nonfiction, used composites in "Joe Is Home Now," a 1944 Life magazine story about wounded soldiers returning from war.

The practice has been continued, defended by some, into the 1990s. Mimi Schwartz acknowledges that she uses composites in her memoirs in order to protect the privacy of people who didn't ask to be in her books. "I had three friends who were thinking about divorce, so in the book, I made a composite character, and we met for cappuccino." While such considerations may be well-meaning, they violate the contract with the reader not to mislead. When the reader reads that Schwartz was drinking coffee with a friend and confidante, there is no expectation that there were really three friends. If the reader is expected to accept that possibility, then maybe that cappuccino was really a margarita. Maybe they discussed politics rather than divorce. Who knows?

Time and chronology are often difficult to manage in complicated stories. Time is sometimes imprecise, ambiguous or irrelevant. But the conflation of time that deceives readers into thinking a month was a week, a week a day, or a day an hour is unacceptable to works of journalism and nonfiction. In his author's note to the best-seller "Midnight in the Garden of Good and Evil," John Berendt concedes:

> Though this is a work of nonfiction, I have taken certain storytelling liberties, particularly having to do with the time of events. Where the narrative strays from strict nonfiction, my intention has been to remain faithful to the characters and to the essential drift of events as they really happened.

The second sentence is no justification for the first. Authors cannot have it both ways, using bits of fiction to liven up the story while desiring a spot on the New York Times nonfiction list.

Contrast Berendt's vague statement to the one G. Wayne Miller offers at the beginning of "King of Hearts," a book about the pioneers of open-heart surgery:

This is entirely a work of nonfiction; it contains no composite characters or scenes, and no names have been changed. Nothing has been invented. The author has used direct quotations only when he heard or saw (as in a letter) the words, and he paraphrased all other dialogues and statements—omitting quotations marks—once he was satisfied that these took place.

The interior monologue, in which the reporter seems to get into the head of a source, is a dangerous strategy but permissible in the most limited circumstances. It requires direct access to the source, who must be interviewed about his or her thoughts. Boston University writer-in-residence Mark Kramer suggests, "No attribution of thoughts to sources unless the sources have said they'd had those very thoughts."

This technique should be practiced with the greatest care. Editors should *always* question reporters on the sources of knowledge as to what someone was thinking. Because, by definition, what goes on in the head is invisible, the reporting standards must be higher than usual. When in doubt, attribute.

Such guidelines should not be considered hostile to the devices of fiction that can be applied, after in-depth reporting, to journalism. These include, according to Tom Wolfe, setting scenes, using dialogue, finding details that reveal character and describing things from a character's point of view. NBC News correspondent John Larson and Seattle Times editor Rick Zahler both encourage the reporter at times to convert the famous Five W's into the raw material of story-telling, so that Who becomes Character, Where becomes Setting, and When becomes Chronology.

But the more we venture into that territory, the more we need a good map and an accurate compass. John McPhee, as quoted by Norman Sims, summarizes the key imperatives:

> The nonfiction writer is communicating with the reader about real people in real places. So if those people talk, you say what those people said. You don't say what the writer decides they said. . . . You don't make up dialogue. You don't make a composite character. Where I came from, a composite character was a fiction. So when somebody makes a nonfiction character out of three people who are real, that is a fictional character in my opinion. And you don't get inside their heads and think for them. You can't interview the dead. You could make a list of the things you don't do. Where writers abridge that, they hitchhike on the credibility of writers who don't.

This leads us to the conviction that there should be a firm line, not a fuzzy one, between fiction and nonfiction and that all work that purports to be nonfiction should strive to achieve the standards of the most truthful journalism. Labels such as "nonfiction novel," "real-life novel," "creative nonfiction" and "docudrama" may not be useful to that end.

Such standards do not deny the value of storytelling in journalism, or of creativity or of pure fiction, when it is apparent or labeled. Which leads us to the Dave Barry exception, a plea for more creative humor in journalism, even when it leads to sentences such as "I did not make this up."

We can find many interesting exceptions, gray areas that would test all of these standards. Howard Berkes of National Public Radio once interviewed a man who stuttered badly. The story was not about speech impediments. "How would you feel," Berkes asked the man, "if I edited the tape to make you not stutter?" The man was delighted and the tape edited. Is this the creation of a fiction? A deception of the listener? Or is it the marriage of courtesy for the source and concern for the audience?

I come to these issues not as the rider of too high a horse but as a struggling equestrian with some distinctively writerly aspirations. I want to test conventions. I want to create new forms. I want to merge nonfiction genres. I want to create stories that are the center of the day's conversation in the newsroom and in the community.

In a 1996 series on AIDS, I tried to re-create in scene and dramatic dialogue the excruciating experiences of a woman whose husband had died of the disease. How do you describe a scene that took place years ago in a little hospital room in Spain, working from one person's memory of the event?

In my 1997 series on growing up Catholic with a Jewish grandmother, I tried to combine memoir with reporting, oral history and some light theology to explore issues such as anti-Semitism, cultural identity and the Holocaust. But consider this problem: Along the way, I tell the story of a young boy I knew who grew up with a fascination with Nazis and constantly made fun of Jews. I have no idea what kind of man he became. For all I know, he is one of the relief workers in Kosovo. How do I create for him—and myself—a protective veil without turning him into a fictional character?

And finally, in 1999 I wrote my first novel, which was commissioned by the New York Times Regional Newspaper Group and distributed by the New York Times Syndicate. It appeared in about 25 newspapers. This 29-chapter serial novel about the millennium taught me from the inside out some of the distinctions between fiction and nonfiction.

There is certainly an argument to be made that fiction—even labeled fiction—has no place in the newspaper. I respect that. Thirty inches of novella a day may require a loss of precious newshole. But do we think less of John McPhee's nonfiction in the New Yorker because it may sit next to a short story by John Updike?

It is not the fiction that's the problem, but the deception.

Hugh Kenner describes the language of journalism as:

> . . . the artifice of seeming to be grounded outside language in what is called fact—the domain where a condemned man can be observed as he silently avoids a puddle and your prose will report the observation and no one will doubt it.

British scholar John Carey puts it this way:

> Reportage may change its readers, may educate their sympathies, may extend—in both directions—their ideas about what it is to be a human being, may limit their capacity for the inhuman. These gains have traditionally been claimed for imaginative literature. But since reportage, unlike literature, lifts the screen from reality, its lessons are—and ought to be—more telling; and since it reaches millions untouched by literature, it has an incalculably greater potential.

So don't add and don't deceive. If you try something unconventional, let the public in on it. Gain on the truth. Be creative. Do your duty. Have some fun. Be humble. Spend your life thinking and talking about how to do all these well.

24
NEWS AS A FORM OF KNOWLEDGE
Robert Ezra Park

I

There are, as William James and certain others have observed, two fundamental types of knowledge, namely, (1) "acquaintance with" and (2) "knowledge about." The distinction suggested seems fairly obvious. Nevertheless, in seeking to make it a little more explicit, I am doubtless doing injustice to the sense of the original. In that case, in interpreting the distinction, I am merely making it my own. James's statement is, in part, as follows:

> *There are two kinds of knowledge* broadly and practically distinguishable: we may call them respectively *knowledge of acquaintance* and *knowledge-about*. . . . In minds able to speak at all there is, it is true, *some* knowledge about everything. Things can at least be classed, and the times of their appearance told. But in general, the less we analyze a thing, and the fewer of its relations we perceive, the less we know about it and the more our familiarity with it is of the acquaintance-type. The two kinds of knowledge are, therefore, as the human mind practically exerts them, relative terms. That is, the same thought of a thing may be called knowledge-about it in comparison with a simpler thought, or acquaintance with it in comparison with a thought of it that is more articulate and explicit still.[1]

At any rate, "acquaintance with," as I should like to use the expression, is the sort of knowledge one inevitably acquires in the course of one's personal and firsthand encounters with the world about him. It is the knowledge which comes with use and wont rather than through any sort of formal or systematic investigation. Under such circumstances we come finally to know things not merely through the medium of our special senses but through the responses of our whole organism. We know them in the latter case as we know things to which we are accustomed, in a world to which we are adjusted. Such knowledge may, in fact, be conceived as a form of organic adjustment or adaptation, representing an accumulation and, so to speak, a funding of a long series of experiences. It is this sort of personal and individual knowledge which makes each of us at home in the world in which he elects or is condemned to live.

It is notorious that human beings, who are otherwise the most mobile of living creatures, tend nevertheless to become rooted, like plants, in the places and in the associations to which they are accustomed. If this accommodation of the individual to his habitat is to

Robert Ezra Park, "News as a Form of Knowledge," *Society: Collective Behaviour, News and Opinion, Sociology and Modern Society* (Glencoe, Ill.: The Free Press, 1955), 71–89. Reprinted with permission of the Free Press, a division of Simon and Schuster. Copyright © 1955; copyright renewed © 1983 by the Free Press.

be regarded as knowledge at all, it is probably included in what we call tact or common sense. These are character[istics] which individuals acquire in informal and unconscious ways; but, once acquired, they tend to become private and personal possessions. One might go so far as to describe them as personality traits—something, at any rate, which cannot well be formulated or communicated from one individual to another by formal statements.

Other forms of "acquaintance with" are: (1) clinical knowledge, in so far at least as it is the product of personal experience; (2) skills and technical knowledge; and (3) anything that is learned by the undirected and unconscious experimentation such as the contact with, and handling of, objects involves.

Our knowledge of other persons and of human nature in general seems to be of this sort. We know other minds in much the same ways that we know our own, that is, intuitively. Often we know other minds better than we do our own. For the mind is not the mere stream of consciousness into which each of us looks when, introspectively, he turns his attention to the movements of his own thoughts. Mind is rather the divergent tendencies to act of which each of us is more or less completely unconscious, including the ability to control and direct those tendencies in accordance with some more or less conscious goal. Human beings have an extraordinary ability, by whatever mechanism it operates, to sense these tendencies in others as in themselves. It takes a long time, however, to become thoroughly acquainted with any human being, including ourselves, and the kind of knowledge of which this acquaintance consists is obviously not the sort of knowledge we get of human behavior by experiments in a psychological laboratory. It is rather more like the knowledge that a salesman has of his customers, a politician of his clients, or the knowledge which a psychiatrist gains of his patients in his efforts to understand and cure them. It is even more the sort of knowledge which gets embodied in habit, in custom, and, eventually—by some process of natural selection that we do not fully understand—in instinct; a kind of racial memory or habit. Knowledge of this sort, if one may call it knowledge, becomes, finally, a personal secret of the individual man or the special endowment of the race or stock that possesses it.[2]

One may, perhaps, venture this statement since the type of intuitive or instinctive knowledge here described seems to arise out of processes substantially like the accommodations and adaptations which, by some kind of natural selection, have produced the different racial varieties of mankind as well as the plant and animal species. One may object that what one means by knowledge is just what is not inherited and not heritable. On the other hand, it is certain that some things are learned much more easily than others. What one inherits therefore is, perhaps, not anything that could properly be called knowledge. It is rather the inherited ability to acquire those specific forms of knowledge we call habits. There seems to be a very great difference in individuals, families, and genetic groups as to their ability to learn specific things. Native intelligence is probably not the standardized thing that the intelligence tests might lead one to believe. In so far as this is true studies of intelligence in the future are, I suspect, more likely to be concerned with . . . the idiosyncrasies of intelligence and the curious individual ways in which individual minds achieve essentially the same results than in measuring and standardizing these achievements.

It is obvious that this "synthetic" (i.e., the knowledge that gets itself embodied in habit and custom, as opposed to analytic and formal knowledge) is not likely to be articulate and communicable. If it gets itself communicated at all, it will be in the form of practical maxims and wise saws rather than in the form of scientific hypotheses. Nevertheless, a wide and intimate acquaintance with men and things is likely to be the bulwark of most sound judgment in practical matters as well as the source of those hunches upon which experts depend in perplexing situations and of those sudden insights which, in the evolution of science, are so frequently the prelude to important discoveries.

In contrast with this is the kind of knowledge that James describes as "knowledge about." Such knowledge is formal, rational, and systematic. It is based on observation and fact but on fact that has been checked, tagged, regimented, and finally ranged in this and that perspective, according to the purpose and point of view of the investigator.

"Knowledge about" is formal knowledge; that is to say, knowledge which has achieved some degree of exactness and precision by the substitution of ideas for concrete reality and of words for things. Not only do ideas constitute the logical framework of all systematic knowledge but they enter into the very nature of the things themselves with which science—natural as distinguished from the historical science—is concerned. As a matter of fact, there seem to be three fundamental types of scientific knowledge: (1) philosophy and logic, which are concerned primarily with ideas; (2) history, which is concerned primarily with events; and (3) the natural or classifying sciences, which are concerned primarily with things.

Concepts and logical artifacts, like the number system, are not involved in the general flux of events and things. For precisely that reason they serve admirably the purpose of tags and counters with which to identify, to describe, and, eventually, to measure things. The ultimate purpose of natural science seems to be to substitute for the flux of events and the changing character of things a logical formula in which the general character of things and the direction of change may be described with logical and mathematical precision.

The advantage of substituting words, concepts, and a logical order for the actual course of events is that the conceptual order makes the actual order intelligible, and, so far as the hypothetic formulations we call laws conform to the actual course of events, it becomes possible to predict from a present a future condition of things. It permits us to speculate with some assurance how, and to what extent, any specific intervention or interference in a present situation may determine the situation that is predestined to succeed it.

On the other hand, there is always a temptation to make a complete divorce between the logical and verbal description of an object or a situation and the empirical reality to which it refers. This seems to have been the cardinal mistake of scholasticism. Scholasticism has invariably tended to substitute logical consistency, which is a relation between ideas, for the relation of cause and effect, which is a relation between things.

An empirical and experimental science avoids a purely logical solution of its problems by checking up its calculation at some point with the actual world. A purely intellectual science is always in danger of becoming so completely out of touch with things that the symbols with which it operates cease to be anything more than mental toys. In that case science becomes a kind of dialectical game. This is a peril which the social sciences, to the extent that they have been disposed to formulate and investigate social problems in the forms in which they have been conventionally defined by some administrative agencies or governmental institution, have not always escaped. Thus investigation has invariably tended to take the form of fact-finding rather than of research. Having found the facts, the agencies were able to supply the interpretations; but they were usually interpretations which were implicit in the policies to which the agencies or institutions were already committed.

These are some of the general characteristics of systematic and scientific knowledge, "knowledge about," as contrasted with the concrete knowledge, common sense and "acquaintance with." What is, however, the unique character of scientific knowledge, as contrasted with other forms of knowledge, is that it is communicable to the extent that common sense or knowledge based on practical and clinical experience is not. It is communicable because its problems and its solutions are stated not merely in logical and in intelligible terms but in such forms that they can be checked by experiment or by reference to the empirical reality to which these terms refer.

In order to make this possible, it is necessary to describe in detail and in every instance the source and manner in which facts and findings were originally obtained. Knowledge about, so far at least as it is scientific, becomes in this way a part of the social heritage, a body of tested and accredited fact and theory in which new increments, added to the original fund, tend to check up, affirm, or qualify, first of all, in each special science and, finally, in all the related sciences, all that has been contributed by earlier investigators.

On the other hand, acquaintance with, as I have sought to characterize it, so far as it is based on the slow accumulation of experience and the gradual accommodation of the individual to his individual and personal world, becomes, as I have said, more and more completely identical with instinct and intuition.

Knowledge about is not merely accumulated experience but the result of systematic investigation of nature. It is based on the answers given to the definite questions which we address to the world about us. It is knowledge pursued methodically with all the formal and logical apparatus which scientific research has created. I might add, parenthetically, that there is, generally speaking, no scientific method which is wholly independent of the intuition and insight which acquaintance with things and events gives us. Rather is it true that, under ordinary circumstances, the most that formal methods can do for research is to assist the investigator in obtaining facts which will make it possible to check up such insights and hunches as the investigator already had at the outset or has gained later in the course of his researches.

One of the functions of this methodical procedure is to protect the investigator from the perils of an interpretation to which a too ardent pursuit of knowledge is likely to lead him. There is, on the other hand, no methodical procedure that is a substitute for insight.

II

What is here described as "acquaintance with" and "knowledge about" are assumed to be distinct forms of knowledge—forms having different functions in the lives of individuals and of society—rather than knowledge of the same kind but of different degrees of accuracy and validity. They are, nevertheless, not so different in character or function— since they are, after all, relative terms—that they may not be conceived as constituting together, a continuum—a continuum within which all kinds and sorts of knowledge find a place. In such a continuum news has a location of its own. It is obvious that news is not

systematic knowledge like that of the physical sciences. It is rather, in so far as it is concerned with events, like history. Events, because they are invariably fixed in time and
located in space, are unique and cannot, therefore, be classified as is the case with things.
Not only do things move about in space and change with time but, in respect to their
internal organization, they are always in a condition of more or less stable equilibrium.

News is not history, however, and its facts are not historical facts. News is not
history because, for one thing among others, it deals, on the whole, with isolated events
and does not seek to relate them to one another either in the form of causal or in the form
of teleological sequences. History not only describes events but seeks to put them in their
proper place in the historical succession, and, by doing so, to discover the underlying
tendencies and forces which find expression in them. In fact, one would not be far wrong
in assuming that history is quite as much concerned with the connections of events—the
relation between the incidents that precede and those that follow—as it is with the events
themselves. On the other hand, a reporter, as distinguished from a historian, seeks merely
to record each single event as it occurs and is concerned with the past and future only in
so far as these throw light on which is actual and present.

The relation of an event to the past remains the task of the historian, while its
significance as a factor determining the future may perhaps be left to the science of
politics—what Freeman calls "comparative politics"[3]—that is to say, to sociology or to
some other division of the social sciences, which, by comparative studies, seeks to arrive
at statements sufficiently general to support a hypothesis or a prediction.[4]

News, as a form of knowledge, is not primarily concerned either with the past or
with the future but rather with the present—what has been described by psychologists as
"the specious present." News may be said to exist only in such a present. What is meant
here by the "specious present" is suggested by the fact that news, as the publishers of
the commercial press know, is a very perishable commodity. News remains news only
until it has reached the persons for whom it has "news interest." Once published and its
significance recognized, what was news becomes history.

This transient and ephemeral quality is of the very essence of news and is intimately
connected with every other character that it exhibits. Different types of news have a different time span. In its most elementary form a news report is a mere "flash," announcing
that an event has happened. If the event proves of real importance, interest in it will lead
to further inquiry and to a more complete acquaintance with the attendant circumstances.
An event ceases to be news, however, as soon as the tension it aroused has ceased and
public attention has been directed to some other aspect of the habitat or to some other
incident sufficiently novel, exciting, or important to hold its attention.

The reason that news comes to us, under ordinary circumstances, not in the form of a
continued story but as a series of independent incidents becomes clear when one takes
account of the fact that we are here concerned with the public mind—or with what is
called the public mind. In its most elementary form knowledge reaches the public not,
as it does the individual, in the form of a perception but in the form of a communication,
that is to say, news. Public attention, however, under normal conditions is wavering,
unsteady, and easily distracted. When the public mind wanders, the rapport, grapevine
telegraph, or whatever else it is that insures the transmission of news within the limits of
the public ceases to function, tension is relaxed, communication broken off, and what
was live news becomes cold fact.

A news item, as every newspaperman knows, is read in inverse ratio to its length. The ordinary reader will read a column and a half of two- or three-line items about men and things in the home town before he will read a column article, no matter how advertised in the headlines, unless it turns out to be not merely news but a story, i.e., something that has what is called technically "human interest."

News comes in the form of small, independent communications that can be easily and rapidly comprehended. In fact, news performs somewhat the same functions for the public that perception does for the individual man; that is to say, it does not so much inform as orient the public, giving each and all notice as to what is going on. It does this without any effort of the reporter to interpret the events he reports, except in so far as to make them comprehensible and interesting.

The first typical reaction of an individual to the news is likely to be a desire to repeat it to someone. This makes conversation, arouses further comment, and perhaps starts a discussion. But the singular thing about it is that, once discussion has been started, the event under discussion soon ceases to be news, and, as interpretations of an event differ, discussions turn from the news to the issues it raises. The clash of opinions and sentiments which discussion invariably evokes usually terminates in some sort of consensus or collective opinion—what we call public opinion. It is upon the interpretation of present events, i.e., news, that public opinion rests.

The extent to which news circulates, within a political unit or a political society, determines the extent to which the members of such a society may be said to participate, not in its collective life—which is the more inclusive term—but in its political acts. Political action and political power, as one ordinarily understands these terms, are obviously based not merely on such concert and consensus as may exist in a herd or in a crowd. It rests ultimately, it seems, on the ability of a political society, aside from whatever of military or material resources it possesses, to act not only concertedly but consistently in accordance with some considered purpose and in furtherance of some rational end. The world of politics, it seems, is based, as Schopenhauer has said of the world in general, on the organic relation of will and idea. Other and more material sources of political power are obviously merely instrumental.

Freeman, the historian, has said that history is past politics and politics is present history. This puts a great deal of truth into a few words, even if the statement in practice needs some enlargement and some qualification. News, though intimately related to both, is neither history nor politics. It is, nevertheless, the stuff which makes political action, as distinguished from other forms of collective behavior, possible.

Among other kinds of collective behavior are the recognized and conventional forms of ceremonial and religious expression—etiquette and religious ritual—which, in so far as they create unanimity and maintain morale, play directly and indirectly an important role in politics and in political action. But religion has no such intimate connection as politics with the news. News is a purely secular phenomenon.

III

There is a proverbial saying to the effect that it is the unexpected that happens. Since what happens makes news, it follows, or seems to, that news is always or mainly concerned with the unusual and the unexpected. Even the most trivial happening, it seems, provided it represents a departure from the customary ritual and routine of daily life, is likely to be reported in the press. This conception of news has been confirmed by those editors who, in the competition for circulation and for advertising, have sought to make their papers smart and interesting, where they could not be invariably either informing or thrilling. In their efforts to instil into the minds of reporters and correspondents the importance of looking everywhere and always for something that would excite, amuse, or shock its readers, news editors have put into circulation some interesting examples of what the Germans, borrowing an expression from Homer, have called *geflügelte Wörter*, "winged words." The epigram describing news which has winged its way over more territory and is repeated more often than any other is this: "Dog bites man"—that is not news. But "Man bites dog"—that is. *Nota bene!* It is not the intrinsic importance of an event that makes it newsworthy. It is rather the fact that the event is so unusual that if published it will either startle, amuse, or otherwise excite the reader so that it will be remembered and repeated. For news is always finally, what Charles A. Dana described it to be, "something that will make people talk," even when it does not make them act.

The fact that news ordinarily circulates spontaneously and without any adventitious aids—as well as freely without inhibitions or censorship—seems to be responsible for another character which attaches to it, distinguishing it from related but less authentic types of knowledge—namely, rumor and gossip. In order that a report of events current may have the quality of news, it should not merely circulate—possibly in circuitous underground channels—but should be published, if need be by the town crier or the public press. Such publication tends to give news something of the character of a public document. News is more or less authenticated by the fact that it has been exposed to the critical examination of the public to which it is addressed and with whose interests it is concerned.

The public which thus, by common consent or failure to protest, puts the stamp of its approval on a published report does not give to its interpretation the authority of statement that has been subjected to expert historical criticism. Every public has its local prejudices and its own limitations. A more searching examination of the facts would quite possibly reveal to a more critical and enlightened mind the naïve credulity and bias of an unsophisticated public opinion. In fact, the naïveté and credulity thus revealed may become an important historical or sociological datum. This, however, is merely another and further illustration of the fact that every public has its own universe of discourse and that, humanly speaking, a fact is only a fact in some universe of discourse.[5]

An interesting light is thrown on the nature of news by a consideration of the changes which take place in information that gets into circulation without the sanction which publicity gives to it. In such a case a report, emanating from some source not disclosed and traveling to a destination that is unknown, invariably accumulates details from the innocent but mainly illicit contributions of those who assist it on its travel. Under these circumstances what was at first mere rumor tends to assume, in time, the character of a legend, that is, something which everyone repeats but no one believes.

When, on the other hand, reports of current events are published with the names, dates, and places which make it possible for anyone concerned to check them, the atmosphere of legend which gathers about and clothes with fantastic detail the news as originally reported is presently dispelled, and what is fact, or what will pass for fact, until corrected by further and later news reports, is reduced to something more prosaic than legend and more authentic than news, i.e., historical fact.

If it is the unexpected that happens, it is the not wholly unexpected that gets into the news. The events that have made news in the past, as in the present, are actually the expected things. They are characteristically simple and commonplace matters, like births and deaths, weddings and funerals, the conditions of the crops and of business, war, politics, and the weather. These are the expected things, but they are at the same time the unpredictable things. They are the incidents and the chances that turn up in the game of life.

The fact is that the thing that makes news is news interest, and that, as every city editor knows, is a variable quantity—one that has to be reckoned with from the time the city editor sits down at his desk in the morning until the night editor locks up the last form at night. The reason for this is that the news value is relative, and an event that comes later may, and often does, diminish the value of an event that turned up earlier. In that case the less important item has to give way to the later and more important.

The anecdotes and "believe it or nots" which turn up in the news are valuable to the editor because they can always be lifted out of the printer's form to make way for something hotter and more urgent. In any case it is, on the whole, the accidents and incidents that the public is prepared for; the victories and defeats on the ball field or on the battlefield; the things that one fears and things that one hopes for—that make the news. It is difficult to understand, nevertheless, considering the number of people who are killed and maimed annually by automobile accidents (the number killed in 1938 was 32,600) that these great losses of life rarely make the front page. The difference seems to be that the automobile has come to be accepted as one of the permanent features of civilized life and war has not.

News, therefore, at least in the strict sense of the term, is not a story or an anecdote. It is something that has for the person who hears or reads it an interest that is pragmatic rather than appreciative. News is characteristically, if not always, limited to events that bring about sudden and decisive changes. It may be an incident like that of the colored family in Philadelphia, Frances and Ben Mason, who won a fortune in the Irish sweepstakes recently.[6] It may be a tragic incident like the battle off the coast of Uruguay which resulted in the destruction of the German battleship, the "Graf Spee," and the suicide of its captain. These events were not only news—that is, something that brought a sudden decisive change in the previously existing situation—but, as they were related in the newspapers and as we reflected upon them, they tended to assume a new and ideal significance: the one a story of genuine human interest, the other that of tragedy, something, to use Aristotle's phrase, to inspire "pity and terror." Events such as these tend to be remembered. Eventually they may become legends or be recorded in popular ballads. Legends and ballads need no date line or the names of persons or places to authenticate them. They live and survive in our memories and in that of the public because of their human interest. As events they have ceased to exist. They survive as a sort of ghostly symbol of something of universal and perennial interest, an ideal representation of what is true of life and of human nature everywhere.

Thus it seems that news, as a form of knowledge, contributes from its record of events not only to history and to sociology but to folklore and literature; it contributes something not merely to the social sciences but to the humanities.

IV

The sociological horizon has recently taken on new dimensions. Social anthropology, no longer interested in primitive society merely, has begun to study not only the history but the natural history and function of institutions. In doing so it has appropriated more and more the field of sociological interest and research. Psychiatry, likewise, has discovered that neuroses and psychoses are diseases of a personality which is itself a product of a social milieu created by the interaction of personalities. Meanwhile there has grown up in the United States and in Europe a sociology of law which conceives as natural products the norms which the courts are seeking to rationalize, systematize, and apply in specific cases. Finally, there have been some interesting recent attempts to bring the subject of knowledge itself within the limits of a sociological discipline.

Theories of knowledge have existed since the days of Parmenides. They have, however, been less interested in knowledge which is a datum than in truth or valid knowledge which is an idea and an ideal. The question with which the sociology of knowledge is concerned is not what constitutes the validity of knowledge—of a statement of principle or of fact—but what are the conditions under which different kinds of knowledge arise and what are the functions of each.

Most of the forms of knowledge that have achieved the dignity of a science are, in the long history of mankind, of very recent origin. One of the earliest and most elementary forms of knowledge is news. There was a period, and not so long ago, either, when there was neither philosophy, history, nor rational knowledge of any sort. There was only myth, legend, and magic. What we now describe as the exact sciences did not exist until the Renaissance. The social sciences have, roughly speaking, only come into existence in the last fifty years. At least they have only begun within the last half-century to achieve, with the wider use of statistics, anything like scientific precision.

News, so far as it is to be regarded as knowledge at all, is probably as old as mankind, perhaps older. The lower animals were not without a kind of communication which was not unlike news. The "cluck" of the mother hen is understood by the chicks as signifying either danger or food, and the chicks respond accordingly.

This is not to suggest that every kind of communication in a herd or flock will have the character of news. What is ordinarily communicated is merely a kind of contagious excitement—sometimes merely a sense of well-being and security in the gregarious association of the herd, at others a sense of unrest or malaise, manifested and often intensified in the milling of the herd. It seems likely that this pervasive social excitement, which is essential to the existence of the herd as a social unit, serves, also, to facilitate the communication of news, or what corresponds to it in the herd.

There is in naval parlance an expression, "the fleet in being," which means, apparently, that the ships which constitute a fleet are in communication and sufficiently mobilized, perhaps, to be capable of some sort of concerted action. The same expression might be applied to a community, a society, or a herd. A society is "in being" when the individuals that compose it are to such an extent *en rapport* that, whether capable of united and collective action or not, they may be described as participating in a common or collective existence. In such a society a diffuse social excitement tends to envelope, like an atmosphere, all participants in the common life and to give a direction and tendency to their interests and attitudes. It is as if the individuals of such a society were dominated by a common mood or state of mind which determined for them the range and character of their interests and their attitudes or tendencies to act. The most obvious illustration of this obscure social tension or state of mind in a community is the persistent and pervasive influence of fashion.

At certain times and under certain conditions this collective excitement, so essential to communication if not to understanding, rises to a higher level of intensity and, as it does so, tends to limit the range of response but to increase the intensity of impulses not so inhibited. The effect of this is the same as in the case of attention in the individual. Exclusive attention to some things inhibits responses to others. This means in the case of a society a limitation of the range and character of the news to which it will either collectively or individually respond.

The rise of social tension may be observed in the most elementary form in the herd when, for some reason, the herd is restless and begins to mill. Tension mounts as restlessness increases. The effect is as if the milling produced in the herd a state of expectancy which, as it increased in intensity, increased also the certainty that presently some incident, a clap of thunder or the crackling of a twig, would plunge the herd into a stampede.

Something similar takes place in a public. As tension arises, the limits of public interest narrows, and the range of events to which the public will respond is limited. The circulation of news is limited; discussion ceases, and the certainty of action of some sort increases. This narrowing of the focus of public attention tends to increase the influence of the dominant person or persons in the community. But the existence of this dominance depends upon the ability of the community, or its leaders, to maintain tension. It is in this way that dictators arise and maintain themselves in power. It is this that explains likewise the necessity to a dictatorship of some sort of censorship.

News circulates, it seems, only in a society where there is a certain degree of rapport and a certain degree of tension. But the effect of news from outside the circle of public interest is to disperse attention and, by so doing, to encourage individuals to act on their own initiative rather than on that of a dominant party or personality.

Under ordinary circumstances—in a time of peace rather than of war or revolution —news tends to circulate over an ever widening area, as means of communication multiply. Changes in society and its institutions under these circumstances continue to take place, but they take place piecemeal and more or less imperceptibly. Under other conditions—in war or revolution—changes take place violently and visibly but catastrophically.

The permanence of institutions under ordinary conditions is dependent upon their ability, or the ability of the community of which they are a part, to adapt themselves to technological and other less obvious changes. But these changes and their consequences manifest themselves not only directly but rather indirectly in the news. Institutions like the Catholic church or the Japanese state have been able to survive the drastic changes of time because they have been able to respond to changes in the conditions of existence, not merely those physically and obviously imposed upon them but those foreshadowed and reflected in the news.

I have indicated the role which news plays in the world of politics in so far as it provides the basis for the discussions in which public opinion is formed. The news plays quite as important a role in the world of economic relations, since the price of commodities, including money and securities, as registered in the world-market and in every local market dependent upon it, is based on the news.

So sensitive are the exchanges to events in every part of the world that every fluctuation in fashion or the weather is likely to be reflected in the prices on the exchanges. I have said that news is a secular phenomenon. But there come times when changes are so great and so catastrophic that individuals and peoples are no longer interested in worldly affairs. In such case men, frustrated in their ambitions and their hopes, turn away from the world of secular affairs and seek refuge and consolation in a flight from the great world into the security of the little world of the family or of the church. The function of news is to orient man and society in an actual world. In so far as it succeeds it tends to preserve the sanity of the individual and the permanence of society.

Although news is an earlier and more elementary product of communication than science, news has by no means been superseded by it. On the contrary, the importance of news has grown consistently with the expansion of the means of communication and with the growth of science.

Improved means of communication have co-operated with the vast accumulations of knowledge, in libraries, in museums, and in learned societies, to make possible a more rapid, accurate, and thoroughgoing interpretation of events as they occur. The result is that persons and places, once remote and legendary, are now familiar to every reader of the daily press.

In fact, the multiplication of the means of communication has brought it about that anyone, even in the most distant part of the world, may now actually participate in events—at least as listener if not as spectator—as they actually take place in some other part of the world. We have recently listened to Mussolini address his fascist followers from a balcony of Rome; we have heard Hitler speaking over the heads of a devout congregation in the Reichstag, in Berlin, not merely to the President, but to the people, of the United States. We have even had an opportunity to hear the terms of the momentous Munich agreement ten seconds after it had been signed by the representatives of four of the leading powers in Europe and the world. The fact that acts so momentous as these can be so quickly and so publicly consummated has suddenly and completely changed the character of international politics, so that one can no longer even guess what the future has in store for Europe and for the world.

In the modern world the role of news has assumed increased rather than diminished importance as compared with some other forms of knowledge, history, for example. The changes in recent years have been so rapid and drastic that the modern world seems to have lost its historical perspective, and we appear to be living from day to day in what I have described earlier as a "specious present." Under the circumstances history seems to be read or written mainly to enable us, by comparison of the present with the past, to understand what is going on about us rather than, as the historians have told us, to know "what actually happened."

Thus Elmer Davis in a recent article in the *Saturday Review* announces as "required reading" for 1939 two volumes: Hitler's *Mein Kampf* and Thucydides' *History of the Peloponnesian War* (431 B.C.). He recommends the history of the Peloponnesian War because, as he says, "Thucydides was not only a brilliant analyst of human behavior both individual and collective" but was at the same time "a great reporter."[7]

One notes, also, as characteristic of our times, that since news, as reported in American newspapers, has tended to assume the character of literature, so fiction—after the newspaper the most popular form of literature—has assumed more and more the character of news.[8]

Emile Zola's novels were essentially reports upon contemporary manners in France just as Steinbeck's *The Grapes of Wrath* has been described as an cpoch-making report on the share-cropper in the United States.

Ours, it seems, is an age of news, and one of the most important events in American civilization has been the rise of the reporter.

NOTES

1. William James, *The Principles of Psychology* (New York: Henry Holt & Co., 1896), I, 221–22.

2. "The biologist ordinarily thinks of development as something very different from such modification of behavior by experience, but from time to time the idea that the basis of heredity and development is fundamentally similar to memory has been advanced. . . . Viewed in this way the whole course of development is a process of physiological learning, beginning with the simple experience of differential exposure to an external factor, and undergoing one modification after another, as new experiences in the life of the organism or of its parts in relation to each other occur" (C. M. Child, *Physiological Foundations of Behavior*, pp. 248–49; quoted by W. I. Thomas in *Primitive Behavior* [New York: McGraw-Hill Book Co., 1937], p. 25).

3. Edward A. Freeman, *Comparative Politics* (London, 1873).

4. The sociological point of view makes its appearance in historcial investigation as soon as the historian turns from the study of "periods" to the study of institutions. The history of institutions—that is to say, the family, the church, economic institutions, political institutions, etc.—leads inevitably to comparison, classification, the formation of class names or concepts, and eventually to the formulation of law. In the process history becomes natural history, and natural history passes over into natural science. In short, history becomes sociology (R. E. Park and E. W. Burgess, *Introduction to the Science of Sociology* [Chicago: University of Chicago Press, 1921], p. 16).

5. A universe of discourse is, as the term is ordinarily used, no more than a special vocabulary which is well understood and appropriate to specific situations. It may, however, in the case of some special science include a body of more precisely defined terms or concepts, which in that case will tend to have a more or less systematic character. History, for example, employs no, or almost no, special concepts. On the other hand, sociology, and every science that attempts to be systematic, does. As concepts assume this systematic character they tend to constitute a "frame of reference."

6. See *Time*, December 25, 1939, p. 12.

7. "Required Reading," *Saturday Review of Literature*, October 14, 1939.

8. See Helen MacGill Hughes, *News and the Human Interest Story* (Chicago: University of Chicago Press, 1940).

Study Guide

TALKING POINTS

I.   Lippmann says that "the press is not constituted to furnish . . . the amount of knowledge the democratic theory of public opinion demands." Is he right? How would you go about assessing such a claim?

II.   John Carey uses the term "objective" negatively and the term "subjective" positively as he discusses "truth" and "authenticity." He says, first, that "eyewitness evidence . . . makes for authenticity" and then goes on to say that such "accounts have the feel of truth because they are quick, subjective and incomplete, unlike 'objective' or reconstituted history, which is laborious and dead." Can you make sense of the unconventional manner in which he uses these terms?

III. Compare and discuss the following statements:

• "Good reportage is designed to make that flight [from the real] impossible. It exiles us from fiction into the sharp terrain of truth." (Carey)

• " . . . in fiction, there is the saving notice on the license: THIS WAS MADE UP. . . . there is one sacred rule of journalism. The writer must not invent. The legend on the license must read: NONE OF THIS WAS MADE UP. The ethics of journalism . . . must be based on the simple truth that every journalist knows the difference between the distortion that comes from subtracting raw data and the distortion that comes from adding invented data . . ." (Hersey)

• "In fiction, the writer's voice matters; in reporting, the writer's authority matters. . . . The serious writer of fiction hopes to achieve a poetic truth, a human truth, which transcends any apparent or illusory 'reality'." (Hersey)

• " . . . there should be a firm line, not a fuzzy one, between fiction and nonfiction and . . . all work that purports to be nonfiction should strive to achieve the standards of the most truthful journalism. Labels such as 'nonfiction novel,' 'real-life novel,' 'creative nonfiction' and 'docudrama' may not be useful to that end." (Clark)

During the course of your discussion, debate the validity of the following writing methodologies: (1) drawing a composite character from a number of real-life models, (2) re-creating dialogue from events that happened in the past, (3) reporting on what a character in a story was thinking, (4) flip-flopping events in time, (5) telescoping time so that several scenes happen at once, (6) reconstructing events in such detail that it appears the author is an eyewitness.

IV.   Discuss the following ideas and terms introduced by James Ettema and Theodore Glasser:

• "Philosophers . . . define knowledge as 'justified true belief' "
• Authorized "knowers"
• "Primitive empiricism"
• "Daily reporters strive for accuracy, not veracity"

- "Preponderance test"
- "Moral certainty."

V.   Discuss Susan Sontag's proposition that "the camera is the ideal arm of consciousness in its acquisitive mood."

VI. Discuss Susan Sontag's observation that "the work photographers do is no generic exception to the usually shady commerce between art and truth." As you discuss her view, return for inspiration to the essay in Part I by Robert Stone on "The Reason for Stories."

VII. "A picture is worth a thousand words" is an old and persuasive axiom. But in what sense is it reliable? Review the essays on photography by Morris and Sontag and then discuss the reliability of photographic images as news evidence.

VIII. Discuss the meaning of the following bedrock statistical concepts described by Victor Kohn: probability; "power" and numbers; bias and confounders; variability; correlation and causation.

IX. Revisit these essays, comparing and contrasting the "scientific method" to the "journalistic method." Discuss what constitutes "reliable evidence" in journalism as compared with science.

X.   Discuss and justify (if you can) the following proposition written by Robert Ezra Park: "The function of news is to orient man and society in an actual world. In so far as it succeeds, it tends to preserve the sanity of the individual and the permanence of society." Now revisit Lippmann's proposition (in Item I) about the press's limitations.

WORKBENCH

I.   Kovach and Rosenstiel argue persuasively that journalism is essentially a discipline of verification. The reporter goes out and finds things out:

- Robert Capa risks his life to show troops landing on the French coast on D-Day.
- David Halberstam and other young reporters in Vietnam attempt to verify the claims of the U.S. government about the success of the war against the evidence of their own eyes and ears.
- Seymour Hersh works to verify that an American soldier will be tried during the Vietnam War for what we now call the "Mylai massacre."
- Michelle Caruso struggles to establish that the police in Boston are following the wrong trails in the Stuart murder investigation.

Kovach and Rosenstiel also argue that this discipline of verification has been displaced in some quarters by a "journalism of assertion." We think this is especially true on twenty-four-hour cable news networks, such as CNN, MSNBC, and Fox. With fellow students watch an hour of prime-time programming on these networks. How much of the journalism you see there is based on reporting—on verification—and how much of it is based on unproved "assertions"? Discuss your findings.

II.   Reread the narrative written by Seymour Hersh on how he got the Mylai story. With a pen, mark each part in the narrative where Hersh describes a particular reporting strategy that he used in his hunt, such strategies as "playing hunches" or "using the phone book." After you've done this, take a journalism story you have written and annotate it in the same way. What kinds of reporting strategies did you use? What kinds of evidence did each strategy produce? Look at each piece of evidence in the story, asking yourself, "Am I sure about that?" and "How do I know that?" What steps could you have taken to strengthen the evidentiary basis of your story?

III. Many journalists are attracted to their profession because of a talent in language or the visual arts, combined with an interest in social issues and public life. Our guess is that few journalists were math majors in college. Yet the world is full of numbers, so the lack of numerical literacy, or numeracy, and ignorance of social-science methods can be impediments to understanding. Interview a professor in a quantitative field such as math, biology, economics, demography, psychology, or political behavior. Ask him or her to evaluate the performance of journalists through the lens of a specialist in quantitative methods. Ask him or her for examples of how journalists get things wrong because they can't count.

IV.   Add terms, phrases, and sentences to your "editor's lexicon." (See Workbench assignments in Part I Study Guide and Part II, Section A.)

V.   Write an investigative piece under the supervision of your professor/editor. Using Seymour Hersh's essay as a model, write an accompanying piece describing the reporting strategies you used and how you collected and corroborated the facts on which it was constructed.

LANGUAGE AND NARRATIVE

INTRODUCTION

The subjects of this section, put simply, are words and story structure. But the context for their consideration is something more complex—namely, democracy and the essential relationship between good writing and a common life.

The hero of the section is the English journalist, essayist, and novelist, George Orwell. No one wrote more eloquently or urgently on these subjects, and no essay of his has been more influential than "Politics and the English Language." So we begin the section with Orwell's essay in the hope that it will promote an appreciation in apprentice journalists of their special place in the architecture of a democracy. For Orwell, who saw vividly "the special connection between politics and the debasement of language," good writers are democracy's stewards and good writing is born in an attachment to such elements as plain language, succinctness, active verbs, original metaphors, and precise diction. These elements are essential to the creation of the common understandings and common consciousness on which democratic life turns.

Orwell's essay is followed by the reflections of the literary critic, Hugh Kenner, who argues that the plain style, of which Orwell was himself a master, "feigns a candid observer." It is a style of writing that cultivates trust. Kenner says, memorably, that you "get yourself trusted by artifice"—that is, by the artifice of the plain style. It seems, he says, "to be announcing at every phrase its subjection to the check of experienced and nameable things." Kenner's argument rescues the language of journalism from the criticisms of those who express the belief that it is too clear, too conventional, too free from metaphor and other forms of figurative language. For generations, journalists could find no place in the literary canon because their simplicity and directness could easily be misinterpreted as simplemindedness or superficiality. Kenner writes to the rescue. Turning hard facts into easy reading takes craft and discipline.

The theme continues in the essay by the semanticist, S. I. Hayakawa, who implies that the heart of journalism—and of its language—is the "report," which should exclude "loaded words" and careless inferences. Hayakawa warns against inferences and other temptations, which color reports and draw them into the territory of opinion. Reports must have an integrity; their job is to make "good maps of the territory of experience." Hayakawa's reflections seem more pertinent than ever in an era when new forms of journalism and the political culture express themselves in terms of unbridled assertion, spin, and ideological bias. Hayakawa reminds us that impartiality is possible, if not in thought, then in disciplined forms of evidence and expression.

The section ends with two essays intended to broaden the vision of the journalist in a way we trust will not contradict the point of view of the first group of essays. We have included, first, a meditation on the nature of narrative by scholars Robert Scholes and Robert Kellog that can be used to show the fit between journalism and other ancient and contemporary narrative forms. We believe that journalists gain much by absorbing the principles of narrative as they develop stories as opposed to reports, articles, and arguments. The study of narrative leads the journalist further down the writer's path.

We conclude with Tom Wolfe, who walked purposely down such a path. We have published his reflections on the New Journalism, a movement associated with his and others' innovations, in which literary devices were used, sometimes aggressively, to enrich not just the language, but also the experience of journalism itself. The plain style, of which Kenner writes, may be barely visible in the self-conscious stylistic experiments that blast off the pages of Wolfe's work like skyrockets, but it is there, expressed in showing concern for the reader and in giving spirit to the concerns of his age.

Speaking of his own work, Wolfe says he used four devices: "scene-by-scene construction," "realistic dialogue," "third-person point of view," and "the recording of everyday gestures, habits . . . and other symbolic details." As it pertains to narrative, Wolfe sought to make the narrator's voice in journalism a livelier spirit—that is to say, not a bore—than he found in much of the journalism from which he was breaking away.

It has been said that journalists surround all innovations as if they were antibodies surrounding a virus. The experiments of Wolfe and the other New Journalists came under attack from the likes of John Hersey (see his essay in Part II, Section B), who often experimented himself with literary forms and language. To Hersey, Wolfe crossed a line into invention, into making stuff up, a line that should never be crossed. To his credit, Wolfe often answered critiques of his work with the evidence of his disciplined reporting strategies.

Our view is that literary devices are as much a part of the journalist's toolbox as the principles of empirical prose. As Rosenstiel and Kovach describe in their book, *The Elements of Journalism*, journalists feel a duty to make the important interesting. Wolfe took interesting risks as he put a literary face on his reports. One payoff was and continues to be an understanding of democracy's nooks and crannies, rather than its formal public life, where humans gather and engage in life's temptations, complexities, and possibilities.

25

POLITICS AND THE ENGLISH LANGUAGE

George Orwell

Most people who bother with the matter at all would admit that the English language is in a bad way, but it is generally assumed that we cannot by conscious action do anything about it. Our civilization is decadent and our language—so the argument runs—must inevitably share in the general collapse. It follows that any struggle against the abuse of language is a sentimental archaism, like preferring candles to electric light or hansom cabs to aeroplanes. Underneath this lies the half-conscious belief that language is a natural growth and not an instrument which we shape for our own purposes.

Now, it is clear that the decline of a language must ultimately have political and economic causes: it is not due simply to the bad influence of this or that individual writer. But an effect can become a cause, reinforcing the original cause and producing the same effect in an intensified form, and so on indefinitely. A man may take to drink because he feels himself to be a failure, and then fail all the more completely because he drinks. It is rather the same thing that is happening to the English language. It becomes ugly and inaccurate because our thoughts are foolish, but the slovenliness of our language makes it easier for us to have foolish thoughts. The point is that the process is reversible. Modern English, especially written English, is full of bad habits which spread by imitation and which can be avoided if one is willing to take the necessary trouble. If one gets rid of these habits one can think more clearly, and to think clearly is a necessary first step toward political regeneration: so that the fight against bad English is not frivolous and is not the exclusive concern of professional writers. I will come back to this presently, and I hope that by that time the meaning of what I have said here will have become clearer. Meanwhile, here are five specimens of the English language as it is now habitually written.

These five passages have not been picked out because they are especially bad— I could have quoted far worse if I had chosen—but because they illustrate various of the mental vices from which we now suffer. They are a little below the average, but are fairly representative samples. I number them so that I can refer back to them when necessary:

> (1) I am not, indeed, sure whether it is not true to say that the Milton who once seemed not unlike a seventeenth-century Shelley had not become, out of an experience ever more bitter in each year, more alien [*sic*] to the founder of that Jesuit sect which nothing could induce him to tolerate.
>
> Professor Harold Laski (Essay in *Freedom of Expression*)

(2) Above all, we cannot play ducks and drakes with a native battery of idioms which prescribes such egregious collocations of vocables as the Basic *put up with* for *tolerate* or *put at a loss* for *bewilder*.

Professor Lancelot Hogben (*Interglossa*)

(3) On the one side we have the free personality: by definition it is not neurotic, for it has neither conflict nor dream. Its desires, such as they are, are transparent, for they are just what institutional approval keeps in the forefront of consciousness; another institutional pattern would alter their number and intensity; there is little in them that is natural, irreducible, or culturally dangerous. But *on the other side*, the social bond itself is nothing but the mutual reflection of these self-secure integrities. Recall the definition of love. Is not this the very picture of a small academic? Where is there a place in this hall of mirrors for either personality or fraternity?

Essay on psychology in *Politics* (New York)

(4) All the "best people" from the gentlemen's clubs, and all the frantic fascist captains, united in common hatred of Socialism and bestial horror of the rising tide of the mass revolutionary movement, have turned to acts of provocation, to foul incendiarism, to medieval legends of poisoned wells, to legalize their own destruction of proletarian organizations, and rouse the agitated petty-bourgeoisie to chauvinistic fervor on behalf of the fight against the revolutionary way out of the crisis.

Communist pamphlet

(5) If a new spirit *is* to be infused into this old country, there is one thorny and contentious reform which must be tackled, and that is the humanization and galvanization of the B.B.C. Timidity here will bespeak canker and atrophy of the soul. The heart of Britain may be sound and of strong beat, for instance, but the British lion's roar at present is like that of Bottom in Shakespeare's *Midsummer Night's Dream*—as gentle as any sucking dove. A virile new Britain cannot continue indefinitely to be traduced in the eyes or rather ears, of the world by the effete languors of Langham Place, brazenly masquerading as "standard English." When the Voice of Britain is heard at nine o'clock, better far and infinitely less ludicrous to hear aitches honestly dropped than the present priggish, inflated, inhibited, school-ma'amish arch braying of blameless bashful newing maidens!

Letter in *Tribune*

Each of these passages has faults of its own, but, quite apart from avoidable ugliness, two qualities are common to all of them. The first is staleness of imagery; the other is lack of precision. The writer either has a meaning and cannot express it, or he inadvertently says something else, or he is almost indifferent as to whether his words mean anything or not. This mixture of vagueness and sheer incompetence is the most marked characteristic of modern English prose, and especially of any kind of political writing. As soon as certain topics are raised, the concrete melts into the abstract and no one seems able to think of turns of speech that are not hackneyed: prose consists less and less of *words* chosen for the sake of their meaning, and more and more of *phrases* tacked together like the sections of a prefabricated henhouse. I list below, with notes and examples, various of the tricks by means of which the work of prose-construction is habitually dodged:

Dying metaphors. A newly invented metaphor assists thought by evoking a visual image, while on the other hand a metaphor which is technically "dead" (e.g. *iron resolution*) has in effect reverted to being an ordinary word and can generally be used without loss of vividness. But in between these two classes there is a huge dump of worn-out metaphors which have lost all evocative power and are merely used because they save people the trouble of inventing phrases for themselves. Examples are: *Ring the changes on, take up the cudgels for, toe the line, ride roughshod over, stand shoulder to shoulder with, play into the hands of, no axe to grind, grist to the mill, fishing in troubled waters, on the order of the day, Achilles' heel, swan song, hotbed.* Many of these are used without knowledge of their meaning (what is a "rift," for instance?), and incompatible metaphors are frequently mixed, a sure sign that the writer is not interested in what he is saying. Some metaphors now current have been twisted out of their original meaning without those who use them even being aware of the fact. For example, *toe the line* is sometimes written *tow the line.* Another example is *the hammer and the anvil,* now always used with the implication that the anvil gets the worst of it. In real life it is always the anvil that breaks the hammer, never the other way about: a writer who stopped to think what he was saying would be aware of this, and would avoid perverting the original phrase.

Operators or *verbal false limbs.* These save the trouble of picking out appropriate verbs and nouns, and at the same time pad each sentence with extra syllables which give it an appearance of symmetry. Characteristic phrases are *render inoperative, militate against, make contact with, be subjected to, give rise to, give grounds for, have the effect of, play a leading part (role) in, make itself felt, take effect, exhibit a tendency to, serve the purpose of, etc., etc.* The keynote is the climination of simple verbs. Instead of being a single word, such as *break, stop, spoil, mend, kill,* a verb becomes a *phrase,* made up of a noun or adjective tacked on to some general-purpose verb such as *prove, serve, form, play, render.* In addition, the passive voice is wherever possible used in preference to the active, and noun constructions are used instead of gerunds (*by examination of* instead of *by examining*). The range of verbs is further cut down by means of the *-ize* and *de-* formations, and the banal statements are given an appearance of profundity by means of the *not un-* formation. Simple conjunctions and prepositions are replaced by such phrases as *with respect to, having regard to, the fact that, by dint of, in view of, in the interests of, on the hypothesis that*; and the ends of sentences are saved by anticlimax by such resounding commonplaces as *greatly to be desired, cannot be left out of account, a development to be expected in the near future, deserving of serious consideration, brought to a salisfactory conclusion,* and so on and so forth.

Pretentious diction. Words like *phenomenon, element, individual* (as noun), *objective, categorical, effective, virtual, basic, primary, promote, constitute, exhibit, exploit, utilize, eliminate, liquidate,* are used to dress up simple statement and give an air of scientific impartiality to biased judgments. Adjectives like *epoch-making, epic, historic, unforgettable, triumphant, age-old, inevitable, inexorable, veritable,* are used to dignify the sordid processes of international politics, while writing that aims at glorifying war usually takes on an archaic color, its characteristic words being: *realm, throne, chariot, mailed fist, trident, sword, shield, buckler, banner, jackboot, clarion.* Foreign words and expressions such as *cul de sac, ancien régime, deus ex machina, mutatis mutandis, status quo, gleichschaltung, weltanschauung,* are used to give an air of culture and elegance. Except for the useful abbreviations *i.e., e.g.,* and *etc.,* there is no real need for any of the hundreds of foreign phrases now current in English. Bad writers, and especially scientific, political, and sociological writers, are nearly always haunted by the notion that Latin or Greek words are grander than Saxon ones, and unnecessary words like *expedite, ameliorate, predict, extraneous, deracinated, clandestine, subaqueous,* and hundreds of others constantly gain ground from their Anglo-Saxon opposite numbers.[1] The jargon peculiar to Marxist writing (*hyena, hangman, cannibal, petty bourgeois, these gentry, lackey, flunkey, mad dog, White Guard,* etc.) consists largely of words and phrases translated from Russian, German, or French; but the normal way of coining a new word is to use a Latin or Greek root with the appropriate affix and, where necessary, the size formation. It is often easier to make up words of this kind (*deregionalize, impermissible, extramarital, nonfragmentary* and so forth) than to think up the English words that will cover one's meaning. The result, in general, is an increase in slovenliness and vagueness.

Meaningless words. In certain kinds of writing, particularly in art criticism and literary criticism, it is normal to come across long passages which are almost completely lacking in meaning.[2] Words like *romantic, plastic, values, human, dead, sentimental, natural, vitality,* as used in art criticism, are strictly meaningless, in the sense that they not only do not point to any discoverable object, but are hardly ever expected to do so by the reader. When one critic writes, "The outstanding feature of Mr. X's work is its living quality," while another writes, "The immediately striking thing about Mr. X's work is its peculiar deadness," the reader accepts this as a simple difference of opinion. If words like *black* and *white* were involved, instead of the jargon words *dead* and *living,* he would see at once that language was being used in an improper way. Many political words are similarly abused. The word *Fascism* has now no meaning except in so far as it signifies "something not desirable." The words *democracy, socialism, freedom, patriotic, realistic, justice,* have each of them several different meanings which cannot be reconciled with one another. In the case of a word like *democracy,* not only is there no agreed definition, but the attempt to make one is resisted from all sides. It is almost universally felt that when we call a country democratic we are praising it: consequently the defenders of every kind of regime claim that it is a democracy, and fear that they might have to stop using the word if it were tied down to any one meaning. Words of this kind are often used in a consciously dishonest way. That is, the person who uses them has his own private definition, but allows his hearer to think he means something quite different. Statements like *Marshal Pétain was a true patriot, The Soviet press is the freest in the world, The Catholic Church is opposed to persecution,* are almost always made with intent to deceive. Other words used in variable meanings, in most cases more or less dishonestly, are: *class, totalitarian, science, progressive, reactionary, bourgeois, equality.*

Now that I have made this catalogue of swindles and perversions, let me give another example of the kind of writing that they lead to. This time it must of its nature be an imaginary one. I am going to translate a passage of good English into modern English of the worst sort. Here is a well-known verse from *Ecclesiastes:*

I returned and saw under the sun, that the race is not to the swift, nor the battle to the strong, neither yet bread to the wise, nor yet riches to men of understanding, nor yet favour to men of skill; but time and chance happeneth to them all.

Here it is in modern English:

Objective considerations of contemporary phenomena compels the conclusion that success or failure in competitive activities exhibits no tendency to be commensurate with innate capacity, but that a considerable element of the unpredictable must invariably be taken into account.

This is a parody, but not a very gross one. Exhibit (3), above, for instance, contains several patches of the same kind of English. It will be seen that I have not made a full translation. The beginning and ending of the sentence follow the original meaning fairly closely, but in the middle the concrete illustrations—race, battle, bread—dissolve into the vague phrase "success or failure in competitive activities." This had to be so, because no modern writer of the kind I am discussing—no one capable of using phrases like "objective consideration of contemporary phenomena"—would ever tabulate his thoughts in that precise and detailed way. The whole tendency of modern prose is away from concreteness. Now analyze these two sentences a little more closely. The first contains forty-nine words but only sixty syllables, and all its words are those of everyday life. The second contains thirty-eight words of ninety syllables: eighteen of its words are from Latin roots, and one from Greek. The first sentence contains six vivid images, and only one phrase ("time and chance") that could be called vague. The second contains not a single fresh, arresting phrase, and in spite of its ninety syllables it gives only a shortened version of the meaning contained in the first. Yet without a doubt it is the second kind of sentence that is gaining ground in modern English. I do not want to exaggerate. This kind of writing is not yet universal, and outcrops of simplicity will occur here and there in the worst-written page. Still, if you or I were told to write a few lines on the uncertainty of human fortunes, we should probably come much nearer to my imaginary sentence than to the one from *Ecclesiastes*.

As I have tried to show, modern writing at its worst does not consist in picking out words for the sake of their meaning and inventing images in order to make the meaning clearer. It consists in gumming together long strips of words which have already been set in order by someone else, and making the results presentable by sheer humbug. The attraction of this way of writing is that it is easy. It is easier—even quicker, once you have the habit—to say *In my opinion it is not an unjustifiable assumption that* than to say *I think*. If you use ready-made phrases, you not only don't have to hunt about for words; you also don't have to bother with the rhythms of your sentences, since these phrases are generally so arranged as to be more or less euphonious. When you are composing in a hurry—when you are dictating to a stenographer, for instance, or making a public speech—it is natural to fall into a pretentious, Latinized style. Tags like *a consideration which we should do well to bear in mind* or *a conclusion to which all of us would readily assent* will save many a sentence from coming down with a bump. By using stale metaphors, similes, and idioms, you save much mental effort, at the cost of leaving your meaning vague, not only for your reader but for yourself. This is the significance of mixed metaphors. The sole aim of a metaphor is to call up a visual image. When these images clash—as in *The Fascist octopus has sung its swan song, the jackboot is thrown into the melting pot*—it can be taken as certain that the writer is not seeing a mental image of the objects he is naming; in other words he is not really thinking. Look again at the examples I gave at the beginning of this essay. Professor Laski (1) uses five negatives in fifty-three words. One of these is superfluous, making nonsense of the whole passage, and in addition there is the slip—*alien* for akin—making further nonsense, and several avoidable pieces of clumsiness which increase the general vagueness. Professor Hogben (2) plays ducks and drakes with a battery which is able to write prescriptions, and, while disapproving of the everyday phrase *put up with*, is unwilling to look *egregious* up in the dictionary and see what it means: (3), if one takes an uncharitable attitude towards it, is simply meaningless: probably one could work out its intended meaning by reading the whole of the article in which it occurs. In (4), the writer knows more or less what he wants to say, but an accumulation of stale phrases chokes him like tea leaves blocking a sink. In (5), words and meaning have almost parted company. People who write in this manner usually have a general emotional meaning—they dislike one thing and want to express solidarity with another—but they are not interested in the detail of what they are saying. A scrupulous writer, in every sentence that he writes, will ask himself at least four questions, thus: What am I trying to say? What words will express it? What image or idiom will make it clearer? Is this image fresh enough to have an effect? And he will probably ask himself two more: Could I put it more shortly? Have I said anything that is avoidably ugly? But you are not obliged to go to all this trouble. You can shirk it by simply throwing your mind open and letting the ready-made phrases come crowding in. They will construct your sentences for you—even think your thoughts for you, to a certain extent—and at need they will perform the important service of partially concealing your meaning even from yourself. It is at this point that the special connection between politics and the debasement of language becomes clear.

In our time it is broadly true that political writing is bad writing. Where it is not true, it will generally be found that the writer is some kind of rebel, expressing his private opinions and not a "party line." Orthodoxy, of whatever color, seems to demand a lifeless, imitative style. The political dialects to be found in pamphlets, leading articles, manifestoes, White Papers and the speeches of undersecretaries do, of course, vary from party to party, but they are all alike in that one almost never finds in them a fresh, vivid, homemade turn of speech. When one watches some tired hack on the platform mechanically repeating the familiar phrases—*bestial atrocities, iron heel, bloodstained tyranny, free peoples of the world, stand shoulder to shoulder*—one often has a curious feeling that one is not watching a live human being but some kind of dummy: a feeling which suddenly becomes stronger at moments when the light catches the speaker's spectacles and turns them into blank discs which seem to have no eyes behind them. And this is not altogether fanciful. A speaker who uses that kind of phraseology has gone some distance toward turning himself into a machine. The appropriate noises are coming out of his larynx, but his brain is not involved as it would be if he were choosing his words for himself. If the speech he is making is one that he is accustomed to make over and over again, he may be almost unconscious of what he is saying, as one is when one utters the responses in church. And this reduced state of consciousness, if not indispensable, is at any rate favorable to political conformity.

In our time, political speech and writing are largely the defense of the indefensible. Things like the continuance of British rule in India, the Russian purges and deportations, the dropping of the atom bombs on Japan, can indeed be defended, but only by arguments which are too brutal for most people to face, and which do not square with the professed aims of political parties. Thus political language has to consist largely of euphemism, question-begging and sheer cloudy vagueness. Defenseless villages are bombarded from the air, the inhabitants driven out into the countryside, the cattle machine-gunned, the huts set on fire with incendiary bullets: this is called *pacification*. Millions of peasants are robbed of their farms and sent trudging along the roads with no more than they can carry: this is called *transfer of population* or *rectification of frontiers*. People are imprisoned for years without trial, or shot in the back of the neck or sent to die of scurvy in Arctic lumber camps: this is called *elimination of unreliable elements*. Such phraseology is needed if one wants to name things without calling up mental pictures of them. Consider for instance some comfortable English professor defending Russian totalitarianism. He cannot say outright, "I believe in killing off your opponents when you can get good results by doing so." Probably, therefore, he will say something like this:

"While freely conceding that the Soviet régime exhibits certain features which the humanitarian may be inclined to deplore, we must. I think, agree that a certain curtailment of the right to political opposition is an unavoidable concomitant of transitional periods, and that the rigors which the Russian people have been called upon to undergo have been amply justified in the sphere of concrete achievement."

The inflated style is itself a kind of euphemism. A mass of Latin words falls upon the facts like soft snow, blurring the outlines and covering up all the details. The great enemy of clear language is insincerity. When there is a gap between one's real and one's declared aims, one turns as it were instinctively to long words and exhausted idioms, like a cuttlefish squirting out ink. In our age there is no such thing as "keeping out of politics." All issues are political issues, and politics itself is a mass of lies, evasions, folly, hatred, and schizophrenia. When the general atmosphere is bad, language must suffer. I should expect to find—this is a guess which I have not sufficient knowledge to verify—that the German, Russian and Italian languages have all deteriorated in the last ten or fifteen years, as a result of dictatorship.

But if thought corrupts language, language can also corrupt thought. A bad usage can spread by tradition and imitation, even among people who should and do know better. The debased language that I have been discussing is in some ways very convenient. Phrases like *a not unjustifiable assumption, leaves much to be desired, would serve no good purpose, a consideration which we should do well to bear in mind*, are a continuous temptation, a packet of aspirins always at one's elbow. Look back through this essay, and for certain you will find that I have again and again committed the very faults I am protesting against. By this morning's post I have received a pamphlet dealing with conditions in Germany. The author tells me that he "felt impelled" to write it. I open it at random, and here is almost the first sentence that I see: "[The Allies] have an opportunity not only of achieving a radical transformation of Germany's social and political structure in such a way as to avoid a nationalistic reaction in Germany itself, but at the same time of laying the foundations of a co-operative and unified Europe." You see, he "feels impelled" to write—feels, presumably, that he has something new to say—and yet his words, like cavalry horses answering the bugle, group themselves automatically into the familiar dreary pattern. This invasion of one's mind by ready-made phrases (*lay the foundations, achieve a radical transformation*) can only be prevented if one is constantly on guard against them, and every such phrase anaesthetizes a portion of one's brain.

I said earlier that the decadence of our language is probably curable. Those who deny this would argue, if they produced an argument at all, that language merely reflects existing social conditions, and that we cannot influence its development by any direct tinkering with words and constructions. So far as the general tone or spirit of a language goes, this may be true, but it is not true in detail. Silly words and expressions have often disappeared, not through any evolutionary process but owing to the conscious action of a minority. Two recent examples were *explore every avenue* and *leave no stone unturned*, which were killed by the jeers of a few journalists. There is a long list of flyblown metaphors which could similarly be got rid of if enough people would interest themselves in the job; and it should also be possible to laugh the *not un-* formation out of existence,[3] to reduce the amount of Latin and Greek in the average sentence, to drive out foreign phrases and strayed scientific words, and, in general, to make pretentiousness unfashionable. But all these are minor points. The defense of the English language implies more than this, and perhaps it is best to start by saying what it does *not* imply.

To begin with it has nothing to do with archaism, with the salvaging of obsolete words and turns of speech, or with the setting up of a "standard English" which must never be departed from. On the contrary, it is especially concerned with the scrapping of every word or idiom which has outworn its usefulness. It has nothing to do with correct grammar and syntax, which are of no importance so long as one makes one's meaning clear, or with the avoidance of Americanisms, or with having what is called a "good prose style." On the other hand it is not concerned with fake simplicity and the attempt to make written English colloquial. Nor does it even imply in every case preferring the Saxon word to the Latin one, though it does imply using the fewest and shortest words that will cover one's meaning. What is above all needed is to let the meaning choose the word, and not the other way about. In prose, the worst thing one can do with words is to surrender to them. When you think of a concrete object, you think wordlessly, and then, if you want to describe the thing you have been visualizing you probably hunt about till you find the exact words that seem to fit it. When you think of something abstract you are more inclined to use words from the start, and unless you make a conscious effort to prevent it, the existing dialect will come rushing in and do the job for you, at the expense of blurring or even changing your meaning. Probably it is better to put off using words as long as possible and get one's meaning as clear as one can through pictures or sensations. Afterward one can choose—not simply *accept*—the phrases that will best cover the meaning, and then switch round and decide what impression one's words are likely to make on another person. This last effort of the mind cuts out all stale or mixed images, all prefabricated phrases, needless repetitions, and humbug and vagueness generally. But one can often be in doubt about the effect of a word or a phrase, and one needs rules that one can rely on when instinct fails. I think the following rules will cover most cases:

(i) Never use a metaphor, simile, or other figure of speech which you are used to seeing in print.

(ii) Never use a long word where a short one will do.

(iii) If it is possible to cut a word out, always cut it out.

(iv) Never use the passive where you can use the active.

(v) Never use a foreign phrase, a scientific word, or a jargon word if you can think of an everyday English equivalent.

(vi) Break any of these rules sooner than say anything outright barbarous.

These rules sound elementary, and so they are, but they demand a deep change of attitude in anyone who has grown used to writing in the style now fashionable. One could keep all of them and still write bad English, but one could not write the kind of stuff that I quoted in those five specimens at the beginning of this article.

I have not here been considering the literary use of language, but merely language as an instrument for expressing and not for concealing or preventing thought. Stuart Chase and others have come near to claiming that all abstract words are meaningless, and have used this as a pretext for advocating a kind of political quietism. Since you don't know what Fascism is, how can you struggle against Fascism? One need not swallow such absurdities as this, but one ought to recognize that the present political chaos is connected with the decay of language, and that one can probably bring about some improvement by starting at the verbal end. If you simplify your English, you are freed from the worst follies of orthodoxy. You cannot speak any of the necessary dialects, and when you make a stupid remark its stupidity will be obvious, even to yourself. Political language—and with variations this is true of all political parties, from Conservatives to Anarchists—is designed to make lies sound truthful and murder respectable, and to give an appearance of solidity to pure wind. One cannot change this all in a moment, but one can at least change one's own habits, and from time to time one can even, if one jeers loudly enough, send some worn-out and useless phrase—some *jackboot, Achilles' heel, hotbed, melting pot, acid test, veritable inferno*, or other lump of verbal refuse—into the dustbin where it belongs.

NOTES

1. An interesting illustration of this is the way in which the English flower names which were in use till very recently are being ousted by Greek ones, *snapdragon* becoming *antirrhinum, forget-me-not* becoming *myosotis*, etc. It is hard to see any practical reason for this change of fashion: it is probably due to an instinctive turning away from the more homely word and a vague feeling that the Greek word is scientific.

2. Example: "Comfort's catholicity of perception and image, strangely Whitmanesque in range, almost the exact opposite in aesthetic compulsion, continues to evoke that trembling atmospheric accumulative hinting at a cruel, an inexorably serene timelessness. . . . Wrey Gardiner scores by aiming at simple bull's-eyes with precision. Only they are not so simple, and through this contented sadness runs more than the surface bittersweet of resignation." (*Poetry Quarterly.*)

3. One can cure oneself of the *not un-* formation by memorizing this sentence: *A not unblack dog was chasing a not unsmall rabbit across a not ungreen field.*

26
THE POLITICS OF THE PLAIN STYLE

Hugh Kenner

Monsieur Jourdain, the Molière bourgeois, was so misguided as to conclude he'd been talking prose all his life, his bogus instructor having defined prose as whatever is not verse. But as nobody talks in rhyme, so nobody talks in prose. Prose came late into every written language, and very late into English. Even Chaucer had few clues to its workings. A special variety, "plain" prose, came especially late. Plain prose, the plain style, is the most disorienting form of discourse yet invented by man. Swift in the eighteenth century, George Orwell in the twentieth are two of its very few masters. And both were political writers—there's a connection.

The plain style has been hard to talk about except in circles. Can plainness, for instance, even lay claims to a style? Swift seems to think so. "Proper words in proper places" is what he has to say about style, not explaining, though, how to find the proper words or identify the proper places to put them into. But Swift is teasing. His readers in 1720 were among the first to feel alarm at the norm of the printed page, the way members of the intelligentsia in the 1950s were alarmed by television. Swift confronts them with their own bewilderment about what *style* may mean on silent paper, where words have not cadences or emphases but places. He is nearly asking if style has become a branch of geometry.

Styles were long distinguished by degrees of ornateness, the more highly figured being the most esteemed. There was a high style in which Cicero delivered his orations and a low style in which he would have addressed his cook. Rhetoricians gave their attention to the high style. The low style was beneath attention. It was scarcely, save by contrast, a style at all.

Evaluation like that has nothing to do with writing. It appeals to the way we judge oral performance. When Cicero spoke with his cook, he was offstage; when he addressed the Senate, he was in costume and in role and in command of a scene carefully pre-scripted. Of the five parts into which the Romans analyzed oratory, two pertained to the theatrics of performance; they were "memory" and "delivery." "Memory" is a clue to something important. Cicero's intricate syntax, its systems of subordination, its bold rearrangements of the natural order of words would have been impossible for an orator to improvise. So he worked them out on paper, memorized them and performed them in a way that made it seem he was giving voice to his passion of the moment. In fact, he was being careful not to let passion master him, lest it overwhelm memory.

Hugh Kenner, "The Politics of the Plain Style" (New York: Oxford University Press, 1990), 183–190 (originally published in *The New York Times Book Review*, September 15, 1988). Reprinted with the kind permission of Mary Anne Kenner.

251

A good public speech is something as contrived as a scene by Shakespeare. Even Lincoln, in what is represented as an address of exemplary plainness, launched it with diction he could only have premeditated: "Four score and seven years ago our fathers brought forth on this continent. . . ." The word *style* pertains to the art of contriving something like that. You contrive it by hand. A stilus was a pointed tool with which Romans wrote on wax tablets, and what you did with its aid was what came to be called your style. It was *you*, like your handwriting. A plain style would seem to be a contradiction in terms. If it's plain, then surely it didn't need working out with a stylus.

But indeed it did. Something so lucid, so seemingly natural, that we can only applaud its "proper words in proper places" is not the work of nature but of great contrivance. W. B. Yeats wrote, on a related theme:

> I said, "A line will take us hours maybe;
> Yet if it does not seem a moment's thought,
> Our stitching and unstitching has been naught."

Here's an intricate instance of writing that's saying it was spoken despite the fact that it rhymes, writing therefore that's inviting us to ponder its own degrees of artifice. Yeats has in mind poetry that has abandoned the high style and is managing to look not only improvised but conversational, even while rhyming. That would be poetry contriving, as T. S. Eliot put it, to be "at least as well written as prose." And it helps us perceive good prose as an art with a new set of norms—feigned casualness, hidden economy.

Since you're feigning those qualities, nothing stops you from feigning much more. George Orwell wrote "A Hanging," an eye-witness account of something he almost certainly never witnessed, as well as "Shooting an Elephant," his first-person recollection of a deed he may or may not ever have done.

We like to have such things plainly labeled fiction, if they are fictions. Then we are willing to admire the artistry—so acutely invented a detail as the condemned man's stepping around a puddle within yards of the rope, which prompts the narrator's reflection on "the unspeakable wrongness of cutting a life short when it is in full tide. This man was not dying, he was alive just as we were alive." That is like John Donne meditating on a sacred text, and we would not welcome news that the text was nowhere in the Bible, that Donne had invented it for the sake of the sermon he could spin. True, we can cite something Orwell wrote elsewhere, "I watched a man hanged once." Alas, that doesn't prove that he watched a man hanged once; it proves only that the author of "A Hanging" (1931) still had such an idea on his mind when he was writing something else six years later. An appeal to other writers may be more helpful. We soon find that Swift wrote a very similar sentence: "Last week I watched a woman *flay'd*."

We could surely find more parallels, and in seeking them we'd be nudging "A Hanging" from reporting into literature, where questions of veracity can't reach it. For we'll half accept the idea that printed words do no more than permute other printed words, in an economy bounded by the page. That gets called the literary tradition, in which statements aren't required to be true.

But if we'll half accept the fictive quality of everything we read, don't we also tend to believe what it says in black and white, what we read in the papers? Of course we do, perhaps because the printed word stays around to be checked, like a stranger with nothing to hide. (Though handwriting does that too, print has the advantage of looking impersonal.)

Plain prose was invented among consumers of print, to exploit this ambiguous response. It seems to peg its words to what is persistently *so*—no matter how words drift about. Couched in plain prose, even the incredible can hope for belief. It's a perfect medium for hoaxes. By publishing the word that a nuisance, an astrologer named Partridge, was dead, Swift caused him vast trouble proving he was alive, and H. L. Mencken's mischievous printed statement that the first American bathtub got installed as recently as December 20, 1842, is enshrined as history in the *Congressional Record*, although Mencken himself tried to disavow it four times. Having grown famous for a baroque manner that advertised its own exaggerations, Mencken may have been surprised to find he could make people believe anything if he simply dropped to the plain style.

The science writer Martin Gardner, whose style is plain to the point of naïveté, had a similar experience when he sought to amuse readers of *Scientific American* by discussing a bogus force that haunted pyramids and could sharpen razor blades. The joke instantly got out of hand. Cultists of pyramid power made themselves heard, and Mr. Gardner has tried in vain to discredit them. Like Mr. Gardner's pyramid and Mencken's bathtub, the novel, which we both believe and don't, has origins inextricable from fakery. Readers in the eighteenth century could savor *The Life and Strange Surprising Adventures of Robinson Crusoe*, who'd been cast away on an island. That was an exotic thought if you lived in crowded London, and exoticism fostered the will to believe. The title page, moreover, said, "Written by Himself," so the account had the merit of firsthand truth. It was a while before "Himself" turned out to be a journalist named Defoe.

Today we handle the question of deception by saying Defoe was writing a novel, a genre of which he would have had no inkling. Defoe had simply discovered what plain prose, this new and seemingly styleless medium, is good for. Nothing beats it as a vehicle for profitable lies, which can entertain people and may even do them good in other ways. Knowing as we do that Defoe, not Crusoe, was the author, we still contrive to read *Robinson Crusoe* as if it were true. The formula "willing suspension of disbelief" was invented to help us accept what we are doing.

The next development was the replacement of the old polemical journalism by journalism of fact, meaning reports you could trust, statement by statement, fact by fact, because they appeared in newspapers. Gradually newspapers gravitated toward the plain style, the style of all styles that was patently trustworthy—in fact, the style of *Robinson Crusoe*, with which Defoe had invented such a look of honest verisimilitude. A man who doesn't make his language ornate cannot be deceiving us; so runs the hidden premise. Bishop Thomas Sprat extolled "a close, naked, natural way of speaking" in 1667; it was the speech, he went on to say, of merchants and artisans, not of wits and scholars. Merchants and artisans are men who handle *things* and who presumably handle words with a similar probity. Wits and scholars handle nothing more substantial than ideas. Journalism seemed guaranteed by the plain style. Handbooks and copy editors now teach journalists how to write plainly, that is, in such a manner that they will be trusted. You get yourself trusted by artifice.

Plain style is a populist style and one that suited writers like Swift, Mencken, and Orwell. Homely diction is its hallmark, also one-two-three syntax, the show of candor and the artifice of seeming to be grounded outside language in what is called fact—the domain where a condemned man can be observed as he silently avoids a puddle and your prose will report the observation and no one will doubt it. Such prose simulates the words anyone who was there and awake might later have spoken spontaneously. On a written page, as we've seen, the spontaneous can only be a contrivance.

So a great deal of artifice is being piled on, beginning with the candid no-nonsense observer. What if there was a short circuit: no observation, simply the prose? Whenever that is suggested, straight-forward folk get upset. But they were never meant to think about it, any more than airplane passengers are meant to brood about what holds them aloft—thin air. The plain style feigns a candid observer. Such is its great advantage for persuading. From behind its mask of calm candor, the writer with political intentions can appeal, in seeming disinterest, to people whose pride is their no-nonsense connoisseurship of fact. And such is the trickiness of language that he may find he must deceive them to enlighten them. Whether Orwell ever witnessed a hanging or not, we're in no doubt what he means us to think of the custom.

His masterly plain style came to full development in *Homage to Catalonia* (1938), an effort to supply a true account of the Spanish Civil War, about which the communists, his one-time allies, were fabricating a boilerplate account. Though their ostensible enemies were the so-called fascists, the communists also figured that much trouble was being made by treasonable Trotskyists, whom they accused of making an alliance with the fascists to subvert genuine revolution. It was in communist so-called news of the mid-1930s that Orwell first discerned newspeak, which penetrated not only *The Daily Worker* but respectable London papers like *The News Chronicle*. What they printed was the news, and it was believed. How to counter what was believed?

Why, by the device of the firsthand observer, a device as old as Defoe, who used it in *A Journal of the Plague Year* to simulate persuasive accounts of things he could not have seen. When newspeak indulges in sentences like "Barcelona, the first city in Spain, was plunged into bloodshed by *agents provocateurs* using this subversive organization," your way to credibility is via sentences like this: "Sometimes I was merely bored with the whole affair, paid no attention to the hellish noise, and spent hours reading a succession of Penguin Library books which, luckily, I had bought a few days earlier; sometimes I was very conscious of the armed men watching me fifty yards away." After you've established your credentials like that, your next paragraphs can ignore the newspeak utterance as mere academic mischief. And it literally doesn't matter whether you read Penguins in Spain or not.

Orwell was alert to all of English literature, from Chaucer to *Ulysses*. A source for the famous trope about some being more equal than others has been found in *Paradise Lost*. He had studied Latin and Greek, and once, when hard up, he advertised his readiness to translate from anything French so long as it was from after 1400 A.D. Yet he is identified with an English prose that sounds native, a codifying of what you'd learn by ear in the Wigan of Orwell's *Road to Wigan Pier*, or in any other English working-class borough. Newspeak, as he defined it in *Nineteen Eighty-Four*, seems to reverse the honesty of all that: War is peace, freedom is slavery, $2 + 2 = 5$. Political discourse being feverish with newspeak, he concocted his plain style to reduce its temperature.

We are dealing now with no language humans speak, rather with an implied ideal language the credentials of which are moral, a language that cleaves to things and has univocal names for them. "Cat" is cat, "dog" is dog. That, in Swift's time, had been a philosopher's vision, and in *Gulliver's Travels* Swift had derided philosophers who, since words were but tokens for things, saved breath and ear by reducing their discourse to a holding up of things.

Examine Orwell's famous examples, and discover an absence of opposite *things*. "War" is not war the way "cat" is cat, nor is "freedom" freedom the way "dog" is dog. Such abstractions are defined by consensus. Once we've left behind "cat" and "dog" and "house" and "tree," there are seldom things to which words can correspond, but you can obtain considerable advantage by acting as if there were. The plain style, by which you gain that advantage, seems to be announcing at every phrase its subjection to the check of experienced and namable things. Orwell, so the prose says, had shot an elephant. Orwell had witnessed a hanging. Orwell at school had been beaten with a riding crop for wetting his bed. The prose says these things so plainly that we believe whatever else it says. And none of these things seem to have been true.

We should next observe that Orwell's two climactic works are frank fictions— *Animal Farm* and *Nineteen Eighty-Four*. In a fiction you address yourself to the wholly unreal as if there were no doubt about it. In *Animal Farm* we're apprised of a convention at which pigs talk to one another. Except for the fact that we don't credit pigs with speech, we might be attending to a report of a county council meeting. (And observe which way the allegory runs; we're not being told councilors are pigs.)

It is clarifying to reflect that the language of fiction cannot be told from that of fact. Their grammar, syntax, and semantics are identical. So Orwell passed readily to and fro between his two modes, reportage and fiction, which both employ the plain style. The difference is that the fictionality of fiction offers itself for detection. If the fiction speaks political truths, it does so by allegory.

That is tricky, because it transfers responsibility for what is being said from the writer to the reader. Orwell's wartime BBC acquaintance William Empson warned him in 1945 that *Animal Farm* was liable to misinterpretation, and years later Empson himself provided an object lesson when he denied that *Nineteen Eighty-Four* was "about" some future communism. It was "about," Empson insisted, as though the fact should have been obvious, that pit of infamy, the Roman Catholic Church. One thing that would have driven Empson to such a length was his need to leave the left unbesmirched by Orwell and Orwell untainted by any imputation that he'd besmirched the left. Empson summoned Orwell's shade to abet the hysteria he was indulging at the moment. He was writing about *Paradise Lost*, contemplation of which appears to have unsettled his mind.

Now, this is an odd place for the plain style to have taken us, a place where there can be radical disagreement about what is being said. "A close, naked, natural way of speaking," Sprat had written: "positive expressions, clear senses . . . thus bringing all things as near to the mathematical plainness as they can." That is terminology to depict a restored Eden, before both Babel and Cicero, when Adam's primal language could not be misunderstood, when words could not possibly say (as Swift mischievously put it) "the thing that was not." That was when Adam delved and Eve span, and they both had the virtues of merchants and artisans—as it were, Wigan virtues.

But the serpent misled them, no doubt employing the high style. and what their descendants have been discovering is that not even the plain style can effect a return to any simulacrum of Paradise. Any spokesman for political decencies desires the Peaceable Kingdom. Books like *Animal Farm* and *Nineteen Eighty-Four* can go awry. *Gulliver's Travels* does; it ends with the hero-narrator longing vainly to be a horse. What the masters of the plain style demonstrate is how futile is anyone's hope of subduing humanity to an austere ideal. Straightness will prove crooked, gain will be short-term, vision will be fabrication and simplicity an intricate contrivance. Likewise, no probity, no sincerity, can ever subdue the inner contradictions of speaking plainly. These inhere in the warp of reality, ineluctable as the fact that the square root of two is irrational. Swift is called mad, Orwell was reviled for betraying the left, and by divulging the secret of the root of two, which was sacred to the Pythagoreans, a Greek named Hippasos earned a watery grave.

27

REPORTS, INFERENCES, JUDGMENTS

S. I. Hayakawa

To exchange information, the basic symbolic act is the *report* of what we have seen, heard, or felt: "It is raining." "You can get those at the hardware store for $2.75." "The solution contains .02% iodine." "The gross profits for December were $253,876.98." We also frequently rely on reports of reports: "The National Weather Service says a tropical storm is developing in the Gulf of Mexico." "According to the Timberlake report, the company lost 23% of its sales in the first quarter of this year." "The papers say there was a four-car accident on Highway 41 near Evansville." Reports adhere to the following rules: first, they are *verifiable*; second, they exclude, as far as possible, *inferences, judgments*, and the use of "*loaded*" words. (These terms will be discussed later.)

VERIFIABILITY

Reports are verifiable. For example, the price of the item at the hardware store may have increased; we could verify the price by calling the store. We can analyze the solution ourselves to verify the percentage of iodine. We could audit the company's books. Sometimes, of course, we may not be able to verify the report's content ourselves. We may not be able to drive to Evansville to see the physical evidence of the crash; we may not

S. I. Hayakawa and Alan R. Hayakawa, "Reports, Inferences, Judgments," Chapter 3 of *Language in Thought and Action* (fifth edition), (New York: Harcourt, 1990). © 1989. Reprinted with permission of Heinle, a division of Thomson Learning: *www.thomsonrights.com*.

have access to the Timberlake report. Nevertheless, the nature of the report is such that, given the proper resources, it can be verified—or, if inaccurate, it can be invalidated.

Even in a world like today's, in which everybody seems to be fighting everyone else, *we still, to a surprising degree, trust each other's reports*. We have agreed to agree, even if roughly, on the names of many things: on what constitutes a "meter," "yard," "bushel," and so on, and on how to measure time. As a result, much of daily life proceeds with little danger of our misunderstanding each other. To a surprising degree, we trust each other's reports. We ask directions of total strangers when we are traveling. We follow directions on road signs without being suspicious of the people who put the signs up. We read books of information about science, mathematics, automotive engineering, travel, geography, the history of costume, and other such factual matters, and we usually assume that the author is doing her best to tell us as truly as she can what she knows. And we are safe in so assuming most of the time. With the interest given today to the discussion of biased reporting and propaganda, and the general mistrust of many of the communications we receive, we are likely to forget that we still have an enormous amount of reliable information available and that deliberate misinformation, except in warfare, still is more the exception than the rule. The desire for self-preservation that compelled people to evolve means for the exchange of information also compels them to regard the giving of false information as profoundly reprehensible.

At its highest development, the language of reports is known as science. By "highest development" we mean greatest general usefulness. Presbyterian and Catholic, worker and capitalist, German and Englishman, *agree* on the meanings of such symbols as $2 \times 2 = 4$, $100°C$, HNO_3, *Quercus agrifolia*, and so on. But how, it may be asked, can there be agreement even about this much among people who are at each other's throats about practically everything else?

The answer is that circumstances *compel them to agree*, whether they wish to or not. If, for example, there were a dozen different religious sects in the United States, each insisting on its own way of naming the time of the day and the days of the year, the necessity of having a dozen different calendars, a dozen different kinds of watches, and a dozen sets of schedules for business hours, trains, and television programs, to say nothing of the effort that would be required for translating terms from one nomenclature to another, would make life as we know it impossible.

The language of reports, then, including the more precise reports of science, is "map" language, and because it gives us reasonably accurate representations of the "territory," it enables us to get work done. Such language may often be what is commonly termed dull or uninteresting reading; one does not usually read logarithmic tables or telephone directories for entertainment. But we could not get along without them. There are numberless occasions in the talking and writing we do in everyday life that require that we state things *in such a way that everybody will agree with our formulation*.

INFERENCES

Writing reports is an effective means of increasing linguistic awareness. Practice in writing reports will constantly provide examples of the principles of language and interpretation under discussion. The reports should be about firsthand experience—scenes the reader has witnessed, meetings and social events he has taken part in, people he knows well. The reports should be of such a nature that they can be verified and agreed upon. For the purposes of the exercise, inferences are to be excluded.

Not that inferences are not important. In everyday life and in science, we rely as much on inferences as on reports. Nevertheless, it is important to be able to distinguish between them.

An inference, as we shall use the term, is *a statement about the unknown based on the known*. On an elementary level, the difference between a report and an inference is demonstrated in the following statement: "He's afraid of women." This statement does not report; it draws an inference from some set of observable data: "He blushes and stammers whenever a woman speaks to him. He never speaks to women at parties."

In some areas of thought, such as geology, paleontology and nuclear physics, reports are the foundations, but inferences—and inferences upon inferences—form the main body of the science. For example, a geologist may use the facts from a report to advise an oil company whether or not to drill in a particular place. The geologist infers from the report that there is oil. A physician making an initial diagnosis examines a patient's symptoms, then makes an inference about an intestinal condition that cannot be seen.

In short, inferences are extremely important. We may infer from the material and cut of a woman's clothes the nature of her wealth or social position; we may infer from the character of the ruins the origin of the fire that destroyed the building; we may infer the nature of the Soviet Union's geopolitical strategy from its actions across the globe; we may infer from the shape of land the path of a prehistoric glacier; we may infer from a halo on an unexposed photographic plate that it has been in the vicinity of radioactive materials.

Inferences may be carefully or carelessly made. They may be made on the basis of a broad background of previous experience with the subject matter or with no experience at all. For example, the inferences a good mechanic can make about the condition of an engine by listening to it are often startlingly accurate, while the inferences made by an amateur may be entirely wrong.

In any case, the common characteristic of inferences is that they are statements about matters that are not directly known, made on the basis of what has been observed. Generally speaking, the quality of inference is directly related to the quality of the report or observations from which it stems and to the abilities of the one making the inference.

JUDGMENTS

Another barrier to clear thinking is the confusion of reports and judgments. By judgments we shall mean expressions of the speaker's approval or disapproval of the occurrences, persons, or objects he is describing. To say, "It is a wonderful car" is not a report; to say, "It has been driven 50,000 miles without requiring repairs" is a report. "Jack lied to us" is a judgment, while "Jack said he didn't have the car keys, but later, when he pulled a handkerchief out of his pocket, the keys fell out" is a report. Similarly, when a newspaper says, "The senator has been stubborn, uncooperative, and defiant," or "The senator courageously stood by his principles," the paper is judging and evaluating rather than reporting.

Many people would regard statements like the following as statements of "fact": "Mary lied to us," "Jerry is a thief," "Robin is clever." As ordinarily employed, however, the word "lied" involves first an inference (that Mary knew otherwise and deliberately misstated the facts) and second a judgment (that the speaker disapproves of what he infers that Mary did). To say, "Jerry was convicted of theft and served two years in San Quentin" is a verifiable report—we could look up the court and prison records. To say a man is a "thief" is to say in effect, "He has stolen *and will steal again*"—which is more a prediction than a report. Even to say, "He has stolen" is to make an inference and simultaneously to pass a judgment on an act about which there may have been a difference of opinion based on the evidence at the time.

Verifiability rests upon the external observation of facts, not upon the heaping up of judgments. If one person says, "Peter is a deadbeat," and another says, "I think so, too," the statement has not been verified. In court cases, considerable trouble is sometimes caused by witnesses who cannot distinguish their judgments from the facts on which those judgments are based. Cross-examinations under these circumstances go something like this:

WITNESS: That scumbag ripped me off.

DEFENSE ATTORNEY: Your honor, I object.

JUDGE: Objection sustained. (Witness's remark is stricken from the record.) Now, try to tell the court exactly what happened.

WITNESS: He ripped me off, the dirty scum.

DEFENSE ATTORNEY: Your honor, I object. (The remark is again stricken.)

JUDGE: Sustained. Will the witness try to stick to the facts?

WITNESS: But I'm telling you the facts, your honor. He did rip me off.

This can continue indefinitely unless the cross-examiner exercises some ingenuity in order to get at the facts behind the judgment. To the witness it is a "fact" that he was "ripped off." Often, long, patient questioning is required before the factual bases of the judgment are revealed.

Of course, many words simultaneously report and judge. For the kind of strict reporting discussed here, these should be avoided. Instead of "sneaked in," one might say "entered quietly"; instead of "politicians," "candidates"; instead of "bureaucrat," "public official"; instead of "bum," "homeless person"; instead of "crackpots," "holders of unconventional views." A newspaper reporter may not write, "A crowd of suckers came to listen to Senator Smith last evening in that rickety firetrap and ex-dive that disfigures the south side of town," but rather, "Between 75 and 100 people heard an address last evening by Senator Smith at the Evergreen Gardens near the southern city limits."

HOW JUDGMENTS STOP THOUGHT

A judgment ("He is a fine boy," "It was a beautiful service," "Baseball is a healthful sport," "She is an awful bore") is a *conclusion*, evaluating a number of previously observed facts. The reader is probably familiar with the fact that many students, when called upon to write "themes," have difficulty in writing papers of the required length because their ideas give out after a paragraph or two. Often, the reason is that those early paragraphs contain so many such judgments that there is little left to be said. When the conclusions are carefully excluded, however, and observed facts are given instead, there is never any trouble about the length of papers; in fact, they tend to become too long, since inexperienced writers, when told to give facts, often give more than are necessary.

Still another consequence of judgments early in the course of a written exercise—and this applies also to hasty judgments in everyday thought—is the temporary blindness they induce. When, for example, a discussion starts with the words, "He was a real Wall Street executive," "She was a typical yuppie," or "Ernest Hemingway was a sexist who had little idea how to portray women in his fiction," the writer must make all later statements consistent with those judgments. The result is that all the individual characteristics of this particular "executive," "yuppie," or even Hemingway as a unique writer with a unique stance toward women are lost entirely; and the rest of the essay is likely to deal not with observed facts, but with the writer's *private notion* (based on previously read stories, movies, pictures, etc.) of what "Wall Street executives" or "yuppies" are like. Premature judgment often prevents us from seeing what is directly in front of us. Even a writer sure at the beginning of a written exercise that the man being described is a "redneck" or that the scene is a "beautiful residential suburb" will conscientiously keep such notions out of his head, lest his vision be obstructed.

SNARL-WORDS AND PURR-WORDS

Language is not an isolated phenomenon. Our concern is with language in action—in the full context of nonlinguistic events which are its setting. The making of noises, like other muscle activities, is sometimes involuntary. Our responses to powerful stimuli, such as to things that make us very angry, are a complex of muscular and physiological events: the contracting of fighting muscles, the increase of blood pressure, a change in body chemistry, *and* the making of noises such as growls and snarls. We are a little too dignified, perhaps, to growl like dogs, but we do the next best thing and substitute series of words such as "You dirty sneak!" "The filthy scum!" Similarly, if we are pleasurably agitated, we may, instead of purring or wagging the tail, say things like "She's the sweetest little girl in all the world!"

Such statements have less to do with reporting the outside world than they do with our inadvertently reporting the state of our internal world; they are the human equivalents of snarling and purring. On hearing "She's the sweetest girl in the whole world," the listener would be wise to allocate the meaning correctly—as a revelation of the speaker's state of mind and not as a revelation about the girl.

Although this observation may seem obvious, it is surprising how often, when such a statement is made, both the speaker and the hearer feel that something has been said about the girl. This error is especially common in the interpretation of utterances of orators and editorialists in some of their more excited denunciations of "leftists," "fascists," "Wall Street," "right-wingers," and in their glowing support of "our way of life." Constantly, because of the impressive sound of the words, the elaborate structure of the sentences, and the appearance of intellectual progression, we get the feeling that something is being said about something. On closer examination, however, we discover that these utterances really say "What I hate ('liberals,' 'Wall Street,') I hate very, very much," and "What I like ('our way of life') I like very, very much." We may call such utterances *snarl-words* and *purr-words*.

On the other hand, if the snarl-words and purr-words are accompanied by verifiable reports (which would also mean that we have previously agreed as to what specifically is meant by the terms used), we might find reason to accept the emotional position of the speaker or writer. But snarl-words and purr-words as such, unaccompanied by verifiable reports, offer nothing further to discuss, except possibly the question "Why do you feel as you do?"

Issues like gun control, abortion, capital punishment, and elections often lead us to resort to the equivalent of snarl-words and purr-words. It is usually fruitless to argue such statements as "Reagan was the great Teflon president—nothing stuck," "She is anti-life," "Wagner's music is just a cacophony of hysterical screeching," "People who don't want to control the purchase of handguns are nuts." To take sides on such issues phrased in such judgmental ways is to reduce communication to a level of stubborn imbecility. But to ask questions relating to the statements (Why do you like or dislike President Reagan? Why are you for or against gun control?) is to learn something about the beliefs of others. After listening to their opinions and the reasons for them, we may leave the discussion slightly wiser, slightly better informed, and perhaps less one-sided than we were before the discussion began.

SLANTING

Not all forms of judgments are as direct as the ones discussed above. In the course of writing reports, despite all efforts to keep judgments out, some will creep in. An account of a man, for example, may read like this:

> "He had apparently not shaved for several days, and his face and hands were covered with grime. His shoes were torn, and his coat, which was several sizes too small for him, was spotted with dried clay."

Though no judgment has been directly stated, one is obviously implied. Let us contrast this with another description of the same man:

> "Although his face was bearded and neglected, his eyes were clear, and he looked straight ahead as he walked rapidly down the road. He seemed very tall; perhaps the fact that his coat was too small for him emphasized that impression. He was carrying a book under his left arm, and a small terrier ran at his heels."

In this example, the impression about the man is considerably changed, simply by the inclusion of new details and the subordination of unfavorable ones. Even if explicit judgments are kept out of one's writing, implied judgments will get in.

How, then, can we ever give an impartial report? The answer is, of course, that we cannot attain complete impartiality while we use the language of everyday life. Even with the very impersonal language of science, the task is sometimes difficult. Nevertheless, we can, by being aware of the favorable or unfavorable feelings that certain words and facts can arouse, attain enough impartiality for practical purposes. Such awareness enables us *to balance implied favorable and unfavorable judgments against each other*. To learn to do this, it is a good idea to write *two* essays at a time on the same subject, both strict reports, to be read side by side: the first to contain facts and details likely to prejudice the reader in favor of the subject, the second to contain those likely to prejudice the reader against it. For example:

FOR	AGAINST
He had white teeth.	His teeth were uneven.
His eyes were blue, his hair blond and abundant.	He rarely looked people straight in the eye.
He had on a clean blue shirt.	His shirt was frayed at the cuffs.
He often helped his wife with the dishes.	He rarely got through drying the dishes without breaking a few.
His pastor spoke very highly of him.	His grocer said he was always slow about paying his bills.
He liked dogs.	He disliked children.

This process of selecting details that are favorable or unfavorable to the subject being described may be termed *slanting*. Slanting gives no explicit judgments, but it differs from reporting in that it deliberately or inadvertently makes certain judgments inescapable. One-sided or biased slanting, not uncommon in private gossip and backbiting and all too common in the "interpretive reporting" of newspapers and magazines, can be described as a technique of lying without actually telling any lies.

DISCOVERING ONE'S BIAS

When a news account tells a story in a way we dislike, leaving out facts we think important and playing up others in a way we think unfair, we are tempted to say, "Look how unfairly they've slanted the story!" Such a statement, of course, is an inference about the story's reporters and editors. We are assuming that what seems important or unimportant to us is equally weighty or trivial to them, and on the basis of that assumption we infer that the writers and editors "deliberately" gave the story a misleading emphasis. Is this necessarily the case? Can the reader, as an outsider, determine whether a story assumes a given form because the editors "deliberately slanted it that way" or because that was the way the events appeared to them?

The point is that, by the process of selection and abstraction imposed on us by our own interests and background, experience comes to all of us—including editors—already "slanted." What is important to a 50-year-old suburban lawyer will likely be different from what is important to a 20-year-old, unemployed, inner-city parent.

The writer who is neither an advocate nor an opponent avoids slanting, except in search of special literary effects. The avoidance of slanting is not only a matter of being impartial; it is even more importantly a matter of making good maps of the territory of experience. The profoundly biased individual cannot make good maps because she can see an enemy *only* as an enemy and a friend *only* as a friend. The individual with genuine skill in writing—and in thinking—can with imagination and insight look at the same subject from many points of view. . . .

28

THE NARRATIVE TRADITION

Robert Scholes
Robert Kellog

For the past two centuries the dominant form of narrative literature in the West has been the novel. In writing about the Western narrative tradition we will in one sense, therefore, necessarily be describing the heritage of the novel. But it will not be our intention to view the novel as the final product of an ameliorative evolution, as the perfected form which earlier kinds of narrative—sacred myth, folktale, epic, romance, legend, allegory, confession, satire—were all striving, with varying degrees of success, to become. Instead, our intention will be almost the opposite. We hope to put the novel in its place, to view the nature of narrative and the Western narrative tradition whole, seeing the novel as only one of a number of narrative possibilities. In order to attempt this it has been necessary to take long views, to rush into literary areas where we can claim some interest and competence but not the deep knowledge of the specialist, and perhaps to generalize overmuch in proportion to the evidence we present. For these and other excesses and exuberances, we apologize, hoping only that the result will justify our temerity in having undertaken such an elaborate project.

The object of this study of narrative art is not to set a new vogue, in either literature or criticism, but to provide an antidote to all narrow views of literature, ancient or modern. In any age in which criticism flourishes, and ours is certainly such an age, a conflict between broad and narrow approaches to literary art is sure to arise. An age of criticism is a self-conscious age. Its tendency is to formulate rules, to attempt the reduction of art to science, to classify, to categorize, and finally to prescribe and proscribe. Theoretical criticism of this sort is usually based on the practice of certain authors, whose works become classics in the worst sense of the word: models of approved and proper literary performance. This kind of narrowing down of the literature of the past to a few "classic" models amounts to the construction of an artificial literary tradition. Our purpose in this work is to present an alternative to narrowly conceived views of one major kind of literature—which we have called narrative.

By narrative we mean all those literary works which are distinguished by two characteristics: the presence of a story and a story-teller. A drama is a story without a story-teller; in it characters act out directly what Aristotle called an "imitation" of such action as we find in life. A lyric, like a drama, is a direct presentation, in which a single actor, the poet or his surrogate, sings, or muses, or speaks for us to hear or overhear. Add a second speaker, as Robert Frost does in "The Death of the Hired Man," and we move toward drama. Let the speaker begin to tell of an event, as Frost does in "The Vanishing Red," and we move toward narrative. For writing to be narrative no more and no less than a teller and a tale are required.

There is a real tradition of narrative literature in the Western world. All art is traditional in that artists learn their craft from their predecessors to a great extent. They begin by conceiving of the possibilities open to them in terms of the achievements they are acquainted with. They may add to the tradition, opening up new possibilities for their successors, but they begin, inevitably, within a tradition. The more aware we are—as readers, critics, or artists—of the fullness and breadth of the narrative tradition, the freer and the sounder will be the critical or artistic choices we make. For mid-twentieth-century readers a specific problem must be overcome before a balanced view of the narrative tradition becomes attainable. Something must be done about our veneration of the novel as a literary form.

With Joyce, Proust, Mann, Lawrence, and Faulkner, the narrative literature of the twentieth century has begun the gradual break with the narrative literature of the immediate past that characterizes all living literary traditions. Specifically, twentieth-century narrative has begun to break away from the aims, attitudes, and techniques of realism. The implications of this break are still being explored, developed, and projected by many of the most interesting living writers of narrative literature in Europe and America. But, by and large, our reviewers are hostile to this new literature and our critics are unprepared for it, for literary criticism is also influenced by its conception of tradition.

Rather than pick out one or a dozen reviewers to exemplify the hostility of contemporary criticism to much that is best in contemporary narrative art, we can take as an example a great scholar and critic, whose views are now acknowledged to be among the most influential in our graduate schools of literature (where the teachers, critics, and even the reviewers of the future are being developed) and whose attitude toward modern literature, for all the learning and sensitivity with which he presents it, is suprisingly similar to that of the most philistine weekly reviews. This scholar-critic is Erich Auerbach, whose book *Mimesis*, in its paperback, English language version, is one of the two or three most widely read and currently influential books in its field. And its field is a broad one: Western narrative literature. It is a great book, but Auerbach's single-minded devotion to realistic principles leaves him unwilling or unable to come to terms with twentieth-century fiction, and especially with such writers as Virginia Woolf, Proust, and Joyce. He finds *Ulysses* a "hodgepodge," characterized by "its blatant and painful cynicism, and its uninterpretable symbolism," and he asserts that along with it, "most of the other novels which employ multiple reflection of consciousness also leave the reader with an impression of hopelessness. There is often something confusing, something hazy about them, something hostile to the reality which they represent."

Auerbach's dissatisfaction with post-realistic fiction is echoed by the dissatisfactions of lesser men, which we meet on nearly every page of current literary reviews and journals, where much of the best contemporary writing is treated with hostility or indifference. And current attitudes toward contemporary literature also carry over into current attitudes toward the literature of the past. The tendency to apply the standards of nineteenth-century realism to all fiction naturally has disadvantages for our understanding of every other kind of narrative. Spenser, Chaucer, and Wolfram von Eschenbach suffer from the "novelistic" approach as much as Proust, Joyce, Durrell, and Beckett do. In order to provide a broader alternative to the novelistic approach to narrative, we must break down many of the chronological, linguistic, and narrowly conceived generic categories frequently employed in the discussion of narrative. We must consider the elements common to all narrative forms—oral and written, verse and prose, factual and fictional—as these forms actually developed in the Western world. While fairly rare, an undertaking of this sort is not without precedent.

Such, in fact, was the aim of the first book in English wholly devoted to the study of the narrative tradition, Clara Reeve's *The Progress of Romance through Times, Countries, and Manners*, which was published in 1785. Clara Reeve, confronted by the common eighteenth-century prejudice against romance, endeavored to provide a pedigree for the form, to show especially that "the ancients" employed it, and to distinguish it from its follower, the novel, without prejudice to either form. Her distinction, indeed, is the one preserved in our dictionaries today, and it is still employed by critics who make any pretensions to discriminating among narrative forms:

> I will attempt this distinction, and I presume if it is properly done it will be followed,—if not, you are but where you were before. The Romance is an heroic fable, which treats of fabulous persons and things.—The Novel is a picture of real life and manners, and of the times in which it is written. The Romance in lofty and elevated language, describes what never happened nor is likely to happen.—The Novel gives a familiar relation of such things, as pass every day before our eyes, such as may happen to our friend, or to ourselves; and the perfection of it, is to represent every scene, in so easy and natural a manner, and to make them appear so probable, as to deceive us into a persuasion (at least while we are reading) that all is real, until we are affected by the joys or distresses of the persons in the story, as if they were our own.

Along with this clear and useful formulation, Miss Reeve made halfhearted attempts at some other categories: a miscellaneous group of "original or uncommon" stories, which included such "modern" works as *Gulliver's Travels*, *Robinson Crusoe*, *Tristram Shandy*, and *The Castle of Otranto*; and another class of "tales and fables," which included everything from fairy tales to *Rasselas*. She also struggled with the problem of separating the Epic from the Romance, tackling such formidable considerations as the Ossianic question. (She hesitated, saying *Fingal* was "an Epic, but not a Poem" and finally located Ossian with the romances.) She made it clear throughout that a romance might be in either verse or prose, but felt that an epic must be poetical. She was also disposed to think of epic as a term of praise, so that a really fine poetic romance such as Chaucer's Knight's Tale (the example is hers) would deserve the title of epic.

For her time, and considering the limits of her education, Clara Reeve was astonishingly well informed and free from prejudice. Her veneration for "the ancients" and her moralistic approach to literary achievement were shared by greater minds than her own. Until quite recently, in fact, very few attempts to deal with narrative literature in her comprehensive way have been made; and her knowledge, balance, and good sense would benefit many a modern book reviewer, could he attain them. Still, the difficulties Clara Reeve encountered in 1785 may be instructive for us in the present. After novel and romance she had trouble reducing other narrative forms to order—and so have modern critics. But even more troublesome is her tendency to attach a value judgment to a descriptive term like "epic." One of the greatest difficulties arising in modern criticism stems from a tendency to confuse descriptive and evaluative terminology. "Tragic" and "realistic," for example, are normally applied to literary works as terms of praise. Such usage can be found in the book and theater review pages of nearly any of our periodicals. A serious drama can be damned for its failure to be "tragic." A narrative can be damned as "unrealistic." But the greatest obstacle to an understanding of narrative literature in our day is the way notions of value have clustered around the word "novel" itself. One reason Clara Reeve could see the progress of romance with such a relatively unprejudiced eye was the fact that she lived before the great century of the realistic novel, the nineteenth.

But now, in the middle of the twentieth century, our view of narrative literature is almost hopelessly novel-centered. The expectations which readers bring to narrative literary works are based on their experience with the novel. Their assumptions about what a narrative should be are derived from their understanding of the novel. And this is true whether the reader is a professor of contemporary literature or a faithful subscriber to one of those ladies' magazines which regale their readers with contemporary fiction. The very word "novel" has become a term of praise when applied to earlier narratives. We are told on dust-jackets and paperback covers that such diverse works as Chaucer's *Troilus and Criseyde*, Geoffrey of Monmouth's *History of the Kings of Britain*, and Homer's *Odyssey* are "the first novel." But if we take these designations seriously, we are bound to be disappointed. Judged as a "novelist" even Homer must be found wanting.

The novel-centered view of narrative literature is an unfortunate one for two important reasons. First, it cuts us off from the narrative literature of the past and the culture of the past. Second, it cuts us off from the literature of the future and even from the advance guard of our own day. To recapture the past and to accept the future we must, literally, put the novel in its place. To do this we need not part with any of our appreciation of realistic fiction. When the novel is in its place the achievements of such as Balzac, Flaubert, Turgenev, Tolstoy, and George Eliot will not lose any of their luster. They may even shine more brightly.

The novel, let us remember, represents only a couple of centuries in the continuous narrative tradition of the Western world which can be traced back five thousand years. Two hundred years of considerable achievement, of course; modern Europe has nothing to be ashamed of where its production of narrative literature is concerned, whatever its failings in other spheres; but still, only two hundred years out of five thousand. The purpose of this study is to examine some of the lines of continuity in this five-thousand-year tradition by considering some of the varieties of narrative literature, by discerning patterns in the historical development of narrative forms, and by examining continuing or recurring elements in narrative art. Our task is incomparably easier than Clara Reeve's. Though the need for a broad approach to narrative art is as pressing now as it was in 1785, the intellectual developments of the intervening years have brought many more of the necessary tools to hand.

From various sources we have learned more in the last hundred years about the prehistory of literature and about pre-modern literature than was ever known before. Vital information that was simply not available to the literary historians and critics of the eighteenth and nineteenth centuries is now available to us. The anthropologists, beginning with Frazer in *The Golden Bough*, have given us priceless information about the relationship between literature and culture in primitive society, opening the way to such literary studies as Jessie Weston's *From Ritual to Romance*. The psychologists—Jung even more than Freud—have given us equally important insights into the ways in which literature is related to an individual's mental processes, making possible a new and fruitful school (despite some excesses) of literary studies—archetypal criticism. The students of oral literature, such as Parry and Lord, have enabled us for the first time to perceive how written and oral literatures are differentiated and what the oral heritage of written narrative actually is. Literary scholars like the classicists Murray and Cornford and the Hebraist Theodore Gaster have shown ways in which some of the new extra-literary knowledge can enhance our understanding of literature. Historians of art and literature, such as Erwin Panofsky and D. W. Robertson, Jr., have made the attitudes and world view of our cultural ancestors more intelligible to us than ever before. And such a brilliant critical synthesizer as Northrop Frye has shown us how it is possible to unite cultural and literary study in such a way as to approach closer to a complete theory of literature than ever before.

Deriving what we could from the example as well as from the techniques and discoveries of such men as these, we have attempted to formulate a theory which would, as clearly and economically as possible, account for the varieties of narrative form and the processes that produce them and govern their interrelationships. Faced with the facts of history, with the various kinds of narrative which have been recognized and classified —often according to different and conflicting systems—and with the "influences," affinities, and correspondences which have been observed, we have tried to do justice to both the intractabilities of fact and the mind's lust for system and order. Our results, with their full and proper range of illustrations and qualifications, are developed in the following chapters. In the remainder of this chapter, we offer a kind of "argument" or gloss for the more elaborate exposition to come. It is a minimal, stripped-down version of our view of the narrative tradition, representing not *a priori* convictions which have shaped our study but rather a pattern we found emerging in the course of it.

The evolution of forms within the narrative tradition is a process analogous in some ways to biological evolution. Man, considering himself the end of an evolutionary process, naturally sees evolution as a struggle toward perfection. The dinosaur, could he speak, might have another opinion. Similarly, a contemporary novelist can see himself as the culmination of an ameliorative evolution; but Homer, could he speak, might disagree. Yet the epic poem is as dead as the dinosaur. We can put together a synthetic epic with a superficial resemblance to the originals, just as we can fabricate a museum dinosaur; but the conditions which produced the originals have passed. God will never recover that lost innocence which He displayed in the creation of those beautiful monsters, nor will man ever again be able to combine so innocently materials drawn from myth and history, from experience and imagination.

Of course, the evolutionary analogy breaks down. The *Iliad* is as great a wonder as a live dinosaur would be. Individual literary works do not always die off, though their forms may cease to be viable. Nor is their reproduction a matter of natural selection. Literary evolution is in some ways more complex than biological evolution. It is a kind of cross between a biological and a dialectical process, in which different species sometimes combine to produce new hybrids, which can in turn combine with other old or new forms; and in which one type will beget its antitype, which in turn may combine with other forms or synthesize with its antitypical originator.

To find a satisfactory means of ordering and presenting the complex processes at work in the evolution of narrative forms is a difficult task. The solution here presented is a compromise between the chaotic and the schematic. It is not offered as a simulacrum of the actual conscious or unconscious mental processes of narrative artists but as a handy way of reducing such processes to manageable terms. Its main purpose is to reveal, by clarifying them, the principal relationships which do exist and have existed historically among the major forms of narrative literature.

Written narrative literature tends to make its appearance throughout the Western world under similar conditions. It emerges from an oral tradition, maintaining many of the characteristics of oral narrative for some time. It often takes that form of heroic, poetic narrative which we call epic. Behind the epic lie a variety of narrative forms, such as sacred myth, quasi-historical legend, and fictional folktale, which have coalesced into a traditional narrative which is an amalgam of myth, history, and fiction. For us, the most important aspect of early written narrative is the fact of the tradition itself. The epic story-teller is telling a traditional story. The primary impulse which moves him is not a historical one, nor a creative one; it is *re*-creative. He is retelling a traditional story, and therefore his primary allegiance is not to fact, not to truth, not to entertainment, but to the *mythos* itself—the story as preserved in the tradition which the epic story-teller is re-creating. The word *mythos* meant precisely this in ancient Greece: a traditional story.

In the transmission of traditional narrative it is of necessity the outline of events, the plot, which is transmitted. Plot is, in every sense of the word, the articulation of the skeleton of narrative. A myth, then, is a traditional plot which can be transmitted. Aristotle saw plot (*mythos* is his word) as the soul of any literary work that was an imitation of an action. Sacred myth, a narrative form associated with religious ritual, is one kind of mythic narrative; but legend and folktale are also mythic in the sense of traditional, and so is the oral epic poem. One of the great developmental processes that is unmistakable in the history of written narrative has been the gradual movement away from narratives dominated by the mythic impulse to tell a story with a traditional plot. In Western literature we can trace this movement twice: once in the classical languages and again in the vernacular languages. In the course of this evolutionary process narrative literature tends to develop in two antithetical directions. A proper understanding of the growth of the two great branches of narrative which emerge as the traditional impulse declines in power is essential to a true appreciation of the evolution of narrative forms. To understand this development properly we must take into account both the nature of the separation between the two great branches of narrative and the interaction and recombination of the two.

The two antithetical types of narrative which emerge from the epic synthesis may be labeled the *empirical* and the *fictional*. Both can be seen as ways of avoiding the tyranny of the traditional in story-telling. Empirical narrative replaces allegiance to the *mythos* with allegiance to reality. We can subdivide the impulse toward empirical narrative into two main components: the *historical* and the *mimetic*. The historical component owes its allegiance specifically to truth of fact and to the actual past rather than to a traditional version of the past. It requires for its development means of accurate measurement in time and space, and concepts of causality referable to human and natural rather than to supernatural agencies. In the ancient world empirical narrative manifests itself first through its historical component as writers like Herodotus and Thucydides carefully distinguish their work from Homeric epic. The mimetic component owes its allegiance not to truth of fact but to truth of sensation and environment, depending on observation of the present rather than investigation of the past. It requires for its development sociological and psychological concepts of behavior and mental process, such as those which inform the characterization of the Alexandrian Mime. Mimetic forms are the slowest of narrative forms to develop. In the ancient world we find the strongest mimetic elements in the Theophrastian Character (a narrative counterpart of the dramatic Mime), in such a realistic "idyll" as Theocritus' *Adoniazusae* (No. 15), and in such a passage as the Dinner at Trimalchio's in Petronius. Mimetic narrative is the antithesis of mythic in that it tends toward plotlessness. Its ultimate form is the "slice of life." Biography and autobiography are both empirical forms of narrative. In biography, which is developed first, the historical impulse dominates; in autobiography, the mimetic.

The *fictional* branch of narrative replaces allegiance to the *mythos* with allegiance to the ideal. We can subdivide the impulse toward fictional narrative into two main components also: the *romantic* and the *didactic*. The writer of fiction is set free from the bonds of tradition and the bonds of empiricism as well. His eye is not on the external world but on the audience, which he hopes to delight or instruct, giving it either what it wants or what he thinks it needs. While empirical narrative aims at one or another kind of truth, fictional narrative aims at either beauty or goodness. The world of romance is the ideal world, in which poetic justice prevails and all the arts and adornments of language are used to embellish the narrative. Where mimetic narrative aims at a psychological reproduction of mental process, romantic narrative presents thought in the form of rhetoric. As the general titles of the two great branches of narrative imply (empirical and fictional) they represent, within the world of narrative literature, an opposition akin to the scientific and the artistic approaches to ultimate truth. In the ancient world, Greek romance, with its alliance between the rhetorical and the erotic, typifies romantic narrative. In the movement from the *Odyssey* to the *Argonautica* we can see the epic becoming more literary and fictional, moving toward such pure romance as the *Aethiopica*. In a modern language such a progression as the *Chanson de Roland*, Chrétien's *Perceval*, and the *Grand Cyrus* reveals the same pattern of evolution.

The didactic subdivision of fiction we may call *fable*, a form which is ruled by an intellectual and moral impulse as romance is ruled by an esthetic one. The human intellect being what it is, fable tends toward brevity in narrative, and is inclined to lean heavily on romance for narrative articulation if the narrative artist has anything like a sustained flight in mind. Aesop's fables are typical of the form, but in its usual combination with romance Xenophon's *Cyropaedia* and the narrative allegories of the Middle Ages and Renaissance are major examples. So-called Menippean satire is fable combined with anti-romance, Lucian's *True History* beginning as a parody of Odysseus' adventures. Literary epic moves from romantic to didactic narrative in Vergil, who did not become Dante's guide in the *Commedia* by accident. Didactic and romantic narrative seek one another out for mutual support and for justification in the face of attacks such as Plato's attack on poetry in the *Republic*. Sidney's *Defense* of literature is made from the fictional side of the great division we have been considering. He defends literature as presenting an ideal, or "golden," world and as instructing through delight. But Fielding's account of his practice in his Preface to *Joseph Andrews* and elsewhere is made from the empirical side of the line, on the basis of his work's truth to general human nature, though he certainly intended to provide delight and instruction as well.

We have been considering the breakdown of the epic synthesis into two antithetical components. We must now consider briefly the new synthesis in narrative which has been the main development in post-Renaissance narrative literature. This was a gradual process, beginning at least as early as Boccaccio, but it is most obviously discernible in Europe during the seventeenth and eighteenth centuries. The new synthesis can be seen clearly in a writer like Cervantes, whose great work is an attempt to reconcile powerful empirical and fictional impulses. From the synthesis he effected, the novel emerges as a literary form. The novel is not the opposite of romance, as is usually maintained, but a product of the reunion of the empirical and fictional elements in narrative literature. Mimesis (which tends to short forms like the Character and "slice of life") and history (which can become too scientific and cease to be literature) combine in the novel with romance and fable, even as primitive legend, folktale, and sacred myth originally combined in the epic, to produce a great and synthetic literary form. There are signs that in the twentieth century the grand dialectic is about to begin again, and that the novel must yield its place to new forms just as the epic did in ancient times, for it is an unstable compound, inclining always to break down into its constituent elements. The disintegration of the novel is much too complicated to consider here in detail, but we can note that it is reflected in the extreme measures taken by such as Joyce and Proust to counteract it, in the return to romance of Isak Dinesen and Lawrence Durrell, in the reduction of naturalism to absurdity by Samuel Beckett, in the rise of science fiction and the nightmare novels of Céline and Hawkes, and even in the best-seller list, which tends to fragment into sociological narrative and spy-adventure tales, Mary McCarthy and Ian Fleming inevitably reminding us of fiction's ancient heritage from Theophrastian Character and Greek romance.

In its instability the novel partakes of the general nature of narrative. Poised between the direct speaker or singer of lyric and the direct presentation of action in drama; between allegiance to reality and to the ideal; it is capable of greater extremes than other forms of literary art, but pays the price for this capability in its capacity for imperfection. The least formal of disciplines, it offers a domain too broad for any single work to conquer, and it continually provokes literary compromise and subterfuge. The greatest narratives are inevitably those in which the most is attempted. Narrative literature provides, as William Faulkner observed, opportunities for cautious success or glorious failure. It has been, historically, the most various and changeable of literary disciplines, which means that it has been the most alive. For all its imperfections it has been—from the epic to the novel—the most popular and influential kind of literature, seeking the widest audience in its culture and being more responsive to extraliterary influences than other kinds of literature. It is this various, complex, and often contradictory nature of narrative art which we shall be exploring in the following chapters.

29

FROM *THE NEW JOURNALISM*

Tom Wolfe

THE FEATURE GAME

I doubt if many of the aces I will be extolling in this story went into journalism with the faintest notion of creating a "new" journalism, a "higher" journalism, or even a mildly improved variety. I know they never dreamed that anything they were going to write for newspapers or magazines would wreak such evil havoc in the literary world . . . causing a panic, dethroning the novel as the number one literary genre, starting the first new direction in American literature in half a century . . . Nevertheless, that is what has happened. Bellow, Barth, Updike—even the best of the lot, Philip Roth—the novelists are all out there right now ransacking the literary histories and sweating it out, wondering where they stand. Damn it all, Saul, the *Huns* have arrived . . .

God knows I didn't have anything new in mind, much less anything literary, when I took my first newspaper job. I had a fierce and unnatural craving for something else entirely. Chicago, 1928, that was the general idea . . . Drunken reporters out on the ledge of the *News* peeing into the Chicago River at dawn . . . Nights down at the saloon listening to "Back of the Yards" being sung by a baritone who was only a lonely blind bulldyke with lumps of milk glass for eyes . . . Nights down at the detective bureau—it was always nighttime in my daydreams of the newspaper life. Reporters didn't work during the day. I wanted the whole movie, nothing left out. . . .

I was aware of what had reduced me to this Student Prince Maudlin state of mind. All the same, I couldn't help it. I had just spent five years in graduate school, a statement that may mean nothing to people who never served such a stretch; it is the explanation, nonetheless. I'm not sure I can give you the remotest idea of what graduate school is like. Nobody ever has. Millions of Americans now go to graduate schools, but just say the phrase—"graduate school"—and what picture leaps into the brain? No picture, not even a blur. Half the people I knew in graduate school were going to write a novel about it. I thought about it myself. No one ever wrote such a book, as far as I know. Everyone used to sniff the air. How morbid! How poisonous! Nothing else like it in the world! But the subject always defeated them. It defied literary exploitation. Such a novel would be a study of frustration, but a form of frustration so exquisite, so ineffable, nobody could

Tom Wolfe, "The Feature Game," "Like a Novel," "Seizing the Power," Chapters 1, 2, and 3 of *The New Journalism*, Tom Wolfe and E. W. Johnson, eds. (New York: Harper and Row, 1973), 3–36. Copyright © 1973 by Tom Wolfe and E. W. Johnson. Reprinted by permission of HarperCollins Publishers Inc.

describe it. Try to imagine the worst part of the worst Antonioni movie you ever saw, or reading *Mr. Sammler's Planet* at one sitting, or just reading it, or being locked inside a Seaboard Railroad roomette, sixteen miles from Gainesville, Florida, heading north on the Miami-to-New York run, with no water and the radiator turning red in an amok psychotic overboil, and George McGovern sitting beside you telling you his philosophy of government. That will give you the general atmosphere.

In any case, by the time I received my doctorate in American studies in 1957 I was in the twisted grip of a disease of our times in which the sufferer experiences an overwhelming urge to join the "real world." So I started working for newspapers. In 1962, after a cup of coffee here and there, I arrived at the *New York Herald Tribune* . . . This must be the place! . . . I looked out across the city room of the *Herald Tribune*, 100 moldering yards south of Times Square, with a feeling of amazed bohemian bliss . . . Either this is the real world, Tom, or there is no real world . . . The place looked like the receiving bin at the Good Will . . . a promiscuous heap of junk . . . Wreckage and exhaustion everywhere . . . If somebody such as the city editor had a swivel chair, the universal joint would be broken, so that every time he got up, the seat would keel over as if stricken by a lateral stroke. All the intestines of the building were left showing in diverticulitic loops and lines—electrical conduits, water pipes, steam pipes, effluvium ducts, sprinkler systems, all of it dangling and grunting from the ceiling, the walls, the columns. The whole mess, from top to bottom, was painted over in an industrial sludge, Lead Gray, Subway Green, or that unbelievable dead red, that grim distemper of pigment and filth, that they paint the floor with in the tool and die works. On the ceiling were scalding banks of fluorescent lights, turning the atmosphere radium blue and burning bald spots in the crowns of the copy readers, who never moved. It was one big pie factory . . . A Landlord's Dream . . . There were no interior walls. The corporate hierarchy was not marked off into office spaces. The managing editor worked in a space that was as miserable and scabid as the lowest reporter's. Most newspapers were like that. This setup was instituted decades ago for practical reasons. But it was kept alive by a curious fact. On newspapers very few editorial employees at the bottom—namely, the reporters—had any ambition whatsoever to move up, to become city editors, managing editors, editors-in-chief, or any of the rest of it. Editors felt no threat from below. They needed no walls. Reporters didn't want much . . . merely to be *stars*! and of such minute wattage at that!

That was one thing they never wrote about in books on journalism or those comradely blind-bulldagger boots-upon-the-brass-rail swill-boar speakeasy memoirs about newspaper days and children of the century . . . namely, the little curlicues of newspaper status competition . . . For example, at the desk behind mine in the *Herald Tribune* city room sat Charles Portis. Portis was the original laconic cutup. At one point he was asked onto a kind of *Meet the Press* show with Malcolm X, and Malcolm X made the mistake of giving the reporters a little lecture before they went on about how he didn't want to hear anybody calling him "Malcolm," because he was not a dining-car waiter—his name happened to be "Malcolm X." By the end of the show Malcolm X was furious. He was climbing the goddamned acoustical tiles. The original laconic cutup, Portis, had invariably and continually addressed him as "Mr. X" . . . "Now, Mr. X, let me ask you this . . ." Anyway, Portis had the desk behind mine. Down in a bullpen at the far end of the room was Jimmy Breslin. Over to one side sat Dick Schaap. We were all engaged in a form of newspaper competition that I have never known anybody to even talk about in public. Yet Schaap had quit as city editor of the *New York Herald Tribune*, which was one of the legendary jobs in journalism—moved *down* the organizational chart, in other words—just to get in this secret game.

Everybody knows about one form of competition among newspaper reporters, the so-called *scoop* competition. Scoop reporters competed with their counterparts on other newspapers, or wire services, to see who could get a story first and write it fastest; the bigger the story—i.e., the more it had to do with the matters of power or catastrophe—the better. In short, they were concerned with the main business of the newspaper. But there was this other lot of reporters as well . . . They tended to be what is known as "feature writers." What they had in common was that they all regarded the newspaper as a motel you checked into overnight on the road to the final triumph. The idea was to get a job on a newspaper, keep body and soul together, pay the rent, get to know "the world," accumulate "experience," perhaps work some of the fat off your style—then, at some point, quit cold, say goodbye to journalism, move into a shack somewhere, work night and day for six months, and light up the sky with the final triumph. The final triumph was known as The Novel.

That was Someday, you understand . . . Meanwhile, these dreamboaters were in there banging away, in every place in America that had a newspaper, competing for a tiny crown the rest of the world wasn't even aware of: Best Feature Writer in Town. The "feature" was the newspaper term for a story that fell outside the category of hard news. It included everything from "brights," chuckly little items, often from the police beat . . . There was this out-of-towner who checked into a hotel in San Francisco last night, bent upon suicide, and he threw himself out of his fifth-story window—and fell nine feet and sprained his ankle. What he didn't know was—the hotel was on a steep hill! . . . to "human interest stories," long and often hideously sentimental accounts of hitherto unknown souls beset by tragedy or unusual hobbies within the sheet's circulation area . . . In any case, feature stories gave a man a certain amount of room in which to write.

Unlike the scoop reporters, the feature writers did not openly acknowledge the existence of their competition, not even to one another. Nor was there any sort of scorecard. And yet everyone in the game knew precisely what was going on and went through the most mortifying sieges of envy, even resentment, or else surges of euphoria, depending on how the game was going. No one would ever admit to such a thing, and yet all felt it, almost daily. The feature writers' arena differed from the scoop reporters' in another way. Your competition was not necessarily working for another publication. You were just as likely to be competing with people on your own paper, which meant you were even less likely to talk about it.

So here was half the feature competition in New York, right in the same city room with me, because the *Herald Tribune* was like the main Tijuana bullring for feature writers . . . Portis, Breslin, Schaap . . . Schaap and Breslin had columns, which gave them more freedom, but I figured I could take the both of them. You had to be brave. Over at the *Times* there was Gay Talese and Robert Lipsyte. At the *Daily News* there was Michael Mok. (There were other contenders, too, on all the newspapers, including the *Herald Tribune*. I am only mentioning those I remember most clearly.) Mok I had been up against before, when I worked on the *Washington Post* and he worked on the *Washington Star*. Mok was tough competition, because, for one thing, he was willing to risk his hide on a feature story with the same wild courage he later showed in covering

Vietnam and the Arab-Israel war for *Life.* Mok would do . . . eerie things. For example, the *News* sends Mok and a photographer out to do a feature on a fat man who is trying to lose weight by marooning himself on a sailboat anchored out in Long Island Sound ("I'm one of those guys, I walk past a delicatessen and breathe deep, and I gain ten pounds"). The motorboat they hire conks out about a mile from the fat man's sloop, with only four or five minutes to go before the deadline. This is March, but Mok dives in and starts swimming. The water is about 42 degrees. He swims until he's half dead, and the fat man has to fish him out with an oar. So Mok gets the story. He makes the deadline. There are pictures in the *News* of Mok swimming furiously through Long Island Sound in order to retrieve this great blob's diet saga for two million readers. If, instead, he had drowned, if he had ended up down with the oysters in the hepatitic muck of the Sound, nobody would have put up a plaque for him. Editors save their tears for war correspondents. As for feature writers—the less said, the better. (Just the other day I saw one of the *New York Times*'s grand panjandrums react with amazement to superlative praise for one of his paper's most popular writers, Israel Shenker, as follows: "But he's a *feature* writer!") No, if Mok had bought the oyster farm that afternoon, he wouldn't even have rated the quietest award in journalism, which is 30 seconds of silence at the Overseas Press Club dinner. Nevertheless, he dove into Long Island Sound in March! Such was the raging competition within our odd and tiny grotto!

At the same time everybody in the game had terrible dark moments during which he lost heart and told himself: "You're only kidding yourself, boy. This is just one more of your devious ways of postponing the decision to put it *all* on the line . . . and go into the shack . . . and write your novel." Your Novel! At this late date—partly due to the New Journalism itself—it's hard to explain what an American dream the idea of writing a novel was in the 1940s, the 1950s, and right into the early 1960s. The Novel was no mere literary form. It was a psychological phenomenon. It was a cortical fever. It belonged in the glossary to *A General Introduction to Psychoanalysis,* somewhere between Narcissism and Obsessional Neuroses. In 1969 Seymour Krim wrote a strange confession for *Playboy* that began: "I was literally made, shaped, whetted and given a world with a purpose by the American realistic novel of the mid- to late-1930s. From the age of fourteen to seventeen, I gorged myself with the works of Thomas Wolfe (beginning with *Of Time and the River,* catching up with *Angel* and then keeping pace till Big Tom's stunning end), Ernest Hemingway, William Faulkner, James T. Farrell, John Steinbeck, John O'Hara, James Cain, Richard Wright, John Dos Passos, Erskine Caldwell, Jerome Weidman, and William Saroyan, and knew in my pumping heart that I wanted to be such a novelist." The piece turned into a confession because first Krim admitted that the idea of being a novelist had been the overwhelming passion of his life, his spiritual calling, in fact, the Pacemaker that kept his ego ticking through all the miserable humiliations of his young manhood—then he faced up to the fact that he was now in his forties and had never written a novel and more than likely never would. Personally I was fascinated by the article, but why *Playboy* was running it, I didn't know, unless it was the magazine's monthly 10 cc. of literary penicillin . . . to hold down the gonococci and the spirochetes . . . I couldn't imagine anyone other than writers being interested in Krim's Complex. That, however, was where I was wrong.

After thinking it over, I realized that writers comprise but a fraction of the Americans who have experienced Krim's peculiar obsession. Not so long ago, I am willing to wager, half the people who went to work for publishing houses did so with the belief that their real destiny was to be novelists. Among people on what they call the creative side of advertising, those who actually dream up the ads, the percentage must have reached 90 per cent. In 1955, in *The Exurbanites*, the late A. C. Spectorsky depicted the well-paid Madison Avenue advertising genius as being a man who wouldn't read a novel without checking out the dust jacket blurb and the picture of the author on the back . . . and if that ego-flushed little bastard with the unbuttoned shirt and the wind rushing through his locks was younger than he was, he couldn't bear to open the goddamn book. Such was the grip of the damnable Novel. Likewise among people in television, public relations, the movies, on the English faculties of colleges and high schools, among framing shop clerks, convicts, unmarried sons living with Mom . . . a whole swarm of fantasizers out there steaming and proliferating in the ego mulches of America . . .

The Novel seemed like one of the last of those superstrokes, like finding gold or striking oil, through which an American could, overnight, in a flash, utterly transform his destiny. There were plenty of examples to feed the fantasy. In the 1930s all the novelists had seemed to be people who came blazing up into stardom from out of total obscurity. That seemed to be the nature of the beast. The biographical notes on the dust jackets of the novels were terrific. The author, you would be assured, was previously employed as a hod carrier (Steinbeck), a truck dispatcher (Cain), a bellboy (Wright), a Western Union boy (Saroyan), a dishwasher in a Greek restaurant in New York (Faulkner), a truck driver, logger, berry picker, spindle cleaner, crop duster pilot . . . There was no end to it . . . Some novelists had whole strings of these credentials . . . That way you knew you were getting the real goods . . .

By the 1950s The Novel had become a nationwide tournament. There was a magical assumption that the end of World War II in 1945 was the dawn of a new golden age of the American Novel, like the Hemingway-Dos Passos-Fitzgerald era after World War I. There was even a kind of Olympian club where the new golden boys met face-to-face every Sunday afternoon in New York, namely, the White Horse Tavern on Hudson Street . . . Ah! There's Jones! There's Mailer! There's Styron! There's Baldwin! There's Willingham! In the flesh—right here in this room! The scene was strictly for novelists, people who were writing novels, and people who were paying court to The Novel. There was no room for a journalist unless he was there in the role of would-be novelist or simple courtier of the great. There was no such thing as a *literary* journalist working for popular magazines or newspapers. If a journalist aspired to literary status—then he had better have the sense and the courage to quit the popular press and try to get into the big league.

As for the little league of feature writers—two of the contestants, Portis and Breslin, actually went on to live out the fantasy. They wrote their novels. Portis did it in a way that was so much like the way it happens in the dream, it was unbelievable. One day he suddenly quit as London correspondent for the *Herald Tribune*. That was generally regarded as a very choice job in the newspaper business. Portis quit cold one day; just like that, without a warning. He returned to the United States and moved into a fishing shack in Arkansas. In six months he wrote a beautiful little novel called *Norwood*. Then he wrote *True Grit*, which was a best seller. The reviews were terrific . . . He sold both books to the movies . . . He made a fortune . . . A *fishing* shack! In *Arkansas*! It was too goddamned perfect to be true, and yet there it was. Which is to say that the old dream, The Novel, has never died.

And yet in the early 1960s a curious new notion, just hot enough to inflame the ego, had begun to intrude into the tiny confines of the feature statusphere. It was in the nature of a discovery. This discovery, modest at first, humble, in fact, deferential, you might say, was that it just might be possible to write journalism that would . . . read like a novel. *Like* a novel, if you get the picture. This was the sincerest form of homage to The Novel and to those greats, the novelists, of course. Not even the journalists who pioneered in this direction doubted for a moment that the novelist was the reigning literary artist, now and forever. All they were asking for was the privilege of dressing up like him . . . until the day when they themselves would work up their nerve and go into the shack and try it for real . . . They were dreamers, all right, but one thing they never dreamed of. They never dreamed of the approaching irony. They never guessed for a minute that the work they would do over the next ten years, as journalists, would wipe out the novel as literature's main event.

LIKE A NOVEL

What inna named christ is this—in the fall of 1962 I happened to pick up a copy of *Esquire* and read a story called "Joe Louis: the King as a Middle-aged Man." The piece didn't open like an ordinary magazine article at all. It opened with the tone and mood of a short story, with a rather intimate scene; or intimate by the standards of magazine journalism in 1962, in any case:

" 'Hi, sweetheart!' Joe Louis called to his wife, spotting her waiting for him at the Los Angeles airport.

"She smiled, walked toward him, and was about to stretch up on her toes and kiss him—but suddenly stopped.

" 'Joe, she said, 'where's your tie?'

" 'Aw, sweetie,' he said, shrugging, 'I stayed out all night in New York and didn't have time—'

" 'All *night!*' she cut in. 'When you're out here all you do is sleep, sleep, sleep."

" 'Sweetie,' Joe Louis said, with a tired grin, 'I'm an old man.'

" 'Yes,' she agreed, 'but when you go to New York you try to be young again.' "

The story featured several scenes like that, showing the private life of a sports hero growing older, balder, sadder. It wound up with a scene in the home of Louis's second wife, Rose Morgan. In this scene Rose Morgan is showing a film of the first Joe Louis-Billy Conn fight to a roomful of people, including her present husband.

"Rose seemed excited at seeing Joe at the top of his form, and every time a Louis punch would jolt Conn, she'd go, 'Mummm' (sock). 'Mummm' (sock). 'Mummm.'

"Billy Conn was impressive through the middle rounds, but as the screen flashed Round 13, somebody said, 'Here's where Conn's gonna make his mistake; he's gonna try to slug it out with Joe Louis.' Rose's husband remained silent, sipping his Scotch.

"When the Louis combinations began to land, Rose went, 'Mummmmm, mummmmm,' and then the pale body of Conn began to collapse against the canvas.

"Billy Conn slowly began to rise. The referee counted over him. Conn had one leg up, then two, then was standing—but the referee forced him back. It was too late."

—and then, for the first time, from the back of the room, from out of the downy billows of the sofa, comes the voice of the present husband—*this Joe Louis crap again*—
  " 'I thought Conn got up in time,' he said, 'but that referee wouldn't let him go on.'
  "Rose Morgan said nothing—just swallowed the rest of her drink."
What the hell is going on? With a little reworking the whole article could have read like a short story. The passages in between the scenes, the expository passages, were conventional 1950s-style magazine journalism, but they could have been easily recast. The piece could have been turned into a non-fiction short story with very little effort. The really unique thing about it, however, was the reporting. This I frankly couldn't comprehend at first. I really didn't understand how anyone could manage to do reporting on things like the personal by-play between a man and his fourth wife at an airport and then follow it up with that amazing cakewalk down Memory Lane in his second wife's living room. My instinctive, defensive reaction was that the man had piped it, as the saying went . . . winged it, made up the dialogue . . . Christ, maybe he made up whole scenes, the unscrupulous geek . . . The funny thing was, that was precisely the reaction that countless journalists and literary intellectuals would have over the next nine years as the New Journalism picked up momentum. *The bastards are making it up!* (I'm telling you, Ump, that's a *spitball* he's throwing . . .) Really stylish reporting was something no one knew how to deal with, since no one was used to thinking of reporting as having an esthetic dimension.

At the time I hardly ever read magazines like *Esquire*. I wouldn't have read the Joe Louis piece except that it was by Gay Talese. After all, Talese was a reporter for the *Times*. He was a player in my own feature game. What he had written for *Esquire* was so much better than what he was doing (or was allowed to do) for the *Times*. I had to check out what was going on.

Not long after that Jimmy Breslin started writing an extraordinary local column for my own paper, the *Herald Tribune*. Breslin came to the *Herald Tribune* in 1963 from out of nowhere, which is to say he had written a hundred or so articles for magazines like *True*, *Life*, and *Sports Illustrated*. Naturally he was virtually unknown. At that time knocking your brains out as a free-lance writer for popular magazines was a guaranteed way to stay anonymous. Breslin caught the attention of the *Herald Tribune*'s publisher, Jock Whitney, through his book about the New York Mets called *Can't Anybody Here Play This Game?* The *Herald Tribune* hired Breslin to do a "bright" local column to help offset some of the heavy lumber on the editorial page, paralyzing snoremongers like Walter Lippmann and Joseph Alsop. Newspaper columns had become a classic illustration of the theory that organizations tend to promote people up to their levels of incompetence. The usual practice was to give a man a column as a reward for outstanding service as a reporter. That way they could lose a good reporter and gain a bad writer. The archetypical newspaper columnist was Lippmann. For 35 years Lippmann seemed to do nothing more than ingest the *Times* every morning, turn it over in his ponderous cud for a few days, and then methodically egest it in the form of a drop of mush on the foreheads of several hundred thousand readers of other newspapers in the days thereafter. The only form of reporting that I remember Lippmann going for was the occasional red-carpet visit to a head of state, during which he had the opportunity of sitting on braided chairs in wainscotted offices and swallowing the exalted one's official lies in person instead of reading them in the *Times*. I don't mean to single out Lippmann, however. He was only doing what was expected of him . . .

In any case, Breslin made a revolutionary discovery. He made the discovery that it was feasible for a columnist to actually leave the building, go outside and do reporting on his own, genuine legwork. Breslin would go up to the city editor and ask what stories and assignments were coming up, choose one, go out, leave the building, cover the story as a reporter, and write about it in his column. If the story were big enough, his column would start on page one instead of inside. As obvious as this system may sound, it was unheard of among newspaper columnists, whether local or national. If possible, local columnists are even more pathetic. They usually start out full of juice, sounding like terrific boulevardiers and raconteurs, retailing in print all the marvelous *mots* and anecdotes they have been dribbling away over lunch for the past few years. After eight or ten weeks, however, they start to dry up. You can see the poor bastards floundering and gasping. They're dying of thirst. They're out of material. They start writing about funny things that happened around the house the other day, homey one-liners that the Better Half or the Avon lady got off, or some fascinating book or article that started them thinking, or else something they saw on the TV. Thank God for the TV! Without television shows to cannibalize, half of these people would be lost, utterly catatonic. Pretty soon you can almost see it, the tubercular blue of the 23-inch screen, radiating from their prose. Anytime you see a columnist trying to squeeze material out of his house, articles, books, or the television set, you've got a starving soul on your hands . . . You should send him a basket . . .

But Breslin worked like a Turk. He would be out all day covering a story, come back in at 4 p.m. or so and sit down at a desk in the middle of the city room. It was quite a show. He was a good-looking Irishman with a lot of black hair and a great wrestler's gut. When he sat down at his typewriter he hunched himself over into a shape like a bowling ball. He would start drinking coffee and smoking cigarettes until vapor started drifting off his body. He looked like a bowling ball fueled with liquid oxygen. Thus fired up, he would start typing. I've never seen a man who could write so well against a daily deadline. I particularly remember one story he wrote about the sentencing, on a charge of extortion, of a Teamster boss named Anthony Provenzano. Early in the story Breslin set up the image of the sun coming through the moldering old windows of the Federal courthouse and exploding off Provenzano's diamond pinky ring:

"It did not seem like a bad morning at all. The boss, Tony Provenzano, who is one of the biggest men in the Teamsters Union, walked up and down the corridor outside of this Federal courtroom in Newark and he had a little smile on his face and he kept flicking a white cigarette holder around.

" 'Today is the kind of a day for fishing,' Tony was saying. 'We ought to go out and get some fluke.'

"Then he spread his legs a little and went at this big guy named Jack, who had on a gray suit. Tony stuck out his left hand so he could throw a hook at this guy Jack. The big diamond ring on Tony's pinky flashed in the light coming through the tall windows of the corridor. Then Tony shifted and hit Jack with a right hand on the shoulder.

" 'Always the shoulder,' one of the guys in the corridor laughed. 'Tony is always banging Jack on the shoulder.' "

The story went on in that vein with Provenzano's Jersey courtiers circling around him and fawning, while the sun explodes off his pinky ring. Inside the courtroom itself, however, Provenzano starts getting his. The judge starts lecturing him, and the sweat starts breaking out on Provenzano's upper lip. Then the judge sentences him to seven years, and Provenzano starts twisting his pinky ring finger with his right hand. Then Breslin wraps it up with a scene in a cafeteria where the young prosecutor who worked the case is eating fried scallops and fruit salad off a tray.

"Nothing on his hand flashed. The guy who sunk Tony Pro doesn't even have a diamond ring on his pinky."

Well—all right! Say what you will! There it was, a short story, complete with symbolism, in fact, and yet true-life, as they say, about something that happened today, and you could pick it up on the newsstand by 11 tonight for a dime . . .

Breslin's work stirred up a certain vague resentment among both journalists and literati during the first year or two of his column—vague, because they never fully understood what he was doing . . . only that in some vile Low Rent way the man's output was *literary*. Among literary intellectuals you would hear Breslin referred to as "a cop who writes" or "Runyon on welfare." These weren't even intelligent insults, however, because they dealt with Breslin's attitude, which seemed to be that of the cabdriver with his cap tilted over one eye. A crucial part of Breslin's work they didn't seem to be conscious of at all: namely, the reporting he did. Breslin made it a practice to arrive on the scene long before the main event in order to gather the off-camera material, the by-play in the make-up room, that would enable him to create character. It was part of his *modus operandi* to gather "novelistic" details, the rings, the perspiration, the jabs on the shoulder, and he did it more skillfully than most novelists.

Literary people were oblivious to this side of the New Journalism, because it is one of the unconscious assumptions of modern criticism that the raw material is simply "there." It is the "given." The idea is: Given such-and-such a body of material, what has the artist done with it? The crucial part that reporting plays in all story-telling, whether in novels, films, or non-fiction, is something that is not so much ignored as simply not comprehended. The modern notion of art is an essentially religious or magical one in which the artist is viewed as a holy beast who in some way, big or small, receives flashes from the godhead, which is known as creativity. The material is merely his clay, his palette . . . Even the obvious relationship between reporting and the major novels—one has only to think of Balzac, Dickens, Gogol, Tolstoy, Dostoyevsky, and, in fact, Joyce—is something that literary historians deal with only in a biographical sense. It took the New Journalism to bring this strange matter of reporting into the foreground.

But these were all matters that came up later. I don't remember a soul talking about them at the time. I certainly didn't. In the spring of 1963 I made my own entry into this new arena, although without meaning to. I have already described (in the introduction to *The Kandy-Kolored Tangerine-Flake Streamline Baby*) the odd circumstances under which I happened to write my first magazine article—"There Goes (Varoom! Varoom!) That Kandy-Kolored (Thphhhhhh!) Tangerine-Flake Streamline Baby (Rahghhh!) Around the Bend (Brummmmmmmmmmmmmmmmmmmm). . . ."—in the form of what I thought was merely a memorandum to the managing editor of *Esquire*. This article was by no means like a short story, despite the use of scenes and dialogue. I wasn't thinking about that at all. It is hard to say what it was like. It was a garage sale, that piece . . . vignettes, odds and ends of scholarship, bits of memoir, short bursts of sociology, apostrophes, epithets, moans, cackles, anything that came into my head, much of it thrown together in a rough and awkward way. That was its virtue. It showed me the possibility of there being something "new" in journalism. What interested me was not simply the discovery that it was possible to write accurate non-fiction with techniques usually associated with novels and short stories. It was that—plus. It was the discovery that it was possible in non-fiction, in journalism, to use any literary device, from the traditional dialogisms of the essay to stream-of-consciousness, and to use many different kinds simultaneously, or within a relatively short space . . . to excite the reader both intellectually and emotionally. I am not laying all those gladiolas on that rather curious first article of mine, you understand. I'm only talking about what it suggested to me.

I soon had the chance to explore every possibility I could think of. The *Herald Tribune* assigned me split duties, like a utility infielder's. Two days a week I was supposed to work for the city desk as a general assignment reporter, as usual. The other three days I was supposed to turn out a weekly piece of about 1,500 words for the *Herald Tribune's* new Sunday supplement, which was called *New York*. At the same time, following the success of "There Goes (Varoom! Varoom!) That Kandy-Kolored (Thphhhhhh!) Tangerine-Flake Streamline Baby (Rahghhh!) Around the Bend (Brummmmmmmmmmmmmmmm). . . ."—I was also cranking out stories for *Esquire*. This setup was crazy enough to begin with. I can remember flying to Las Vegas on my two regular days off from the *Herald Tribune* to do a story for *Esquire*—"Las Vegas!!!!"—and winding up sitting on the edge of a white satin bed in a Hog-Stomping Baroque suite in a hotel on the Strip—in the decor known as Hog-Stomping Baroque there are 400-pound cut-glass chandeliers in the bathrooms—and picking up the phone and dictating to the stenographic battery of the *Trib* city desk the last third of a story on demolition derbies in Long Island for *New York*—"Clean Fun at Riverhead"—hoping to finish in time to meet a psychiatrist in a black silk mohair suit with brass buttons and a shawl collar, no lapels, one of the only two psychiatrists in Las Vegas County at that time, to take me to see the casualties of the Strip in the state mental ward out Charleston Boulevard. What made it crazier was that the piece about the demolition derbies was the last one I wrote that came anywhere close to being 1,500 words. After that they started climbing to 3,000, 4,000, 5,000, 6,000 words. Like Pascal, I was sorry, but I didn't have time to write short ones. In nine months in the latter part of 1963 and first half of 1964 I wrote three more long pieces for *Esquire* and twenty for *New York*. All of this was in addition to what I was writing as a reporter for the *Herald Tribune* city desk two days a week. The idea of a day off lost all meaning. I can remember being furious on Monday, November 25, 1963, because there were people I desperately needed to talk to, for some story or other, and I couldn't reach them because all the offices in New York seemed to be closed, every one. It was the day of President Kennedy's funeral. I remember staring at the television set . . . morosely, but for all the wrong reasons.

Yet in terms of experimenting in non-fiction, the way I worked at that point couldn't have been more ideal. I was writing mostly for *New York*, which, as I say, was a Sunday supplement. At that time, 1963 and 1964, Sunday supplements were close to being the lowest form of periodical. Their status was well below that of the ordinary daily newspaper, and only slightly above that of the morbidity press, sheets like the *National Enquirer* in its "I Left My Babies in the Deep Freeze" period. As a result, Sunday supplements had no traditions, no pretensions, no promises to live up to, not even any rules to speak of. They were brain candy, that was all. Readers felt no guilt whatsoever about laying them aside, throwing them away or not looking at them at all. I never felt the slightest hesitation about trying any device that might conceivably grab the reader a few seconds longer. I tried to yell right in his ear: *Stick around!* . . . Sunday supplements were no place for diffident souls. That was how I started playing around with the device of point-of-view.

For example, I once did a story about the girls in jail at the Women's House of Detention in Greenwich Village at Greenwich Avenue and the Avenue of the Americas, an intersection known as Nut Heaven. The girls used to yell down to boys on the street, to all the nice free funky Village groovies they saw walking around down there. They would yell every male first name they could think of—"Bob!" "Bill!" "Joe!" "Jack!" "Jimmy!" "Willie!" "Benny!"—until they hit the right name, and some poor fool would stop and look up and answer. Then they would suggest a lot of quaint anatomical impossibilities for the kid to perform on himself and start laughing like maniacs. I was there one night when they caught a boy who looked about twenty-one named Harry. So I started the story with the girls yelling at him:

" 'Hai-ai-ai-ai-ai-ai-ai-ai-ai-ai-ai-ai-ai-ai-ai-ai-ai-ai-ai-ai-ai-ai-ai-ai-ai ai-ai-ai-ai-ai-ai-ai-ai-ai-ai-ai-ai-ai-ai-ai-ai-ai-ai-aireeeeeeeeeeeeeeeeeeee!' "

I looked at that. I liked it. I decided I would enjoy yelling at the little bastard myself. So I started lambasting him, too, in the next sentence:

"O, dear Sweet Harry, with your French gangster-movie bangs, your Ski Shop turtleneck sweater and your Army-Navy Store blue denim shirt over it, with your Bloomsbury corduroy pants you saw in the *Manchester Guardian* airmail edition and sent away for and your sly intellectual pigeon-toed libido roaming in Greenwich Village—that siren call really for you?"

Then I let the girls have another go at it:

" 'Hai-ai-ai-ai-ai-ai-ai-ai-ai-ai-ai-ai-aireeeeeeeeeee!' "

Then I started in again, and so on. There was nothing subtle about such a device, which might be called the Hectoring Narrator. Quite the opposite. That was precisely why I liked it. I liked the idea of starting off a story by letting the reader, via the narrator, talk to the characters, hector them, insult them, prod them with irony or condescension, or whatever. Why should the reader be expected to just lie flat and let these people come tromping through as if his mind were a subway turnstile? But I was democratic about it, I was. Sometimes I would put myself into the story and make sport of me. I would be "the man in the brown Borsalino hat," a large fuzzy Italian fedora I wore at the time, or "the man in the Big Lunch tie." I would write about myself in the third person, usually as a puzzled onlooker or someone who was in the way, which was often the case. Once I even began a story about a vice I was also prone to, tailor-made clothes, as if someone else were the hectoring narrator . . . treating *me* in a flippant manner: "Real buttonholes. That's it! A man can take his thumb and forefinger and unbutton his sleeve at the wrist because this kind of suit has real buttonholes there. Tom, boy, it's terrible. Once you know about it, you start seeing it. All the time!" . . . and so on . . . anything to avoid coming on like the usual non-fiction narrator, with a hush in my voice, like a radio announcer at a tennis match.

The voice of the narrator, in fact, was one of the great problems in nonfiction writing. Most non-fiction writers, without knowing it, wrote in a century-old British tradition in which it was understood that the narrator shall assume a calm, cultivated and, in fact, genteel voice. The idea was that the narrator's own voice should be like the off-white or putty-colored walls that Syrie Maugham popularized in interior decoration . . . a "neutral background" against which bits of color would stand out. *Understatement* was the thing. You can't imagine what a positive word "understatement" was among both journalists and literati ten years ago. There is something to be said for the notion, of course, but the trouble was that by the early 1960s understatement had become an absolute pall. Readers were bored to tears without understanding why. When they came upon that pale beige tone, it began to signal to them, unconsciously, that a well-known bore was here again, "the journalist," a pedestrian mind, a phlegmatic spirit, a faded personality, and there was no way to get rid of the pallid little troll, short of ceasing to read. This had nothing to do with objectivity and subjectivity or taking a stand or "commitment"—it was a matter of personality, energy, drive, bravura . . . style, in a word . . . The standard non-fiction writer's voice was like the standard announcer's voice . . . a drag, a droning . . .

To avoid this I would try anything. For example, I wrote a story about Junior Johnson, a stock car racer from Ingle Hollow, North Carolina, who had learned to drive by running moonshine whiskey to Charlotte and other distribution points. "There ain't no harder work in the world than making whiskey," Junior would say. "I don't know of any other business that compels you to get up at all times of night and go outdoors in the snow and everything else and work. H'it's the hardest way in the world to make a living, and I don't think anybody'd do it unless they had to." Now, as long as Junior Johnson was explaining the corn liquor industry, there was no problem, because (a) dialogue tends to be naturally attractive, or involving, to the reader; and (b) Johnson's Ingle Hollow lingo was unusual. But then I had to take over the explanation myself, in order to compress into a few paragraphs information that had come from several interviews. So . . . I decided I would rather talk in Ingle Hollow accents myself, since that seemed to go over all right. There is no law that says the narrator has to speak in beige or even New York journalese. So I picked up the explanation myself, as follows: "Working mash wouldn't wait for a man. It started coming to a head when it got ready to and a man had to be there to take it off, out there in the woods, in the brush, in the brambles, in the muck, in the snow. Wouldn't it have been something if you could have just set it all up inside a good old shed with a corrugated metal roof and order those parts like you want them and not have to smuggle all that copper and all that sugar and all that everything out here in the woods and be a coppersmith and a plumber and a cooper and a carpenter and a pack horse and every other goddamned thing God ever saw in the world, all at once.

"And live decent hours—Junior and his brothers, about two o'clock in the morning they'd head out to the stash, the place where the liquor was hidden after it was made . . . ."

I was feigning the tones of an Ingle Hollow moonshiner, in order to create the illusion of seeing the action through the eyes of someone who was actually on the scene and involved in it, rather than a beige narrator. I began to think of this device as the *downstage voice*, as if characters downstage from the protagonist himself were talking.

I would do the same thing with descriptions. Rather than just come on as the broadcaster describing the big parade, I would shift as quickly as possible into the eye sockets, as it were, of the people in the story. Often I would shift the point of view in the middle of a paragraph or even a sentence. I began a story on Baby Jane Holzer, entitled "The Girl of the Year," as follows:

"Bangs manes bouffant beehives Beatle caps butter faces brush-on lashes decal eyes puffy sweaters French thrust bras flailing leather blue jeans stretch pants stretch jeans honeydew bottoms eclair shanks elf boots ballerinas Knight slippers, hundreds of them, these flaming little buds, bobbing and screaming, rocketing around inside the Academy of Music Theater underneath that vast old moldering cherub dome up there—aren't they super-marvelous!

" 'Aren't they super-marvelous!' says Baby Jane, and then: 'Hi, Isabel! Isabel! You want to sit backstage—with the Stones!'

"The show hasn't even started yet, the Rolling Stones aren't even on the stage, the place is full of a great shabby moldering dimness, and these flaming little buds.

"Girls are reeling this way and that way in the aisle and through their huge black decal eyes, sagging with Tiger Tongue Lick Me brush-on eyelashes and black appliqués, sagging like display-window Christmas trees, they keep staring at—her—Baby Jane—on the aisle."

The opening paragraph is a rush of Groovy clothes ending with the phrase "—aren't they super-marvelous!" With this phrase the point-of-view shifts to Baby Jane, and one is looking through her eyes at the young girls, "the flaming little buds," who are running around the theater. The description continues through Jane's eyes until the phrase "they keep staring at—her—Baby Jane," whereupon the point-of-view shifts to the young girls, and the reader is suddenly looking through *their* eyes at Baby Jane: "What the hell is this? She is gorgeous in the most outrageous way. Her hair rises up from her head in a huge hairy corona, a huge tan mane around a narrow face and two eyes opened—swock!—like umbrellas, with all that hair flowing down over a coat made of . . . *ze*bra! Those motherless stripes! Oh, damn! Here she is with her friends, looking like some kind of queen bee for all flaming little buds everywhere."

In fact, three points-of-view are used in that rather short passage, the point-of-view of the subject (Baby Jane), the point-of-view of the people watching her (the "flaming little buds"), and my own. I switched back and forth between points-of-view continually, and often abruptly, in many articles I wrote in 1963, 1964, and 1965. Eventually a reviewer called me a "chameleon" who instantly took on the coloration of whomever he was writing about. He meant it negatively. I took it as a great compliment. A chameleon . . . but exactly!

Sometimes I used point-of-view in the Jamesian sense in which fiction writers understand it, entering directly into the mind of a character, experiencing the world through his central nervous system throughout a given scene. Writing about Phil Spector ("The First Tycoon of Teen"), I began the article not only inside his mind but with a virtual stream of consciousness. One of the news magazines apparently regarded my Spector story as an improbable feat, because they interviewed him and asked him if he didn't think this passage was merely a fiction that appropriated his name. Spector said that, in fact, he found it quite accurate. This should have come as no surprise, since every detail in the passage was taken from a long interview with Spector about exactly how he had felt at the time:

"All these raindrops are *high* or something. They don't roll down the window, they come straight back, toward the tail, wobbling, like all those Mr. Cool snowheads walking on mattresses. The plane is taxiing out toward the runway to take off, and this stupid infarcted water wobbles, sideways, across the window. Phil Spector, 23 years old, the rock and roll magnate, producer of Philles Records, America's first teen-age tycoon, watches . . . this watery pathology . . . it is *sick, fatal.* He tightens his seat belt over his bowels . . . A hum rises inside the plane, a shot of air comes shooting through the vent over somebody's seat, some ass turns on a cone of light, there is a sign stuck out by the runway, a mad, cryptic, insane instruction to the pilot—Runway 4, Are Cylinder Laps Mainside DOWN?—and beyond, disoriented crop rows of sulphur blue lights, like the lights on top of a New Jersey toothpaste factory, only spreading on and on in sulphur blue rows over Los Angeles County. It is . . . disoriented. Schizoid raindrops. The plane breaks in two on takeoff and everybody in the front half comes rushing toward Phil Spector in a gush of bodies in a thick orange—*napalm!* No, it happens aloft; there is a long rip in the side of the plane, it just rips, he can see the top ripping, folding back in sick curds, like a sick Dali egg, and Phil Spector goes sailing through the rip, dark, freezing. And the engine, it is *reedy*—

"Miss!"

"A stewardess is walking to the back to buckle herself in for the takeoff. The plane is moving, the jets are revving. Under a Lifebuoy blue skirt, her fireproof legs are clicking out of her Pinki-Kinki-Panti Fantasy—"

I had the feeling, rightly or wrongly, that I was doing things no one had ever done before in journalism. I used to try to imagine the feeling readers must have had upon finding all this carrying on and cutting up in a Sunday supplement. I liked that idea. I had no sense of being a part of any normal journalistic or literary environment. Later I read the English critic John Bayley's yearnings for an age when writers had Pushkin's sense of "looking at all things afresh," as if for the first time, without the constant intimidation of being aware of what other writers have already done. In the mid-1960s that was exactly the feeling I had.

I'm sure that others who were experimenting with magazine articles, such as Talese, began to feel the same way. They were moving beyond the conventional limits of journalism, but not merely in terms of technique. The kind of reporting they were doing struck them as far more ambitious, too. It was more intense, more detailed, and certainly more time-consuming than anything that newspaper or magazine reporters, including investigative reporters, were accustomed to. They developed the habit of staying with the people they were writing about for days at a time, weeks in some cases. They had to gather all the material the conventional journalist was after—and then keep going. It seemed all-important to *be there* when dramatic scenes took place, to get the dialogue, the gestures, the facial expressions, the details of the environment. The idea was to give the full objective description, plus something that readers had always had to go to novels and short stories for: namely, the subjective or emotional life of the characters. That was why it was so ironic when both the journalistic and literary old guards began to attack this new journalism as "impressionistic." The most important things one attempted in terms of technique depended upon a depth of information that had never been demanded in newspaper work. Only through the most searching forms of reporting was it possible, in non-fiction, to use whole scenes, extended dialogue, point-of-view, and interior mono-logue. Eventually I, and others, would be accused of "entering people's minds" . . . But exactly! I figured that was one more doorbell a reporter had to push.

Most of the people who eventually wrote about my style, however, tended to concentrate on certain mannerisms, the lavish use of dots, dashes, exclamation points, italics, and occasionally punctuation that never existed before :::::::::: and of interjections, shouts, nonsense words, onomatopoeia, mimesis, pleonasms, the continual use of the historical present, and so on. This was natural enough, because many of these devices stood out even before one had read a word. The typography actually *looked* different. Referring to my use of italics and exclamation points, one critic observed, with scorn, that my work looked like something out of Queen Victoria's childhood diary. Queen Victoria's childhood diaries are, in fact, quite readable; even charming. One has only to compare them with the miles of official prose she laid on Palmerston, Wellington, Gladstone in letters and communiqués and on the English people in her proclamations to see the point I'm making. I found a great many pieces of punctuation and typography lying around dormant when I came along—and I must say I had a good time using them. I figured it was time someone violated what Orwell called "the Geneva conventions of the mind" . . . a protocol that had kept journalism and non-fiction generally (and novels) in such a tedious bind for so long. I found that things like exclamation points, italics, and abrupt shifts (dashes) and syncopations (dots) helped to give the illusion not only of a person talking but of a person thinking. I used to enjoy using dots where they would be least expected, not at the end of a sentence but in the middle, creating the effect . . . of a skipped beat. It seemed to me the mind reacted—*first!* . . . in dots, dashes, and exclamation points, then rationalized, drew up a brief, with periods.

I soon found that people loved to parody my style. By 1966 the parodies began to come in a rush. I must say I read them all. I suppose it's because at the heart of every parody there is a little gold ball of tribute. Even hostile parodies admit from the start that the target has a distinct voice.

It is not very often that one comes across a new style, period. And if a new style were created not via the novel, or the short story, or poetry, but via journalism—I suppose that would seem extraordinary. It was probably that idea—more than any specific devices, such as using scenes and dialogue in a "novelistic" fashion—that began to give me very grand ideas about a new journalism. As I saw it, if a new literary style could originate in journalism, then it stood to reason that journalism could aspire to more than mere emulation of those aging giants, the novelists.

SEIZING THE POWER

I have no idea who coined the term "the New Journalism" or even when it was coined. Seymoar Krim tells me that he first heard it used in 1965 when he was editor of *Nugget* and Pete Hamill called him and said he wanted to write an article called "The New Journalism" about people like Jimmy Breslin and Gay Talese. It was late in 1966 when you first started hearing people talk about "the New Journalism" in conversation, as best I can remember. I don't know for sure. . . . To tell the truth, I've never even liked the term. Any movement, group, party, program, philosophy or theory that goes under a name with "New" in it is just begging for trouble. The garbage barge of history is already full of them: the New Humanism, the New Poetry, the New Criticism, the New Conservativism, the New Frontier, il Stilo Novo . . . The World Tomorrow. . . .

Nevertheless, the New Journalism was the term that caught on eventually. It was no "movement." There were no manifestos, clubs, salons, cliques; not even a saloon where the faithful gathered, since there was no faith and no creed. At the time, the mid-Sixties, one was aware only that all of a sudden there was some sort of artistic excitement in journalism, and that was a new thing in itself.

I didn't know what history, if any, lay behind it. I wasn't interested in the long view just then. All I knew was what certain writers were doing at Esquire, Thomas B. Morgan, Brock Brower, Terry Southern and, above all, Gay Talese . . . even a couple of novelists were in on it, Norman Mailer and James Baldwin, writing nonfiction for *Esquire* . . . and, of course, the writers for my own Sunday supplement, *New York*, chiefly Breslin, but also Robert Christgau, Doon Arbus, Gail Sheehy, Tom Gallagher, Robert Benton and David Newman. I was turning out articles as fast as I could write and checking out all these people to see what new spins they had come up with. I was completely wrapped up in this new excitement that was in the air. It was a regular little league they had going.

As a result I never had the slightest idea that any of it might have an impact on the literary world or, for that matter, any sphere outside the small world of feature journalism. I should have known better, however. By 1966 the New Journalism had already been paid literary tribute in its cash forms: namely, bitterness, envy and resentment.

This had all come bursting forth during a curious episode known as *The New Yorker* affair. In April of 1965, in the New York *Herald Tribune*'s Sunday magazine, *New York*, I had made what I fancied was some lighthearted fun of *The New Yorker* magazine with a two-part article entitled "Tiny Mummies! The True Story of the Ruler of 43rd Street's Land of The Walking Dead!" A very droll *sportif* performance, you understand. Without going into the whole beanball contest I can tell you that there were many good souls who did not consider this article either lighthearted or *sportif*. In fact, it caused a hulking furor. In the midst of it the kentucky colonels of both Journalism and Literature launched their first attack on this accursed Low Rent rabble at the door, these magazine writers working in the damnable new form. . . .

The longest attacks came in two fairly new but highly conservative periodicals. One was mounted by what had already become the major organ of traditional newspaper journalism in the United States, the *Columbia Journalism Review*, and the other by the major organ of America's older literary essayists and "men of letters," *The New York Review of Books*. They presented lists of "errors" in my piece about *The New Yorker*, marvelous lists[1] as arcane and mystifying as a bill from the body shop—whereupon they concluded that *there* you had the damnable new genre, this "bastard form," this "Parajournalism," a tag they awarded not only to me and to my magazine *New York* and all its works but also to Breslin, Talese, Dick Schaap and, as long as they were up, *Esquire*.[2] Whether or not one accepted the lists, the strategy itself was revealing. My article on *The New Yorker* had not even been an example of the new genre; it used neither the reporting techniques nor the literary techniques; underneath a bit of red-flock *Police Gazette* rhetoric, it was a traditional critique, a needle, an attack, an "essay" of the old school. It had little or nothing to do with anything I had written before. It certainly had nothing to do with any other writer's work. And yet I think the journalists and literati who were so furious were sincere. I think they looked at the work a dozen or so writers, Breslin, Talese and myself among them, were doing for *New York* and *Esquire*, and they were baffled, dazzled. . . . This *can't* be right. . . . These people must be piping it, winging it, making up the dialogue. . . . Christ, maybe they're making up whole scenes, the unscrupulous geeks (I'm telling you, Ump, those are *spit*balls they're throwing). They needed to believe, in short, that the new form was illegitimate . . . a "bastard form."

Why newspaper people were upset was no mystery. They were better than railroad men at resisting anything labeled new. The average newspaper editor's idea of a major innovation was the Cashword Puzzle. The literary opposition was more complex, however. Looking back on it one can see that what had happened was this: the sudden arrival of this new style of journalism, from out of nowhere, had caused a status panic in the literary community. Throughout the twentieth century literary people had grown used to a very stable and apparently eternal status structure. It was somewhat like a class structure on the eighteenth-century model in that there was a chance for you to compete but only with people of your own class. The literary upper class were the novelists; the occasional playwright or poet might be up there, too, but mainly it was the novelists. They were regarded as the only "creative" writers, the only literary artists. They had exclusive entry to the soul of man, the profound emotions, the eternal mysteries, and so forth and so on. . . . The middle class were the "men of letters," the literary essayists, the more authoritative critics; the occasional biographer, historian or cosmically inclined scientist also, but mainly the men of letters. Their province was analysis, "insights," the play of intellect. They were not in the same class with the novelists, as they well knew, but they *were* the reigning practitioners of nonfiction. . . . The lower class were the journalists, and they were so low down in the structure that they were barely noticed at all. They were regarded chiefly as day laborers who dug up slags of raw information for writers of higher "sensibility" to make better use of. As for people who wrote for popular ("slick") magazines and Sunday supplements, your so-called free-lance writers—except for a few people on *The New Yorker*, they weren't even in the game. They were the lumpenproles.

And so all of a sudden, in the mid-Sixties, here comes a bunch of these lumpenproles, no less, a bunch of slick-magazine and Sunday-supplement writers with no literary credentials whatsoever in most cases—only they're using all the techniques of the novelists, even the most sophisticated ones—and on top of that they're helping themselves to the insights of the men of letters while they're at it—and at the same time they're still doing their low-life legwork, their "digging," their hustling, their damnable Locker Room Genre reporting—they're taking on *all* of these roles at the same time—in other words, they're ignoring literary class lines that have been almost a century in the making.

The panic hit the men of letters first. If the lumpenproles won their point, if their new form achieved any sort of literary respectability, if it were somehow accepted as "creative", the men of letters stood to lose even their positions as the reigning practitioners of nonfiction. They would get bumped down to Lower Middle Class. . . . This was already beginning to happen. The first indication I had came in an article in the June, 1966, *Atlantic* by Dan Wakefield, entitled "The Personal Voice and the Impersonal Eye." The gist of the piece was that this was the first period in anybody's memory when people in the literary world were beginning to talk about nonfiction as a serious artistic form. Norman Podhoretz had written a piece in *Harper's* in 1958 claiming a similar status for the "discursive prose" of the late Fifties, essays by people like James Baldwin and Isaac Rosenfeld. But the excitement Wakefield was talking about had nothing to do with essays or any other traditional nonfiction. Quite the contrary; Wakefield attributed the new prestige of nonfiction to two books of an entirely different sort: *In Cold Blood*, by

Truman Capote, and a collection of magazine articles with a title in alliterative trochaic pentameter that I am sure would come to me if I dwelled upon it.

Capote's story of the life and death of two drifters who blew the heads off a wealthy farm family in Kansas ran as a serial in *The New Yorker* in the Fall of 1965 and came out in book form in February of 1966. It was a sensation—and a terrible jolt to all who expected the accursed New Journalism or Parajournalism to spin itself out like a fad. Here, after all, was not some obscure journalist, some free-lance writer, but a novelist of long standing . . . whose career had been in the doldrums . . . and who suddenly, with this one stroke, with this turn to the damnable new form of journalism, not only resuscitated his reputation but elevated it higher than ever before . . . and became a celebrity of the most amazing magnitude in the bargain. People of all sorts read *In Cold Blood*, people at every level of taste. Everybody was absorbed in it. Capote himself didn't call it journalism; far from it; he said he had invented a new literary genre, "the nonfiction novel." Nevertheless, his success gave the New Journalism, as it would soon be called, an overwhelming momentum.

Capote had spent five years researching his story and interviewing the killers in prison, and so on, a very meticulous and impressive job. But in 1966 you started seeing feats of reporting that were extraordinary, spectacular. . . . Here came a breed of journalists who somehow had the moxie to talk their way inside of any milieu, even closed societies, and hang on for dear life. A marvelous maniac named John Sack talked the Army into letting him join an infantry company at Fort Dix, M Company, 1st Advanced Infantry Training Brigade—not as a recruit but as a reporter—and go through training with them and then to Vietnam and into battle. The result was a book called *M* (appearing first in *Esquire*), a nonfiction *Catch-22* and, for my money, still the finest book in any genre published about the war. George Plimpton went into training with a professional football team, the Detroit Lions, in the role of reporter playing rookie quarterback, rooming with the players, going through their workouts and finally playing quarterback for them in a pre-season game—in order to write *Paper Lion*. Like Capote's book, *Paper Lion* was read by people at every level of taste and had perhaps the greatest literary impact of any writing about sports since Ring Lardner's short stories. But the all-time free-lance writer's Brass Stud Award went that year to an obscure California journalist named Hunter Thompson who "ran" with the Hell's Angels for eighteen months—as a reporter and not a member, which might have been safer—in order to write *Hell's Angels: The Strange and Terrible Saga of the Outlaw Motorcycle Gang*. The Angels wrote his last chapter for him by stomping him half to death in a roadhouse fifty miles from Santa Rosa. All through the book Thompson had been searching for the single psychological or sociological insight that would sum up all he had seen, the single golden *aperçu*; and as he lay sprawled there on the floor coughing up blood and teeth, the line he had been looking for came to him in a brilliant flash from out of the heart of darkness: "Exterminate all the brutes!"

At about the same time, 1966 and 1967, Joan Didion was writing those strange Gothic articles of hers about California that were eventually collected in *Slouching Towards Bethlehem*. Rex Reed was writing his celebrity interviews—this was an old journalistic exercise, of course, but no one had ever quite so diligently addressed himself to the question of, "What is So-and-so *really* like?" (Simone Signoret, as I recall, turned out to have the neck, shoulders and upper back of a middle linebacker.) James Mills was pulling off some amazing reporting feats of his own for *Life* in pieces such as "The Panic in Needle Park," "The Detective," and "The Prosecutor." The writer-reporter team of

Garry Wills and Ovid Demaris was doing a series of brilliant pieces for *Esquire*, culminating in "You All Know Me—I'm Jack Ruby!"

And then, early in 1968, another novelist turned to nonfiction, and with a success that in its own way was as spectacular as Capote's two years before. This was Norman Mailer writing a memoir about an anti-war demonstration he had become involved in, "The Steps of the Pentagon." The memoir, or autobiography . . . , is an old genre of nonfiction, of course, but this piece was written soon enough after the event to have a journalistic impact. It took up an entire issue of *Harper's Magazine* and came out a few months later under the title of *The Armies of the Night*. Unlike Capote's book, Mailer's was not a popular success; but within the literary community and among intellectuals generally it couldn't have been a more tremendous *succès d'estime*. At the time Mailer's reputation had been deteriorating in the wake of two inept novels called *An American Dream* (1965) and *Why Are We In Vietnam?* (1967). He was being categorized somewhat condescendingly as a journalist, because his nonfiction, chiefly in *Esquire*, was obviously his better work. *The Armies of the Night* changed all that in a flash. Like Capote, Mailer had a dread of the tag that had been put on him—"journalist"—and had subtitled his book "The Novel as History; History as the Novel." But the lesson was one that nobody in the literary world could miss. Here was another novelist who had turned to some form of accursed journalism, no matter what name you gave it, and had not only revived his reputation but raised it to a point higher than it had ever been in his life.

By 1969 no one in the literary world could simply dismiss this new journalism as an inferior genre. The situation was somewhat similar to the situation of the novel in England in the 1850's. It was yet to be canonized, sanctified and given a theology, but writers themselves could already feel the new Power flowing.

The similarity between the early days of the novel and the early days of the New Journalism is not merely coincidental. . . . In both cases we are watching the same process. We are watching a group of writers coming along, working in a genre regarded as Lower Class (the novel before the 1850's, slick-magazine journalism before the 1960's), who discover the joys of detailed realism and its strange powers. Many of them seem to be in love with realism for its own sake; and never mind the "sacred callings" of literature. They seem to be saying: "Hey! Come here! This is the way people are living now— just the way I'm going to show you! It may astound you, disgust you, delight you or arouse your contempt or make you laugh. . . . Nevertheless, this is what it's like! It's *all* right here! You won't be bored! Take a look!"

As I hardly have to tell you, that is not exactly the way serious novelists regard the task of the novel today. In this decade, the Seventies, The Novel will be celebrating the one-hundredth anniversary of its canonization as *the* spiritual genre. Novelists today keep using words like "myth," "fable" and "magic." (Appendix II.) That state of mind known as "the sacred office of the novelist" had originated in Europe in the 1870's and didn't take hold in the American literary world until after the Second World War. But it soon made up for lost time. What kind of novel should a sacred officer write? In 1948 Lionel Trilling presented the theory that the novel of social realism (which had flourished in America throughout the 1930's) was finished because the freight train of history had passed it by. The argument was that such novels were a product of the rise of the bourgeoisie in the nineteenth century at the height of capitalism. But now bourgeois society was breaking up, fragmenting. A novelist could no longer portray a part of that society and hope to capture the Zeitgeist; all he would be left with was one of the broken pieces. The only hope was a new kind of novel (his candidate was the novel of ideas). This theory caught on among young novelists with an astonishing grip. Whole careers were altered. All those writers hanging out in the literary pubs in New York such as the White Horse Tavern rushed off to write every kind of novel you could imagine, so long as it wasn't the so-called "big novel" of manners and society. The next thing one knew, they were into novels of ideas, Freudian novels, surrealistic novels ("black comedy"), Kafkaesque novels and, more recently, the catatonic novel or novel of immobility, the sort that begins: "In order to get started, he went to live alone on an island and shot himself." (Opening line of a Robert Coover short story.)

As a result, by the Sixties, about the time I came to New York, the most serious, ambitious and, presumably, talented novelists had abandoned the richest terrain of the novel: namely, society, the social tableau, manners and morals, the whole business of "the way we live now," in Trollope's phrase. . . . There is no novelist who will be remembered as the novelist who captured the Sixties in America, or even in New York, in the sense that Thackeray was the chronicler of London in the 1840's and Balzac was the chronicler of Paris and all of France after the fall of the Empire. Balzac prided himself on being "the secretary of French society." Most serious American novelists would rather cut their wrists than be known as "the secretary of American society," and not merely because of ideological considerations. With fable, myth and the sacred office to think about—who wants such a menial role?

That was marvelous for journalists—I can tell you that. The Sixties was one of the most extraordinary decades in American history in terms of manners and morals. Manners and morals *were* the history of the Sixties. A hundred years from now when historians write about the 1960's in America (always assuming, to paraphrase Céline, that the Chinese will still give a damn about American history), they won't write about it as the decade of the war in Vietnam or of space exploration or of political assassinations . . . but as the decade when manners and morals, styles of living, attitudes toward the world changed the country more crucially than any political events . . . all the changes that were labeled, however clumsily, with such tags as "the generation gap," "the counter culture," "black consciousness," "sexual permissiveness," "the death of God," . . . the abandonment of proprieties, pieties, decorums connoted by "go-go funds," "fast money," swinger groovy hippie drop-out pop Beatles Andy Baby Jane Bernie Huey Eldridge LSD marathon encounter stone underground rip-off. . . . This whole side of American life that gushed forth when postwar American affluence finally blew the lid off—all this novelists simply turned away from, gave up by default. That left a huge gap in American letters, a gap big enough to drive an ungainly Reo rig like the New Journalism through.

When I reached New York in the early Sixties, I couldn't believe the scene I saw spread out before me. New York was pandemonium with a big grin on. Among people with money—and they seemed to be multiplying like shad—it was the wildest, looniest time since the 1920's . . . a universe of creamy forty-five-year-old fashionable fatties with walnut-shell eyes out on the giblet slab wearing the hip-huggers and the minis and the Little Egypt eyes and the sideburns and the boots and the bells and the love beads, doing the Watusi and the Funky Broadway and jiggling and grinning and sweating and sweating and grinning and jiggling until the onset of dawn or saline depletion, whichever came first. . . . It was a hulking carnival. But what really amazed me was that as a writer

I had it practically all to myself. As fast as I could possibly do it, I was turning out articles on this amazing spectacle that I saw bubbling and screaming right there in front of my wondering eyes—New York!—and all the while I just knew that some enterprising novelist was going to come along and *do* this whole marvelous scene with one gigantic daring bold stroke. It was so ready, so *ripe*—beckoning . . . but it never happened. To my great amazement New York simply remained the journalist's bonanza. For that matter, novelists seemed to shy away from the life of the great cities altogether. The thought of tackling such a subject seemed to terrify them, confuse them, make them doubt their own powers. And besides, it would have meant tackling social realism as well.

To my even greater amazement I had the same experience when I came upon 1960's California. This was the very incubator of new styles of living, and these styles were right there for all to see, ricocheting off every eyeball—and again a few amazed journalists working in the new form had it all to themselves, even the psychedelic movement, whose waves are still felt in every part of the country, in every grammar school even, like the intergalactic pulse. I wrote *The Electric Kool-Aid Acid Test* and then waited for the novels that I was sure would come pouring out of the psychedelic experience . . . but they never came forth, either. I learned later that publishers had been waiting, too. They had been practically crying for novels by the new writers who must be out there somewhere, the new writers who would do the big novels of the hippie life or campus life or radical movements or the war in Vietnam or dope or sex or black militancy or encounter groups or the whole whirlpool all at once. They waited, and all they got was the Prince of Alienation . . . sailing off to Lonesome Island on his Tarot boat with his back turned and his Timeless cape on, reeking of camphor balls.

Amazing, as I say. If nothing else had done it, that would have. The—New Journalists—Parajournalists—had the whole crazed obscene uproarious Mammon-faced drug-soaked mau-mau lust-oozing Sixties in America all to themselves.

So the novelists had been kind enough to leave behind for our boys quite a nice little body of material: the whole of American society, in effect. It only remained to be seen if magazine writers could master the techniques, in nonfiction, that had given the novel of social realism such power. And here we come to a fine piece of irony. In abandoning social realism novelists also abandoned certain vital matters of technique. As a result, by 1969 it was obvious that these magazine writers—the very lumpenproles themselves!—had also gained a technical edge on novelists. It was marvelous. For journalists to take Technique away from the novelists—somehow it reminded me of Edmund Wilson's old exhortation in the early 1930's: Let's take communism away from the Communists.

If you follow the progress of the New Journalism closely through the 1960's, you see an interesting thing happening. You see journalists learning the techniques of realism —particularly of the sort found in Fielding, Smollett, Balzac, Dickens and Gogol—from scratch. By trial and error, by "instinct" rather than theory, journalists began to discover the devices that gave the realistic novel its unique power, variously known as its "immediacy," its "concrete reality," its "emotional involvement," its "gripping" or "absorbing" quality.

This extraordinary power was derived mainly from just four devices they discovered. The basic one was scene-by-scene construction, telling the story by moving from scene to scene and resorting as little as possible to sheer historical narrative. Hence the sometimes extraordinary feats of reporting that the new journalists undertook: so that they could actually witness the scenes in other people's lives as they took place—and record the dialogue in full, which was device No. 2. Magazine writers, like the early novelists, learned by trial and error something that has since been demonstrated in academic studies: namely, that realistic dialogue involves the reader more completely than any other single device. It also establishes and defines character more quickly and effectively than any other single device. (Dickens has a way of fixing a character in your mind so that you have the feeling he has described every inch of his appearance—only to go back and discover that he actually took care of the physical description in two or three sentences; the rest he has accomplished with dialogue.) Journalists were working on dialogue of the fullest, most completely revealing sort in the very moment when novelists were cutting back, using dialogue in more and more cryptic, fey and curiously abstract ways.

The third device was the so-called "third-person point of view," the technique of presenting every scene to the reader through the eyes of a particular character, giving the reader the feeling of being inside the character's mind and experiencing the emotional reality of the scene as he experiences it. Journalists had often used the first-person point of view—"I was there"—just as autobiographers, memoirists and novelists had. . . . This is very limiting for the journalist, however, since he can bring the reader inside the mind of only one character—himself—a point of view that often proves irrelevant to the story and irritating to the reader. Yet how could a journalist, writing nonfiction, accurately penetrate the thoughts of another person?

The answer proved to be marvelously simple: interview him about his thoughts and emotions, along with everything else. This was what I had done in *The Electric Kool-Aid Acid Test*, what John Sack did in *M* and what Gay Talese did in *Honor Thy Father*.

The fourth device has always been the least understood. This is the recording of everyday gestures, habits, manners, customs, styles of furniture, clothing, decoration, styles of traveling, eating, keeping house, modes of behaving toward children, servants, superiors, inferiors, peers, plus the various looks, glances, poses, styles of walking and other symbolic details that might exist within a scene. Symbolic of what? Symbolic, generally, of people's *status life*, using that term in the broad sense of the entire pattern of behavior and possessions through which people express their position in the world or what they think it is or what they hope it to be. The recording of such details is not mere embroidery in prose. It lies as close to the center of the power of realism as any other device in literature. It is the very essence of the "absorbing" power of Balzac, for example. Balzac barely used point of view at all in the refined sense that Henry James used it later on. And yet the reader comes away feeling that he has been even more completely "inside" Balzac's characters than James's. Why? Here is the sort of thing Balzac does over and over. Before introducing you to Monsieur and Madame Marneffe personally (in *Cousine Bette*) he brings you into their drawing room and conducts a social autopsy: "The furniture covered in faded cotton velvet, the plaster statuettes masquerading as Florentine bronzes, the clumsily carved painted chandelier with its candle rings of molded glass, the carpet, a bargain whose low price was explained too late by the quantity of cotton in it, which was now visible to the naked eye—everything in the room, to the very curtains (which would have taught you that the handsome appearance of wool damask lasts only three years)"—everything in the room begins to absorb one into the lives of a pair of down-at-the-heel social climbers, Monsieur and Madame Marneffe.

Balzac piles up these details so relentlessly and at the same time so meticulously—there is scarcely a detail in the later Balzac that does not illuminate some point of status—that he triggers the reader's memories of his own status life, his own ambitions, insecurities, delights, disasters, plus the thousand and one small humiliations and the status coups of everyday life, and triggers them over and over until he creates an atmosphere as rich and involving as the Joycean use of point of view.

I am fascinated by the fact that experimenters in the physiology of the brain, still the great terra incognita of the sciences, seem to be heading toward the theory that the human mind or psyche does not have a discrete, internal existence. It is not a possession locked inside one's skull. During every moment of consciousness it is linked directly to external clues as to one's status in a social and not merely a physical sense and cannot develop or survive without them. If this turns out to be so, it could explain how novelists such as Balzac, Gogol, Dickens and Dostoevsky were able to be so "involving" without using point of view with the sophistication of Flaubert or James or Joyce. . . .

I have never heard a journalist talk about the recording of status life in any way that showed he even thought of it as a separate device. It is simply something that journalists in the new form have gravitated toward. That rather elementary and joyous ambition to show the reader *real life*—"Come here! Look! This is the way people live these days! These are the things they do!"—leads to it naturally. In any case, the result is the same. While so many novelists abandon the task altogether—and at the same time give up two thirds of the power of dialogue—journalists continue to experiment with all the devices of realism, revving them up, trying to use them in a bigger way, with the full passion of innocents and discoverers.

Their innocence has kept them free. Even novelists who try the new form . . . suddenly relax and treat themselves to forbidden sweets. If they want to indulge a craving for Victorian rhetoric or for a Humphrey Clinkerism such as, "At this point the attentive roader may wonder how our hero could possibly . . ."—they go ahead and do it, as Mailer does in *The Armies Of The Night* with considerable charm. In this new journalism there are no sacerdotal rules; not yet in any case. . . . If the journalist wants to shift from third-person point of view to first-person point of view in the same scene, or in and out of different characters' points of view, or even from the narrator's omniscient voice to someone else's stream of consciousness—as occurs in *The Electric Kool-Aid Acid Test*—he does it. For the gluttonous Goths there is still only the outlaw's rule regarding technique: take, use, improvise. The result is a form that is not merely *like a novel*. It consumes devices that happen to have originated with the novel and mixes them with every other device known to prose. And all the while, quite beyond matters of technique, it enjoys an advantage so obvious, so built-in, one almost forgets what a power it has: the simple fact that the reader knows *all this actually happened*. The disclaimers have been erased. The screen is gone. The writer is one step closer to the absolute involvement of the reader that Henry James and James Joyce dreamed of and never achieved.

At this point, as I have already discovered, the student of literature tends to say: Even if I grant you that, what about the *higher* accomplishments of the great fiction writers? You haven't even mentioned the creation of character, much less such matters as psychological depth, a sense of history, the struggle of ideas, the moral consciousness of man, the great *themes* of EngLit, in short. To which I would say: I am talking about technique; as for the rest, from character to moral consciousness (whatever that may be), it depends upon the writer's experience and intellect, his insights, the quality of his emotions, his ability to see into others, his "genius," to use the customary word—and this remains so whether he is working in fiction or in journalism. My argument is that the genius of any writer—again, in fiction or in nonfiction—will be severely handicapped if he cannot master, or if he abandons, the techniques of realism. The psychological, moral, philosophical, emotional, poetic, visionary (one may supply the adjectives as needed) power of Dickens, Dostoyevsky, Joyce, Mann, Faulkner, is made possible only by the fact that they first wired their work into the main circuit, which is realism.

Novelists have made a disastrous miscalculation over the past twenty years about the nature of realism. Their view of the matter is pretty well summed up by the editor of the *Partisan Review*, William Phillips: "In fact, realism is just another formal device, not a permanent method for dealing with experience." I suspect that precisely the opposite is true. If our friends the cognitive psychologists ever reach the point of knowing for sure, I think they will tell us something on this order: the introduction of realism into literature by people like Richardson, Fielding and Smollett was like the introduction of electricity into machine technology. It was *not* just another device. It raised the state of the art to a new magnitude. The effect of realism on the emotions was something that had never been conceived of before. No one was ever moved to tears by reading about the unhappy fates of heroes and heroines in Homer, Sophocles, Molière, Racine, Sydney, Spenser or Shakespeare. But even the impeccable Lord Jeffrey, editor of the *Edinburgh Review*, had cried—actually blubbered, boohooed, snuffled and sighed—over the death of Dickens' Little Nell in *The Old Curiosity Shop*.

One doesn't have to admire Dickens or any of the other writers who first demonstrated this power in order to appreciate the point. For writers to give up this unique power in the quest for a more sophisticated kind of fiction—it is as if an engineer were to set but to develop a more sophisticated machine technology by first of all discarding the principle of electricity. In any case, journalists now enjoy a tremendous technical advantage. They have all the juice. This is not to say they have made maximum use of it. The work done in journalism over the past ten years easily outdazzles the work done in fiction, but that is saying very little. All that one can say is that the material and the techniques are now available, and the time is right.

The status crisis that first hit literature's middle class, the essayists or "men of letters," has now hit the novelists themselves. Some have turned directly to nonfiction. Some, such as Gore Vidal, Herbert Gold, William Styron and Ronald Sukenick, have tried forms that land on a curious ground in between, part fiction and part nonfiction. Still others have begun to pay homage to the power of the New Journalism by putting real people, with their real names, into fictional situations. . . . They're all sweating bullets. . . . Actually I wouldn't say the novel is dead. It's the kind of comment that doesn't mean much in any case. It is only the prevailing fashions among novelists that are washed up. I think there is a tremendous future for a sort of novel that will be called the journalistic novel or perhaps documentary novel, novels of intense social realism based upon the same painstaking reporting that goes into the New Journalism. I see no reason why novelists who look down on Arthur Hailey's work couldn't do the same sort of reporting and research he does—and write it better, if they're able. There are certain areas of life that journalism still cannot move into easily, particularly for reasons of invasion of privacy, and it is in this margin that the novel will be able to grow in the future.

When we talk about the "rise" or "death" of literary genres, we are talking about status, mainly. The novel no longer has the supreme status it enjoyed for ninety years (1875–1965), but neither has the New Journalism won it for itself. The status of the New Journalism is not secured by any means. In some quarters the contempt for it is boundless . . . even breathtaking. . . . With any luck at all the new genre will never be sanctified, never be exalted, never given a theology. I probably shouldn't even go around talking it up the way I have in this piece. All I meant to say when I started out was that the New Journalism can no longer be ignored in an artistic sense. The rest I take back. . . . The hell with it. . . . Let chaos reign . . . louder music, more wine. . . . The hell with the standings. . . . The top rung is up for grabs. All the old traditions are exhausted, and no new one is yet established. All bets are off! the odds are canceled! it's anybody's ball game! . . . the horses are all drugged! the track is glass! . . . and out of such glorious chaos may come, from the most unexpected source, in the most unexpected form, some nice new fat Star Streamer Rockets that will light up the sky.

NOTES

1. Prepared, in both instances, by *New Yorker* staff members, if one need edit.

2. The first of two *New York Review of Books* articles on "Parajournalism" (August, 1965) said: "The genre originated in *Esquire* but it now appears more flamboyantly in the New York *Herald Tribune*" . . . "Dick Schaap is one of the *Trib*'s parajournalists". . . . "Another is Jimmy Breslin . . . the tough-guy-with-the-heart-of-schmaltz bard of the little man and the big celeb". . . . Later the piece spoke of "Gay Talese, an *Esquire* alumnus who now parajournalizes mostly in *The Times*, in a more dignified way, of course". . . . "But the king of the cats is, of course, Tom Wolfe, an *Esquire* alumnus who writes mostly for the *Trib*'s Sunday magazine, *New York*, which is edited by a former *Esquire* editor, Clay Felker. . . ."

Study Guide

TALKING POINTS

I.   George Orwell says those who believe that the reform of language is impossible share "the half-conscious belief that language is a natural growth and not an instrument which we shape for our own purposes." What do you believe? While you are discussing this, consider Hugh Kenner's assertion that the plain style is artifice and that it "seems to be announcing at every phrase its subjection to the check of experience and nameable things."

II.   Explore the implications of Kenner's claim that "[i]f fiction speaks political truth, it does so by allegory."

III. Discuss Orwell's belief that there is a connection between debased language and the quality of political life. Is it possible to think of democracy as—substantially and fundamentally—a linguistic phenomenon? What is the place of journalism in the architecture of democracy?

IV.   What does S. I. Hayakawa mean by the term "map" language and the assertion that there is a responsibility to use the report to make "good maps of the territory of experience"? How do such notions figure into your picture of journalistic language and responsibility?

V.   What do you make of the definition of narrative offered by Robert Scholes and Robert Kellog? They write: "By narrative we mean all those literary works which are distinguished by two characteristics: the presence of a story and a story-teller."

VI.   Consider the meanings of the following terms and the place of each in the discussion of narrative:

- Romance
- Fable
- Legend
- Folktale
- Myth

VII.   Is Tom Wolfe right when he says the "modern notion of art is an essentially religious or magical one" that fails to acknowledge the role of reporting? What is the role of reporting in fiction writing?

VIII. Wolfe observes that the narrator's voice in nonfiction typically assumes "a calm, cultivated . . . genteel voice" or that, as he then puts it, "a well-known bore" (or "pallid little troll") with "a pedestrian mind" routinely turns up to perform the narrative tasks. With these and other hearty insults in mind, ask yourself if the neutral voice of the narrator in journalism could actually be a good thing. Is it possible—is it sometimes desirable—to construct a more lively narrator as a presence in narrative journalism?

IX.   Reread Hersey's critique of Wolfe's work in Hersey's essay, "The Legend on the License" in Part II, Section B and discuss Wolfe's claims in light of Hersey's assessments.

X.   Assess the following four literary devices that Wolfe describes and imports into his nonfiction:

- Scene-by-scene construction
- Realistic dialogue
- Third-person point of view
- Recording of symbolic details

WORKBENCH

I.   Identify examples from sample essays, speeches, or articles and then discuss in detail each of the following:

- Dying metaphors
- Operators or verbal false limbs
- Pretentious diction
- Meaningless words

(While you are at it, collect and reflect on examples from your own work.)

II.   In your next assignments, follow carefully the advice Orwell offers: "A scrupulous writer, in every sentence that he writes, will ask himself [these] questions . . . : What am I trying to say? What words will express it? What image or idiom will make it clearer? Is this image fresh enough to have an effect? . . . Could I put it more shortly? Have I said anything that is avoidably ugly?" At the same time see if you can follow these injunctions:

- Never use a metaphor, simile, or other figure of speech that you are used to seeing in print.

- Never use a long word where a short one will do.

- If it is possible to cut a word out, always cut it out.

- Never use the passive where you can use the active.

- Never use a foreign phrase, a scientific word, or a jargon word if you can think of an everyday English equivalent.

- Break any of these rules rather than say anything outright barbarous.

III.   Analyze a manageable selection of newspaper or magazine articles with a view to spotting loaded words and unwarranted inferences, judgments, and conclusions.

IV.   Scholes and Kellog describe a kind of evolution of narrative forms in Western culture. A study of journalism history reveals that news writing has also "evolved." That evolution can be drawn from short public notices and business items in eighteenth-century newspapers to multimedia productions on the Web sites of our own time. Using the essays in this book and your knowledge of journalism history, compile a list of as many news narrative forms as you can think of. Write a one-paragraph description of each form on your list. Begin with these: the inverted pyramid report, the human-interest story, the investigative report, the "New Journalism"-style feature.

V.   In an era when accusations of news media bias are common, S. I. Hayakawa offers a set of standards on the reliability of reports. Reports, he argues, must be verifiable, and they must be as free as possible from inferences, judgments, and "loaded words." Go on a hunting expedition in your own journalism. Be on the lookout for any of the elements that undercut its reliability. Can you find in your work any evidence of bias? Now apply the same methods of study to a newspaper or a news broadcast. Where is there evidence of bias? Where are the inferences, judgments, and loaded words?

VI.   Make additions to your "editor's lexicon."

VII.   Using a person, place, or event from your beat, write two radically different versions of the same story. Your first version should be scrupulously neutral—let's call it a "report." Write it with special care to make sure all the elements are verifiable. Try to liberate your report from the distorting effects Hayakawa warns of and strive for the clarity Orwell calls for. Then put aside your report. Now write a version of the same story using techniques described by Wolfe that place us on the scene. Think of plot, character, and setting.

INTERPRETATION

INTRODUCTION

As a democratic craft, journalism arises out of the impulse to bring important and interesting matters in the here and now to the attention of citizens—and then to make sense of these matters. This act of making sense is cognitive, a way of knowing and understanding. In reporting, it may begin with the literal: a description of what actually happened expressed in a common language, a discourse that is plain and concrete, meaningful and comprehensible.

But in addition to the cognition that comes from unadorned literalism, writers add layers of meaning. They enlarge what they see through a variety of magnifying lenses. Let us call all these layers of sense-making by a single name: "interpretation." We could have called it "analysis" or something more muscular—something that might require wearing a lab coat. Instead, we chose "interpretation" because it is a more general and inclusive term and because it directs attention to matters central to the book as a whole.

The term "interpretation" describes not just analytical methods, which we have chosen to feature in this section, but also all the devices of making sense we have already discussed. Meaning is inscribed onto events by using original figures of speech and analogies (the fresh images Orwell praised, for example, in his essay "Politics and the English Language"), by stretching the vision of news (as Max Ways did in his essay "What's Wrong with News?"), or by writing narratives in the languages and archetypes of ancient myths. Journalistic stories on pollution in the Everglades borrow from stories of the apocalypse; stories of human failure remind us of Sisyphus. So the conferral of meaning may come from aligning current events to familiar myths or by stitching—here we are squarely in the domain of analysis—the explanatory devices of history or the social sciences into journalistic narratives. This concluding section of the book contains reflections on this process.

Jordan Peterson, a Canadian writer, reminds us that "the world can be validly construed as a forum for action, or as a place of things."[1] In their narrative art, journalists try to make sense of action, leaving to scientists the task of making sense of things. We use the narrative arts—humanities, literature, mythology, and journalism—to make sense of this world of motion and action. So although journalists might borrow from science to form hypotheses, measure elements, and adduce evidence, they normally stitch their interpretations into a narrative structure containing literary and even poetic devices. A master journalist is a master of both the literary and analytical dimensions of the craft.

The first essay is from the report of the Hutchins Commission on Freedom of the Press (1947), a classic reference in journalism studies. It includes a clear statement of the overarching goals of journalism and reminds us that journalists are not only obliged to circulate facts, but to promote understanding by providing context and interpretation. The essay is a final reminder of journalism's public and democratic mission. It provides a backdrop to the essays that follow.

The second essay for consideration is by James Carey, who explores in detail the manner in which the concepts of "how" and "why" figure in journalistic storytelling. The "why" is one of the five Ws of journalistic method in which journalists are expected, in order to render full accounts, to provide answers to these questions: Who? What? Where? When? Why? And then how? Professor Carey remarks that "[h]ow and why are the most problematic aspects of American journalism: the dark continent and invisible landscape." Despite the best and declared intentions of journalists, he says, why and how "are what we most want to get out of a news story and are least likely to receive or what we must in most cases supply ourselves."

In journalism, the "why" and "how" questions are often conspicuous by their absence, missing because—this is Carey's language—they are "properties of the whole, not the part." They are pieces of a larger narrative that unfolds over time. Explanations answering the "why" and the "how" of events are difficult to achieve under the burden of deadline, but they can emerge as the arc of the whole story becomes visible. As Carey remarks, "[t]o expect the dramatic unity of a three-act play in a twelve-paragraph story in a daily newspaper is to doom oneself to perpetual disappointment. . . ."

When journalists do seek answers to the questions of why and how, according to Carey, they are too dependent upon explanations and story frames that refer to motives. In government writing, for example, reporters cleave too routinely to theories of political motive and special interest. But, as he notes, other explanatory devices are available that would locate journalists intellectually in richer soil. He is clearly thinking of some of the methods of formal disciplines such as political science, sociology, economics, literary theory, or classics. To call a fallen political hero a "tragic figure" is to draw upon ideas of character and dramatic narrative that can be traced back to Aristotle.

We turn next to an essay by Paul Starobin and Pamela Varley, who reflect on the phenomenon of "The Conceptual Scoop." These authors point to examples of journalism that involve, as Tom Rosenstiel has noted, "scoops of perception." The "conceptual scoop" is a "fresh interpretation of the political landscape" that in a Lippmannesque fashion connects "dots into big pictures." According to Starobin and Varley, Ron Brownstein of the *Los Angeles Times* is a noted practitioner of this style of writing. Brownstein says that traditional practice calls on journalists "to collect as many pieces of information" as he or she can. His goal, he says, is "to build a box around the information —some sort of conceptual framework."

Another practitioner is Thomas Edsall of *The Washington Post*, who has successfully used categories such as race, class, and gender—staples of social-science explanatory method—to illuminate current events. Yet another is John B. Judis of *The New Republic*, who, the authors say, "has a knack for using history as a lens for examining contemporary politics." And yet another is E. J. Dionne, also of *The Washington Post*, who has a background in political science and polling. The texts produced by such writers reveal that they possess a theorized understanding of human behavior and social systems —theories that shed light and meaning on the news—and, further, an understanding of the evidentiary methods that support such theories.

We believe that the study of journalism would be strengthened if more attention and time in the curriculum were turned over to the study of the methods of formal interpretation that have been incubated within university disciplines. We are seeking to enlarge journalism so that it incorporates more routinely knowledge and methods generated by historians, social scientists, anthropologists, and critics. If this were to happen, journalism could be seen not just for its current strengths, but also for its application of the forms of knowledge generated in the academy to an understanding of the here and now.

NOTE

1. Jordan Peterson, *Maps of Meaning: The Architecture of Belief* (New York: Routledge, 1999), xxi.

30

THE REQUIREMENTS

Commission on Freedom of the Press

If the freedom of the press is freighted with the responsibility of providing the current intelligence needed by a free society, we have to discover what a free society requires. Its requirements in America today are greater in variety, quantity, and quality than those of any previous society in any age. They are the requirements of a self-governing republic of continental size, whose doings have become, within a generation, matters of common concern in new and important ways. Its internal arrangements, from being thought of mainly as matters of private interest and automatic market adjustments, have become affairs of conflict and conscious compromise among organized groups, whose powers appear not to be bounded by "natural law," economic or other. Externally, it has suddenly assumed a leading role in the attempt to establish peaceful relationships among all the states on the globe.

Today our society needs, first, a truthful, comprehensive, and intelligent account of the day's events in a context which gives them meaning; second, a forum for the exchange of comment and criticism; third, a means of projecting the opinions and attitudes of the groups in the society to one another; fourth, a method of presenting and clarifying the goals and values of the society; and, fifth, a way of reaching every member of the society by the currents of information, thought, and feeling which the press supplies.

Commission on Freedom of the Press, "The Requirements," Chapter 2 of *A Free and Responsible Press* (Chicago: University of Chicago Press, 1947), 20–29. Reprinted by permission of the University of Chicago Press.

The Commission has no idea that these five ideal demands can ever be completely met. All of them cannot be met by any one medium; some do not apply at all to a particular unit; nor do all apply with equal relevance to all parts of the communications industry. The Commission does not suppose that these standards will be new to the managers of the press; they are drawn largely from their professions and practices.

A TRUTHFUL, COMPREHENSIVE, AND INTELLIGENT ACCOUNT OF THE DAY'S EVENTS IN A CONTEXT WHICH GIVES THEM MEANING

The first requirement is that the media should be accurate. They should not lie.

Here the first link in the chain of responsibility is the reporter at the source of the news. He must be careful and competent. He must estimate correctly which sources are most authoritative. He must prefer firsthand observation, to hearsay. He must know what questions to ask, what things to observe, and which items to report. His employer has the duty of training him to do his work as it ought to be done.

Of equal importance with reportorial accuracy are the identification of fact as fact and opinion as opinion, and their separation, so far as possible. This is necessary all the way from the reporter's file, up through the copy and makeup desks and editorial offices, to the final, published product. The distinction cannot, of course, be made absolute. There is no fact without a context and no factual report which is uncolored by the opinions of the reporter. But modern conditions require greater effort than ever to make the distinction between fact and opinion. In a simpler order of society published accounts of events within the experience of the community could be compared with other sources of information. Today this is usually impossible. The account of an isolated fact, however accurate in itself, may be misleading and, in effect, untrue.

The greatest danger here is in the communication of information internationally. The press now bears a responsibility in all countries, and particularly in democratic countries, where foreign policies are responsive to popular majorities, to report international events in such a way that they can be understood. It is no longer enough to report *the fact* truthfully. It is now necessary to report *the truth about the fact*.

In this country a similar obligation rests upon the press in reporting domestic news. The country has many groups which are partially insulated from one another and which need to be interpreted to one another. Factually correct but substantially untrue accounts of the behavior of members of one of these social islands can intensify the antagonisms of others toward them. A single incident will be accepted as a sample of group action unless the press has given a flow of information and interpretation concerning the relations between two racial groups such as to enable the reader to set a single event in its proper perspective. If it is allowed to pass as a sample of such action, the requirement that the press present an accurate account of the day's events in a context which gives them meaning has not been met.

A FORUM FOR THE EXCHANGE OF COMMENT AND CRITICISM

The second requirement means that the great agencies of mass communication should regard themselves as common carriers of public discussion.[1] The units of the press have in varying degrees assumed this function and should assume the responsibilities which go with it, more generally and more explicitly.

It is vital to a free society that an idea should not be stifled by the circumstances of its birth. The press cannot and should not be expected to print everybody's ideas. But the giant units can and should assume the duty of publishing significant ideas contrary to their own, as a matter of objective reporting, distinct from their proper function of advocacy. Their control over the various ways of reaching the ear of America is such that, if they do not publish ideas which differ from their own, those ideas will never reach the ear of America. If that happens, one of the chief reasons for the freedom which these giants claim disappears.

Access to a unit of the press acting as a common carrier is possible in a number of ways, all of which, however, involve selection on the part of the managers of the unit. The individual whose views are not represented on an editorial page may reach an audience through a public statement reported as news, through a letter to the editor, through a statement printed in advertising space, or through a magazine article. But some seekers for space are bound to be disappointed and must resort to pamphlets or such duplicating devices as will spread their ideas to such public as will attend to them.

But all the important viewpoints and interests in the society should be represented in its agencies of mass communication. Those who have these viewpoints and interests cannot count on explaining them to their fellow-citizens through newspapers or radio stations of their own. Even if they could make the necessary investment, they could have no assurance that their publications would be read or their programs heard by the public outside their own adherents. An ideal combination would include general media, inevitably solicitous to present their own views, but setting forth other views fairly. As checks on their fairness, and partial safeguards against ignoring important matters, more specialized media of advocacy have a vital place. In the absence of such a combination the partially insulated groups in society will continue to be insulated. The unchallenged assumptions of each group will continue to harden into prejudice. The mass medium reaches across all groups; through the mass medium they can come to understand one another.

Whether a unit of the press is an advocate or a common carrier, it ought to identify the sources of its facts, opinions, and arguments so that the reader or listener can judge them. Persons who are presented with facts, opinions, and arguments are properly influenced by the general reliability of those who offer them. If the veracity of statements is to be appraised, those who offer them must be known.

Identification of source is necessary to a free society. Democracy, in time of peace, at least, has a justifiable confidence that full and free discussion will strengthen rather than weaken it. But, if the discussion is to have the effect for which democracy hopes, if it is to be really full and free, the names and the characters of the participants must not be hidden from view.

THE PROJECTION OF A REPRESENTATIVE PICTURE OF THE CONSTITUENT GROUPS IN THE SOCIETY

This requirement is closely related to the two preceding. People make decisions in large part in terms of favorable or unfavorable images. They relate fact and opinion to stereotypes. Today the motion picture, the radio, the book, the magazine, the newspaper, and the comic strip are principal agents in creating and perpetuating these conventional conceptions. When the images they portray fail to present the social group truly, they tend to pervert judgment.

Such failure may occur indirectly and incidentally. Even if nothing is said about the Chinese in the dialogue of a film, yet if the Chinese appear in a succession of pictures as sinister drug addicts and militarists, an image of China is built which needs to be balanced by another. If the Negro appears in the stories published in magazines of national circulation only as a servant, if children figure constantly in radio dramas as impertinent and ungovernable brats—the image of the Negro and the American child is distorted. The plugging of special color and "hate" words in radio and press dispatches, in advertising copy, in news stories—such words as "ruthless," "confused," "bureaucratic"—performs inevitably the same image-making function.

Responsible performance here simply means that the images repeated and emphasized be such as are in total representative of the social group as it is. The truth about any social group, though it should not exclude its weaknesses and vices, includes also recognition of its values, its aspirations, and its common humanity. The Commission holds to the faith that if people are exposed to the inner truth of the life of a particular group, they will gradually build up respect for and understanding of it.

THE PRESENTATION AND CLARIFICATION OF THE GOALS AND VALUES OF THE SOCIETY

The press has a similar responsibility with regard to the values and goals of our society as a whole. The mass media, whether or not they wish to do so, blur or clarify these ideals as they report the failings and achievements of every day.[2] The Commission does not call upon the press to sentimentalize, to manipulate the facts for the purpose of painting a rosy picture. The Commission believes in realistic reporting of the events and forces that militate against the attainment of social goals as well as those which work for them. We must recognize, however, that the agencies of mass communication are an educational instrument, perhaps the most powerful there is; and they must assume a responsibility like that of educators in stating and clarifying the ideals toward which the community should strive.

FULL ACCESS TO THE DAY'S INTELLIGENCE

It is obvious that the amount of current information required by the citizens in a modern industrial society is far greater than that required in any earlier day. We do not assume that all citizens at all times will actually use all the material they receive. By necessity or choice large numbers of people voluntarily delegate analysis and decision to leaders whom they trust. Such leadership in our society is freely chosen and constantly changing; it is informal, unofficial, and flexible. Any citizen may at any time assume the power of decision. In this way government is carried on by consent.

But such leadership does not alter the need for the wide distribution of news and opinion. The leaders are not identified; we can inform them only by making information available to everybody.

The five requirements listed in this chapter suggest what our society is entitled to demand of its press. We can now proceed to examine the tools, the structure, and the performance of the press to see how it is meeting these demands.

Let us summarize these demands in another way.

The character of the service required of the American press by the American people differs from the service previously demanded, first, in this—that it is essential to the operation of the economy and to the government of the Republic. Second, it is a service of greatly increased responsibilities both as to the quantity and as to the quality of the information required. In terms of quantity, the information about themselves and about their world made available to the American people must be as extensive as the range of their interests and concerns as citizens of a self-governing, industrialized community in the closely integrated modern world. In terms of quality, the information provided must be provided in such a form, and with so scrupulous a regard for the wholeness of the truth and the fairness of its presentation, that the American people may make for themselves, by the exercise of reason and of conscience, the fundamental decisions necessary to the direction of their government and of their lives.

NOTES

1. By the use of this analogy the Commission does not intend to suggest that the agencies of communication should be subject to the legal obligations of common carriers, such as compulsory reception of all applicants for space, the regulation of rates, etc.

2. A striking indication of the continuous need to renew the basic values of our society is given in the recent poll of public opinion by the National Opinion Research Center at Denver, in which one out of every three persons polled did not think the newspapers should be allowed to criticize the American form of government, even in peacetime. Only 57 per cent thought that the Socialist party should be allowed, in peacetime, to publish newspapers in the United States. Another poll revealed that less than a fourth of those questioned had a "reasonably accurate idea" of what the Bill of Rights is. Here is widespread ignorance with regard to the value most cherished by the press—its own freedom—which seems only dimly understood by many of its consumers.

31

THE DARK CONTINENT OF AMERICAN JOURNALISM

James W. Carey

> Men can do nothing without the make-believe of a beginning. Even Science,
> the strict measurer, is obliged to start with a make-believe unit, and must fix on
> a point in the stars' unceasing journey when his sideral clock shall pretend
> that time is at Nought. . . . No retrospect will take us to the true beginning:
> and whether our prologue be in heaven or on earth, it is but a fraction
> of that all-presupposing fact with which our story sets out.
> —GEORGE ELIOT, *Daniel Deronda*

Journalists are writers of stories and, after hours, tellers of stories as well. The stories they tell are of stories they missed, stories they got, stories they scooped, and cautionary little tales that educate the apprentice to the glories, dangers, mysteries, and desires of the craft. One such story—one that might be called the "quest for the perfect lead"—features Edwin A. Lahey, a legendary reporter of the *Chicago Daily News*. Like most stories invoking legends, it is perhaps apocryphal, but its significance is less in its truth than in the point it attempts to make.

The story begins with a celebrated murder case of 1924, the Leopold-Loeb case. Nathan Leopold and Richard Loeb were teenage graduate students at the University of Chicago when they killed fourteen-year-old Bobby Franks in an attempt to commit the perfect crime. They made one mistake—a pair of Leopold's eyeglasses was found at the scene of the crime. They were arrested, brought to trial, and defended by the famous barrister Clarence Darrow. He had them plead guilty but successfully argued against the death penalty. Both were sentenced to life terms for the murder plus ninety-nine years for the kidnapping.

Nathan Leopold was paroled in 1958 and finished his life in Puerto Rico doing volunteer medical work. Richard Loeb was killed in Stateville Penitentiary in 1936 after making a homosexual advance toward another prisoner. Eddie Lahey, who covered the story for the *Daily News*, began his report with this lead:

> Richard Loeb, the well-known student of English, yesterday ended a sentence with a proposition.

Even if invented, the well-knownness of the story tells us something of the imagination and desires of American journalists. What makes the lead so gorgeous is not only the

James Carey, "The Dark Continent of American Journalism," *Reading the News; A Pantheon Guide to Popular Culture*, Robert Karl Manoff and Michael Schudson, eds. (New York: Pantheon Books, 1986), 146–196. Reprinted with the kind permission of the author.

way in which it encapsulates most of the elements of the news story—the five *W*'s and the *H*—but does so through a delightful play on words—journalistic prose brushing up against poetry, if only in the ambiguity it celebrates. The lead also illustrates a necessary condition of all good journalism: a profound collaboration between the writer and his audience.

Lahey marks this collaboration by the assumptions he makes about the knowledge his audience brings to the story: that they were constant readers who would remember Richard Loeb as an actor in a twelve-year-old drama; that they would remember who Loeb was at the time of the 1924 crime and therefore catch the irony of the "well-known student of English"; that they could appreciate from the drills of schoolmasters the play on preposition and proposition; and, finally, they would grasp the dual meaning of "sentence" in the sentence.

If the assumptions Lahey makes about his audience and the cleverness of his language set this lead apart, the desire it expresses and the elements contained within it make it emblematic of all journalism. All writing, all narrative art depends upon dramatic unity, bringing together plot, character, scene, method, and purpose. The distinctive and tyrannical aspect of daily journalism is the injunction that the elements be assembled, arrayed, and accounted for in the lead, the topic sentence, or at best—here is where the inverted pyramid comes in—the first paragraph. The balance of the story merely elaborates what is announced at the outset. (The long, often interminable stories of the *Wall Street Journal*, and many similar feature stories, are the exception; they, as T. S. Eliot said of Swinburne, diffuse their "meaning very thinly throughout an immense verbal spate.")

In Lahey's lead, the character, as is usual with American journalism, has pride of place: Richard Loeb is both the subject of the story and the sentence. The scene, when and where, is given in the Stateville dateline (conveniently both a place *and* a prison) and in the commonest word in any lead, "yesterday." The plot, the what, is cleverly implied, though left undeveloped, by the action and reaction—"ended a sentence with a preposition." Only the how is omitted from the lead (he was killed with a razor) and awaits another sentence.

And where is the why, the explanation of the act, the elucidation of the purposes, however misaligned, of the actors? Why did Richard Loeb make an advance, if indeed he did? Why did James Day, for that was his name, murder Richard Loeb, if that is what he did? No one, certainly not Eddie Lahey, knew. The why was merely an insinuation. It would be established, if at all, only by the courts. James Day, in fact, was acquitted on grounds of self-defense. Was it all an elaborate mistake, a behavioral ballet of misunderstood intentions? Lahey merely insinuates a why—he appeals to his readers' commonsense knowledge of what goes on in prisons, of what men are like in captivity. We must read the why into the story rather than out of it: Richard Loeb as a prisoner of sexual desire as well as of the prison itself.

The omission of the how and the insinuation of the why is absolutely unremarkable: indeed, it is the standard practice of daily journalism. How could it be otherwise? At one level, how merely answers the question of technique: in this case, the killing was accomplished with a razor. In other cases, how tells us that interest rates were lowered by increasing the money supply, the football victory was achieved via a new formation, the political candidate won through superior precinct organization. The how is clearly of less importance than the what and, in our culture, the who, and can be relegated safely to subsequent sentences and paragraphs.

At another, and deeper, level, answering how requires detailing the actual sequence of acts, actors, and events that leads to a particular conclusion. How fills in a space; it tells us how an intention (the why) becomes an accomplishment (the what). How puts the reader in touch with the hard surfaces of human activity, the actual set of contingent circumstances. Loeb did this; Day did that—a blind chain of events, finally detailed for a jury, leading to a hideous outcome. When the description becomes fine-grained enough, how merges into why: a description becomes an explanation.

Why answers to the question of explanation. It accounts for events, actions, and actors. It is a search for the deeper underlying factors which lie behind the surfaces of the news story. "A story is worthless if it doesn't tell me why something happened," says Allan M. Siegal, news editor of the *New York Times*. Well, Mr. Siegal goes too far. If we threw out all the stories in the *Times* that failed to answer the question "why," there wouldn't be much newspaper left beyond the advertisements. Nonetheless, the why element attempts to make things sensible, coherent, explicable. It satisfies our desire to believe that the world, at least most of the time, is driven by something other than blind chance.

How and why are the most problematic aspects of American journalism: the dark continent and invisible landscape. Why and how are what we most want to get out of a news story and are least likely to receive or what we must in most cases supply ourselves. Both largely elude and must elude the conventions of daily journalism, as they elude, incidentally, art and science. Our interest in "what's new," "what's happening," is not merely cognitive and aesthetic. We want more than the facts pleasingly arranged. We also want to know how to feel about events and what, if anything, to do about them. If they occur by luck or blind chance, that is a kind of explanation, too. It tells us to be tragically resigned to them; indeed, luck and chance are the unannounced dummy variables of journalistic thought, as they are of common sense. We need not only to know but to understand, not only to grasp but to take an attitude toward the events and personalities that pass before us. But to have an understanding or an attitude depends upon depth in the news story. Why and how attempt to supply this depth, even if honored every day largely in the breach.

The fact that news stories seldom make sense in this larger context is the most frequent, punishing, and uncharitable accusation made of daily journalism. Listen to one comment, this about daily reporting from Washington, among the many that might be cited:

> The daily news coverage travels over surfaces of words and events, but it rarely reaches deeper to the underlying reality of *how* things actually happen. Its own conventions and reflexes, in large measure, prevent the news media from doing more. Until this changes too, citizens will continue to be confused by the daily slices of news from Washington. Periodically, they will continue to be shocked by occasional comprehensive revelations of what's really happening, *deeper accounts which explain the events* they thought they understood.

This obsessive criticism of daily journalism is true as far as it goes, though it is unforgivably self-righteous. What it overlooks is that depth—the how and the why—are rarely in any individual story. They are properties of the whole, not the part; the coverage, not the account. To expect the dramatic unity of a three-act play in a twelve-paragraph story in a daily newspaper is to doom oneself to perpetual disappointment. But if a story can be kept alive in the news long enough, it can be fleshed out and rounded off. Journalists devote much of their energy to precisely that: keeping significant events afloat long enough so that interpretation, explanation, and thick description can be added as part of ongoing development. Alas, management and the marketing department devote much of their energy to precisely the opposite—making each front page look like a new chapter in human history.

Journalism must be examined as a corpus, not as a set of isolated stories. The corpus includes not only the multiple treatments of an event within the newspaper—breaking stories, follow-ups, news analysis, interpretation and background, critical commentary, editorials—but also the other forms of journalism that surround, correct, and complete the daily newspaper: television coverage, documentary and docudrama, the newsweeklies and journals of opinion and, finally, book-length journalism. It is a decade after the Vietnam War that its why is being established in books such as Loren Baritz's *Backfire*. The story of busing and racial desegregation in Boston—the how and the why—cannot be found in the *Boston Globe*'s massive coverage that won the paper a Pulitzer Prize. The story wasn't remotely complete until the publication of J. Anthony Lukas's *Common Ground*, though even that remarkable book subordinated the why of the busing story to the how—to the closegrained, personified flow of events. The story behind the story was that there was no story at all. All the standard explanations—racism, bureaucratic incompetence, political manipulation, journalistic irresponsibility—ebb away under the relentless detail of Lukas's narrative. Similarly, the story of apartheid in South Africa can never be adequately described or explained in the *New York Times* no matter how many stories are devoted to it or how relentlessly Anthony Lewis bangs away at it in his columns. Joseph Lelyveld's *Move Your Shadow* deepens our understanding beyond that provided in breaking stories of this riot or that, this government action or that, but it hardly explains either the origins or trajectory of that political system. If anything, the book makes apartheid politically more ambiguous, as it deepens our moral revulsion.

Journalism is, in fact, a curriculum. Its first course is the breaking stories of the daily press. There one gets a bare description: the identification of the actors and the events, the scene against which the events are played out and the tools available to the protagonists. Intermediate and advanced work—the fine-grained descriptions and interpretations—await the columns of analysis and interpretation, the weekly summaries and commentaries, and the book-length expositions. Each part of the curriculum depends on every other part.

It is a weakness of American journalism that the curriculum is so badly integrated and cross-referenced that each story starts anew as if no one had ever touched the subject before. It is also a weakness of American journalism that so few of the students ever get beyond the first course. But keep things in perspective. It is similarly a weakness, say, of American social science that the curriculum is incoherent and badly cross-referenced and so few of the students take more than the introductory course. It is worse. Most students think the introductory course is the curriculum, and this naive assumption is reinforced by the pretensions of teachers and textbook writers.

The weaknesses of American journalism are systemic; they are of a cloth with the weaknesses of American institutions generally, including education. Both journalism and education assume the constant student and the constant reader. American journalism assumes the figure who queues up every day for his dose of news and beyond that the commentary, analysis, and evidence that turn the "news" into knowledge. American education assumes the "constant student" who engages in lifelong learning; who, unsatisfied by the pieties and simplicities of Sociology I, goes on to explore subjects in depth and detail and along the way acquires a mastery of theory and evidence. This is both wrong and self-serving. But, to rephrase Walter Lippmann, more journalists and scholars have been ruined by self-importance than by liquor.

I

Many of the relations between the course and curriculum of American journalism, and many of the problems of description and explanation, are exemplified by an episode within the "big story" of recent years, the story of the American economy. Since at least 1980, we have been treated to a daily saga of runaway budget deficits, high unemployment, tax reform and reductions, roller-coaster stock market prices, corporate takeovers and consolidations, mounting trade deficits, rapidly rising military expenditures, and high, though moderating, interest rates.

An instructive episode in this larger story opened in January 1982 when William Greider, then of the *Washington Post*, published a long essay in *The Atlantic* entitled "The Education of David Stockman." The piece was based on eighteen "off-the-record" interviews with the then director of the Office of Management and Budget taped during the first nine months of the presidency of Ronald Reagan. The essay revealed Stockman's growing doubts about the wisdom of the economic policy Reagan was pursuing. Stockman early recognized that no matter how cleverly numbers were massaged, the president's economic policy would produce massive budget deficits and the economic stimulus from tax reduction would not generate sufficient revenue to offset increased expenditures for defense. The doctrines of supply-side economics on which Reagan had conducted his successful campaign were, in Stockman's estimation, naively optimistic or "voodoo economics," as George Bush had called them during the heat of the Republican primaries. The supply-side tax reduction of Ronald Reagan turned out to be no different from the demand-side tax reduction of President John Kennedy, except it was much more skewed toward the rich and powerful. Reagan's economic policy was a return to traditional Republican "trickle down" economics that helped the poor by first benefiting the rich.

Greider's essay revealed in stark terms the considerable pulling and hauling within the administration and Congress over economic policy. It underscored the compromises and trade-offs, the caving in to special interests, the triumph of expediency over principle that is inevitable in putting together a revenue and expenditure program. It set out the terms on which the private debate among presidential advisers was conducted and defined in "brutal terms" the genuine problems which Congress and the president would have to confront. It took us behind the calm exterior of the federal bureaucracy into a war of conflicting opinions where political choices were made amid ambiguity and uncertainty. To a certain extent, it demystified the process of budget-making by demonstrating that the experts had no magic wand or profound insight into the economy. They turned out to be pretty much like everyone else: confused about what was going on in the economy; badly divided among themselves as to remedies; not much more in control of the situation than the rankest amateurs. The piece revealed as well, at least as Greider saw it, an awesome paradox: Reagan's stunning legislative victories, which had dominated the news during the first months of his term, trapped him in the awesome fiscal crisis with which we still live. At least one of the roots of the paradox was in the Greider-Stockman revelation that the one impregnable, offlimits part of the budget was defense. This was the biggest peacetime arms buildup in the history of the republic—one which in five years would more than double the Pentagon's annual budget.

Despite the picture of conflict, indecision, and uncertainty over economic policy the *Atlantic* essay revealed, Reagan himself presented a confident image on television and in the newspaper: an image of fiscal control and responsibility, of a new era of stable growth, balanced budgets, stock market expansion, and lowered inflation: a calm and eloquent reassurance despite privately held doubts of many of his advisers, including Stockman.

For anyone familiar with bureaucracies, Greider's article rang true, particularly in contrasting the smooth and reassuring exterior of certainty and an interior space of policy-making dominated by conflict and disarray. But did the article explain anything? Hardly. It did account for Stockman's position on economic policy by showing something of the ideological commitments from which it derived. The essay, however, was primarily an answer to the question "how," a thick description of the actual process of policy-making, an etching of the space between intention and accomplishment that eludes so much of daily journalism. Greider's publisher, E. P. Dutton, described the essay this way when it reprinted it in book form: "*The Education of David Stockman* is a narrative of political action with overtones of tragedy as the idealistic young conservative reformer discovers the complexities of the political system and watches as his moral principles are undermined by the necessities of compromise." It sounds like a soap opera; indeed, the sentence has the cadence of the introduction to the old radio soap opera "Our Gal Sunday." And it is, in a way, a soap opera. While the essay is flat-footed and straightforward, it does have a strong narrative line. It opens with its one literary twist: a tour of the Stockman farm in western Michigan, situating the protagonist in his native habitat, among the conditions and people that formed him. The essay thereby sets up a contrast between a quasi-heroic protagonist who has learned solid ideological lessons in the outlands and the administration insiders who defeat him in the cloakrooms and boardrooms of Washington. The essay's revelatory power is in its consistent narrative focus—from David Stockman's point of view—and a dramatic line—from Michigan innocence to Washington defeat—which, while an exaggeration, makes the entire episode coherent and the descriptive detail informing.

But the story had an additional twist. Although the Greider-Stockman conversations were "off-the-record" (not for publication in any form), certain details were put on "background" (for anonymous publication only). *Washington Post* reporters pursued the leads the private discussions opened up and published the results. They found White

House sources to corroborate important information in the Stockman interviews so they could write independent stories. Other Washington journalists were covering and writing about these same matters. Therefore, the essential facts in the Greider essay appeared in the daily press attributed to those ubiquitous characters of Washington journalism: administration sources, senior officials, senior White House aides, key congressional aides, Defense Department advisers, etc. The key point, in Greider's mind, was that the *Atlantic* essay contained nothing that was not widely known among Washington journalists, nothing that had not already appeared in the daily press. Nonetheless, the article created one of those brief storms typical of a Washington season: a squall of comment, charges, and recriminations that dissipates as quickly as it appears. Stockman was called into the president's woodshed for a licking and emerged striking his breast intoning many *mea culpas*. Greider was pilloried for betraying principles of the press. He had, so it was charged, withheld information from his own paper and the public to publish it where it would get more attention.

When the *Atlantic* article appeared, Greider was transformed from a reporter to a source: he was now a who, the subject of a story. Some reporters who called for interviews obviously hadn't read the piece and wanted Greider to summarize it. They showed little interest in the substance of the article—the depiction of the process of policy-making, the specific policies developed, the paradox of legislative triumph and fiscal crisis—but much interest in the specific personalities inhabiting the story. They wanted to know about motive: Why did Stockman give the interviews? Why did Greider conduct them? Why did Stockman tell Greider the things he did? Why did Greider withhold such information from his own paper?

Greider tried to explain the ground rules for the interviews and the content of the article, but he found that sophisticated explanations did not hold up well in telephone interviews with reporters writing to deadline and in search of a pithy lead. Press accounts of the article by journalists who had read it were "brutal summaries" that sacrificed psychological nuance, character, plot, subtlety, and ambiguity—all those qualities which Greider thought made his piece distinctive and useful.

As I said earlier, the perplexing thing about the controversy was that the essential information contained in the *Atlantic* piece had been earlier reported in the daily press, though attributed to "senior budget officials." All Greider had done was to thicken the narrative and put Stockman's name in place of the anonymous source. It was now Stockman revealing his private doubts about the administration program. But if the information was already available, why the controversy? The answer is simple: in American journalism, names make news, and explanations in the news pretty much come down to the motives of the actors in the political drama.

Greider concluded that the conventions of daily journalism "serve only a very limited market—the elite audience of Washington insiders—while obscuring things for the larger audience of ordinary citizens." Such insiders can read names into the anonymous sources and can ferret out motives from the interests lying behind the innocence of the text. The text may answer how and why, but in ways accessible only to those who already know the rules of Washington and the reportorial game, those who already understand the background of government policy-making: the players and interests at loose in the process, the alliances that exist between officials and reporters. Greider came to believe that his *Atlantic* article refuted the simple and shallow version of reality that the news created when complex episodes were carved into daily slices. He also rediscovered an old lesson of journalism, a lesson recently restated by the journalist-turned-historian Robert Darnton: journalists write not for the public but for one another, for their editors, for their sources, and for other insiders who are part of the specialized world they are reporting. It is in this context that the deeply coded text of the daily news story develops. Such stories provide a forum in which "participants in political debates can argue with each other in semipublic disguises, influencing the flow of public dialogue and the content of elite opinion without having to answer directly for their utterances." Journalists and other insiders become so adept at the deep reading of veiled messages that they forget they are unintelligible to the ordinary reader, or, if intelligible, convey an entirely different message. Washington news is valued precisely because it is an insider's conversation, one interest group speaking to another, with reporters acting as symbol brokers coding stories into a conversation only the sophisticated few can follow. Greider summarizes:

> This inside knowledge provides a continuing subtext for the news of Washington; very little of it is conveyed in intelligible terms to the uninformed. The "rules" prevent that, and so also do the conventions of the press, how a story is written, and what meets the standard definition of what is news. The insiders, both reporters and government officials, will read every news story with this subtext clearly in mind. Other readers are left to struggle with their own translation.

The *Atlantic* article broke through this coded text; it presented the "unvarnished private dialogue of government" that was supposed to remain private, implicit, known only to insiders capable of penetrating the bland, reassuring rhetoric of the official news story and the official handout. By making the private public, the Greider piece diminished the value of every insider's knowledge and revealed the rules of the game to a wider audience. Greider attempted, in short, to give a lesson in how to read the daily news and how to add description and explanation to accounts that regularly omit them. In doing so, his piece contradicted the reassuring image of order and progress conveyed by breaking stories.

What are the lessons to be learned from the Greider-Stockman episode? First, daily journalism offers more description and explanation than one would ordinarily think, but they are not transparently available on the surface of the text. Despite the commitment of journalists to objectivity and facticity, much of what they have to report is obliquely stated, coded deeply into the text, and recoverable only by "constant readers" who can decode the text and who bring to it substantial knowledge of politics, bureaucracy, and, as here, budgets. Second, the most important descriptions and explanations of journalism are lost when they are sliced into daily fragments, thin tissue cultures of reality, disconnected from a narrative framework. Third, the reader can discover such descriptions and explanations only when the separate stories are reintegrated into a more coherent framework and when the episodes of the news have a narrative structure that contains elements of drama, nuances of character, and precise chronological order. Finally, the episode demonstrates how overwhelmingly dependent American journalism is on explaining events by attributing motives. What the essay displays throughout are the motives, purposes, and intentions of the actors in the budget struggle and, then, in the newspaper accounts, the motives of Stockman and Greider themselves. The origins of these habits, including the habit of relying on motives for explanations, is revealed in some commonplace history of American journalism. . . .*

III

The conditions of journalistic practice and the literary forms journalists inherited together strictly limit the degree to which daily journalism can answer how and why. How something happens or how someone accomplishes something demands the journalist's close, detailed attention to the flow of facts which culminate in a happening. The dailiness and deadline of the newspaper and the television news show usually preclude the opportunity to adequately etch in the detail which intervenes between an intention and an accomplishment, a cause and its effect. Moreover, the journalist's typical tools, particularly the telephone interview, are inadequate to a task that demands far more varied resources. Journalists cannot subpoena witnesses; no one is required to talk to them. As a result, "how," the detail, must await agencies outside of journalism such as the grand jury, the common trial, the blue-ribbon commission, social surveys, congressional investigating committees, or other, more leisured and wide-ranging forms of journalistic inquiry: the extended series, magazine article, or book.

Explanation in daily journalism has even greater limits. Explanation demands that the journalist not only retell an event but account for it. Such accounting normally takes one of four forms: determining motives, elucidating causes, predicting consequences, or estimating significance. However, the canons of objectivity, the absence of a forum or method through which evidence can be systematically adduced, and the absence of an explicit ideological commitment on the part of journalists renders the task of explanation radically problematic, except under certain well-stipulated conditions.

First, the problem of objectivity. Who, what, when, and where are relatively transparent. Why is invisible. Who, what, when, and where are empirical. Why is abstract. Who, what, when, and where refer to phenomena on the surface of the world. Why refers to something buried beneath appearances. Who, what, when, and where do not mirror the world, of course. They reflect the reality-making practices of journalists. Answering such questions depends upon conventions that are widely shared, even if infrequently noted. The other essays in this volume attest to the conventionality of these elements. We no longer, for example, identify figures in the news by feminine nouns: poetess, Negress, Jewess, actress. The who, the identification, now obeys a different set of conventions which attempt to depress the importance of "race" and gender, conventions which journalists both use and legitimate. But for all the conventionality of who, what, when, and where, they are accessible and identifiable because our culture widely shares a gradient against which to measure them. As Michael Schudson's essay demonstrates, the notion

---

*A second section of this essay concerns the events that influenced the development of American journalism practices. We pick up this theme at the beginning of the essay's third section—the editors.

of when, of time in journalism, is not as transparent as phrases like "recent," "immediate," or "breaking" seem to suggest. Nonetheless, time in journalism is measured against a standard gradient of tense, of past, present, and future, which is widely shared in the culture.

There is no accessible gradient for the measurement of causes, the assessment of motives, the prediction of consequences, or the evaluation of significance. No one has seen a cause or a consequence; motives are ghostly happenings in the head; and significance seems to be in the eye of the beholder. Explanations do not lie within events or actions. Rather, they lie behind them or are inferences or extrapolations that go well beyond the commonsense evidence at hand. Explanation, then, cuts against the naive realism of journalism with its insistence on objective fact.

The first injunction of journalists is to stay with the facts; facts provide the elements of the story. But causes, consequences, and motives are not themselves facts. Because journalists are above all else empiricists, the why must elude them. They lack a framework of theory or ideology from which to deduce evidence or infer explanations. To explain is to abandon journalism in the archetypal sense: it is to pursue soft news, "trust me" journalism. Explanatory journalism is, to use an ugly phrase, "thumbsucker journalism": stories coming from the journalist's head rather than the facts.

Something is philosophically awry about all this, of course. While the first law of journalism is to stick to hard surfaces, the essays in this volume present enough evidence for the mushiness of all facts. The facts of the case are always elaborate, arbitrary cultural constructions through which who, what, when, and where are not only identified but judged, not only described but evaluated. But such constructions and identifications can be pinned down by ordinary techniques of journalistic investigation. Not so with why. For it, one must go outside the interview and the clip file. It drives one to the library, the computer, government documents, historical surveys. But there are no conventions to guide journalists in sifting and judging evidence from such sources and no forum in which conflicting evidence can be weighed.

More than the organization of the newsroom, the nature of journalistic investigations and the professional ideology of journalism suppress a journalism of explanation. The basic definitions of news exclude explanation from the outset. News focuses on the unusual, the nonroutine, the unexpected. Thus, it necessarily highlights events that interest us precisely because they have no explanation. This is part of the meaning of human interest: deviation from the accepted routine of ordinary life. News of novel events must strain causality and credibility. News is when man bites dog. Unfortunately, no one knows what possessed the man who bit the dog; even psychiatrists are not likely to be much help.

Much of journalism focuses on the bizarre, the uncanny, the inexplicable. Journalism ritualizes the bizarre; it is a counterphobia for overcoming objects of fear. Such stories of the bizarre, uncanny, horrible, and unfathomable are like roller coasters, prizefights, stock car races—pleasurable because we can be disturbed and frightened without being hurt or overwhelmed. Where would we be without stories of UFOs and other such phenomena, stories at once intensely pleasing and intensely disturbing? In the age of the partisan press, such stories were consigned to folklore, the oral tradition, and other underground modes of storytelling. With the penny press, they came into the open and took up residence in newspapers as the unexplained and unexplainable desiderata of our civilization.

The impossible French have even given such stories a name: *faits-divers*. This most easily translates as "fillers," but we might better render it idiomatically as "random, uncanny occurrences." Such stories, according to Roland Barthes, preserve at the very heart of modern society an ambiguity of the rational and the irrational, of the intelligible and the unfathomable. In his essay, Carlin Romano cited one such story: "Guest Drowns at Party for 100 Lifeguards." But think of some other newspaper staples: "Chief of Police Kills Wife"; "Psychiatrist's Son Commits Mayhem"; "Burglars Frightened Away by Other Burglars"; "Thieves Sic Their Police Dog on Night Watchman." We are here in the realm of perversity, chance, accident, coincidence. "Man and Wife Collide with One Another in Auto Accident"; "Father Runs Over His Child in the Driveway"; "Man Drinks Himself to Death at Party to Celebrate His Divorce." Every such story is a sign at once intelligent and indecipherable.

The factors of coincidence, unpredictability, and the uncanny float some events to the surface of the news from the many which fit a type, explaining why a few murders get reported of the many committed, a few accidents detailed of the many occurring.

Consider this from the Associated Press:

> A confirmed AIDS victim who allegedly spat on four police officers during a traffic arrest was charged Friday with assault with intent to murder.
>
> John Richards of Davison, Ohio, was charged with the felony warrant because "it appears the man knows he has AIDS and was trying to transmit it by spitting on the officers," said Assistant Genesee County Prosecutor John McGraw.

What is going on here? This is of course the season for stories about AIDS because of the menacing potential of the disease. But what did Mr. Richards think he was up to? And what, even more, was going on with the police? It is precisely the bizarre and inexplicable quality of the event that makes it a story. It gives new meaning to the phrase "deadly weapon"; it conjures up a time when our saliva will be registered.

Or, consider the following from the *Chicago Sun-Times* of January 7, 1986:

Tale of True Love
He Expects Death, Gives Girlfriend His Heart

PATTERSON, Calif. (AP) A 15-year old boy who learned that his girlfriend needed a heart transplant told his mother three weeks ago that he was going to die and that the young woman should have his heart.

Felipe Garza Jr., who his half-brother said had seemed to be in perfect health, died Saturday after a blood vessel burst in his head.

His family followed his wishes, and Felipe's heart was transplanted Sunday into Donna Ashlock.

His half-brother, John Sanchez, 20, said Felipe told their mother, Maria, three weeks ago: "I'm going to die, and I'm going to give my heart to my girlfriend."

This is the type of story that *faits-divers* defines; as a result, it appeared everywhere: the straight press; the weekly tabloids; television news, national and local; the news-weeklies; even many of the prestige papers. It is the generality of its distribution and the uncanniness of its content that makes it so informing an example. Naturally, as the story travels from the most to the least respectable journal, the bizarre elements in the story become more pronounced. But its appeal and significance are universal.

Stories like those cited appear in the daily press, where they are oddment and filler. They are the main news of the tabloid weeklies. In the *National Enquirer*, the *Star*, and the *Weekly World News*, the limits of the bizarre are pushed out one standard deviation, but the type is common to the press in general. From the tabloid weeklies: "She Became Great Granny Three Times in One Day"; "Dog Eats Boy's Nose"; "Chinese Genius is Only Five and Ready for College"; "I Won't Be a Fat Farm Flop—700 Pound Behemoth Vows." What is filler in the straight press is feature in the tabloids. What is filler in the evening news, often designed to give an upbeat if totally improbable ending to a half hour of mayhem and melancholy, is feature for Charles Kuralt's "On the Road." As we shall see, the same instructive relation between the straight press and the weekly tabloids occurs in the realm of motives.

The world of the inexplicable contrasts sharply with the foreground of daily news, the world of politics and economics. In the latter domains, we are unwilling to leave events to chance or dismiss happenings as bizarre, mysterious, or coincidental. The world of politics and economics is a world of threat in which we can lose our lives, our possessions, our freedom, our entire sense of purpose. In that world, we seek reassurance that someone or something is in control. We are intolerant of mystery in politics even when politics is mysterious, for this is the sphere of the menacing. Whenever such threat and reward systems confront us, we demand explanation, coherence, significance, and intelligibility. So once we leave the realm of *faits-divers*, the how and why get answered by one device or another despite the limitations of daily journalism.

IV

We start from this proposition: when matters of fundamental importance surface in the news, they cannot be treated as secular mysteries and left unexplained. They must be accounted for, must be rendered sensible. The economy and the political system form the sacred center of modern society. With them, we are unwilling to sit about muttering "It's fate" or "So be it." We insist that the economy and the polity be explicable: a domain where someone is in control, or natural laws are being obeyed, or events are significant and consequential, or that despite all the bad news of the moment, the signs in the headlines augur well for the future.

The importance of economics and politics to each individual's life chances guarantees that people will come up with explanations—ideological explanations—even if the press and the politicians are silent on these issues. As a result, explanation is an arena of struggle within journalism, a struggle to control the natural ideological forces set in motion by the appearance of disturbing and perplexing events. The press explains such events by elucidating motives, demonstrating causes, predicting consequences, or divining significance. The order of these forms of explanation is logical, not chronological. Different events are explained in different ways; any given story will mix these forms of explanation together; and the same story will be subjected at different times to different forms of explanation. But the order of explanation runs as follows: if you can find a motive, state it; if you can't find a motive, search for a cause; if you can't find a motive or a cause, look for consequences; if you can find none of the above, read the tea leaves of the event for its significance. Motive explanations, however, dominate American journalism and create, as we shall see, all sorts of havoc.

To unpack these complicated matters, I will use one extended example. In March 1985, the Department of Commerce issued its monthly report on the balance of payments of the American economy. These monthly statements had regularly shown a deteriorating American position in the international economy. The March statement was unexceptional; indeed, it was a considerable improvement over the report of the previous October. Here is the AP story which opened this chapter in the trade crisis:

> The nation's trade deficit climbed to $11.4 billion in February, the worst showing since September, as export sales fell 7.7 per cent, the government reported Thursday.
>
> The deficit was 11 percent higher than the $10.3 billion deficit in January and was the biggest monthly imbalance since the $11.5 billion deficit in September, the Commerce Department said.

Then, after one more paragraph of description, the story offered this unattributed explanation:

> The poor performance has been blamed in part on the dollar's high value, which makes U.S. goods more expensive and harder to sell overseas while whetting Americans' appetite for a flood of cheaper exports.

This explanation undoubtedly came from the Department of Commerce briefing, but interestingly it did not carry the argument a step further: the high value of the dollar could have been blamed on the large federal deficit, continuing high interest rates, the need for enormous federal borrowing, and the influx of foreign currency chasing investments.

The monthly stories of the trade deficit normally do not receive much attention beyond the business and financial press and usually disappear within a day or two. However, the March 1985 report showed, among other things, a further worsening of our trade balance with Japan. This story might have disappeared except that the voluntary import restrictions on Japanese automobiles were about to expire. The question on the political agenda was whether the import restrictions should be kept at the same level, raised, lowered, or eliminated altogether. Action on automobile import restrictions was but a prelude, however, to overall trade policy on a number of American products—shoes, textiles, steel—that had been faring badly in international trade. The Reagan administration generally supported free trade, but it was also negotiating with the Japanese to gain greater access to Japanese markets for American manufacturers of, among other things, telecommunications products. The second matter which made the March Commerce Department report of greater-than-normal significance was that planning was under way for an early May "economic summit" in Bonn, West Germany, between Japan, the United States, and the other major Western countries. At that conference, trade policy was to be a principal item of discussion.

The story of the balance of payments and trade policy was continuously at the "front" of the news from early March until it was pushed aside by the controversy surrounding President Reagan's visit to the Bitburg cemetery containing the graves of

World War II German soldiers, including the burial sites of members of the SS. The trade story declined in prominence through an odd conjunction of circumstances: the attention to German-American relations symbolized by the cemetery visit offended President Mitterrand of France, who largely sabotaged attempts to plan a series of future meetings on trade policy.

One of the early reactions to the trade crisis was a 92–0 vote in the Senate condemning the Japanese for restrictive trade practices. A flurry of charges and countercharges allowed journalists to keep the trade story alive for a protracted period and to examine it from every conceivable angle. Many other interest groups also wished to keep the story in the headlines, and there was considerable behind-the-scenes struggle to define and explain the trade crisis. The struggle was an attempt to control public sentiment toward the Japanese and toward tariff and trade policy generally.

The question facing journalists was this: why was there an increasingly negative balance of payments with Japan and other countries? The significance of the journalist's attempt to answer the questions was this: the answer arrived at would be one of the central elements determining the course of government economic policy.

The first explanation offered was based upon motives. Such stories pitted wily Japanese against innocent Americans. The Japanese in their desire to dominate international markets were playing by unacceptable rules of the game. Through a variety of devices, they were securing access to American markets and technology, engaging in unfair competitive practices, and excluding American products and producers from Japan.

This explanation was advanced by leaders of declining industries, Senators Robert Packwood and John Danforth, and congressmen from districts economically depressed by the flood of imports. Senator Packwood wrote in the *New York Times* that, to cite the headline, "Japan's Not Entitled to 'Free Lunch.'" He argued that "America can successfully compete in the Japanese market—if we can get into it. The problem is the jaded Japanese bureaucracy." The *Chicago Tribune* reported a speech by Lee Iacocca, the Chrysler Corporation chairman, in which he demanded that the "Japanese Play Fair With Us." He claimed that "Americans see it as a one-way trade relationship, a well-ordered plan by Japan to take as much as it can and put very little back." Joseph A. Reaves of the *Chicago Tribune* reported from Tokyo that "Americans see the Japanese as conniving protectionists who want to get rich exporting their goods around the world while buying only Japanese products at home." The troubles of individual industries in dealing with the Japanese were reported. James Mateja, the automotive writer of the *Chicago Tribune*, interviewed a representative of the automotive replacement parts industry who argued that neither low quality nor high price kept his industry out of the Japanese market. It was restrictive trade practices: ". . . if you have equal access to specifications, and if you can retain business at the best price, then our prices would knock their socks off. I don't know how they accept price quotes now." A consensus position offered on Japanese motives was summarized by a *Tribune* business writer: "They [U.S. officials in Tokyo] say the Japanese simply aren't playing fair in the trade game. American companies trying to do business in Japan face an impenetrable wall of government-imposed barriers designed to protect Japanese firms."

The "motive story" of trade was not restricted to analyzing the Japanese. Clyde Farnsworth of the *New York Times* reported that pressing "trade issues are reshaping the political lineup in the United States as Democrats and Republicans maneuver for

advantage while trying to deal with an influx of imports from Japan and other countries."
He claimed that "Democrats now smell blood on the issue" and were going after twenty-
two Republican Senate seats. The Democrats were going to tie trade problems to
Republican free market economic policy that was causing an overvalued dollar.

Farnsworth's story hints at a shift in the form of explanation of the trade crisis story:
from motives to causes. It was the Japanese themselves who pointed out not only the
restrictive trade practices of the United States but, more importantly, that the trade deficit
was caused by the overvalued dollar, the poor quality of American goods, the taste standards of the Japanese market, or the fact that the strength of the recovery of the American
economy set unprecedented demand by Americans for foreign products. The explanation,
in other words, did not reside in the motives of the Japanese or in individual Americans
but in collective international economic conditions: the more or less natural laws of
modern economics or the unintended consequences of normal economic activity.

Ronald Yates of the *Chicago Tribune* reported the comments of Toshiaki Fujinami,
president of a small Japanese paper products company: U.S. senators "are just trying to
shift the blame for the declining American economy away from the huge U.S. budget
deficit and the over-valued dollar to Japan." Edwin Yoder in the Providence *Journal*
warned against "Misreading Causes of the U.S. Trade Deficit" and claimed that
"Reagan-Congress fiscal policy" and the ludicrous budget deficit of $200 billion a year
"is the sword we throw ourselves on every day." He offered his own quick explanation:

> The budget deficits generate historically high "real" interest rates, adjusted for inflation.
> They suck prodigious sums of foreign capital into the United States, keeping the dollar
> drastically overvalued against other major currencies.
>
> The stark weighting of the terms of trade to our disfavor functions as an export tax
> on U.S. goods, an import subsidy to foreign goods and an incentive to U.S. employers to
> move plants "offshore" if they can. Those that can't move close. In this witch's brew,
> one partner's trade practices, even Japan's, are a piddling ingredient—the equivalent of
> one eye of newt.

Chicago Tribune editorials and editorial columns by Stephen Chapman pointed out
that the "real" motives of Lee Iacocca and others like him were less in gaining access to
Japanese markets and more in restricting foreign competition. They pointed out that
Japan's trade restrictions are "just handy excuses for American ones." Chapman argued
that the Japanese had not refused to buy American goods. "American exports to Japan
had risen by 9 per cent last year." What, then, caused the trade deficit? The strong dollar.
"Foreigners, including the Japanese, are eager to buy a share of our booming economy.
As long as foreigners invest more here than Americans invest abroad, Americans
will have to import more goods than they export. That's not bad trade." Another reason:
the American economy recovered faster than Japan's and Western Europe's. "Consequently, American businesses and consumers have more money to spend than their
foreign counterparts. So the U.S. imports more than they do."

Hobart Rowen of the *Washington Post* reported that a study by the Institute of
International Economics showed that each country had roughly equivalent barriers to
trade. The study attributed trade tension to the distorted relation between the dollar and
the yen. Rowen noted that the institute's conclusion "conflicts with frequent assertions

by administration officials and business executives that the imbalance in trade is a result of Tokyo's barriers to U.S. imports."

As this example shows, journalists writing about causes depend upon "experts," "think tanks," and other organizations attempting to influence policy. Journalists can often handle motive explanations based upon only their own knowledge or a few well-placed sources. But with causes, journalists are largely at the mercy of others, not because the subject is necessarily more technical but because the form of the explanation is one in which social scientists specialize and therefore have an overwhelming advantage.

United States and international economic conditions were not the only causes cited for the trade deficit. A slowly emerging crop of stories admitted to Japanese trade barriers but rooted those barriers not in the motives and intentions of Japanese leaders but in Japanese cultural habits. The *New York Times's* Nicholas Kristof argued that "even without intentional restrictions the Japanese market remains more elusive than most because of deep cultural differences—the way Japan organizes its society, arranges its economy, and views the world." Kristof suggested that the cultural barriers to trade "cannot be easily negotiated away." Even Japanese often have difficulty breaking into the Japanese market. He cited Jon K. T. Choy, an economist at the Japan Economic Institute in Washington, who explained that the "Japanese system doesn't simply discriminate against foreigners—it discriminates against newcomers." The Japanese "place a premium on a long-term relationship with suppliers, doing business with those who have faithfully performed their obligations in the past. This is what makes it difficult even for new Japanese companies to break into the market." Even more: Americans don't speak Japanese, whereas the Japanese speak English and understand American culture; the Japanese resist foreign goods because they consider their own superior; American products have incomprehensible instructions and are not sized and detailed to the Japanese market. (Pampers, for example, were inappropriately shaped to the Japanese bottom.)

The cultural cause of the trade deficit was elaborated in other articles which examined the shopping habits of the Japanese ("The Wary Shoppers of Japan," *New York Times*) and Japanese attitudes toward everything foreign ("The Hideous Gaijin in Japan," *Newsweek*).

There was something disingenuous about cultural explanations of trade deficits. Most of those reporting such explanations were advocating free trade in one way or another. However, the theory of free trade assumes the absence of cultural barriers to trade. Buyers and sellers in Japan and the United States are assumed to operate in terms of a purely rational model of economic activity where price and quality govern the terms of trade.

While such stories increasingly emphasized the causes of the trade deficit, other reports continued to analyze motives. The motives in question were those of the Reagan administration. A long wrap-up story in the *Chicago Tribune* relied on an expert on Japan, Chalmers Johnson of the University of California. He linked the trade deficit to the fact that "U.S. foreign policy is controlled by the State Department which, like Reagan, sees Japan more in terms of the Soviet-American rivalry than in its economic role." As long as Prime Minister Nakasone was seen as a firm ally against the Soviets, "his inability to produce real Japanese concessions on trade will be forgiven." Similarly, the economist Robert Solow, writing in the *New York Times*, suggested that the Reagan administration did not really care about the economic effect of budget deficits. The

Reagan administration did not really favor investment, productivity, or growth. "Its goal is to shrink the Federal Government, to limit its capacity to provide services, at least civilian services, or to redistribute income to the poor or to regulate private activity." In other words, the trade crisis was a nonstory because the budget deficits driving the terms of trade derived from Reagan's intention to reshape domestic politics.

These multiple explanations of the trade deficit, and the blizzard of stories reporting them, were made more complicated by two other types of stories concerning Japanese-American relations. First were stories about the personal relations of Reagan and Nakasone, a "Ron" and "Yasu" show: two embattled leaders trying to control angry forces of economic warfare at loose beneath them, sending delegations from one capital to the other to soothe relations. The other set of stories transmitted messages between the Japanese and American bureaucracies: charges, recriminations, demands for concessions, threats of what was ahead if this practice or that was not abandoned.

The causes of an event are intimately linked to its consequences. Therefore, every story that explains an event by elucidating causes also states, more or less directly, the consequences that flow from it. If the balance of payment problem is caused by budget deficits, and if the budget deficits are to continue for some time, then a train of consequences follows—at least until the Gramm-Rudman deficit controls kick in. But the Gramm-Rudman mechanisms have their own consequences. Causes are usually emphasized more than consequences because consequences are in the future and thus as much a matter of prophecy as of knowledge. Even so, many stories cited the predicted consequences of the trade imbalance for employment, basic manufacturing industries, regional economic development, and even the future of United States—Japanese relations. Edwin Yoder's piece, previously cited, evoked a reenactment of World War II: "Only fools underrate the mischief of . . . cultural barriers in history and the teaching of this sad history is that the United States and Japan have had difficulty understanding one another before. . . . No one is looking for a reprise of those old enmities. . . ."

If all else fails, find the significance in the event. What does the trade crisis tell us about ourselves? What is the larger meaning of the event? Bill Neikirk in the *Chicago Tribune* told us: "Here is what's happening: They [the Japanese] sacrifice more than we do. . . . They anticipate and manage better than we do. . . . Their system of compensation promotes worker loyalty and holds down welfare payments . . . they have maintained higher efficiency . . . better management and lower wages . . . we have been outperformed." In short, the real significance of the trade crisis is that ours is a declining economy and civilization, having lost the habits of character that made us once a great nation.

V

I have argued that "why" is the question most often left unanswered, or answered with an insinuation. Attempting to answer "why" places American journalists on soft ground, where they are subjected to and reliant on experts. When explanations do appear, they are of particular types consonant with American culture as a whole. That should not surprise us. Despite everything said about the political biases of American journalists, they are, John Chancellor says, "pretty much like everyone else in their basic beliefs."

I earlier suggested that American journalism always begins from the question of "who." Although I exaggerate, you will not go far wrong assuming that "names make news." The primary subject of journalism is people—what they say and do. Moreover, the subject is usually an individual—what someone says and does. Groups, in turn, are usually personified by leaders or representatives who speak or act for them, even when we know this is pretty much a fiction. Edward Kennedy speaks for liberals, Jesse Jackson for blacks, Gloria Steinem for liberated women. Sometimes a composite or a persona speaks for a leaderless or amorphous group: "scientists say"; a suicide note from a teenager stands for all unwritten notes. Their sayings and doings are representative of a class. If journalists cannot find a representative individual, they more or less invent one, as leaders were invented or selected by the press during the 1960s for the student and antiwar movements.

Because news is mainly about the doings and sayings of individuals, why is usually answered by identifying the motives of those individuals. Why tells us why someone did something. This is the sense in which American culture is "individualistic": We assume that individuals are authors of their own acts, that individuals do what they do intentionally, they say what they say because they have purposes in mind. The world is the way it is because individuals want it that way. Explanation in American journalism is a kind of long-distance mind reading in which the journalist elucidates the motives, intentions, purposes, and hidden agendas which guide individuals in their actions.

This overreliance on motive explanations is a pervasive weakness of American journalism. Motive explanations are too easy. It takes time, effort, and substantial knowledge to find a cause, whereas motives are available for a phone call. And motives are profoundly misleading and simplifying. Motive explanations end up portraying a world in which people are driven by desires no more complicated than greed.

Journalism is not the only forum in which motives are established. The courtroom is the great American scene in the drama of motives. To compare journalism to the courts is not farfetched. The adversary model of journalism, with the press as prosecutor and public representative, is clearly derived from the courts. The journalist is the detective, the investigator, trying to establish the facts of the case and the motives of the actors. The "detective story" and the journalism story have developed in tandem since the emergence of the penny press.

A *New Yorker* cartoon of a few years back featured two quizzical detectives staring at a corpse. One remarked to the other that "it is an old-fashioned crime—it has a motive." The cartoon is testimony to a demand we make of the courtroom and the press: they present little episodes in what Max Weber called the "quest for lucidity," the demand that the world make sense.

In a murder trial, for example, there will be two points of contention. First, what was the act and was it committed by the accused? But the answer to those questions depends critically on a third: what was the motive? The nature of the act and the assignment of guilt cannot be made until the act is motivated, until a statement of intention is attached to it that makes it intelligible to us. In fact, to make acts intelligible is the greatest demand of the courtroom. We make acts intelligible by showing the grounds a person had for acting. These grounds are, however, not the cause of an act. If I make a person's murderous act intelligible by portraying his motive, I do not mean the motive caused the murder. After all, many people have such motives, but they do not commit murder. The motive makes intelligible but it does not cause; it is understanding action without understanding causation. Because I understand the motive behind a murderous act, I do not necessarily approve of it. It merely means that the motive is a plausible ground for the act. Acts must be placed within learned interpretive schemes so that we might judge them as being murder, suicide, manslaughter, self-defense, first degree, etc. And those terms are not exactly unambiguous.

Let us take the matter a step further. Suppose in our hypothetical crime a husband murders his wife. What interpretations might be made of his behavior? How will it be motivated? How will the action be made intelligible to us (which is also an attempt, let us remember, to make it intelligible to the accused)? We have a standard typology of motives we can bring to bear. He did it for her money—a technically rational motive in a utilitarian culture. He did it because he found her sleeping with another man—the motive of honor. He did it out of anger—it was an act of passion, of emotion. Finally, we might even imagine that he did it because this is what men always do in this society under such circumstances—it is explained by tradition.

This example illustrates a number of things. First, the courtroom is simply a compacted scene of the most ordinary and important aspects of social life: it consists of interpreting experience, attaching explanations to ambiguous phenomena, using cultural resources—standard typologies of motives, for example—to explain human activity.

Similarly, American journalists explain actions by attributing motives. The motives they attribute are, in the first instance, rational, instrumental, purposeful ones. We can understand murder for money much better than murder for honor. Similarly, journalists attribute rational motives to politicians. In 1980, the *New York Times* explained that Jimmy Carter was opening his campaign on Labor Day in the South because of what Mr. Carter's campaign advisers "concede to be a serious effort by Ronald Reagan to win votes here." Carter had many reasons to begin in the South: tradition, his affection for his native region, the honor he wished to bring to his associates. Nonetheless, the motive selected was the one that showed it was a rational act designed solely to win the election.

The explanation of conduct by rational motives is a literary and cultural convention. Just how conventional it is is revealed when we encounter, for example, Soviet journalism, where stories are framed in terms of large collective forces—capitalism, history, imperialism—rather than individual motives. Individuals merely personify these larger forces which are in the saddle driving the actions of individuals. But for us, individuals act. Individuals make history. Individuals have purposes and intentions. Therefore, to answer the question "why" in American journalism, the journalist must discover a motive or attribute one to the actor.

Explanation by rational motives is the archetype of journalism as it is of the culture. But such explanations are often too arbitrary. William Greider, for example, was dismayed when journalists asked about the motives behind his *Atlantic* article rather than about the substance of the article itself. Similarly, the questions put to political candidates are less about what the candidate is saying than why he is saying it, leading to the well-known complaint that no one writes about the issues anymore. It is simply assumed that everything a candidate does is designed to win the election, and that pretty much exhausts the meaning of what is said. Indeed, it seems at times that journalists and political candidates are in a silent conspiracy to focus attention on the hidden states of mind and intentions of politicians and away from what they are concretely up to and saying.

When a story breaks this mold, it is often refreshing in its candor. A *New York Times* story from Moscow by Serge Schmemann on December 10, 1985, was striking precisely because it reported directly on what Gorbachev said about U.S.-Soviet relations without one word of speculation as to motives:

> Mikhail S. Gorbachev told 400 American business executives today that while the Geneva summit meeting had opened the way to better Soviet-American relations, trade would remain limited until Washington lifted "political obstacles."
>
> "I will be absolutely frank with you," the Soviet leader told the representatives of about 150 American companies in Moscow . . . , "so long as those obstacles exist . . . there will be no normal development of Soviet-U.S. trade and other economic ties on a large scale. This is regrettable but we are not going to beg the United States for anything."
>
> . . . Mr. Gorbachev held out the carrot of "major long-term projects and numerous medium and even small business deals." But first, he said, Washington would have to lift the restrictions imposed on trade with the Soviet Union.
>
> The obstacles he listed included legislation denying most favored nation status and export-import credits to Moscow unless it permitted emigration of Jews and restrictions on high-technology exports. Mr. Gorbachev also cited what he called "the policy of boycotts, embargoes, punishments and broken trade contracts that has become a habit with the United States."

The story conveys the sense of Russian rhetoric that is, one imagines, the real substance of summit diplomacy.

Motive explanations are not only arbitrary but easy. They deflect attention rather too quickly and casually away from the what and onto the why. Sometimes the motive is incorporated into the very definition of the who, as when the *New York Times* in a breaking story from Japan mentions that "saboteurs today knocked out key rail communications and signal systems, forcing the shutdown of 23 commuter trains. . . . The saboteurs, described by authorities as left-wing extremists . . ." Similarly, Bernhard Goetz quickly became known as the "subway vigilante," an identification that told us immediately what he did and why he did it. More to the point, journalists approach the action of politicians as drama critics at a play, looking for a subtext in the script. The *Wall Street Journal* tells us that Representative Daniel Rostenkowski, chairman of the House Ways and Means Committee, had "several motives" behind his enthusiasm for tax reform: "He isn't eager to get ambushed by the White House again; tax revision can be a vehicle to reassert his committee's and his own imperatives"; the average voter supports tax simplification; and it is "an issue that can move the Democratic party closer to the political center." In short, Rostenkowski is interested in everything but tax reform.

This tendency to focus on motive explanations led Leon Sigal to complain that news stories focus on the who rather than the what and the why of disputes. As he said, journalists tend to ask who was responsible for an event rather than what was the cause. It is not that journalists substitute who for why but rather that they substitute one kind of why—a motive statement—for another kind of why—a cause statement.

In continuing stories, motives are often reduced to boilerplate, a continuing thread of standard interpretation inserted in every story. Since 1969, for example, we have had a steady stream of stories about political violence in Northern Ireland. A recent one was carried in the *Times* from the AP:

BELFAST, Northern Ireland, Jan. 1—Just one minute into the new year, Irish Republican Army guerrillas killed two policemen and wounded a third in an ambush that the I. R. A. said opened a renewed campaign against British security forces.

After five paragraphs describing the killings, the following boilerplate paragraph was inserted:

The predominantly Roman Catholic I. R. A. is fighting to drive the British from Northern Ireland and unite the Protestant-dominated province with the overwhelmingly Catholic Irish Republic.

That paragraph appears in virtually every story from Northern Ireland with little or no variation. It is the explanatory paragraph, the motive paragraph, the paragraph that sets the story in context. The trouble is that it is a gross, oversimple, and unchanging explanation for complex and changing events. Not even the IRA is that simple, internally unified, or unchanging. The boilerplate acts to select stories as well as to select explanations. Stories from Ireland are selected, at one point in the transmission system or another, that fit into the one overarching boilerplate explanation available for all events in the province.

Rational explanations by motives—and here the IRA is rational on an American model—commit journalists to viewing individuals, particularly political actors, as possessing far clearer and more articulate purposes than they usually do. As a result, they create a picture that renders politics far more orderly and directed than it ever is for the participants. Journalists introduce a clarity into events that rarely exists for those caught up in the muddled flow of happenings, the ambiguities of situations, and the crosscutting and contradictory nature of purposes and intentions.

That motives obey literary and even legal conventions rather than simply mirroring what is going on can be seen in the contrasting treatment of two New York killings. In December 1985, Paul Castellano and Thomas Bilotti were gunned down on a mid-Manhattan street. Before the blood was dry on the sidewalk, the *Times* had identified the killer and the motive. "John Gotti, a fastidious, well-groomed forty-five-year-old resident of Queens, is believed by law-enforcement officials to be a central figure in an internal fight for leadership of the Gambino crime family." The law enforcement officials were then quoted to round out the explanation: "John Gotti is a major organized crime figure in the Gambino crime family and heir apparent. . . . Gotti will emerge as the head of the other capos—that's what this struggle is all about. Bilotti was Gotti's rival and he's gone, and there may well be some more killings before it's settled." Well, we know why members of the Mafia commit murder, and they normally do not bring libel suits.

That case contrasts nicely with a more mysterious one. In June 1985, a seventeen-year-old Harlem resident, Edmund Perry, a graduate of Phillips Exeter Academy, a member of the freshman class at Stanford, was killed by an undercover police officer near St. Luke's Hospital on Manhattan's Upper West Side. It was an improbable killing, and the *Times* covered the case very circumspectly. The paper was cautious in attributing motive, was hesitant to convict anyone involved. The case did not fit the type. Racism is one nonrational motive we all understand. As a result, the episode was dramatically awry. It should have been the racism of the police officer that motivated the killing. Why should a successful black youth on his way to great things mug and attempt to rob an undercover officer as alleged? The killing did not fit an acceptable, sensible pattern of motivation, and so the *Times* awaited the grand jury investigation and, even when charges were dismissed against the officer, was careful not to resolve the case for its readers.

Motive explanations work only when they fit a certain ideal type of rational, purposeful action. But when they are made to fit the type, they are often too simple or radically misleading or generate an unnecessary cynicism. In anticipation of the first celebration of Martin Luther King's birthday as a national holiday, NBC reported that President Reagan was to visit a school named after the slain civil rights leader. It described it as "part of his attempt to improve his image among blacks," an image, we were told, that was "on the rise." Even Ronald Reagan is more complicated than that.

It is not the literal truth of the motives journalists unmask that is in question. Surely, people are driven by self-interest. But that is not the only motive that drives them; all self-interested action is knotted into and contained by other, larger, and often more honorable motives. The real problem is that the motives journalists describe and report are the motives that we live. The notion of the "hidden agenda" is now so destructively widespread in the culture because we have so unfailingly described our political leaders as possessed by undisclosed and manipulative intentions. Paradoxically, Marxism has become the ideology of late bourgeois America because our vocabulary of motives pretty much comes down to "whose ox gets gored." Therefore, journalism becomes the unmasking and revealing of the "true" motives behind appearances. Power, wealth, control become the primary objects of people's actions because we assume that everyone is driven by selfish interest. This compulsive explanation excludes the possibility that anyone can be motivated by the common good or the public interest, and so we should not be surprised if individuals are not so motivated. Greed, in the most general sense, explains everything. The one state of mind with which we feel comfortable is the rational, instrumental one. Actions which do not fit this scheme largely confuse and befuddle us.

The final and most unfortunate aspect of motive explanations is the overwhelmingly technical bias they give to journalism. If people are uniformly out to better their own self-interest, and what they say and do is designed to further that end, the only sensible questions are: Are they successful? Are their means well adapted to their ends? Are they pursuing a rational course of action? We therefore ask: How is pacification going in Vietnam? What is the body count? Who is winning the election? What do the opinion polls say? Is the antiwar movement gaining or losing ground? Technique becomes all-important because we assume that all individuals, groups, and institutions care about is winning and that the technical success of their strategies is all that is in question. All life becomes a horse race in which the press reports the progress of the contestants to the wire and announces the winners and the losers. Meanwhile, everyone forgets what the race is about and the stakes we have in the outcome.

It is often said that the press reduces politics to a clash of personalities, wills, and ambitions. The only purpose of politics becomes the desire to win elections. The real meaning of objectivity is that the press takes that desire, and all such rational desires, as given and assesses everything a politician does in its light. We get, therefore, stories of success or failure, victory or defeat, cleverness or ineptness, achievement or mismanagement, defined by technical expertise, not by the content of character or nobility of purpose.

Journalists pretty much keep their own counsel on rational motives. Sources are used to "objectify" what the journalist already knows. Other actions and other motives cannot be fully explained because, while conscious, they are not rational or believable. The old saw that men kill for money and women for love simply argues that while both men and women are motivated by conscious motives, men are motivated by reason, women are not. Claus von Bülow, innocent, makes sense; Jean Harris, guilty, does not. If individuals announce they are motivated by honor, loyalty, duty, or other nonrational motives, the journalist cannot quite take them seriously, nor can we; therefore, they have to be unmasked. Actions motivated by tradition, values, and affections pretty much escape our understanding and end up as the human interest exotica which fill the space between the self-interest stories and provide the features for the *National Enquirer* and Charles Kuralt.

When we move to nonrational motives, we move, in fact, into the domain of causes. Nonrational motives move people as irresistible forces over which they have no control. To deal with them, journalists must call on the experts. Experts play the same role in journalism as they do in the courts. They straighten out minor technical matters such as ballistics and resolve major matters of cause and interpretation. If journalists cannot find a rational motive, they have to bring in psychiatrists, psychologists, sociologists, and other experts on national character and the behavior of strange people to provide an irrational one. English rioting in Brussels, blacks rioting in Brixton, terrorists "rioting" everywhere pretty much fall outside rational assessment, so only the experts can make them comprehensible. This is particularly pronounced on television, where breaking stories on the evening news are explained by experts on "Nightline" or the morning news. Unfortunately, the experts do not always agree, and it usually comes down to whom the journalist chooses to trust.

If the irrational is the first domain of causal explanations, the statistical is the second. Explanation by causes is particularly well adapted to the periodic reports of government and the significant findings that turn up in scientific journals. Youth suicide is up, and the *New England Journal of Medicine* has an explanation based on the "rate" of depression in all age groups. Child abuse is on the rise, and a sociologist tells us of the disorganization of the American family. Mortgage rates hit a six-year low, and an economist informs us of the money supply and the Federal Reserve Board. Auto sales are down 15 percent, and an expert in consumer behavior tells us about the psychology of consumer expectations. The homeless are filling up the city, and a bureaucrat reminds us of the consequence of "de-institutionalizing" the mentally ill.

Stories of causation turn the journalist to the experts, even though the experts are not always disinterested. In fact, organizations are often created for the sole purpose of providing journalists with explanations. When a new and perplexing report comes out, someone has to be found with an explanation, and, therefore, "institutes of explanation" are available for every problem affecting the national interest.

A few years back, there was a move afoot to increase the amount of what Philip Meyer called "precision journalism," the application of social science methods to the problems journalists regularly report. Precision journalism was designed to get at aggregate motives of large numbers of people so that journalists would not be always guessing at the motives of voters, or of racial groups or other subclasses of the population. It was also designed to free journalists from relying on experts by making them more self-sufficient investigators of large-scale problems for which statistics and computers provide the only answers: problems of population, migration, collective behavior, or problems of analyzing public records from the courts, the police, and the assessors's office. The movement has pretty much come to naught, except that newspapers conduct horse race polls in elections. Otherwise, given the nature of breaking news, journalists still pretty much rely on experts for the stipulation of causes.

Causal stories are often personified, of course. The growth of population, shifts in migration patterns, changes in the composition of the labor force or the mix of occupations are often exemplified in individuals and the reasons they have for migrating, changing jobs, having children, etc. For example, the increasing rate of suicide among young males is often rendered by focusing on a particularly tragic death or a group of suicides in a community overcome by grief. But such suicides represent a class of acts that must be accounted for by larger historical forces than simply the motives of individuals.

When a farmer in Hills, Iowa, killed three people and then committed suicide, the *New York Times* headlined the story "Deaths on the Iowa Prairie: Four New Victims of the Economy." The deaths were "but the latest in a series of violent outbursts across the Middle West" caused by the sagging farm economy.

The reverse side of cause stories are consequence stories, and they frequently are embedded one in the other. Youth suicide, falling interest rates, and declining sales all have consequences in addition to causes. They are fateful signs with which to read the future of the community and the nation. When Chrysler and Mitsubishi signed an agreement to build a new joint production plant in Bloomington, Illinois, the newly formed company, the Diamond Star Motors Corporation, announced that the workers to be hired would be recent high-school graduates. A television story of the announcement did not emphasize the motives of the company—new workers are cheaper and less given to unionization—or the cause of the policy—the problems of training older workers without automotive experience. Instead, the story emphasized the consequence: The opening of the plant would not reduce unemployment. It would merely siphon off new entrants to the job market.

A decision to emphasize consequence over causes and motives is a decision to emphasize the future over the past. Consequences are predictions of what will happen rather than a recounting of what has happened. They open up the future and often unintended consequences of events. As they are as much matters of prophecy as prediction, consequence stories also throw the journalist into the arms of the expert: the futurologists of one kind or another who are able to divine the far horizons of human life.

The final form of explanation in journalism is significance. Events surface all the time which are in no way the result of intentional human acts nor the result of vast historical causes. Their consequences are opaque and unknowable. They are, nonetheless, signs that must be read, portents of something larger, events to be prized and remembered as markers, as peculiar evidence of the state of civilization, or the dangers we face or the glories we once possessed.

Any event can be read for its significance. Carlin Romano calls these "symbolic events" and cites the spate of stories about President Reagan on horseback following his surgery for cancer of the colon. Such stories show that the presidency continues, the ship of state, forgive the pun, rests on an even keel. At such a moment, only the most cynical ask why he is on horseback. People treat it for what it is—a sign full of meaning for the body politic.

The murder and suicide victims in Hills, Iowa, mentioned earlier, were treated by the *Times* as casualties of the economy. The *Iowa City Press-Citizen* admitted that explanation but tried to see in the event a larger, tragic significance:

> There are accounts of bank transactions and economic explanations and other hypotheses as the murder and suicide story unravels. But that's not what it is really all about. It's about people—alone, desperate, and powerless with nowhere to turn. . . .
>
> Target prices, price supports, ceilings, sealing crops. The terminology doesn't matter. It's welfare. Farmers know it. And farmers are proud people. Nobody really wants to live that way. But for now there is no choice. . . .
>
> But if there's one thing that is clear from Monday's tragic series of murder and suicide, it is that the farm crisis is *not* numbers and deficits and bushels of corn. It is people and pride and tears and blood.
>
> The time has come for the state and the country to reach out to farmers who are suffering—not because they are failed businessmen and women but because they are human beings whose lives are falling apart—fast.

Significance can be found in a grain of sand—indeed, in any episode, however minor, that surfaces in a community. But as a form of explanation, significance is most manifest in stories of deaths, birthdays, anniversaries, inaugurals, coronations, weddings—in, to twist a phrase of Elihu Katz, the high holy days and the high holy events of the press. The inauguration of a president, the death of a beloved public figure, the two-hundredth anniversary of the Revolution or the Constitution, the commemoration of the onset of World War II or the invasion of Normandy—these become rituals of reflection and recollection: symbols of unity and disunity, triumph and tragedy, hope and despair. They are marked by an altered role for the journalist. While writing about them, he abandons his pose as critic, adversary, and detective and becomes a member of the communty, a citizen: reverent and pietistic. In these events, he aids us in the search for meaning rather than motives, consolation rather than causes, symbolism rather than consequences.

Two events of the recent past demonstrate aspects of the search for significance. The first was the tenth anniversary of the evacuation of Saigon and the "loss" of the war in Vietnam. The war is still too close, the memory still too green, to completely abandon the question of why we lost the war. Nonetheless, the widespread and often enormously expensive coverage of the anniversary took the form of a stocktaking: Where were we ten years later? What did we learn from it? What does it reveal to us about ourselves?

The second event says something about the struggle over significance rather than its mere elucidation: the visit of Reagan to the cemetery at Bitburg. In one sense, this was a harmless ceremonial event amid a busy European tour. But it came to bear significance as a gesture of contrasting meaning: a gesture of final reconciliation with an old enemy now a valuable ally and, simultaneously, a gesture of forgiveness for that which could not be forgiven—the Holocaust. The struggles over whether Reagan should make the ceremonial stop and over the meaning of going or not going reveal the power of presidential gestures and the way in which the press collaborates in the quest for meaning while innocently reporting the news.

Perhaps the best and most revealing recent example of a "significance story" started out as a far more ordinary event. In the late fall of 1984, a seventeen-year-old black man was shot on the South Side of Chicago. The murder perhaps wouldn't have been reported or have received any particular play except that Ben Wilson happened to be one of the best high-school basketball players in the country. Destined for stardom, he had already signed a tender with the basketball program at the University of Illinois. He was about to embark on an education, an escape from the ghetto, and perhaps a life of fame and riches.

The first stories concentrated on what had happened on a Friday afternoon after school: Who killed him and why did he do it? Was Wilson responsible in any way for his own death?

Between the time of the stories of the murder of Ben Wilson and the stories of the trial, conviction, and sentencing of his killer, the fate of this young man gave rise to other kinds of stories.

At first, Ben Wilson became the personification of the problems of growing up black, of the constant threat of gang violence, and of the toll taken by ghetto life. Wilson became a "news peg," a tragic death to be explained by the impersonal causes of poverty, unemployment, ignorance, illiteracy, and hopelessness. Ben Wilson's death, in a way, explained his killer. Distinguished reporting of these conditions even had an effect. Gang violence was reported to be down 40 percent in the wake of Wilson's death and the coverage of it.

The coverage, however, also looked for the significance of the death of this young man. The significance was found in public forgetfulness a generation after the civil rights struggle and a half generation after the War on Poverty. In an era of affluence, concern for private gratification, and disinterest in the problems of public life, stories of the "ghetto" were not in. The *Chicago Tribune* used the death of Ben Wilson to forcefully remind its readers of the meaning of life in urban America. The tragedy of the stories was that it took the misfortune of Ben Wilson to bring these persistent concerns and problems back into the newspaper.

VI

I have emphasized throughout this essay that journalism is a curriculum and not merely a series of news flashes. Everything can be found in American journalism, generously understood, but it is disconnected and incoherent. It takes an astute and constant reader—such as journalists are themselves—to connect the disconnected, to find sense and significance in the overwhelming and overbearing glut of occurrences.

American journalism is deeply embedded in American culture. Its faults and its triumphs are pretty much characteristic of the culture as a whole. The forms of story-telling it has adopted are those prized and cultivated throughout much of our literature. The explanations it offers are pretty much the same offered in the intellectual disciplines. As journalists move from explanations by motives to causes to consequences to significance, they roughly mirror the movement of scholars from utilitarian to causal to functional to hermeneutic explanations. Journalists, however, obsessively rely on motive explanations and thereby weaken the explanatory power of their work.

Journalists, because of their professional ideology and the industrial conditions under which they work, offer thick descriptions pretty much between the lines. They explain events by insinuating, often sotto voce, motives typical of our obsessively practical culture. Otherwise, they rely on experts, not always of their own choosing, to supply them with causes and consequences, or they sum up the folk wisdom and commonsense significance of the community. This renders journalists active participants in reality making and not merely passive observers. It also makes them frequent victims of the forces around them rather than defenders of a public interest or a common good.

As a wise man once said, journalism has taken its revenge on philosophy. As the unloved child of the craft of letters, journalism concentrates on the new, novel, transient, and ephemeral. Philosophy, the crown of the literary craft, once concentrated on the eternal, enduring, momentous, and significant. Journalism's revenge has been to impose the cycle of the news on philosophy, indeed, on all the literary arts. Everyone looks for their subject in today's headlines.

Many have argued that the overriding problem of American culture is that it has no sense of time. American managers administer for the short run; American politicians look no further than the next election. Whether one looks at the fashionability of our scholarship, the transience of our interests, the length of our memories, the planning of our institutions, or even, Reagan aside, the tenure of our presidents, everything seems to have the life span of a butterfly in spring.

The daily news bulletins report this spectacle of change: victories, defeats, trends, fluctuations, battles, controversies, threats. But beneath this change, the structures of society—the distribution of income and poverty, the cleavages of class and status, race and ethnicity, the gross inequalities of hardships and life chances—remain remarkably persistent.

If you look at the entire curriculum of journalism, you will find much reporting of the enduring and persistent, the solid and unyielding structures of social life. It is the part of journalism that offers genuine description and explanation, compelling force and narrative detail, and yet it is not the part of journalism we generally honor. At some lost moment in our history, journalism became identified with, defined by, breaking news, the news flash, the news bulletin. When that happened, our understanding of journalism as a democratic social practice was impossibly narrowed and our habits of reading, of attention, of interpretation were impaired. Journalists came to think of themselves as being in the news business, where their greatest achievements were defined by being first rather than best, with uncovering the unknown rather than clarifying and interpreting the known. Scholars too often take journalists at their word and neither read nor analyze anything beyond the wire services. They are as ignorant of the curriculum of journalism as the most addled teenager. We are then doubly betrayed. To restore a sense of time to both journalism and scholarship is going to take a lot of work and a lot of luck. All of us might begin by reading more wisely.

32

THE CONCEPTUAL SCOOP

Paul Starobin with Pamela Varley

When Ronald Brownstein of the *Los Angeles Times* explains what animates him as a political reporter, it is clear why a colleague calls him "The Great Analyzer." "My dominant interest in politics," he says, is "figuring out the evolution of the arguments between and within the parties and how that reflects changes in the country." The traditional approach to political journalism, Brownstein says, is "to collect as many pieces of information as you can," but his own is "to build a box around the information—some sort of conceptual framework."

Brownstein is ever in pursuit of the conceptual scoop—a fresh interpretation of the political landscape, a new way of connecting dots into big pictures. Shortly after the 1994 congressional elections, for example, he got a lot of attention with an in-depth piece that compared the triumphant Republicans with turn-of-the-century Populists. It was a smart take and far ahead of the curve. Four months later, *Business Week* ran a cover story on "The New Populism."

Brownstein isn't alone. As Campaign '96 heats up and reporters look for alternatives to traditional horserace coverage of elections, he faces growing competition in his search for the conceptual scoop.

Conceptual journalists are more interested in figuring things out than in finding things out—their impulse is to explain, to interpret, to move from the particular fact to the general proposition. What they do is no substitute for shoe-leather or what-happened-yesterday stories. But it can help people make sense of the torrent of raw data in "an Internet world," says Peter G. Gosselin, a domestic policy reporter for *The Boston Globe*. And the focus of conceptual journalists on political ideas and culture is particularly well suited for an era of crumbling paradigms about the role of government. "People are clearly hungry for this," says political reporter Thomas B. Edsall of *The Washington Post*. "It's a period of extraordinary upheaval in politics."

The genre also holds considerable appeal for journalists, offering an intellectual challenge and tantalizing status-and-prestige rewards. Leading practitioners, such as the *Washington Post* editorial writer and columnist E. J. Dionne, write scholarly books that win them acclaim as public intellectuals, right up there with highbrow academics.

Besides, this brand of journalism is fun—reporters get to make up catchy labels for their conceptual packages. "I basically invented a group of Republicans," *Newsweek*'s Howard Fineman proudly declares, referring to his coining of "Volvo Republicans" to

Paul Starobin with Pamela Varley, "Covering Campaign '96, the Conceptual Scoop," *Columbia Journalism Review*, Vol. 34, No. 5, February 1996, 21. Copyright © 1996 by Columbia Journalism Review. Reprinted by permission.

encapsulate a new cluster of GOP leaders with a libertarian approach on social and economic policy. "The fact that you can trademark this kind of journalism makes it extremely attractive," adds Jonathan Rauch, a visiting writer at *The Economist* who came up with "Demosclerosis" to describe the petrifaction of Washington government. (And just so I don't get accused of infringement, I heard the term "conceptual scoop" from the *Globe*'s Gosselin; Tom Rosenstiel, who covers politics for *Newsweek* and writes often about the media, noted in 1994 that reporters were talking about "scoops of perception.")

But more skeptical journalists point out that a snazzy conceptual take can camouflage a multitude of sins, including slack reporting and embedded bias, and serve the dubious function of packaging old ideas in shiny new wrappers. "The search for a conceptual scoop can be a contrived game," says political reporter James A. Barnes of the *National Journal*. "Sometimes there's more sizzle than steak."

The Genre A conceptual orientation in political and other types of journalism has a long history in books, magazines like *The New Republic* and *The Nation*, and the newspaper opinion sections, where opinions and prescriptions are wrapped around the analytical take. In the mainstream press, it used to be a narrow specialty for the likes of Walter Lippmann—columnists and essay writers, often drawn from academia, with an ability to write for non-specialists. For most political reporters, the paradigm was Theodore White's *Making of the President* series, beginning with the 1960 presidential election-behind-the-scenes reportage on the operations of a political campaign. The tradition was followed by such reporters as Jack Germond and Jules Witcover of the *Baltimore Sun*.

But in the 1990s, a growing number of mainstream political reporters began migrating toward a conceptual brand of coverage, a trend that was embodied by Dionne's influential 1991 book, *Why Americans Hate Politics*. Dionne formulated a theory: the electorate was turned off to politics, according to his "false choices" thesis, because the two parties had become overly polarized and thus were failing to address the mass of voters in the political center. Dionne described the project as an "interpretative history of thirty years of political ideas." That's a far cry from Teddy White journalism.

One reason the conceptual scoop is in the ascendancy these days is television, with its virtual monopoly on breaking news. "The era of the pure scoop is long gone," political reporter Paul Taylor of *The Washington Post* says. "To the extent that there is a competitive nature to this business, it's trying to arrange the known facts in the most intelligent, prescient way. That's where you get your job satisfaction." And *Newsweek* editor Maynard Parker says the "newsmagazine" tack increasingly taken by daily newspapers including the Post and *The New York Times* puts a "high premium" on *Newsweek* and its magazine brethren "to be faster to spot trends and move on them."

Another reason is that after the frustrating 1992 campaign, many reporters were looking for alternatives to horserace and strategy coverage. The campaign was "a humbling experience" for the press, says Gerald F. Seib, *Wall Street Journal* political reporter and editor and former defense and foreign-policy reporter. "The whole Perot phenomenon showed that there was a group of issues and a particular populist approach to issues that wasn't really reflected in the conventional political dialogue or the conventional political journalism."

After the election, the *Journal* and the *Los Angeles Times* created for Seib and Brownstein, respectively, what might be called the conceptual column. Both Seib's "Capital Journal" and Brownstein's "Washington Outlook" run on the news pages, not

the opinion pages. Both strive for more depth and intellectual adventure than the traditional day-after-the-big-event sidebar news analysis. Their goal is to bundle the facts into
new interpretive takes, shorn of the opinions and prescriptions of the editorial and op-ed
pages. A recent Seib entry, for example, offered a new twist on popular discontent with
the federal government, commonly reported as a narrowly channeled suspicion of
Washington. Drawing on public opinion research findings that Americans were also very
worried about a spate of mergers that were producing large, remote corporations, he suggested that the real problem runs broader and deeper than distrust of government—it was
"fear of big," whether the institution was a government, a business, or even a large labor
union. He came up with a conceptual tag—a "culture of suspicion"—that encompassed
such sentiments.

Edsall of the *Post* gravitated toward a conceptual approach when he became
convinced that "news stories don't tell the truth—there may be things taking place in
a traditional hard-news story that cannot be described, encompassed or conveyed to
the reader." In particular, Edsall's longstanding, political-science focus on the nexus
between American politics and race, class, and gender equips him with a kind of conceptual flashlight that can illuminate the shadows, or subtext, of events, yielding stories that
sometimes elude less conceptually oriented reporters.

Another factor behind the emergence of the conceptual genre is the white-collarization
of journalism: the craft's growing share of educationally credentialed reporters who resisted
their parents' pleas to go to law school—high achievers who are confident of their ability
to synthesize complicated matters, stimulated by the intellectual challenge, eager to
establish marks as thinkers and have a voice in the policy arena. Check out Dionne's
resume. As a Harvard undergraduate (class of 1973), he learned the techniques of public-
opinion analysis from teachers including William Schneider, now a political analyst (with
a conceptual bent) for CNN. His first job was to help set up *The New York Times*/CBS
News Poll; he earned a doctorate in political sociology from Oxford and was a political
reporter for the *Times* before joining the *Post*. Dionne is also typical of the political reporter
pool of which the conceptualizers are members—they are a mostly white male crew.

The shift toward conceptual coverage of politics is paralleled and fostered by the
growing influence of conceptually oriented strategists in the political arena-big-picture
intellectual types such as Republican gum William Kristol, the ex-Harvard political
scientist and Bush White House staffer who's the editor of *The Weekly Standard*, and
Democratic pollster Stanley B. Greenberg, the ex-Yale political scientist who's an
adviser to President Clinton. Different milieus breed different kinds of reporters; in the
Teddy White era, when hard-boiled party chairmen ran the political world, the political-
reporting crew was more hard-boiled too. Brownstein says his Rolodex is "not great on
county chairmen" but that's no longer such a handicap.

Not everyone on the Campaign '96 bus views the conceptual scoop as the ultimate
prize. "I get more excited over breaking some kind of story that reveals an underside
of American politics in stark detail that the American public was not aware of," says
Richard L. Berke, chief political correspondent for *The New York Times*. He sometimes
writes conceptually oriented pieces for the Sunday "Week in Review" section but is
better known for such gumshoe efforts as his page-one expos of how fiercely Dick
Morris, Clinton's controversial political guru, had criticized Clinton's character when he
was working for Republicans.

However, many of Berke's colleagues, including the *Time*'s Michael Wines and others, are happily stepping into a void left by professional academics, who have tended to write on ever-narrower topics for ever-more-specialized audiences. The conventional wisdom is that academics tend to know the right questions but have no idea how to get the answers, and traditional journalists tend to know how to get the answers but have no idea what the right questions are. Alan Ehrenhalt, executive editor of *Governing* magazine, says conceptual journalism can bridge this gap, and not only in political coverage. For example, James Fallows and Nicholas Lemann of *The Atlantic Monthly* (both began at *The Washington Monthly*) have long specialized in ambitious conceptual pieces on a variety of subjects. Lemann has explored the workings of American meritocracy for years, and, in a kind of sociological fashion, has identified alternative paths to success.

And conceptual journalists can also counteract too-facile reporting about complex ideas. In a recent *New Republic* cover piece on "Newt's Not-So-Weird Gums," John B. Judis, an ex-graduate student in philosophy at Berkeley, traced the philosophical evolution of futurists Alvin and Heidi Toffler (beginning with an embrace of Marxism in the 1950s) and showed that the Tofflers aren't the nutball conservatives they had been depicted as in the press and have, in fact, been prescient about a lot of changes in work and society. Judis has a knack for using history as a lens for examining contemporary politics. Formerly a reporter for *In These Times*, he says he was "intellectually raised as a Freudian, a Wittgensteinian, and a Marxist."

Many academics welcome the dialogue with journalists. "When I have conversations with leading journalists I might as well be talking to my brighter colleagues," says Everett Carll Ladd, a political scientist at the University of Connecticut who's also the executive director of the Roper Center for Public Opinion Research. Since he took over the center in 1977, Ladd adds, there has been "a continuing enlargement of the reach and range of questions" he gets from journalists and a shift toward "academic" sorts of discussions.

The *Washington Post*'s veteran team of political journalists is a mini-political-science department unto itself—even to the extent of a publish-or-perish imperative. Dionne is wrapping up a new book on the promise of a new kind of progressive politics. Inspired by his late father-in-law, political theorist Karl W. Deutsch, Edsall has written books on race and class in American politics and is now writing a third one on gender; he's a frequent contributor to *The New York Review of Books*. Reporter/columnist David Broder's voluminous oeuvre includes a book on the decline of political parties; reporter Dan Balz has just finished writing a book with the *L. A. Times*'s Brownstein on how the evils of Big Government replaced communism as the centralizing organizing force for the post-cold war Republican party. The *Post* gives its staff plenty of leeway to stretch their intellectual muscles on academic fellowships and leaves; Dionne was a resident scholar in 1994 at the Woodrow Wilson International Center for Scholars and reporter Taylor spent half his time this fall on the Princeton campus teaching a course on the press and politics.

DANGERS

Conceptual journalism is easy to do sloppily and hard to do well—the journalistic equivalent of brain surgery, it requires a delicate touch. The danger is a genre that marries the worst features of journalism and the academy—journalistic shallowness and academic isolation from the real word.

"A thoughtful critic needs four things—intellect, special expertise, time for reflection, and an attitude of judiciousness," says Ted J. Smith H.I., a journalism professor at Virginia Commonwealth University. "If you wanted to pick a group of people who are almost uniquely unfit for that role, you'd pick journalists."

Journalists themselves say they're not sure what the standards are. "There is a certain level of high-wiredness in all of this," Brownstein says. The possible missteps:

Bias and Overstepping. The interpretive approach lends itself to prescribing and editorializing, as critics including Rosenstiel have pointed out. For example, *Newsweek*'s Joe Klein didn't stop at offering a diagnosis of the "radical middle" in American politics—he suggested four ways for politicians to reach these voters, which he implicitly endorsed. Journalists aren't political consultants; when they're not writing explicit opinion columns or essays, the conceptualizers best serve their readers by aspiring to an analytic neutrality. A neutral tack is particularly valuable these days as a counterweight to the proliferation of conceptual pieces by partisans like Kristol of *The Weekly Standard*.

Trickle-Down Journalism. Senior editor Jerry Adler says *Newsweek* often gets its ideas from writers at "little magazines" like *The New Republic*, *The Atlantic Monthly*, and *Harper's*, and "with our reporting resources we can package them for a larger market. . . . There's some value added in what we do." Or value subtracted. Last July, *Newsweek* ran a cover story on "The Overclass," a term adapted from *The Next American Nation*, a high-concept book by *New Republic* senior editor Michael Lind. Lind warned of the growth of a "white overclass" of rich managers and professionals ominously "gazing down on America from gated communities or the more exclusive suburbs." *Newsweek* put that into the blender, combined it with a new analysis of the American meritocracy by Lemann of *The Atlantic*, and served up a gee-whiz *People*-magazinish spread that featured "The Overclass 100"—a list of yuppie high-achievers, including many non-whites, in the arts and media, business, finance and law, politics and government, and the like. There was even an "Overclass Pop Quiz"—with such questions as, "True or false: You can tell the difference between a Manet and a Monet."

"I was appalled by it," Lind says. "It shows how, when somebody even attempts serious intellectual journalism, it gets totally denatured and debased to fit into preexisting categories of thought. By the way," he adds, "they left me out of the Overclass 100." *Newsweek* editor Parker retorts: "Although we took his term, we're not signing onto everything he said." Minorities, Parker says, can be members of an overclass, adding, "I think we can have a little fun with this concept."

New Republic-itis. The danger of conceptual scoops, Dionne says, "is to try to put a clearer definition on things than actualy exists." Boutique magazines like *The New Republic* do this in an almost formulaic fashion in their roles as intellectual provocateurs. A grand, often contrarian, thesis is presented and argued with verve—for example, Lind's *TNR* cover piece in August on "The Incredible Growing Presidency," which challenged the conventional wisdom that Congress had captured power at the expense of the White House. Such stuff can be good fun to read but often suffers from thin reporting and a carts-before-horses problem—headline first, story later.

Peter Braestrap, a former military correspondent for *The Washington Post*, deplores what he calls "hypothesis" stories by "the indoor boys"—whiz kids "who have never been shot at." And Brownstein says, "The biggest risk in all of this is that you get to a point where you stop talking to people—because you're more interested in what you think than what people have to say."

Shiny New Wrappers. Sometimes the impulse to invent labels for every contour on the political landscape results in the mere repackaging of old news. In 1994, *Los Angeles Times* magazine staff writer Nina J. Easton coined "Retro-cons" to describe a supposedly new cluster of Republican thinkers hostile to the welfare state, including William Bennett and Charles Murray, who she said took their cues from conservative philosophers of earlier centuries. But a generation of conservative thinkers have done so, and it's not obvious how the "Retro-cons" differ from the cluster of thinkers widely known as "neo-conservatives" who cropped up in the '60s and '70s. Back in 1971, the godfather of neo-conservatism, Irving Kristol, was warning of "the fundamental problems of our welfare system" and urging policy makers to re-read Alexis de Tocqueville.

Close Conceptual Quarters. The ties of intellectual community spun by practitioners of the conceptual genre pose tricky problems for peer-group and source relationships. At the same time that Brownstein and the *Post*'s Balz were competing with each other as political reporters for rival newspapers, they were also co-writing an ambitious book on the Republican political ascendancy. And should Brownstein have agreed to read and critique the manuscript of pollster Greenberg's new book, *Middle Class Dreams*? He doesn't see any impropriety—and he may be right. "I wouldn't read a Greenberg memo to Clinton and say, "You're giving him the wrong advice," Brownstein says. "This was something for the public." But he asked another close conceptual source, Peter Wehner, policy director at the conservative advocacy group Empower America, to critique a chapter of his and Balz's manuscript. Wehner says he views Brownstein as "an intellectual" with whom he can have "a real conversation" at a level few other journalists meet. Intellectual fellowship is a valuable thing, but at the end of the day, Greenberg advises the president, Wehner tries to advance the conservative ball, and Brownstein covers politics for the *L. A. Times*.

The shift into the Knowledge Era is changing what it means to be a political reporter. The conceptualizers are postmodem journalists—more interested in subtext than in text.

Entry into the intellectual class is a mixed blessing for journalists: already, as *The Economist*'s Jonathan Rauch notes, the conceptualizers face unhealthy pressures to produce books in order to show they're more than "just" reporters. Still, by deconstructing the political dialogue, these journalists can meet what Dionne calls a need for "an investigative reporting of ideas" in political life. And they can aid a public swamped with information but starved for explanation.

Study Guide

TALKING POINTS

I. Examine four examples of news journalism by focusing on the elements in the pieces that provide the "who," the "what," the "when," the "where," the "how," and the "why." What does such an audit reveal about routine journalism?

II. Put together a portfolio of current pieces of journalism that may qualify as "conceptual scoops." Examine them with the following questions in mind:

- Do they actually work?
- Are they "good fun to read but [suffer] from thin reporting"?
- If they work, say why.
- If they fail, say why.

III. Discuss in detail the following statements written by James Carey:

- "How fills in space: it tells us how an intention (why) becomes an accomplishment (the what). How puts the reader in touch with the hard surfaces of human activity, the actual set of contingent circumstances."

- "Why answers to the question of explanation. It accounts for events, actions, and actors. It is a search for the deeper underlying factors which lie behind the surfaces of the news story."

- "Journalism is . . . a curriculum."

- "Motive explanations are not only arbitrary but easy. They deflect attention rather too quickly and casually away from the what onto the why . . ."

- ". . . [journalists] substitute one kind of why—a motive statement—for another kind of why—a cause statement."

- "As journalists move from explanations by motives to causes to consequences to significance, they roughly mirror the movement of scholars from utilitarian to causal to functional to hermeneutic explanations. Journalists, however, obsessively rely on motive explanations and thereby weaken the explanatory power of their work."

- ". . . they rely on experts . . ."

WORKBENCH

I. Review a portfolio of your writing, then write a short essay evaluating your work with the title "The Undiscovered Why." In your essay, emphasize those stories that have unfulfilled potential because they lack analysis or a conceptual framework.

II. Work with your editor/professor to develop a writing assignment—an act of journalism—that allows you to benefit from the specific knowledge gained in an academic discipline other than journalism, preferably your minor. As you report your story, use the professors in your minor field as resources. For example, if your interest is psychology and are writing a story about a criminal trial, ask your psych professor to review and analyze the psychological aspects of character and the specific details of criminal behavior.

III. Study the work of one of the conceptual reporters described in Starobin's essay, journalists such as Nicholas Lemann and E. J. Dionne. Discuss examples of this work with your colleagues. Analyze specific passages in their work. Note which parts of the work rely on straight reporting and which parts are analytical. Notice the writer's narrative strategies. How much of the work presents information? How much involves storytelling? How much requires interpretation? What fields of study does the author depend upon: Economics? Political science? Gender studies?

IV. Focus on a news event of current importance: a war, a national election, a high-profile court case. Using a variety of media platforms, study the many contexts in which this event is described or analyzed. Write an essay describing the media landscape you have explored.

V. Continue to make additions to your "editor's lexicon."

VI. Under the supervision of your editor/professor, write a piece of explanatory journalism related to an event or process in your beat or area of specialization.

PART III
SUMMATION

INTRODUCTION

The English poet W. H. Auden, to whom we referred in the preface, described a poem in his essay "Making, Knowing, Judging" as a contraption with a guy inside of it. In a real sense, journalism can be described the same way. Journalism is a device, a made thing, "a contraption," if you will, with a person hiding inside. The contraption may be a story, an editorial, a photo, a television documentary. The guy or gal inside is the journalist: the reporter, the editorial writer, the photojournalist, the videographer.

The architecture for this textbook was built upon two cornerstones. One concerns the made thing, the other concerns the maker. It should be clear by now that we see journalism as an act of culture, a democratic craft, worthy of study, analysis, and debate. We see the journalist as someone motivated by a sense of mission and purpose and educated to impart to citizens and communities useful and reliable versions of the world.

Some history: Stuart Adam was invited in the mid-1980s to judge a journalism contest in Canada and found it at first difficult to differentiate the good work from the merely good, the best from the almost best. So he called on his instincts as a classroom teacher and a marker of student work to make such distinctions. On a piece of paper, he created a scoring grid that denoted categories within which each submission was evaluated. They included news judgment, reporting, language, narrative, and analysis. These categories helped him evaluate the works in the contest, but they did something much more powerful. They provided the seeds for Stuart's working definition of journalism as a democratic craft.

He formalized the categories subsequently in a seminar and then in an essay he produced for the Poynter Institute in the early 1990s. Stuart offered the seminar, "Towards a Philosophy of Journalism," to members of the institute in the winter and spring of 1991 when he was a visiting scholar and Roy Clark was the academic dean. As a result of Roy's encouragement, the essay—"Notes towards a Definition of Journalism"—was published two years later in a series titled the "Poynter Papers."

"Notes towards a Definition of Journalism" does what the title promises: it defines journalism. The essay starts by asserting calmly that journalism is "an invention or form of expression used to report and comment in the public media on events and ideas as they occur." Some of that may be self-evident. What may be unfamiliar or surprising in the definition are the references to "invention" and "form of expression." Such terms could steer discussion away from the more routine concerns that dominate the minds of most journalists. But we believe there are payoffs associated with their use. These terms put human expression, of which journalism is an important form, squarely into the foreground.

They direct attention to journalism's master texts—and the ideas of craft they embody—rather than to the media systems in which they appear.

So the essay starts by locating journalism in a congenial landscape. It provides a context for the study of journalism out of reflections on the nature of the imagination, the sources of public consciousness, and the concept of culture, which in democracies includes independent journalism. To put the matter directly, journalism is a cultural practice or invention involving a clear set of methods and protocols for forming consciousness of the here and now. The custodians of this practice—the guys and the gals inside of it—are journalists who follow the protocols and thereby make news judgments, engage in reporting, and explain in their stories and articles how and why things happen in our world.

The section of "Notes towards a Definition of Journalism" that theorizes about journalism, art, and the imagination ends with the following statement: "[Journalism] is the aspect of culture that inspires and directs the work of every journalist, or to put it differently, it is the aspect of culture that is more or less immanent in the personal culture of every journalist and, correspondingly, immanent in the institutional culture of every publication or broadcast unit." In other words, journalism is an imaginative and creative act inherent in the soul of the journalist and inherent in the culture of the newsroom.

This idea, after it has been thoroughly digested, opens the door to a particular view of teaching. The instructor's task is to ensure that the protocols of journalism become immanent in the personal culture of every apprentice journalist. The method for achieving this goal is to build that culture in stages through an orderly system and agenda. Thus the essay's main portion introduces and discusses each of the elements of journalism —news judgment, reporting and evidence, language, narration, and interpretation— that now forms the building bricks of this larger book. After years of discussing and elaborating on the operations of this system, we believe that the careful examination of these topics encourages a student to look at journalism like a poet might look at poetry or a novelist might look at prose fiction before engaging in his or her own forms of composition.

"Notes towards a Definition of Journalism" provides an explanation and a summation of the subjects with which this book is concerned. We offer it as a method of integrating the readings in the book and concluding the discussion.

33

NOTES TOWARDS A DEFINITION OF JOURNALISM

G. STUART ADAM

I. THE EDUCATION OF JOURNALISTS

I have taken my title from T. S. Eliot's *Notes Towards the Definition of Culture*, knowing, of course, that Eliot would shudder at the thought that his title and subject had in any way inspired mine. His shock would be well earned. Eliot was concerned in that work with the definition and preservation of a particular cluster of impulses and inventions out of which British culture was composed. As usual, he was on high ground, defending art, religious belief, and a caste society.[1]

My task is much more humble. Although I may be tempted into some of the conceits of art, I do not intend to involve God; and to the extent persons are on my mind as I write, they are a cast of characters, not a social caste. They are the reporters, writers, and critics who labor in the nation's newsrooms, magazine offices, and film documentary units, or who operate as free-lancers out of their own dens, and who are more commonly blamed, as Eliot might blame me, for being philistines rather than agents of culture. But I am pleased nevertheless to borrow part of his title. Like him, I am starting something, knowing full well that I cannot finish it. I am eager to make sense of my subject, but am yet unsure of where it will take me. Accordingly, these are my "notes towards a definition of journalism."

What follows is a discussion in which I identify, locate, and analyze the properties of journalism. I begin by providing a simple definition of journalism and then proceed to elucidate the concept of the Imagination in order to associate journalism with forms of expression, particularly fiction, that are intellectual or aesthetic or both. I conclude by identifying and analyzing the primary elements—news, reporting, language, narrative, and interpretative method—that mark it and together distinguish it from other forms of expression.

I have several goals in mind, but first and foremost I want to lift the study of journalism in the university out of what I regard as a state of limbo. I want to define journalism in a way that will enable schools to participate more actively in its reform. I want to inspire a belief that journalism can be and often is an art form.

More specifically, my motives are those of a reformer, a teacher, and a scholar. To begin with, I believe that journalism is a fundamentally democratic art and through it,

G. Stuart Adam, *Notes towards a Definition of Journalism: Understanding an Old Craft as an Art Form* (St. Petersburg: Poynter Institute for Media Studies, 1993). © G. Stuart Adam. Reprinted by permission of the Poynter Institute.

as others have observed, a free society engages in conversation with itself. So as a democrat, I want to protect and defend journalism as a free activity. But as a reformer, I want to strengthen journalism practices, and because I believe that we can only change what we understand, I am obliged to create a deeper understanding of what it is. As a teacher, I am required to do something that is alien to practitioners, and that is to bring to consciousness elements of craft that, once learned and incorporated, are barely recognized. A teacher must recognize such elements so that he or she can organize and communicate efficiently his or her knowledge. I must make explicit what is implicit, and that requires the creation of a language that describes comprehensively journalism's elements and dimensions.

As a scholar, I am interested in placing the field of journalism studies on what I regard as its proper ground. I have written about this elsewhere and argued, in summary, that the practical study of journalism in universities has been based on a notion of journalism that is too narrow, and that research wings of journalism schools have been dominated for too long by the social sciences.[2]

These goals, motives, and roles are not truly divided or separate. They reflect a point of view I have developed in faculty meetings and conferences where the discussion has turned to the purposes and quality of journalism education. The focus of these discussions has usually been curriculum and research, and the context has been, for the most part, a consideration of the beliefs my colleagues express that professors should teach something called reporting, that students should receive an education in something called the liberal arts, and that it is in the interests of students to study a field, which is taught in the schools by scholars rather than practitioners, called mass communication or media studies.

No sensible person would deny the utility of reporting, liberal arts, and mass communication studies as categories to guide the development of a curriculum. But they are one thing as categories and another as operations. My disagreement with my colleagues turns on a consideration of how these beliefs have been operationalized, and so I have argued that reporting is defined far too narrowly to guide the development of an ambitious writer, and that the liberal arts are not necessarily liberal anymore, and that the research and teaching conducted under the rubric of mass media studies or mass communication tend to deflect interest in journalism and direct attention to systemic, technological, or social concepts that are not immediately relevant.

In a nutshell, I believe that much of journalism teaching—whether it is concerned with professional practices or with social and political effects—is too functional and too divorced from the higher reaches of authorship and thought. Professional practitioners are inclined to define journalism in terms of limited newsroom conceptions and thus jettison any consideration of journalism's poetics or its ambitious forms; sociologists, communicologists, and political scientists are inclined to read journalism functionally rather than intrinsically and thus contribute to the leveling impulse that originates with the practitioners. Neither the practitioners nor the social scientists are sufficiently inclined to lift journalism out of the bureaucratic settings in which journalists are likely to operate and imagine journalism as the best journalists do as they make news judgments, engage in reporting, and compose accounts of the world. In the meantime, the liberal arts are organized for the most part within disciplines rather than across disciplines, and they contribute only randomly to the student's real education. The dividend of all this considered together is that students in journalism schools are too likely to end up stunted in their moral, intellectual, and aesthetic capacities, and too formed by bureaucratic needs rather than journalistic possibilities and obligations. Put a little differently, I believe that the language and concepts of traditional journalism instruction are either too lean or too bureaucratic to inspire passion or to encourage the creative spirit. A great opportunity is lost.

This is not a radical position. It is consistent with the findings of Everette Dennis and his highly influential *Oregon Report*, which was published in 1984, and it is more or less consistent with the point of view that led to the formation of a task force on journalism education by the Association for Education in Journalism and Mass Communication later in the decade. It published its report in 1989.[3]

The stronger of the two reports was the earlier one. Dennis and his colleagues simply declared that journalism education had failed to live up to the expectations that accompanied the foundation of the first university school of journalism at Missouri in 1908. Among other things, the report said that although "journalism schools had begun with lofty ideals . . . many were little more than trade schools . . . following industry, not leading it," that "there is little connection between the [schools] . . . and the rest of the university," and that the "paradigm of journalism education has not changed much in 40 years despite massive changes in mass communication."[4]

These reports mapped out a series of recommendations aimed at reforming the curriculum within the schools and strengthening the relationship between the schools and the wider university. But the prescriptions for change left the narrow definitions of journalism in place. I concluded as I examined them that until there was a clear philosophical foundation for the study of journalism and some measure of consensus about the coordinates of this philosophy, the field would continue to be marked by a sense of failure and/or the uncertainty expressed in the reports.

So this paper has been conceived to provide a remedy for what seems to afflict journalism education. It is intended to put journalism studies on firm methodological foundations by putting the concept of journalism squarely into the foreground and placing institutional and systemic concepts like media, press, and social structure into the background. I am promoting what I imagine is a more orderly approach to the practical and theoretical study of journalism in the academy by recommending that the study should begin with a searching interrogation of the concept of journalism itself.

So what are we referring to when we speak of journalism? The answer to this question is the principal subject of this paper and a recommended starting point for the organization of the field of journalism studies.

II. JOURNALISM, ART, AND THE IMAGINATION

A preliminary definition might go like this: Journalism is an invention or a form of expression used to report and comment in the public media on the events and ideas of the here and now. There are at least five elements in such a definition: (1) a form of expression that is an invention; (2) reports of ideas and events; (3) comments on them; (4) the public circulation of them; and (5) the here and now.

Let me comment on each of these elements, but save the first of them until the end so that I can dwell at greater length on the ideas of invention and what I think is invention's sponsor—namely, the Imagination. As noted, the idea of the Imagination is central to the argument of this paper.

In the most fundamental sense, journalism involves reporting on ideas and events as they occur—the gathering and presentation of information on subjects that may vary each day from dogs that bite children to developments in ideas about the universe. The variety and range of journalistic subjects and treatments is suggested by a partial inventory of what was published in single editions of a daily, a weekly, a bimonthly, and a monthly in June 1991: *The New York Times* on June 11, *The Economist* in the week of June 15–21, *Rolling Stone* on June 13, and the June edition of *Harper's*.

Page one of *The New York Times* included stories on the ticker-tape parade honoring the troops who fought in the Persian Gulf War, on the problems in the U.S. banking industry, on the decision to award professional baseball franchises to Miami and Denver, and on the decision by the Supreme Court to hear an appeal of a case originating in Minnesota involving a statute outlawing the display of symbols of racial hatred.

The Economist published "Leaders" on the problems of economic growth, Iraq in the aftermath of the war, Japanese finance, confusing food labels, and civil liberties in Hong Kong; and, in the department its editors call "American Survey," it published stories on health care reform and on Japanese-bashing at the Central Intelligence Agency.

Other stories in other departments included an account of Poland's "anomalous" parliament, the debate in Germany over the venue of its capital, a feature with the diverting headline "Squid Are People Too," and another with the poetic headline "Arsenic and Cold Places."

Rolling Stone ran a story on the savings and loan problems, a step in the direction of the mainstream. But characteristically, its focus was on the entertainment scene, with notes on the musical group R.E.M., a feature on a writer Mike Sager described as the "Pope of Pot," and a long and raunchy Q&A interview by Carrie Fisher with Madonna— a follow-up on the release of her film documentary on herself, *Truth or Dare*. The Madonna interview included views on oral and heterosexual sex.

Harper's published, as it regularly does, a set of "Readings," not all of which, speaking precisely, were journalistic. But two essays, one on banks and bankers and another entitled "Reading May Be Harmful to Your Kids," and its regular index of absurdities and puzzles represented its editor's method of keeping Americans abreast of current issues.

Whatever else this journalism may be, some of it originating in the United States and some in Britain, it is the product of reporting—the gathering and presentation of slices and bits of human experience and thought selected from what N. K. Llewellyn once called the "aperceptive mass of behavior."[5]

So journalism involves, and is defined to some extent by, reporting. But it also involves criticism, or editorializing, or the conferral of judgments on the shape of things. Each of the items in the foregoing inventory—some more consciously than others— involved a judgment or an assessment of the significance or value or worth of the actions of its subjects. The situation of the savings and loans banks was not only a debacle but a "scandal"; Madonna, not to mention her opinions, was "important"; R.E.M. makes good music; baseball and civil liberties matter. So journalism involves the application of the values we use to judge things, and those values are reflected in the selection of subjects and in the judgments conferred by journalists on how well the world they reveal is working. In other words, the concept of journalism embraces and gives a place to notions of commentary, judgment, and criticism.

Journalism is also public. We distinguish in our minds between voices that are specialized or private, as in correspondence, and voices conceived for public consumption. Journalism, along with novels, short stories, speeches, and proclamations, is created for public consumption. Thus its voice and vocabulary are colored by didactic responsibilities—by explicitness, by an absence of allusions that have meaning only in the private sphere, and by the absence of a vocabulary that has meaning solely within a specialized discourse such as science.

If journalism is marked by its public voice, it is marked equally by its relation to the here and now. Michael Oakeshott, a British philosopher, once defined "the world of history [as] the real world as a whole comprehended under the category of the past."[6] The world of journalism, by contrast, may be the real world as a whole comprehended under the category of the present. I'll come to that later. In the meantime, may it be noted that journalism is avowedly about the present, not the past.

So the preliminary definition of journalism contains at least these four elements: reporting, judging, a public voice, and the here and now. These elements are straightforward—at least they arise out of a commonplace view of how journalism should be defined. But let me now turn to the first element of the original definition. I said journalism is a form of expression that is an invention. I will put it differently. It is a creation—a product of the Imagination—in both an individual and a cultural sense. It is a form of expression in which the imaginative capacities both of individuals and of a culture are revealed. The idea here is that although individual journalists speak individually in journalism, they speak through a cultural form that, although it is an invention, they did not invent.

I have used the words "invention," "creation," and particularly "imagination" in a way that may seem jarring. Journalism, after all, is about reality, not fantasy; there are no fairies or dreams in journalism, only the contours of nature and the dreary but familiar faces and words of our fellow beings. But I have chosen my words carefully and note that others connected to similarly earthly and empirical concerns have done so as well. C. Wright Mills, one of America's most accomplished sociologists, entitled one of his best books *The Sociological Imagination*;[7] R. G. Collingwood, a British historian and philosopher, devoted a section to "The Historical Imagination" in his book *The Idea of History*.[8] Their points of view have inspired me, as have the points of view of such writers as Northrop Frye, the Canadian literary critic who wrote *The Educated Imagination*.[9] They each refer broadly to parts of human consciousness that are formed initially by what Michael Oakeshott in his essay, *The Voice of Poetry in the Conversation of Mankind*, calls the "primordial activity" of imagining and completed by elaborate and culturally sanctioned methods for framing such images.[10]

Oakeshott says that the self is activity and this activity is "imagining: the self making and recognizing images. . . ." So the not-self is composed of images, many of them: trees, chewing gum, cigarette butts, department stores, gas stations, dogs, cats, students, and colleagues. In order to see ourselves, he argues, we must see that before anything else we form images, and then through language or other forms of representation we create what he calls arrest[s] in experience.[11] We give those images and thus consciousness specificity. This activity, he says, is primordial, and by this he means there is nothing antecedent to it. And so even sophisticated forms of representation—art and science, for example—are expressions of a primordial activity. Each of these are complex systems that bestow method and thus past experience on what in origin is a primordial activity.

So the forms of expression, whether sociological, historical, poetic, literary, or journalistic, are methods we use to form such consciousness. C. Wright Mills was interested in how and in the name of what sociologists form images of society; Collingwood and Oakeshott, among other things, were interested in how historians form images of the past; Frye was interested in how literature builds images of the spirit and provides a home for the soul. I am interested in how journalists frame experience and form consciousness—in short, how a method is attached to the experience of the here and now.

A clue to how journalists form consciousness has been recorded by the distinguished American journalist and novelist Joan Didion. Her account of her own work corresponds nicely with Oakeshott's conceptions of the self's imagining:

> I write entirely to find out what I'm thinking, what I'm looking at, what I see and what it means. . . .
>
> When I talk about pictures in my mind I am talking, quite specifically, about images that shimmer around the edges. There used to be an illustration in every elementary psychology book showing a cat drawn by a patient in varying stages of schizophrenia. This cat had a shimmer around it. You could see the molecular structure breaking down at the very edges of the cat: the cat became the background and the background the cat, everything interacting, exchanging ions. . . . I am not a schizophrenic . . . but certain images shimmer for me. Look hard enough, and you can't miss the shimmer. It's there. You can't think too much about these pictures that shimmer. You just lie low and let them develop. . . . you try to locate the cat in the shimmer, the grammar in the picture.[12]

It is the "grammar in the picture" that suggests most vividly the journalist's impulse to construct an edifice of words on a primordial image.

Didion's novels and journalism provide examples of what she described in her essay on writing. Her reports on Miami, for example, published first in *The New York Review of Books* and then in a single volume, included the observations that

> . . . the entire tone of the city, the way people looked and talked and met one another, was Cuban. The very image the city had begun presenting of itself, what was then its newfound glamour, its "hotness" (hot colors, hot vice, shady dealings under the palm trees), was that of prerevolutionary Havana, as perceived by Americans. There was even in the way women dressed in Miami a definable Havana look, a more distinct emphasis on the hips and decolletage, more black, more veiling, a generalized flirtatiousness of style not then current in American cities.[13]

It is the images of the women's styles, more than the picture of the city, that suggest the shimmer. But all of it works. It calls to mind the words of Joseph Conrad in his famous manifesto on the art of writing. "My task," he wrote, "which I am trying to achieve is, by the power of the written word, to make you hear, to make you feel—it is, before all, to make you see."[14] Didion's vision is clear and her use of language correspondingly vivid. She enables her readers to see.

One might say that it is tendentious to argue for a particular view of journalism by pointing to the achievements of Joan Didion. Her gifts are extraordinary; she is a poet of the craft—an artist. What about the routine and the commonplace—the five-paragraph story on the city page that records a vote in the local council on the municipal tax rate, or the brief that notes the submission of the annual report of the Humane Society? What about AP style, the inverted-pyramid story, or the filler on page two that says that the production of sisal hemp on the Yucatan Peninsula has risen by 10% in the last six months? What about the breathless accounts of shootings, stabbings, fires, accidents, traffic jams, and earthquakes?

There are at least three answers to such questions. But before answering them, it is necessary to do some owning up. Journalists work under varying conditions and deadlines. Some have much more time than others. But more to the point, just as the imaginative gifts of poets and novelists are unequal, so too are the imaginative gifts of journalists. Some are much more creative than others. Some are artists, which means they can invent with the invention, and some are bureaucrats, which means they can reproduce the invention without inventing. But all are imaginative in the sense in which Oakeshott uses the word. They imagine and they fabricate images. With this admission and its qualification out of the way, the questions can be addressed.

First, the same principles of clarity, although perhaps not of complexity, apply in every story. A carefully constructed news story that follows the rules of narration we call the inverted pyramid can be a work of sculpture akin in its principles of rhythm and composition to Joan Didion's account of Miami. The problems are not always so complex, and do not necessarily call for such penetration; but clarity is always a requirement.

Second, from the point of view of the storyteller the most interesting stories come after proclamations announcing an accident, a disaster, or an earthquake. The day-after "follos" on the earthquake in California in October 1989 included this story by Jennifer Warren and George Ramos of the *Los Angeles Times*:

> For James Bess, the horror of Tuesday's earthquake peaked right around 8 P.M. It was then that the surgeon reached a frightened boy named Julio Berumen after slithering 20 meters on his belly through a one-meter crawl space in the wreckage of a crumpled Nimits Freeway.
>
> Julio, 6, was pinned in a car, the weight of his mother's dead body upon him. After a quick look around, Betts and paramedics knew what had to be done . . .[15]

Most readers would know by now what is coming—the removal by surgical means of a boy from under the corpse of his mother. It is difficult; it fills us with shame and sorrow. But as Joseph Conrad once noted, "there is not a place of splendour or a dark corner of the earth that does not deserve . . . if only a passing glance of wonder or pity."[16] Journalism has many styles: the bulletin, the proclamation, and the announcement are only three of them. Lying in wait are more engaging narrative techniques and avenues of exploration that lead to the territories of splendor and of terror.

The third answer pulls us back clearly into the view that the analysis of Oakeshott's philosophy promotes and Didion's work illustrates. It is that the world is born in our imaginations. This is not to say that acts of nature do not have an objective existence. It is to say that the experience of them—consciousness, in other words—is the work of the

Imagination in both its rudimentary and its artistic incarnations. It means that the transfer of consciousness from one human being to another through a story, any story—from a journalist to an audience, in other words—produces the forms of public consciousness that make collective existence possible. What is initially private becomes public, and so in journalism society is born and reborn every day. But this brings us to the functions of journalism—what journalism does rather than what it is. I want to concentrate on what it is.

We have touched now on styles and techniques, the devices and instruments of imagining, showing, and telling, and this suggests, as noted above, that there is more to journalism than simply a display of the imaginative qualities of single journalists. There are also styles to choose from or narrative procedures to adopt, and all of these belong to this broadly conceived form of expression we call journalism. Its elements and principles of design are a legacy of past experience, and although they must be reproduced and reconceived every time a journalist writes, the working journalist is never working in a vacuum. He or she is shaping new experience to established forms. Journalism is an imaginative form, like the poem or the novel, within which individual imaginations function.

I will discuss the properties of this expressive form in detail shortly, but note here that the history of journalism as we know it begins in the early seventeenth century in Europe's cities, particularly in London, where so-called corantos were first published in 1621.[17] It is possible, although it is a complex task, to map the evolution of the form from that time by following initially the contents of newspapers and tracing reportorial, narrative, and analytical methods through broadcasting to the present day. Seventeenth-century journalism was marked by the news brief and, during the discontents at midcentury, the violent essay. Journalism in Britain in the eighteenth century evolved into something extraordinarily rich. It included the literary essays of Addison and Steele; the polemical writing of Lord Bolingbroke, Cato, and Junius; the legislative reports of Dr. Johnson in *The Gentleman's Magazine*; and, later, of Woodfall, one of the first Gallery reporters, in *The Public Advertiser*. By 1790, there were 14 dailies and nine triweeklies in London alone.[18] So there was lots of journalism published, and much of it in form and content that an American or Canadian in the late twentieth century can read with pleasure and insight. The modern world was being made and journalism was being made with it. Not only that. The modern world was being made and through journalism imagined in a modern way.

The world that was being made and imagined had two fundamental—one might even say mythic—properties that provided firm coordinates for journalism's content. One was the democratic state and thereby the democratically constituted legislature; the other was the community of citizens. The journalism of the eighteenth century in Britain and in North America reflected initially a fundamental interest in the civic domain and the activities of the people's representatives. The legislature and its affairs were very much in the foreground through the device of the political report. The journalism of the nineteenth century, while continuing to cast up images of the state and the legislatures, added more textured images of the community through the device of the human interest story. An invention mainly of American journalists and editors, the human interest story began the important phase of its career in the United States when the penny papers were launched in the 1830s. Together, as we will see, the civic and the human interest stories continue to provide the foundations for modern journalism. The world that they reflect is like the world imagined by journalists from the beginning; and the way that they have imagined it has been consistently modern. From the beginning, the world was imagined by journalists through empirical techniques, just as the natural world was being imagined by those who were deserting religious myths and adopting scientific practices in the same period. These techniques, however crude and haphazard, grew into consolidated methods of reporting and generating facts.

Let me summarize what I have said about the Imagination and journalism. W. H. Auden says that a poem is a contraption with a guy inside of it.[19] Journalism is something like that. Each report, essay, editorial, or narrative documentary, however displayed in a publication by an editor or played in a broadcast by a producer, is the creation normally of an individual. Each item, however long or short, however simple or complex, is a composition in which experience is apprehended and rendered in narrative form by an individual. So journalism may be thought of in its particulars and in its various manifestations as single products of the imaginations of single individuals. There's a guy or a gal inside of it.

But it is also a contraption. This means that journalism is a creation in the broader—cultural—sense. The contraption is a form of expression, the templates of which reside in the culture and the principles of which have been invented and developed in the English-speaking world since the second decade of the seventeenth century. In other words, it is a form of expression that, along with the novel, narrative film, and modern social science, resides in the cultural storehouse where we put the procedures and techniques for creating public consciousness. It is the aspect of culture that inspires and directs the work of every journalist, or to put it differently, it is the aspect of culture that is more or less immanent in the personal culture of every journalist and, correspondingly, more or less immanent in the institutional culture of every publication or broadcast unit. Considered culturally, journalism is a contraption with a method or a set of procedures and principles inside of it. So what are the elements or essential principles of this contraption? This is the question to which I will now turn.

III. THE ELEMENTS OF JOURNALISM

I have used the words "form" and "element" and am about to use the word "principle" to assist in this account of what I think journalism is. I am not married to such words, although for the moment they seem helpful. "Form" refers simply to a type or class of thing—a genus, in this case, of expression—that has an internal structure and functions distinct from the internal structures and functions of other types of expression. As I have already said by way of illustration, poetry is a form of expression; so too is journalism. In poetry, there are sonnets, epics, limericks, and free verse; in journalism, there are news stories, sidebars, editorials, news features, backgrounders, think pieces, columns, narrative documentaries, and reviews. I am not identifying the subforms of journalism by reference to various media. I have referred to items that could be published in a newspaper or magazine, or broadcast on radio or television. In other words, I am trying to define journalism in terms of what it is rather than by the medium through which it is circulated. Now I am prepared to commit myself.

There are minimally five elements or principles of design in any piece of journalism that, although journalism may share some of these with other forms of expression and although the elements may be unequally represented in individual pieces, together mark and define it. In my view, journalism comprises distinctive elements or principles (1) of news, (2) of reporting or evidence-gathering, (3) of language, (4) of narration, and (5) of meaning.

I have used the words "element" and "principle" of design synonymously. Speaking precisely, it is best to see them in this context as two sides of the same coin. A principle of design becomes an element when it is acted upon, operationalized, and embodied in a work of journalism. Put differently, the elements in the text reveal the principles that have guided its creation. It would be possible to write a full essay and then some on each of these elements or principles. Here, I will discuss each briefly in order to illustrate what I have in mind.

News: A Shift in the State of Things

At the core of what we call news are journalistic conceptions of events, time, and subject matter. That is, journalism is concerned with events in time or, to use the language I have already introduced, events in the here and now. Often these events are defined narrowly and in terms of conflict or, as the textbooks remind us, of the prominence of the major actors or the consequences for individuals in society.[20] The greater the consequences, the lesson goes, the higher the news value. But the starting point for journalism is an event, regardless of the scale of values on which it may be weighed, and regardless of the breadth of meaning that we may give to the notion of an event.

By "event," I am not referring to anything that happens. There are boundaries to the subjects and thereby to the events that journalism embodies. For example, the subjects of news and fiction are different, not only because one is documentary and the other pure invention, but because they operate in different territories. William Faulkner once said that the proper subject of fiction is the "human heart in conflict with itself."[21] He meant that fiction is primarily concerned with the interior lives of the characters an author imagines. In order to write a novel, an author has to do what a journalist can never do, and that is, as one commentator has observed, to "suspend the blur of events, to make passion an object for contemplation."[22] So the novelist follows a subject beyond the boundary of acts and events into the inner regions of mind and soul. A journalist normally stops at that boundary. Journalism does not suspend the blur. In a sense it is the blur. Journalism is primarily about the events that the mysteries of passion or a competition or love or hating produce—a fight, a foreclosure, a marriage, a war. It is about the manifest rather than the hidden, the objective rather than the subjective. News represents a shift or change in the state of the objective world, and a news story is an inquiry into this new state.

Furthermore, in the world of the manifest and the objective, at least two kinds of stories can be distinguished: the civic, having to do with politics, the conduct of public business, and the administration of society's major institutions and systems; and the human interest, having to do with events in the lives of individuals and the community of souls. Civic stories dominate the front page of *The New York Times*. For example, the edition of Tuesday, July 16, 1991, included the following headlines: "Big Bank Merger to Join Chemical, Manufacturer"; "Commerce Dept. Declines to Revise 90 Census Counts"; and "AIDS Tests Urged for Many Doctors." Each headline and story resonates with the idea of public business rather than private emotion. Not so with the human interest story.

The most obvious and natural setting for human interest stories is the tabloid, although I hasten to add that all major news organizations, including *The New York Times*, carry them. Human interest stories are constructed, for the most part, out of what humans do to each other beyond the boundaries of organized society and the state. Their motive, above all, is to divert by stirring emotions. Thus *The Chicago Sun-Times* of January 7, 1986, told "A Tale of True Love: He Expects Death, Gives Girlfriend His Heart." The dateline was Patterson, California, and the story, from AP, started with the words, "A 15-year-old boy who learned that his girlfriend needed a heart transplant told his mother three weeks ago that he was going to die and that the young woman should have his heart." The boy died; the transplant surgery followed. The girl survived.[23]

So the events that journalism records have boundaries of sorts. Journalism's view of the "pageant of creation" is, to start with, the view of a spectator to the manifest.[24] But as already noted, "the governing gaze," to borrow from Janet Emig, is not only directed at manifest events, either civic or human interest, but situated in the here and now.[25]

The clue to this is to be found in what functions as the news lead in hard news stories or the news points, which may or may not be the basis for the lead, in stories that are sometimes referred to as soft.

In a hard news story, narration begins normally in the lead and the lead embodies the notion of the latest. Thus, "Iraq on *Sunday* [my italics] delivered a new list of its nuclear facilities to U.N. inspectors" is the lead to a hard news story. The rest, which appeared on the front page of the *St. Petersburg Times* on Monday, July 15, 1991, is commentary and detail, not so much by the journalist who wrote it, but by President Bush of the United States and President Mitterand of France, who said "they might use military force if Iraq fails to disclose and then destroy its nuclear weapons. . . ."

If this had been my story, I probably would have led on the threat by the two presidents rather than on the delivery of the note to U.N. inspectors by Iraq. My reasons would have been partly because of the relative weight I would give to the two events recorded here—the delivery of the note and the utterance of the threat—and partly because of timeliness. As far as I can see, the threats followed the delivery of the note. The news is often nothing more than the last thing that happened in a chain of events.

So time counts. The lead in the story on Iraq incorporated the word "Sunday." A second story at the bottom of the page on a computerized directory of the 3.5 million soldiers who fought in the Civil War turned on the time-word "soon." It said, "Visitors to Civil War battlefields *soon* [my italics] will be able to ask a computer if their ancestors were Yankees or Rebels."

The elements of time and event are always present even when the boundaries of the event are blurred and the notion of time functions on a different calendar. Consider, for example, Pete Hamill's article on the Everglades that appeared in *Esquire* in October 1990. A contribution to the magazine's "American Journal," the article was titled "The Neverglades." As with all of Hamill's writings, this piece was evocative and powerful.

At one stage in the narrative, Hamill recorded his memory of the wildlife when, as a youth, he first countenanced the Everglades:

I heard them, far off, almost imperceptible at first: thin, high, and then like the sound of a million whips cutting the air. They came over the edge of the horizon and then the sky was black with them. Birds. Thousands of them. Tens of thousands. Maybe a million. I shivered in fear and awe. . . . And then the vast dense flock was gone. The great molten ball of the sun oozed over the horizon.

Much later, he noted:

I wasn't the first human to see the sky blacken with birds, I only felt that way. Once they came in the millions; dozens of species, including flamingos, great white herons, ibis, snowy egrets, pelicans, roseate spoonbills, and bald eagles with seven-foot wingspans, living in nests that were nine feet deep.

These passages appeared before and after the article's news point. It came in the 119th line and said, "The Everglades are in trouble." The detail of the news point's meaning was that a clash between developers and nature—an event of sorts—was being resolved or is being resolved *now* in favor of the developers. That's the news; the story, with all that powerful imagery, provides the detail.

I don't want to belabor this point unnecessarily, but it takes work to tune into the news and write it. The news is different from a story's subject. Subjects are one thing; the news is another. The Everglades can be thought of as a subject; that it is in trouble is news. Similarly, Michael Landon is a subject; his sickness and then his death were news.[26]

The news is a hook into journalism's subjects, regardless of what they are. Its weight is judged in relation to the weight of the facts and news involved in other events and in relation to the other facts of the story for which it provides the hook. It occurs when there is a change in the state of things—in the economy or politics or business or human relationships. To put it in words borrowed from Joan Didion, news is part of journalism's basic grammar. Without it, journalism itself is impossible to imagine.

Reporting: Facts and Information

If it is impossible to imagine journalism without imagining a principle of news, it is equally impossible to imagine it without reporting or, to put it in the language of my earlier list, without the principle and the operations of fact-gathering and assessment. Journalists are concerned with facts and information, and they follow, however crudely and randomly, an epistemological procedure. They construct a picture of fact and information.

The American writer Robert Stone has observed that a writer assumes, "above all, the responsibility to understand."[27] There are many ways to achieve understanding and belief. A psychoanalyst does it one way; a moral philosopher does it another way; a scientist does it in yet another way. The Czech novelist Milan Kundera has written that the "novel is a meditation on existence as seen through the medium of imaginary characters."[28] If we take Kundera as the authority, the writer of fiction "meditates" whereas a journalist reports. A journalist might meditate as well, but only after, and on what, he or she reports.

What journalists hear or see or smell is the authority for what they write. In this sense they are lock step in the empirical tradition we associate with science and with one strand of philosophy. John Hersey put it this way in a review that challenged some of the conceits of the so-called New Journalism and the "numbed acceptance of the premise that there is no difference between fiction and nonfiction. . . ."[29] He had been dismayed by the liberties Tom Wolfe, Norman Mailer, and Truman Capote had taken in *The Right Stuff*, *The Executioner's Song*, and "Handcarved Coffins," a story in Capote's larger collection titled *Music for Chameleons*. Among other things, Hersey said:

> I will assert that there is one sacred rule of journalism. The writer must not invent. . . .
> The ethics of journalism must be based on the simple truth that every journalist knows
> the difference between the distortion that comes from subtracting observed data and the
> distortion that comes from adding invented data.[30]

Hersey used the verb "observe" for good reason. Observation is a central device of the reporter, one that the British critic John Carey makes the principle of inclusion in his book *The Faber Book of Reportage*. He notes in the introduction that "for my purposes reportage must be written by an eye witness. . . ." He goes on to say that "eye-witness evidence . . . makes for authenticity."[31] There is something to such a claim. Much of what is rich and authoritative in journalistic writing—think of Pete Hamill's description of the Everglades or Joan Didion's account of the dress of Cuban women in Miami—is the product of such observation.

However, every practitioner knows that much of what is published or broadcast originates in the analysis and summary of documents, whether published previously in newspapers and available on request from databases, or published in books and magazines, or broadcast on television and radio, or found in public records offices.

From the point of view of the investigative reporter, public records are gold mines. They include simple things such as phone books and city directories; they also include files in county courthouses where a journalist can often get access to the records of lawsuits, divorce files, wills and guardianship agreements, marriage licenses, real estate records (including deeds, mortgages, foreclosure notices, and tax records), and criminal records. City and county governments are likely to have records of auto and boat licenses, voter registration, hunting and fishing records, and so on.

An investigative reporter such as Jeff Good of the *St. Petersburg Times*, from whom this list was taken, has mastered forensic techniques that would humble a professional detective. As he notes, when all else fails, there is always the device of the state or federal freedom of information act—a slow but nevertheless useful method for getting at well-buried material.

The opportunities created by the federal act are evident in a story published in June 1991 in the *St. Petersburg Times* on the investigation by J. Edgar Hoover and the FBI on the politics and connections of Claude Pepper, a congressional representative from Florida who throughout his career was an outspoken advocate of the rights of the elderly and the poor. Hoover and his colleagues evidently thought Pepper was a Communist and worked hard, but failed, to find a way to put him out of business. Written by Lucy Morgan, the story noted that the request for information dated from October 1989, shortly after his death. The documents were supplied in April 1991 and published, as noted, in June 1991.

If observation and the study of documents are primary devices of the reporter, so too is the interview. In fact, the interview is the primary, although probably the least reliable, instrument. It would take some time to document this, but I would guess that most of what is published as news and most of what is factually wrong in newspapers is based on interviews. Regardless, many major stories, including the story of the Watergate cover-up, are based on interviews—in this case, with Deep Throat. Bob Woodward, one of the authors of *The Washington Post* articles that exposed the scandal in the executive branch of the U.S. government, is a prodigious interviewer. In an appendix to his book *Wired*, an account of the life of John Belushi, Woodward provides a list of more than 200 individuals he interviewed in order to construct his portrait of Belushi.[32]

Similarly, Gail Sheehy noted in the preface to her book *Character: America's Search for Leadership*, a collection of stories on candidates in the 1988 presidential campaign, that

> I build my portrait of an individual on evidence culled from interviewing thirty, forty, or fifty people who have known him at different stages of his life—a parent, an uncle, a rivalrous brother, schoolmates; I seek the significant teacher, the high-school coach who forged him into a competitor, the first wife . . .

To construct her portrait of Gary Hart—it appeared first in *Vanity Fair* in September 1987—she interviewed, among others, Ann Warren, a high school date; Ralph Hartpence, Hart's uncle; and Aunt Emma Louise, Hart's mother's sister.[33]

The interview is at the heart of the practice of journalism. Sometimes interviews are conducted carelessly; sometimes they are conducted with a dedication to truth that would surprise the best historians or lawyers. And sometimes they are incorporated into systems of fact-gathering and discovery that would please the best empirical social scientists. I am thinking here of survey research published in newspapers, especially at election time. The random selection of interviewees and the preparation of questionnaires represent, in a sense, add-ons in reporting methods to the interview.

Acts of observation, the analysis of documents, and interviewing in journalism are intended to provide authoritative facts. They represent the operations of the principle of reporting. It is often necessary to check and crosscheck, to corroborate and double-corroborate in order to assert a fact with confidence. But in journalism, regardless of what some journalists might say or do, the principle requires that facts are authoritative. As John Hersey has said, "In fiction, the writer's voice matters; in reporting, the writer's authority matters."[34]

Language: The Plain Style

The clue that journalism has its own voice and style—that there are distinctive linguistic principles at work in journalism—is revealed by the fact that there are dictionary definitions of something called "journalese." *Webster's New World Dictionary* says that journalese is "a style of writing and diction characteristic of many newspapers, magazines, etc." Journalists can live with that. But the entry goes on to say that it is "a facile or sensational style, with many clichés." That's a little harder to accept.

Journalists who are proud of their craft are proud of their command of the language and endorse the point of view, inspired as much by George Orwell as by anyone, that they have an obligation to protect the language and guard it against its enemies. This means that they must resist using clichés, or what Orwell called "dying metaphors," or any inclination to numb the intellect's sharpness.[35] John Carey has said, in an extended commentary, that the "power of language to confront us with the vivid, the frightening or the unaccustomed is equaled only by its opposite—the power of language to muffle any such alarms."[36] John Carey is right. I think all journalists must face up to the fact that there is a tension between the cognitive obligations the language is supposed to perform and the conditions under which it is used. The former inclines journalism to clarity, the latter to clichés.

There is also a tension between the need of journalism to sell itself and the need to provide a judicious reading of the day's events. The need to sell inclines the language to hyperbole; the need for judiciousness inclines the language to a kind of monotone— spare and efficient word choice to a fault. Good journalists know that these tensions must be resolved and the use of language turned into an art. Many succeed, but always within certain limits.

The limits are imposed by the public. Whatever else might be said about the language of journalism, it is fair to say that it is disciplined by its public and empirical character. Its vocabulary is the vocabulary of public discourse. It may strive to represent scientific ideas or the abstract notions of philosophy, but it does not adopt the vocabularies of those disciplines. It always uses a vocabulary that can be understood in the street or in the marketplace. Furthermore, it is always explicit in its references; it is laced with nouns, adjectives, and proper names; it is concrete, powerfully descriptive, and light on, although not devoid of, metaphors and similes. That does not mean it is devoid of beauty. It may well be beautiful. It has its own aesthetics—an aesthetics of originality, form, and efficiency, the last of these a product of the practical work it must do for us.

Hugh Kenner sums up these attributes by calling them together "the plain style."[37] It marks not journalism alone but much of prose fiction as well. But to say that it is plain is not to say that it is natural. Like the other forms of rhetoric, journalism is a contrivance, an artifice with its own palette pointing to the concrete and the experiential. Its great merit is that it is trustworthy. "The plain style," Kenner notes, "seems to be announcing at every phrase its subjection to the check of experience and namable things."[38] And so, "[h]andbooks and copy editors now teach journalists how to write plainly, that is, in such a manner that they will be trusted. You get yourself trusted by artifice."[39]

Narrative: The Story and the Storyteller

What applies to language applies with equal force to the operations of the narrative principle in journalism. But as with linguistic principles, there is more to the matter than meets the eye. To speak of narrative is to speak, as Scholes and Kellogg have reminded us, of a story and a storyteller.[40] The journalist creates both.

The storyteller in newspapers and news magazines is often disguised behind the device of an anonymous third person. That third person may be the Publisher, the persona in the mind of the writer who states authoritatively that the war has ended or has been declared, or that the election campaign has begun or the vote tallied. *Time* magazine, when it was published by Henry Luce, was written in a uniform style so that it would appear, despite the many hands at work, that there was a single writer and a single voice—Mr. Luce's. That voice was clever, male, and a bit chummy, conferring judgments with the wisdom and insight of a true insider and expressing them confidently in an accessible prose style.

The New York Times in its way and the Associated Press in its also strive for uniformity and consistency in their news voices. The narrator in such organizations is likely to be less of an inside-dopester than a public authority with quasi-official status. True to its origins in seventeenth-century English gazettes, much of twentieth-century news journalism in the English-speaking world retains elements of officialdom. The announcements from the White House and the results of a criminal trial each turn the narrator in journalism into an official of sorts who functions as a town crier or herald once did, but now with a stylized, published, and routinized voice.

Of course, sometimes in journalism—when the journalist rather than the institution is speaking—the narrator is the journalist himself or herself. Occasionally, he or she appears as "this writer" or "this reporter" or simply as "I" or "me." Pete Hamill was an "I" in the aforementioned story on the Everglades, as was Joan Didion in *Miami*. So the narrator is sometimes official-like and a part of the establishment; sometimes he or she is in an adversarial relationship to the same establishment; sometimes he or she is simply the journalist—his or her subjectivity revealed. But in every case the narrator is a presence who guides the reader through a story. He or she shows, tells, and explains.

The devices the narrator in journalism uses are those used by all storytellers: plot, characterization, action, dialogue, sequencing, dramatization, causation, myth, metaphor, and explanation. This may be understood simply by considering what all newspaper editors conventionally require in stories filed by apprentice reporters. They require, they say, five W's—a who, a what, a where, a when, and a why. The *who* guides the writer to construct characters, the *what* to action, the *where* to sites, the *when* to a time line, and the *why* to motive or meaning.[41] The characters may exist simply as names attached to institutions—what James Ettema and Theodore Glasser call "authorized knowers"—or as carefully described individuals with clear voices, personalities, and physical shapes.[42] The action may be rendered in an abbreviated or sustained form, the sites only alluded to, and the motive barely canvassed. The treatments may be shallow or profound, cursory or thorough. But in every case, the narrative the journalist constructs will contain these elements.

There are some twists. Stories in prose fiction normally begin at a beginning, and the middles and the ends fall into place according to the sequencing required by conventional time lines. In hard news, by contrast, the endings of events mark the beginnings of the stories. The lead is a conclusion of sorts and the rest is background.

It is not always so. Features very often start with setting shots—either physical or psychological. Narrative documentaries like "South of Heaven," a seven-part series by Tom French published in the *St. Petersburg Times* in May 1991, is a good example. It was inspired as much by portraiture as by narrative, and the result was a story replete from the beginning with site and character descriptions.

"South of Heaven" is one of the most ambitious pieces of journalism ever published in a newspaper. French, a staff reporter with the *Times*, spent a year with the students and staff of a high school in Largo, a community north of St. Petersburg, Florida. A major theme of his documentary, implicit from the beginning, was that much more than academic learning goes on in high schools. Romance, ambition for status, confusion, and personal despair are as common as poems, foreign languages, and calculus. French's account revealed that high schools are in trouble because the society is in trouble and teachers are often required to be parents to a generation that includes too many orphans. He built his portrait by drawing detailed pictures of teachers, students, and parents and by weaving their individual stories into a single narrative. It is an impressive achievement.

It is fair to say that the operations of the principle of narrative are normally less complex in newspaper journalism than they are in French's piece. That journalism is a public discourse inclines it, in narrative terms, to simplicity and explicitness. For example, efficiency and clarity are the principles that shape the construction of the hard news story, which stands at the opposite end of the spectrum. In narrative terms, the hard news story comprises actors, actions, and time sequences without the benefit of carefully drawn setting shots, scenes, character development, and suspenseful plot lines. But it is wrong to imagine journalism's narrative approaches as limited by the inverted pyramid. Between the inverted pyramid and the narrative documentary, a journalist may choose from many approaches.

Much of it will be underdeveloped from the point of view of the serious student of narrative. But it is useful then to shift ground and consider that the short, short stories in newspapers and broadcasts are stories within unfolding stories. Stories in newspapers and daily broadcasts especially are guided and constructed by reference to a meta-narrative that at the most general level reveals society's story. At a less general level, they are guided by society's yet incomplete stories. They call for, as Andre Codrescu has noted, a follow-up that answers the childlike question, "What happened afterward? . . . What happened to the man who wrote the Hitler diaries or the man who faked the autobiography of the Pope?"[43] To these we might add: What happened to the economy? What happened to women after the Supreme Court reconsidered Roe v. Wade? What happened to President Bush after he met concerned citizens on the lawn of the White House to discuss the state of the nation?

These events are marked by stories, follow-ups, and commentaries. The last of these may be discourses by editorialists on how we should evaluate such things. But they all fit together in meta-narratives about society's progress, however many hands are engaged in rendering the descriptions and interpretations, however incomplete they may seem at the time. James Carey has noted that it is useful to think of the newspaper as a curriculum— to be judged, in other words, by how it follows a story day by day or month by month rather than by the character and substance of each story.[44] The curriculum fleshes out the detail and substance of a story—a narrative.

Meaning: Myth, Metaphor, Explanation

"South of Heaven" is compelling reading for a variety of reasons. It is carefully constructed and narrated; its imagery and characters are vivid and memorable; but more centrally, it contains an intellectual structure or principle of meaning that is, well, meaningful or persuasive. The principle of meaning is the last of my five elements.

The stories and the characters of "South of Heaven" are exquisitely aligned to a compelling idea that is the news of the series—namely, that the social system is disintegrating. Put differently, the lives of the individuals described in the series reflect the forces of disintegration outside of the school—in the family, in race relations, and in the economy. The disintegration of failing individuals or the conflicts of successful ones, and the therapeutic and compensatory efforts of the teachers, are each an expression of such a theorized picture of society.

A similar idea organized Joan Didion's "Slouching Towards Bethlehem," an eloquent description written in 1967 of the comings and goings of the youthful inhabitants of Haight-Ashbury in San Francisco.[45] Didion's inspiration for that report and its principle of meaning was derived from "The Second Coming," a poem by W. B. Yeats in which the words "slouching towards Bethlehem" are part of its powerful cadence. In this poem, Yeats wrote gloomily that as the mythic gyre turns and widens, "things fall apart" and "the center cannot hold."

Didion secularized the notion of the gyre but held on to the observation that anarchy and "atomization" were everywhere. She said that the youths of Haight-Ashbury were hardly the bearers of a new communal vision, as they had sometimes been described in the press. Rather, they were the victims of America's disintegrating social system. The evidence for her belief was the halting and abstract language the flower children used. For Didion it was still an axiom that "the ability to think for one's self depends upon one's mastery of the language. . . ."[46] What she saw and reported, then, was the "desperate attempt of a handful of pathetically unequipped children to create a community in a social vacuum."[47]

Like all storytellers, journalists inscribe meaning on the facts and events they describe. The devices they use may vary. Some depend on myth—the myth of evil, for example,—and/or metaphor. (Valentine stories are based on the metaphor of the heart.) Others depend on the secular explanatory devices of modern social scientists. Such devices are prominent in modern journalism.

For the most part, journalists are not highly conscious of the explanatory techniques they use. In this vein, James Carey has argued that while the answers to the how and the why of daily journalism are almost always hidden, daily journalists have nevertheless a fairly fixed view of the causes of human behavior. "Because news is mainly about the doings and sayings of individuals," he says, "why is usually answered by identifying the motives of those individuals."[48] Rational motive is assumed to be the primary cause of behavior. Missing from the picture is a consideration of causes that transcend individuals and their motives and reflect deeper impulses in society and culture.

Such wider theories are not always missing. A reading of contemporary journalism that embraces more than the news pages reveals that there is as much variation in the intellectual cosmologies of journalists as there is in the cosmologies of social scientists and literary critics. I will identify four theories of human behavior in order to illustrate how the principle of meaning functions in contemporary journalism.

A first type, the interpretative method James Carey has identified, is an example of rational individualism. It is a theory that reads the world in terms of individuals and their mainly rational calculations. There is a kinship between this theory and traditional utilitarianism. That such a theory is dominant in a liberal-utilitarian culture is hardly surprising.

I would call a second type simply sociological. In the sociological method, events and behavior are explained primarily in the light of the composition of the social world as distinct from the unique psychological composition of individuals. The sociological method requires that the investigator read the impulses on which individuals act as the result of forces external to such individuals. These forces are to be found primarily in the domain of social organization and the structure of power. Individual actors are likely to be unaware—or to be falsely conscious—of the primary causes of their actions.

The third is a bit like the first. It works out of the category of the individual; however, it emphasizes the nonrational. Dr. Freud's presence may be noticed here. The unconscious, which is the product of experience and discovered in the detail of biography, is regarded as the source of the impulses that govern much of behavior. Individuals act out of unremembered psychic wounds that their current lives trigger.

The fourth is cultural—the method of Didion's "Slouching . . ." is a vivid example— and it is idealist in the technical sense. In Didion's cosmology, individuals are the embodiment of ideas and impulses that dwell in the culture. As in the sociological and the psychological, individuals are more the expressions of things than they are the source of things. But the things they are the expression of are to be found not so much in the society's organization or in an individual's psychic wounds, but in society's texts and language.

I have said all that needs to be said about rational individualism. In any case, Carey's article covers it nicely. In the world of journalism that Carey analyzes, human actors are possessed of conscious motives and purposes and human acts can be understood in light of them. Individual accounts of behavior are taken at face value. Human beings do what they intend for the reasons that they give.

The unconscious or falsely conscious mark the other examples. An example of the "sociological" was published in the *St. Petersburg Times* of February 12, 1992, in an analysis of the reason why Mike Tyson, the former world boxing champion, was convicted of rape while William Kennedy Smith, the nephew both of a senator and of a former president, was acquitted of a similar charge two months earlier. The story begins with these statements:

> William Kennedy Smith is a free man, about to walk through the halls of a university as a first-year medical student.
>
> Mike Tyson is living on borrowed time, out on bail awaiting a sentence that could put him in a prison cell for the rest of his life.

There were actually several approaches to the *why* of the acquittal and the conviction in this analysis. One approach took account of the evidence presented at the respective trials; another focused on the differences in the victims. (In the Kennedy case, the victim was picked up in a bar and was a 28-year-old single mother; the other was a Sunday school teacher and barely 18.) Yet another approach spoke of the skill of the respective prosecutors and lawyers for the defendants. However, the various approaches were themselves subject to an understanding provided in a single proposition attributed to Martha Burt, "a researcher for the Urban Institute, a non-profit policy and research organization in Washington." Ms. Burt said: "Smith is white, rich and a Kennedy. . . . Tyson is not white, not a Kennedy. He's rich, but he wasn't born into it."

So the primary way to understand these findings, according to the *St. Petersburg Times* writers, is to move from the categories of class and race to the fate of these single individuals. Marx, Weber, Michels, Pareto, and Mosca in their various ways have inscribed this explanatory method on the minds of social scientists and their disciples in the field of journalism. The jurors may have thought they were dispensing justice; to the writers of the *Times*, or at least to Ms. Burt, their actions embodied the predictable impulses of a society marked by racial divisions.

If Marx and Weber et al. in their various ways inhabited the minds of these St. Petersburg journalists and one of their principal sources, Sigmund Freud, developmental psychologists and anthropological notions of a subculture provided the intellectual coordinates for Gail Sheehy's analyses of presidential candidates that she published in *Vanity Fair* starting in September 1987. In the introduction to the book in which the articles were republished, Sheehy wrote candidly that as a journalist, she had been covering campaigns since 1968, but that as an author she had concentrated "on character and psychological development. In 1984, these two parallel tracks . . . came together. *Vanity Fair* magazine asked me to find out who Gary Hart really was. . . ."[49]

Sheehy was lucky, because by the time she was ready to publish Gary Hart's story, Hart's philandering and tastes in recreation had been discovered. She made "character" the true subject of her inquiry into Hart's life and sought, therefore, to ascertain what was most fundamental to his personality and behavior. She worked with complex intellectual materials.

> Character . . . refers to the enduring marks left by life that set one apart as an individual. Commonly, [they] are carved in by parental and religious imprinting, by a child's early interactions with siblings, peers at school, and authority figures. The manners of one's social class and the soil in which one grows up often remain indelible, and certain teachers and coaches or books and ideas may leave a lasting impression. . . . [W]hat matters . . . in a would-be leader, is how many of the passages of adult life have been met and mastered, and what he or she has done with the life accidents dealt by fate.[50]

It would be possible to argue with the results of Sheehy's analyses or to compare them to Didion's theories. But it is not possible to deny that in these articles she operated both as a journalist and a theorist with a carefully developed intellectual system. She operated as a journalist by interviewing former teachers, friends, parents, coaches, lovers, and associates in order to put together factual accounts of the lives of her subjects. But she also used the diagnostic techniques of a thoughtful psychologist. The pictures she formed of the characters of such individuals were pictures that the subjects themselves could not compose. For example, Hart was undoubtedly unconscious of the impulses that drove him and gave him, as Sheehy was to conclude, "a pathological deficit of character [that] riddled the public man as thoroughly as it ruled the private one."[51] Sheehy argued that the impulses were established in his personality when, as a youngster in Ottawa, Kansas, he was cut off from normal friendships and the pleasures he might have derived from them by a cold and demanding mother who insisted that he conform to the strict codes of the Nazarene Church. Sheehy constructed a portrait of Hart in which the adult Hart could not escape the child who longed for forbidden pleasures. So regardless of his accounts of himself, the *why* of his behavior was to be found in the character of the child locked up in his soul.

By contrast, Didion's method of explanation focuses on the cultural as distinct from the psychological. For Didion, what is unconscious resides not in the soul, as it did in Sheehy's Hart, but in society's primary texts or media. What is unconscious in human beings is ambient in the culture. Didion's meditation on Haight-Ashbury illustrates this method. But there is a better example of it in "Some Dreamers of the Golden Dream," a report published in the same collection. The site is the San Bernardino Valley in California. She writes:

> The future always looks good in the golden land, because no one remembers the past. Here is where the hot wind blows and the old ways do not seem relevant, where the divorce rate is double the national average and where one person in every thirty-eight lives in a trailer. Here is the last stop for all those who come from somewhere else, for all those who drifted away from the cold and the past and the old ways. Here is where they are trying to find a new life style, trying to find it in the only places they know to look: the movies and the newspapers. The case of Lucille Marie Maxwell Miller is a tabloid monument to the new life style.[52]

Lucille Miller was a murderer who discarded a husband in order to get a new one. She was unhappy. She did what the culture's axiology says you should do when you are finished with one thing and want another.

The study of all the major journalists and critics—from Walter Lippmann to Lewis Lapham—reveals something similar. Each works out of intellectual systems that shape both what they see and how they see it. They are not, of course, limited to theories of human action akin to the ones I have described. Their theories embrace, as it were, all that requires explanation. Typically, the systems contain conceptual templates that have been inscribed by such intellectual figures as John Stuart Mill, Max Weber, or Sigmund Freud. Sometimes they are grounded in the mythic and the metaphoric and can therefore be read more as literature than as social science. Thus, the operations of the principle of meaning in journalism vary according to who is writing and according to the explanatory or mythic systems that guide description and analysis. If there is a dominant method in daily journalism for conferring meaning, it is through the devices James Carey points to, in which causes and effects are read in terms of individuals possessed of motives acting more or less rationally. Such theorizing eschews references to social categories or even mythic notions of evil and virtue. But many journalists—some have been cited here—work in deeper intellectual cosmologies and thus confer meaning on their subjects in richer and more persuasive ways.

IV. CONCLUSION

Let me end by summarizing the case I have tried to make and by suggesting some of the benefits that arise from reading journalism in my way. I have argued, first, that journalism is a form of expression that is the product of something called the Imagination. I have used the term "Imagination" in two carefully blended senses. In the first sense, the Imagination is a property of individual human beings; it is, in short, their spontaneous consciousness-forming faculty. In the second sense, the Imagination is a property of culture. In this sense, it is made up of the methods and practices established in the culture for framing experience and forming consciousness. Language itself—but more relevant to the understanding I am attempting to promote—art, social science, fiction, and journalism are each examples of methods in culture for forming consciousness. In these various incarnations, the Imagination conceived as a property of culture connects the imaginations of individuals to society's consciousness-forming projects. Individual works of journalism comprise inquiries by individuals into the state of things. So journalism is a cultural practice, a section or part of the modern Imagination that in its broadest and most comprehensive sense includes all the devices we use to form consciousness. Journalism—or more precisely, the Journalistic Imagination—is the primary method of framing experience and forming the public consciousness of the here and now. Its principles are immanent, more or less, in every journalist and in every journalistic institution.

Second, I have named and analyzed the five principles of design that mark every piece of journalism. They are (1) news or news judgment, (2) reporting or evidentiary method, (3) linguistic technique, (4) narrative technique, and (5) method of interpretation or meaning. Clearly each of these principles of design is operationalized differently by different individuals and different institutions. But in my view, all journalists work off a palette composed of these principles. They exist in relation to the journalist as the principles of form and color exist in relation to painters, and they are embodied as elements, however inchoately, in every piece of journalism.

What is the use of all this? There are several uses, and I will conclude with a brief review of some of them. The first is that it enriches our vision of what journalism is. Whatever else the conception adumbrated in these remarks may be, it is richer than most, perhaps all, of the analyses of journalism. Most of what passes for the analysis of journalism—whether it is written by journalists themselves or by social scientists—takes the journalism of the newsroom as a starting point and argues for its worth or meaning or significance in terms of what it does rather than what it is. The analysis of all the detail and especially the analysis of the work of journalism's poets or artists enable us to see truly what is going on. The payoff that comes from including journalism's more ambitious forms in the analysis is that it is possible to see more clearly what is inchoate in its less ambitious forms.

This broadening of the subject gives rise to a second benefit. By expanding the world of reference, it is easier to locate journalism in the territory of art and the humanities. Journalism is made; it doesn't just happen. So the language we use to see it and to teach it must be akin to the language of art. The language of art encourages students to enter the imagination of the artist and meditate on how the artist does what he or she does. In this sense, what I have written is simply a meditation on what I do. I am a journalist. I have tried in this piece to create a language that expresses what I and other journalists are doing as we work off our palettes. With the words and concepts I have used in this piece, I can say why I have written a news lead in a particular way, or why I have chosen to put this story on page one and another on page eight. I can say why one human interest story is a delight and another is not. I can tell you why a fact is authoritative, why a particular set of words are apposite, why a narrative line works, and why I see an event's meaning in a certain way.

A third benefit is that it enables us to be better critics of journalism. This system of analysis provides a straightforward guide to an analysis of journalistic achievements. It guides the critic to an assessment of the quality of news judgment in a journalistic piece, the authority of its facts, the clarity and originality of the language, the utility and success of its narrative technique, and the degree to which the journalist has penetrated and thereby interpreted the materials he or she has brought to light. Put differently, it engages the critic in the work of the editor rather than the work of the politician or bureaucrat. An editor measures achievements according to what is truly possible. A politician or bureaucrat measures impacts or effects, extrinsic rather than intrinsic goods.

What is good for the critic is good for the educator. As I noted at the outset, two major reports were written in the 1980s by American journalism educators on curriculum and teaching, and both contained critiques and suggestions for reform. It strikes me that neither hit the mark because the authors started and ended with both a limited view of journalism and an uncritical understanding of the broader university and its culture. For reasons I have already suggested, journalism education will look profoundly different when teachers of journalism add the perspectives of the artist and critic to the perspectives of the news journalist and the social scientist. In the schools themselves, such a cast of mind should encourage more systematic teaching of the elements of journalism in the class and lecture rooms and less reliance on hit-and-miss apprenticeship teaching in newsrooms. As important as the newsroom is—there is no implication here that it is not important—the class or lecture room is also important, and the systematic exploration of the language of journalism is best dealt with in the latter.

It should also encourage a more thoughtfully constructed set of connections with the other departments of the university. For example, historians put the past into perspective and encourage the development of a capacity to judge what matters; information scientists are in the business of finding facts, and historians, lawyers, and social scientists are in the business of assessing them; literary and composition theorists examine words, sentences, paragraphs, metaphors, rhythm, diction, dialogue, narrative, characterization, and dramatization; philosophers analyze systems of meaning. So the five principal elements of journalism may be imagined as starting points for laying out a curriculum that connects study in the schools and departments of journalism to classical disciplines and courses in the university at large. The task of journalism education in the university is to transmit journalism's principles—to see to it that these principles are immanent or, to put it differently, represented strongly in the mental equipment of novice journalists. In my view, the connection to the classical disciplines is direct and clear, and ought to be strengthened.

Finally, the approach I am recommending puts first things first. It is not journalists on their own who have written skimpy accounts of the journalistic palette and thereby diminished both the craft and what is necessary through curriculum to the formation of good journalists. My reading of journalism education has lead me to conclude that social scientists have been likewise helpful. What I would construe as social science—the analysis of systems of interaction rather than the analysis of acts or methods through which artifice is produced—seems to have dominated the research wings of journalism schools. I am talking not just of the division between those who say they engage in quantitative as opposed to qualitative scholarship. I am talking, as I have already indicated, of the division between the analysis of the systems through qualitative or quantitative means, on the one hand, and the analysis of the creative acts of single individuals, on the other. Such acts may in turn give birth to systems, and they too may be studied. In the meantime, it is time to start at the beginning, to incorporate an understanding of the creative process more fully into the study of journalism, and to equip students with more appropriate capacities of execution and judgment.

To conclude, the study of journalism practices should be invigorated by the spirit of art and the humanities. The humanities, properly understood, celebrate creation more than power. They celebrate the highest achievements of the human imagination and meditate on them as starting points for civilized life and discourse. Journalism education and practice can benefit from a recasting within such a world. Put differently, as journalism is taught, it should be bathed in the light of the Imagination and the idea that journalism can be and often is one of our highest arts.

NOTES

1. T. S. Eliot, *Notes Towards the Definition of Culture*, (London: Faber and Faber, 1954). I am using the indefinite article in my title to suggest that the definition I am proposing may not be the only one.

2. G. Stuart Adam, "Thinking Journalism," in *Content for Canadian Journalists*, July/August, 1988; a version of this article appeared in the *Canadian Journal of Communication*, Vol. 14, no. 2, May 1989, under the title "Journalism Knowledge and Journalism Practice: The Problems of Curriculum and Research in University Schools of Journalism"; see also "Journalism and the University: Reporters, Writers and Critics," in Kathleen Jaeger (ed.), *The Idea of the University: 1789–1989* (Halifax: Institute for Advanced Study, University of King's College, 1990); and "The World Next Door: A Commonwealth Perspective," *Gannett Center Journal*, Vol. 2, no. 2, Spring 1988.

3. *Planning for Curricular Change: A Report on the Future of Journalism and Mass Communication Education*, School of Journalism, University of Oregon, 1984 (Oregon Report); "Challenges and Opportunities in Journalism and Mass Communication Education: A Report of the Task Force on Journalism and Mass Communication Education," (AEJMC Task Force) in *Journalism Educator*, Vol. 44, no. 12, Spring 1989.

4. Oregon Report; pp. 5, 10, 11.

5. N. K. Llewellyn, *The Bramble Bush* (New York: Oceana Publications, 1930); p. 56. Llewellyn, who was a lawyer, was quoting a psychologist.

6. Michael Oakeshott, *Experience and Its Modes* (London: Cambridge University Press, 1978); p. 124.

7. C. Wright Mills, *The Sociological Imagination* (New York: Oxford University Press, 1957).

8. R. G. Collingwood, *The Idea of History* (New York: Oxford University Press, 1959).

9. Northrop Frye, *The Educated Imagination* (Toronto: Canadian Broadcasting Corporation, 1980).

10. Michael Oakeshott, *The Voice of Poetry in the Conversation of Mankind, An Essay* (London: Bowes and Bowes, 1959); p. 17.

11. Michael Oakeshott, *Experience and Its Modes* (London: Cambridge University Press, 1978); p. 32.

12. Joan Didion, "Why I Write," in *The Writer and Her Work*, Janet Steinberg (ed.), (New York: W. W. Norton, 1980); p. 20.

13. Joan Didion, *Miami* (New York: Simon and Schuster, 1987); p. 52.

14. Joseph Conrad, "Preface" to *The Nigger of the Narcissus, Typhoon and Other Stories*, (Hammondsworth, Middlesex: Penguin, 1986); p. 13.

15. Jennifer Warren and George Ramos (of the *Los Angeles Times*), "Devastation and Heroism," in *The Ottawa Citizen*, Thurs., Oct. 19, 1989; p. D1.

16. Conrad; p. 12.

17. Joseph Frank, *The Beginning of English Newspapers, 1620–1660* (Cambridge, Mass.: Harvard University Press, 1961).

18. A. Aspinall, "Statistical Accounts of the London Newspapers in the Eighteenth Century," *English Historical Review*, Vol. LXIII, 1948; pp. 201–232; see also Stanley Morison, *The English Newspaper, Some Account of the Physical Development of Journals* (London: Cambridge University Press, 1963); p. 197.

19. W. H. Auden, "Making, Knowing, Judging," in *The Dyer's Hand and Other Essays* (New York: Random House, 1962); p. 51.

20. I first encountered this formulation in Curtis MacDougall's *Interpretative Reporting* (New York: Macmillan, 1972); another source for it is in Melvin Mencher's *News Reporting and Writing* (Dubuque: Wm. C. Brown, 1977).

21. This quote comes from an essay by Thomas Gavin, "The Truth Beyond Facts: Journalism and Literature," in *The Georgia Review*, Vol. XLV, no. 1, Spring 1991; p. 45.

22. Gavin; p. 45.

23. The story is recorded in "The Dark Continent of American Journalism," by James Carey in *Reading the News*, edited by Robert Karl Manhoff and Michael Schudson (New York: Pantheon, 1987); p. 170.

24. The phrase "pageant of creation" is George Kelly's and it is quoted in Janet Emig's *The Web of Meaning, Essays on Writing, Teaching, Learning and Thinking* (Upper Montclair: Boynton/Cook, 1983); p. 165.

25. Emig; p. 160.

26. Landon's struggle with cancer of the pancreas was the cover story of *People* magazine of May 6, 1991.

27. Robert Stone, "The Reason for Stories, Toward a Moral Fiction," in *Harper's Magazine*, June, 1988; p. 71.

28. Milan Kundera, *The Art of the Novel* (New York: Harper and Row, 1986); p. 83.

29. John Hersey, "The Legend on the License," *The Yale Review*, Vol. 75, no. 2, Feb. 1986; p. 296.

30. Hersey; p. 290.

31. John Carey, *The Faber Book of Reportage* (London: Faber and Faber, 1987); p. xxix.

32. Bob Woodward, *Wired* (New York: Pocket Books, 1984).

33. Gail Sheehy, *Character America's Search for Leadership*, (New York: William Morrow and Co., 1988); p. 18.

34. Hersey; p. 308.

35. George Orwell, "Politics and the English Language," in *The Collected Essays, Journalism and Letters of George Orwell*, Vol. 1, edited by Sonia Orwell and Ian Angus (London: Secker and Warburg, 1968).

36. John Carey, p. xxxi.

37. Hugh Kenner, "The Politics of the Plain Style," in Norman Sims (ed.), *Literary Journalism in the Twentieth Century* (New York: Oxford University Press, 1990).

38. Kenner; p. 189.

39. Kenner; p. 187.

40. Robert Scholes and Robert Kellogg, *The Nature of Narrative* (New York: Oxford University Press, 1966).

41. I heard this first from Roy Clark, Dean of the Faculty at The Poynter Institute for Media Studies, who said that he first heard the idea of journalistic narrative formulated this way from a journalist who works in Seattle.

42. James Ettema and Theodore Glasser, "On the Epistemology of Investigative Journalism," *Communication*, Vol. 8, No. 2, 1985; p. 188.

43. Andre Codescru, "Of unknown endings and new beginnings," *The Globe and Mail*, Monday, Oct. 19, 1987; p. A7.

44. James Carey, "The Dark Continent . . ."; p. 151.

45. Joan Didion, "Slouching Towards Bethlehem," in a book with the same title (New York: Dell, 1967).

46. Didion, "Slouching . . ."; p. 123.

47. Didion, "Slouching . . ."; p. 122.

48. James Carey, p. 180.

49. Sheehy; p. 11.

50. Sheehy; p. 15.

51. Sheehy; p. 39.

52. Joan Didion, "Some Dreamers of a Golden Dream," in *Slouching Towards Bethlehem*; p. 4.

Study Guide

TALKING POINTS

I. Stuart Adam writes that journalism is "a form of expression that is an invention." Borrowing from W. H. Auden, he goes on to say it is a "contraption" with a guy or a gal inside of it. Are you comfortable with these propositions? What about the rest of the definition that says that this form of expression "is used to report and comment in the public media on events and ideas" as they occur?

II. Revisit and reflect on the categories marking journalism—news, evidence and fact, language and narrative, and analysis. Are these categories sufficiently comprehensive to capture the subject? What would you add?

III. Discuss the following: ". . . the world is born in our imaginations. This is not to say that acts of nature do not have an objective existence. It is to say that the experience of them—consciousness in other words—is the work of the Imagination. . . . It means that the transfer of consciousness through a story, any story—from a journalist to an audience in other words—produces the forms of public consciousness that make collective life possible."

IV. What about the following? "[J]ournalism is the aspect of culture that inspires and directs the work of every journalist . . . it is the aspect of culture that is more or less immanent in the personal culture of every journalist and, correspondingly, more or less immanent in the institutional culture of every publication or broadcast unit."

V.   Does it make sense to analyze journalism "in terms of what it is rather than by the medium through which it is circulated"?

VI. In summary, do you agree with the basic assumption of this essay that journalism "is made; it doesn't just happen" and the conclusion that it "can be and often is one of our highest arts"?

WORKBENCH

I. Complete your "editor's lexicon."

CONTRIBUTORS

G. Stuart Adam is the Journalism Scholarship Fellow at the Poynter Institute for Media Studies and a professor emeritus of journalism at Carleton University, Ottawa, Canada. He has worked as a reporter and desk editor for *The Toronto Star*, as a reporter and editorial writer for *The Ottawa Journal*, and as a contract producer and writer for the Canadian Broadcasting Corporation.

He was born in Toronto in 1939 and received his primary and secondary education in Ontario schools. He attended Carleton University, Ottawa, where he earned degrees in journalism and Canadian studies, and Queen's University, Kingston, where he earned a doctorate in political science.

From 1973 to 1987, Adam was director of the School of Journalism at Carleton University, Ottawa. After his term as Carleton's director, he became founding chair of the Center for Mass Media Studies in the School of Journalism at the University of Western Ontario. He returned to Carleton's permanent faculty in 1989 and later became dean of the faculty of arts and then vice president (academic) and provost, a position from which he retired in June 2003.

In 1990–1991, he took a twelve-month leave from Carleton to be Scholar in Residence at the Poynter Institute for Media Studies in St. Petersburg. His association with the institute dates from that time.

Adam has written extensively on the philosophy of journalism, freedom of expression, and the Canadian legal system. He is author (with Robert Martin) of *A Sourcebook of Canadian Media Law* and author of *Notes towards a Definition of Journalism*. His academic and research essays have appeared in such publications as the *Journal of Mass Media Ethics*, the *Australian Journalism Review*, *Journalism: Theory, Practice, Criticism*, *Media Studies Journal*, and the *Canadian Journal of Communication*.

Maya Angelou is best known for her autobiographical books: *All God's Children Need Traveling Shoes*, *The Heart of a Woman*, *Singin' and Swingin' and Gettin' Merry Like Christmas*, *Gather Together in My Name*, and *I Know Why the Caged Bird Sings*, which was nominated for the National Book Award. The author, poet, playwright, stage and screen producer, and performer was born Marguerite Johnson in St. Louis, Mo., on April 4, 1928, and grew up in St. Louis and Stamps, Ark. Among her volumes of poetry are *A Brave and Startling Truth*, *The Complete Collected Poems of Maya Angelou*, *Wouldn't Take Nothing for My Journey Now*, *Now Sheba Sings the Song*, *I Shall Not Be Moved*, *Shaker, Why Don't You Sing?*, *Oh Pray My Wings Are Gonna Fit Me Well*, and *Just Give Me a Cool Drink of Water 'fore I Diiie*, which was nominated for the Pulitzer Prize.

Angelou read her poem "On the Pulse of Morning" at the inauguration of President Bill Clinton in 1993.

Daniel Boorstin (1914–2004) was a historian, Pulitzer Prize-winning author, and the librarian of Congress. He also served as director of the National Museum of American History and senior historian of the Smithsonian. Boorstin was born in Atlanta in 1914 and raised in Tulsa, Okla. He took his first degree at Harvard, received his doctorate from Yale, and was a Rhodes scholar at Balliol College, Oxford, before joining the faculty of the University of Chicago, where he taught history for twenty-five years. In 1974 he won the Pulitzer Prize for history for *The Americans: The Democratic Experience*. He was a two-time nominee for the National Book Award. Boorstin received many other honors and was awarded a number of honorary degrees. His other works include *The Image, The Discoverers, The Creators, The Genius of American Politics, Democracy and Its Discontents*, and *The Lost World of Thomas Jefferson*.

James W. Carey is the CBS Professor of International Journalism in the graduate school of journalism at Columbia University and adjunct professor at Union Theological Seminary, both in New York City. He previously served as dean of the College of Communications at the University of Illinois at Urbana-Champaign and has held the George H. Gallup Chair at the University of Iowa. In addition, Carey has been president of the Association for Education in Journalism, president of the American Association of Schools and Departments of Journalism, a fellow at the National Endowment for the Humanities, a fellow at the Gannett Center for Media Studies, a member of advisory board for the Poynter Institute for Media Studies, a member of the board of directors of the Public Broadcasting System, and a board member of the Peabody Awards for Broadcasting. His other works include *Media, Myth and Narratives: Television and the Press, Communication as Culture*, and *James Carey: A Critical Reader*.

John Carey is a fellow of the British Academy and an emeritus professor at Oxford. Born in 1934, the distinguished literary critic, professor, and journalist twice has chaired the Man Booker prize panel for fiction. His books include *Milton, The Violent Effigy: A Study of Dickens' Imagination, Thackeray: Prodigal Genius, John Donne: Life, Mind and Art, The Intellectuals and the Masses*, and *Pure Pleasure: A Guide to the Twentieth Century's Most Enjoyable Books*. He also is the editor of several anthologies, including *The Faber Book of Reportage, The Faber Book of Science*, and *The Faber Book of Utopias*.

Roy Peter Clark is vice president and senior scholar at the Poynter Institute. He has worked full-time at Poynter since 1979 as director of the writing center, dean of the faculty, and associate director.

Clark was born in 1948 on the Lower East Side of New York City and raised on Long Island, where he attended Catholic schools. He was graduated from Providence College in Rhode Island with a degree in English and earned a Ph.D. from the State University of New York at Stony Brook, specializing in medieval literature. He taught writing, language, and literature at Auburn University at Montgomery, Alabama.

In 1977 Clark was hired by the St. Petersburg Times to become one of America's first writing coaches and worked with the American Society of Newspaper Editors (ASNE) to improve newspaper writing nationwide. Because of his work with ASNE, Clark was elected as a distinguished service member.

Clark has worked with journalists and taught writing in more than forty states and five continents and is widely considered one of America's most influential writing coaches. He is the founding director of the National Writers' Workshops, regional conferences that attract more than five thousand writers annually.

Clark has edited seven volumes of *Best Newspaper Writing*, the annual collection of ASNE writing award winners. He is the author of *Free to Write: A Journalist Teaches Young Writers*, published by Heinemann. With Don Fry, he wrote *Coaching Writers: Editors and Reporters Working Together*, published by Bedford/St. Martin's Press. With Christopher Scanlan he is the editor of the twenty-year anthology *America's Best Newspaper Writing*, published by Bedford/St. Martin's Press. He is the author of the Poynter Paper titled "The American Conversation and the Language of Journalism" and edited nine other Poynter Papers, a collection of which has been published by the University Press of Florida under the title *The Values and Craft of American Journalism*. With Raymond Arsenault he has edited an inspirational collection of newspaper columns under the title *The Changing South of Gene Patterson: Journalism and Civil Rights, 1960–1968*.

From 1977 to 1978 Clark wrote news, features, and reviews for the *St. Petersburg Times*. In 1996 he began writing serial narratives for newspapers, including "Three Little Words," "Sadie's Ring," "Her Picture in My Wallet," and "Ain't Done Yet," a serial novel syndicated by *The New York Times*. He is the author of "The Line between Fact and Fiction," published in the journal *Creative Nonfiction*.

Victor Cohn (1920–2000) was a science and medical reporter for the *Minneapolis Tribune* for twenty years and then science editor, science and medical reporter, and health columnist for *The Washington Post* for twenty-five years. In 1959 Cohn cofounded the Council for the Advancement of Science Writing, and he served as president of the National Association of Science Writers. He was the first triple winner of the Society of Professional Journalists' Sigma Delta Chi Award for newspaper reporting and the first two-time winner of the American Association for the Advancement of Science Award.

The **Commission on Freedom of the Press** published *A Free and Responsible Press, A General Report on Mass Communication: Newspapers, Radio, Motion Pictures, Magazines, and Books* in 1947. The chair of the commission was Robert M. Hutchins, president of the University of Chicago, and the report is widely known as the "Hutchins Commission," not only because he was its chair, but also because of the extent of his influence on its contents. The other commissioners were Zechariah Chaffee Jr., professor of law, Columbia University, who was vice chairman; John M. Clark, professor of economics, Columbia University; John Dickinson, professor of law, University of Pennsylvania; William E. Hocking, professor of philosophy emeritus, Harvard University; Harold D. Laswell, professor of law, Yale University; Archibald MacLeish, former assistant secretary of state; Charles E. Merriam, professor of political science emeritus, University of Chicago; Reinhold Neibuhr, professor of ethics and philosophy of religion, Union Theological Seminary; Robert Redfield, professor of anthropology, University of Chicago; Beardsley Ruml, chairman, Federal Reserve Bank of New York; Arthur M. Schlesinger, professor of history, Harvard University; and George N. Shuster, president, Hunter College.

Joan Didion is a freelance writer whose works include fiction and nonfiction. She has been an editor and columnist for *Vogue, The Saturday Evening Post, Life*, and other national magazines. She was born in Sacramento, Calif., and graduated from the University of California at Berkeley. She contributes regularly to *The New York Review of Books* and *The New Yorker*. Didion also collaborated with her late husband, writer John Gregory Dunne, on screenplays. Her novels include *Run River, A Book of Common Prayer, Play It as It Lays, Salvador, Democracy*, and *The Last Thing He Wanted*. Her collections of essays and nonfiction include *Slouching toward Bethlehem, The White Album, After Henry, Political Fictions*, and *Where I Was From*.

James S. Ettema is chairman of the department of communication studies at Northwestern University. He received bachelor's and master's degrees from the University of Minnesota and worked as a writer, filmmaker, and photographer before completing his doctoral studies at the University of Michigan. He is the editor, with D. Charles Whitney, of *Individuals in Mass Media Organizations: Creativity and Constraint* and *Audience Making: How the Media Created the Audience*. His book *Custodians of Conscience: Investigative Journalism and Public Virtue*, written with Theodore L. Glasser of Stanford University, won the Frank Luther Mott-Kappa Tau Alpha Award from the National Journalism and Mass Communication Honor Society, the Bart Richards Award for Media Criticism from Penn State University, and the Sigma Delta Chi Award for research on journalism from the Society of Professional Journalists.

Theodore L. Glasser is director of the graduate program in journalism at Stanford University. He received his doctorate from the University of Iowa and taught in the University of Minnesota's School of Journalism and Mass Communication before going to Stanford in 1990. Glasser has also served as president of the Association for Education in Journalism and Mass Communication. His book *Custodians of Conscience: Investigative Journalism and Public Virtue*, written with James S. Ettema of Northwestern University, won the Frank Luther Mott-Kappa Tau Alpha Award from the National Journalism and Mass Communication Honor Society, the Bart Richards Award for Media Criticism from Penn State University, and the Sigma Delta Chi Award for research on journalism from the Society of Professional Journalists. Other books include *Public Opinion and the Communication of Consent*, edited with Charles T. Salmon; *Media Freedom and Accountability*, edited with Everette E. Dennis and Donald M. Gillmor; and *The Idea of Public Journalism*, an edited collection of essays.

David Halberstam is a reporter and commentator. He was born in New York in 1934 and graduated from Harvard University in 1955. He started his career writing at the *Daily Times Leader* in West Point, Miss., and was a reporter for the Nashville *Tennessean* before moving to *The New York Times*. In 1964, at age thirty, Halberstam earned a Pulitzer Prize for his international reporting from Vietnam. His books include *The Unfinished Odyssey of Robert Kennedy, The Making of a Quagmire—America and Vietnam during the Kennedy Era, Ho, The Best and the Brightest, The Powers That Be, The Amateurs—The Story of Four Young Men and Their Quest for an Olympic Gold Medal, The Reckoning, Summer of '49, The Next Century, The Fifties, October Nineteen Sixty-Four, Freedom Rider, The Children, Playing for Keeps—Michael Jordan and the World He Made, Sports on New York Radio—A Play-by-Play History, War in a Time of*

Peace—Bush, Clinton, and the Generals, Firehouse, and *The Teammates*. He also is the editor of *Defining a Nation: Our America and the Sources of Its Strength*.

S. I. Hayakawa (1906–1992) was a professor, semanticist, and writer who served as a U.S. senator from California from 1977 to 1983. He was born in Vancouver, British Columbia, received his undergraduate degree from the University of Manitoba in Winnipeg, a master's in English from McGill University, Montreal, and a doctorate from the University of Wisconsin. He taught at the Illinois Institute of Technology before moving to the University of Chicago in 1950. In 1955, the year he became a U.S. citizen, he moved to San Francisco State College (now San Francisco State University), and in 1968 Hayakawa became president of the college. From 1970 to 1976 he was a columnist for the *Register & Tribune* Syndicate. In 1976 Hayakawa was elected to the U.S. Senate and became known for his efforts to promote English as the nation's official common language. Hayakawa was the founder and editor of *ETC*, a journal published by the International Society for General Semantics, and he edited *Language, Meaning and Maturity* and *Our Language and Our World*, both books comprising essays published initially in *ETC*. Other works include *Modern Guide to Synonyms and Related Words*.

John Hersey (1914–1993) was an American writer and journalist who won the Pulitzer Prize for his novel *A Bell for Adano*. Hersey was born in China, where his parents were serving as missionaries. He graduated from Yale University and became a correspondent for *Time* magazine in the Far East. As a correspondent for *Time*, *Life*, and *The New Yorker*, he covered fighting during World War II in Europe and Asia. Hersey was one of the first Western journalists to arrive in Hiroshima after the atomic bomb was dropped there in 1945. *The New Yorker* article he wrote, "Hiroshima," was later turned into a book. Other nonfiction works include *The Algiers Motel Incident* and *Blues*. Other novels include *The Wall, The War Lover, The Child Buyer, Letter to the Alumni, The Conspiracy*, and *Antonietta*. Collections of his short stories include *Fling and Other Stories* and *Key West Tales*.

Seymour Hersh is an investigative reporter and author who won the Pulitzer Prize for international reporting for exposing the MyLai massacre and its cover-up during the Vietnam War. He was born in 1934 and began his career in journalism in 1959 as a police reporter for the City News Bureau of Chicago. He was also a correspondent for United Press International and the Associated Press before joining *The New York Times*. A regular contributor to *The New Yorker*, Hersh won a 2004 National Magazine Award for public interest for his work on intelligence and the Iraq war. He has also been awarded four George Polk Awards, the National Book Critics Circle Award, and more than a dozen other prizes. Other books include *The Price of Power—Kissinger in the Nixon White House, The Dark Side of Camelot, The Target Is Destroyed—What Really Happened to Flight 007 and What America Knew about It*, and *Chain of Command: The Road from 9/11 to Abu Ghraib*.

Helen MacGill Hughes was born in 1903 in Vancouver, British Columbia. She studied sociology at the University of Chicago, where she was a student of Robert Park. She was an active partner with her husband, Everett Cherrington Hughes, at the University of Chicago and later at Brandeis University. Her books include *News and the Human*

Interest Story, Inquiries in Sociology, and *Racial and Ethnic Relations*. Other publications with her husband include *Where Peoples Meet: Racial and Ethnic Frontiers, Men and Their Work*, and *Twenty Thousand Nurses Tell Their Story: A Report on Studies of Nursing Functions Sponsored by the American Nurses' Association*.

Robert Kellog (1929–2004) was an educator who developed expertise in areas ranging from the Middle Ages to James Joyce and Icelandic literature. He received his bachelor's degree from the University of Maryland and master's and doctoral degrees from Harvard University. Kellog taught at the University of Virginia starting in 1957 and retired as dean of the College of Arts & Sciences in 1985. He also served as chair of the board of trustees of the Leifur Eiríksson Foundation at the University of Virginia.

Hugh Kenner (1923–2003) was a professor of English and a literary critic best known for his research and writing on Ezra Pound and James Joyce. Kenner studied at the University of Toronto under Marshall McLuhan. His first teaching post was at Santa Barbara College (now University of California at Santa Barbara). Subsequently, he moved to Johns Hopkins University and then to the University of Georgia. He wrote on subjects as diverse as geodesic mathematics, the cartoons of Chuck Jones, and the effect of modern technology on literary imagery. Other works include *Paradox in Chesterton* (with a foreword by Marshall McLuhan), *The Poetry of Ezra Pound, Dublin's Joyce, The Pound Era, Bucky: A Guided Tour of Buckminster Fuller, Geodesic Math and How to Use It*, and *Chuck Jones: A Flurry of Drawings*.

Bill Kovach is a journalist, writer, and founding director of the Committee of Concerned Journalists. He began his career in Tennessee at the *Johnson City Press Chronicle* and later served as a reporter for the Nashville *Tennessean*. He joined *The New York Times* as a reporter and later became chief of the *Times* Washington bureau. He also served as editor of the *Atlanta Journal-Constitution* and curator of the Nieman Fellowships at Harvard. Other books include *Warp Speed: America in the Age of Mixed Media*, written with Tom Rosenstiel. He is a contributor to *The Prevailing South: Life and Politics in a Changing Culture, The Art of Writing Non Fiction*, and *Assignment America*. His writing has also appeared in such publications as *The New York Times Sunday Magazine, The Washington Post*, and the *New Republic*.

Walter Lippmann (1889–1974) was a writer, editor, and nationally syndicated columnist. He was associate editor of the *New Republic* in its early days and served as assistant secretary of war in the Wilson administration. He joined the staff of the *New York World* after the war and become editor in 1929. He moved to the *New York Herald Tribune* after the *World* closed. For thirty years he wrote his column, *Today and Tomorrow*, and received a special Pulitzer Prize citation in 1958. His books include *A Preface to Politics, A Preface to Morals, The Phantom Public, U.S. War Aims, The Cold War, Isolation and Alliances*, and *Western Unity and the Common Market*.

Christopher Lydon is an author, media personality, and pioneer in audio blogging. He was a statehouse reporter for *The Boston Globe* and covered several presidential campaigns for *The New York Times*, where he worked for eight years. He anchored public television news on WGBH-TV in Boston and founded *The Connection*, a radio show that was carried by public radio stations around the country. He also has collected sounds, voices, and ideas for "The Whole Wide World with Christopher Lydon," an audio blog.

John G. Morris is a former a picture editor and photographer who edited many of the images of an era, from photos of the London air raids and the D-Day landing during World War II to the assassination of Robert Kennedy. Morris also has edited pictures for *Life* magazine, Magnum Photos, *Ladies' Home Journal*, *National Geographic*, *The Washington Post*, and *The New York Times*.

Frank Luther Mott (1886–1964) was a Pulitzer Prize-winning author and journalism professor who guided the school of journalism at the University of Iowa and was dean of the journalism school at the University of Missouri. His parents published the weekly paper in his hometown of What Cheer, Iowa. Mott worked for his father from age ten until he graduated from college. He worked his way through college as a reporter for his father on the *Daily American* in El Reno, Okla. By 1914 he had become editor and publisher of the *Grand Junction Globe*. With John T. Frederick he edited and published the *Midland*. He served as editor of *Journalism Quarterly* for five years. Other works include *American Journalism*, the four-volume *A History of American Magazines*, for which he was awarded the Pulitzer Prize in American history in 1939, and *Time Enough*, a collection of his autobiographical essays.

V. S. Naipaul is a novelist and essayist, with works that range from short stories and novels to political essays and international analysis. He was born in Trinidad and graduated from University College, Oxford. He worked briefly for the BBC as a writer and editor, but for most of his career he has written fiction and nonfiction. He received the Booker Prize for Fiction in 1971, the T. S. Eliot Award for Creative Writing in 1986, and the Nobel Prize for Literature in 2001. His novels include *The Mystic Masseur*, *A House for Mr. Biswas*, *In a Free State*, *Guerrillas*, *A Bend in the River*, *Half a Life*, and *Magic Seeds*. His nonfiction includes three books about India—*An Area of Darkness*, *India: A Wounded Civilization*, and *India: A Million Mutinies Now*—and two books about Islamic societies—*Among the Believers: An Islamic Journey* and *Beyond Belief: Islamic Excursions*. Collections of his essays include *The Overcrowded Barracoon and Other Articles*, *The Return of Eva Peron*, *The Writer and the World: Essays*, and *Literary Occasions*.

"George Orwell" (1903–1950) was the pen name of Eric Blair, an English writer and journalist who chronicled much of the history of the twentieth century. He was born in Bengal, India, attended Eton, and then served with the Indian imperial police in Burma. He returned to Europe five years later, living first in France and then England, where he began writing under the name "George Orwell." In 1936 he fought against Franco in the Spanish civil war. During World War II he worked for the BBC and then left to work as literary editor of the *Tribune*. Later he contributed regularly to the *Manchester Evening News*. His best–known works of fiction are the sociopolitical novels *Animal Farm* and *Nineteen Eighty-Four*. Other fiction includes *Down and Out in Paris and London*, *Burmese Days*, *The Road to Wigan Pier*, *Homage to Catalonia*, *A Clergyman's Daughter*, *Keep the Aspidistra Flying*, and *Coming Up for Air*. His collections of essays include *Dickens, Dali and Others*, *Shooting an Elephant*, and the *Collected Essays, Journalism, and Letters of George Orwell*.

George Plimpton (1927–2003) was a writer, editor, and one of the founders of *The Paris Review*. He was born in New York City and attended Harvard University, where he was an editor of the *Harvard Lampoon*. Under the early guidance of Plimpton and writers

H. L. Humes and Peter Matthiessen, *The Paris Review* featured the work of new authors as well as interviews with established writers that focused on the craft of writing. In addition, Plimpton participated in sports and other events, writing about them in magazines and books. Those books include *Paper Lion*, *Open Net*, *Bogey Man*, *One More July*, and *The Curious Case of Sidd Finch*, a novel that was an extension of a *Sports Illustrated* article about a fictitious baseball pitcher.

Tom Rosenstiel is director of the Project for Excellence in Journalism and vice chairman of the Committee of Concerned Journalists. He worked as a journalist for more than twenty years, serving as the media critic for the *Los Angeles Times* and MSNBC's *The News with Brian Williams* and working as chief congressional correspondent for *Newsweek* magazine. His work has appeared in such publications as *Esquire*, the *New Republic*, *The New York Times*, *Columbia Journalism Review*, and the *Washington Monthly*, He also is the author of *Strange Bedfellows: How Television and the Presidential Candidates Changed American Politics* and co-editor of *Thinking Clearly: Cases in Journalistic Decision Making*. Other books include *Warp Speed: America in the Age of Mixed Media*, written with Bill Kovach.

Salman Rushdie is an author best known for *Midnight's Children* and *The Satanic Verses*, which Iran's spiritual leader, Ayatollah Ruhollah Khomeini, proclaimed as sacrilegious. Khomeini issued a faatwa against Rushdie in 1989, forcing him into hiding. (The fatwa was formally lifted in 1998.) He was born in Bombay and educated at Cambridge University. He worked as an advertising copywriter in London until he achieved success with his novels. Other fiction includes *The Moor's Last Sigh*, *The Ground beneath Her Feet*, and *Fury*. His nonfiction includes *The Jaguar Smile*, *Imaginary Homelands*, *The Wizard of Oz*, *Mirrorwork*, and *Step across This Line: Collected Non-Fiction, 1992–2002*.

Robert Scholes is professor emeritus of English, comparative literature, and modern culture and media at Brown University. Scholes has contributed articles and book reviews to journals, literary magazines, and weekly reviews, including *Yale Review*, *Georgia Review*, *Iowa Review*, *Semiotica*, and *American Journal of Semiotics*. His books and articles include *The Rise and Fall of English: Reconstructing English as a Discipline*, *Protocols of Reading*, *Textual Power: Literary Theory and the Teaching of English*, *The Practice of Writing*, with Nancy R. Comley and Janice Peritz, and *Text Book: Writing through Literature*, with Nancy R. Comley and Gregory L. Ulmer.

Susan Sontag (1933–2004) was a writer, critic, and human rights activist. She grew up in Arizona and California and studied philosophy at the University of Chicago, Harvard, and Oxford. As an activist, Sontag served from 1987 to 1989 as president of the American Center of PEN and staged Beckett's *Waiting for Godot* in the summer of 1993 in besieged Sarajevo. She later was named an honorary citizen of the city. Her work includes the novels *The Benefactor*, *Death Kit*, *The Volcano Lover*, and *In America*; a collection of short stories, *I, etcetera*; several plays, including *Alice in Bed* and *Lady from the Sea*; and nonfiction, including *Against Interpretation*, *Illness as Metaphor*, *Where the Stress Falls*, and *Regarding the Pain of Others*. Her stories and essays appeared in such publications as *The New Yorker*, *The New York Review of Books*, *The Times Literary Supplement*, *Art in America*, *Antaeus*, *Parnassus*, and *The Nation*. In

2000 she won the National Book Award for her historical novel *In America*, and she was a MacArthur fellow from 1990 to 1995.

Paul Starobin is a contributing editor of *The Atlantic Monthly* magazine and a staff correspondent for *National Journal*. He previously served for four years as the Moscow bureau chief for *Business Week*. In addition, he is a contributor to *The Real State of the Union*, a collaboration between *The Atlantic Monthly* magazine and the New America Foundation, which features essays about facets of the well-being of citizens of the United States.

Robert Stone is an award-winning author. Stone grew up in New York and served in the U.S. Navy. After leaving the Navy, Stone lived in New York, working the night shift as a copy boy at the *Daily News* while writing and reading poetry. In 1962 he received a Stegner fellowship to the creative writing program at Stanford University. He was briefly a correspondent in Saigon (now Ho Chi Minh City) during the Vietnam War, forming the basis for his best-known novel, *Dog Soldiers*, which was filmed as *Who'll Stop the Rain*. His other works include *A Hall of Mirrors*, *A Flag for Sunrise*, *Children of Light*, *Outerbridge Reach*, *Damascus Gate*, *Bay of Souls*, and *Bear and His Daughter: Stories*.

Max Ways (1906–1985) was a close associate of Henry Luce. He joined *Time* in 1945 after serving as a senior analyst in the Foreign Economics Administration in Washington. Before the war he had worked for the *Baltimore Sun* and *Philadelphia Record*. At *Time* he served as national editor, foreign news editor, and chief of the London bureau. Later in his career he was associate managing editor of *Fortune* magazine.

Tom Wolfe is a journalist and novelist who is considered to be one of the founders of the New Journalism. He attended Washington and Lee University as an undergraduate and received a doctorate in American studies from Yale University. He worked as a reporter for the *Springfield Union*, *The Washington Post*, and the *New York Herald Tribune*, and his writing also has appeared in *New York* magazine, *Esquire*, and *Harper's*. His journalistic works include *The Kandy-Kolored Tangerine-Flake Streamline Baby*, *The Electric Kool-Aid Acid Test*, *Radical Chic and Mau-mauing the Flak Catchers*, *The Right Stuff*, *From Bauhaus to Our House*, and the anthology *Hooking Up*. His novels include *The Bonfire of the Vanities*, *A Man in Full*, and *I Am Charlotte Simmons*.

INDEX

Note: Numbers for footnotes and endnotes are indicated by "n."

380